Managing Major Sports Events

The hosting of major sporting events can be a key tool in the development of cities and countries around the world. If carried out effectively these events can not only bring prestige to an area, but can leave the local population with a legacy of improved infrastructure and facilities. *Managing Major Sports Events: Theory and Practice* is a complete introduction to the principles and practical skills that underpin the running and hosting of major sports events, from initial bid to post-event legacy.

The book draws closely on the authors' personal practical experiences of day-to-day management during the 2010 Winter Olympics in Vancouver, now widely regarded as the gold standard of Olympic organization. Drawing on the latest research from across multiple disciplines, it covers every key area in the event management process, including:

- bidding, leadership and planning
- venue implementation
- communications (e.g. media, marketing and sponsorship, technology)
- functional area considerations (e.g. sport, protocol, security and risk management)
- Games-time considerations
- ceremonies
- legacy and sustainability.

Each chapter contains a unique combination of theory, practical decision-making exercises and case studies of major sports events from around the world, helping students and practitioners alike to understand and prepare for the reality of executing major events on an international scale. *Managing Major Sports Events: Theory and Practice* is an essential textbook for any course on sports event management, or international sports management and an invaluable resource for all sport management researchers and professionals.

Milena M. Parent is an Associate Professor in the School of Human Kinetics, University of Ottawa, as well as an invited Professor at the Norwegian School of Sport Sciences. She holds a Government of Ontario Early Researcher Award and is a Research Fellow of the North American Society for Sport Management.

Sharon Smith-Swan has an international private consulting and coaching practice in Vancouver, British Columbia, home of the 2010 Olympic and Paralympic Winter Games. She has delivered hundreds of speeches and seminars related to her management experience in the strategic, tactical, and organizational aspects of business and held executive volunteer positions in sports, arts, and cultural organizations.

Managing Major Sports Events

Theory and Practice

Milena M. Parent and Sharon Smith-Swan

Routledge
Taylor & Francis Group

LONDON AND NEW YORK

First published 2013
by Routledge
2 Park Square, Milton Park, Abingdon, Oxon OX14 4RN

Simultaneously published in the USA and Canada
by Routledge
711 Third Avenue, New York, NY 10017

Routledge is an imprint of the Taylor & Francis Group, an informa business

British Library Cataloguing in Publication Data
A catalogue record for this book is available from the British Library

Library of Congress Cataloging in Publication Data
Parent, Milena M.
Managing major sports events : theory and practice/Milena M. Parent and
Sharon Smith-Swan.
   p. cm.
   1. Sports–Management. 2. Sports administration. I. Smith-Swan, Sharon.
   II. Title.
   GV713.P37 2013
   796.06'9–dc23   2012022400

ISBN: 978-0-415-67228-3 (hbk)
ISBN: 978-0-415-67233-7 (pbk)
ISBN: 978-0-203-13237-1 (ebk)

Typeset in Perpetua and Bell Gothic
by Wearset Ltd, Boldon, Tyne and Wear

Contents

Contents

Contents

Figures

Tables

Expert case study contributor information

Michael A. Chambers LLP
Sport affiliations: President, Canadian Olympic Committee 2001–2010; Member, Board of Directors, Canadian Olympic Committee; Member, Board of Directors, VANOC 2003–2010; Member, Board of Directors, TO2015 Organizing Committee; Member, Executive Council, Association of National Olympic Committees; Member, Executive Committee, Pan American Sports Organization.
Other Affiliation: LLP Maclearn Corlett.

Sally Rehorick
Former title: Director of International Client Services, VANOC 2010.
Current: Professor Emerita, University of New Brunswick, Canada.

Dr Kristin M. Johannsdottir, PhD
Former title: Manager Language Services, VANOC 2010.
Current: Researcher, University of Iceland.

Donna Wilson
Former title: Senior Vice President of Human Resources & Sustainability, VANOC 2010.
Current: V.P., Industry Services and Sustainability WorkSafe B.C.

Dana Ellis, MA
Current: PhD candidate, University of Ottawa.

Christian Akamp
Former title: Manager of Protocol, VANOC 2010.
Current: Lead Venue Protocol Manager, London Organising Committee of the Olympic Games and Paralympic Games.

Contributor information for the Sport and Sport Production expert case for the lecturer's section of the website:

Kyla Denisuik Dickey
Former title: Assistant Manager of Sport & Sport Production, VANOC 2010.
Current: Development Officer, University of Manitoba.

Joel Fitzpatrick
Former title: Rugby News Service Project Manager, Infostrada Rugby World Cup 2011.

Aurelia Ruetsch
Former title: Protocol Manager, VANOC 2010.
Current: Lead Venue Protocol Manager, London 2012 Olympic Games.

Rick Antonson
Current: President and CEO, Tourism Vancouver.

Walt Judas
Current: Vice President of Marketing Communications & Member Services, Tourism Vancouver.

Robert G. McDowell
Former title: Protocol Manager, Ceremonies, VANOC 2010.
Current: Managing Director, International Governance Associates Inc.

Daryl Wiebe, MA
Former title: Venue Commander, VANOC 2010.
Current: Superintendent, Vancouver Police Department.

Bethany Saunders
Former title: Venue Human Resources Manager, VANOC 2010.

Leah M. Hill, PE
Former title: Protocol Manager, VANOC 2010.
Current: Personal Coach.

Melissa Harder
Former title: Executive Assistant to the Vice-President Corporate Strategy, and Partner Relations, VANOC 2010.
Current: Government Relations Consultant.

Taleeb F. Noormohamed
Former: Vice-President, Corporate Strategy and Partner Relations, VANOC 2010.
Current: DPhil candidate, Oxford University.

Becca Leopkey
Current: PhD student, University of Ottawa.

Dr Eric W. MacIntosh, PhD
Current: Associate Professor, School of Human Kinetics, University of Ottawa.

Foreword

Information is power only when it is used wisely.

From a distance, big-event management can look effortless – close up it can be daunting. Under a microscope, its countless moving parts beg to be calibrated and massaged into perfect symmetry. Even for the most experienced it can be mystifying. *Managing Major Sports Events: Theory and Practice* breaks it all apart and stitches it back together in a form that even a naive rookie can embrace. The book lays out a strong blend of theoretical concepts and real-life experiences over the course of a major sports event's lifecycle. If it's likely to happen, has happened or could happen, then it's in here. The planning and execution of sports events should always be about the athlete experience, so the book is centred on what really matters.

This book lays out for sport event management researchers and practitioners a contextual foundation, examining events from a multi-dimensional perspective. It provides researchers and practitioners with concept and subject information, without turning it into a dull, standard to-do list often found scattered throughout event management books. The theory, practice, case studies, decision-making exercises (on the website), and additional suggested readings allow the reader to take away what they need to supplement their existing knowledge. Whatever you know or think you know, this gem will give you a lift, and it will give you added confidence. There is a nice balance here.

It is a thoughtful, researched, practical and sometimes entertaining work, which makes a significant contribution to the theory and practice of major sports events. It will surely become a seminal, must-read book for researchers and practitioners alike. A pocket book or cheat sheet on the edge of your desk ready to help get you through the next dilemma and the one after that. A lot better than winging it and a whole lot more reliable. Read and enjoy it.

John A. Furlong
Chief Executive Officer, Vancouver Organizing Committee for the 2010
Vancouver Olympic and Paralympic Games

Preface

Major sports events are a global phenomenon. There is an exponentially growing field of research associated with sports events. Researchers are trying to understand various aspects of sports event, such as planning, marketing, volunteers, economic impact, and legacy. Journals, academic books, and articles on this topic are proliferating. It is time to start synthesizing some of this research into one book.

Hitting the ground running, having very little training time, doing more with less, constantly dealing with change, and only having one shot to get it right is the reality of major sports event managers. Many major sports events (e.g. Olympic Games, FIFA World Cup, and Super Bowl) have books written by the event owners and/or managers. Usually, they are personal opinions of one person for one event. It is time to synthesize this information, these best practices, into one book.

Both researchers and sport event managers – whether or not this is their first major sports event – try to not see past events' (usually costly) mistakes repeated. Many areas remain to be examined by sport event researchers. We have combined our theoretical and practical strengths to offer a unique approach to this book on managing major sports events, by providing a solid theoretical and practical foundation for event managers, which we hope will "get theorists and practitioners talking", which could also foster research in underdeveloped areas within sport event management. We hope that this book helps to synthesize key literature in the sport event management field and provides suggestions for new avenues of research, while also providing managers with food for thought and best practices garnered from research and past event experience.

To do so, chapters begin with illustrative examples. Key theory on the chapter's topic is then provided. Practitioner considerations follow to emphasize areas of the chapter's topic which may or may not have been studied by researchers. Chapters include case studies from experts. Case and chapter questions, as well as the suggested further readings, allow the reader to engage with the material.

Finally, the book has a companion website (see www.routledge.com/cw/parent) for the reader/student, as well as a section for lecturers using the book for their classes. The student section includes multiple-choice questions to help test knowledge of each chapter, while the lecturer's section includes essay questions, PowerPoint slides for teaching purposes, and decision-making exercises (DMX) and answers. These DMX (also called table-top exercises) are based on true situations; they help students and event managers think through various scenarios and discuss/determine the best course of action(s). These DMX are often (and should be) used by event managers as good planning and training exercises to prepare for Games-time.

Milena Parent
Sharon Smith-Swan

Acknowledgements

We would like to thank the expert case contributors in order of their chapter contributions: Michael Chambers, Sally Rehorick, Kristin Johannsdottir, Donna Wilson, Dana Ellis, Christian Akamp, Kyla Denisiuk Dickey, Aurelia Ruetsch and Joel Fitzpatrick, Rick Antonson and Walt Judas, Robert McDowell, Daryl Weibe, Bethany Saundres, Leah Hill, Taleeb Noormohamed and Melissa Harder, Becca Leopkey, and Eric MacIntosh. We thank them for providing their personal perspectives on the topics at hand; the cases truly help to bring to life the theory and arguments made in the chapters. Thanks to all our colleagues and friends from the 2010 Vancouver Olympic Winter Games. We are thankful to our publisher, Routledge, editor, Simon Whitmore, and editorial assistant, Joshua Wells, for having provided us with the opportunity to see our theory–practice book idea materialize.

Milena would like to thank Sharon, her co-author, for her keen insights into the managerial world. She would especially like to thank her fiancé, John, and his girls, Sarena and Kate, for their patience and encouragement throughout the process. Finally, she would like to thank the Social Sciences and Humanities Research Council of Canada – Interdisciplinary and Multidisciplinary Studies Committee (grant number 410-2009-0523) for the opportunity to go to the Vancouver 2010 Games to be a secondee and undertake research on the Games.

Sharon is thankful to her co-author Milena, a gifted intellect and infinitely patient colleague. Appreciation and gratitude go to friends and family who know who they are, for their unwavering support

Abbreviations

3Cs	consumer, company, competition
4G	fourth generation
4Ps	product, price, place, promotion
5Ws	who, what, when, where, why
AIOWSF	Association of International Olympic Winter Sport Federations
AISTS	Académie Internationale des Sciences et Technologies du Sport
ANOC	Association of National Olympic Committees
ASLF	Amateur Sport Legacy Fund
ASOIF	Association of Summer Olympic International Federations
BOCOG	Beijing Organizing Committee for the Olympic Games
BOH	back-of-house
BRIC	Brazil, Russia, India, China
CAD	computer-assisted (or -aided) design
CAS	Court of Arbitration for Sport
CBA	cost–benefit analysis
CBSA	Canada Border Services Agency
CC	corporate citizenship
CCTV	closed-circuit television
CEFR	Common European Framework of Reference
CEO	chief executive officer
CF	Canadian Forces
CFC	chlorofluorocarbon
CGA	Commonwealth Games Association
CGE	computable-general-equilibrium model
CGF	Commonwealth Games Federation
COC	Canadian Olympic Committee
CONCACAF	Confederation of North, Central America and Caribbean Association Football
CP	communications protocol
CRM	Commercial Rights Management
CSIT	Confédération Sportive Internationale du Travail
CSPR	Corporate Strategy and Partner Relations

CSR/CSR$_1$	corporate social responsibility
CSR$_2$	corporate social responsiveness
CSR$_3$	corporate social rectitude
CSS	Centre for Sport and Sustainability
CWG	Commonwealth Games
DMO	destination marketing organization
EBITA	earnings before interest, taxes, and amortization costs
EFD	earliest finish date
EMBOK	Event Management Body of Knowledge
EQ	emotional intelligence
ESD	earliest start date
EURO	UEFA European Football Championships
EVS	event services
F&B	food and beverage
FA	functional area
FCC	Federal Communications Commission
FIFA	Fédération Internationale de Football Association
FINA	Fédération Internationale de Natation
FISU	International University Sports Federation
FOH	front-of-house
GDP	gross domestic product
GOT	Games Operating Trust
GPS	Global Positioning System
GRI	Global Reporting Initiative
HR	human resources
HRM	human resource management
IAAF	International Association of Athletics Federations
IBC	international broadcast centre
ICS	International Client Services
IF	international (sport) federation
IFEA	International Festivals & Events Association
ILBI	intelligent local-based information
IOA	input–output analysis
IOC	International Olympic Committee
IPC	International Paralympic Committee
IPP	international protected person
ISES	International Special Events Society
ISU	International Skating Union
KSF	key success factor
LAOOC	Los Angeles Olympic Organizing Committee
LBDQ	Leadership Behaviour Description Questionnaire
LEED	Leadership in Energy and Environmental Design
LEF	Legacy Endowment Fund
LFD	latest finish date

LMX	leader–member exchange
LOCOG	London Organising Committee of the 2012 Olympic and Paralympic Games
LPC	least preferred co-worker
LSD	latest start date
MEMOS	Executive Masters in Sport Organization Management
MESGO	Executive Masters in European Sport Governance
MMC	main media centre
MOU	Memorandum of Understanding
MPA	Multi-Party Agreement
MPC	main press centre
MSSC	Motivation Scale for Sport Consumption
NBS	Network for Business Sustainability
NFC	near-field communications
NFL	National Football League
NHL	National Hockey League
NOC	National Olympic Committee
NPC	National Paralympic Committee
NSF	national sport federation
OAC	Officials Assessment Commission
OBS	Olympic Broadcast Service
OCA	Olympic Council of Asia
OCOG	Organizing Committee for the Olympic Games
OGI	Olympic Games Impact
OGKM	Olympic Games Knowledge Management
ONS	Olympic News Service
OPMA	Olympic and Paralympic Marks Act
PASO	Pan American Sports Organization
PEA	prime event access
PERT	Programme Evaluation and Review Technique
PEST	political, economic, social, technological
PMBOK	Project Management Book of Knowledge
PPS	Project Performance Scorecard
QUANGOs	quasi autonomous non-government organizations
RCMP	Royal Canadian Mounted Police
RFID	radio frequency identification
RFP	request-for-proposals
ROI	return on investment
RSS	really simple syndication
SARS	severe acute respiratory syndrome
SCSA	Supreme Council of Sport in Africa
SII	Sports Interest Inventory
SOCOG	Sydney 2000 Organizing Committee for the Olympic Games
SPEED	Socialization, Performance, Excitement, Esteem and Diversion

STEAM	Sport Tourism Economic Assessment Model
STP	segmentation, targeting, positioning
SWOT	strengths, weaknesses, opportunities, threats
TOP	The Olympic Partners
UBC	University of British Columbia
UEFA	Union of European Football Associations
UNCED	United Nations Conference on Environment and Development
Vancouver2010-ISU	Vancouver 2010 Integrated Security Unit
VANOC	Vancouver Organizing Committee for the 2010 Olympic and Paralympic Winter Games
VGM	venue general manager
VIK	value in-kind
VIP	very important person
VMT	venue management team
VoIP	voice over internet protocol
VPD	Vancouver Police Department
VTeam	venue team
WADA	World Anti-Doping Agency
WBS	work breakdown structure
WLS	Whistler Legacies Society
WOP	Whistler Olympic Park
WSL	Whistler Sport Legacies
YOG	Youth Olympic Games
YOGINN	Youth Olympic Games Laboratory for Youth and Innovation
YVR	Vancouver International Airport

Chapter 1

Introduction: The world of major sports events

OBJECTIVES

- To understand the world of major sports events and the different types of events
- To understand that there are different theoretical perspectives which can be used to examine major sports events
- To understand the lifecycle of major sports events

ILLUSTRATIVE CASE: HOW WE ENTERED THE GAMES WORLD

Milena M. Parent's experience

During her undergraduate studies, Milena was certain she would go into sports medicine. All of her courses were in physics, chemistry, biology, physiology, and biochemistry – except for one. In the first year of her Masters in Cellular and Molecular Medicine she realized, as she was toiling on a 24-hour experiment, that she no longer wanted this career. What she also discovered while doing some web research for a requirement of her Masters programme was a Faculty of Health Sciences, School of Human Kinetics link and a prompt to Sport Administration. As a former competitive figure skater, coach, volunteer, and administrator, her interest was piqued.

Fast-forward eight months; she started an internship with the 2001 Games of La Francophonie. She realized that there was a lack of resources for understanding how to do her job; this led to an idea for a doctoral thesis. She was also bitten by the Games bug. As a Professor at the University of Ottawa, she still looked regularly for an opportunity to return to a Games experience. In November 2009 she was seconded for four months to the 2010 Vancouver Olympic Winter Games. This book is a result of her personal hands-on experience with the protocol planning and venuization for the Olympic Family, which included athletes, heads of state and government, international and domestic dignitaries, and special guests who visited the various sport venues of the 2010 Olympic Winter Games; her collaboration with her co-author and dozens of experts she worked with; as well as her academic/expert knowledge of managing major sport events.

Sharon Smith-Swan's experience

There has never been a straight line in Sharon's career. Her goal was to become a tenured professor of English at one of the two universities in her hometown of Ottawa, Ontario, Canada.

To fast-track her ambition, she decided to work for one year at Bell Canada and earn enough money to attend university with no semester breaks. The trajectory of her career changed radically when she was identified as a "female with potential". She received extensive management training and development, and rotated through customer service, training, and computer communications. A self-imposed move to British Columbia awakened her entrepreneurial spirit. She became the first female Phone Power consultant in western Canada within the telephone industry; and after two years she left to start her own training and communications business.

Over 25 years she has provided consulting, management, training, and coaching services to all sectors of business: non-profit, private, and public in communications, client sales and service, and self development. She volunteers extensively and has held the position of President of the Vancouver Special Olympics. In 2009 she was invited to join the protocol team for the 2010 Olympic and Paralympic Games in a paid position. Putting her consulting practice on hold, she immersed herself for seven months with a high-performance, fast-paced team of professionals to deliver service to the Olympic Family at all of the sport venues. One of her colleagues was Dr Milena Parent. They determined that their combined knowledge, skill set, experience, and access to "experts" could create a useful, interesting and instructive book on managing major sports events.

WHY THIS BOOK AT THIS TIME?

There is always a need for knowledge transfer and opportunity to share. However, it is frequently inadequate or incomplete because of language barriers (e.g. translation for the next organizing committee is costly and time intensive); the motivation diminishes with the completion of the event; the organization is collapsed immediately following completion; and most resource people are long gone. It became evident during our tenure with the 2010 Olympic Winter Games that there was always a lack of available resources. The expectation most frequently was to do more with less. Based on our experiences, we determined that there were processes, checklists, and exercises that could enhance the effort of any organizing committee. Our combined hands-on experience fuelled our premise that there was an opportunity to contribute to the sports world at large in both generic and specific ways.

The 2010 Vancouver Olympic Winter Games was arguably the most successful Winter Games in the history of the Olympic Games. We have tried to capture the components of that success, and combine them with examples, case studies, and experts from other major sport events to create a book for studying and for managing a successful event.

WHAT ARE EVENTS, SPORTS EVENTS, AND FESTIVALS?

Much has been written in terms of classifying events and, more specifically, sporting events and festivals. Terms such as mega-event, hallmark event, major sporting event, large-scale sporting event, and special event have all been used, sometimes interchangeably.

Most researchers in this field will start by referring to Ritchie's (1984) definition of a hallmark event being an event that can be one-time or recurring, but of a temporary nature, and whose significance provides awareness, appeal, or any other potential benefit to the host region. It is also an event which is outside the normal pattern of everyday life. Here, hallmark events are the overarching concept for all other types of events. Since then, authors such as Hall (1989, 1992, 2001) and Getz (1997) have modified that definition to include or exclude special events, mega-events and community events, as well as distinguishing one-time events from recurring (e.g. annual) events. These changes include different combinations of size, geographic span, economic return, length of event, and identification to place. Most conceptual research is of a logical/deductive nature (i.e. typologies) and/or comparisons between previous definitions, often with a focus on festivals more than sporting events (e.g. Hall, 1992). Interestingly, an overview of the definitions provided by Hall (1989, 1992, 2001) shows an evolution from very defined and specific terms to the various terms essentially becoming synonymous. Therefore, whether the terms should be separated or combined is a key question that remains unanswered, with the answer having possibly profound effects on research into such events (e.g. generalizability).

Nevertheless, some key parameters should be set for the rest of this book. In this book, we will focus first on planned (as opposed to unplanned or unforeseen) events, which are a unique combination of programme (sport in our case), people and place (Higham and Hinch, 2003; Getz, 2005). Planned events, like projects, have a pre-determined lifecycle; we know when they will start and end. These planned events are temporary in nature, and consequently, so are their organizing committees. However, there are events that fall under pulsating organizations. Pulsating organizations are those which are enduring (i.e. not finite) and have periodic (weekly, monthly, yearly, bi-annual) events they hold as a manifestation of their existence. The annual academic conference of the European Association for Sport Management would be an example of such an event.

We then limit ourselves to special events. These events are special because it could be a one-time event outside an organization's normal routines or outside participants' normal, daily lives (Getz, 2005). They typically remember the event as being singular, special, unique, etc. Events can be considered "special" if they have a combination of factors, which could include: authenticity, uniqueness, festive spirit, quality, tradition, hospitality, theme, symbolism, multiple goals, international attention, significant attendance levels, image/pride improvements to the host region (Getz, 2005; Jago and Shaw, 1999).

As well, we will focus on major sporting events, as opposed to more local/community-based sporting events, which have comparatively low levels of attendance or interest by media at large, or festivals (Jago and Shaw, 1998). Festivals are a form of cultural event or public/themed celebration (Getz, 2005). Major events include recurring hallmark events (events that are tied to a place), such as Wimbledon, and one-time mega-events, such as the Olympic Games or the FIFA (Fédération Internationale de Football Association) World

Cup. Hallmark events, such as the Calgary Stampede, are typically embedded within a community and provide it with a competitive advantage by being hosted annually. They are imbued with tradition and quality. In turn, mega-events, such as the World Expositions (e.g. Expo 2012 Yeosu, Korea) or the NFL's (National Football League) Super Bowl, are defined as those events which by their size or significance will provide significant media attention, financial/economic impact, attendance/tourism, and prestige to the host region, venue, and/or organization (Getz, 2005). Major sporting events also include other large-scale sporting events, such as the Commonwealth Games (CWG), Jeux de la Francophonie, or Pan American Games. These events are of international nature, attract many delegations and international media, and provide benefits/legacies for the host region. These types of events are increasingly popular with host regions as they are smaller than mega-events (easier to host logistically speaking), yet provide many of the same types of legacies and benefits. Examples of large-scale sporting events now include niche market events such as the Winter World Transplant Games, the X Games, the World Dwarf Games, the World Police & Fire Games, the Military World Games, the Muslim Women's Games, the World Peace Games, the Journalist World Games, the World Masters Games, as well as "regional" events such as the Asian Games, the All-Africa Games, the Asian Beach Games, and the Pan Arab Games. While such large-scale sporting events might not attract as many spectators as the Olympic Games or the FIFA World Cup, they can attract an equal or sometimes greater number of participants. For example, the 2011 World Police & Fire Games in New York City had 15,000 athletes (2011 World Police & Fire Games, 2011) and the 2009 Sydney World Masters Games attracted 30,000 participants (Torino 2013 World Masters Games, 2009)! In comparison, the 2008 Beijing Olympic Games attracted 10,942 athletes (International Olympic Committee, 2010a). Regardless, concepts presented in this book for major sports events can also usually be applied to smaller events or festivals. Figure 1.1 provides a typology of sports events, which stems in part from Jago and Shaw (1998) and Getz (2005).

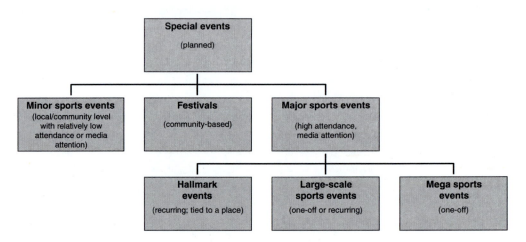

Figure 1.1 A typology of major sports events.

THEORIES AND APPROACHES USED TO STUDY SPORTS EVENTS

In academia, many approaches can be used to study sporting events. These include:

- *Anthropology*: Here, the celebratory aspect of events is often showcased and the community is often a focus (see, for example, Carey *et al.*, 2011; Chalip, 2006; O'Brien and Chalip, 2008; O'Brien, 2007).
- *Economics*: This popular approach focuses on economic impacts of events on tourism, residents and the host community/region/country more broadly, but also on leveraging events (see, for example, Chalip and Leyns, 2002; Crompton, 1995; Matheson, 2009; Preuss, 2005, 2006; Taks *et al.*, 2011).
- *Geography*: Researchers using this approach typically examine spatial patterns and resource needs, temporal patterns (e.g. a calendar of events in a community), and an event's impact on the community and the environment (see, for example, Dawson, 2011; Gibson *et al.*, 2005; Giulianotti and Klauser, 2010; Oliver, 2011).
- *History*: Here, evolution, lifecycles, and developments of aspects of events – or events as a whole – are typically the focus (see, for example, Bridges, 2011; Gupta, 2009; Legg *et al.*, 2009; Mangan, 2011; McCartney and Osti, 2007).
- *Management and marketing*: This popular approach includes organizational theory and behaviour, as well as strategic management concepts such as leadership, marketing and sponsorship, ambush marketing and branding, human resource management, decision making, organizational structure, and stakeholder management (see, for example, Parent, 2008, 2010; Parent *et al.*, 2009a; Parent and Séguin, 2007, 2008; Séguin and O'Reilly, 2008; Xing and Chalip, 2009).
- *Political science*: This approach examines the politicians and the politics of wanting and bidding for events (see, for example, Burbank *et al.*, 2001; Emery, 2002; Gillon, 2011).
- *Psychology*: Researchers using this approach typically examine participants' motives for attending events, using theories associated with needs, wants, and motives (see, for example, Jarvis and Blank, 2011; Nelson, 2009; Roy *et al.*, 2010; Snelgrove *et al.*, 2008; Uhrich and Koenigstorfer, 2009).
- *Sociology*: This popular approach examines events as mini-societies, as impacting (or being impacted by) society/the community, often from a political or cultural perspective (see, for example, Gyongyi and Krawczyk, 1982; Lenskyj, 1996, 2000; Ndlovu-Gatsheni, 2011a; Whitson and Macintosh, 1993, 1996).

Sport event management researchers are using a combination of these approaches to study events. They also use different theories such as the resource dependence perspective and the decision-making literature (e.g. Theodoraki, 2001), regime theory (e.g. Burbank *et al.*, 2001), Elias' game theory and more general critical theory approach (e.g. Lenskyj, 1996, 2000), and the literature on temporary and pulsating organizations (e.g. Hanlon and Cuskelly, 2002; Pipan and Porsander, 2000; Porsander, 2000). In addition, researchers looking at volunteers have used the literature on (volunteer) motivation, satisfaction and commitment to describe why they get involved in such events, how they stay committed and how happy they are (e.g. Costa *et al.*, 2006; MacLean and Hamm, 2007; Treuren, 2009).

While the literature is on the right track regarding the use/application of theories from other fields, research pertaining to sports events is still relatively young. Some researchers are using theories to understand certain aspects of sports events as noted above, and some researchers are trying to develop theories related to other aspects of events. However, most researchers are still employing a rather descriptive and/or definitional approach. More important, though, is the fact that there are many functions within events that remain under-researched, if at all. Our hope with this book is that new avenues of research can be explored and theory developed.

Before getting into these different functions in the upcoming chapters, we provide an overview of the sport event management world and the lifecycle of major sports events.

THE SPORT EVENT MANAGEMENT WORLD

With the variety of sports events in the world, no single entity directs the industry. Instead, it is a combination of different rights holders and other stakeholders (e.g. sport federations, sponsors, and broadcasters), as well as professional associations, which provide the parameters for the events and event managers.

Within the international sport world, we find the International Olympic Committee (IOC; www.olympic.org/), rights holder of the Olympic Games and Olympic Winter Games. The IOC sets out the rules for inclusion of sports within the Games, and accreditation parameters for the various stakeholders. The IOC also oversees the general preparations for each edition of its Olympic Games through its coordination commissions. The International Paralympic Committee (IPC; www.paralympic.org/IPC) has the same responsibilities as the IOC but for the Paralympic Games. While the Olympic Games and Paralympic Games are two distinct events, today they are awarded simultaneously to the same host city and organized by the same organizing committee. The IOC and IPC are international, non-profit organizations. They are represented in each country by their respective National Olympic/Paralympic Committees (NOC, NPC).

In order to promote sport and foster athletic excellence, the IOC created the Pan American Games, the Asian Games, and the All-Africa Games. The Pan American Games are held under the auspices of the Pan American Sports Organization (PASO), the Asian Games under the Olympic Council of Asia (OCA), and the All-Africa Games under the Supreme Council of Sport in Africa (SCSA).

While the IOC and IPC are the rights holders for the Olympic and Paralympic Games, it is the international sport federations (IFs) who determine athletes' eligibility for the Olympic and Paralympic Games. Each IF is in charge of the worldwide governance of its sport, including rules, regulations and competition structures. IFs also choose the locations of their world championships and world cup events. IFs can be single-sport or multi-sport in nature. IFs typically acknowledge only one national sport federation (NSF) per country for their sport. In the case of aquatic sports in Canada, which include Swimming Canada, Diving Canada, Synchro Canada, and Water Polo Canada, the Fédération Internationale de Natation (FINA) cannot recognize all of these NSFs. Thus, the Aquatic Federation of Canada was formed to be the voice of Olympic aquatic sports nationally and internationally. As well, most of the national sport organizations, federations, and/or associations have some form of state, provincial, local/municipal organizational representation. This could be in the form of a local sport organization (e.g. local figure skating club) or be within the school system.

Similarly to the IOC, some IFs have created continental sport federations. For example, FIFA created six continental football/soccer federations, such as the Confederation of North, Central America and Caribbean Association Football (CONCACAF, www.concacaf.com/page/Home/0,,12813,00.html), to assist in the administration and promotion of the sport.

The popularity of international major sports events has led to the creation of a multitude of other Games with their respective international rights holding organization. For example, we have the Commonwealth Games Federation (CGF; www.thecgf.com) and its CWG, the Organisation Internationale de la Francophonie (www.jeux.francophonie.org) and its Games of La Francophonie, and the International University Sports Federation (FISU, www.fisu.net/en/Accueil-950.html) and its Universiades. Other increasingly popular Games include the Confédération Sportive Internationale du Travail (CSIT, www.csit.tv/en/menu_main/about-us) and its CSIT World Sports Games (or Workers' Games), the Arctic Winter Games (www.arcticwintergames.org), the Military World Games (www.cism-milsport.org/eng/001_HOME/001_homepage.asp), the World Masters Games (www.imga.ch), and the Mediterranean Games (www.cijm.org.gr/en/home). We also find Games related to the Sport for All movement (www.fispt.org) and the Special Olympics (www.specialolympics.org).

Besides these international, regional/continental sport federations and Games organizations, we find a variety of international sport federation/organization assemblies and associations. For example, the World Anti-Doping Agency (WADA; www.wada-ama.org) ensures the promotion, coordination, and monitoring of doping in sport. The Court of Arbitration for Sport (CAS; www.tas-cas.org/news) is the highest tribunal for resolving sport-related disputes. We also find assemblies of NOCs and IFs, such as in the Association of National Olympic Committees (ANOC), Association of Summer Olympic International Federations (ASOIF), and Association of International Olympic Winter Sport Federations (AIOWSF). Finally, many, if not all, of the preceding organizations are also part of Sport-Accord (www.sportaccord.com/en), an umbrella organization created to unite, support, and promote its Olympic and non-Olympic sports members.

Thus, we see that the international sport event context includes a variety of single-sport and multi-sport organizations, federations, assemblies, and associations. All of these organizations, it is worth noting, can be influenced (to varying degrees) by external stakeholders, notably their sponsors, the media, and the general public. Figure 1.2 provides an illustration of the various components of the international sport event world.

Nevertheless, sports events require (sport) event managers. While we may not have demographics specific to event managers – a potential area of study – we do have some information on the broader meeting planners (though these demographics likely differ from sport event managers based on our own personal experience and observations): (1) gender: there seems to be a larger percentage in Europe and especially North America of women; (2) age: most planners fall within the 25–54 age range, with most planners being between 35 and 44 years of age; (3) education and experience: most planners had industry-based (as opposed to academic) training, with an average of ten years of experience (Robson, 2011).

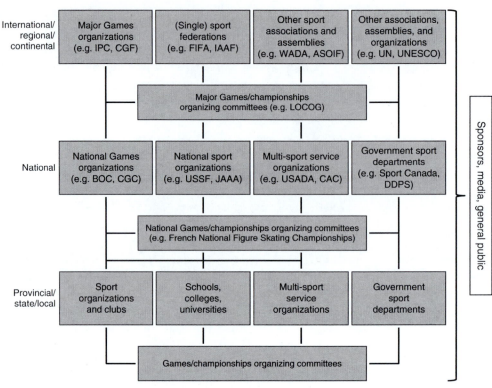

Legend:
IPC: International Paralympic Committee; CGF: Commonwealth Games Federation;
FIFA: Fédération Internationale de Football Association; IAAF: International Amateur Athletic Federation;
WADA: World Anti-Doping Agency; ASOIF: Association of Summer Olympic International Federations; UN: United Nations;
UNESCO: United Nations Educational, Scientific and Cultural Organization; LOCOG: London 2012 Organizing Committee for the Olympic and Paralympic Games; BOA: British Olympic Association; CGC: Commonwealth Games Canada;
USSF: United States Soccer Federation; JAAA: Jamaican Amateur Athletic Association; ISADA: United States Anti-Doping Association;
CAC: Coaching Association of Canada; DDPS: Swiss Federal Department of Defence, Civil Protection and Sport

Figure 1.2 The international sport event world.

While there are no sport event-specific certifications (yet), sport event managers have a variety of options for skills learning, training, and certification. The International Special Events Society (ISES; www.ises.com) and the International Festivals & Events Association (IFEA; www.ifea.com/joomla1_5/index.php) both provide event manager certification programmes. As well, given that sports events are often seen as mega projects, the Project Management Institute offers a variety of certification programmes for project management, programme management professionals, and risk management professionals, over and beyond its popular Project Management Book of Knowledge (PMBOK) global standards guide. There is now an event-specific body of knowledge, the Event Management Body of Knowledge (EMBOK) created by the International EMBOK society (www.embok.org/index.php), which provides an overview of core values, processes, and phases, as well as five core domains or functional areas (FAs). Table 1.1 offers an overview of all four components of the EMBOK. Finally, an interesting resource is William O'Toole's website (www.epms.net); O'Toole is a 30-year event management veteran and offers a variety of tools and information for event managers through his event project management system.

Table 1.1 Overview of the event management body of knowledge

Component	Aspects	
Phases	Initiation; planning; implementation; the event; closure	
Processes	Assess; select; monitor; document; communicate	
Core values	Creativity; strategic (thinking); continuous improvement; ethics; integration	
Domains	Administration	Financial management; human resource management; information management; procurement management; stakeholder management; systems management; time management
	Design	Catering; content; entertainment; environment; production; programme; theme
	Marketing	Marketing plan management; materials management; merchandise management; promotion management; public relations management; sales management; sponsorship management
	Operations	Attendee management; communications management; infrastructure management; logistics management; participant management; site management; technical management
	Risk	Compliance management; decision management; emergency management; health and safety management; insurance management; legal management; security management

Source: Based on www.embok.org/index.php; Silvers and Nelson, 2009.

An increasing number of sport organizations are also aligning themselves with universities to offer Executive Masters' programmes for sport managers. The IOC recognizes, for example, the International Olympic Academy (Olympia, Greece; www.ioa.org.gr), which offers a Masters' programme (with the University of Peloponnese) and a post-graduate seminar, as well as the Executive Masters in Sport Organizations Management (MEMOS; www.idheap.ch/MEMOS) delivered by professors from over ten universities worldwide. FIFA has the FIFA Masters (www.cies.ch/cies/fifa-master) in collaboration with the International Centre for Sport Studies through three European universities. Finally, a few European sport organizations are partners in the Executive Masters in European Sport Governance (MESGO; www.mesgo.org) along with five European universities.

Of course, one can also learn on the job. This is often the case with sport event managers who were athletes and/or officials/referees before; they therefore know the athlete's/official's perspective of an event. As well, one may also learn by being a volunteer for a small- or large-scale sports event. Finally, being an employee of a major sports event allows an individual to become a highly sought-after consultant or even a "Games gypsy". A Games gypsy is one who has been "bitten by the Games bug", and seeks that Games-time adrenaline-rush experience by going from one Games to another (Olympic or otherwise). These individuals are full of useful knowledge on Games planning and operations for newcomers to the event world.

THE LIFECYCLE OF A SPORTS EVENT

Parent (2008) described the lifecycle of a major international sports event from beginning to end. There are three modes through which an organizing committee passes. First, we find the planning mode. This mode starts with the bid phase, which typically lasts 1–3 years, depending on the exact event. If the bid committee is successful in obtaining the right to host the event, then a transition happens, transforming the bid committee into the organizing committee. A successful transition should take about six to eight months. During this time, a leader is chosen, and he or she will create the overall strategic plan and organizing committee chart. At this point the organizing committee is in its business plan phase. The operational plan phase is next. It highlights the responsibilities to be fulfilled by each FA. The operational plan is an extension of the terms of reference from the business plan; it provides more detail, and it keeps an eye on the budget. The organizing committee then "breaks up" the operational plan into the divisional plans phase or work packages phase for each FA (mini-versions of the operational plan).

Most of the second half of its life is spent in the implementation mode. The implementation mode starts with the venuization of the divisional plans into venue plans. The venue plans phase sees the combination of the various divisional plans into each of the venues, providing for a "day in the life of" perspective. The organizing committee then moves into the actual Games-time phase, which can last upwards of 17 days (for an Olympic Games) or even a month (for a FIFA World Cup), including venuizing the members (moving from headquarters to the venues).

Once the closing ceremonies are completed, the organizing committee enters its third and final mode, the wrap-up mode. This mode typically lasts between six months and one year. During this time, the remaining members of the organizing committee – most members' contracts finish by the end of the closing ceremonies – get together to write the final report(s) and manage the event's legacy.

Of course, this is an ideal lifecycle; but it still provides a general guide for sport event managers. The transition is particularly important, as is the planning mode, since both provide the foundation for the actual hosting of the event. Figure 1.3 provides an illustration of the event lifecycle over a hypothetical Olympic Games. The rest of the book provides details for each of the planning, implementation, and wrap-up modes.

OVERVIEW OF THE BOOK

This book is not meant to be a how-to encyclopaedia for organizing sports events. Nevertheless, the collection of chapters covers the broad span of a major sports event's lifecycle using a comprehensive set of themes, functions, and issues dealt with by sport event managers. As well, the book is meant to present current research pertaining to the various topics at hand, and promote research where none or little currently exists. Thus, the book provides a combined theory–practice approach.

Each chapter will start with an illustrative case/story/example, followed by the existing theory behind the topic. The theory will then be supplemented by the practitioner's perspective, that is, aspects a manager should pay particular attention to which have yet to

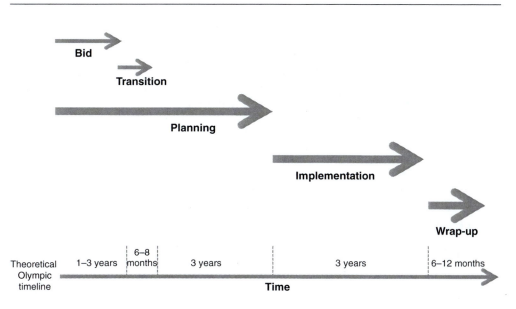

Figure 1.3 The major sports event lifecycle.

emerge in the literature. Each chapter will conclude with a summary, a case provided by an expert (with questions), general questions on the theory and practice pertaining to the topic at hand, and suggestions for further reading and knowledge development for both researchers and practitioners.

FURTHER READING

For further readings on the management of sport organizations, events, and on the Olympic governance system, we suggest:

Chappelet, J.-L. & Kübler-Mabbot, B. (2008) *The International Olympic Committee and the Olympic system: The Governance of World Sport*, London, Routledge.

Page, S. & Connell, J. (2011) *The Routledge Handbook of Events*, London, Routledge.

Slack, T. & Parent, M. M. (2006) *Understanding Sport Organizations: The Application of Organization Theory*, Champaign, IL, Human Kinetics.

Chapter 2

Bidding for an event

OBJECTIVES

- To understand the bid process, reasons for undertaking a bid, and what is required of a successful bid
- To understand the stakeholders, considerations, and issues involved in a bid process
- To understand the importance of the leader in a bid process

ILLUSTRATIVE CASE: LONDON VERSUS PARIS FOR THE 2012 OLYMPIC GAMES BID

When the 2012 Olympic Games candidate cities were first evaluated, London was in third place, behind Paris and Madrid, due in part to its "obsolete" (Fraser, 2005: 1), problematic transportation system. So for 14 months London had to play catch-up if it wanted to win. Bring in Lord Sebastian Coe, two-time Olympic gold medallist, and London chief executive Keith Mills. They put on an "aggressive" (Keogh and Fraser, 2005: 1) international campaign to win over IOC members. Lord Coe also addressed the transportation system problem.

By the time of the next evaluation, it became a two-man, or rather a two-city, race of two old rivals for the right to host the 2012 Olympic Games: Paris with its high evaluation scores (almost nothing to critique – BBC Sport, 2005) and London with its much stronger evaluation and some momentum. Paris was still the favourite going into the 6 July 2005 vote in Singapore. Madrid also had an excellent bid and was a rival during most of the voting. But, ultimately, London won by a vote of 54–50 against Paris. So what made London the winner?

There seems to be a general agreement that the "Lord Coe factor" (with Keith Mills) was significant. Lord Coe was said to have delivered "a stunning performance, it was statesman-like" (BBC correspondent John Rawling, as quoted by Fraser, 2005: 1) Lord Coe was also smart in his approach during the final presentation: he brought his passion and history/experi-ence with the Games. He focused his message on youth (the future of the Olympic Games and a key interest of the IOC with its new Youth Olympic Games (YOG)) – having 30 of a possible 100-member delegation in the room during the presentation be local youth – and on legacy, another key interest of the IOC. This legacy came in the form of a venue plan which would reinvigorate London's East End, resulting in forecasted social and sport benefits.

London's plan was for a compact but also non-wasteful/non-white elephant Games (white elephants being a critique of many past Games), where temporary venues would be used and then moved post-Games to regions elsewhere in the UK that had need of these venues. The total estimated cost for the London Games was also lower than for Paris. In addition, for London to win, it had to find a chink in the nearly flawless Paris armour. One such chink could be the French habit of having workers' strikes during the summer; if London had the unions on side to say that they would not strike, then that would be a point in their favour.

Nevertheless, it is important to know that we cannot know for sure what was in each IOC member's mind when they voted in the secret ballot. But London was the winner and host of the 2012 Olympic Games.

THE THEORY BEHIND BIDDING FOR EVENTS

While most research in sport event management focuses on the planning, Games-time, and/ or outcomes, researchers have started to examine the bid phase. It is worth noting that more needs to be done in this area, but figuring out how to predict who will win should not be a central focus as the vote casting is ultimately done by human beings in a secret manner. Thus, we will likely never truly know what goes on in each member's mind the moment they cast their ballots in each of the different voting rounds. This does not mean, however, that we cannot examine the components of a "quality" bid and help bid committee members in their tasks. The following provides an overview of what we currently know about bidding for major sports events, including: the bid process, reasons for bidding, stakeholders involved in the bidding and hosting of events, and other bid considerations.

The bid process

Bid processes usually start with someone having an idea such as "Wouldn't it be great if we were able to host . . .!" The bid founders will conceptualize the idea and establish objectives for the bid and the subsequent event. Ideas about the who (bid/event partners, other stake-holders to involve, other stakeholders who would be impacted by the event), what (event), when (timeline), where (location), and why (reasons and benefits) are determined. An initial analysis of the situation and of potential competitors (if there is a formal bid procedure) is also needed (Masterman, 2004). A fit between the event, the location/host region, and the people to do the event is important as well. Often, an initial business plan may be created or needed. If the business plan is needed, then aspects such as the details of the event, management team, marketing, and finances (with a case for financial assistance if needed) are important and need to be included (Getz, 2005).

The next step is to do a feasibility study. A City of Winnipeg (Canada) manager once noted (interview, 8 November 2003) that their feasibility requirements included the following: a facility review and assessment; the event fit-out requirements (e.g. electronics, mechanical, retail, decoration works); hosting capability (e.g. accommodation for athletes/participants, hotels, food preparation and distribution, volunteer requirements, very important persons (VIP) requirements); internal and external transportation capability (i.e. within the host region (public transportation), to the host region (e.g. airport capacity), and by the event organizers, that is, the Games transportation system); community support; sport expertise (e.g. officiating, equipment); and economic impact projections.

Economic impact analyses are still a highly debated process in the sport event management literature. When and how to do the data collection, which multipliers to use, who to include (e.g. tourists only versus including some residents), what to do about time switchers, what to do about the infrastructure built for the event but that would have been built anyway at a later date, what to do about the use of full-year employment equivalents, what to include in terms of participant expenditures, and what kind of leakages to include are all debated issues for an economic impact analysis done post-event. Moreover, the outcome is often inflated towards the positive (sometimes up to ten times what it truly is), and consulting firms who undertake such analyses often do not provide their full methodologies, thus making their results questionable due to the lack of transparency. For more information on economic impact analyses, we direct the reader to Chapter 14.

So, if it is hard to actually analyse the economic impact of an event when it has just ended, imagine trying to forecast what that impact would be for an event one, two, four, seven, or ten years down the road. Very detailed data must be obtained from the previous edition of the event, as well as from the local context – as multipliers, for example, are not only industry-dependent but also location-dependent – in order to begin to forecast an economic impact. Such an analysis also requires one to be good at predicting what the economy will look like when the event takes place. The organizers of the 2010 Vancouver Olympic Winter Games, for example, could not have foreseen the worldwide economic recession that hit in 2007 when they were planning the bid in 2001–2003, as the economic indications at that time were very positive.

Instead of relying on traditional economic impact analyses, potential event bidders can opt to do a cost–benefit analysis (Taks et al., 2011). Késenne (2005) suggested that only a cost–benefit analysis can provide governments with the desired information to argue for an event. Essentially, this type of analysis compares the consumer surplus and expenditures of the local population (consumption) with the production and opportunity costs. The consumer surplus is the difference between what a consumer is willing to pay for an event and the amount he must pay to attend that event. In turn, the opportunity costs should include such elements as crowding out (e.g. losing regular tourists because rooms are reserved for Games-specific participants or tourists), importing leakages, and impacts on the local (un) employment rate (e.g. is the event taking employees from somewhere else – which would be a cost – or from the unemployed). In Késenne's (2005) opinion, the different approaches for economic impact analyses are "all a bit fuzzy" when compared to a cost–benefit analysis.

After potential event bidders have completed their feasibility study, and assuming the cost–benefit analysis is positive, the next step is to find support from the host region's politicians and businesses. If there is no formal bidding procedure, obtaining support from the local politicians and businesses marks the end of the "bid"; organizers can start preparing for the event (see also Masterman, 2004, 2009).

If there is a formal bidding process – meaning the need to formally obtain the right to host the event from the rights holder (e.g. national or international sport organizations) – bid managers enter into the formal bid process at this point. A formal bidding process typically takes 1–3 years to complete. There may be a:

- regional/provincial competition (for regional/provincial and national events);
- national competition (for national and international events); and
- international competition (for international events).

Should the bid be successful, the bid committee will obtain the rights and/or be given a sanction (a good thing in this case) to host the event and attract the appropriate and desired athletes. The bid committee will then enter a transition period (usually no more than 6–8 months) in which the bid organization officially ceases to exist and the organizing committee is created.

Reasons for bidding

Throughout the bidding process, bid managers must determine and present their (and the region's) reasons for bidding. Emery (2002) suggested that the main reasons for organizations to get involved in the hosting of a major sports event include: the promotion of sport (ranked as the most important in his study); economic development (second most important); heightening the area's profile (third most important); increasing facilities, health and fitness, and stimulating tourism. Black and Peacock (2011) add that for developmental states like the BRIC countries (Brazil, Russia, India, China), bids are used by countries to signal concepts of modernity, legitimacy, and success to the international community. The bid should tell the world: "We have arrived."

These are standard reasons seen for many different sports events. It is worth noting, however, that it is a myth to argue for an event on the basis of increasing sport participation as there is currently no evidence that this occurs in a significant, lasting way. At best we can say that there is a temporary, local increase; but this increase is highly dependent on facility and sport organization capacities – both of which are often unprepared for any heightened sport participation interest. Similarly, the sport-for-development reason has been critiqued for its limitations such as low sport participation rates for girls, lack of substance in programmes, and contradictions between stated goals of the programmes and the on-the-ground reality (see Levermore, 2011).

In turn, Turner and Westerbeek (2004; Westerbeek et al., 2002) have argued that there are four macro-level components (political, economic/tourism, architecture/planning, and psychological/community aspects) and eight related key success factors for bids: accountability, political support, relationship marketing, ability to organize, infrastructure, bid team composition, communication and exposure, and existing facilities. They are described in Table 2.1.

While the above reasons are relatively standard and accepted in the literature, as well as being relatively rational reasons for wanting to host a sporting event, Emery (2002) noted that local politicians typically selected and sanctioned bids through an informal process. This may be due, however, to the fact that few cities, regions, and/or nations have had official event-hosting policies in the past – this situation is changing though (see Leopkey et al., 2010 for more information). Emery added that these politicians have typically been driven by political reasons, not detailed/objective analyses in their responses. Politicians were more likely to approve a bid if there was image synergy between the region and event, a good media profile (especially television), low financial costs, and the potential for

Table 2.1 Macro-components and key success factors for event bidding

Macro-component	Key success factor (KSF)	KSF description
Political Enhancing destination image and ideology, enhancing politicians' positions	Bid team composition	The need for a mix of talented (experts) and influential people on the bid committee
	Political support	Increased government involvement in bid processes (securing resources, political stability and financial stability)
Economic/tourism Direct and indirect economic benefits, tourism increases	Communication and exposure	The combination of the host region's reputation with communication/technological systems for national/global media exposure
	Ability to organize	Event organization and management expertise
Psychological/community Competency, self-efficacy, sense of pride of the community, tourists, and participants	Accountability	The dependent relationship the event bidder has with the event owner and the general public
	Relationship marketing	The power the people forming the bid committee have and their related influence on key decision-makers
Architectural Venue and accommodation analysis/allocation, transportation requirements, media services	Infrastructure	Location and accessibility of the proposed sites for the event
	Existing facilities	Pre-existing high-quality facilities related to spectator accommodation and other established facilities

community involvement. Turner and Westerbeek (2004) also noted that the strength of government support for a bid can be notably seen in the level of spending, but also in having special government agencies/groups involved in securing the bid.

Stakeholders involved in bidding and hosting events

So far, we have mentioned different stakeholders (e.g. local politicians/governments, businesses, IFs) as we discussed the bid process. When bidding for and preparing a sports event, the organizing committee has a number of stakeholders with which to deal. Stakeholder theory (see notably Donaldson and Preston, 1995; Friedman *et al.*, 2004; Freeman, 1984; Kaler, 2006; Parent and Deephouse, 2007; Phillips *et al.*, 2003) traditionally argues that the "focal organization" would be the top management or board of directors, and anyone else needs to be managed.

Turner and Westerbeek (2004: 350) suggested that the bid organization needs to show the event owner has "a highly specialized network of relationships", which is determined by the macro-components and key success factors noted earlier. They argued that the key or focal relationship during the bid is between the event owner – who has the event rights and therefore ultimate decision-making power – and the event bidder(s). The media, sponsors, and event participants influence this relationship. As well, the media, sponsors, government/politicians, city, facilities, consumer/community, and NSFs all have dyadic relationships with the event bidder. Turner and Westerbeek added that special interests groups present an indirect influence on these relationships. However, these suggestions are theoretical in nature, remaining to be empirically verified. For example, are they truly dyadic relationships or is the network of these relationships more integrated or coupled? Is this the only governance structure that can lead to a successful bid outcome or are there different options of governance structures? These are only some of the questions that remain to be answered about event bidding processes by the researchers.

From a more general perspective, Parent (2008; Parent and Deephouse, 2007) argued that organizing committees of major sports events deal with a key set of stakeholder groups. The staff and volunteers are the first (internal) stakeholder group. Externally, we find the various levels of government, the media, the community (residents, community groups and schools, and activists) and local business and tourism organizations, national and international sponsors (for larger sports event), the sport organizations (federations and other sport organizations, such as other event organizing committees as well as professional leagues for the "use" of professional players at the Olympic Games like golf, tennis, basketball, ice hockey), and the delegations. Other stakeholders can also be involved, such as consultants and international non-governmental agencies like the United Nations (see Parent, 2012). Figure 2.1 illustrates this stakeholder map (partly based on Parent, 2008, 2012; Parent and Deephouse, 2007). While this map presents a dyadic view of stakeholder relationships with the organizing committee, research is needed to understand the degree to which we find dyadic ties or more tightly coupled network-like relationships (i.e. more relationships between the different stakeholders).

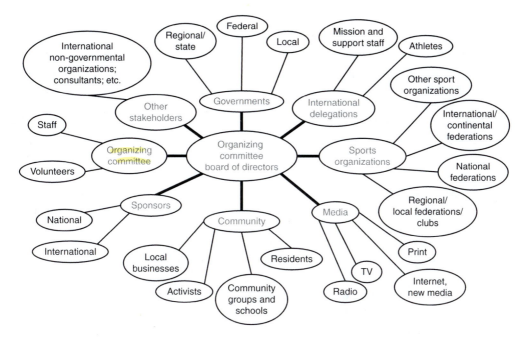

Figure 2.1 A major sports event's stakeholder map.

Nevertheless, what is important to note is that the stakeholder map is dependent on the event manager's own cognitive map or perception of who is seen to be legitimate and therefore seen as a stakeholder. This is an issue especially for activists, as managers within an organizing committee often dismiss activists as pesky annoyances, but they can cause problems for the organizing committee if they are not properly managed. One way to do so would be to co-opt them into the organizing committee, such as the Sydney 2000 Organizing Committee for the Olympic Games (SOCOG) did with Greenpeace for the 2000 Olympic Games, thereby essentially stopping them from being able to criticize the organizing committee as they were now part of it. Notwithstanding, a sport event manager's cognitive (stakeholder) map will depend on where the manager sits in the hierarchy (top-, middle-, or lower-level manager), on the individual's roles and responsibilities (e.g. sport operations versus government relations), as well as on personal characteristics (e.g. past experience, network of contacts) (Parent and Deephouse, 2007).

Bid considerations

Various factors are found to assist in successfully obtaining the right to host a major sports event. We group them into internal, process, and external factors (see Emery, 2002; Merkel and Kim, 2011; Turner and Westerbeek, 2004; Walters, 2011):

- Internal factors:
  - maximizing bid team composition to ensure the inclusion of experts with relevant professional credibility;
  - showing the capability to host the event (e.g. based on past event hosting by the members and by the region);
  - number of past bid attempts.
- Process factors:
  - having a complete understanding of the requirements and of formal and informal decision-making processes (i.e. knowledge of networks, people, politics, and processes);
  - not assuming that decision-makers are experts, or that they use rational criteria for selection;
  - customizing (in)tangible products/services for the event and exceeding expectation of the event owners.
- External factors:
  - knowing the bid's strengths and weaknesses relative to the bid committee's competition;
  - agendas and influences of different stakeholders;
  - local, regional, and/or national policies (governments and sport federations).

One of the key aspects here is to truly know the formal and informal networks, people, and processes to understand how the politics of bidding occur. Thus, both formal and informal processes are equally important.

Questions to ask when preparing a bid

Related to the above factors, a set of questions needs to be asked when preparing a bid to ensure that it is the "right thing to do" and that the bid committee has a chance of being successful in obtaining the right to host the event (based on Emery, 2002; Lenskyj, 1996; Xing *et al.*, 2008):

■ Has the bid already been won by another (i.e. is there an implicit favourite)?
■ Is this "only" the first try for this event? Is this a "practice run"?
■ Is the bid a serious strategic decision for the host region or is it just a political ploy?
■ Does the city/region/country actually need to win the bid to garner the benefits?
■ What does the urban regime look like? How supportive is the community? How involved are the community and the other local stakeholders?
   – Is there a need for a plebiscite/referendum?
   – Should alliances be built between local political parties and/or with other stakeholders?
■ Are there formal structures that facilitate activism (or a history of activism in the region)? Can they be co-opted into the bid process?
■ What is the fit between the image/description of the city and that of the event?
■ What is the bid's marketing strategy?

Issues faced by a bid committee

Throughout the bid process, the bid committee will face different issues. Parent (2008) and Xing *et al.* (2008) suggest a number of them, including:

■ politics: power plays, politicians' involvement for personal reasons, government support, inter-city competition, egos, and protocol consideration;
■ relationships, participation, and interdependence: building relationships, involving different stakeholders as partners (e.g. aboriginal community) in the bid process versus keeping them at arm's length (e.g. activists), discussing/negotiating with stakeholders, managing expectations, coordination between stakeholders, communication, and information management;
■ finance: budget forecasting/creation, sponsorship considerations, and marketing considerations;
■ planning and organizing: planning, structure, decision-making process, deadlines, effectiveness;
■ infrastructure, operations, and logistics: public transportation, choosing to use existing facilities, proposing venues and facilities, proposing ceremonies/cultural events, security and contingencies, Games transportation plans, accommodation plans, tourism considerations, weather considerations, and municipal service needs;
■ legacy: legacy suggestions, new facilities, knowledge-management processes;
■ media and visibility: gaining media support and coverage, reputation and image building, and public/corporate support;

■ human resources: staff and volunteer needs, choice and use of bid/Games ambassadors and experts, choice of leadership, motivation, teamwork.

THE PRACTITIONER'S PERSPECTIVE ON BIDDING

When Vancouver, British Columbia won the bid to host the 2010 Olympic Winter Games in 2003, 64 per cent of the residents had agreed in a referendum to support them. The IOC indicated that a deciding factor was the agreement of a major special interest group, the Four Host First Nations, on whose traditional and shared-traditional lands much of the Games would be hosted. There were dissident factions that continued to protest despite the referendum results. The CEO (chief executive officer) who led the bid process, John Furlong, had the unwavering support of the Chairman of the bid committee's and organizing committee's board of directors, Jack Poole.

The tireless work of the bidding process is realistically just the beginning. Significant to the process is choosing the right person at the right time for the bid's leadership position and simultaneously managing the resistance in the communities that will host the venues. From a practitioner's perspective, there are therefore quite a few issues to consider for a bid: support for a bid, activists and social issues, bid votes, and human resource choices. Each is described below.

Support for a bid

The support of the residents of a region/country has been deemed an important and potentially defining part of the bid process. However, can we trust the bid country's survey statistics? The bidders of the 2008 Beijing (summer) Olympic Games indicated they had 99 per cent support from their population during their bid process. The politics of the country suggest that residents would not dare disagree. In an attempt to balance potentially skewed results, the IOC now conducts its own independent surveys.

Support should be built early and swell during the bid process. The bid corporation is typically staffed by volunteers with the requisite competencies and driven by successful charismatic and influential businesspersons. Vancouver's bid for 2010 was spearheaded by Jack Poole, who was well known and respected in the business community. He appointed his protégé, John Furlong, as CEO. This formidable duo was staggeringly successful in co-opting and gaining support, building momentum, and managing challenges before and during the Games.

Part of the support needs to also come from the (host) governments. As mentioned in the theory section, such support is often not based on rational decisions. Notwithstanding, a key part of the decision to support a bid is a financial one. The budget size, potential for economic return, and the current world and/or country economic situation all impact the choice to support – or withdraw – a bid. The withdrawing of support was seen in the Italian government deciding not to provide financial backing guarantees for Rome's 2020 Olympic Games bid because of the country's economic difficulties in 2011–2012. This forced the bid committee to withdraw its bid from the 2020 race.

Activists, social issues, and bids

In countries where activists have been better organized, there is an opportunity to work with them to mitigate potential backlash during the planning period and at the time of the Games. Vancouver did a satisfactory job with both activists and unions. The public sector employee contract was negotiated with a due date after the 2010 Games and employees accepted because of incentives that were offered during the bargaining process. Cooperation from the First Nations tribes was confirmed when they were invited to become an important part of the Cultural Olympiad. Moreover, co-opting or gaining the cooperation of groups which initially oppose a bid can actually strengthen the bid as these groups can point to flaws in the proposed plans which can be addressed before the final bid submission. It is an opportunity to bring different groups together within a community to strengthen the community.

There are some issues that will galvanize and likely not be solved, but can be rationalized. The displacement of the disenfranchised, health care, and social welfare spawn the argument that the dollars could be better spent. The reality is that the money would likely not be available were it not for the major sports event occurring. There still remains, as was mentioned in the theory section, the argument that some existing programme dollars are now being rerouted to the sports event.

Bids, leaders, and votes

Before the bid document is submitted, it needs to be vetted by experts so that the message is impeccable and transcends the presenter. Ultimately, it is the personal decision of each event-owner (e.g. the IOC for the Olympic Games) member regarding how and why they cast their individual vote for a city. No vote is guaranteed before the members cast their ballot, and no one ever knows for sure how each individual member voted, because it is a confidential process. If the message is impeccable, the charismatic influence of the presenter could tip the scales as it did for London 2012. Lord Sebastian Coe had highly leveraged relationships, and he lobbied diligently in his network in a discreet fashion. Due diligence was conducted to focus on the areas of youth and legacy; and when his powerful presentation was delivered, it resulted in London, the underdog, winning the bid. It is important to note that if the lobbying and solicitation for votes is not discreet, as was the case of Pyeongchang (South Korea) in Salt Lake City in 2002 for the 2010 bid competition, it can result in both failure for the bid and disapproval from the event owner. In this case they had erected huge banners promoting themselves, which is against the rules of promotion, and which likely influenced the unsuccessful outcome.

Should heads of state and governments be present at the bid voting meeting? It would seem the answer is that you are dammed if you do and dammed if you don't. US President Barack Obama travelled to Copenhagen (Denmark) to support Chicago's bid for the 2016 Olympic Game vote, and they lost. Contrast that with Vladimir Putin's (alternatively Russian President or Prime Minister) non-attendance for the 2014 bid for Sochi, which they won. However, the British Prime Minister was in attendance for the 2012 vote (as was the French President, though Paris did not win). It is a subjective decision that the bid committee needs to make as one of the strategies, but not the defining one, towards a winning bid.

Human resource choices: the experts and the leaders

The experienced human resource is the key to the bid process. It is imperative to involve from the beginning people who have been through the process. They come with processes and valuable tacit knowledge. They can prevent and often eliminate the need to "reinvent the wheel". The focus they bring allows the bid team to function efficiently and effectively. Transfer of knowledge from one Olympic Games to the next has often been less than adequate in the past, so the need for people who have Games experience is essential.

As a final statement relative to the success of a bid, there must be a belief to the core of the committee, and especially the presenter, that the Olympics can be good for the country, the city, its people, the athletes, for financial, social, cultural, and legacy reasons. Both Lord Sebastian Coe for London 2012 (London Organising Committee of the 2012 Olympic and Paralympic Games – LOCOG) and John Furlong for Vancouver 2010 (Vancouver Organizing Committee for the 2010 Olympic and Paralympic Winter Games – VANOC) were brilliant at communicating the "goodness" of the Olympic Games during their bids. Votes were gained and success was the outcome of their unshakeable confidence that the Olympic Games would benefit their cities, and ultimately honour the tenants of the Olympic Brand.

CHAPTER SUMMARY

In this chapter we examined the informal and formal bid processes for major sports events, including: bid conceptualization, feasibility study, political and business support, and the regional/national/international bid competition. We present reasons for bidding (e.g. sport promotion, economic development, and facilities), questions to ask oneself when wanting to submit a bid, and various bid considerations (including internal, process, and external factors). We also explored the various stakeholders that surround bid and organizing committees. Finally, we described some issues bid committees face, notably politics, relationship/participation/interdependence, finance, planning and organizing, infrastructure/operations/logistics, media and visibility, and human resources.

From a practitioner's perspective there is a list of considerations for a bid process which includes: support from both political and sports circles; appetite of the citizens, including activists groups, for the event; choice of leader for the bid committee; access to power players and ability to leverage those relationships to influence votes; strategic decisions of who to send to the bid voting meeting; votes being confidential; and the compelling role of subjectivity in the outcome of the bid. While there are hundreds of smaller decisions to be made, this list covers some of the most important aspects of a bid for a major sports event.

EXPERT CASE: THE CANADIAN OLYMPIC COMMITTEE'S BIDDING EXPERIENCE

In the context of the Americas, there are five major multi-sport, multi-nation Games that require NOC support and endorsement as a precondition to the presentation of a bid to a Games rights holder. These are the Olympic Games (or Games of the Olympiad, commonly referred to as the Summer Olympics), the Olympic Winter Games, the Summer YOG, the

Winter YOG – all properties owned by the IOC – and the Pan and ParaPan American Games – owned by PASO – which are a summer sport competition limited to the 42 NOCs of the Americas and Caribbean. The Paralympic Games, properties owned by the IPC, that take place following but in conjunction with the Olympic Games and Olympic Winter Games by agreement between the IOC and the IPC are a part of those Games bid packages. The ParaPan component of the Pan American Games, first added to these Games at the Rio de Janeiro 2007 Games and modelled on the Olympic Games format, although part of a bid city's proposal, lacks the ownership and relationship clarity of the IOC/IPC agreement.

With these many Games to consider, an NOC must determine whether it wishes to pursue a Games, and if it does, which Games ought to be pursued. Although many factors go into such a decision, fundamental to every decision on the part of an NOC to seek or not to seek a Games opportunity will be a measure of the legacy and short- and long-term revenue-generation possibilities. A bid for a Games, particularly in pursuit of an Olympic Games or Olympic Winter Games, is a very costly and resource-diverting exercise. An NOC will seek to therefore assure itself that a particular Games opportunity is one that has a reasonable and realistic chance of success, and payback in legacy and revenue generation, before embarking with a selected city on a bid journey. This first hard look perspective works against a YOG since existing facilities are expected to be used and revenue generation is certainly a challenge.

An NOC will first consider whether a particular Games is one – having regard to what has and is happening internationally with the awarding of a particular Games – that can be won with a bid from the NOC's country. This is sometimes referred to as the "alignment of the stars". More art than science, this exercise will take a good look at the geo-politics, international sport politics, and historic Games award patterns to decide if these factors would be weighing so heavily against a bid that any bid effort would be bound to be futile.

Should the NOC determine that a given Games is a realistic pursuit, whether the idea arose from within the NOC itself or from an approach of interest by a city or cities, the NOC must then decide how it will go about selecting the city that will actually be endorsed to bid for the Games. This can be done either by direct strategic selection of a city by the NOC or by means of a domestic competition among interested cities. Although there is no IOC or PASO requirement that an open competition take place, an NOC is most often inclined to hold a competition among cities to promote, through the spirit of competition, the presentation of the best possible bid not only from an international bid competition perspective, but also from the perspective of the best possible proposals for domestic legacy and revenue generation for sport. This is not always the chosen route, however, particularly when circumstances are such that the city to be selected is clearly known in advance. This was the case, for example, with the selection of Toronto to bid for the 2015 Pan and ParaPan American Games. With Toronto and the Greater Golden Horseshoe Area seen to be in critical need of new summer sport infrastructure facilities and a retrofit on many others, the Canadian Olympic Committee (COC) decided that it would pursue these Games specifically to address this need. In this circumstance, no open competition was held among Canadian cities and Toronto was selected and endorsed by the COC to present what turned out to ultimately be a successful bid for these Games.

The NOC must be careful in this regard, however. A bid requires support, financial and governmental, from the federal government. Both the IOC and PASO require correspondence to this effect from the head of the provincial and federal governments. There may be reluctance on the part of the federal government – or perhaps a provincial government should there be interest from more than one city in the province – to throw its support behind a bid in the absence of an open and fair national competition. A good case needs to be made for the selection of a city by the NOC without an open competition. As mentioned earlier, on balance, in most cases there is much to be gained by an NOC and its NSF members having a bid city come out of an open competitive process.

In the absence of an open competition domestically to win the right for a city to pursue a bid, it is of critical importance that the "sole sourced bid" be accompanied with a credible and verifiable business plan to be considered by the NOC prior to endorsement of the bid. The federal and provincial governments will also insist on review of, and comfort with, the proposed bid's business plan prior to their required endorsements. In a competitive process, the process itself and comparative evaluation of the competing cities generates the information needed to ensure that a city chosen to bid has a solid business case for its bid. When, exceptionally, only one city is to be considered, a realistic business plan must be available to the NOC so that it can assure itself that the bid, and the Games if secured, can in fact achieve the end results intended.

An important element of the pre-bid city selection process that an NOC must be careful to address is the development of a comprehensive Bid City Agreement, a precursor to a Games Multi-Party Agreement (MPA) if the right to host the Games is won, which will map out once in place the respective rights and obligations of the bid committee and the NOC. It will also set the basic framework and structure of the organizing committee and the transition to it should the right to host the Games be won. The NOC is never in a better bargaining position than it is at this time to deal with these and other Games-related issues, and a competition among cities only enhances its position. This is another factor that militates against the selection of a city without a competition.

Once a bid city is selected by an NOC, it must work to ensure that it, the NOC, works hand in glove with the city in the presentation of the bid to those who will ultimately be deciding upon the host city for the Games. A well-crafted Bid City Agreement will go a long way to ensuring that this is the case. It must be the case, and must appear to be the case, that the NOC and the bid committee, once established, have a close and interconnected working relationship. IOC members expect to see the NOC and bid committee standing together. Bid committees and organizing committees come and go. Not so for NOCs. The NOC is the constant in the eyes of the IOC. This is even more so when in pursuit of a Pan and ParaPan American Games through PASO, where it is not the IOC members from the Americas and Caribbean, but rather the NOCs of those countries, who by their votes decide on host cities.

With the above accomplished and in place, the NOC and bid city embark upon the bid journey, always with a watchful eye on the alignment of the stars.

With the clarity of hindsight, the stars were not aligned for the Toronto 2008 Olympic Games bid. With the turn of the millennium, and the recognition of China's ever-increasing prominence in the world's economic and political order, combined with the historic fact that the Games had never been hosted by the world's most populous nation, the IOC was unlikely to turn down Beijing a second time, having already done it once in 2003, when it selected Sydney over Beijing in the contest for the right to host the 2000 Olympic Games. The Games had not been hosted in Asia since the 1988 Seoul Olympic Games. In the meantime, they had been awarded to Europe twice – Barcelona in 2002 and the Athens 2004 Games, although not yet held, had been awarded in 1997 – North America with the 1996 Atlanta Games, and Oceania with the Sydney 2000 Games. From a technical perspective, Toronto's bid proposal might be argued to have been the best of the lot, but this was "Beijing's [China's] time" and it was not to be denied. That said, had there been some particularly acute political issue that befell Beijing's bid, this may have opened up the race to the other bidders; but for the Beijing bid for 2008, Toronto was in a strong position to win. However, Beijing did not falter and was awarded the Games.

A fortuitous circumstance led to the COC being able to negotiate a good and strong Bid City Agreement with the city of Toronto, notwithstanding that it was the only city asking the COC for endorsement of the right to bid for the 2008 Games. Although the host city for the 2010 Olympic Winter Games would not be decided until 2003, two years after the 2008 Olympic Games decision in 2001, the COC had decided in 1998 to pursue a 2010 Olympic Winter Games bid. Its reasoning was that its candidate for 2010, thought at this point to likely be Quebec City in a repeat of its bid for the 2002 Olympic Winter Games, ought to get out ahead of the pack to start the process of relationship building with the IOC members. The COC invited cities in Canada to bid domestically for the right to bid for the 2010 Games. Domestic bids came in from Quebec City, Calgary, and Vancouver. With the help of the competitive approach of these three domestic bids, the COC was able to negotiate a good and strong Bid City Agreement. Thus, when Toronto came along soon after expressing interest in a bid for the 2008 Games, the COC had the Bid City Agreement that had been agreed to by the now-selected city of Vancouver to present as the accepted framework for the agreement that now needed to be negotiated with Toronto. The two agreements were ultimately very similar in content.

Toronto was the only city that approached the COC to bid for the 2008 Games, and was also the only city approached by the COC to bid to host the 2015 Pan and ParaPan American Games. This being a single-city consideration, there was close review and consideration of a business plan for the 2015 Games by the COC, the provincial government, and the federal government prior to their respective endorsements of the bid. The bid committee recognized the need to project itself as one with the COC and did so successfully, winning the right to host the Games in convincing fashion in October of 2009.

By Michael A. Chambers, Immediate Past President, Canadian Olympic Committee; Board Member, Toronto 2015; Executive Committee Member, PASO; Executive Council Member, ANOC

Case questions

1 What factors does an NOC consider when bidding for an Olympic Games?

2 Do you think that Canada's decision to open up the bid process for the 2010 Olympic Winter Games prior to an IOC decision for the 2008 Olympic Games hindered Toronto's chances? Explain.

3 When do you think your country would be in the best position to host an Olympic Games? Reference the factors an NOC considers when bidding for a major Games. If you do not think it can host an Olympic Games, explain your position.

CHAPTER QUESTIONS

1 Describe the bidding process for an event, noting the informal and formal aspects of the bid process.

2 Which reasons for bidding do you believe would apply more to mega-events like the FIFA World Cup than smaller sports events like a national table tennis championship?

3 What would make you decide to not proceed with a bid?

4 What would an organization chart look like for a typical bid committee?

5 What are some of the key factors in deciding if a head of state or government should attend the bid vote meeting?

FURTHER READING

For further readings on bids, we suggest the following:

Chappelet, J.-L. (ed.) (2005) *From Initial Idea to Success: A Guide to Bidding for Sports Events for Politicians and Administrators*, Lausanne: IDHEAP.

Furlong, J. & Mason, G. (2011) *Patriot Hearts: Inside the Olympics that Changed a Country*, Vancouver, BC: Douglas & McIntyre.

Mason, D. S., Thibault, L., & Miserner, L. (2006) An agency theory perspective on corruption in sport: The case of the International Olympic Committee. *Journal of Sport Management*, 20, 52–73.

Chapter 3

Leading and setting up an organizing committee

OBJECTIVES

- To understand the different theories that can be applied to leaders of major sports events
- To understand what makes a good leader for a major sports event
- To understand how to set up an organizing committee (its organizational structure)
- To understand the managerial differences between a temporary organization like a major sports event organizing committee and other more traditional (enduring) organizations

ILLUSTRATIVE CASE: THE LEADERSHIP OF THE 2010 DELHI CWG

The 2010 Delhi CWG Organizing Committee had an executive board which was the ultimate decision-making power (other organizing committees have boards of directors). The link between the sub-committees/functional areas and the executive board was with the four-member executive management team (other committees often have a CEO/Director General and (executive) vice-presidents), which was composed of a chairman, vice-chairman, secretary general, and treasurer. These were the organizing committee leaders. The chairman was the executive head and was responsible for overseeing and executing all policies and directives provided by the Games' executive board. The vice-chairman was the link between the organizing committee and the Commonwealth Games Associations (CGAs) around the world. The secretary general was in charge of technical aspects and sub-committee coordination. Finally, the treasurer was in charge of financial matters and coordinating the finance and revenue sub-committee (Organizing Committee Commonwealth Games 2010 Delhi, 2010).

By the opening ceremonies of the 2010 Delhi CWG, these leaders had been plagued with credibility issues, from alleged sponsorship scandals, to workforce problems (e.g. child labour, health and safety problems of construction workers and of venues, such as faeces in the athletes' village), to construction problems (e.g. huge delays meaning increased costs, a main bridge collapsing days before teams were scheduled to arrive). While all venues were ready by the time the Games started, it left a bad taste in people's mouths as the crowd at the opening ceremonies booed the chairman of 2010 Delhi when he came to give his speech, because he was the embodiment of the organizing committee that was giving India a bad image and reputation.

In contrast, the President of India was greatly cheered. Together with the President of the CGF, the President of India "whipped the organizing committee into shape", got venues cleaned up, built (in the case of the bridge, with the help of the army), and generally ready for the Games. She became the embodiment of what India was capable of by putting her power, her leadership into action.

THE THEORY BEHIND LEADING AND SETTING UP AN EVENT

The top-tier management of a major sports event is typically the board of directors, which is made up of the various sport, government, and community partners who have a major stake in the Games. Their first task is to hire the key figurehead or leader of the Games, a paid staff position called by various names – president, CEO, or executive director. Hiring such an individual is often done through a head-hunting company to obtain the "best" person possible, who may or may not be from the host region. This is a more transparent process than the often used favouritism route (i.e. the brother-in-law of..., the business associate of...). The exact process will depend on the needs and desires of the board of directors, but also on the host region/country's political/governance structure and process. For example, Australians would wonder to see a "brother" of the prime minister become head of an organizing committee; however, this may not be as surprising in an autocratic emerging country. Regardless of the manner in which the leader is chosen, she or he has a huge task ahead. The following provides a description of the various theories that can be used to examine leadership in major sports events, as well as comments on organizational structure options for the leader.

Applicable leadership theories

There are a variety of leadership theories that could be applicable to major sports events. The trait approach was really the first in the leadership literature. People who follow the trait approach believe that leaders are born; individuals cannot be trained to become leaders (see Katz, 1955; Stogdill, 1948, 1974). McLennan (1967) argued that a leader's skills depend on an organization's nature and size, and on the degree to which decision-making is centralized.

Following the trait approach, there was the style and behavioural approaches, mainly seen within the Ohio State and Michigan studies. These approaches are primarily interested in how leaders/managers treat their employees to increase their effectiveness. The Ohio State studies (e.g. Fleishman and Harris, 1962; Fleishman et al., 1955; Halpin, 1957; Halpin and Winer, 1957) provided us with the Leader Behavior Description Questionnaire (LBDQ) and a focus on considerations (e.g. trust in relationship) and initiation structure (e.g. work structure to meet organizational goals). In turn, the Michigan studies (e.g. Katz et al., 1950, 1951; Taylor and Bowers, 1972) focused on high-performing organizational units, which had differentiated roles, were employee-centred, provided latitude to their employees, developed cohesiveness within the unit, and received general (instead of close) supervision.

28

Leadership stemming from the Michigan studies included four dimensions: support, interaction facilitation, goal emphasis, and work facilitation.

Since these approaches, leadership theories have evolved. We will consider a few key ones and then examine what the sport event management literature says about sport event leaders.

Contingency/situational theories

Four contingency/situational theories are of interest to us: path–goal theory, situational leadership theory, least-preferred co-worker (LPC), and leader–member exchange (LMX).

The following applies to path–goal theory (e.g. Bass, 1990a; Evans, 1970; House, 1971, 1977; Jermier, 1996):

- theory is focused on subordinates;
- effective leadership depends on the situation;
- leaders act as guides – there are four leadership options: supportive, instrumental, participative, and achievement;
- effective leaders are seen as a (present or future) source of satisfaction;
- there is weak empirical support for the theory.

Regarding situational leadership theory (Hersey and Blanchard, 1984):

- leader behaviour is described as task behaviour (work structure) and relationship behaviour (employee support, open communication);
- a subordinate's level of maturity will mediate the relationship between a leader's behaviour and effectiveness;
- a subordinate's maturity is described as job maturity (technical ability) and psychological maturity (self-confidence, self-respect);
- little empirical work has been done to determine the theory's effectiveness.

For LPC (e.g. Bluedorn, 1991; Fiedler, 1967, 1978; Hooijberg et al., 1997; House and Aditya, 1997, Peters et al., 1985, Rice, 1978):

- theory is focused on the interpersonal relationship between the leader and their followers;
- situational variables or favourability include the task structure, leader–member relations, and the leader's power position;
- taken together, this situational favourability leads to leader effectiveness;
- the leader's score is based on the leader thinking about their LPC and assessing that person on 16 bipolar descriptors;
- there has been mixed empirical support for the theory.

For LMX (Graen and Uhl-Bien, 1991, 1995):

- theory is focused on leader–subordinate group interaction dyads;
- theory is interested in communication and high-quality exchanges;

- the goal of subordinates is to be an "in-group" member (to be part of the group, as opposed to outside);
- subordinates should work to get along with the leader and want to expand their responsibilities;
- effective leadership is seen when leader–subordinate communication leads both parties to gain respect, mutual trust, and commitment.

Transactional leadership

Transactional leadership (see Bass, 1990b; Bass and Avolio, 1990a; Doherty, 1997; Doherty and Danylchuk, 1996; Kuhnert and Lewis, 1987) is about leaders exchanging rewards for subordinates' efforts. So it is about the leader–subordinate exchange relationship. Past approaches described above that fall within this exchange relationship perspective are argued to be part of transactional leadership (Bryman, 1992; Burns, 1978; Doherty and Danylchuk, 1996). The rewards noted relate to lower-order needs such as affiliation, recognition, and security (see Maslow, 1954). Transactional leaders appeal to subordinates' self-interests by pursuing values linked to the exchange process, such as fairness, reciprocity, responsibility, and honesty. As we will see later in this book, these needs and values can certainly be in line with reasons for being part of a major sports event's organizing committee.

Charismatic and transformational leadership

By the 1990s there was a move away from transactional approaches towards what we now call charismatic and transformational leadership approaches.

Charismatic leadership (e.g. Avolio and Yammarino, 1990; Conger and Kanungo, 1987; Gardner and Avolio, 1998; House, 1977; Shamir and Howell, 1999; Wang *et al.*, 2005) is thought to be essentially divinely inspired; this type of leader is perceived by followers to possess exceptional traits/qualities, which are a natural gift, like super human, mystical powers (Wang *et al.*, 2005; Weber, 1947). This leader can be narcissistic but is usually very popular with others. Thus, this approach focuses on the leader's (top management) qualities. Charismatic leaders typically emerge during a crisis. They have a radical vision; they attract people with their vision; and they usually experience some degree of success, which shows that the vision is "attainable" (Parent *et al.*, 2009b). The effective charismatic leader is seen as being extraordinary.

Transformational leadership (e.g. Bass, 1990b; Bass and Avolio, 1990a, 1990b; Doherty, 1997; Keegan and Den Hartog, 2004; Keller, 2006; Kuhnert and Lewis, 1987; Ozaralli, 2003; Parent *et al.*, 2009b) is somewhat different than charismatic leadership. Here, the leader is more of a guide, gaining commitment of followers to a shared vision or objectives. The transformational leader empowers her followers to accomplish their shared vision by appealing to moral values and emotions, thereby raising their consciousness about ethical issues. This allows followers to mobilize their resources and "transform" the institutions. Thus, in contrast to charismatic leadership, the focus is on the followers. Transformational leadership has yet to receive sufficient empirical support to say that it is superior to other leadership theories, however.

Other leadership styles

While the preceding provides the core leadership approaches/theories popular in management, Getz (2005) suggested other leadership styles that could also apply to event managers:

- Artistic: this leader's *modus operandi* is creativity; specifics and operations are for everyone else in the organizing committee.
- Autocratic: this leader makes all the key decisions and expects his orders to be obeyed.
- Bureaucratic: this leaders uses a committee for all decisions in order to know all options and consequences, and sets up an extensive set of rules and regulations.
- Democratic: this leader requires votes for everything (there is little "true" leadership).
- Entrepreneurial: this leader is focused on the bottom line; decisions are about money.
- Technocratic: this leader is the opposite of the artistic leader; the technocratic leader is focused on details – there is not a creative bone in his body.

Parent *et al.* (2009b) examined different leadership approaches/theories for the leaders of a major sports event, the 2005 FINA World Aquatic Championships, and found that the multiple-linkages theory (Yukl, 1971, 1981, 2002) was the most appropriate and complete theory for describing the leadership of this event. The multiple-linkages theory has not truly been tested empirically, in part due to its complexity. It focuses on the leader (top management or supervisor), with attention paid to both subordinates and stakeholders, thus fitting with the open-system view of a major sports event organizing committee. This contingency theory also focuses on four types of variables: managerial, intervening, criterion, and situational:

- Managerial behaviours: actions the leader may take to deal with deficiencies in the intervening variables.
  - Short-term leader behaviour examples include offering special incentives or giving inspiring talks so that subordinates work faster/produce higher-quality work; reducing task confusion in order to increase subordinates' abilities; re-organizing or coordinating the work to be done in a different, more efficient manner; or acquiring additional needed informational, human, or material resources to do the work.
  - Long-term leader behaviour examples include gaining more control over resource acquisition or the unit's product/service demands; initiating "new, more profitable activities for the work" (Yukl, 2002: 226); initiating personnel/equipment and programme improvements; and modifying the organizational culture.
- Intervening variables mediate the leader behaviour–unit effectiveness relationship:
  - Task commitment: members' desire to attain high performance levels and the degree of their personal commitment to the group/unit's objectives.
  - Ability and role clarity: members' understanding of their individual job responsibilities, degree to which they know what to do and have the skills to do it.
  - Organization of the work: use of effective performance strategies for reaching objectives and how work is organized for efficient use of personnel, facilities, and equipment/material resources.

- – Cooperation and mutual trust: degree of members' trust, information/ideas sharing, and mutual help, as well as identification to the unit/group.
- – Resources and support: degree to which members have access and can use the necessary resources (budgetary funds, tools/equipment, personnel, facilities, information) and assistance from other units.
- – External coordination: the degree of interdependence between the unit/group's work and the work in other units/groups, as well as outside the organization.
- ■ Criterion variables: criteria related to unit effectiveness
- ■ Situational variables:
  - – Situational variables constrain managerial behaviour by moderating the relationship between leader behaviour and unit effectiveness (e.g. they can neutralize the effect).
  - – They influence intervening variables by acting as substitutes.
  - – Examples are: formal reward systems; the work's intrinsic motivating properties; recruitment and selection systems; task structure; external dependencies; type of technologies used; competitive strategy of the organization; size of the group; membership stability; department interdependence; and current economic conditions.

The intervening and situational variables are the most important of the four types of variable. As little empirical research has been done to test this leadership theory, we have few details relating to the different variables and their impact on specific criterion variables, more long-term and proactive leader behaviour (versus short-term and reactive), and the interactions between the different intervening variables. Nevertheless, Parent *et al.* (2009b) did find that the breadth of the variables noted in this theory provided a greater frame for understanding leadership in major sports events.

While the multiple-linkages theory has been found to fit the world of major sports events, that is not to say that no other theory does. Emerging leadership theories include authentic leadership (see Avolio and Gardner, 2005; Ilies *et al.*, 2005; Ladkin and Taylor, 2010; Walumbwa *et al.*, 2008), servant leadership (see Dierendonck, 2011; Greenleaf, 2002; Spears, 1995), and flexible and adaptive leadership theory (see Yukl and Mahsud, 2010). Authentic leadership is about being true to one's self, transparent, and open, which helps leaders build trust within themselves and with their followers. Authentic leaders "know who they are and what they believe" (Yukl, 2010: 424). Servant leadership in the workplace is described as "about helping others to accomplish shared objectives by facilitating individual development, empowerment, and collective work that is consistent with the health and long-term welfare of followers" (Yukl, 2010: 419). Finally, as its name may indicate, flexible and adaptive leadership theory sees leadership behaviour as changing over time in order to adapt to various and changing circumstances. Indicators of flexible and adaptive leadership include the taking on/adaptation to new responsibilities, how the individual reacts/responds to crises, the ability to balance competing values, and the ability to transition from one position to another (Yukl and Mahsud, 2010). These three leadership theories may provide insight into major sports event leaders; this can therefore become a fruitful future research direction.

Key leadership qualities

While we know that organizing committees of major sports events evolve through three modes (Parent, 2008), is this the same for leadership? In their work on leadership qualities for major sports events, Parent et al. (2009a) argued that this is true. In the planning mode, networking (for building relationships), access to resources, human resource management skills, credibility, and communications/public relations are key leadership qualities. During the implementation mode, networking, human resource management skills, and organization are key leadership qualities. During the wrap-up mode, networking (for maintaining relationships), recognition, human resource management skills, financial skills, and legacy management skills are key leadership qualities.

What we see from the above is the predominance of networking as the key quality. This stands somewhat in contrast to what the previous literature would deem most important in a leader, such as having a vision, a magnetic personality, and the drive to get the project done (cf. Basefsky et al., 2004; Laios et al., 2003; Tait, 1996). Parent et al.'s (2009a) research seems clear that the leader needs to be able to network in order to reach the organizing committee's goals. This links the leadership skills of the bid phase (e.g. understanding formal and informal political processes) with that of preparing the major sports event. The leader's networks should include political actors, but also business and sport actors. A leader could have the best network in the world, but if the network does not have actors within the host region/community, then the leader's network may be less effective. Another point to note is that the "leader" may not be one person but a group of two or three individuals, as was the case for the 2005 FINA World Aquatics Championships, where one person had the local political network (as mayor), one had the sport network (as Formula 1 race owner), and one had the business network (as president of a major media company). Combined, these three individuals had the necessary network to achieve their goals of successfully hosting the event.

Parent and Séguin (2008) associated these three networks with specific skill sets the leadership group should have, namely: political/networking skills; business/management skills; and sport/event skills. Political/network skills are those associated with personal and professional relationships with the different event stakeholders (i.e. sport, business, and politics – Parent et al., 2009a). But this skill also refers to negotiating skills, and understanding the stakeholders' needs and wants. The business/management skills are the standard financial, communication, strategic planning, and human resource management skills. The sport/event skills are more technical in nature – that is, how to run an event and/or a sport. We can see how linked specific leadership skills and networks seem to be.

Parent et al. (2009a) actually indicated that some of the skills/qualities noted above acted as antecedents to networking or were seen as consequences of networking activity. More precisely, antecedents included good communication, organization, human resource management, and financial skills. In turn, networking allowed for the easier development of the following skills: public relations, credibility, recognition, relationship maintenance, access to resources, and legacy management. Many of these "consequences", however, are required during the planning mode – thus the importance of choosing a leader or leaders with an already established network.

Organizational structure

The appointed leader has two key tasks to undertake: (1) start the planning, including the mission, vision, and values of the organizing committee (see Chapter 4); and (2) setting up the organizing committee's structure (Parent, 2008).

Major and mega sports organizing committees are typically incorporated as non-profit organizations. The exact structure, however, will depend on the national context, desires, and responsibilities of the partners or key stakeholders, and the exact nature of the event (see Getz, 2005). That is, the partners, such as municipal and federal governments as well as the NSF/Olympic committee, may decide to enter into a loose alliance. Alternatively, one key partner, such as the national organization holding the rights to the event, may lead efforts and enter into sub-contracts with other organizations for specific tasks or responsibilities. A third option is for an event-hosting organization to take over the hosting of another event with its "sub-event" associated organization. However, the most popular and likely option is the creation of a new organization to lead the efforts by the event's "alliance" of key partners (see also Parent et al., 2009c). In this case, the key partners and rights holders will have representatives sit on the board of directors of the new non-profit event organization, which means that there can be many people around the table. The board of directors may choose to organize itself into standing (sub)committees, which can deal with specific dossiers, such as finance or human resources, based on the expertise of the individuals around the table.

Headed by the chairman, the board of directors' roles and responsibilities include establishing the main vision, values, and goals of the organization, formulating the general policies, acquiring and allocating important resources for the event, overseeing major or critical issues/problems, and standing united for the event (Getz, 2005). The board members are therefore more interested in the broad governance of the event than specific, operational tasks, as they are typically volunteers and only meet every three or four months. The board of directors' first key decision is to hire the first paid staff member, who can be called the president, CEO, and/or director general. This person, the leader, will then create the structure for the rest of the organization and will head the operational, day-to-day activities. This leader's tasks include preparing/implementing the budget (which is ultimately approved by the board of directors), supervising and evaluating the staff, strategic planning, operationalizing the policies and procedures, dealing with the board of directors and external stakeholders (Getz, 2005), and generally being the face of the Games.

Typically, the leader will have a staff of vice-presidents and/or Executive vice-presidents heading the different divisions, departments, or committees. These divisions are typically organized by function, such as sport, marketing and communications, legal, international and domestic relations, human resources, finance, venue construction, and media. The number of divisions will vary from one event to the next, and some can be "mega" divisions, in that they hold a range of portfolios within their purview. For example, it may be decided that human resources includes the hiring and training of not only paid staff, but also volunteers, as well as including the portfolio of official languages interpretation and translation. Another leader may alternatively decide that the volunteer portfolio is so large that it should be a stand-alone division. Thus, the exact number of divisions will vary greatly. If there are mega-divisions, then they are more likely to be headed by executive vice-presidents, who will then have two or more vice-presidents under their direction, each heading different portfolios, departments, or FAs (i.e. specific functions). Nevertheless, key (executive) vice-presidents – such as the human resources, finance, marketing/communications, and legal vice-presidents – will also form an executive committee headed by the leader to make critical (high-impact, far-reaching, and/or fast) decisions.

Under the executive vice-presidents (if any) and vice-presidents, we find a series of directors, managers, and coordinators for each specific FA. While the directors are often hired within a two-year period of the start of the organizing committee's life (especially for Olympic Games) – thus in the planning mode – the managers and coordinators are often hired only within the last 2–2.5 years, with the coordinators often hired only within the last year (during the implementation mode – see Parent, 2008). The hiring of the final set of staff during the implementation mode sees the highest number of hirings for the organization in a given timeframe. As Parent and Séguin (2010: 12) noted, "The quick growth of the organization is a new experience for most members, and it still involves all the 'growing pains' an enduring organization may face, only in a more compressed timeline." For major international multi-sport events, all these positions are usually filled by paid staff. The volunteers will come into play at Games-time and be led by the managers and/or coordinators. We will discuss workforce (human resource) management in Chapter 5.

The trend over the past 15 years has been to have this hierarchical type of structure in place until the event takes place. However, come Games-time, the trend has been to then create mini-organizing committees for each venue if the event is a multi-venue event. These venue teams, or VTeams, are headed by venue general managers. By Games-time, the FA coordinators move from reporting to their FA managers to also reporting to their venue general manager. This can create tensions or conflicts if responsibilities and communication patterns are not planned appropriately beforehand. Nevertheless, it allows venues to work almost independently, as a representative from each key FA sits at the table for that venue and can therefore make decisions for the FA – assuming they are given the decision-making power to do so, of course. This VTeam approach is therefore more of what is called a matrix structure. Thus, we can argue that the same organization moves from a functional structure to a matrix structure.

Figure 3.1 provides an overview of the generic structure of a major multi-sport event that includes multiple competition and non-competition venues.

After the Games end, most coordinators' contracts end, with those of the managers ending a few weeks or couple of months later. The final duties of the organizing committee, which are to complete the accounting, write the final reports and manage the legacies (if another organization has not been set up to do so – see Chapters 14–15), are completed by the senior levels of the organizing committee (directors and/or vice-presidents/executive vice-presidents with the leader).

Theodoraki (2001) was the first to explicitly examine organizational configurations or designs of Organizing Committees of Olympic Games (OCOGs), arguing that if one understood how OCOGs are structured, then they can understand how organizational aspects and activities are interrelated, as well as figuring out where inefficiencies lie. A key configuration

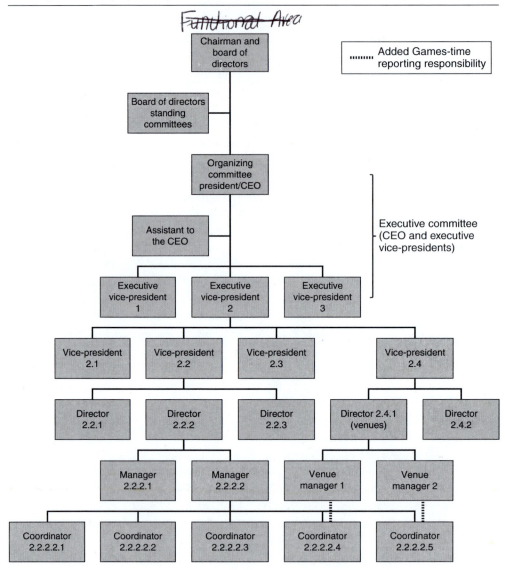

Figure 3.1 Example of a generic major sports event organizing committee structure.

theorist, Henry Mintzberg (1979), suggested five distinct organizational configurations and one hybrid configuration:

1   *Simple structure*: the focus is on the owner, and there are few employees. The employees are directly supervised by the owner, yet everything is relatively centralized.
2   *Machine bureaucracy*: the focus is on the standardization of work processes (think factory) and formalized communication procedures, so the technostructure (IT specialists, engineers, analysts, accountants, etc.) is key. There is a clear centralized hierarchy.
3   *Professional bureaucracy*: the focus is on the standardized skills of the professionals who form the operating core of the organizations. These individuals are experts so the tasks are decentralized to them as they want autonomy.

4   *Divisionalized structure*: the focus is on standardized outputs. As the middle-line managers want some autonomy to direct their own divisions as they see fit, the focus is on this middle line. These managers run somewhat autonomous organizations under the umbrella of a corporate headquarters.

5   *Adhocracy*: the focus is on the support staff in this core organic organization, which has little formalization or structured hierarchy. As decentralization is key in this flexible organization, coordination is undertaken through mutual adjustment.

6   *Missionary organization*: the focus is on the ideology more than the workers. This type of organization is about trust, so we find it to be decentralized, though much of the power is given to its leader. As such it is somewhat of a hybrid organization between the simple structure (for the leader) and the professional bureaucracy (for the decentralization and trust). Work is coordinated through socialization (i.e. standardized norms).

Theodoraki (2001) associated the OCOGs' lifecycle stages to Mintzberg's different configurations. More precisely, within the first year, Theodoraki hypothesized that the OCOGs are simple structures given their small size. During the second to sixth year (out of seven), Theodoraki hypothesized that the OCOGs are like professional bureaucracy as they grow and rely on the hired staff. As OCOGs move into their seventh and final year, they are thought to be like divisionalized structures with the VTeams. During Games-time, Theodoraki suggests that OCOGs are a mix of the divisionalized structure (because of the VTeams), adhocracy (because of the decentralization and flexibility), and missionary organization (because of the ideology and socialization aspects). Theodoraki then postulated that the post-Games period sees OCOGs resembling missionary organizations when most staff are gone and the primary task becomes one of closing the books and the organization itself. Thus, we see a relationship between the OCOG situation (age and size) and structure. However, this relationship is a theoretically driven, structurally based framework for researchers to examine OCOGs and their efficiencies.

Taking a somewhat different approach, Parent and Séguin (2010) explored second-tier major sports events (i.e. not the Olympic Games or FIFA World Cup). This resulted in two organizational structural designs proposed to be specific to major sports event organizing committees: headquarters-centred and venue-centred. That is, before the managers and coordinators are hired, the organization has a design that is *headquarters-centred* as the structure is relatively flat (only senior-level staff) and the tasks are "executive" or strategic in nature (e.g. creating the organization-wide plans, policies/procedures, and budgets, setting up the organization's structure). In this design, the senior staff are concerned with the general direction of the organization and with finding and acquiring the key resources, both financial (e.g. sponsorship money) and human (e.g. finding the managers, coordinators, and volunteers). As such, the staff in this design and at this stage of the hosting process are undertaking ostensive routines, which are "the abstract, generalized idea of the routine, or the routine in principle" used prospectively (as in this case) or retroactively (Feldman and Pentland, 2003: 101). This is observed through artefacts such as policies and procedures.

Once the managers and coordinators have been hired, the organizing committee is in the implementation mode and moves into a *venue-centred*, matrix organizational design with its VTeams (Parent and Séguin, 2010). Here, the staff and volunteers enact the ostensive routines (the plans, policies, and procedures) during Games-time, thereby undertaking performative routines, "the specific actions taken by specific people at specific times" and in specific places (Feldman and Pentland, 2003: 101). Finally, as the staff and volunteers leave, the organizing committee moves back into a headquarters-centred organizational design. However, in this wrap-up mode, the remaining staff members are still enacting the plans made years back, except those pertaining to reporting and legacy management specifically. As such, the remaining organizational members are argued to be undertaking performative routines (Parent and Séguin, 2010). It seems relatively easy to extrapolate these findings for an OCOG. However, the suggested organizational designs would have to be tested at the mega-event level, as well as smaller events.

As such, it is clear that more work needs to be undertaken to examine organizational structure and design elements of organizing committees if we are to understand how they work and provide suggestions for improving their efficiency and effectiveness.

THE PRACTITIONER'S PERSPECTIVE ON LEADING AND SETTING UP AN EVENT

Leadership style not only informs and impacts the outcome of a sports event, it imprints each and every person with one common goal – the Games! Every person who is part of organizing and executing the event must adapt to varying degrees to the leader's management style. There is a saying: "As the leader goes, so goes the organization." There are differences in the way that the leadership of an enduring organization manifests itself with employees. First, let's look at some of the obvious contrasts between defined, ephemeral organizations like a major sports events and a business with longevity, which will be referred to as an enduring business.

Enduring businesses allow employees to follow an evenly paced learning curve that matches their ability to perform functions and absorb new information. With ephemeral organizations, employees hit the ground running with the skills they have and then play catch-up. If individuals are not able to adapt quickly to the changes and the steep learning curve that often involves a "teach yourself" mentality (because the transfer of knowledge from previous similar events is often lacking), they are quickly replaced. If event employees want to stay with the organization and there is another area with an opening, they can possibly be redeployed. It's all about timing and availability. However, second chances are not the norm.

Enduring business employees have the luxury of knowing that there is a transition period allowed for learning and making mistakes. If they make a decision that does not work, there will likely be a second and even third chance because time is on their side. Ephemeral organizations demand that decisions be "right" the first time, because the urgency of every task does not allow for a graduated learning curve and experimentation. Mistakes will be made, but not many are tolerated. Damage control is expected and demanded as soon as possible and efforts are redoubled to always consider collateral damage with every decision.

Ephemeral organizations require employees to adapt quickly to a steep learning curve contrary to employees of an enduring business who, if they have performance issues or are not a right fit, are given time to improve their performance and/or be reassigned to a position that may better suit their skills and abilities. Enduring business employees are oriented and trained step-by-step. There is an existing tried-and-tested pool of knowledge that protects them from needing to re-invent the wheel. In an ephemeral organization, individuals do not get second chances and are quickly replaced if they are not performing. While there is effort made to transfer people to another FA, it must be a convergence of timing and skill; and if that is not present, employment will be terminated. Ephemeral organizations add employees in waves as the Games draw near, and the "race horses" are brought on board. These are the people who thrive on the adrenalin rush of a fast-paced, high-performance environment, and could perhaps be described as "Indiana Jones" types who love making it up as they go along! The "wave hiring" process will be discussed more fully in Chapter 5, which focuses on the workforce.

For a leader in both types of organizations, there is usually an intermittent challenge of not enough human resources. However, when delivering a successful sports event, there is a relentless, constant challenge of stretched and skinny human resources. It is important, therefore, that each person must feel, at some level, a connection to the leader. That connection will permit the individual to draw on their inner resources, and mirror the characteristics and behaviour that is necessary to handle just-in-time changes, unforeseen challenges, and sometimes disasters that are an inevitable part of every event.

This connection is most easily facilitated by the leader modelling, for people to see and mimic, the behaviour and speech that best represents their leadership style. At the 2010 Olympic Winter Games the leader, John Furlong, was a quadruple threat with regard to this modelling: (1) he was a former competitive athlete and coach, and planned fitness into his daily schedule, working out regularly in the head office fitness facility; (2) he was a charismatic and inspiring speaker, and his content guidelines were less-is-more and leave them wanting more; (3) he was consistent in critical ways – he inverted the organizational chart to position the athlete at the top, and he valued equally the contribution of volunteer and paid employees by having every single person who delivered the Games wear the same uniform; and (4) he "walked the talk", never asking anyone to do what he was not prepared to do himself. An example of that was delivering a short and very inspiring Christmas message acknowledging most of the employees who would be working during the Christmas break. He announced that he, too, would spend Christmas working on the road with the torch relay team, encouraging and supporting them and their efforts to engage all Canadians in the Games. These demonstrations of involved leadership translated into seemingly unwavering support and devotion to Furlong that was palpable in the streets, at the venues, and in the hearts and minds of the VANOC team as employees and volunteers could speak and function as an extension of the leadership they experienced and observed in Furlong.

There is always one person who is identified as the voice and identifiable figurehead of a sports event. However, sometimes there are behind-the-scenes leaders who are necessary for a variety of reasons, including having skills/highly leveraged relationships that are integral to the success of securing the event, and for their own reasons do not want to publicly take on the leader role for the organization and execution of the event. The bid committee chairman of the Vancouver 2010 Olympic Winter Games, Jack Poole, had the requisite skill set and was a networker *par excellence* – but did not want the CEO position. He instead insisted that the bid committee's chief executive, John Furlong, be appointed CEO of

VANOC. Poole had mentored Furlong during the three-year journey to a successful bid. He continued to provide powerful and steady leadership when Furlong stepped into the role of CEO. Poole exerted his considerable influence and behind-the-scenes leadership, along with powerful rhetoric when some members of the government and sport community expressed concern that Furlong may not have the necessary skills. Poole remained a mentor and role model as he guided and supported his protégé behind the scenes. Furlong grew in stature and experience into a powerful, well-respected leader; and when Poole sadly passed away a couple of months before the Opening of the Games, the transition to a new chairman was essentially seamless.

Leadership is complex and sometimes complicated. What we know for sure is that it can make or break an event. As the leader goes, so goes the organization. Leaders must have a vision and lead with purpose to make it to the goal line, regardless of what happens. Their ability to make decisions and accept the responsibility on behalf of their team/organization is mandatory for the duration of the event. They need the respect and support of the thousands of stakeholders. The physical and mental stamina of the leader is paramount so that they are seen as fit and able to handle the relentlessly long days and punishing barrage of challenges that make up those days.

In conclusion, leaders are born and leaders can be shaped. There are qualities that are necessary for the leader of a sports event that are specific to the nature and brand of the event. Individual skill and experience can be transferred to fit a sports event. Intrinsic to the leadership role is the ability to be seen and heard, it is the ability of the leader to project confidence and competency on a consistent basis that determines the success of the organization. At the same time, employees of a defined ephemeral event are expected to buy into the mission statement and philosophy of the organization and perform in challenging, constantly changing, and sometimes hostile environments with competency and consistency. There is little or no wiggle room for learning experiences and mistakes. The consequence of performance that does not meet these expectations is usually swift. Event managers must be flexible and adaptable, as well as able to self-manage in an arena where hand-holding is not available.

CHAPTER SUMMARY

In this chapter we examined the leadership of an organizing committee and how an organizing committee is structured or organized. We discussed a variety of leadership approaches (and their associated theories) which could be used to understand a major sports event's leader, including: the trait approach, style/behavioural approaches, contingency/situational approaches, and transactional, charismatic and transformational approaches. We also explored certain researchers' suggestions of other theories or styles, including: the artistic, autocratic, bureaucratic, democratic, entrepreneurial, and technocratic styles, as well as the multiple-linkages theory and other potential theories which could be applicable in a major sports event setting. Also presented were key skills and abilities the leader of a major sports event should have, focusing particularly on the importance of networks.

We then examined the structure of organizing committees, noting the presence of the chairman/board of directors, the key paid staff person (alternatively called a CEO, president, director general), the (executive) vice-presidents – who together with the key paid staff person form the executive committee – and the directors, managers, coordinators, and volunteers. We then explored different configurations that help to describe the evolution of the organizing committee's structure, including the headquarters-centred and venue-centred designs.

From a practitioner's perspective, we contrasted some obvious differences between the employees of ephemeral and enduring businesses to highlight the importance of hiring the right people for the right job at the right time. We also emphasized the function of the leader to constantly perform as a role model and inspire employees, because there is little or no time for second chances.

EXPERT CASE: LEADERSHIP AS VIEWED THROUGH THE LENS OF SIX OLYMPIC WINTER GAMES

I have participated in all six Olympic Winter Games from 1992 to 2010. In each of these Games, I had completely different leadership roles located in widely dissimilar pockets of this enormously complex undertaking.

Albertville 1992. The lens: team leader for the Canadian figure skating team

It was only at subsequent Games that I realized Albertville was really just a first glimpse into a key characteristic of leadership within an Olympic environment: the multiple constituent groups or stakeholders present at the Games, all with an important role in staging a successful event, are led by people who are used to making decisions quickly and effectively within their own environment. A single team leader of one sport from one country is just one of many trying to get things done.

Lillehammer 1994. The lens: Assistant Chef de mission for the Canadian team

As Assistant Chef de mission, I was part of the leadership team of the COC's mission staff and therefore responsible for the athletes and team members of all sports. Thus I went from being an expert in one sport to being a novice in many. The leadership responsibilities extended also to the 100 or so members of the mission staff, whose roles varied from medical doctors and physiotherapists to administration officers to logistics, ticketing, and hospitality staff. The Assistant Chef de mission needs to be knowledgeable in the larger issues affecting the Canadian team as a whole: questions about team selection and the high standards set by the COC; our anticipated number of medals; the method for selecting the flag bearer for the opening ceremonies; appeal procedures for all the sports; protocols for anti-doping and the "what-if" scenarios of positive drug tests; and Canada's position on femininity tests. With this larger perspective, I also gained insights regarding the various sport NSFs, the IFs governing the various disciplines, and some of the functions of the Norwegian Olympic Games Organizing Committee (NOC services, for example).

41

Nagano 1998. The lens: judge for the men's event in figure skating

It is the pinnacle of all judges' careers to be named to judge the Olympic Games. At the Nagano Games, I felt the pressure and the excitement of being responsible for helping to choose the Olympic men's champion, remaining at all times neutral and impartial according to International Skating Union (ISU) rules. The ISU Medical Commission was conducting physiological research in Nagano on how judges experience the Games. I had always been aware of my level of anxiety before judging major events, but I couldn't have imagined that my heart rate would nearly double from its resting rate of 67 beats per minute to 127 beats during the hour before the men's short programme. My experience as a judge for these Games informed my sense of Games leadership in an indirect but important way: managing stress is an essential component of all leadership positions at the Games.

Salt Lake City 2002: Chef de mission for the Canadian team

Named Chef de mission 27 months before the Games, I had time to plan and shape the direction of the team on several fronts. At the time, I thought that Canadians were feeling a little blasé about the Olympics in general. Salt Lake fell fairly closely on the heels of the 2000 (summer) Olympic Games in Sydney and many people didn't even realize that there was another Olympic Games coming in the near future. If they remembered at all, it was with the thought that Salt Lake had been associated with a bribery scandal that implicated both the Salt Lake organizers and the IOC. Moreover, there was a sense of disappointment in the medal results of the Sydney Games, as well as the feeling that there are always doping scandals that taint Canadian athletes. My response to this general malaise was to establish a key message for the Salt Lake Games through my vision for the Canadian team; I wanted people to focus back on the sports and, more importantly, on the athletes themselves. The requirements to be focused, flexible, resourceful, determined, and visible guided all my decisions before, during, and after the Games.

Nowhere were these skills more needed than when I faced a major pre-Games challenge: the terrorist attacks of September 11, 2001 (9/11) in the United States. Occurring as they did some few months before the Olympics, these events caused a rupture in our planning of major proportions. Not only were there deeply felt emotions of everyone associated with our planning, but the very real fears that the Games would be a target for terrorists, or that the Games would be cancelled, or that team members would opt out of the Games for personal reasons were omnipresent. With our staff orientation seminar occurring in Calgary a scant week-and-a-half after 9/11, I had to determine an immediate course of action. I wrote a letter to all mission staff 48 hours after the events in New York City, indicating that although we had no information about the Games at that point, we were proceeding with the seminar and adjusting its content to include additional presentations on security. The backbone of our Emergency Preparedness and Response Plan was a detailed communications network that would ensure a quick way to keep in touch with the team, and a way for family and friends to contact team members and stay informed in the event of a crisis. As leader of the Canadian team, I needed to be assured that I could know where each of the 325 team members was within 30 minutes of any incident.

These events of 9/11 notwithstanding, the pairs figure skating remains one of the defining moments for these entire Games. Due to a dishonest judge, the Canadian team of Jamie Sale and David Pelletier was denied first place. My approach to rectifying the clearly wrong decision to award the Russian team the gold medal involved, in the first instance, ensuring that our pair team's silver medal was appropriately celebrated, that their privacy was protected both within and outside the athletes' village, and that they could continue to enjoy the Games. I was the chief spokesperson for the team, and as such, was very vocal right from the beginning in describing why the result was erroneous from a technical standpoint. I called for an external review of the judging of the event and a second gold medal to be awarded to Sale and Pelletier. I also kept my promise to the whole team to support them all as, far from being a negative influence on the team, this series of events seem to serve as a catalyst for solidarity.

Torino 2006. The lens: member of the Officials Assessment Commission (OAC) for the figure skating events

The effects of the pairs figure skating scandal in Salt Lake on the sport were far-reaching. The ISU acknowledged a flawed judging system and, within one year, completely changed the judging system from a rank-order system to a system that awarded points for exactly what the skaters accomplished during their performances. A three-person commission, appointed by the ISU without regard to national representation, was tasked with observing and "judging" the events and with filing in-depth reports on the judges' performances. I was named by the ISU to the first OAC. Thus, I was placed in a position where I had to manage and lead through change at a time when my sport was in danger of being eliminated from the Games altogether.

Vancouver 2010. The lens: Director of International Client Services (ICS); Director of Official Languages for Translation Services

I was a volunteer for the five Olympic Winter Games described above. When VANOC offered me the position of Director of ICS, I was delighted to be part of the regular staff and also to be a member of the senior leadership team. My responsibilities for this position included protocol, Olympic and Paralympic Family services and hotels, venue protocol and operations, dignitary management (domestic and international), and language interpretation services. Of the 52 FAs, ICS was one of seven to have direct responsibility for the well-being of an entire client group – the Olympic Family. The other groups included athletes (and the support team around the athletes), the Canadian public, spectators, broadcasters, the press, and sponsors. Early on in the strategic planning process at VANOC, the members of the executive team established a rank order of importance for the seven client groups. The clients of ICS were last on the list of priorities.

From the IOC's standpoint, VANOC was merely the wedding planner: it was the IOC's wedding and they would be in charge of the invitation list. The job of the OCOG was to plan and execute the celebration according to the wishes of the IOC. The leadership challenge for me was to satisfy both organizations.

Two months before the Games, I was asked to take on the role of Director of Official Languages for Translation Services. My main task was to finalize an agreement with the federal government to provide assistance in translating the predicted five million words still to come from November 2009 until the end of March 2010. The project was fraught with political overtones and underlying suspicions; resilience was needed, and I had to adapt my leadership style to be much more highly directive than I had been with the ICS department.

The sheer size and complexity of an Olympic Games mean that it is very difficult to be aware of its entire scope, either before or during the actual Games-time period. My lenses were laparoscopic compared to the wide-angle lens through which the general public viewed the events. In each of the leadership roles I filled, I was fully involved in one component of the whole. The Games are not a single entity, but a kaleidoscope of multiple constituents each with their own leaders and leadership styles. The OCOG itself is only one of these constituents. For me, providing leadership in this environment meant anchoring my decisions on the athletes themselves and continually asking myself how my decisions affected their well-being. The courage, daring, grace, and determination of the athletes served to guide me in all my work.

By Sally Rehorick, Olympic and World Judge, Referee and Technical Controller, ISU; Professor Emerita, University of New Brunswick

Case questions

1 Based on this chapter and your own experience, do you think there should be a definitive list of leadership qualities for a major sports event? Explain your answer.

2 How does leadership express itself differently in different types of sports events? Explain and give an example.

3 For each of the following, determine whether each statement is true or false:
   a If you are working a Games, you often do not see what the public sees.
   b Every person working the Games can take on a leadership role.
   c The ability to make decisions instantly without all the information is critical for leadership at major sports events.
   d Many decisions at sports events are guesstimates and subjective judgement calls.

CHAPTER QUESTIONS

1 How would leading a community-level sports event differ from leading an international event?

2 Think of a major sports event leader you know or have seen in the media. Describe the leader using the different theories presented in this chapter.

3   What is the difference between pre-Games and Games-time organizing committee structures?

4   What are the differences between an enduring organization and ephemeral organization regarding leadership, staffing, and structure?

5   What does the leader of an ephemeral organization need to manage the organization effectively?

FURTHER READING

If you are interested in leadership and organizing, we suggest the following:

Czarniawska, B. (2008) *A Theory of Organizing*, Cheltenham: Edward Elgar.

Northouse, P. G. (2007) *Leadership: Theory and Practice*, Thousand Oaks, CA: SAGE Publications.

Scott, W. R. & Davis, G. F. (2007) *Organizations and Organizing: Rational, Natural, and Open System Perspectives*, Upper Saddle River, NJ: Pearson Education.

Chapter 4

Planning major sports events

OBJECTIVES

- To understand the different types of plans created and used by organizing committees
- To understand the basic tenets of project management
- To understand how a major sports event is financed and what its financial management entails

ILLUSTRATIVE CASE: BUSINESS PLANS ARE CONTEXT DEPENDENT

The president and CEO of the 1999 Pan American Games in Winnipeg, Canada, noted that once the rights to hold the event were won in July 1994, he had prepared the business plan, which he then had to significantly change six months later because the situation was not as he had anticipated (personal communication, 5 December 2003). This is not an atypical situation. Even when everything is going "well", the business plan has to be updated. One key difficulty is forecasting up to seven years in advance how the situation will look for the organizing committee. VANOC circulated its 2007 updated business plan (two years after the initial version). One could see positive and negative changes in many areas. Part of the changes were due to the general situation in which VANOC found itself, as well as to a greater understanding of specific operational needs stemming from the divisional plans having been completed in November 2006 (Vancouver Organizing Committee for the 2010 Olympic and Paralympic Winter Games, 2007).

While VANOC kept saying that it was "on time and on budget", the world had other ideas. When the economic recession hit, only months after VANOC had released its revised business plan, VANOC saw its revenues dwindle, putting the "on time, on budget" mantra in jeopardy. A key problem was that the funding for the salaries of some of the paid staff to be hired within the last year was to come from the interest earned by revenues currently in VANOC's bank accounts. As the interest dropped down to being essentially non-existent, the number of paid staff needed to be decreased, even if the work was still to be done. One creative solution VANOC used was to ask its partners for employee secondments (loaning). The impact of the recession was reflected in VANOC's 2009 updated budget (Vancouver Organizing Committee for the 2010 Olympic and Paralympic Winter Games, 2009).

THE THEORY BEHIND PLANNING MAJOR SPORTS EVENTS

Within the organizing committee's planning mode, we find the bid process (Chapter 2), the hiring of the leader (Chapter 3), and the preparation of the business, operational, and divisional plans. Besides discussing these plans, we will examine what the literature has said about this mode, including project management considerations and financing.

Plans, plans, and more plans

As you saw in the illustrative case, the business plan is an important document, one which is continuously revised. But the business plan is not the only necessary plan when preparing and hosting a major sports event. The overall operational plan and the specific divisional/ functional area plans are also critical. We will examine each type of plan in turn.

The business plan

The business plan is the first major document that the leader(s) of the organizing committee must create. Taking the vision, ideas, and plans from the bid book, the leader will set out:

- the organizing committee's vision, mission, values, and goals;
- an overview of agreements and contract information (e.g. venue agreements, communications and marketing agreements, and host city contracts), as well as key assumptions (financial or otherwise). These provide a context for the business plan;
- the organizing committee's terms of reference, which provide the scope of the "project" at hand, and include:
  - the organizing committee's legal incorporation (i.e. non-profit or other);
  - the organizational structure;
  - the different stakeholders and their roles/responsibilities;
  - the success factors;
  - the key risks and how to mitigate them;
  - the resources needed;
  - the benchmarks, timeline, and key dates/milestones (the "calendar").
- the budget and the financial planning and control mechanisms;
- an overview of the key senior management team;
- an overview of the marketing and sponsorship plan, strategic plan, human resource management (HRM) plan, language requirements and plan, cultural event plan, legacy and sustainability plan, health services plan, and evaluation plan.

The 2010 Vancouver Olympic Games' second business plan is a good example of a relatively complete business plan (Vancouver Organizing Committee for the 2010 Olympic and Paralympic Winter Games, 2007).

Early on, few of the details of the marketing/sponsorship, strategic, HRM, and other plans are available, and the budget is likely not very detailed as the respective FA directors (those who will head each specific function) are not yet in place to provide the "meat on the bone". That is why, for major sporting events at least, you will see more than one iteration of the business plan, with each successive iteration becoming more specific and likely voluminous. Also, as you approach the date of the opening ceremonies, some activities (e.g. venues constructed, test events conducted) will have been completed, providing photos and tangible proof of progress and success. While business plans are often used as proposals to approach potential sponsors and other partners and can therefore be asked to be 40 pages or less, it is easy to see that for a major sports event, where the key stakeholders are there from the outset (see Getz, 2005), the business plan will likely be larger as its main purpose is not only to sell the idea of the event to potential partners/stakeholders and show the competency of the senior management team, but also to act as a guide for each division/function as they develop their respective plans.

During the business plan phase, the organizing committee will face a number of issues, and four in particular (Parent, 2008). First, politics predominate, and include: power plays, lobbying, and government support issues. Second, given the need to plan, create the organizational structure and the management team, and set the timeline, planning and organizing issues also dominate. Third, when creating the business plan, the leaders will have to manage expectations while building relationships with their stakeholders and key Games partners (i.e. rights holders, governments, sponsors), and communicate, coordinate, and discuss the business plan with others (e.g. IFs, governments, and other Games partners). So the organizing committee has to deal with relationship and interdependence issues. Finally, the creation of the budget means financial issues are of course at the forefront.

The operational plan

According to Parent (2008), the organizing committee's operational plan highlights the responsibilities to be fulfilled according to each FA. The following information should be included: what has to be done; who will do it and who will assist; when it will be done; where it will be done; and how it will be done. Essentially, the operational plan is an extension of the terms of reference (business plan); it just provides more detail, and keeps an eye on the budget.

For the business plan, politics, organizing, financial, and interdependence are key issues. However, the detailing required in the operation plan means that other issues come to the forefront. Operational issues are, of course, at the forefront because venues and facilities must be built, and accreditations, security, technology, cultural events, opening and closing ceremonies, contingencies, and in-house Games transportation (as opposed to public transportation) must be planned. The public transportation and other municipal services must also be examined, which means that infrastructure issues are important. Finally, human resources issues are also important as you must plan for the growth of the organization, following the overall planned structure; this means thinking about numbers, roles, and responsibilities, as well as thinking about recruitment, selection, and training procedures (Parent, 2008).

The divisional plans

As FA directors are hired, they will take the business and operational plans and create their own divisional plan or work package. The divisional plan will have to detail the work to be completed, exclusions, provisional timelines, major contracts, and overall costs. The divisional plans will form the basis of the cost and project control systems. Other related systems that the organizing committee should have at this point include (Parent, 2008, 2010; Getz, 2005):

- risk analysis system (to anticipate the potential problems);
- contingency plans (for all eventualities, including budget shortfalls);
- emergency procedures (for security, health, and safety);
- training (staff and volunteers are prepared, confident, and empowered);
- information and marketing (to inform everyone of changes).

During the divisional plans phase, the organizing committee will face the same kinds of issues it has dealt with so far – politics, relationships and interdependence, finance, and infrastructure and operations (Parent, 2008).

Project management considerations

By virtue of the fact that major sports events have pre-defined start and end dates, they are similar to projects. In fact, event managers use many project management tools while planning for their sports event. VANOC made use of work breakdown structures and critical paths in their efforts to host the Games. Does every event use project management tools? No. Should they? Yes. Project management tools allow for anyone coming into the organizing committee at any point in time to see what has been done, where the organizing committee is, where it is going, what needs to be done, and by when. We will go through the basic elements including tasks, work breakdown structure (WBS), critical path, and milestones.

Tasks are the basic unit of the WBS, which in turn is the list of all tasks or activities for a project. A task is one specific activity that needs to be undertaken. It is usually found in the form of a verb and object combination, such as "recruit volunteers". All activities related to one topic are grouped together. The title of that group is the summary task or "parent", while each specific activity is a subtask or "child". For example, all subtasks pertaining to recruiting volunteers, such as doing a needs assessment, writing the job descriptions, interviewing the volunteers, selecting the volunteers, training the volunteers, etc., would constitute one group under the summary task (parent) "recruit volunteers". A rule within the WBS is to not have a single child under a parent; there must be at least two tasks for each parent. Besides the volunteers' group, there would likely be similar tasks to be undertaken for paid staff, contractors, and secondees. Each summary task would fall under the major heading of perhaps "manage human resources". The left-hand side of Figure 4.1 provides a hypothetical basic WBS for paid staff and volunteers, and the parent–children relationships, for the 2014 Sochi Olympic Winter Games and its human resources activities/needs.

ID	Task Mode	Task Name	Duration	Start	Finish	Predecessors
1		**Recruit paid staff**	**803 days**	**Thu 03/02/11**	**Mon 03/03/14**	
2		Do needs assessment	1 mon	Thu 03/02/11	Wed 02/03/11	
3		Create job descriptions	1 mon	Thu 03/03/11	Wed 30/03/11	2
4		**Recruit managers**	**301 days**	**Thu 31/03/11**	**Thu 24/05/12**	
5		Post manager positions	6 mons	Thu 31/03/11	Wed 14/09/11	3
6		Hire managers	8 mons	Fri 16/09/11	Thu 26/04/12	5
7		Train managers	1 mon	Fri 27/04/12	Thu 24/05/12	6
8		**Recruit coordinators**	**210 days**	**Mon 03/09/12**	**Fri 21/06/13**	
9		Post coordinator positions	6 mons	Mon 03/09/12	Fri 15/02/13	7
10		Hire coordinators	4 mons	Mon 18/02/13	Fri 07/06/13	9
11		Train coordinators	2 wks	Mon 10/06/13	Fri 21/06/13	10
12		Thank paid staff	7 days	Sun 23/02/14	Mon 03/03/14	11
13		**Recruit volunteers**	**455 days**	**Mon 28/05/12**	**Sun 23/02/14**	
14		Do needs assessment	1 mon	Mon 28/05/12	Fri 22/06/12	7
15		Create job descriptions	2 wks	Mon 25/06/12	Fri 06/07/12	14
16		Post volunteer positions	3 mons	Mon 09/07/12	Fri 28/09/12	15
17		Select volunteers	3 mons	Mon 01/10/12	Fri 21/12/12	16
18		**Train volunteers**	**290 days**	**Mon 24/12/12**	**Fri 31/01/14**	
19		Give general volunteer training	2 mons	Mon 24/12/12	Fri 15/02/13	17
20		Give job-specific volunteer training	6 mons	Wed 01/05/13	Tue 15/10/13	19
21		Give venue-specific volunteer training	35 days	Mon 16/12/13	Fri 31/01/14	20
22		Supervise volunteers	3.2 wks	Mon 03/02/14	Sun 23/02/14	21
23		Thank volunteers	15 days	Tue 04/02/14	Sun 23/02/14	22FF
24		Celebrate one-year post-Games	1 day	Tue 03/02/15	Tue 03/02/15	12,23

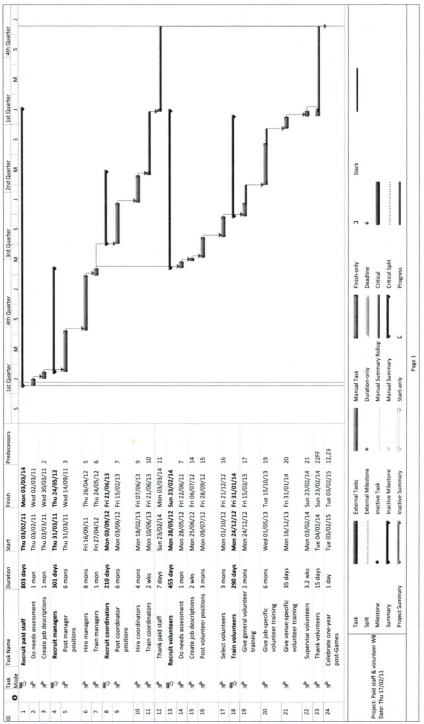

Project: Paid staff & volunteer WB
Date: Thu 17/02/11

Task
Split
Milestone
Summary
Project Summary

External Tasks
External Milestone
Inactive Task
Inactive Milestone
Inactive Summary

Manual Task
Duration-only
Manual Summary Rollup
Manual Summary
Start-only

Finish-only
Deadline
Critical
Critical Split
Progress

Slack

Figure 4.1 Hypothetical paid staff and volunteers WBS and Gantt chart for Sochi 2014.

The WBS is done using MS Project, a software program that makes it easy to create and track projects of all kinds – it is a good idea for sport event managers to familiarize themselves with this program. A trial version of the current version of MS Project can be downloaded from Microsoft; Microsoft also offers online resources and an easy-to-follow tutorial to get started with MS Project.

There are therefore many activities that can fall within the simple idea of needing volunteers for your event. And volunteers are only one small part of preparing a mega-event like the Olympic Games. The idea of the WBS is to sit down and reflect upon all the activities that need to be undertaken for the event, starting with major categories and then breaking them down into specific sub-categories, and finally even more specific tasks (the children). Next, tasks need to be ordered, to figure out what needs to be done before what. For example, volunteers must be selected before they are trained. Thus, selecting volunteers would be a *predecessor task* to training volunteers. There will of course be some tasks that can be done at the same time; these are called *concurrent tasks*. For example, recruiting volunteers and paid staff (e.g. coordinators) can be done concurrently. Also, venue construction, marketing planning, and other FAs' tasks will also be done concurrently with many HRM tasks as different people will be doing these tasks.

This brings us to resources. Once predecessor and concurrent tasks are determined, tasks need to have their necessary resources assigned. Of course, human resources need to be assigned. As a manager assigns people, this will impact the timeline. More precisely, managers have to determine if a person needs to do one task only (e.g. huge, important project requiring much work and time by the individual, such as overseeing the construction of a venue) or can take on more tasks (e.g. a coordinator scheduling her volunteers and creating necessary Games-time policies and procedures). This will have an impact on the timing of tasks, when they can start, and the overall project. A second resource is material resources. These can be stationary, building materials, etc. Another important resource to consider is finance. Here, the manager needs to consider the overall Games budget (determined by the leader and senior management staff), as well as purchasing costs, promotional costs, insurance and legal costs, etc.

An organizing committee's senior management team should prepare the basic framework for the WBS with the key milestones, and the division heads and department/function directors and managers will be able to provide the more specific tasks. The key milestones – dates when certain tasks need to be completed – will often be determined in conjunction with the Games rights holder (e.g. the IOC and its Games coordination committee for the Olympic Games). Key milestones can include: when all staff members are hired, when venues are completed, when test events are completed, the opening ceremonies, the closing ceremonies, and the end of the organization's existence. Some milestones are unmovable dates, such as the dates of the opening and closing ceremonies. This will help determine timelines; that is, the milestones will help the organizing committee work backwards from key unmovable milestones to know how long they have to complete certain tasks. Each task should be assigned a start and end date. There are two ways to determine the start and end dates:

1 Earliest start and finish dates (ESD, EFD): starting from the beginning of the project, and knowing how long each task needs to take, including predecessor and concurrent

tasks, one can figure out the earliest they can start a task and, consequently (adding the length of time a task is projected to take), the EFD. This is undertaken for the first task, before then proceeding to the next task.

2   Latest start and finish dates (LSD, LFD): starting from the end of the project, and knowing how long each task needs to take, including predecessor and concurrent tasks, one can figure out the latest they can finish the last task and, consequently (subtracting the length of time the task is projected to take), the latest start date for that task. This is done for each task, working backwards from one task to the preceding one.

Once all tasks have their ESD/EFD or LSD/LFD, there should be a difference between the projected end of the last task and end of the project or the start of the project and projected start of the first task. This difference is called the slack, float, or spare time. It is the project manager's wiggle room. Slack or float can be determined by the following formulas:

$$LFD - EFD = float$$

$$LSD - ESD = float$$

The organizing committee then completes the WBS. While the WBS lists the tasks, the Gantt chart combines the WBS with each task's associated timelines and resources, as well as a diagram depicting this same information (see the right-hand side of Figure 4.1). A variation on the Gantt chart is the PERT, the Program Evaluation and Review Technique. Depicting a PERT can be done in two ways: activity-on-arc, where tasks and their length are placed on arrows linking one key activity category or milestone to another (depicted by a node or circle); and activity-on-node, where tasks are in the nodes. Initially, PERTs were depicted using activity-on-arc, but more and more often, PERTs are depicted using activity-on-node.

The PERT allows the project manager to verify that they follow some basic rules of project management:

1   If using activity-on-arc, they number the nodes in increments of five or ten to allow for more tasks to be added later, without needing to change all the numbering.

2   All arrows are made to go from left to right. They avoid *looping*, which is a task whose subsequent task is actually to be undertaken earlier. In other words, they avoid arrows going from right to left when linking two tasks.

3   All tasks should be dependent on a previous and be a predecessor to another. Project managers avoid *dangling*, which is when a task (other than the finishing/last task) does not have a subsequent task.

The Gantt chart and PERT allow project managers to figure out the critical path. The critical path is the longest path with the least amount of float. It likely hits more milestones as well. Essentially, it is the path that the manager must keep an eye on for the project to be completed on time and within the stated resources. Figure 4.2 illustrates the PERT activity-on-node format, and the critical path (hexagon nodes) for the earlier Sochi 2014 paid staff and volunteers WBS and Gantt from Figure 4.1.

The above information on tasks, WBS, PERTs, and the critical path provide the reader with an overview of the basics of project management pertinent to major sports events. For more information on Gantt charts, PERTs and critical paths, we suggest the reader consult MindTools (2012) or the PMBOK guide and standards (www.pmi.org/PMBOK-Guide-and-Standards.aspx).

Financing

A key part of the planning process of a major sports event is the financial planning. Financial planning truly starts with the event owners or rights holders' (e.g. FIFA, CGF) goals and objectives, which are then incorporated to varying degrees in the bid/organizing commit-tees' vision, mission, and goals (see Chapter 2 and the business plan section in this chapter). The rights holders, as well as the organizing committee, will then make strategic, long-term decisions for the event generally, and for an edition of the event more specifically (e.g. growth of the brand, entering new markets such as the Middle East with FIFA). Next, spe-cific operational decisions are considered (see the operational plan earlier in this chapter) to understand what the previously determined objectives mean, on the ground, for a given edition of the event. This is where the budget comes into play as it will help define what is involved in turning those operational decisions into reality in terms of costs. Finally, there will be the monitoring and correction (ongoing evaluation, tracking) where individuals will be assigned the responsibility for specific revenues and/or expenditures (Masterman, 2004, 2009; Berry and Jarvis, 2006). This is where financial controls come into play. Before getting into financial controls, we will examine the different sources of funding available to major sports events, as well as the different aspects found within a budget.

Sources of funding

As Getz (2005) noted, there are six typical sources of funding for sports events and festivals: fundraising, grants, food and beverage sales, tickets (and other pricing structures), merchan-dising and licensing, and sponsorship. While Getz (2005) provides an overview of each source, in the case of major/mega sports events, fundraising as traditionally understood (e.g. doing charity dinners) is of less interest; so we will focus on the other five sources. Also, the IFs include broadcasting as another funding source that we will also examine.

1   *Grants*: financial grants can be obtained from philanthropic organizations, foundations, or governments. In the case of major sports events, governments would be the key source of grants. The increasing popularity of and benefits believed to accrue from hosting major sports events have led municipal, regional/provincial/state, and national governments to establish policies that provide accountability guidelines to potential organizing committees, but also parameters and conditions if the governments will support (read: help finance) a major sports event on their territory (Leopkey *et al.*, 2010). For example, in its hosting policy, the government of Canada (Sport Canada, 2008) states that bid/Games projects must meet minimum requirements found within a number of federal policies (e.g. on doping in sport, environmental assessments,

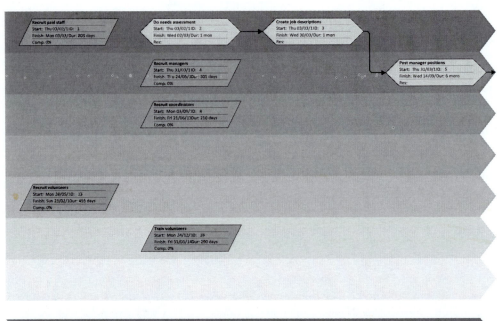

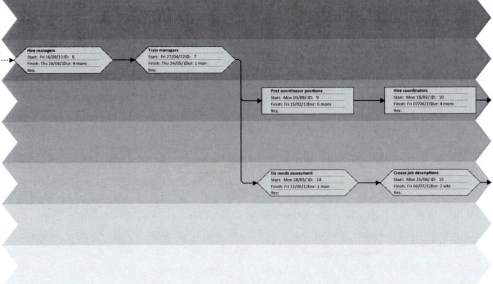

Figure 4.2 PERT and critical path for hypothetical paid staff and volunteer WBS.

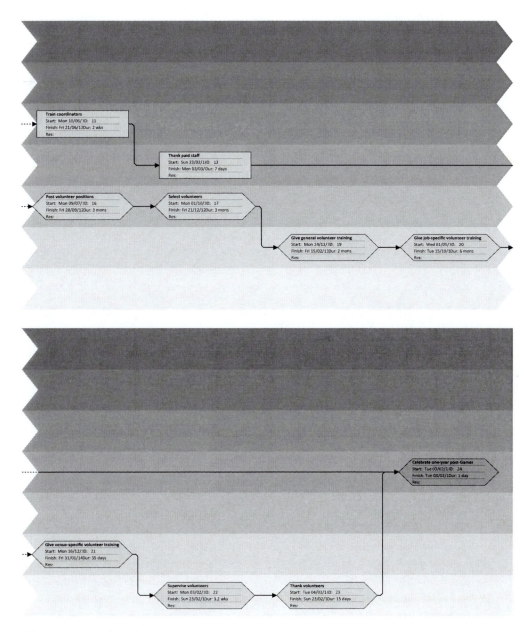

Figure 4.2 continued.

tobacco sponsorship, and official languages) and respect bid/hosting procedures set out by the International Sport Events Coordination Group (e.g. meeting deadlines, application requirements, and following memorandums of understanding and agreements). The bid/Games projects are also to follow "sound use of federal funds" (p. 5), which includes contribution limits, legacy and sport-development provisions, no allowance for deficit funding, demonstrated feasibility and good management capacity, sound financial and human resource management, and acknowledgement of the government of Canada's support and access to information.

2   *Food and beverage sales*: food and beverage sales come during Games-time and are a key part of attendees' and participants' direct event-related spending (cf. Case *et al.*, 2010; Gratton *et al.*, 2000). Food and beverage concessions are not typically provided by the organizing committee of a major sports event, but are instead outsourced, which is not seen as an issue by potential customers (cf. Mowen *et al.*, 2009). Depending on the contract signed with the food and beverage service providers, you can have three different delivery settings, which can have either set service (eating/drinking) times (e.g. during an event) or be open continuously (e.g. in the athletes' village):

a   beverage and food booths (no sitting) – highly popular in concourse areas of venues;
b   beverage tents (e.g. beer tent) and other enclosed areas – popular in gathering areas (e.g. live sites);
c   cafés, restaurants, canteens (more formal, full-service areas) – popular in athletes' villages, VIP areas.

Some IFs, as well as the IOC through its TOP (The Olympic Partners) sponsorship programme (e.g. Coca-Cola, McDonald's), have long-term agreements with key food and beverage sponsors, which can limit an organizing committee's choice of delivery format. As well, if existing venues are used, they may have prior agreements with food and beverage providers (e.g. Aramark) that the organizing committee may have to follow. In such cases, one important thing to consider will be to ensure a certain level of consistency and standard of quality from one venue to the next.

3   *Tickets (and other pricing structures)*: while smaller sports events and festivals may have a variety of options in terms of ticketing and pricing options (e.g. free general admission, donation entry charges, sponsor-provided discounts, multi-visit passes), major sports events are a little more limited or, more appropriately, can charge for tickets. Thus, tickets are the prime form of pricing structure. The 2012 Olympic Games 6.6 million tickets ranged from £20 to £2,012 (top tickets for the opening ceremonies – see Cutler, 2011a). Tickets can be offered in single-event form or as packages. Organizing committees will only have a relatively small portion of tickets that they can sell to the general public, sometimes as little as 30 per cent of a venue for an Olympic Games, for example. VANOC sold 97 per cent of its 1.54 million available tickets to the tune of CAN$269.5 million (The Vancouver Organizing Committee for the 2010 Olympic and Paralympic Winter Games, 2010a; International Olympic Committee, 2010b). The rest of the seats are reserved for the media, dignitaries, athletes and coaches, as well as sponsors. These sponsors can turn around and give away tickets to clients, customers (e.g. through promotions, giveaways, raffles, competitions), business partners, etc. We discuss Games-time

ticketing issues in Chapter 13. Notwithstanding, for smaller major sports events like the YOG, there may be opportunities to offer free admission. This is typically done to help boost attendance (and spending in other areas, like food and beverages or merchandising).

4   *Merchandising and licensing*: as organizing committees typically do not have the capacity to produce and sell a wide range of goods (merchandise), they enter into contracts with suppliers and other companies by giving them a licence to produce and sell a type of merchandise (e.g. clothing/apparel, equipment, jewellery). Major sport event organizing committees can essentially license almost any form of merchandise to promote their events and brand. The 2010 Vancouver Olympic Winter Games merchandise spectrum included, for example, T-shirts, sweaters, pants, outwear, scarves, accessories and stationery (e.g. key chains, mugs, drinking and shot glasses, pens), caps, toques, ice hockey pucks, posters, snowboards and skies, jewellery, stuffed toys, computer games, maple syrup, and *the* souvenir of the Games, the red mittens. Revenues from merchandise and licensing garnered CAN$54.6 million for VANOC (The Vancouver Organizing Committee for the 2010 Olympic and Paralympic Winter Games, 2010a). According to Getz (2005), merchandising and licensing allows the organizing committee to garner revenue but also a positive image. Others (e.g. Alexander, 1995; Cobbs and McKelvey, 2009) add that while licensing provides an important source of revenue, organizing committees must be strategic in their choice of licensees to ensure fit with the event and brand (see also Parent and Séguin, 2008).

5   *Sponsorship*: sponsors for major sports events are typically companies – through they can also be individuals or groups – that provide the organizing committee with financial and/or value in-kind (VIK) resources in return for visibility and other benefits (returns on investments). While we will talk more about sponsorship in Chapter 6, suffice it to say here that for organizing committees of major sports events, sponsorship is now a large part of their revenues. The IOC's TOP programme is an international-level sponsorship programme where companies buy the right to be the official exclusive worldwide sponsor in a given product or service category for a four-year period (International Olympic Committee, 2010b). The TOP programme allows organizing committees to have a good approximation (in advance) of how much revenue they will obtain from this source, thereby facilitating their budgeting somewhat. To illustrate, VANOC received CAN$173.5 million from the TOP programme and garnered another CAN$730.2 million from domestic sponsorship (The Vancouver Organizing Committee for the 2010 Olympic and Paralympic Winter Games, 2010a). As Getz (2005) noted, other benefits of sponsorship include greater marketing reach through the sponsors' own cross-promotions, stakeholder network growth for the event, and positive image boost when associated with good companies and brands.

6   *Broadcasting*: within the world of major sports events, broadcasting includes television, mobile, and internet media. Broadcast rights are sold in advance by the Games rights holders (e.g. the IOC, FIFA) and so, as for international-level sponsorship, organizing committees of major sports events should know how much revenue they will receive from broadcasting rights. The IOC provided $CAN479.7 million in broadcasting rights revenues to VANOC (The Vancouver Organizing Committee for the 2010 Olympic and Paralympic Winter Games, 2010a).

57

From an IOC marketing revenue-generation perspective, broadcasting and sponsorship are the main revenue sources at 47 per cent and 45 per cent, respectively. Ticketing accounts for only 5 per cent, while licensing offers only 3 per cent (International Olympic Committee, 2009a). Thus, we see the importance in major sports events of sponsorship and broadcasting. This importance certainly warrants further research into these sources, especially broadcasting, as well as its link with sponsorship, as major revenue sources for organizing committees. We also suggest bringing in different perspectives with marketing, such as finance/economics, legal, organization studies, and policy.

Budgets

In this section we will go over some basic terminology related to budgeting, leaving specific budgeting issues and considerations for the practitioner's section. Our reasoning here is that, somewhat surprisingly, sport event management research has not truly focused on budgets and financial controls. Instead, research has incorporated budgeting and financial control aspects within topics such as risk management (e.g. one risk to manage is the financial aspect, Leopkey and Parent, 2009a) and event hosting policies (Leopkey et al., 2010). For example, the government of Canada requires financial statements and annual reports as part of those supported organizing committees' sound fiscal management procedures (see Sport Canada, 2008). Also, we can find budgeting and financial management/control skills as key qualities for effective sport event leaders and managers (cf. Parent et al., 2009a; Emery, 2010). From a broader sport management perspective, budgeting and financial management have tended to be found as part of a broader analysis of sport organizations' resources and organizational efficiency/effectiveness/performance (e.g. Armstrong-Doherty, 1996; Časlavova and Berka, 2005; Frisby, 1986; Kaczynski and Crompton, 2006; Maynard et al., 2005; Wadongo et al., 2010), sponsorship (e.g. Copeland et al., 1996), security (e.g. Giulianotti and Klauser, 2010), participation in sport (e.g. Jung, 2004), sport facilities (e.g. Rafoss and Troelsen, 2010), or trends in the sport industry (e.g. Mahony and Howard, 2001). In contrast, in the broader management literature, we find fruitful research avenues for budgeting and financial management/controls, which can be applied in the context of major sports events. Management, and perhaps more appropriately, accounting and finance researchers, are examining:

- appropriate budget accounting for non-profit organizations – for example, Pineno and Tyree (2006) review category and line items for non-profit organization budgets. They also illustrate the use of activity-based costing.
- how to forecast/estimate the future and display this information in current financial statements. The argument is that asset and liability measures should reflect current economic conditions as well as future expectations, with future estimates' incorporation into financial statements being dependent on asset/liability definitions and attributes. However, such up-to-date asset/liability definitions provide for expected inflows/outflows of economic benefits as well as control over expected benefits. While estimated future income measures would differ from present income, such an approach allows for "better information for making economic decisions" (Barth, 2006: 271). Rasmus (2009) also examined speculation and finance in relation to the recent economic downturn.

■ attitudes toward budget processes and pay. Montemayor (1995) examined individual values in a situation of budgetary constraint, specifically in regards to merit pay, suggesting that measuring individual values is important for understanding this situation. In turn, Ritchie *et al.* (2004) examined executives' individual characteristics and their impact on non-profit organizations' financial measures. Finally, Cheng-Li and Mien-Ling (2009) argued that organizations should foster more positive attitudes in managers towards budgetary processes by increasing their involvement in the process, which in turn will decrease budgetary slack behaviour.

■ the role of budgeting in a context of uncertainty and a need for flexibility. When there is high uncertainty, as there is for major sports event financial planning, Frow *et al.* (2010) suggested continuous budgeting as a means for managers to use their discretion when faced with unexpected events through the integration of budgeting uses within other management controls. It is suggested that this integration allows for flexibility as well as financial discipline. In turn, Mulvey and Shetty (2004) provided a framework for modelling financial planning under conditions of uncertainty.

■ the roles of the non-profit board of directors. The trend in non-profits has been to increasingly adopt for-profit business practices. However, as Judge and Zeithaml (1992) argued, non-profits (as are most major sports event organizations) should be cautious when doing so given that non-profit boards are typically more involved in the organization's strategic decisions than for-profit boards. Thus, the governance structure needs to be considered when making decisions regarding for-profit-like business practices (e.g. financial management processes). Parker (2008) also examined board operations and financial control.

As the reader can see from the above, there are many areas yet to be studied in major sports events regarding budgeting and financial management/control. We will now briefly turn to some basics of budgeting, lists, and tools, details of which can be found in numerous other textbooks (e.g. Getz, 2005; Masterman, 2004; Shone and Parry, 2004; Van der Wagen and Carlos, 2005).

First, a *budget* is one type of plan, one which is focused on the financial aspect. In major sports events, you will often hear of two types of budgets: (1) the *operating budget* is the budget for the organizing committee, excluding capital costs (venue construction); and (2) the *capital budget* is the budget for capital expenditures only. This division is often done because governments (and/or other stakeholders) may have control or contribute only to the building/renovating of venues and other Games infrastructure, making it sometimes easier management-wise to separate the two budgets. Nevertheless, both types of budgets have two core entries: the *revenues* (what comes in, i.e. inflow of assets) and the *expenses* or expenditures (what goes out, i.e. outflow of assets). Examples of revenues include ticketing, sponsorship, and marketing royalties; examples of expenses include salaries, communication, and promotion costs (e.g. advertising, printing posters), and technology equipment and other procurements. *Assets* are broader than revenues and include anything that is owned, fabricated, and/or donated to the organizing committee (e.g. venues, signs, VIK equipment), which will give the organizing committee future economic gain (e.g. when leftover sport equipment is sold). In turn, *liabilities* can include such things as borrowing costs/reimbursements, exchange-rate changes, and revenues not yet received. Liabilities can be seen as future economic sacrifices (e.g. if exchange rates change, sponsorship monies received in euros and needing to be converted to American dollars may be affected if the currencies come to par, as there would be "less" American money received), or past or present obligations such as paying interest on a bank loan (see also AccountingStudy.com, n.d. for more on assets, liabilities, and other financial statement terms such as equity, gains, and losses).

Given the difficulty of predicting circumstances 5–10 years down the road, fiscally responsible sport event managers will include a *contingency fund* to cover, as the name indicates, contingencies. Examples of contingencies to consider include potential natural-event problems (e.g. earthquakes, floods, or major storms), increased venue construction costs, health epidemics (e.g. H1N1, SARS, and mad-cow disease), unfavourable exchange-rate changes, economic downturns, or not reaching sponsorship or ticket sale targets. Should the contingency fund not be used, which is the hope of all sport event managers, then it can be converted into a financial legacy post-Games.

Each type of asset/revenue and liability/expense is typically represented by a line in the budget, for what is referred to as a line-item budget (Getz, 2005). Table 4.1 provides an example of the line-item final operating budget of the 2010 Olympic Winter Games. What we can notably see in this budget is that the budget should be balanced, at least if there are no extra revenues to provide as financial legacy. To set up a line-item budget, senior event staff need the assistance of the FA directors/managers. The directors/managers will receive guidelines and constraints from senior staff (e.g. a range within which they can fall for their part of the budget, economic constraints on the overall budget). Using research data (typically from past Games), the directors/managers will then build their FA's part of the line-item budget and provide justifications for each number provided. All FA line-item budgets are then sent back to the senior staff for integration into the full Games budget, which must ultimately be approved by the event's board of directors (this is a form of financial control).

When speaking about expenses, sport event managers should know the term *cost centre*. A cost centre is one type of management or programme activity. For example, salaries may fall under the staffing cost centre and petrol for the Games car fleet would fall under the transportation cost centre. Salaries and petrol would be considered *cost objects* (Getz, 2005). When a staff member pays for an organization-related expense (e.g. pays for the petrol for a fleet car), they can get reimbursed but must do so from the appropriate cost centre. Cost centres are a form of organizing the expenses and of controlling the finances.

There are two types of costs: direct and indirect (Masterman, 2009). *Direct costs* are those that fall under one specific cost centre; thus they are attached to a specific programme or activity. These costs can also be called variable costs, as they are typically dependent on the number of attendees (Games participants, spectators, etc.). For example, the more athletes there are, the more beds are needed, the more food is needed, the more cleaning is needed. *Indirect costs*, sometimes also called fixed costs or overheads, are those costs that do not change based on the number of attendees. They typically fall under more than one cost centre. For example, it does not matter if you have 10,000 or 12,000 media representatives attending your venue, the cost of renting the main media centre's designated building remains the same. Ideally, event managers want to keep their fixed costs as low as possible.

Table 4.1 2010 Vancouver Olympic Winter Games final operating budget

	For the period of 30 September 2003 to 31 July 2010 (in thousands of CAN$)
Operating revenues	
Government of Canada contribution	74,401
Government of British Columbia contribution	113,395
Ticket sales	269,459
Merchandising and licensing	54,618
International Olympic Committee TOP sponsorship	173,558
Domestic sponsorship	730,157
International Olympic Committee contribution (e.g. broadcast revenues)	479,742
Marketing rights royalties	(186,759)
Other	175,558
Total operating revenues	1,884,129
Operating expenses	
Finance	115,074
Revenues, marketing, and communications	167,704
Services and Games operations	723,043
Sport and Games operations	287,972
Technology	452,425
Workforce and sustainability	129,954
Foreign exchange net loss	7,957
Total operating expenses	1,884,129
Balance	0

Source: Adapted from The Vancouver Organizing Committee for the 2010 Olympic and Paralympic Winter Games, 2010a.

Two other financial terms should be familiar to sport event managers: *cash flow* and *break-even analysis*. Major sports events need up-front money to be able to hire the staff and start building the venues; yet, few revenues are available up-front, creating a negative cash flow situation (especially when many large venues must be built). Essentially, sport event managers must be prepared to work "in the red" for a while. This is where obtaining sponsors early (especially financial institutions) and receiving broadcast revenues up-front (if possible) come in handy. There will be expenses for which the attached revenues will only come later; for example, merchandise must be created and salaries paid before merchandise and tickets can be sold. Come Games-time, however, the organizers should (hopefully) find themselves in a positive cash flow situation as there are fewer expenses and more revenues coming in. Shone and Parry (2004) describe a Games cash flow situation in greater detail.

A *break-even analysis* is useful to sport event managers for determining ticket pricing (Getz, 2005; Shone and Parry, 2004). If managers know their total costs (fixed plus variable), they know how much revenue they need to generate to break even. Assuming also that they know the total broadcasting and sponsorship amounts as well, then the managers can deduce how much revenue is needed from tickets, merchandise/licensing, and other sources. For the tickets specifically, managers will need to know how many seats are available in each venue, as well as how much the market is willing to pay for a given ticket. For example, the London 2012 Olympic Games organizers knew that the opening ceremonies would be the top event, meaning that a higher price could be asked for prime seats. In contrast, the opening round of the equestrian events may not be as popular; thus, tickets would have to be lower. Organizers can promote certain less-popular sports by offering cheap tickets (e.g. £20). Having certain tickets at a low cost also allows organizers to say that the Games are accessible to lower-income individuals. Nevertheless, using a simplified example, if the total costs for the 100-metre sprint event were £1 million and there were 30,000 seats available in the stadium for ticket holders from the general public (i.e. 30,000 tickets for sale), then on average, tickets should be £33.33 each for the organizers to break even on that event. Given the popularity of this specific event, organizers will likely charge more for tickets, thus allowing them to make a profit and perhaps offset losses in a less-popular event. Charging a little more can also help offset tickets that are not sold. For example, SOCOG sold 92.4 per cent of its tickets; the Beijing Organizing Committee for the Olympic Games (BOCOG) sold 95.6 per cent of its tickets; and VANOC sold 97 per cent of its tickets (International Olympic Committee, 2008, 2010b). LOCOG would have been aware of this fact when creating its pricing strategy to ensure that it at least broke even.

Financial controls

In this section we cover some basic forms of financial controls (see also Masterman, 2009; Getz, 2005): budget authority; requests-for-proposals and contracts; cost centres and reimbursements; annual reports, budget revisions, and cash flow analyses; VIK; scrip, meal tickets, and designated credit cards; and inventory control. The various forms of control are interrelated and typically work together as a financial management system:

- *Budget authority*: organizing committees will usually designate different individuals as having the responsibility for certain parts of the budget. Responsibility is typically split along two lines: by area and by level of expense. More precisely, directors will usually be held responsible for expenses incurred within their FA. However, responsibility is offered often only to a certain level of expense – for example, anything under US$5,000. Expenses between US$5,000 and US$10,000 may have to be approved at the vice-president level, whereas expenses between US$10,000 and US$25,000 may have to be approved at the executive vice-president level. Anything above this amount would then have to be approved at the board of directors level, either the whole board or the board's finance committee. While these are hypothetical examples, they give an idea that the larger the expense, the more likely responsibility will rest with a higher managerial level.

■ *Requests-for-proposals and contracts*: associated with the above financial control, organizing committees will typically tender major jobs (i.e. outsource) by requesting proposals. The best candidate for each request for proposal (RFP) is chosen (hopefully not only on cost but also on quality, experience, and reputation) and a contract is signed. RFPs also allow for fairness instead of seeing conflicts of interest or patronage (e.g. choosing the CEO's brother-in-law's construction company because he is family). Within this contract, the organizing committee can help control costs by paying for services rendered or output instead of by time. This comes in especially handy for venue construction, an area known for delays and cost increases. Thus, if the organizing committee pays the contractor by milestone (foundations complete, walls up, interior finished, etc.), then the organizing committee decreases its likelihood of seeing its construction costs sky-rocket if the contractor incurs delays (thus needing to pay more for labour, for example) or the cost of materials increases.

■ *Cost centres and reimbursements*: as mentioned earlier, using a cost centre approach allows for financial control as the organizing committee can categorize expenses and follow them more easily. The organizing committee's financial director or vice-president can track which cost centres are on track (on or under budget) and which are not (over budget), and take the appropriate measures before the organizing committee's financial situation becomes dire. Cost controlling using cost centres is also important for reimbursements. Travel expenses, for example, need to be categorized as such, and separated from venue construction expenses or transportation, for accounting purposes.

■ *Annual reports, budget revisions, and cash flow analyses*: granting agencies (e.g. governments) and rights holders typically require annual reports. This is an opportunity to review the budget and update the cash flow analysis. While the organizing committee may not undertake a full budget revision, it will at least need to provide some form of tracking/performance analysis. Nevertheless, revising the budget will be necessary every two or three years, given the different externalities and contingencies that may (or may not) occur, such as economic downturns or economic booms. For example, VANOC provided a budget of CAN$1.507 million in the bid book (The Vancouver Organizing Committee for the 2010 Olympic and Paralympic Winter Games, 2003). An initial budget appeared in VANOC's first business plan dated July 2005; however, the detailed FA analyses had not yet been undertaken. When these plans were completed, a second business plan was published in May 2007, which showed a revised operating budget of CAN$1.629 million (The Vancouver Organizing Committee for the 2010 Olympic and Paralympic Winter Games, 2007). VANOC planned to have the third edition of its business plan and revised budget out in 2008. However, the economic downturn heavily impacted VANOC's activities; as a consequence, a revised budget of CAN$1.756 million was published in January 2009 (The Vancouver Organizing Committee for the 2010 Olympic and Paralympic Winter Games, 2009). VANOC's final financial statement, published on 17 December 2010, showed a balanced budget of CAN$1.884 million. It is not uncommon to see budgets increase from bid to final report; in fact, it is more the norm, and it is somewhat understandable given the seven-year span from initial bid proposed budget to Games-time.

63

- *Value-in-kind*: given the negative cash flow situation at the beginning, to alleviate expenses organizing committees have recourse to VIK. These are non-financial sponsorships (e.g. ACER computers, Samsung phones, Workopolis internet job posting capabilities). Accountants will nevertheless assign a realistic value to the VIK for budgetary line-item purposes (i.e. what it would have cost the organizing committee to buy this equipment or service).

- *Scrip, meal tickets, and designated credit cards*: major sports events are typically held in more than one venue at the same time. Money handling will therefore occur on each site, making it more difficult to control than when it was all centralized at headquarters. Besides designating spending authority to venue managers, organizing committees can use scrip – fake or "funny money" – in order to avoid too much direct handling of actual cash. Scrip is exchanged at the end of the event for actual money. As Getz (2005) notes, this increases the honesty and accuracy of vendors and users. For example, volunteers may be given meal tickets to exchange at meal time. This controls who gets food but also how many times the individual can get food (thus controlling food costs as well). Another way to control expenses is to provide selected individuals with company credit cards to allow them to spend up to a maximum amount, similar to petty cash. This provides flexibility for the cardholder and can speed up approval processes during crunch time or during emergencies.

- *Inventory control*: major sports events are full of materials and potential memorabilia. It therefore becomes important for the budget and the proper functioning of the event to carefully control inventory, be it food, beverage, merchandise, technological equipment, or any other material or "thing". Imagine a manager going to work one day and finding their computer has been stolen. It is therefore common to have expensive equipment (walkie-talkies, computers, etc.) locked down, locked in a room, or controlled through signing in and out. When a manager or coordinator takes control of a space at Games-time, she will typically receive a list of all equipment and materials in her space, which she will have to sign off on to (1) approve the state of the equipment; and (2) take responsibility for it during the Games. All must be returned to the organizing committee upon completion of the Games for subsequent legacy distribution. This is admittedly a difficult task as people are always looking to take home a piece of the Games.

In this finance section we have covered a specific type of plan, the budget, including various revenue sources and financial control mechanisms. We now turn to the practitioner's perspective.

THE PRACTITIONER'S PERSPECTIVE ON PLANNING MAJOR SPORTS EVENTS

Handling the intricacies of planning an event is much like piecing together a puzzle. Not only are there the obvious hard pieces – which include budgets, project management, financial controls, RFPs, and annual reports – there are the soft pieces that include competencies and expertise: Games vs. non-Games; experience vs. inexperience; EQ (emotional intelligence), learning intelligence vs. previous title or designation; leadership and communication skills vs. technical knowledge. All pieces of the puzzle eventually must fit together for the event to be successful; and at every step of the planning stage, all pieces need to be considered. If any of the puzzle pieces are changed, it can alter or drastically affect the overall picture (i.e. the business plan and the operating budget). If we look at BOCOG, for example, their bid book planning promised open access to the internet and media, but we see in retrospect that they did not keep to their plan and we question whether or not they ever really intended open access. It became obvious that their initial promises were not going to be kept despite the IOC's strong urgings to honour their bid book plan. This change (movement of the puzzle piece) became a major issue with a significant impact for the key stakeholders of the Games, including: media, broadcasters, sponsors, and athletes. We will cover practitioner aspects of planning for the unknown, project management, and financing of the Games in this section.

Planning for the unknowns

When the business plan for a major sports event is conceived, it reflects the "what is" in the present and the best possible guesstimates relative to financial, political, and social factors in both local and global environments. Historical data are analysed, and experts are consulted for future projections to assist in mitigating crises and disasters both before and during the Games. There are always unknowns that you don't know (aka "unknown unknowns") during the planning period. The examples below demonstrate how financial, social, and political factors have impacted major sports events.

The location of the 2014 Sochi Olympic Winter Games is in an exclusive seaside resort, not easily accessible. As the planning began, there was little or no transportation system to the area, no infrastructure of existing facilities, no local workforce – in essence, everything needed to be created from scratch. The Russian government spent billions just to create the physical municipal infrastructure, on top of which Games infrastructure would have to be added. The initial financial plan anticipated these known factors, but they did not consider the impact of a lack of infrastructure on the recruitment of the workforce (the *unknown*). What was not anticipated (socially) is that many previous "Games gypsies" (a workforce that migrates from major sports event to major sports event) would not be interested in working in such a remote location without access to established infrastructure, services, and entertainment. Work fell behind schedule, and the budget of the Games escalated as the organizing committee attempted to use signing bonuses and increased salaries to attract a competent, experienced, ex-pat workforce to build the Olympic facilities, including accommodation and transportation.

Even one factor, on its own, can be enough to derail an event. For example, the political factor affected the Formula 1 racing event in Bahrain in 2011. Continued civil unrest caused so much fear and concern within the international racing teams that the race was cancelled.

Next, if the political climate changes, a medical or health issue occurs, an economic downturn happens or a union situation develops, the security and safety planning of the event will likely be escalated and changed. Contingency plans are always a part of planning a major event, with human and financial resources as key considerations. An example was the

H1N1 flu epidemic in Canada six months before the 2010 Olympic Winter Games in Vancouver. All employees were "strongly encouraged" to have the flu vaccine provided free of charge on VANOC's premises. In preparation for these same Winter Games, contracts were negotiated with government employees before the Games. Bonuses were offered in exchange for agreement that their union would not strike during the Games. It was estimated that not only was money saved, but the security of knowing there would be no labour disruption reduced stress for all concerned and helped enhance Vancouver's international reputation as a responsible and effective organizing committee. This example illustrates how proactive planning can be far reaching and contributes to the success of an event long before it occurs. Nevertheless, both business and operating plans have been modified significantly as a result of these unknowns.

One obvious take-away from these examples is that we live in a changing world and cannot possibly know with any degree of certainty how changes in financial, social, and political arenas will impact the bottom line. We just have to be prepared for the fact that such factors will likely change the Games budget and plans.

Project management

Project management is key for an organizing committee to be on time, on budget, and efficiently integrate the constant arrival of new team members. The WBS and PERT described earlier allow new members to hit the grounding running by knowing the current status of activities in all functional areas. The critical path is particularly necessary for leaders to ensure they reach milestones on time and on budget. A formal online project management process for tracking activity is critical to ensuring that changes in dates and budgets are quickly received by all the FAs affected so they can effect revisions and adjustments to drop dead dates and that they can still meet the milestones. It is worth considering a certification in project management as part of the prerequisite for hiring in this position or providing the opportunity for a project management course. This could provide a solid foundation for meeting the rigorous challenges of developing a project execution plan that integrates contingency plans, allocates and shares resources, and resolves conflict through accurate monitoring of multiple projects. It is essential to understand the principles of project management if one is going to be successful in creating a solid plan.

Financing the games

Specific to the Olympic Games, sponsorship and broadcasting revenues account for the biggest pieces of the pie. So that begs the question: which is most important – the consumer who buys the tickets and merchandise or the sponsors and broadcasters who provide the bulk of the financing to be able to execute the Games?

Revenues as double-edged swords

Organizing committee managers have to understand that each revenue source is a double-edged sword. For example, because of pre-existing relationships, sponsorship is good, in the sense that it provides guaranteed revenue sources that are already known when the budget planning occurs. However, it also limits the organizing committee managers' range of potential revenue sources because of exclusivity clauses in sponsorship contracts and programmes.

In turn, broadcasting's major contribution to the IOC and Olympic Movement's coffers provides a source of revenue for many Olympic programmes. However, it also gives the media a certain power to influence the decisions that managers make during the planning sessions. To illustrate, NBC's power influenced competition schedules during the 2008 Beijing Olympic Games. The schedule for the swimming finals, for example, was changed from late evening to early morning to fall within NBC's prime-time spots back home in the United States. This significantly impacted athletes' training plans and possibly their performance.

In contrast, there is a mismatch of expense and effort vs. revenue from ticket sales, because they account for a maximum of 30 per cent of income at any major event. There is always debate and discussion in the planning stages about how many tickets will be delivered to the public for events, even though the relative income and impact to the bottom line is so much less than the sponsorship and broadcast revenue. Is there an opportunity for Games messaging to the public to reflect these facts and impact public rhetoric on this subject? Moreover, if the consumer was more accurately informed, would that more positively affect the discourse and gossip about tickets for the public? These questions could be reflected on further by researchers.

Financial planning

Financial information and budget details are disseminated through numbers. Numbers tell a story depending on how they are shaped and disseminated. For example, traditional businesses are described as before or after EBITA (earnings before interest, taxes and amortization costs). Success is determined by profitability. However, EBITA is not an appropriate measure for major sports events – organizing committee managers are temporary owners who relinquish everything when an event is finished: assets are sold or folded into legacy groups. There is no amortization, and earnings are revenue against expenses where they hope to break even. If there is a surplus at the end of a major sports event, it is distributed in the form of bonuses for employee loyalty during the life of the bid and organizing committee – in the case of the Olympics an average of 11 years – or in the form of financial legacies for the host region.

While major sports events would be thrilled with a profit, they usually spend the life of the event from planning to wrap-up attempting to prove they are on budget and will finish with no debt. Stakeholders are not looking for dividends on their investment – their return is in the form of leveraging by association of their social or business status; increased market share; and favours in the form of future considerations. None of this gets reflected in the traditional bottom line, it is subjective ROI (return on investment).

A budget detail which can be controversial is VIK, the in-kind contributions. These are goods and services that the organization is given. The organizing committee does not pay for them. The provider may and is often given consideration, advertising, accreditation for access to events, and promotion in exchange for their goods and services. While no money has changed hands, in-kind contributions are shown as an expense or as income, depending on what will most positively impact the budget. It is defended as an expense, because it is argued that if they had to be purchased, there would have been a cash outlay, so it is therefore an expense. It is also in other cases defended and recorded as income because it has value and that value must be reflected in some way, so the VIK contribution is assigned a cash value and recorded as income on the budget. The challenge in both cases is that there is no cash in hand because real money has not been exchanged. This is a common practice in business to attach a value to goods and services received; and the rationale is that they were needed and if not donated would have had to be purchased. The grey area in all of this is that if it is recorded as revenue it looks like cash in hand for spending. Perhaps it could more appropriately appear on another line in the budget that reflects goods in hand that have a value in themselves but no cash value, so there is an acknowledgement of the value to the organization, but it is not perceived as cash that can be spent. Budgets are complex because they can be prepared years in advance (requiring forecasting skills on the part of the managers) and are affected and informed by stakeholders, Games partners, the politics of sports, and the role of politicians as conduits to the budget. With multiple stakeholders, including the media and the general public, there is a need for transparency so that stakeholders in turn can make informed decisions for their own organization, but also to assist the organizing committee in its efforts.

Also Milena's E-mail!

CHAPTER SUMMARY

In this chapter we examined different types of plans used by major sports events. We first looked at the business plan, which should include the organizing committee's vision, mission, values, and goals; an overview of agreements, contract information, key assumptions; the organizing committee's terms of reference; the budget and financial planning and control mechanisms; and an overview of the key senior management team, as well as any other plans (marketing, HRM, etc.). Following the business plan, the overall operational plan should be created and explain what has to be done, who will do it and who will assist, when it will be done, where it will be done, and how it will be done. The divisional plans are the FAs' specific operational plans. Next, we examined basic project management concepts. We described what tasks are, what slack or float is, how to create a WBS, what a Gantt chart is, how to draw a PERT, and how to determine the critical path.

In addition, we examined financing. This included reviewing the different sources of funding for major sports events (grants, food and beverage sales, tickets and other pricing structures, merchandising and licensing, sponsorship, and broadcasting) and budgeting. For budgeting, we first examined what can be found within the literature. We then turned to the budget itself, describing assets/revenues, liabilities/expenses, cost centres, cash flow, and break-even analyses. Finally, we examined different forms of financial control, including budget authority; RFP and contracts; cost centres and reimbursements; annual reports, budget revisions, and cash flow analyses; VIK; scrip, meal tickets, and designated credit cards; and inventory control.

From the practitioner's perspective, we made the reader aware that there are both hard and soft aspects to the planning process and they need to fit like pieces of a puzzle. Factors were identified (political, social, financial, health, security/safety) that affect planning and can fall into the category of unknown unknowns. Examples illustrated the effect on both business and operational planning. The importance of using and executing project management at every level of management was mentioned. Finally, the double-edged sword of revenue sources was explained and the need to be transparent with all stakeholders during the complex budgeting process was noted.

EXPERT CASE: PLANNING A MAJOR SPORTS EVENT'S LANGUAGE SERVICES

In world Games, such as the Olympics, athletes come from all over the globe, speaking various languages, not always able to communicate with the different functions they need to interact with, such as the media, doping control, sport production, etc. In order to secure the success of the Games, an organizing committee has to make language resources available to these athletes, first and foremost in the form of language interpretation.

In some cases, providing language services is necessary, in others, just good business. One of the functions that most rely on the service of interpreters, and one that couldn't be without it, is doping control. In every Olympic Games the medal-ranking athletes are tested for illegal substances and the procedure is quite complicated. Questions need to be answered, forms need to be filled out. It is vital that the athlete understands the process to the fullest, for if he or she fails the test and then claims not to have been given adequate language assistance, the results can be tossed out.

When it comes to the media, another big client of language services, the service is not necessary for the legality of the Games, but hugely important for its delivery. The media are vital in the perceived success of the Games; and so the more access the media have to the medal-winning athletes, the more positive messages reach the consumers.

But how is it possible to provide language services for all the athletes speaking some dozen languages? Simply said, it is not, except with extreme cost, importing interpreters from other countries. So what the organizing committee needs to do is focus on the medal-winning athletes and, early on, guesstimate the most likely winners of each sport. Based on an educated estimation from language services and sport FAs, a relatively small number of languages are chosen for each venue, intended to cover the medal-winning athletes only, in addition to the most likely runner-ups. During the Vancouver 2010 Olympic and Paralympic Winter Games, ten languages were provided for: Czech, French, German, Japanese, Korean, Mandarin, Russian, Slovak, and Spanish, and at one venue Lithuanian. Of these, the three Asian languages and Russian were by far the most used. This was partly due to the success of those four nations, but also because athletes from these nations were less likely to speak English than athletes from many of the other nations participating in the Games. In contrast, no language service was, for instance, provided for the Nordic nations (e.g. Norway, Denmark, Sweden), even though they tend to be extremely successful in Nordic (ski) events. This is because their athletes almost always speak excellent English.

In order to keep the cost of language services down, professional interpreters were only used for major press conferences at the venues, all press conferences at the main media centre (MMC; where interpretation was required), as well as at various meetings (such as

IOC meetings, Chef de Mission meetings, the medical commission, etc.). In all other places and for all other purposes, volunteers provided language services. The volunteers were not trained interpreters, but simply people that happened to know both English and the target language. They were given minimal orientation, which included one day of interpreter training, some reading material, and good advice, before being put to the task.

Not everyone evaluates their own language abilities in the same way, and someone who might say they are fluent in English might not speak the language well enough to interpret at a press conference. At the Vancouver 2010 Games the original application question where volunteers ranked their language skills as mother tongue, fluent, conversational, and beginner were followed up with two different test methods. First they received the CEFR (Common European Framework of Reference) self-evaluation grid where the user selects the scale that most describes their language ability. This was followed up with a standardized online language test, evaluated by professional language evaluators. The goal was to ensure that the linguistic knowledge of each volunteer was high enough for both target and source language.

Contrary to popular belief, volunteers are not a free resource for an organizing committee. They need to be fed and clothed, both of which cost considerable amounts of money, and scheduling many volunteers with different availabilities is a huge task. In some ways, language volunteers can be seen as particularly expensive volunteers as their service is not always needed and sometimes not at all. For example, let's say that a Czech skater is particularly good and almost guaranteed to win a medal. He speaks no English, and it is therefore hugely important that language services provide an interpreter for the days this skater competes, which, in this example, covers three days. If the volunteer is at the venue only to interpret for this one skater, his role is very limited and he is only needed for three short shifts. He would nevertheless have to get the same training and the same uniform as an interpreter who works 12 full shifts. If the volunteer can be used in some other way as well, however, the cost can be said to go down.

Combining language services with other functions can, therefore, be hugely successful. At the Vancouver 2010 Games, as well as at some previous Games, the role of language services was integrated with venue protocol in such a way that, while the volunteer was not interpreting, he was helping venue protocol with tasks such as managing the Olympic Family lounge and seating area. This was not only economical for VANOC but also much more enjoyable for the volunteer, who did not have to wait around while they were not interpreting.

In some venues this is not possible, such as at the MMC, where minimal protocol service is provided. And yet there, as in other venues, the situation can arise where language service is not needed either for a certain time period or for a specific language. During such periods it is up to the language services managers to be creative in order to make use of the available workforce as well as to keep the volunteers happy. This happened on frequent occasions at the MMC during the Vancouver 2010 Games. What the managers did then was to offer up services to other functions such as the press, event services (EVS), and whoever was in need of extra manpower. Examples of tasks the language services volunteers took on in such cases were: preparing the press kits, taking shifts at the information desk, escorting members of the press around the building, as well as assistance to EVS in patrolling the area around the

Olympic cauldron. Few language volunteers resisted the dual responsibility because most people want to be kept busy. It was communicated to them in advance of accepting the language role that they would be required to assist as protocol volunteers.

Using volunteers instead of professional interpreters can be hugely useful and cost saving in straightforward situations. Using volunteers to interpret for major press conferences should only be done as a substitute for professional interpreters. An example was the Czech and Slovak languages at the Vancouver 2010 Games.

Language volunteers were, however, frequently used for non-medal round press conferences. The consideration is once again a risk, and not all volunteers are comfortable being in that position. At the Vancouver 2010 Games, there was an occasion where shortly before a press conference was to start, the French volunteer got cold feet and refused to interpret. That time, it was fortunate that the language services manager was a francophone who stepped in and interpreted the press conference. Had this happened to the only Lithuanian speaker in the group, the first step would have been to ask among the Lithuanian group whether anyone spoke English and was comfortable interpreting, and if not there would be nothing to do except to tell the press that no interpretation could be provided. This happened during one of the sport events leading up to the Vancouver Games, where Korean interpretation was lacking at the snowboard venue, which resulted in no interviews with the Korean medal-winning athletes. Such a situation is unavoidable, particularly if an athlete not expected to do well wins a medal. Games planning may not have included that athlete's language. If the athlete makes the podium, the option is to contact an over-the-phone interpreter, which is less than effective as they often do not have the proper context for the interpretation, but it is an option nonetheless.

With the increasing use of the English language, and general acceptance that it is the global language (especially in sport), more and more athletes speak English. This may in the future diminish the role of language services; but until that happens, language services need to be provided for those that need interpretation.

By Dr. Kristín M. Jóhannsdóttir, Researcher, University of Iceland

Case questions

1   What kind of operation plan would a language services manager need to create? What would be the main costs?

2   Why are language services important in a major sports event?

3   To what extent should an organizing committee provide language services (e.g. to everyone – including athletes, officials, VIPs, spectators – to athletes only, for press conferences only)?

CHAPTER QUESTIONS

1   What is the difference between an organizing committee's business plan, operational plan, and the divisional plans?

2   Explain why project management tools are useful for sport event planning.

3   Think about where you want to be in five years. With this image in mind, think about what you need to do to get to that point (tuition for further education, buying a car, buying a house, money for marriage, etc.). Now prepare a budget to reach that goal. Will you be able to reach your goal? If not, what would you need to change in order to reach that goal?

4   What factors can impact a major sports event's planning and budgeting exercises? Which of those factors which can constitute "unknowns"?

5   Describe how the different major sports event revenue sources can be double-edged swords.

FURTHER READING

If you are interested in planning, we suggest the following:

Canadian Sport Tourism Alliance (2011) *Business Plan Template (Version 3)*. Online. Available at http://canadiansporttourism.com/industry-tools/business-plan-template.html (accessed 27 February 2012).

Mingus, N. (2002) *Project Management in 24 Hours*, Madison, WI: CWL Publishing.

Stewart, B. (2007) *Sport Funding and Finance*, Oxford: Butterworth-Heinemann.

Chapter 5

Workforce management: Building high-functioning organizing committees

OBJECTIVES

- To understand the different types of workforce members involved in a major sports event
- To understand what it takes to manage both paid staff and volunteers in a major sports event
- To understand how to build a high-functioning organizing committee

ILLUSTRATIVE CASE: HOW MANY PEOPLE DOES IT TAKE TO HOST A MAJOR SPORTS EVENT?

Most major sports events are predominantly executed by volunteers; however, paid professionals are critical in developing the plans and assisting in the Games delivery. The following gives you an idea of different major sports events' workforce sizes:

1   1984 Los Angeles Olympic Games: 20,000 paid employees and 50,000 volunteers (McDonald, 1991);

2   2000 Sydney Olympic Games: 142,748 accredited workforce members, including 2,972 paid staff and 46,967 volunteers (International Olympic Committee, 2009d; Parmenter, 2000; Sloman, 2000);

3   2002 Salt Lake City Olympic Winter Games: 51,200 accredited workforce members including 1,500 regular employees and 22,000 volunteers (International Olympic Committee, 2009c; SLOC, 2002);

4   2008 Beijing Olympic Games: over 266,000 accredited workforce members, including 16,337 paid employees and 74,202 volunteers (BOCOG, 2008; International Olympic Committee, 2009b);

5   2010 Vancouver Olympic Winter Games: 93,650 accredited workforce members, including 9,384 staff and 20,704 volunteers (VANOC, 2010);

6   2010 Singapore Youth Olympic Games: 50,688 accredited workforce members, including 2,601 staff and 20,000 volunteers (International Olympic Committee, 2010c; Singapore 2010 Youth Olympic Games, 2010);

73

7   2011 New Zealand Rugby World Cup: upwards of 500 paid staff and 5,500 volunteers (Joel Fitzpatrick, personal communication, 31 October 2011; Rugby New Zealand 2011 Ltd., 2011);

8   2012 Innsbruck Winter Youth Olympic Games: approximately 100 paid staff and 1,440 volunteers (Martin Schnitzer, personal communication, 9 March 2012; Innsbruck 2012, 2011).

THE THEORY BEHIND WORKFORCE MANAGEMENT

Within major sports events we typically speak of the workforce to designate those paid employees, consultants, contract workers, secondees, and unpaid volunteers who form the human resources of a given organizing committee. There are some differences between the types of workforce:

- employees: regular, typically full-time, paid workforce members;
- consultants: short- or long-term paid (part- or full-time) workforce members;
- contract workers: short-term, paid workforce members;
- secondees: short- or long-term workforce members paid by their originating employer – they are on loan to the organizing committee and thus not usually paid by it;
- volunteers: short- or long-term unpaid workforce members.

Managing the workforce is part of the HRM processes, which are very well developed in the broader management and sport management literatures (e.g. Alvesson and Kärreman, 2007; Chelladurai, 1999; Dessler and Cole, 2010; Goslin, 1996; Gratton, 1994; Greenwood, 2002; Nord and Durand, 1978). We direct the reader to these (and other) readings for further examination of basic HRM processes. Suffice it to say here that HRM refers to the coherent, strategic approach to managing "an organization's most valued assets: the people working there who individually and collectively contribute to the achievement of its objectives" (Armstrong, 2003: 3). HRM includes the demonstration of a strategic fit between the business part and the people part; a coherent and supporting system of employment policies, procedures, and practices; increasing employees' commitment to the organization's mission and philosophy/values; ensuring that employees and employers have mutual interests; and ensuring line managers are those who are ultimately responsible for HRM delivery and performance (Armstrong, 2003). HRM practices, combined with human assets (e.g. paid employees, volunteers) and individual differences (e.g. personality, abilities) lead to various outcomes, such as commitment and satisfaction (Chelladurai, 1999).

HRM considers all types of human assets. In sport, we find two main types of human assets, the professionals (paid employees, consultants, etc.), and the unpaid volunteers. Both are equally important. To be considered a "professional", one must have a combination of education, training, and experience, which is recognized by a certifying body of the given field (e.g. event management). There must be a body of knowledge associated with this field, a code of ethics determined by the certifying body, a certification process, and government sanctioning (Getz, 2005). Sport event management is not yet a full profession as most governments don't consider (sport) event management as a profession like they do dentistry or psychology, and thus do not typically have sanctions, rules, and regulations to follow. There are a multitude of associations and bodies which can provide certification, some of which were noted in the introduction chapter. Nevertheless, people who make a career of being managers in sports events want the same thing as professionals: a relative degree of autonomy in the undertaking of their tasks and duties (cf. Chelladurai, 1999; Getz, 2005). In contrast, as we will see later in this chapter, volunteers want different things in exchange for the time they put into the organization.

As the illustrative case at the beginning of this chapter demonstrates, the largest percentage of workforce members in major sports events is usually formed by the volunteers, followed by the employees and then other types of workforce members. The exact size of the workforce will depend on a number of factors, including (Shone and Parry, 2004):

- event size: attendance numbers, likelihood of demand;
- staffing type balance: volunteers versus full-time versus part-time versus contract versus secondees, etc.; it depends partly on the budget and the type of work (e.g. less exciting, isolated work is better undertaken by a paid employee);
- event activity location and staff concentration needs at key points;
- method of provision (e.g. catering hall versus concession, in-house capability versus the need to outsource);
- demand patterns and staff scheduling needs; and
- required expertise.

The large percentage of volunteers is but one unique aspect of major sports event HRM. We also find that the organizing committee must have a strong relationship with its host community and stakeholders in order to recruit volunteers; both employees and volunteers often have to interact directly with paid staff from other organizations or stakeholders; some volunteers are staff from key stakeholders and/or sponsors; and there is often a greater emphasis placed on informal, direct, interpersonal leadership and control methods instead of through formal personnel systems (Getz, 2005).

Most workforce members only come onboard within the last year, if not on the first day the venues open for business. Thus, we see a significant spike in the size of the workforce a year before and then when the Games begin. Nevertheless, all workforce members should follow a similar path of recruitment, training, and integration/socialization. Human resources (HR) managers have to balance the different types of human assets with each person's individual differences. Personality is determined in part by cultural influences and in part by social and family groups (Chelladurai, 1999). Table 5.1 outlines personality aspects (part of individual differences) and essential HRM activities a HR manager must balance. The goal of HRM practices is to enhance outcomes of motivation, commitment, and satisfaction, which can be defined as follows:

- Motivation: the willingness to exert a persistent and high level of effort toward organizational goals, conditioned by the effort's ability to satisfy some individual need. The key elements in our definition are intensity of effort, persistence, direction towards organizational goals, and needs (Robbins, 1997: 388).

Table 5.1 Personality aspects and HRM activities

Personality aspects	HRM activities
Attitude towards authority (person's wish for freedom/autonomy vs. willingness to be controlled and directed by others)	Planning (job design, task definition, etc.)
Attitude towards individualism (person's preference for working alone vs. with others)	Staffing (recruitment, screening/evaluation, and hiring of candidates)
Authoritarian personality (person's degree of respect of authority, order, rules, and regulations)	Orientation, training, and ongoing development of the staff
Bureaucratic orientation (person's degree of preference for self-subordination, compartmentalization, impersonalization, rule conformity, and traditionalism)	Health and safety issues, working conditions
Locus of control (person's degree of belief that they are the ones in control of the events in their lives)	Labour relations
Machiavellianism (degree of manipulative behaviour when interacting with others)	Performance appraisals
Managerial potential (degree of managerial effectiveness)	Rewards (compensation, recognition, and benefits)
Positive and negative affectivity (active, achievement-oriented, interpersonal and self-efficacious versus having a negative view of themselves and their environment)	Discipline and termination
Problem-solving style (sensation vs. intuitive; thinking vs. feeling)	Counselling and outplacement assistance
Service orientation (person's level of social skills, willingness to follow rules, good adjustment, interest in customers, and courtesy)	Organizational change programmes
Tolerance for ambiguity (person's wish for change and/or new/unusual activities vs. routine/structured activities)	Organizational justice

Source: For more information, see Chelladurai, 1999; Getz, 2005.

■ Commitment: "The relative strength of an individual's identification with and involvement in a particular organization" (Mowday *et al.*, 1982: 27). A member who is highly committed should believe and accept their organization's mission, vision, and values; the member should be willing to exert significant effort on behalf of their organization; and the member should wish to maintain their association with the organization (Chelladurai, 1999; Mowday *et al.*, 1982).
■ Satisfaction: "An attitude people have about their job" (Chelladurai, 1999: 230).

Within the planning part of HRM, job design and task definition are important pieces of the HR manager's responsibilities to ensure the motivation, commitment, and satisfaction of their counterparts. Job design can include job simplification, rotation, enlargement, enrichment, and feedback. Task definition includes task attributes, variety, variability, autonomy, identity, and significance (Chelladurai, 1999). There are also different types of tasks (Carron and Chelladurai, 1981):

- Independent tasks: tasks which a member doesn't need anyone else to complete.
- Coactively dependent tasks: these tasks depend on outside, common sources to initiate and control them.
- Proactively–reactively dependent tasks: one member initiates the tasks and another completes them.
- Interactively dependent tasks: these tasks require interaction with other organizational members for the tasks to be completed.

Besides planning, a key aspect of HRM is the staffing. Staffing goes beyond the focusing on the job (i.e. the needs assessments, job analysis, and job descriptions) to include a focus on the people and career considerations. Focusing on people refers to the recruitment, screening, hiring, orientation/training, and integration of staff (Chelladurai, 1999; Getz, 2005). Some of these processes have to be tailored to the type of workforce member to be recruited. For example, paid employees can be recruited through an agency (e.g. Workopolis) that will manage the job advertising and submission process, whereas volunteers would more likely be recruited through word-of-mouth and networking (Shone and Parry, 2004). The type of workforce member may also affect the method of integration; to wit, contract workers would more likely receive tender induction documentation and be asked to take part in a team/organizational culture-building activity, whereas full-time regular employees would undertake induction processes in the organizing committee's headquarters during their in-house office-based orientation session (Hanlon and Cuskelly, 2002). Research has found differences in workforce management across major sports events, notably regarding the degree of systematic/tailored practices and guidance; Hanlon and Stewart (2006) suggest that sport event managers provide detailed documentation to the different types of workforce managers, but also offer proper guidance throughout the event's lifecycle. Part of this documentation, guidance, and training, should include safety, emergency, health, security, and risk management procedures for all workforce members (Getz, 2005; Hanlon and Cuskelly, 2002; Van der Wagen and Carlos, 2005), the specific details of which will depend on each member's exact duties and responsibilities. Moreover, providing documentation and guidance should be extended into Games-time, such as through daily staff briefings (Van der Wagen and Carlos, 2005). Next, career considerations include the organization's career systems and mentoring activities (Chelladurai, 1999). These can be part of the induction and integration process of new members (i.e. mentoring being used to integrate a new member), as well as to progress through the ranks of the organization and/ or set someone up to take up a higher position in a future event by assisting this person with gaining additional skills and abilities.

A third key aspect of HRM is performance appraisals. These appraisals should include both developmental and administrative appraisals. Developmental appraisals are there to assist the organizational member in their development, whereas the administrative appraisals are associated with the meeting of organizational goals. Appraisals will evaluate job-specific task performance (e.g. written/oral communication, supervision/leadership activities, and management/administration activities) and non-job-specific task performance (e.g. effort, facilitation of peer/team performance, personal discipline). Performance criteria will be either outcome- or behaviour-based. The appropriate time to undertake the evaluations will depend on the type of appraisal: ongoing for development (if possible), and typically at the end of a task or activity for the administrative appraisals (Chelladurai, 1999).

Based on the appraisals, the organizational member can receive rewards, another important aspect of HRM. The purpose of rewards is to attract and retain good employees, reduce absenteeism, motivate members to enhance their performance, develop members' skills, facilitate organizational culture and strategic organizational objectives, and define/reinforce the organization's structure (Chelladurai, 1999). Rewards can be based on the job, the skill, seniority, and/or performance. There are different types of rewards as well (Chelladurai, 1999):

- intrinsic versus extrinsic rewards
- financial vs. non-financial rewards
- career vs. social rewards
- direct vs. indirect compensation
- performance vs. membership rewards
- work schedules as rewards.

Finally, it is worth noting that "as custodians of socially sanctioned enterprises" (Chelladurai, 1999: 214), sport event managers should also concern themselves with organizational justice. Organizational justice is composed of three parts:

1   Distributive justice: the perception of the outcomes which are received by individuals/ groups in comparison to others. It includes concepts of equity, equality, and need.
2   Procedural justice: this is about the decision procedures, that is perceived bias, fairness, consistency, accuracy, ethicality, correctibility, and representativeness.
3   Interactional justice: how decisions are communicated. This includes the explanation, respect, warmth, and concern expressed by the member.

Ultimately, the key is to form high-performing teams and groups so that the organization (the organizing committee in our case) may achieve its goals. To do so, managers should consider the following within their HRM plans and procedures (Hackman et al., 1975):

- the formation of natural work units;
- the establishment of client relationships;
- the degree of discretion or control over how one performs their tasks; and
- the openness of feedback channels.

As we will not go further into the great body of literature associated with HRM, we direct the reader to the HRM texts cited in this chapter and the multitude of others available in libraries and bookstores. However, as it pertains to sport event management, we note that the HRM process should be one that follows the principles outlined in the broader literature. Thus, we propose Figure 5.1 to illustrate the HRM path followed in major sports events. One addition we have made is the assistance of an organizing committee, which should be provided to its employees for their (future) career and its development/options

78

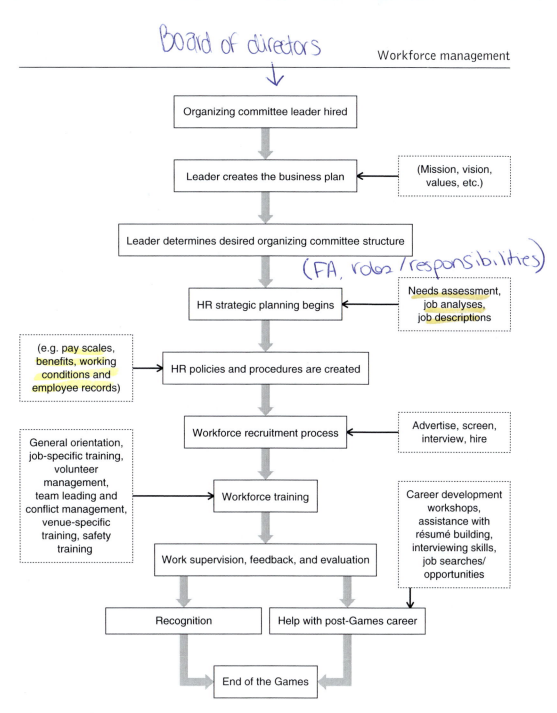

Figure 5.1 The HRM process in major sports events.

through help with résumé building, interviewing skills, job searches, and opportunities (see the practitioner section of this chapter for more information).

Within sport event management research, there is a significant amount of literature associated with volunteers, their motives and management. But we also find a burgeoning literature associated with other aspects, such as employee perceptions and organizational culture, which we outline below.

Volunteers

Major sports events would not happen without the hard work of volunteers. It is therefore fitting that much research has focused on event volunteers, their motivations to volunteer, their commitment to the event, and their satisfaction with their experience and the event. To this end, different motivation, satisfaction, and commitment theories have been directly or indirectly used, notably: Maslow's need hierarchy theory (Maslow, 1943), Hertzberg's two-factor theory (Herzberg, 1968; Herzberg *et al.*, 1959), McGregor's Theory X and Theory Y (McGregor, 1960), Adam's Theory of Inequity (Adams, 1963, 1965), Skinner's behaviour modification (Skinner, 1974), Vroom's expectancy theory (Vroom, 1964; Vroom and MacCrimmon, 1968) (see also Chelladurai, 1999; Getz, 2005 for more information). In this chapter we present three perspectives that are emerging in the field: Meyer and Allen's (1991) three-component (affective, continuance, and normative) commitment model, psychological contract theory, and self-determination theory. We describe these three theories and then move on to understanding event volunteers (their motivations) and volunteer management programme key success factors.

Meyer and Allen's (1991) three-component commitment model

Support is mounting for the three-component model presented by Meyer and Allen (1991) as three independent yet related concepts (Meyer *et al.*, 1993, 2002). *Affective* commitment, also described as desire or want, is an individual's emotional attachment to an organization (Cuskelly *et al.*, 1998; Meyer and Allen, 1991; Meyer and Herscovitch, 2001). Antecedents of affective commitment include personal characteristics, work experience, and organizational structure (Meyer and Allen, 1991; Meyer *et al.*, 2002). The second component of Meyer and Allen's (1991) three-component model of organizational commitment is *continuance* commitment. This component, referring to the perceived costs that are associated with leaving an organization, is usually composed of the loss of investments/side bets and the lack of alternatives (Meyer and Allen, 1991; Meyer and Herscovitch, 2001). Side bets can be work or non-work related and can include the following if a decision is made to leave the organization: the loss of attractive benefits, a feeling of time wasted on non-transferable skills, the loss of seniority privileges, and the loss of personal relationships (Meyer and Allen, 1991). The third and final component of organizational commitment is *normative* commitment. This type of commitment encompasses the perceptions or feelings of obligation towards staying committed to the organization; it is related to socialization (cultural, familial, and organizational norms), benefits and reciprocity norm exchanges, organizational investments, and psychological contracts (Meyer and Allen, 1991; Meyer and Herscovitch, 2001). Normative commitment, as its name infers, is the unwritten feeling of duty or responsibility towards the organization that is formed before entry into it (e.g. familial pressure) or following entry; it may also be a feeling of debt towards the organization if, for example, the organization provided an extra incentive or reward (such as paying for accommodations) in advance. The employee then feels a need to return the favour by staying with the organization (Meyer and Allen, 1991).

According to Meyer and Allen (1991), the likelihood that an individual will leave an organization (turnover) decreases as any one of the three components of organizational commitment increases in strength. However, on-the-job behaviour (i.e. willingness to contribute to organizational effectiveness) depends on the specific component of commitment studied. More precisely, if the person–environment fit is great (i.e. an individual enjoys their work environment), then the person will feel a desire to contribute to the organization in a positive way by increasing their performance, decreasing absenteeism, and increasing organizational citizenship. Here, organizational citizenship refers to an individual's discretionary behaviour (usually not explicitly/directly recognized by the organization's formal reward system) which contributes to the organization's efficiency and/or effectiveness (Organ et al., 2006). In contrast, the continuance commitment–behaviour relationship will depend on the features of the individual's perception about the nature of the behaviour–employment link. Specifically, an individual with high continuance commitment (i.e. continued employment is a necessity) will increase their performance if employment is dependent on performance. If not, then the individual's performance will be low. In such a case, absenteeism will increase and citizenship will be low. In terms of normative commitment, on-the-job behaviour will depend on reciprocity since normative commitment is based on obligation. For instance, if an employer pays an individual a very large sum of money, then the individual may feel obligated to perform at a high level as opposed to an individual being paid the minimum wage for the same task. If the feeling of obligation is high, then absenteeism may decrease and citizenship increase until such time as the individual feels that the "debt" has been paid.

Research on organizational commitment has examined both volunteers and paid staff. Volunteer commitment, as we will see below, has also been examined within the event management literature. The Meyer and Allen (1991) model has been used, although more indirectly or in passing (e.g. MacLean and Hamm, 2007). Allen and Shaw (2009) highlight the concept of volunteer autonomy as needing to be supported by event managers, so that volunteers may feel that their skills and competence, and their sense of association, are fostered. Using the three components of the Meyer and Allen model allows researchers to touch on emotional, intention to stay/leave, and normative (ethical, right thing to do, socialization) aspects of volunteering. The strength of the model warrants further use for examining sport event volunteers' commitment.

Psychological contract theory

The desire to maintain membership within an organization, the need to do so, and the obligation to do so are all perceptions of the individual. Such perceptions can be related to the perceived psychological contract the individual has with the organization. Rousseau (1989) described a psychological contract as an individual's beliefs concerning the terms and conditions of an exchange agreement with another party (either another individual or an organization). The individual has an (often unwritten) obligation of reciprocity. Such terminology immediately can be related to normative commitment. The psychological contract involves the issue of trust; when the psychological contract is violated, there is a strong emotional reaction (e.g. shock, outrage, anger, resentment). The trust and emotional reaction to contract violation can be closely related to affective commitment. Organizational commitment and psychological contracts may be correlated, but they are two distinct concepts (Rousseau,

1989). Spoiling an individual's psychological contract with an organization is thought to likely result in reduced organizational commitment (Guest, 1998).

Psychological contracts can be categorized on a continuum from transactional to relational psychological contract. A largely transactional psychological contract is one that is related to an individual's job and its requirement, while a largely relational psychological contract refers to the emotions such as loyalty and support (Morrison and Robinson, 1997; Rousseau and McLean Parks, 1993). Transactional contracts are positively correlated to careerism, a lack of trust in the employer, and greater resistance to change. Relational contracts show opposite correlations (see Rousseau, 1998). Intuitively, a transactional psychological contract should be closely related to continuance commitment and therefore negatively correlated to affective and normative commitment. In contrast, the relational psychological contract, which deals with emotions, would be more closely related to affective commitment and (most likely) to normative commitment but less so with continuance commitment.

Farmer and Fedor (1999) argued that the psychological contract approach highlights the level of support volunteers believe they receive from the organization, which can in turn foster commitment and decrease intentions to leave. Nichols and Ojala (2009) used psychological contract theory to show that volunteers' expectations include quality personal relationships, flexibility of engagement, contribution recognition, and clearly communicated expectations. Volunteer autonomy is highlighted in such studies.

Self-determination theory

Because volunteering is done by choice, free will, or self-determination, Allen and Shaw (2009) suggest that self-determination theory (see Deci et al., 1989; Deci and Ryan, 1985, 2002) is an appropriate theory for understanding volunteers in sports events. Self-determination theory distinguishes between intrinsic and extrinsic motivations. Intrinsic volunteer motivations would be associated with volunteering for the inherent sake or goodness of volunteering (the activity), whereas extrinsic volunteer motivations would be associated to a distinct outcome (e.g. expected material gains). Importantly, extrinsic motivations can vary in their degree of free choice. For example, clearing snow may be a task given to a volunteer. If a volunteer does it only because someone told them to do it, then there is little free will; conversely, if the volunteer feels that doing this will make the venue safer and so chooses to do the task, then there is a degree of free will. Thus, we see a sort of behavioural regulation continuum. High self-determination extrinsic motivations garner similar positive outcomes to intrinsic motivations (e.g. enjoyment, enhanced performance, engagement, persistence, and well-being). In contrast, low self-determination extrinsic motivations have negative outcomes (e.g. little enjoyment or persistence, stress, and anxiety). Motivations to volunteer for an event have been found to include both intrinsic and self-determined extrinsic motivations (Allen and Shaw, 2009). There is a desire by volunteers to choose the organization/event, venue(s), and sport(s) (Hoeber, 2010).

Volunteer motivations and commitment

Individuals are seen to want to volunteer in events for various reasons. For example, women, more than men, seem to want to volunteer at major sports events to increase their personal and social capital (Downward *et al.*, 2005). Different taxonomies or typologies have been created with overlapping terms for describing event volunteer motivations. Here, we summarize them into six categories (cf. Pauline and Pauline, 2009; Strigas and Jackson Jr, 2003; Thoits and Hewitt, 2001; Treuren, 2009; Wilson, 2000):

- Egoistic: tangible or intangible gains focused on the ego.
- External: factors outside volunteers' direct control (e.g. family tradition).
- Instrumental, material, or utilitarian: expected gains (e.g. in social status, gifts, wages).
- Leisure: the need for leisure choices.
- Purposive, normative, altruistic, or associative-supportive: desire to give back, "desire to support and ensure the success of an event [and/or sport] . . . by direct involvement . . . and personal attachment to the activity or event" (Treuren, 2009: 687).
- Solidary: need for interpersonal relationships, social interaction, self-actualization.

The purposive motive is seen as quite dominant in event volunteers (Treuren, 2009). There is support for the idea that sport event volunteers are the same as other types of volunteers (Downward *et al.*, 2005). However, Olympic volunteers are thought to be different than other event volunteers, with Olympic subculture, solidary, and purposive motives dominating (Fairley *et al.*, 2007; Giannoulakis *et al.*, 2008). At least, Olympic volunteers seem to be consistent from one Games to the next. Kemp's (2002) analysis of the volunteers at the 1994 Lillehammer Olympic Winter Games and the 2000 Sydney Olympic Games demonstrates that beyond the traditional volunteer's motivations, both sets of Olympic volunteers demonstrated national and cultural pride and the need for social contact and friendship. To the above Olympic volunteer motives, Fairley *et al.* (2007) added nostalgia and the desire to share and be recognized for their expertise as reasons for individuals to travel abroad to volunteer at an Olympic Games.

Whereas motivation refers to the motives behind the desire to volunteer for an event, commitment refers to the longer-term responsibility, association, or loyalty to the organization and/or event. MacLean and Hamm (2007) suggested that motivation to volunteer is associated more to being part of a community (e.g. the organizing committee, fellow volunteers), while commitment is associated more to sport-specific factors within the event. Motivation and commitment are closely linked factors, which warrant further investigation (e.g. similarity in antecedents, causal relationships, links to psychological contracts, links to intentions to leave). In fact, the feeling of being part of a community (associated to motivation) seems to have a positive effect on event volunteers' pride and commitment levels to the organizing committee, which in turn had an effect on their job satisfaction (Costa *et al.*, 2006; Kim *et al.*, 2010). Satisfaction can include feelings of accomplishment, of having provided a valuable contribution, of having garnered valuable experience/skills, and of having been supported by one's colleagues (Mei, 2009). This feeling of satisfaction has been found to depend not only on the attributes of the event organization itself, but also on the

83

attributes of the venue(s) where the volunteer is posted, perceived stress levels, and volunteer recruitment and management (Farrell *et al.*, 1998; Kim *et al.*, 2010; Mei, 2009). The future intention to volunteer is also associated with motivation and commitment, community involvement, and extrinsic rewards, as well as role flexibility (Bang *et al.*, 2009; Lockstone *et al.*, 2010).

A number of volunteers come from out of town. These volunteers "perceive themselves to be a tourist . . . [and wish to] take part in tourism activities, in addition to their volunteer activities" (Jarvis and Blank, 2011: 129). What is interesting in this regard is that these volunteers can be seen as an untapped source of potential future tourists to the host region where they volunteered (if not their home region). The case can be made that individuals who travel to a region to volunteer become potential future return tourists to the region if their experience was satisfactory (Ralston *et al.*, 2005). However, tapping into such a market requires that tourism organizations work closely with the organizing committee to promote the region to potential volunteers, as well as ensure the capacity for volunteers to return to the region as tourists. Moreover, sport event managers should remember that during the event, these volunteers consider volunteer-based motives to be "more important than the tourism-based considerations" (Jarvis and Blank, 2011: 129).

Successful volunteer management programmes

As our understanding of event volunteers' motives, commitment, and satisfaction grows, we can build better volunteer management programmes for the Games-time period. Key success factors for volunteer management programmes in major sports events include (see, for example, Chanavat and Ferrand, 2010; Costa *et al.*, 2006; Kemp, 2002; Kim *et al.*, 2009; Shaw, 2009):

- creating an effective brand for the volunteer programme;
- promoting and developing the volunteer recruitment campaign with an eye to the local host region;
- tailoring the programme (e.g. process, training, types of gifts) to the type of volunteers desired (based on the volunteer motives, commitment, and satisfaction factors noted above), building on volunteers' sense of self-worth and self-esteem, as well as the opportunity to build and/or use valuable skills, network, and experience;
- determining appropriate programme planning and operations aspects (e.g. define standards, allow for flexibility, volunteer role rotation, use past Games/volunteer experience, train paid staff in volunteer management techniques), and implement them with precision;
- treating volunteers as customers (service quality, attention during volunteer meetings);
- offering generic, role-specific, and venue-specific volunteer training;
- training volunteers to build a sense of community between them and with the rest of the workforce;
- communicating frequently with the volunteers and engaging them before the event;
- integrating volunteers and paid staff together – do not distinguish between types of workforce or even types of volunteers;

- monitoring volunteers' motivation and morale and ensuring that their time is spent wisely (not wasted waiting around doing nothing);
- recognizing volunteers' efforts during and after the event through volunteer activities and gifts.

Managing the paid staff–volunteer relationship

While volunteers give their time without asking for financial remuneration (Chelladurai, 1999), employees get paid for their time and services. This can create frictions. Some research considers this relationship, its processes, tensions, and managerial implications (e.g. Parent and Slack, 2007). Parent and Slack (2007) found that to foster productive paid staff–volunteer relationships, the following aspects should be considered:

1   Organizational design: to balance differences in motivation and commitment, as well as decrease potential negative conflict:

- strong leadership to coordinate all types of workforce members;
- clarity and effectiveness of organizational structure, task division (departments/divisions), and the ensuing ratio of paid staff to volunteers based on the department/division's responsibilities (e.g. volunteers vs. construction);
- clear definitions for paid staff and volunteer roles and responsibilities and accountability from the outset;
- defining who has control and when;
- determining who has ultimate authority to resolve conflicts between paid staff and volunteers (e.g. a liaison);
- managing transitions (e.g. from headquarter-centred to venue-centred at Games-time).

Parent and Slack (2007) suggest that paid staff be responsible for the day-to-day operations and resource management, while volunteers should still have positive control/operational responsibilities before (for pre-Games volunteers) and during (for Games-time volunteers) the event.

2   Communication:

- information flow, pattern, and time between paid staff and volunteers (usually easier between volunteers or between paid staff than between volunteers and paid staff);
- information before, during, and after the event (e.g. be part of the evaluation for knowledge transfer).

3   Coordination and cooperation: fostering a spirit of compromise and good faith, a team approach.

4   Personal resources: individuals' competencies, contacts, knowledge, skills, and abilities.

While the preceding allows us to combine organizational theory (e.g. organizational design) and organizational behaviour (e.g. workforce relationships) towards enhancing the motivation, commitment, satisfaction, and productivity of paid staff and volunteers in major sports events, more work is certainly needed on this important relationship.

Employee perceptions

In a novel study, Xing and Chalip (2009) examined OCOG lower-level employees two years before the 2008 Beijing Olympic Games. They found four themes that undercut employees' daily work experiences:

1   the mundane nature of daily work;
2   the bureaucratic nature of BOCOG;
3   the privileged nature of privilege; and
4   the nurturing nature of members' immediate working environment.

To mitigate some of the issues, BOCOG employees used different coping strategies such as confronting or adjusting to the situation, using the opportunity to work for BOCOG to develop one's skills and abilities, seeing the working opportunity as one which was representative of a passionate life filled with idealism and one which allowed the employee to be a part of history. This study also breaks down certain myths about working for Olympic Games, such as:

1   It may be exciting to work for an OCOG but the daily work can still be mundane.
2   The organizing committee may be in constant evolution and change, yet it is still bureaucratic (sometimes seeming even more bureaucratic than governments).
3   Anyone can work for an OCOG; who you know actually matters to get you prime positions.
4   Everyone is out for themselves as there is no time for anything else; while somewhat true, a well-built team will provide a nurturing environment for its members.

We see that "social support, the symbolic significance of the event, and learning through event work mitigate the stresses of working to host a mega-event" (Xing and Chalip, 2009: 210). As for the paid staff–volunteer study, more research is needed on organizing committee employees of different managerial levels (i.e. top, middle, lower level), of different sports events, and at different time points so as to understand their full experience from beginning to end.

Organizational culture

As it is commonly understood, successful organizations need successful organizational cultures. These cultures, built through means of stories, rituals, artefacts, symbols, myths, heroes, rites, ceremonies, language, physical setting, power structures and hierarchy, dress codes, control methods, etc. (Johnson and Scholes, 2002; Shone and Parry, 2004; Slack and Parent, 2006), usually take some time to develop. They begin with the owner and/or top leader of the organization and evolve as organizational members come onboard and leave.

Given that organizing committees only exist for a short time, is an organizational culture still important? The short answer is yes. To enhance motivation, commitment, and satisfaction, reduce turnover and absenteeism, and facilitate the achievement of the organizing committee's goals, a strong organizational culture – and hopefully strong subcultures within divisions, departments, and/or groups – is needed. Yet, very little research on this topic in major sports events actually exists.

A notable exception is the work by McDonald (1991) on the creation of the 1984 Los Angeles Olympic Organizing Committee's (LAOOC) organizational culture, incorporating 20,000 employees and 50,000 volunteers. The author described her experience as an employee of the LAOOC by painting a picture of the physical setting (the LAOOC headquarters, its exterior and interior décor, the café, the store), the security measures for entering the building, the key messages (e.g. organizational goals, values, structure) delivered during the formal orientation, the employee badge procedures and meaning, and other aspects of culture building such as symbols and staff meeting experiences. Employees were encouraged to be a part of/play a part in history. They were also assigned a country to know inside-and-out in case someone from that country showed up in Los Angeles and the top management needed information on that country. Stories and myths surrounding this assignment are also described. Formal training was brief, so organizational learning stemmed mainly from informal interactions with colleagues. McDonald also describes the feeling of the frenzied pace within the LAOOC, the dominance of sponsor products, the look/colours of the Games, and the discussions surrounding the post-Games job prospects. She highlights the presence of a departmental culture, socialization, and integration.

Thus, we see that managing a major sports event workforce includes many aspects of HRM, dealing with both paid staff and volunteers, and building a successful organizational culture. However, most of our information on the workforce processes comes from other settings than sports events; thus, much future research is still needed on this topic. We now discuss some aspects in the practitioner section which can be taken as starting points for future research studies.

THE PRACTITIONER'S PERSPECTIVE ON WORKFORCE MANAGEMENT

From the practitioner's perspective, some key issues to consider regarding workforce management include work conditions, leadership, managing momentum, performance and evaluations (including the issues of weak links and recognition), and preparing for the end of the Games.

Work conditions

The workforce is a very interesting blend of skills, competencies, motivations, and personal situations. Because of the privilege of working for a major sports event, people will sacrifice time and money to be associated with it. While salaries are generally commensurate with those of national sports organizations, they are less than what the individual would likely make in the same job in enduring businesses. So people make a choice to work long hours for less money because of what they consider an opportunity of a lifetime or the leveraging opportunity in their business or personal life. The jobs they end up performing could be mundane and/or in less than comfortable conditions. They may never get close to or inside a venue because of their assigned duty – like parking lot attendants, logistics, administration, and parts of EVS, etc. There can be a chasm between the perception of what the experience could be and the actual experience. Volunteers will use their holidays, pay their own transportation and accommodations to be part of such an event. Likewise, employees of major sports events consistently work long days and put their "regular" life on hold to be part of a sporting event, often to the detriment of the relationship with their significant other and/or children – spouses, partners, and children need to be very understanding of the work patterns, time, effort, and dedication needed by the event workforce. It is normal to see managers in major sports events have an average age in the thirties, as such an environment is often better suited to younger and less "attached" (read: without families) individuals.

While every effort is made to provide employees and volunteers with all of the tools they need to do their jobs, staff and volunteers can be in situations where space and equipment, especially technological, is in short supply. This requires people to become resourceful, creative, and very accepting of the "what is" situation. The "skinny" resources can contribute positively to a very cohesive team in which comments are easily heard and chunks of information are communicated simultaneously. This allows just-in-time, spontaneous meetings to occur to clarify and accelerate activity and increase productivity. Teams bond, and a culture of commitment unfolds. Deadlines on deliverables happen more seamlessly and motivation is high. Given that most teams have some level of dysfunction or emotional immaturity, this workshop type of environment can either absorb these factors by osmosis or create an opportunity for people to step up like they have never done before. Time is of the essence, and if someone does not fit, there is little or no time for remedial action. Options include finding a more suitable position (if possible) or immediate exit.

It is an awe-inspiring task for any HR professional to design a strategy, recruit, orient, train, and then exit a temporary workforce. Enduring organizations have time on their side. With a major sports event there are start and finish dates, so the decisions of what to collapse, merge, and let go of relative to a traditional HR programme are critical and very challenging. The workforce is transitioned into the organization in waves, which presents unique challenges and pressures for managers to adequately and quickly prepare them to perform effectively and quickly and for the employee/volunteer to absorb information and processes and assimilate immediately. Traditional businesses' HR processes therefore have to be adapted to the temporary nature of the event, but also to the wave hirings.

Intentions of the organizing committees are honourable with respect to hours of work, scope of responsibilities, and benefits. In reality, many people work long hours, reshaping their original job description to include what is necessary to get the job done. People can be moved within an FA or transferred to a different FA with little notice. The person follows the work rather than the reverse.

It is not that best practices and traditional HR processes are not in place to guide employees and volunteers. Rather, the fast-paced, high-performance demands of a constantly changing environment create situations where subjective decisions must be made in the moment, often disregarding the "rules" in favour of expediency.

Leadership

There is general consensus that leaders can be developed within organizations. Again, the time constraints of an event demand that managers are already effective leaders. While experience in this environment enhances a leader's ability, there is no time to "train" leaders. A common pitfall in recruitment is to assume that management experience equates to leadership skills. Because managing people is so much more complex than managing information, places, or things, there can be some interesting challenges with sometimes unexpected results when it is discovered that some managers do not have the requisite leadership skills and/or their experience of constant change has not been sufficient for the needs of the event environment. Team building is critical, egos must be parked dozens of times each day, and picking up the slack of the weakest link is a hourly task sometimes undertaken without the direction of a manager without strong leadership.

It may happen that managers hire coordinators (the lower level of employees) during the run-up and delivery of the event who have skills that the managers do not hold. To illustrate, international client services managers may not have a high degree of international experience, but they may hire individuals who are international in culture, formally educated with deep subject-related experience and high achievers. In one sense, it is smart of the managers (as leaders) to hire such people so that the FA's tasks can be completed successfully. In another sense, however, the group of coordinators may not have the direction they would normally have and therefore have to find ways of performing their tasks, such as deciding to manage themselves and to solve their problems within their peer group through collaboration, discussion, and majority rules. In such a situation, if the group can take an "ask for forgiveness instead of permission" axiom, their collective stress and complaining may be significantly reduced. The group can become extraordinarily cohesive and effective. It allows help to be freely given to any team member, and to see egos easily kept in check as the group moves towards the goal of delivering the event. Such an approach can allow respect and dignity to be retained by both the managers and group members.

Managing momentum

Managing momentum can be viewed as two prongs. The employees who are hired and start to work immediately are one prong. The other prong belongs to the volunteers, who for most events, are recruited well in advance. Both groups are part of the workforce, and both need to be engaged and the momentum sustained. Both groups require orientation, job-specific training, and venue-specific training including safety, security, health, and emergency procedures, which takes place both face-to-face and through documentation. It is the timing of the delivery that differs. Paid workforce members have the advantage of day-to-day involvement, so training can be planned and mandated. Volunteers have lives and jobs, which means all of their time is "volunteered"; and training must be regular enough to keep them engaged and not so far away from the event that retention of knowledge and momentum has been lost. Volunteer communication must be constant, and delivery methods need to vary between email, telephone, team website, and face-to-face meet-and-greet get-togethers. Volunteers and their paid workforce managers need to socialize and start the team building long before the group arrives on the physical site of the event, allowing momentum to build.

Because of the relentless pace of activity to deliver an event, there is an ongoing challenge to attempt to assist people in managing not only their momentum, but also their fatigue. As an organization, there is a de facto responsibility to organize events, provide strategies, services, and support for the entire workforce. For employees, team-building exercises and retreats that include play and remove people from their normal work environment are very effective. Access to exercise facilities and alternative services like massage, acupuncture, and reflexology give temporary relief. Lunch-and-learn seminars that teach stress management and nutrition can educate and empower people so that they build endurance and mental resilience without burning out. In turn, with volunteers, regular job rotation to offer variety, providing the opportunity for feedback and comments, and constantly expressed appreciation assist with fatigue.

Performance and reputation

There are usually (perhaps unfortunately) no performance evaluations of event managers per se. Instead, an indirect performance evaluation is undertaken based on stakeholders' perceptions of the degree of success and quality of delivery of a given major sports event. If stakeholders perceive the event to have been successful, event managers gain a positive reputation pertaining to event management capabilities and therefore indirectly receive a good performance review, even if a particular event manager was a weak worker. Conversely, if the event process and outcome was perceived as being negative by stakeholders (e.g. the 1996 Atlanta Olympic Games, the 2010 Delhi CWG), then those event managers' reputations are negatively affected, and they obtain a negative performance review even if they did a stellar job themselves.

Weak links

The weak link can be defined as someone who does not have the requisite skills and abilities to perform their tasks and contribute to the group, or someone who does have the skills and abilities but is lazy in their use (e.g. waits for others to take on tasks, acts as a victim). They appear as though they are there for the ride – they freeload (cf. Thompson, 2011). Often, it is a habit they have, or they are not motivated in that particular environment to perform.

In enduring businesses, there is time for remedial action or additional training and development. With temporary organizations, there is once again the constraint of time. Considering the demands of shoring up the weakest link, employees of an event must be maximally empowered to make decisions so they can resolve situations and take action in an effective and timely manner. There are situations when there is no choice but to pick up the slack or prop up the weakest link. Examples of these situations include: until the weak link can be replaced; until the weak link can be reassigned to another FA; when there is no time to replace the weak link because you are at the point of no return – that is, the event is in motion; or until the person can be "dehired" or fired.

Recognition

The number-one reason people leave an organization is because they do not feel valued or recognized (Branham, 2004). In a temporary organization that is delivering an event with a large percentage of the workforce essentially comprising volunteers and the pressing need for continuity with full-time employees and contractors, this statistic cannot be tolerated. To guard against the statistic becoming a reality, a layered formal plan of recognition must be part of the HR process. Some strategies include: verbal and written recognition; milestones of service being acknowledged with branded accessories being given as mementoes; bonuses being offered to employees at the completion of the event to motivate them to stay until the end; certificates or letters of appreciation being awarded to both employees and volunteers; and organized social events with volunteers to recognize contribution and continue building rapport with each other and for future events. You can never say thank you enough – these two words delivered authentically can inspire people to move mountains, accomplish the impossible, and stay with you till the job gets done.

Preparing for the end of the games

Because of the work environment intensity of a temporary organization like an organizing committee of a major sports event, the exit strategy is vastly different to an enduring organization, where exit often means that the person has been "dehired" or fired and it is an unplanned and unknown occurrence. Exactly the opposite happens with an event. Because start and finish dates are finite, people who have been part of a high-performance, fast-paced environment can crash hard after its conclusion. With proper planning, it is possible to transition the workforce by communicating what to expect and helping them prepare for the end. The obvious is an end-of-event celebration and recognition gathering. Other activities include one-on-one or group feedback sessions, where people can express their opinions and ideas and once again be connected with their teams and reconnected through conversation with the experiences of the event. In addition, the HR division managers can assist their colleagues with the post-Games job issue: career development, résumé building, and interviewing skills seminars and workshops, assisting with job searches, and even facilitating job opportunities with Games partners and stakeholders.

Consistent contact is a simple plan that can be implemented post-event and layers the foundation that the HR recruitment process started. This is a continuation of the experience, where lasting memories can positively linger long after the event is finished; and to a degree, it preserves the acquired skills and knowledge the person received during the event. Post-games technology has made it possible to stay connected on social networks, which not only complement end-of-games strategies, but also become a database for recruiting for future events.

CHAPTER SUMMARY

In this chapter we explored the different types of workforce members that can be found in major sports events. We also examined HRM processes as they pertain to major sports events:

- planning: job design and task definition;
- staffing: focus on the job (needs assessments, job analysis, and job descriptions) and people (recruitment, screening, hiring, orientation/training, and integration of staff);
- performance appraisals: both developmental and administrative appraisals;
- organizational justice: distributive, procedural, and interactional justice.

We briefly considered aspects of high-performing organizations, as found in the management literature. Such organizations have natural work units, client relationships, a degree of discretion or control over how one performs their tasks, and open feedback channels. We then focused on volunteers, a key part of the sport event management literature, examining their motivations, commitment, and satisfaction. We also proposed components of a successful volunteer management programme based on the literature. Finally, we explored two other emerging aspects in the literature: organizing committee employee perceptions and organizational culture.

From a practitioner's standpoint, we examined the differences in enduring and temporary organizations regarding work conditions and the link to the concept of leadership – why that dictates the need for an empowered workforce. Other elements of the Games pertaining to HRM were discussed separately and again compared to enduring organizations. They include: managing momentum and fatigue for the whole workforce, performance and reputation, weak links, recognition and reward, and preparing for the end-of-Games, including the importance of post-Games career development and contact with and between workforce members.

EXPERT CASE: BUILDING A HIGH-FUNCTIONING TEAM FOR THE 2010 OLYMPIC WINTER GAMES

VANOC's approach to HR was driven by John Furlong, VANOC's CEO. He wanted a team culture, a trust culture. As such, the first step in creating the HRM piece was to crystallize the vision, mission, and values of the Games. This was done five years before the Games, included the 30–50 people within VANOC, and was vetted through its board of directors. A key aspect was the values, which included: team, trust, creativity, sustainability, and excellence.

The next step was to create strategic objectives for the planning of the work. For example, Furlong wanted venues which had areas of play that enabled athletes to perform at their best; this created a priority around venue location and field-of-play decisions. There was also a people-based objective that focused on a *one-team* culture. This objective set the course for HRM within VANOC. The next step was to institutionalize and operationalize these objectives. One impact of this objective was orientation. Everyone needed to be on board and believe in the one-team concept and in what VANOC was doing; thus, everyone went through orientation, from vice-presidents to volunteers. Another consequence was for employee compensation. Given the one-team culture approach, a decision was made to situate VANOC salaries in the mid-range in comparison to other organizations and have performance pay scales for managers, not distinguishing between pre-Games and Games-time.

However, as Ms Wilson, VANOC's executive vice-president for human resources and sustainability, found out, there are differences between pre-Games and Games-time. While the idea that one's pay would be based on an experience scale did work for pre-Games employees being hired individually, it did not necessarily work for groups of individuals being hired "together" for Games-time roles. These groups of individuals are used to working together and being paid the same rate regardless of individuals' experiences/backgrounds, which caused some problems with HR policies that had been put in place.

There are also recurring themes associated with HR for organizing committees of major sports events in contrast to enduring organizations that should be considered. First, HRM within major sports event organizing committees must be undertaken with the end (of the organization) in mind. Since the organization is to end, time, speed, entrepreneurial spirit, and nimbleness are key in such temporary organizations. Second, while HR plans are typically built starting with research on best practices, this process changes for organizing committees. The best practices used in that event in other locations or other events in the current location are used as a starting point to determine "best-for-us" practices given the temporal, event, and contextual/spatial factors.

The finite nature of the event impacts organizing committees of major sports events differently than for enduring organizations. In major sports events, HRM and other procedures must be built quickly, nimbly, and they must be able to be taken apart at the end. The finite nature of the event impacts HR procedures, such as the recruitment process. For example, the desire to hire the best and the brightest must be tempered with the lack of time to train or develop skills in hirees. Therefore, individuals hired in major sports events have to already possess the necessary skills to perform a given job – there is no time for additional technical training. Also, the desired culture must be embedded within the organization within the first three years.

In addition, the finite nature of the organizing committee means that there will be a fast HR growth. For VANOC, the HR numbers doubled every year for the first three years, and then multiplied tenfold by the time the last year arrived. This fast growth results in strains on HR policies and procedures. For example, while every member needed to undertake orientation, the length of orientation decreased (from one week initially to only a few hours nearer to Games-time) as the number of hirees grew and time sped up. VANOC decided to use the tipping-point theory to mitigate some of the consequences of fast growth. More precisely, organization development can typically deal with about 200 individuals/hires; they can inculcate culture, procedures, etc., in these individuals. But beyond that number, it becomes difficult. Thus, the organization (the organizing committee in this case) needs to rely on those 200 individuals to train the next 200, who will then train the next 200, and so on. This ensures that the message is consistent.

Besides the differences between pre-Games and Games-time, there are two other takeaways which HR executives should bear in mind. First, volunteer workforce planning is more short-term and highly operational in nature. It does not necessarily need to be found within the HR FA. Nevertheless, it does need a strong leader who can question the different FAs with regard to their stated volunteer needs. A leader with previous Games experience combined with strong credibility is best suited for this role as they can objectively call into question the requests for volunteer resources that are beyond reasonable. Many FA leaders will overstate their resource requirements to ensure that they provide "great" service at Games-time. The "Head of Workforce Planning" needs to be able to objectively keep the resource numbers within budget. Second, the one-team approach works for organizing committees; it allows all members to feel empowered and not differentiate between paid staff and volunteers or between FAs, thereby avoiding potential alienation or disengagement. This empowered culture also allows everyone to feel equally excited and foster a sense that everyone can and should pitch in and help regardless of whether they are a volunteer or an executive vice-president.

Finally, a comment on the concept of high-functioning teams in major sports events is needed. It is possible to have high-functioning teams if the process is started five years before with the executive team. In the final 12 months, the stress and strains on the executive vice-presidents and everyone else are so great that they may not seem to be performing like a high-functioning team. But there should be enough muscle built (i.e. the foundation of the high-functioning team) that it will get the individuals/ teams through the difficult period. Moreover, the stress of the final 90 days is such that the HR executive must be prepared to be and have prepared a safe place for the other executives, those who are not supposed to break down, whether male or female, to feel supported. The HR executive must be ready to play this role in the final lead-up to the Games. However, there was no one to take care of Ms Wilson. What carried her was the collective resolve of the senior executive team, which had been built with the thousands of decisions that brought them to the opening of the Games. The resilience they now had together transformed into a sheer determination that they would not allow the Games to fail – it's what got them all through the final planning. They had an ingrained, unshakeable belief in their vision to "Build a stronger Canada through passion for sport, culture and sustainability."

Based on a conversation with Donna Wilson, Executive Vice-President, Human Resources & Sustainability, 2010 Vancouver Olympic Winter Games, currently Vice-President, Industry Services and Sustainability, WorkSafeBC.

Case questions

1   How does the leader of a major sports event impact HRM?

2   What are key take-aways for a HR executive of a major sports event?

3   Who should support the HR executive when he or she is supporting everyone else in the organizing committee, especially the other executives?

CHAPTER QUESTIONS

1   Name the different types of workforce members in a major sports event organizing committee and explain how they are different.

2 Using one of the theories presented in this chapter, describe how you would foster motivation, commitment, and satisfaction in your event volunteers.

3 What are key volunteer management programme components?

4 What is the traditional HRM path for the recruitment of workforce members for sports events?

5 What are some of the differences in HRM practices between traditional, enduring organizations and major sports event organizing committees?

FURTHER READING

For further reading on workforce management and HRM, we suggest the following:

Blanchard, K., Carew, D., & Parsi-Carew, E. (2000) *One Minute Manager Builds High Performing Teams* (revised edn), New York: William Morrow and Company, Inc.

Cuskelly, G., Hoye, R., & Auld, C. (2006) *Working with Volunteers in Sport: Theory and Practice*, London: Routledge.

Van Der Wagen, L. (2006) *Human Resource Management for Events: Managing the Event Workforce*, Oxford: Butterworth Heinemann.

Chapter 6

Marketing, sponsorship, and look-feel

OBJECTIVES

- To understand the various concepts associated with marketing a major sports event and the host region
- To understand consumer considerations associated with the marketing of a major sports event
- To understand the various aspects of branding, sponsorship, and ambush marketing

ILLUSTRATIVE CASE: AMBUSHING MAJOR SPORTS EVENTS

There are repeated examples of companies trying to ambush major sports events. Ambushing refers to companies who make it look like they are sponsors of an event when they are not (they have not paid for the right to be so). For example, during the 2010 FIFA World Cup, 36 women were thrown out of their country's (Holland) game against Denmark for allegedly ambushing the World Cup by wearing orange dresses, the colour of Holland's team but also the colour of the Bavaria Beer Company. At the time, Bavaria denied being responsible for this ambush strategy despite their history of providing Bavaria orange pants to spectators as "gifts" during the 2006 FIFA World Cup (Madison, 2009; *Guardian*, 2010). In addition, during the 2011 Rugby World Cup in New Zealand, Wellington retailers were refusing to remove references to the national team, the "All Blacks", such as a local clothing store which had a small sign for an "All Black Rack" or a local strip club's "All Black" uniforms, despite the potential threat of legal action (Nichols, 2011a, 2011b).

However, one-off sports events are not the only setting for ambush marketers. For example, 24,000 cans of Pringles chips were distributed to fans arriving at Wimbledon on 1 July 2009. The Pringles cans were modified to make them look like cans of tennis balls: they were green and had a tennis ball in the middle, around which was the phrase "These are not tennis balls!" (Vassout, 2009).

THE THEORY BEHIND MARKETING, SPONSORSHIP, AND LOOK-FEEL

As the cost of mega sports events continues to increase, so too does the need for organizers to ensure a high level of marketing competency in order to guarantee the financial success of

 96

their event. Marketing serves not just to ensure that there is awareness and energy surrounding the event, but also to ensure that it receives vital external funding though sponsorship. The American Marketing Association (2007:1) defined marketing as "the activity, set of institutions, and processes for creating, communicating, delivering, and exchanging offerings that have value for customers, clients, partners, and society at large". It has often been argued that value is the key concept around which everything else is focused; but O'Reilly and Séguin (2009) suggested that the exchange process, utility, needs and wants, relationships, and applied sociology are all vital to the understanding and practice of marketing.

When discussing sport marketing, it is important to realize that it occurs in two ways: marketing through sport and marketing of sport. Marketing through sport refers to the use of sport as a vehicle for marketing by a non-sport based company, such as McDonald's leveraging of the Olympic Games as a marketing tool for their fast-food business. Marketing of sport refers to the practice of marketing as it occurs within a sport organization, or in this case, event, for example the marketing tasks that take place within the Olympic Movement. Another key unique feature of marketing sport events relates to the degree of consumer connection that is generated. O'Reilly and Séguin (2009: 7) noted that more so than any other product or service, sport is "about more than the needs and wants [of consumers]; it is about connecting to emotions, building passion and leveraging images". The ability of sport events to tap into the emotion and passion of consumers offers the marketer unparalleled opportunity to connect with them at a personal level, but can also be a hindrance as it is arguably harder to influence decisions made at a purely emotional level.

In this chapter we will examine the theory within the field of sport event marketing, and then move on to discussing the following key topics in more detail: key concepts in marketing strategy, communications and public relations, spectator considerations, marketing research, destination marketing and auditing, branding, sponsorship, and ambush marketing.

Sport event marketing theory

Unquestionably, sport and marketing are complex topics of study individually; and as such, sport marketing is a complex area of study as a singular topic (Schwarz and Hunter, 2008). Despite this, the use and creation of theory as a way to understand and explain sport event marketing concepts is restricted. However, it must be noted that this is not limited to sport event marketing, but is rather a function of the fields of marketing and sport marketing as a whole. The marketing of sport events is an area that covers a wide variety of practices and incorporates the theories and concepts of several scholarly fields of study; but at its core, it has a highly practical and descriptive research base. This is not to say that theory does not exist within the field of sport event marketing; rather, as mentioned above, the use of theory tends to be limited to the application of various existing theories in extraneous fields of study – for example, theories associated with psychology, consumer behaviour, brand equity, organization theory and sociology. In addition, as a result of the vastly descriptive and empirical focus on the applied aspects of research in the field (Pitts, 2002), there is a tendency towards the use of acronyms, categorization, and process development as the field's "conceptual frameworks".

Key concepts in marketing strategy

The key concepts associated with marketing strategy are discussed below. They include: environmental analysis, situational analysis, market segmentation, and the marketing mix, which lead to the concept of marketing strategy.

Environmental analysis

The environmental analysis includes internal and external components. An internal environment analysis involves examining what is termed the 3Cs or the consumer, company, and competition. Consumer behaviour will be discussed in greater detail later, but for the purpose of this section it is important to note that despite the difficulty in understanding exactly what goes on in the mind of consumers (Stotlar, 2001), an organization must attempt to comprehend the factors and reasoning behind consumer decision-making. These factors are likely to be either individual or environmental, and may include factors such as family, social and cultural norms, age, gender, and geography (Mullin *et al.*, 2000). In examining their own company, marketers must evaluate their internal strengths and weaknesses, and create a strategy which minimizes weaknesses and maximizes strengths. The values, goals, and objectives of the organization, as well as their unique characteristics, must play an important role in this evaluation, as what may be seen as a weakness for one organization could be classified as a strength in another given what they are trying to achieve. Finally, marketers must take a close look at their competition. It is vital that they accurately identify those organizations or events which could be considered as competition. For sports events, competitors could include any business providing consumers with an entertainment product, such as theatres and concerts, as well as other events locally, nationally, and internationally. Once their competitors have been determined, marketers should examine these businesses to evaluate their competition's market positioning and strategy, their perceived strengths and weaknesses, their product characteristics, and their probable response to any actions taken by the marketer's organization (Stotlar, 2001).

An external environmental analysis consists of four components forming the acronym PEST, which stands for *political*, *economic*, *social*, and *technological*. An examination of the political environment would discuss such mechanisms as government structures, regulatory environment, and laws and their perceived impact on sport event marketing. For instance, anti-ambush marketing legislation has been passed in many mega-event host cities, which offers the organizing committee the ultimate weapon to protect sponsor exclusivity. External economic elements that must be considered may include such things as the global and local economies. For example, much mega-event funding comes from sponsors; and if the global economy is in recession, it may impact the willingness of organizations to spend large sums of money on event sponsorship opportunities. Social (or demographic) factors must also be considered and may include such elements as the age of the population or their average annual income. These are important considerations for marketers as they may allow them to better identify the potential target markets as well as any limits or opportunities they may face with regards to pricing and cultural expectations. Finally, marketers should also appreciate the technological factors that may impact them. This can include such issues as advances in social media, online streaming, and new ways to generate messaging plat-forms. For example, with so many different forms of online technology available today, sport event property owners have to be increasingly specific with regards to sponsorship category differentiation. For instance, the Olympic Games sponsorship programme has exclusive sponsorship agreements with competitors Panasonic and Samsung; however, they are distinguished by the products they can represent in their advertisements relating to the Olympic Games and their designations with regards to their official sponsor status.

Situational analysis

In addition to the internal and external analysis of an organization's environment, the stra-tegic sport marketing process involves the use of a situational analysis incorporating both the internal and external contingencies (Shank, 2005). This process is described as a SWOT analysis, where SWOT stands for strengths, weaknesses, opportunities, and threats. In scru-tinizing strengths and weaknesses of their event, marketers examine internal, controllable contingencies, while opportunities and threats represent external, potentially uncontrollable contingencies (Shank, 2005). For example, within a sport event organizing committee strengths and weaknesses which may be examined include: resources (e.g. human, financial, information), image and reputation, while opportunities and threats which might be identi-fied may include: consumer demand, climate, and legal structures. The specific elements which should be examined are dependent on the goals and objectives of the organization and must be considered when formulating marketing strategies.

Market segmentation

Market segmentation refers to how an event should be positioned in relation to the com-petition and based on the abovementioned environmental analysis. Market segmentation is broken down into three parts: segmentation, targeting, and positioning, represented by the acronym STP.

Segmentation

O'Reilly and Séguin (2009: 101) described the process of segmentation in a sport organiza-tion as "The delineation of a customer, fan, spectator, participant, or business to business . . . group or groups with homogenous needs and/or wants which the marketing function of the sport organization has the ability to successfully satisfy." The purpose of such an exercise is to ensure that marketing strategies are both efficient and effective. That is, it allows mar-keters to focus their resources on marketing to those consumers they believe will be most receptive to their offering, those who will be profitable and reachable (O'Reilly and Séguin, 2009). This is especially important in sports events where time and money are limited. It also means that the actual process of segmentation must make sense from a financial per-spective; the cost of investing valuable resources in segmenting the market must be less than the potential return (O'Reilly and Séguin, 2009). Shank (2005) suggested that there are six common bases of segmentation which are: demographic, socioeconomic, psychographic, geographic, behavioural, and benefits. A marketer may incorporate more than one criterion from each of these categories in defining their market.

Another model which has examined segmentation comes from Bourgeon and Bouchet (2001), who created a model of sport event segments, and Bouchet *et al.* (2011a), who refined the typology. They argued that there are four sport event segment behaviours:

1   Opportunist: opportunist behaviour is seen when there is the hope of receiving rewards. An opportunist usually only openly participates in the event as part of a show of group support, otherwise only showing neutrality.
2   Aesthete: the aesthete, as the name suggests, takes pleasure in the aesthetic aspect of sport such as beauty, fair play, sporting excellence, and drama.
3   Supporter: supporter behaviour shows a more direct connection to the athletes; the consumer wants to feel as though they have a part in producing the spectacle and will demonstrate this through involving themselves vocally or physically.
4   Interactive: interactive behaviour is based on the reaction and interaction of the consumer to the sport event, with the key elements being the shared emotion among other consumers and the athletes, as well as a sense of entertainment.

Targeting

At its most basic level, targeting involves taking the data gathered during the segmentation process and determining which of the identified segments will be targeted within the event's marketing strategy. While there are many ways of accomplishing this, it typically comes down to an evaluation of which group(s) will allow event marketers to achieve their objectives in the most efficient and effective manner. The characteristics that might be evaluated to determine the appropriate target market include: profitability, size, reach, behavioural variation, and measurability (O'Reilly and Séguin, 2009; Shank, 2005). When examining profitability, the most important element is the sustainability of a target market's profitability. Other questions that might be asked in this area pertain to such issues as the organization's ability to attain competitive advantage within a particular segment, and whether the organization has the required resources to be successful within this segment (O'Reilly and Séguin, 2009). When considering the size of a target market, it is important for marketers to focus on future growth in addition to the current size (Shank, 2005). It is vital that marketers not be fooled by what is known as the majority fallacy, which refers to the mistaken belief that the biggest market segment is always the best for targeting (Shank, 2005). While it may offer the most consumers, it can also offer the greatest competition for their purchasing dollar, and thus may not offer marketers the most efficient use of marketing resources. A measure of the reachability of the target market includes examining how accessible it is through already existing, or easily acquired, channels of communication (O'Reilly and Séguin, 2009). The efficiency and effectiveness of a marketing strategy can be deeply affected if there is no direct way to access the selected target market. Marketing messages that are not being delivered are not effective, and those that are only delivered at great cost are not efficient. The behavioural variation of a target market refers to the degree to which consumers within the targeted group demonstrate similar behaviours, attitudes, and lifestyle approaches and the extent to which those characteristics are unique to that particular group of consumers (Shank, 2005). Finally, the measurability of a target group examines the ability of the marketers to gather information about and evaluate the above criteria (size, reach, profitability, and behavioural variation) with regards to each of the potential target groups. For example, a group whose accessibility through various communication channels is unknown presents a risk, as a company may spend millions of dollars creating and implementing a marketing strategy only to find that there is no way to communicate it directly to their chosen target market. The importance of measurability is often cited as the reason many marketers choose demographic targeting techniques (Shank, 2005), as demographic information is easy to come by through many different primary and secondary sources and includes much useful detail.

Positioning

The final step in the segmentation process involves positioning the event. O'Reilly and Séguin (2009: 101) described this as "how . . . we want the selected target(s) to perceive our offering versus the offerings of our competitors". This step is in part the culmination of the concepts that have been discussed earlier in this chapter. In order to determine appropriate positioning, marketers will examine all internal and external environmental factors as well as any other pertinent information they may have gathered during segmentation and targeting to decide how they will establish and maintain their desired image, relative to those that are put forth by other events that they feel are competitors (Getz, 2005). A marketer can create a position simply by virtue of the sport event's characteristics, or through such strategies as pricing, advertising, and/or promotional messages. Any changes to the core product must be examined in the context of the positioning strategy to ensure that they continue to portray the desired image and not create consumer confusion (Mullin *et al.*, 2000). One strategy that can be used to visually depict market positioning is the creation of a perceptual map. This allows marketers to compare their market positioning strategy with those of their competitors graphically, based on the chosen dimensions of importance for their product and target market. Figure 6.1 provides an example of a perceptual map which shows how a sport event might try to position itself in relation to the perceived positioning of the competition.

Marketing mix

The key acronym to describe the marketing mix is the 4Ps, *product, price, place,* and *promotion*. While some may argue that there are more than just four Ps – for example, Mullin *et al.* (2000) include public relations as a fifth P – the four that are discussed here represent the most well known and widely used grouping. The use of the marketing mix involves manipulating each element in order to find the right combination so as to meet the needs and wants of consumers, and ultimately gain a competitive advantage (Pitts and Stotlar, 1996). As with all other concepts described above, the marketing mix itself is much more a practical concept than theoretical one; however, within each individual element, some research can be noted with regards to sports events.

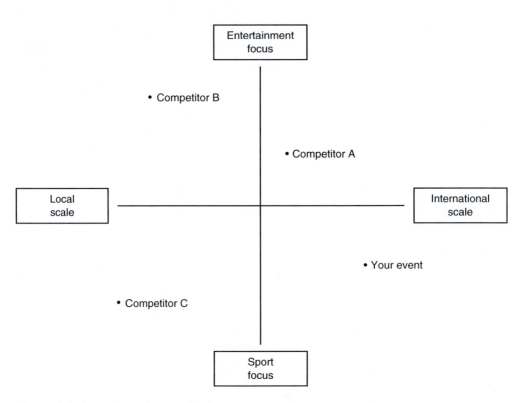

Figure 6.1 A sport event perceptual map.

Product

When discussing the product in the context of the marketing mix, it is taken to mean the development and mental positioning of a company's product. Positioning has been discussed in the segmentation section above and refers to how the product is situated in the minds of consumers, while development can be described as all those aspects that go into making an event what it is. This may include such elements as research, design, and advertising (Mullin *et al.*, 2000). More specifically, Schwarz and Hunter (2008) suggested that when discussing the sport event product, it is important for a marketer to consider branding strategies, appropriate brand extensions, the establishment of a licensing programme, the required product protections (i.e. copyrights and marks of protection), sponsorship fit, concerns regarding product lifecycle, and packaging, which for a sport event means the spectacle and atmosphere that may surround the event.

The product is an especially important consideration with regards to sport event marketing as it is distinctive from typical marketing in many ways. Generally, the sport product can be defined as "any good, service, person, place or idea with tangible or intangible attributes that satisfy consumer sport . . . needs" (O'Reilly and Séguin, 2009: 125). It can be argued that the sport event product is the core sport product which drives the production of all other sport products. The larger the event, the greater the influence the core product (the sport event) has on the overall emergence of other sport-related products. O'Reilly and Séguin (2009) suggested that the primary products include the core product in addition to the athletes, teams, leagues, and clubs. These primary products expand derivative products, including: facilities, the media (press, broadcasters), merchandise and licensing, and skilled services (e.g. health, social, and psychological support team members for the athletes). The derivative products in turn support the primary products.

The sport event product is also unique in its characteristics in the following ways (Mullin *et al.*, 2002):

- intangible and subjective
- inconsistent and unpredictable
- simultaneously produced and consumed
- both a consumer and industrial product
- perishable and must be pre-sold
- incomparable in the emotional attachment and personal identification it provides to consumers
- able to pervade all elements of life and enjoy almost universal appeal.

These characteristics are well documented in the literature and have a large impact on the way marketing is approached in a practical sense. For example, the inconsistent and unpredictable nature of a sport event must be considered when developing a marketing strategy. Despite being the favourite to win a medal, anything may befall an athlete before or during an event to change that predicted outcome, so sponsors must ensure that the success of their marketing campaign is not solely dependent on such an unpredictable outcome.

Price

Price is the second P, and is a concept that is intimately linked to the marketing concepts of value and exchange. According to Shank (2005), price is simply a statement of value; a way to quantify the value of sports objects being exchanged. In the case of an event, this exchange involves organizers providing a sport spectator an experience in exchange for the price of a ticket. With regards to value, Mullin *et al.* (1993) noted that price should be representative of the consumer's perception of the value of the product. Shank (2005: 398) offers the following formula to explain the interaction between value and price within consumer perceptions:

$$value = \frac{\text{perceived benefits of sports product}}{\text{price of sports product}}$$

With the goal of pricing being to provide value to the consumer so they will consider purchasing the good or service, the consumer's perception of perceived benefits (both tangible and intangible) must be balanced according to other internal and external factors and considerations when a marketer is determining the price of a product. Price is a concept that is, at least partially, determined by the decisions made with regards to the other marketing mix elements of product, place, and promotion (Masterman, 2009). It is also directly affected by consideration of the internal and external factors discussed, including, but not limited to (Armstrong and Kotlar, 2005; Mullin *et al.*, 1993):

- efficiency
- fairness
- positive user attitudes
- maximum product exposure
- profits
- demand
- competition
- law
- economy
- technology.

In addition to being highly influenced by several factors, pricing is also arguably the most often and easily manipulated of the marketing mix elements. Ultimately, this is due to the fact that it offers more immediate results than other marketing mix elements when changes are made to pricing strategy. In addition, price is recognized as the easiest element to change; and any changes made to it are easy to convey and noticeable to consumers, allowing them to either keep or change their perceptions as required by the reformed strategy (Mullin *et al.*, 1993). Overall, in a marketplace where demand may be elastic, price can be identified as the most efficient and effective tool for adjusting strategy (Mullin *et al.*, 1993).

Conceptually, price is linked with economic concepts such as supply, demand, elasticity, and fixed and variable costs. While there is research within the sport management literature which deals with theory and pricing strategy (e.g. Berrett *et al.*, 1993), there is little with regards specifically to the pricing of sports events. One exception is Solberg's (2001) study on event income generated through price bundling of tickets. Using the concept of bundling (Guiltinan, 1987), Solberg considered three alternatives with regards to pricing policy: pure component, pure bundling, and mixed bundling. Pure component refers to goods or services that are priced individually and sold separately. Pure bundling means goods or services that are combined with other goods and services and sold at one price. Mixed bundling is when goods and services are available either packaged at a discount, or individually. Results demonstrated that sport event organizers will realize added benefits from a mixed bundling strategy. It was also found that this was applicable in cases where marketers had overestimated event attendance and set price too high (Solberg, 2001).

Place

Place refers to "where and how a company gets a product from its production . . . to a place where the targeted consumer can have access to it" (Pitts and Stotlar, 1996: 89). Different from positioning, it is the actual physical placement and distribution of a sport good or service. While much literature in this area focuses on distribution concepts, such as single versus multiple distribution channels, supply chains, degrees of market coverage and sports retailing, the sport event is unique in that the core product, the event, is simultaneously produced and consumed at the "place' of distribution (Shank, 2005). Sports events require that the marketer draw the consumer to the product rather than take the product to the consumer. With this in mind the components of place that should be examined with regards to sport event marketing strategy include: the athletic facilities themselves, which can be as much of a draw for consumers as the event in some cases, host city and/or country considerations, transportation and accommodation infrastructure, and the creation of a "hype" around the event. Mullin *et al.* (2000) identified eight key components of "place" with regards to the physical location where a sport event happens. They are:

1   accessibility
2   amenities
3   design/layout
4   parking
5   drawing radius
6   personnel
7   security
8   surrounding areas

Schneider and Bradish (2006) used these elements to examine the success of Detroit as host of the XL Super Bowl. In their article they identified several "place" consideration best practices for sport managers and marketers in sports events, such as:

■   the need to ensure that supporting infrastructure is available in order to maximize the place offerings within the host city;
■   the need for organizers and marketers to be creative in their place offerings;
■   the need to maximize the current and future flexibility of the event place(s).

It is also important to note the secondary place considerations related to sports events – mainly ticket distribution and media distribution. They are secondary in that they do not directly refer to the core "place" (i.e. the sport venue), but nevertheless they are vitally important to the marketing function and success of an event. Shank (2005) noted that ticket distribution has become a more complex enterprise which involves such responsibilities as: marketing the event, sales force management and operations, advertising, technical support and customer services. The difficulties related to ticketing at a major sports event were explored by Thamnopoulos and Gargalianos (2002) in their study on the ticketing strategies, objectives, and issues faced by SOCOG. From this, they developed a list of best practices in this area to try and avoid a similar situation in the future, including: attempting to reduce overall complexity, having clear internal communications structures in place, providing the public with clear messages regarding ticket allocation, and encouraging early finalization of venue planning and ticket requirements.

Media distribution is another important secondary place consideration. While not all spectators are lucky enough to attend major events such as the FIFA World Cup or Olympic Games in person, they are still able to access the product through media distribution channels. In this case, the consumer's home has become the "place" and their experience of the event is partially shaped by the ways in which they can access and interact with the event. The advent of digital technology is currently having a drastic impact on the way consumers are able to turn their home, or given mobile technology, wherever they may be, into the sport event place through media distribution. Turner (2007) investigated the impact of technology on sport broadcasting, including mega-events, and identified specific digital distribution system components that are emerging for sport supply networks. After examining the effect of these components on the regulatory, market, and economic consideration of sport event organizers, he suggested that "the sport manager who can understand the developments and opportunities that are emerging alongside the supply and demand associated with digital delivery systems, will be better placed to guide their sporting organization into the future" (Turner, 2007: 359). In addition, Green et al. (2011) argued that the size, placement, and active links found on websites impacted the websites' usability for consumers.

Promotion

Promotions are often mistakenly identified as being tantamount to marketing, as they offer the most publicly perceptible manifestation of the marketing mix (Mullin et al., 2000; Stotlar, 2001). Mullin et al. (2000: 184) defined promotions as "the vehicles through which the marketer conveys information about product, place and price. More importantly, promotion is a critical mechanism for positioning a product and its image in the mind of the consumer". As this definition highlights, promotion is intimately linked with all other elements of marketing strategy that have already been described, which may also explain why it is so often incorrectly thought to be synonymous with the larger concept of marketing. The goals of promotion are multi-faceted and include generating awareness of an event, building, strengthening, positioning, or repositioning an image, building brand loyalty, and increasing product credibility.

The primary components of an event's promotional mix are (Pitts and Stotlar, 1996; Schwarz and Hunter, 2008; Shank, 2005):

- advertising
- publicity
- public relations
- sales promotions (contests and sweepstakes)
- sponsor activation programmes
- personal selling
- licensing
- incentives
- atmospherics.

While these elements can be used independently, typically they are not used in isolation but simultaneously to enhance and support each other. Key in the use of multiple promotional strategies is the articulation of a clear and consistent message which supports the objectives of the sport organization.

At its core, a promotion is a communication strategy that aims to inform and/or encourage action among consumers (Pitts and Stotlar, 1996). Pitts and Stotlar (1996) identified four essential elements of promotional communications. The first is the *sender*, which refers to the source of the information which is to be communicated; in the case of an event, this is likely the organizing committee or sponsor. The sender is responsible for placing a clear, precise message in the appropriate communications channels in order to ensure the success of the promotion. It is also likely that the credibility of the sender will have a major impact on the success of the promotion. The second element of promotional communications is the *message*. This is literally the words and symbols chosen for the promotion, by the sender, to accurately inform the consumer or encourage their actions. The words and symbols should be reflective of the objectives of the promotional campaign as well as the overall organizational values and objectives. The *medium* is the third element of promotional communications and can be described as the channels through which the aforementioned message is related to its intended audience. Promotional mix components, such as advertising and sales promotions, are examples of mediums, as is the media in all its forms (i.e. newspapers, television, online, etc.). Picking the correct medium for a particular target market is key to any successful promotional activity. Virtual advertising, for example, has been recently added as a medium (see Sander and Altobelli, 2011, for details). The *receiver* is the fourth and final element of promotional communications. The receiver is the intended audience for any messages sent through promotional efforts. As part of a fully realized marketing plan the target audience identified during segmentation is likely to be the intended receiver of a promotional message. With this in mind, if the correct message is going to be sent to the correct group of consumers in order to have the desired result, the specifically identified characteristics of that target market must be considered when developing the message and determining the medium through which it will be communicated.

In the literature, there is not a lot of focus on event-specific promotions. One way in which the topic has been approached involves examining specific ways a marketer might promote an event to the best effect. For instance, using the sociological concepts of subculture and sport, identity, and consumption, Green (2001) proposed that by basing promotions on identifying and leveraging the subcultural attachments and identity associations of certain consumers to the sport on offer, rather than more typical product elements like entertainment or fun, marketers could more effectively promote their events. Other research on promotions is more closely tied to related aspects of marketing, which will be discussed later in this chapter, such as how promotions may impact consumer perceptions of a sponsor (McCarville *et al.*, 1998) or how the use of specific narratives, genres, and symbols in the promotion of sporting events may impact spectator considerations (Chalip, 1992).

Marketing strategy

The development of an event's marketing strategy, in its simplest form, can be described as shown in Figure 6.2. Each element of situational and environmental analysis, as well as the segmentation process, not only impacts on each other, but will also have an effect on and provide the foundation for the application of the marketing mix to develop the marketing

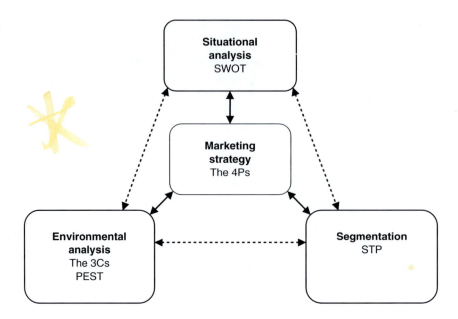

Figure 6.2 The development of a marketing strategy.

strategy. It is important that no area of analysis is neglected and each is considered within the context of the other. This may be a lengthy and resource-consuming project for events that are just getting started; however, it will ultimately prove beneficial to the success of any marketing programme that is implemented.

Communications and public relations

Communications are the means through which an event organizing committee informs their internal and external stakeholders, creating a body of knowledge and images about their event within these groups in the hope of influencing their behaviours. The management of communications as a part of the event marketer's function is described by Schwarz and Hunter (2008: 200) as "the planning, supervising, evaluation and modification of the various methods of communication internal and external to a sport organization". We have chosen to separate communications and public relations from the promotional mix, although some scholars would go so far as to include public relations as the fifth P in the marketing mix (Mullin *et al.*, 2000). With this in mind, it is important to note that communications and public relations are intimately tied to many other aspects of event marketing such as brand management, sponsorship, and most perceptibly the promotional mix. This interconnection is also played out in the management of communications. It is often noted that one key to a successful marketing communications programme is the careful integration of communications messaging throughout both the organization and all elements of the promotional mix. From an organizational perspective, this means that from the top to the bottom of the organizing committee, everyone involved must be conscious of the key messages and ensure they inform all decision-making and public contact (O'Reilly and Séguin, 2009). This presents stakeholders with a clear and consistent idea of the images and information that the organizing committee hopes to portray. From a promotional perspective, integrated marketing communications and public relations means ensuring that elements of the promotional mix and elements of the communications mix are used in combination to support and reinforce each other and the key marketing messages of the event.

Shank (2005) identified three types of communications and public relations strategies that event managers might use: general publicity, producing materials, and lobbying. Within each of these strategies there are numerous communications tools at the disposal of marketers, many of which have been outlined by Getz (2005) as particularly useful for events. General publicity accounts for much of the communications mix and includes such tools as press conferences, new releases, sponsorship leveraging, publicity stunts, VIP and celebrity visits, online and social media content, and unpaid media visibility (e.g. new coverage, athlete interviews, etc.). Producing materials involves the creation of such documents as media kits, audio-visual materials, posters/banners, brochures, and websites. Finally, lobbying can include activities like personal calls and hospitality.

Within an event, there are numerous functions of the communications and public relations aspect. It is usually the case, however, that depending on the particulars of the event (i.e. objectives, timing, etc.) and the specific strategies that are being employed, some functions will be more important than others at any given time. In an event context, the roles of communications and public relations are arguably the following (Mullin et al., 2000):

- provide information to various groups (internal and external)
- image creation/enhancement/modification
- community relations
- employee relations – current and potential (i.e. recruiting)
- educational efforts
- feedback
- crisis management.

There are also obvious interconnections between each of these functions. For instance, the type of information provided will help with education programmes, or previously excellent community relations may help or be a foundation for crisis management programmes.

Events can offer marketers particular challenges in the area of communications, and it is important that they are understood and taken into consideration when formulating a communications plan. Getz (2005) suggests five in particular which must be understood and accounted for. The first is that because events take place over a set period of time (e.g. Olympic Games are 17 days), the intensity and concentration of marketing communication efforts is increased over a similarly set time period rather than a more constant flow. Related to that, a second consideration is the need to achieve event awareness at an early stage and then coordinate the programme so that it reaches its height at a very particular time, usually timed to happen with the beginning of an event (Getz, 2005). It is also the case that, even though the largest events are typically running on a very tight and inflexible budget, this will cause limitation to any promotional mix item; communications are no different. In such cases, tools such as unpaid media visibility, sponsor leveraging, and online social networking become increasingly important to exploit. Budget limitations also complicate the next chal-lenge, which is the need for event marketers to integrate their communications with mul-tiple stakeholders and over various platforms (Getz, 2005). This is particularly important given the rate at which digital platforms for communication are expanding and offering new opportunities to engage the consumer more directly. Finally, the community relations aspect of event communications is arguably more important than it might be in other types of organizations (Getz, 2005). Major sports events in particular are thoroughly integrated with the community and, at times, can be viewed as taking over. A good community rela-tions strategy can not only aid in getting the community to volunteer and become involved, but can also help build positive opinions in the community, making it easier to develop long-term support for recurring events.

Research related directly to communications and public relations in sport events is sur-prisingly limited given the unique characteristics and considerations outlined above. The concept of integrated marketing communications strategies does appear more than once in discussions related to anti-ambush marketing strategies (McKelvey and Grady, 2008; Séguin and O'Reilly, 2008). Likewise, the use of the internet as a communications platform has also been a subject of more than one investigation. In the sport industry more generally, Brown (2003) found that online marketing was most often used to meet the communication objectives of awareness and information distribution. Specific to sport events, Filo *et al.* (2009) examined whether website communications impact consumer attitudes and motiva-tions, and found that they do, leading them to suggest that the strategic use of online com-munications might be one way for event organizers to alter consumer behaviours. Lastly, the effectiveness of television and the internet as communications channels towards brand awareness, sponsorship effectiveness, and purchase intentions (Choi and Yoh, 2011), as well as the success of a particular event communications programme on building awareness and sponsorship success (Bennett *et al.*, 2006a), have also been discussed in the sport event literature.

Consumer (spectator) considerations

Arguably the greatest use of theory in the field of sport event marketing comes within the area of spectator considerations. The principles and theories of consumer behaviour are among those most often used, and they are done so both as general marketing theories and as those which can be identified as sport-marketing-specific theories and concepts. There is also an obvious overlap with many other areas of sport event marketing, such as sponsorship and strategy, which will be articulated in the discussions of sport event consumer research. Spectator considerations are important to marketers as the process and reasoning behind consumer decision-making must be understood before any real strategy to reach/attract can be conceived.

A comprehensive discussion of consumer considerations offers enough material for a textbook in its own right, and so is beyond the scope of this section. We therefore concen-trate on four key areas: consumer definitions; personality and motivations; processes and learning; and outcomes. Each of these areas will be discussed to provide an overview of sport event consumer considerations and some related theories and concepts; however, it is vital to recognize that each of these areas are profoundly interconnected and typically build on each other. This relationship is outlined in Figure 6.3, and will become evident when examining current research in each area. This interconnection is also evident in a detailed explanation of sport consumer behaviour by Funk (2008: 4):

> A desire to seek out a consumption experience reflects a desire to satisfy internal need and receive benefits through acquisition. . . . The amount of time and money individuals devote to sport and events represent behavioural outcomes of some experiential journey [*re: consumer definition and personality/motivations*]. This journey corresponds to the specific sport or event pathway an individual travels to seek out experiences that provide positive outcomes [*re: consumer processes and learning*]. From this perspective, sport consumer behaviour and consumption activities that occur at sport event destinations signify the completion of the journey [*re: consumer outcomes*].

Consumer personality and motivations

Consumer personality and motivation refer to the characteristics and situational factors which go towards explaining why consumers act as they do. In the case of a major sports event, this is associated with why they may choose to attend the event or what they feel they are getting from it which answers to a need or want. Beliefs, attitudes, socialization, involvement, and commitment of the consumer are all examples of ways in which a consumer personality can be described and serve as potential motivators (Schwarz and Hunter, 2008). The processes and outcomes of consumer considerations are arguably a function of the interaction of consumer personality and motivations.

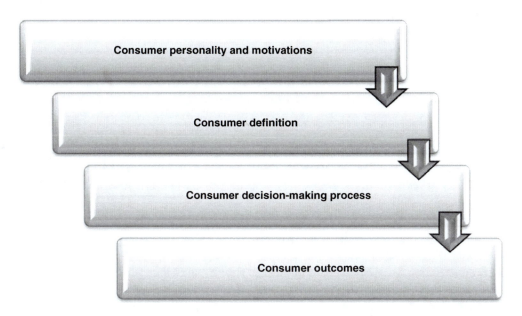

Figure 6.3 Interconnection of consumer considerations.

With regards to the consumer personality element, Freudian theory is one approach that has been used to examine this topic. This perspective argues that purchases (event ticket, merchandise, etc.) made by a consumer are a reflection of their personality, which Freud breaks down into three elements: the id, the super ego, and the ego. The id refers to the entirely unconscious, primitive and instinctive needs of a person in search of base gratifications (Shwarz and Hunter, 2008). Sport events can provide this through such experiences as the pleasure gained watching an athlete win a gold medal for one's country. The super ego is the ethical framework which informs a person's values and beliefs (Schwarz and Hunter, 2008). The Olympic Games do an excellent job in tapping into the value system, and therefore the super ego, of consumers by promoting their espoused positive values, such as respect and friendship, as key to the Olympic experience. The ego provides the balancing element between the id and the super ego – that is the purely instinctive and the purely moral (Schwarz and Hunter, 2008). It is both conscious and unconscious and at least partially formed by ideals of social acceptability and the need for delayed gratification. Ultimately, the ego accounts for the individual differences and situational factors which exist in reality and balances them with the instinctive needs and perceived moral obligations of the individual (Lantos, 2011). In a sport event context, the id's innate desire for aggression can be satisfied in a socially acceptable way which meets the super ego's moral standards through attending a football match and yelling at the opposing team, rather than acting out violently. By understanding these components of a consumer's personality, a marketer can achieve the optimum balance between each aspect and draw the consumer to a purchase decision by satisfying the conscious and unconscious needs and wants of each element as needed (Schwarz and Hunter, 2008).

Funk (2008) classified consumer motivations into two categories: utilitarian and hedonic. Utilitarian motivations are functional, objective, and tangible (Funk, 2008). Typically they are identified with product and/or place attributes; for instance, in a major sports event context, utilitarian motives for consumption may be the venue amenities offered or the chance to see the best athletes in the world all in one place. On the other hand, hedonic motivations are more closely related to the subjective emotions and experiences found in the higher-order aspects of Maslow's hierarchy of needs (i.e. belonging, esteem, and self-actualization); it is within these aspects that sport can contribute to a person's basic needs, and can therefore motivate them to goal-oriented action (Funk, 2008). In a sport event context, hedonic motivations might include having the opportunity to experience the patriotic atmosphere of the Olympic Games or the prestige of having a ticket to the FIFA World Cup final.

The most common theories that have emerged in relation to sport-specific consumer personality and motivations are scales, which have been developed in an attempt to determine consumer motivations. Such scales include, among others: the Sports Interest Inventory (SII) (Funk et al., 2001, 2002, 2003), the Motivation Scale for Sport Consumption (MSSC) (Trail and James, 2001; James and Ridinger, 2002), and the SportWay or SPEED scale, which lists socialization, performance, excitement, esteem, and diversion as the core facets of motivation for sport event attendance (Funk, 2008; Funk et al., 2009). It should be noted, however, that while each of these areas may be applicable to major sports events, they are typically discussed in the literature with regards to sport events more generally (i.e. individual Games) with the exception of the SII, which was originally developed through research on the Women's World Cup in 1999 and has since been expanded to generalized sport events (Funk *et al.*, 2001). In addition to the testing and development of motivational scales, research in the area of consumer motivation also deals with their application in the context of specific elements of marketing strategy. Some research in this area includes how website communications impact consumer motivations and attitudes (Filo *et al.*, 2009), the power of polysemic event characteristics such as multiple narratives, embedded genres, and layered symbols to impact fan interest and the related marketing strategy considerations (Chalip, 1992), or the variation in marketing communication strategies for motivating locals versus visitors to attend an event (Snelgrove *et al.*, 2008).

Consumer definition

Consumer definition relates specifically to elements of the segmentation process discussed earlier in the chapter and how they are applied and researched with regards to the sport event consumer. Within this area, there is an obvious overlap with consumer personality and motivations as it might be the case that consumers are segmented based their motivations. However, this merely covers part of the psychographic variables of segmentation; and so it is important to discuss other aspects of segmentation. Consumer definition refers to the more descriptive aspects of segmentation. While not specific to sport events, Tkaczynski and Rundle-Thiele (2011) examined general event segmentation research, including mega-sport event research. They organized their study on Kotlar's (1980) four bases of segmentation: demographic, geographic, psychographic, and behavioural. The authors found 24 main characteristics within these categories used for segmentation studies in the area. A list of these characteristics is found in Table 6.1. Of the 24, the top five most frequently used were all descriptive characteristics, with four of the five being the demographic variables of age, gender, education, and income, and the only non-demographic variable in the top five being origin/residence, which is classified as a geographic variable.

Table 6.1 Consumer segmentation variables in event studies

Demographic variables	Geographic variables	Psychographic variables	Behavioural variables
Age	Origin/residence	Motivations	Experience
Gender		Purpose	Expenditure
Education		Perceptions	Length of stay
Income		Satisfaction	Frequency
Employment		Involvement	Information sources
Group set		Activities	Repurchase intentions
Travel party composition			Distance travelled
Marital status			Accommodation types
Ethnicity (race)			

Source: Adapted from Tkaczynski and Rundle-Thiele, 2011.

While there are numerous studies on the segmentation of events generally, as discussed above, there are fewer which relate directly to major sports events. Those that can be found tend to be related to the area of tourism and destination marketing research, as major sports events typically seek to draw a large number of tourists as a portion of their targeted consumers. For instance, Kaplanidou (2007) examined how Olympic travellers' intentions were impacted by certain consumer characteristics and what this means for event marketers. Similarly, Kim and Chalip (2004) examined how motives, interests, constraints, and the background characteristics of age, gender, income, education, and previous attendance influenced interest in travelling to a mega-event and the perceived constraints in doing do.

Other studies in the area of consumer definitions examine more specific variables and their impact on consumer intentions. While Preuss *et al.*'s (2007) study focused on examining segmentation of sport mega-event visitors as it directly applies to their potential effect on economic impact, their findings show age and gender have an impact on people's attraction to various different sports, and as such, could be used to improve the effectiveness of event marketing strategies aimed at specific groups. Likewise, Pons *et al.* (2001) and Armstrong (1998, 2008) each examined ethnographic variables to determine how they may shape consumers' considerations of the event and therefore how marketers may segment and target consumers with regards to these characteristics.

Consumer decision-making processes

As with each section on consumer considerations, space does not allow for a full discussion of all consumer decision-making processes. It should be noted, then, that this discussion only touches on one particular theory that has previously been discussed in a sport event marketing context. Funk (2008) provided a sport consumer decision-making sequence (see Figure 6.4) which involves three steps: inputs, throughputs, and outputs. Each of the consumer considerations discussed in this section falls into one or more of these steps, and so the interconnection of the decision-making process with other consumer considerations should be noted.

Inputs refer to external forces that are coming to bear on the decision-maker and will ultimately have an effect on their processing of information about the event, their evaluation of what benefits the event can offer them, and the needs/wants which may be fulfilled by attending the event. The two environmental information categories outlined by Funk (2008) include sociological influences and the marketing activities of event organizations. Sociological influences refer, in part, to second-hand information about potential benefits, or lack thereof, which may come about as a result of event attendance (Funk, 2008). This information may be passed to the consumer from such sources as word-of-mouth or critical reviews. Also among the sociological influences are such factors as geography, climate, social class, gender, and social class, many of which were discussed as part of consumer definition (Funk, 2008), and which describe the consumer's state of being. The marketing activities of the organizing committee refers to the programmes that have been undertaken by event organizers with the implicit purpose of creating a specifically crafted opinion of the event and its offerings in the mind of potential consumers. For instance, if an event's chosen target market is families, their promotional and marketing activities should seek to provide

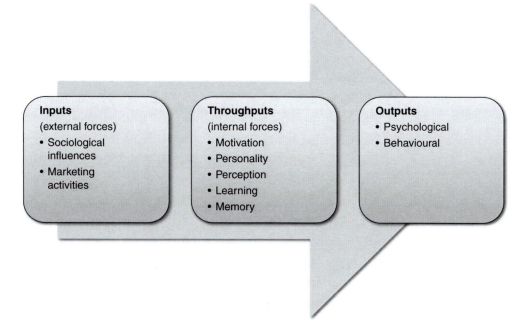

Figure 6.4 Sport consumer decision-making sequence (source: adapted from Funk, 2008).

information to potential consumers on the benefits a family might receive from attending their event. They may position it as a lovely day out and an opportunity to share in the experience of world-class athletic achievement.

The second step in Funk's (2008) decision-making process is throughput, that is, the internal processing. This area is broken down into several internal forces which seek to explain how a consumer's internal characteristics interact with the external information they have received about an event and allows them to make a judgement on the value of the event in helping them meet certain needs and wants. The internal forces that are argued to shape evaluations of external information are: motivation, memory, learning, perception, and personality. While it is beyond the scope of this chapter, there are numerous theories and concepts within each of these areas which could be discussed. For instance, the concepts of personality and motivations were discussed in earlier sections. Schwarz and Hunter (2008) argued that to effectively reach a sport consumer, marketers must have knowledge of theories of learning which can be further divided into behavioural and cognitive learning theories. Evidence of such theories in the literature is particularly prevalent in event sponsorship studies that use learning theories as a lens through which to examine how elements such as image fit might affect a consumer's response to sponsorship, and ultimately their purchase intentions (cf. Koo *et al.*, 2006; Speed and Thompson, 2000).

The final step in Funk's (2008) decision-making sequence is outcomes; these are further divided into interconnected psychological and behavioural outcomes. Put simply, psychological outcomes are the creation of distinct consumer attitudes about an event. An attitude is recognized by Funk (2008: 40) as having three "classes of evaluative responses: cognitive, affective and behavioural intent that occur in a linear structure". A description of each response is outlined in Figure 6.5. The behavioural outcomes (which are distinct from behavioural intent) are the physical and discernible responses of a consumer resulting from the attitude they formed towards the sport event product (Funk, 2008). Behavioural outcomes can be discussed based on the frequency and complexity of a consumer's engagement in consumption behaviours (Funk, 2008). As consumer outcomes are the last key area of importance in the consumer considerations section they will also be discussed in more detail below.

Consumer outcomes

There are five proposed types of sport event outcomes that are sought after by marketers and examined in the literature:

1   purchase intent (event attendance)
2   return intent (with regards to destination from a sport tourism perspective, and for a recurring event)
3   consumer satisfaction
4   sponsorship success
5   event brand creation/awareness/modification.

These elements are not mutually exclusive, meaning that not only can they impact on each other, for instance consumer satisfaction might lead to sponsorship success, but it also means that most marketers would hope for not just one outcome but all to result from consumer decision-making with regards to an event.

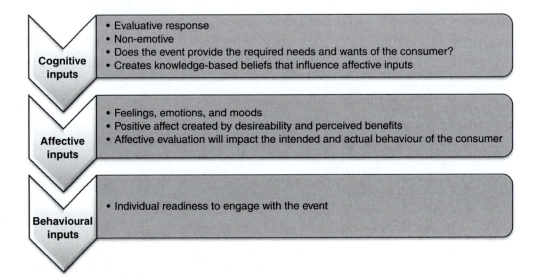

Figure 6.5 Psychological outcomes (source: adapted from Funk, 2008).

In the literature, there are no clear distinctions between studies that involve each of the identified outcomes; and, in fact, many articles touch on more than one outcome due to the already mentioned interconnections. Similarly, much of the related research could also be discussed in other sections of this chapter, such as sponsorship and, more prominently, the previously outlined consumer considerations and their related conceptual frameworks. It is the case that almost every article that examines consumer outcomes also incorporates other elements of consumer considerations and discusses the link between the considerations and the outcomes. One approach in the literature has been to examine how specific consumer characteristics might impact outcomes and therefore also how that outcome then might inform consumer segmentation. For instance Close *et al.* (2006) showed how the community-minded nature of consumers could ultimately have an impact on their purchase intentions with regards to an event sponsor's product. Finally, certain facets of the event experience and their role in impacting consumer outcomes is another way outcomes have been approached in the literature. Service quality and its relationship to satisfaction and future intentions, such as revisiting an event (Shonk and Chelladurai, 2008) or, from the sport tourism perspective, revisiting a host city after the event has moved on (Tsuji *et al.*, 2007) is one such facet.

Market research

It is important at the beginning of this section to make the distinction between market research and research in sport marketing. This section will discuss market research, which is a function of the sport event marketing process and should be carried out by marketers to help guide their decision-making. Sport event market research is the process of organizing committees collecting, analysing, interpreting, evaluating, and reporting data that can assist them in amassing information on such concerns as: the sport event industry, the sport event product generally, their own event product, the effectiveness of their marketing strategies, their competition, economic trends, their consumers, technological advances, and potential risks. All of this information should then be used to make informed and timely decisions about event marketing strategies in order to, hopefully, gain a competitive advantage (O'Reilly and Séguin, 2009).

While conducting market research is viewed as a vital part of most successful marketing strategies, Mullin *et al.* (2000) contended that it is done very poorly within the field of sport marketing. They argued that not only is there too little time and money spent on market research, but also that when it is done, it fails to properly take into consideration the unique features of sport and their potential impact on market research considerations. They state that such research lacks "sportsense" (Mullin *et al.*, 2000: 11). The process of conducting sport event market research can be broken down in many different ways. Figure 6.6 provides an illustration of the steps as they are outlined by several authors.

The types of questions that are answered by market research will vary greatly, depending on the individual event; but, as with much research, marketers typically seek to answer questions related to the 5Ws (who, what, when, where, why) and how. The following provides examples of the types of questions along these lines, which might be asked for an event:

117

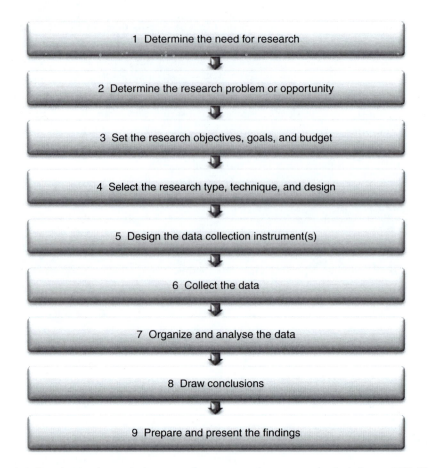

Figure 6.6 Sport event market research process (source: adapted from O'Reilly and Séguin, 2009; Schwartz and Hunter, 2008; Shank, 2005).

- Who is the event's target market?
- What does my consumer want from the event?
- Where does my consumer learn information about my event?
- When is the event most accessible to consumers?
- Why are my consumers interested in the event?
- How do consumers perceive my event relative to competitors?

Obviously, there are an infinite number of questions which could be asked given the diversity of sport events, so determining those which are most appropriate for meeting the objectives of a market research project is a vital step in the process outlined in Figure 6.6.

There are three different types of research that are used for market research purposes: exploratory, descriptive, and causal. Step 4 of the sport event market research process involves choosing the type of research that is appropriate given the objectives of the research and the questions that marketers are hoping to answer. Exploratory research is chosen when very little is known about the problem and there is no clear direction to take. It is typically just used as a starting point for more detailed descriptive and causal research. The purpose is to gather ideas, insights, and details (O'Reilly and Séguin, 2009) while formulating hypotheses, clarifying problems, and forming a list of research priorities (Schwarz and Hunter, 2008). Ultimately, it is hoped that a clearer picture of the threats and opportunities which should be examined will emerge. Descriptive research follows the identification of specific research questions. This type of research provides answers that are very factual, accurate, analytic, often statistical, and typically answers the who, what, when, where, and how questions (O'Reilly and Séguin, 2009; Schwarz and Hunter, 2008; Shank, 2005). Causal research is the final type; its purpose is to determine the cause-and-effect relationships which exist among the variables discussed in the descriptive research. That is, causal research aims to answer the why question, with the ultimate hope of discovering a relationship between two variables that will help predict future events (O'Reilly and Séguin, 2009). For example, while descriptive research might tell a marketer that 57 per cent of those people who attended the Olympic bobsledding event were pleased with the experience, causal research will explain *why* they were pleased and what that might mean for future attendance.

Once the type of research that will be conducted has been decided, the marketer must choose what type(s) of data will be used; secondary data or primary data, or a combination of the two. Secondary data is information that is not created by those carrying out the research, but rather has been previously collected by other researchers yet can be analysed to provide information to help answer the sport event research problem. This data might come from such sources as a census, specialized sport market research company (e.g. IEG, TrojanOne) reports, academic journals, and professional associations. Primary data, on the other hand, is much more labour intensive as it involves designing the research project and personally collecting data specifically for the purposes of answering the sport event market research question(s) (O'Reilly and Séguin, 2009). Depending on such particulars as the goals and objectives of the research, or resource restrictions (human, time, financial), primary data can be collected through a variety of methods; eight of the most common are:

1 experiments
2 surveys/questionnaires
3 interviews (with stakeholder groups)
4 observations
5 focus groups
6 expert surveys/interviews
7 test marketing
8 secret shopping.

Academic research in the area of market research is scarce. While Getz (1998) argued that practitioners could contribute to sport event tourism marketing research by conducting their own market research, there is little else that explicitly discusses market research in the literature. It is the concepts and processes offered by general sport marketing textbooks which provide students and practitioners with the majority of knowledge.

Destination marketing

Unique to event marketing, particularly around mega-events, is the related concept of destination marketing. Here, destination marketing refers to the process of a host city and/or country leveraging the imagery and awareness created by the event to further their own marketing strategies, either through direct coordination with the event organizing committee or independently. Like the field of event marketing generally, destination marketing uses theory and concepts from a wide variety of fields, including sociology, event tourism, marketing, and branding.

The nature of the interaction between the sport event and the destination brand is unique to every situation and depends on a number of factors. Chalip and Costa (2005) proposed a conceptual framework for determining the proper role for an event in destination branding. They began by defining three ways an event and a destination might combine in destination branding (Chalip and Costa, 2005):

- *Co-branding*: co-branding can take place when an event has its own distinct image or brand in the source market. For example, the Olympic Games have their own very clear and recognizable set of images, values, and beliefs which are typically associated with the Games. From the perspective of the destination brand, the purpose of co-branding would be to try and transfer the positive brand images and associations of an event like the Olympics onto the destination (i.e. the host city or country). Chalip and Costa (2005) suggest that the best way to accomplish co-branding is to strategically combine media communications, publicity, and advertising messages by building the sport event into destination promotional efforts and vice versa. A successful co-branding strategy should ensure that key messages which speak to both the event and destination marketer's "desired associations" (Chalip and Costa, 2005: 225) are highlighted with clarity and consistency. Ultimately it is an approach which requires a high level of coordination and integrated marketing communications between the event and the destination.
- *Brand extension*: events which are a better fit as a brand extension are those which do not have a distinct brand image, but rather are intimately tied to and, in some cases, unable to be separated from, the destination brand. They are categorized by Chalip and Costa (2005: 227) as being "explicitly part of the destinations brand range". Part of a brand extension relationship may also be seen in the sharing of features between the event and the destination – for instance, a well-known facility can represent a draw for both an event and a destination (Chalip and Costa, 2005). Similar to co-branding, there is the same two-way transfer of images between the event and the destination, but this should be facilitated through highlighting the existing links between the event and the destination in marketing communications rather than creating a new co-branded link (Chalip and Costa, 2005).
- *Destination feature*: a sport event brand that does not have distinction or influence among the target market of a destination but can still be promoted and leveraged as a positive attribute of the city or country might have a role as a destination feature, providing a physical demonstration of the characteristics, values, and/or images that are already promoted in their destination branding strategies (Chalip and Costa, 2005).

It is important to note that not all events offer the opportunity to provide destination branding outcomes, and marketers must ensure that such relationships are not forced, or they risk doing more damage than good with those associations. Even in the case that an event meets one of the criteria provided by Chalip and Costa (2005) and can potentially play a role in destination branding, there are other considerations which much be taken into account with regards to creating successful partnerships between a sport event and destination brand. Jago et al. (2003) noted several factors which event and destination marketing experts suggest play a role in determining the appropriateness and/or success of a marketing partnership between an event and a destination:

- community support for the event
- ability of the event to differentiate itself from other events
- longevity/tradition of the event
- the use of cooperative and synergistic planning between the event and the destination
- consideration of how the event interacts with other destination events
- the importance of fit
- media support/management.

While each of these factors may be important, it is the significance of event–destination image fit (e.g. Drengner et al., 2011; Hallmann and Breuer, 2010; Xing and Chalip, 2006) and media support/management (e.g. Chalip et al., 2003; Getz and Fairley, 2003) that appear to receive the most attention in the literature. While the event management, sport management, and sport and event tourism fields offer an abundance of research in these areas, the following sections will specifically focus on two aspects of sport event-based destination marketing programmes that are important for sport event marketers to understand: the potential effects of an event on destination image considerations; and consumer behavioural intentions. These aspects are typically linked in a linear causal fashion, as shown in Figure 6.7, with the image considerations directly and indirectly affecting consumer behaviours, meaning much of the research in these areas can be discussed in both sections.

Event effects on destination brand/image

As outlined in Figure 6.7, there are two main impacts an event might be able to have on destination brand and image considerations. The first is increasing destination brand exposure/awareness, which has been examined in the literature by many authors (e.g. Green et al., 2002; Mangan et al., 2011; Ritchie and Smith, 1991). Green et al. (2002) specifically looked at the nature and extent of television exposure a destination might receive during a major sports event, and found that there was minimal direct exposure for destination brand images during a telecast, but that the event logo was shown more often; thus, opportunities were not maximized (Green et al., 2002). They therefore suggested several tactics a destination marketer might attempt to provide the desired destination brand exposure:

- The integration of event and destination logos.

121

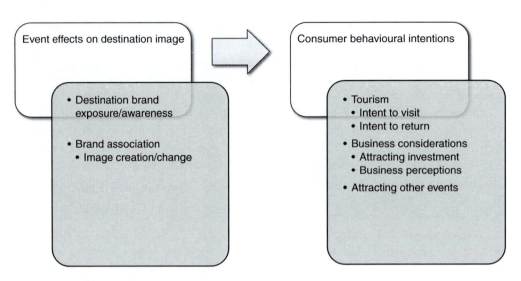

Figure 6.7 Destination brand impacts.

■ Destination marketers should work closely with the broadcasters themselves, creating relationships with announcers to make them aware of what the city has to offer, and then provide them with a clear-cut and straightforward set of information and facts that the announcers can then use to talk about the destination on the air.

■ The destination marketer should highlight the unique and iconographic characteristics and attributes of the city by providing broadcasters with images of the host city, its differentiating characteristics, or perhaps athletes enjoying the attributes of the city, which can then be shown as background during a telecast (Green *et al.*, 2002).

The second impact an event might have on destination brand image considerations is with regards to brand associations. Brand associations are defined by Aaker (1991: 109) as "anything linked in memory to a brand". This includes all tangible and intangible symbols, values, and feelings. As Chalip and Costa (2005) noted, many destinations hope that the associations consumers have with a sport event might be transferred to the destination as well. The Olympic Games provide a good example of this as it is not unbelievable to think that a destination would hope for such Olympic brand associations as friendship and cultural acceptance to be transferred onto themselves and associated with their brand in the mind of consumers. An example from the literature comes from Smith (2006), who, in examining three major UK cities and their efforts to leverage sport events for image effects, found that the events appeared to increase positive associations related to modernity, progress, and vitality, while generating positive cultural meanings.

Closely linked to the idea of brand associations is another potential impact of a sport event on destination brand considerations: image creation and/or change. This involves the specific creation of a link between the sport event and destination brand for the purposes of changing consumer perceptions. This might be the case if: the destination has no brand of its own prior to hosting the event; they have a brand but it is unintentional and based on a bad reputation; or they are simply looking to re-brand and differentiate themselves from an out-dated image. Gripsrud *et al.* (2010) provided an example of research in this area as they examined how the 2006 Winter Olympic Games in Turin, Italy may have impacted consumer images of the host country. It was found that a mega-event might be able to change country image perceptions among those that already had a high level of interest in sport (Gripsrud *et al.*, 2010). However, it was also noted that this did not always mean the change in image was positive, as a negative image could also develop based on how the event unfolds (Gripsrud *et al.*, 2010). While this study has its limitations, it does provide information for destination marketers about the potential for a mega-event to assist in image change or creation and the importance of ensuring the event is well run so as to avoid negative image impacts.

Consumer behavioural intentions

Typically, the desire for positive image impacts is related to the desire to influence consumer behaviour. This is no different with regards to the relationship between events and destination images, and this is clearly shown in the literature. Figure 6.7 outlines several consumer behavioural outcomes that might be hoped for; the literature reinforces the relationship between image considerations and some of these potential outcomes, as is discussed below.

According to research, tourism outcomes that might be sought after include the intention to visit, either for the first time for those who only watched an event on TV or the intent to return for those that experienced the event as a spectator or participant. Research demonstrates that the portrayal by sport event media of certain destination images can positively affect intention to visit, but this is subject to contextual factors that must be considered; thus, marketers' approaches must be educated and strategic (Chalip *et al.*, 2003). The effect of image considerations on intention to return has also been investigated, among both spectators and participants. For instance, Kaplanidou (2007) suggested that perceived excitement and pleasantness of the destination would impact return intentions for spectators who travelled to the 2004 Athens Olympic Games, whereas Hallmann and Breuer (2010) stated that while the sport event image on its own was not a predictor for participant intent to return, image fit between the destination and the sport event could be used a predictor, albeit with hesitation.

Finally, event effects on destination image and the related impacts on business considerations have also been discussed in the literature. Jun and Lee (2008) examined how positive perceptions of the 2006 FIFA World Cup in Germany led to positive visit intentions; they also noted that favourable attitudes towards Germany, as a country, as created by the sport event, would lead to a more positive perception of German companies. Preuss and Alfs (2011) also found evidence of a perceived impact of events on destination images and business considerations in examining China's signalling to external stakeholders during their hosting of the 2008 Beijing Olympic Games. They found that China seemed to focus the destination image messages on influencing potential business partners and/or investors. While the study does not make assumptions about the success of this strategy, it does highlight the fact that Chinese marketers may have felt a sport mega-event, such as the Olympic

Games, offered a platform for producing appealing images of their country that would speak to the global corporate community.

Figure 6.7 also lists attracting other events as a potential outcome from event and destination brand image considerations; but as of yet, there seems to be little research that deals directly with this outcome, suggesting this is perhaps an area for future research to consider.

Sport event brands

The previous section began to touch on some elements of brands and brand strategy with regards to destinations and events. This section will begin a more detailed discussion of brands as they relate to the creation and management of an event brand. Aaker (1991: 7) defined a brand as a

> distinguishing name and or symbol (such as a logo, trademark, or package design) intended to identify the good or services of either one seller or a group of sellers, and to differentiate those goods or services from those of competitors.

A brand consists of tangible and intangible elements, both of which are important to the overall success of the brand. Tangible elements include such things as the trademarks or logos that are used to identify the event – for instance, the five coloured rings of the Olympic Movement. The intangible elements of a brand – for example the values associated with the Olympic Movement such as peace, fair play, and friendship – are the associations which exist in the minds of consumers with regards to the event and are at least as important to the overall brand (O'Reilly and Séguin, 2009). As sport is a unique context, however, it can even be argued that the intangible and emotional aspects are even more important than the tangible. Richelieu (2004) suggested that the highly emotional element of sports may positively affect trust and loyalty towards a sport brand, which means that by tapping into emotional elements of the brand, marketers are more likely to elicit a strong positive reaction towards the brand by consumers.

From a marketing perspective, having a strong brand can arguably be an event's biggest asset, as a strong brand is typically equated with competitive advantage (Aaker, 1991), particularly with regards to consumer behavioural responses. Additionally, event brand loyalty can be leveraged to sell supplementary goods (e.g. event merchandise) and services such as event sponsorship (Gustafson, 2001). In fact, it is often the case that the value of a sport event brand will outlast the event itself. This is particularly the case with regards to the potential positive impact a well-known sport event brand might have on destination image, as discussed in the destination marketing section. A strong brand can be identified as having achieved brand equity, the ultimate goal of the branding process.

Brand equity is a "set of assets and liabilities linked to a brand, its name and symbol that add to or subtract from the value provided by a product or service to a firm and/or to that firm's customers" (Aaker, 1991: 12). Figure 6.8 outlines the five assets or liabilities that have been identified as contributing to brand equity. A sport event which has high perceived quality and brand awareness, positive brand associations, brand loyalty among consumers,

and additional proprietary assets is thought to have achieved brand equity. It is also important to note that each of these assets may impact on the others as well as on overall brand
equity. Perceived quality simply refers to the consumer's perception of the event's quality,
and may or may not be based on actual experience. At a major sports event, perceived
quality might be based on the level of competition on offer or something as symbolic as the
price of tickets, as high ticket prices might signal to potential consumers that the event is of
high quality. Brand awareness is defined as "the likelihood with which a brand name will be
recalled or recognized" (O'Reilly and Séguin, 2009: 155). Awareness is the foundation of
all other elements of brand equity, as without awareness there is little chance that consumers will have any perceptions regarding quality or any particular brand associations. Brand
associations connote the already mentioned intangible assets of brand, the characteristics or
attitudes that consumers link to the brand. O'Reilly and Séguin (2009) classify brand associations as either experiential or symbolic and note that they are closely related to brand
image considerations. While consumer brand associations may or may not reflect reality,
they must be understood by marketers so that positive associations can be leveraged and
negative associations altered in order to help attain brand equity. Brand loyalty is often
thought to be the most important element of brand equity as it directly links to the potential
for profit (Aaker, 1991). If an event achieves brand loyalty, it means that consumers are still
likely to attend that event even in the face of a more attractive set of attributes at a competitor's event. It is a measure of brand attachment that all marketers should strive towards, as
it not only impacts brand equity but also decreases the long-term marketing communications requirements of the event, as maintaining loyal consumers is much easier than creating
loyal consumers (Aaker, 1991).

Brands and brand equity are concepts that have been discussed in detail in the sport literature (e.g. Gladden *et al.*, 1998; Gladden and Milne, 1999), but are only emerging within
major sports events. A notable exception is Séguin and O'Reilly (2008), who discussed the

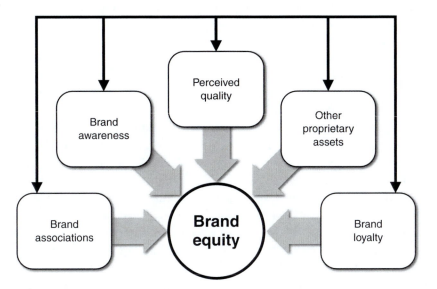

Figure 6.8 Brand equity (source: adapted from Aaker, 1991).

concept of sport event brands as it applies to the Olympic brand and the importance of event brand management for reducing ambush marketing and clutter.

The concept of brand creation is one area that is arguably receiving more attention in the literature lately. Given the difficult circumstances one-off events often face in creating and marketing a brand in the short period of time between when they are awarded hosting responsibilities and when the event takes place, Parent and Séguin (2008) put forward a proposed model for brand creation. Very briefly, they argue that three factors are key in event brand creation:

1   a leadership group whose characteristics fit with the identity of the sport event brand and who possess political/networking skills, business/management skills, and sport/event skills;
2   the context, or internal and external environmental realities of the sport event and host city/country, which moderates the impact of the leadership factor; and
3   the nature of the event – for instance, the brand strength of the governing sport body who franchises the event (Parent and Séguin, 2008).

It is the interaction of these factors, along with the appropriate application of differing two-way brand communications strategies for particular internal and external stakeholders, that create the basis for successful one-off event brand creation. This model has also been used as a framework to examine brand creation in recurring sports events (see Parent *et al.*, 2012). It was found that the three factors outlined above were also key in the brand creation of recurring international sport events. The overall model was altered, however, based on the findings that the organizing committee's core values and culture were also vital to the creation of an event brand. Furthermore, given the different circumstances of a recurring event versus a one-off event, this study found that in a recurring event the experience of leadership also moderated the effects of leadership characteristics/skills and that longstanding relationships between the NSFs and the event host organization impacted the branding process (Parent *et al.*, 2012).

Sponsorship

As with other topics in this section, sponsorship could easily fill a book on its own. While this section only provides a very brief overview of event sponsorship and the related literature, it will discuss some key concepts as well as the key areas of research within the literature to provide a broad overview of the topic. The importance of sponsorship to sport event marketing can hardly be overstated. For example, at the 2010 Olympic Winter Games in Vancouver, sponsorship accounted for about 43 per cent of VANOC's overall operating budget. In total, VANOC had 54 of its own sponsors/suppliers in addition to the ten international sponsors who provide money through the IOC. While such figures are obviously not the norm for every major sports event, most events are just as dependant on the influx of sponsorship dollars to provide the majority of their funding.

Sponsorship is defined as "a cash and/or in-kind fee paid to a property in return for access to the exploitable commercial potential associated with that property" (IEG as cited in Getz,

2005: 255). The provided access to the exploitable commercial assets of the property is partially what differentiates sponsorship from philanthropy; it is the leveraging of those assets by the sponsor that completes the differentiation. Sponsorship leveraging or activation is an important concept. It refers to the marketing and promotional activities of the sponsor as they try to generate awareness and benefits from their association with the event and its related trademarks and images. Leveraging is often argued to be the most important thing a sponsor can do to reap the benefits of a sponsorship and fight against such issues as clutter and ambush marketing. In fact, most researchers will contend that the amount of money spent on leveraging should be many times that spent on the original sponsorship rights. The leveraging of sponsorships also provides the event with needed marketing exposure, which leads to another key concept with regards to sponsorship, and that is its mutually beneficial nature.

A properly leveraged sponsorship can provide many benefits to the event itself, beyond just the initial cash outlay to put towards operating expenses. Getz (2005) stated that events with successful sponsorship programmes stand to realize such benefits as: increased marketing scope through collateral promotions, as mentioned above; growth of event constituencies (supporters, contacts, etc.); knowledge and human resources gain through sponsors' expertise; and image enhancement through connections with well-known and well-respected companies. Similarly, there are numerous benefits which sponsors stand to realize from such partnerships, including: media exposure; increased sales (return on their investment); opportunity for corporate hospitality programmes; image transfer; increased brand awareness; access to specific target markets; employee engagement opportunities; business-to-business marketing opportunities (the ability to interact and form networks with other sponsors); and differentiation from competitors (Getz, 2005; O'Reilly and Séguin, 2009). However, it is equally important for both partners in an event sponsorship to realize that there are also some dangers which should be recognized and accounted for. These include: ambush marketing; clutter; the threat of perceived over-commercialization of the event; too many tickets going to sponsors rather than fans; sponsor interference in how the event is run; and the potential for negative image transfers (due to scandals, etc.). As with any mutually beneficial partnership, both sides also have individual responsibilities to ensure that they are both maximizing the potential benefits and minimizing the potential risks of the situation. Table 6.2 outlines some of the responsibilities of event organizers and sponsors.

Table 6.2 Sponsorship responsibilities

Event organizer responsibilities	Sponsor responsibilities
Service sponsors	Leverage the sponsorship
Educate consumers	Fully incorporate sponsorship into their marketing and communications mix
Under-promise and over-deliver on sponsors' expectations	Actively engage all employees and brands within the company in the sponsorship (horizontal and vertical integration)
Integrate the sponsorship into their communications and public relations	
Protect sponsors	

127

The amount and wide-ranging nature of research in the area of sport event sponsorship is almost unparalleled among other sport event marketing topics. As with sponsorship itself, it is impossible to cover it all in a single section of a chapter, but for the purposes of this book, six key areas of research will be discussed: sponsorship valuation, sponsorship motivations, benefits of sponsorship (including image transfer and consumer behaviour considerations), sponsorship effectiveness, image fit, and sponsorship evaluation. As always, these areas offer some level of interconnection both with each other and with other sections of this marketing chapter. For instance, image transfer could be discussed merely as one type of sponsorship benefit, while consumer behaviour considerations have already been discussed in depth earlier in the chapter. Each of these will be briefly discussed individually here; however, as they represent a trend in the research that has been, and is continuing to be, conducted in the field of event sponsorship.

Sponsorship valuation is a topic which has not received much attention in the literature and is typically noted as being an intimidating undertaking for academics, sponsors, and property owners alike. As such, assigning value to sponsorships is generally a guessing game which leaves both parties open to great risk and the potential for loss. As always the concept of value is open to interpretation; and it can be argued that a sponsorship is always worth as much as one is willing to pay. However, in the context of tight negotiations over sponsorship fees, added knowledge for each party in this area would no doubt be beneficial. One example in the literature of how event sponsorship valuation has been approached is provided by Miyazaki and Morgan (2001), who used the economic model of event study analysis to examine how the media announcement of a company's Olympic sponsorship affected the movement of that company's stock price. They argued that stock price is an accurate reflection of perceived value of the firm in the eyes of investors; and as such, a change in this value in and around the media announcement of Olympic sponsorship is arguably a result of investors' perceived value of the sponsorship (Miyazaki and Morgan, 2001). Using this method, they found that there was indeed value in Olympic sponsorship; however, it can be argued that this is a very limited notion of value and much more research in this area would undoubtedly be useful.

Sponsorship motivations refer to the reasons why an organization may choose to sponsor an event. This also includes the objectives organizations might set for the sponsorship, as it can be argued that their motivation in sponsoring is directly related to their belief that they can achieve stated objectives. McCarville and Copeland (1994) used exchange theory to provide propositions based on the principals of rationality, marginal utility, and fair exchange. Unsurprisingly, they suggest that event sponsors choose to involve themselves with the sponsorship opportunities that offer the best benefits and most chance of success. Somewhat less intuitive, however, were their additional propositions which contended that past sponsorship success, the inclusion of those elements of past agreements which were successful in new agreements, a balanced power relationship between the sponsor and property owner, and multiple reward options would be positively associated with decisions to sponsor, while ambush marketing has the ability to diminish the likelihood of long-term partnerships (McCarville and Copeland, 1994). While their propositions have to be tested empirically, Apostolopoulou and Papadimitriou (2004) interviewed executives of sponsoring companies in order to examine the motivations of the 2004 Olympic Grand National sponsors. They found that gaining a competitive advantage was not the overarching motivation for becoming involved with the Games; rather, it was a desire to help their country, be part of a major event, link themselves to the Olympic Games, support corporate development, and fulfil a corporate obligation befitting their size and reputation within the country that drove them to invest in the national sponsorship effort (Apostolopoulou and Papadimitriou, 2004). While competitive advantage did not figure strongly in the sponsor's motivations, it was arguably evident in their noted overall objectives. The goals of increasing sales and market share, corporate image enhancement, increasing corporate awareness and recognition, and to a lesser degree developing community involvement and employee relations were all found to be important to the sponsoring companies (Apostolopoulou and Papadimitriou 2004). These findings are supported by Kang and Stotlar's (2011) examination of TOP sponsors' motives for participating in the 2010 Vancouver Olympic Winter Games. They found brand equity enhancement, corporate reputation building, and increased sales as the primary motives, followed by corporate social responsibility (CSR) motives.

While there are examples of research that discusses other sponsorship benefits such as the impact of long-term sponsorship on long-term residual brand awareness (Mason and Cochetel, 2006) or, from the sport event property side, the development of brand value through image dimensions and the impact of multiple sport sponsorships (Chanavat et al., 2010), for the most part benefits of sponsorship have been examined with regard to (1) the impact they have on image transfer and (2) consumer behavioural considerations. First, research on image transfer tends to focus on those elements of a sponsorship which act as moderators for the support or hindrance of the image transfer between the event and the sponsoring company. Several authors have examined this topic from both a conceptual (Gwinner, 1997) and empirical direction (Gwinner and Eaton, 1999; Grohs and Reisinger, 2005). For example, Gwinner (1997) put forward a model which suggested that the degree of similarity between the property and sponsor brands, the level of sponsorship (i.e. amount of clutter and offered exclusivity), event frequency, and the consumers' previous involvement and attitudes towards a sponsor's product will all affect the strength of image-transfer outcomes. Empirically, it has been noted that there is in fact support for the belief that sponsorship can lead to image transfer (Gwinner and Eaton, 1999), and that event–sponsor fit (Gwinner and Eaton, 1999; Grohs and Reisinger, 2005) and event involvement seemed to have an effect on image transfer, while the level of sponsorship exposure did not (Grohs and Reisinger, 2005). Second, as consumer behaviour has been discussed generally in more detail earlier in the chapter, this section will only touch on some of the research links to sponsorship-related outcomes, specifically the concepts of consumer recall and response.

Consumer recall refers to the ability of a consumer to call to mind the sponsoring company when asked – for example, the ability of the consumer to single out McDonald's or Visa if asked who sponsors the Olympic Games. Research in this area includes studies by Barros et al. (2007), who studied certain characteristics (i.e. demographics, event, and sponsor perceptions, etc.) to determine their relative influence on the probability of brand recall at the 2004 European Soccer Championships in Portugal. In addition, Pitts (1998) analysed sponsorship recall at the Gay Games, providing insight into the effects presented in sponsorship consumer outcomes, such as unusually high recall and niche events. One way consumer response has been approached is by examining certain consumer perspectives that might influence consumer response to sponsorship. Specifically, Lee *et al.* (1997) proposed that consumers' attitudes towards the event (i.e. their enjoyment, support, and the perceived quality), their attitude towards commercialization of the event, and their inclination towards action based on sponsorship status will impact their response to sponsorship efforts. Roy and Cornwell (2004), on the other hand, examined how the level of knowledge a consumer has about an event might impact their response to event sponsorship.

With the huge amounts of money tied up in sponsorship, the issue of effectiveness is obviously an area of interest; and this is reflected in the literature. While some studies simply attempt to examine its overall effectiveness with regards to certain events (e.g. Nufer and Bühler, 2010; Ozturk *et al.*, 2004), others take a more focused approach to identify practices that might influence effectiveness (however effectiveness is defined). For instance, Lacey *et al.* (2010) discussed the roles of consumer knowledge and perception of sponsors' CSR on positive sponsorship outcomes. Likewise, Papadimitriou and Apostolopoulou (2009) suggested that using multiple methods of activation, the inclusion of leveraging strategies that tap into the unique set of emotions generated by the event, providing tangible and interactive benefits for consumers, and ensuring the proper capabilities and finances are in place to leverage a mega-event to its potential are all strategies that might help increase the effectiveness of sponsorships in attaining competitive advantage for sponsors.

The most developed area of research that is arguably tied to sponsorship effectiveness, however, is the concept of image fit. Image fit refers to the level of congruence that consumers perceive exists between the sponsor and the event, and might refer to images, associations, or objectives, among other things (O'Reilly and Séguin, 2009). Research has examined both elements which impact perceptions of fit, and the impact of perceived fit on sponsorship outcomes. With regards to elements impacting perceptions of fit, Roy and Cornwell (2003) proposed that the positive brand equity of a sponsor would be linked to a greater perception of sponsorship fit among consumers. For example, it was posited that the dominance of a sponsor like Ford in their product category would lead consumers to perceive a better fit with an event for sponsorship purposes. While this was found to be supported in the case of two product categories, it was not supported for a third, which raises the question of how the product category attributes might moderate this effect (Roy and Cornwell, 2003). This study also examined the second element of event sponsorship fit research, which is the impact of perceived fit on sponsorship, namely the effectiveness of the consumer behaviour outcomes of sponsor recall and response. Studies by Roy and Graeff (2002/2003) and McDaniel (1999) support the idea that consumer response to sponsors is positively impacted by a perceived fit between the sponsor and the event, while Koo *et al.* (2006) found that the probability of a consumer correctly recalling an event sponsor was positively impacted by the perceived image fit between the event and the sponsor brand. All of this suggests that sponsors and event marketers could both benefit from seeking out sponsorship arrangements where the event and sponsor brands have some level of congruence.

The final area of sport event sponsorship research which will be touched on is the concept of sponsorship evaluation. Like sponsorship valuation, the task of evaluating a sponsorship is often viewed as a vital but difficult undertaking. Different contexts and sponsor objectives require different methods and measurements of success and/or effectiveness. Despite the recognized importance of evaluating sponsorship, little research could be found that directly related to the provision or discussion of sport event sponsorship evaluation metrics. One instance can be found in a study by Ludwig and Karabetsos (1999), who found that sponsors of the 1996 Olympic Games in Atlanta evaluated their sponsorships using internal sources and external agencies, based on four key areas: (1) hospitality, (2) sales, (3) media coverage, and (4) image and public perceptions. Another example of research in sport event evaluation was completed by O'Reilly *et al.*(2007), who, among other things, demonstrated the difficulties faced by sponsors in evaluating sponsorship by using certain measures to evaluate in-stadium advertising effectiveness during the 2004 Grey Cup. Overall, this dearth of research in such an important area suggests that it may be a key topic for future investigation.

Ambush marketing

Ambush marketing is an increasingly important concern within sponsorship for property owners and sponsors, and the abundance of research in the area suggests it is a highly popular field of study for academics as well. The most frequently used definition of ambush marketing is that of Sandler and Shani (1989: 9), who defined it as "a planned effort (campaign) by an organization to associate itself indirectly with an event in order to gain at least some of the recognition and benefits that are associated with being an official sponsor". While this definition is often used, it is well documented that there are issues with clearly defining the concept in a way which suits all stakeholders and academics. As with many contentious topics, both the tone and the wording of the definition are typically dependent on the role within the ambush situation of the person providing the definition. For example, those with a vested interest in protecting the Olympic brand and the sponsors who have paid to associate with it will typically take a negative tone, while a marketing executive of a non-sponsor may describe it as opportunistic and creative. In fact, it has been argued that perhaps there is not meant to be a single definition. As will be discussed later, there are a wide variety of ambush marketing strategies, many of which fall into an ethically grey area; it has been suggested that ambush marketing is best described by many different definitions along a continuum (Hoek and Gendall, 2002). Further elaboration on this idea has, so far, not been undertaken in the literature.

The main objective of an ambush marketing campaign is said to be the creation of consumer confusion, thus allowing the ambusher to gain the benefits of association without paying for the rights to do so, and weakening the impact of a competitor being the exclusive sponsor of an event (Sandler and Shani, 1989). There are numerous strategies a company might use to ambush an official sponsor; in fact, it has been noted that such strategies are really only limited by the creativity of the marketers. Examples of ambush marketing strategies include sponsoring media coverage of the event, sponsoring individual athletes or teams involved in the event, activating over and above the given product category rights, and creating thematic advertising and promotions that avoid using trademarks but clearly link to the event. While the ambushers will argue that in utilizing such strategies they are meeting the needs of their shareholders and partaking in good business practices, the property owners take a bleaker view. They argue that not only is ambush marketing unethical, but that it threatens the very sport events and sport systems they are taking advantage of. Particularly within the Olympic Movement, it is threatened that ambush marketing has the potential to endanger the vitality of the event by decreasing the value of sponsorships. As the Games continue to grow, so too does the cost of hosting the event; and if a sponsor can no longer be assured they are receiving the benefits of exclusivity, they may be less willing to invest huge sums of money in sponsorship. While this has yet to come to fruition, it is deeply concerning to many major sports event property owners. In order to try and avoid a loss of sponsorship value and protect their sponsors from ambush marketing, such tactics as naming and shaming an ambusher in the media, education programmes, and legal action have been used. However, these are, for the most part, reactive strategies, and with the short lifecycle of an event, much damage can be done by a well-executed ambush campaign before any action can be taken.

Within the field of ambush marketing, there is a highly descriptive literature base with little integration or development of theory. Six key areas of research have been identified, however, which describe much of the research that has taken place to date. The first involves attempts to define and describe the concept of ambush marketing (e.g. Crow and Hoek, 2003; Meenaghan, 1998; Payne, 1998; McKelvey and Grady, 2008). While this may seem to be a straightforward idea, the grey area that much ambush marketing represents and the previously mentioned impact of a person's position on their view of the practice has continued to make this an important area of study. A second key topic in the ambush marketing literature is the investigation of consumer perceptions of, and attitudes towards, ambush marketing. This is a topic which has received much attention, and like other areas of discussion within this chapter. There is a great deal of ambush marketing research which applies some theories and concepts from consumer behaviour and branding (e.g. Portlock and Rose, 2009). However, there has been little consensus in the research within this area, with some studies showing that consumers find ambush marketing unacceptable (e.g. Séguin *et al.*, 2005), others finding mostly consumer indifference and apathy towards the practice (e.g. Lyberger and McCarthy, 2001; Sandler and Shani, 1993; Shani and Sandler, 1998), and others showing consumer perceptions to be dependent on the type of ambush involved (e.g. Moorman and Greenwell, 2005).

The fourth trend in ambush marketing research is the examination of the ethical issues involved in ambush marketing (e.g. Crompton, 2004a). For instance, O'Sullivan and Murphy (1998) used four different ethical frameworks to examine the concept of ambush marketing: utilitarianism, duty-based ethics, stakeholder analysis, and virtue ethics. It can be argued, however, that depending on the strategy, the way it is approached, and the role of the person making the ethical judgement, such frameworks can contribute to arguments on both sides of the ethical debate. The fifth type of research involves investigating various strategies and remedies aimed at fighting and preventing ambush marketing (cf. Burton and Chadwick, 2009; Crow and Hoek, 2003). One example of such research comes from Séguin and O'Reilly (2008), who specifically looked at the roles and responsibilities of each invested party with regards to protecting the Olympic brand from ambush marketing and clutter. Among other things, some of the strategies that were put forth include the need for a worldwide integrated public relations plan, education programmes for consumers and other stakeholders, the creation of legislation for brand protection, clearer sponsorship product category structure at all levels, and increased sponsorship activation (Séguin and O'Reilly, 2008).

Finally, the most recent trend in the area of ambush marketing research is the examination of the practice from a legal perspective (cf. Bhattacharjee and Rao, 2006; Ellis *et al.*, 2011a; Scassa, 2008), particularity regarding the question of the necessity and potential risks of such measures (e.g. Ellis *et al.*, 2011b; Grady *et al.*, 2010; Scassa, 2011).

In sum, there is a significant body of research conducted in sport event marketing, but there remain many avenues for future research, as noted above, as well as in the following section.

THE PRACTITIONER'S PERSPECTIVE ON MARKETING, SPONSORSHIP, AND LOOK-FEEL

While there may be much written on the topic of interest, there are a couple of areas which event marketers should pay attention to that are not discussed in depth in the literature. These are the look and feel of an event, as well as timelines and taglines. We will also briefly discuss some ticketing and tourism issues associated with marketing.

While the look is associated with physical demonstrations of the event (posters, signage, pictures, banners, flags, etc.), the feel is the intangible atmosphere that is created. The look and feel of an event starts internally within an event, years before it actually takes place. Because the organizing committee lives, breathes, eats, and sleeps an event from conception to delivery, it can feel to that group, because of the appearance within headquarters, that the message is being adequately communicated. Their physical surroundings and conversations are ubiquitous with messages of the coming event. So the look and feel, for them, is covered. Conversely, the messaging and marketing efforts externally can be lacking until the momentum builds to a pre-determined countdown phase, when messages and marketers converge on the marketplace to blanket the look and feel of the event in the host region. It can seem like, overnight, an event went from all talk to a visceral feeling that the Games will actually be happening, because of the synergy of everything coming together. It is important for marketers to see the look of the Games around the city as a seamless, natural extension and physical demonstration of their branding and colouring efforts. However, event marketers and communications/public relations managers must also foster an atmosphere for the event in the host region as it is part of the experience, the spectacle, for the event participant – be they spectator, dignitary, tourist, athlete, or someone else.

An anecdotal comment two years out from the 2010 Olympic Winter Games was made by a couple who were former residents of the city and now reside in Jeddah (Saudi Arabia). They visit annually and travel to the ski resort of Whistler, as well as a ten-day stay in a hotel in the heart of the city. They were flabbergasted at what they perceived to be the lack of tangible signage and product to promote the Games two years out. They commented regularly during their stay to service people, friends, and acquaintances about this. One could argue here that although much activity was taking place behind the scenes, it was not obvious enough for these folks; there seemed to be no "natural marketing" (word of mouth) from the service people and residents they interacted with. Yet within a few weeks of the Games, signage went up around the city and in the venues, and the torch relay was completing. These activities combined to create a look and feel (atmosphere) for the event. Still, some individuals criticized the organizing committee for not doing more signage – perhaps a function of the tough economic times. Notwithstanding, the value of natural marketing and its power to influence may be underrated. Would more information earlier, particularly to the service industry, positively impact on a larger scale because these folks were armed with information? We have all experienced the conversation where a person, place, or event is either positively or negatively affected because of the rippling effect of people talking.

Next, each stakeholder group has different timelines for their specific event marketing efforts, depending on their goals and objectives. Taglines are developed to connect the Games and the marketing programmes. If there are too many to absorb, the consumer can become confused. It is important to connect in a strong cohesive way the messaging internally that is meant to sell the workforce on the event, and the messaging that will create the look and feel for all other external stakeholders of the event, including spectators and broadcast media, special interest groups, athletes, etc. Taglines should be a part of the selling of the event and depict in only a few words what the look and feel of the event is supposed to be, and be associated in some way to the mission and/or vision of the event. For example, the 2010 Olympic Winter Games chose "With Glowing Hearts" as their tagline, a line taken from the Canadian national anthem, to depict what the Games were about, how the workforce should act, and how all other stakeholders (most notably the athletes and spectators) should feel/act. This was associated to the desire the organizing committee had of garnering pride within Canadians about the Games and their athletes.

Finally, the marketing of tickets outside the region where the event is being held is a contentious and hotly debated issue. Does exposure to a new geography through attendance at or marketing of a major sports event offer the potential for increased tourism and commerce with other people and countries? The answer seems more qualitative than quantitative, despite the fact that dollar amounts are assigned and projected on the financial pages of related organizations. There is certainly a national pride in being able to say you live in a place where a globally watched sports event has or is taking place. Perhaps it is the skill of the past and present marketers that have convinced us that the bottom line is not as important as bragging rights. This is associated with the id of marketing. Supply and demand are integral parts of marketing strategies and direct price and placement. Major sports events have a finite amount of tickets; and many times, it is all about what the market will bear, as well as protecting, where possible, the vulnerable ticket buyer from the scalpers. The head of ticketing for a major sports event must work in close collaboration with the marketing department, communications and public relations, technology (for online ticket purchases, for example), as well as the legal department. Coordination and integration are key.

CHAPTER SUMMARY

As can be seen, there is a large body of literature on the marketing and sponsorship of major sports events. We have only provided the core, basic yet essential information on this topic, leaving the reader to further explore specific details of interest. The topics we have covered involved concepts associated with marketing a major sports event and the host region such as: the internal and external environmental analyses, the situational analysis, market segmentation, the marketing mix, marketing strategy, communications and public relations, market research, and marketing. We also provided an overview of an event's effects on the destination's brand/image, as well as consumer behavioural intentions. In addition, we reviewed consumer (spectator) considerations for a major sports event. We then focused on branding before moving on to sponsorship, leveraging, and ambush marketing. From a practitioner's perspective, we focused on some additional thoughts related to the look and feel of a Games, timelines and taglines, and the role of marketing in ticket sales and tourism.

EXPERT CASE: AMBUSH MARKETING AND VANCOUVER 2010

Ten years before hosting the 2010 Olympic Winter Games, the Vancouver bid committee began putting together a package to present to the IOC in the hopes of being awarded the honour. Right from the beginning, the issue of ambush marketing was an overt concern for the IOC; as such, one of the requirements of the Vancouver bid was, as it now is with all bids, to provide a guarantee from the Canadian government that anti-ambush marketing legislation would be passed should Vancouver be chosen as host. Sticking to their guarantee, the Canadian government passed the *Olympic and Paralympic Marks Act* (OPMA) in 2007, but this merely represented one measure on hand for organizers in the fight against ambush marketing. This case will discuss not just other measures and remedies which were used by VANOC to fight ambush marketing, but will also examine the reasons why it was viewed as such a concern, specific campaigns that took place during the Games, and the outcomes of VANOC's anti-ambush marketing operation.

VANOC took control of the exclusive rights to the Olympic brand in Canada starting on 1 January 2005 and retained control until after the Games ended and the rights passed back to the COC. Within the formal structure of VANOC, the job of protecting the Olympic brand fell to the Commercial Rights Management (CRM) division, under the higher authority of Revenue, Marketing and Communications. Within CRM, there were nine full-time employees and many more volunteers, short-term employees, and third-party agencies which came on board closer to the event. The need to protect Vancouver's sponsors from ambush marketing was based on several, mostly economic, long-term and immediate considerations. In addition to the previous mentioned requirement for legislated protection and with regards to the immediate concerns, first and foremost the argument was made that given that the operating budget of the Games was around US$1.75 billion, with over 50 per cent of that money provided by domestic and international (TOP) sponsors, first-rate protection from ambush marketing had to be assured in order to secure enough money to host the Games in the spectacular style that had been promised. VANOC felt the business community needed to feel confident that if they invested, their investment would be protected. It was also noted that much legacy planning for the Canadian Sport System had been done with the assumption of a surplus; and so in order to ensure this would happen, sponsors must be seen to be protected so as to encourage greater investment now and in the future. Finally, the observation and experience of organizers with regards to past Games and past ambushers, such as Imperial Oil in 2006, showed them that the threat of ambush marketing was real and something that needed to be dealt with. Long term, the need to encourage sponsors (new and existing) to continue investing in Canadian athletes, Canadian sport, and the wider Olympic Movement were said to be dependent on them feeling protected from ambush marketing during their sponsorship of the Games.

In their remedies and measures to fight against ambush marketing, VANOC sought to take an approach which balanced the needs of their marketing stakeholders and the rights of the community to engage in the Games. VANOC's success in doing this has been debated, but its overall approach seems to be reflective of this idea. VANOC's main proactive strategies involved passing legislation (OPMA) and engaging and educating various stakeholder groups. The legislation offered two key advantages: first, it allowed for the ultimate last-ditch power play when dealing with non-compliant ambushers; second, and arguably more important, organizers felt it served as a deterrent for those considering ambush marketing but not willing to potentially be caught up in legal action. Given that the legislation was barely used by the CRM team, it seems deterrence may have been its main function. Education and engagement was by far the most widely used proactive strategy. It was felt that by ensuring people were aware of what was at stake and where the lines were drawn with regards to what would, or would not, be considered ambush marketing, they would be more likely to respect the guidelines and engage in the event in a way that did not infringe on sponsors' rights. By starting this process early and making it clear that national pride and engagement in the event were not on lockdown, they attempted to balance the needs of many groups. Education programmes took the form of online interactive information, print media, direct mail, conferences, and one-on-one meetings. These efforts were directed at target groups such as NSFs, consumers, the media, the general public, community institutions, and the wider business community.

Despite the proactive strategies, there was inevitably some ambush which took place around the event. When this happened, the CRM team did not just sit back and let it go; they also had reactive strategies for mitigating the threat. The first and most obvious given the above discussion was the use of legislative action. However, this was rarely used. The most common strategies for dealing with such situations seemed to be a letter and personal discussion between VANOC and the offender, or if need be, the use of media strategies such as naming and shaming. This was the strategy used with two of the most widely recognized ambushers at the Vancouver Olympic Winter Games: Scotiabank and Lululemon.

The Royal Bank of Canada is a long-term partner of the Olympic Games in Canada and was a Grand National Sponsor of the Vancouver Games. In the lead-up to the Games, one of their main competitors, Scotiabank, launched a promotion entitled "Show Your Colours". While the promotion did not involve the use of any prohibited Olympic symbols or words, it featured former Olympic gold medallist Cassie Campbell and imagery showing Canadians dressed in red and white cheering on their country. These elements combined with the timing of the promotion led VANOC to feel it infringed on the thematic space of the Olympic Games and might lead consumers to believe Scotiabank was a sponsor. As a result, VANOC came out in the media and spoke of their concerns regarding the campaign; both trying to educate consumers about the situation and put increased pressure on Scotiabank to make concessions, being careful, however, not to be seen as attacking the company. Ultimately, through discussion with VANOC, Scotiabank did scale back the programme but refused to postpone the campaign as VANOC wished.

Lululemon is a Canadian yoga apparel brand that calls Vancouver home; as a result, it felt it could not let the Games pass without a response. Lululemon had bid to be the official clothing supplier for the Canadian Olympic Team before the 2006 Games, but was beaten out by the Hudson's Bay Company; as a result it turned to the strategy of ambush marketing. Lululemon was much more overt about its recognition of the ambush guidelines that were in place and went so far as to poke fun at them when naming its Olympic-related clothing line. Narrowly skirting the legally protected words, Lululemon created country-based clothing (e.g. a Canadian design, an American design, etc.) and called it the "Cool Sporting Event Which Takes Place in British Columbia Between 2009 and 2011 Edition". Likely as a result of the mocking tone adopted by Lululemon, the public media campaign carried by VANOC in this instance was much more aggressive. They called into question the moral standards of the company, highlighting their disappointment, a perceived lack of sportsmanship, and the potential damage being done to the Olympic Movement in general and athletes more particularly. While such an aggressive stance had it critics, and seemed to do little to deter Lululemon from continuing to run its campaign, it showed a willingness on the part of VANOC to come out forcefully against ambushers, even in the case of those who have not fallen foul of legal restrictions.

By Dana Ellis, Doctoral Candidate, Ambush Marketing Expert

Case questions

1   Why was ambush marketing viewed as a concern in this case?

2   What proactive and reactive strategies were used by VANOC to protect against ambush marketing?

3   Is the legislative strategy truly effective and efficient? What are its potential consequences for event organizers, sponsors, potential ambushers, and the general public, today and in the future?

CHAPTER QUESTIONS

1   What is the difference between the following sets of concepts:
    a   Marketing a sport event vs. market research?
    b   Sponsorship vs. ambush marketing?

2   What is included within the marketing strategy?

3   Distinguish between the concepts of brand, brand equity, brand associations, brand awareness, perceived quality, and brand loyalty.

4   How is a brand created within a major sports event?

5   What is the look and feel of a sports event and where does it fit within the overall marketing strategy?

FURTHER READING

If you are interested in aspects of marketing, sponsorship, or look-feel of a major sports event, there is a large body of literature to which you can turn. We recommend the following:

Crompton, J. L. (1993) Sponsorship of sport by tobacco and alcohol companies: A review of the issues. *Journal of Sport & Social Issues*, 17, 148–167.

Ferrand, A., Chappelet, J.-L., & Séguin, B. (2012) *Olympic Marketing*, London: Routledge.

Séguin, B., Parent, M. M., & O'Reilly, N. (2010) Corporate support: A corporate social responsibility alternative to traditional event sponsorship. *International Journal of Sport Management & Marketing*, 7, 202–222.

Chapter 7

Venues and venuization

OBJECTIVES

- To understand the difference between site planning, operations, logistics, and overlay
- To understand the venuization process
- To understand characteristics of venues and key FAs

ILLUSTRATIVE CASE: QATAR WINS THE RIGHTS TO THE 2022 FIFA WORLD CUP BY PROPOSING NINE NEW EXPENSIVE STADIA

FIFA sent shockwaves through the football world on 2 December 2010 when it selected Qatar as the host of the 2022 FIFA World Cup, beating out the United States, Australia, Japan, and South Korea. A key part of Qatar's successful bid was the fact that the Middle East had yet to host the World Cup. Another part of the successful bid was the nine new proposed stadia, plus three renovated stadia, at a cost of US$4 billion – this is only for the capital budget (sportcal.com, 2010). Ten of the 12 stadia are to be set within a 30 km radius, making access to multiple matches on the same day possible for ticket holders. The stadia are inspired by, among other things, marine animals, "dhow" (local fishing boats), a local old fort, and traditional Arabian tents (*Sports Illustrated*, 2010). The top tiers of the modular-built stadia bowls are proposed to be dismantled and sent to developing countries.

In the summer, Qatar's temperatures can reach 50°C. To mitigate against such extreme temperatures for the players and spectators, Qatar proposes to have all of its venues be air conditioned so that spectators and players enjoy a comfortably 27°C environment (Bisson, 2010). The question remains: how will these open-air stadia be cooled? The answer, apparently, is solar-powered, carbon-neutral cooling equipment. How (and if) this will be implemented remains to be seen.

THE THEORY BEHIND VENUES AND VENUIZATION

Proper venue planning and management is essential for the successful hosting of major sports events. Parent (2008) indicated that there are key issues an organizing committee must consider during the creation of the venue plans: politics, participation and interdependence, operations and infrastructure, human resources, and sport. Moreover, all Games functions must integrate seamlessly and flawlessly together in the various venues for participants to have a positive experience. The 2002 Salt Lake City Olympic Winter Games, being the first sport mega-event post 9/11, resulted in repeated security checks and "bizarre attention to detail", which saw the 2002 Salt Lake City Olympic Winter Games be given the moniker "the Unfriendly Games" (McCrory, 2002: 79). Integration of different FAs is therefore key. However, before the venue experience there is the move of workforce members from headquarters to the various venues. This transition period is called venuization, an important, stressful period which we will also discuss in this chapter.

Sport event researchers are beginning to examine venue/facility management. New journals are emerging in sport event management but also other fields (engineering, geography, etc.); two notable dedicated journals are the *Journal of Facility Management* (started in 2002) and the *Journal of Venue and Event Management* (started in 2009). We will first review pertinent research in sport event management but also the broader literature associated with three main concepts: site planning, operations, and logistics.

Site planning

Site planning refers to the look and function of venues (Getz, 2005); *overlay* refers more specifically to the temporary aspects of facilities and other installations for a Games (extra seating, tents, the colours, banners, signage, etc.). Site planning starts with choosing venues. As Shone and Parry (2004: 121) noted, when finding the appropriate venue(s), event organizers should ask themselves: (1) "what location is required?" (which should be linked to the event's objectives); and (2) "what are the available venues within that location?", which should meet the event's given selection criteria. These location criteria include size/capacity, accessibility, centrality, clustering (closeness to other venues), appropriateness, cost, support function requirements (e.g. logistics, power, water, snow, concessions, toilets, drop-off and parking areas, locker rooms, waste, and administration), and perceived atmosphere/image (Getz, 2005).

Organizers have different event setting options (Getz, 2005):

- activity-based: outdoor (e.g. baseball complex) or indoor (e.g. ice arena);
- assembly (e.g. meeting and conference rooms);
- processionnal (e.g. parade routes);
- linear-nodal (e.g. marathon route plus staging and ceremony areas);
- open space (e.g. outdoor festival amphitheatre, park, Games outdoor live celebration site);
- exhibition/sale: where attendees can buy goods and services (e.g. wine-and-food show, Christmas craft show).

As you can see, these venue types are interrelated. That is, a venue will often fit more than one type, such as a marathon competition venue which would be outdoor activity-based and linear-nodal. However, for major sports events, venues are typically divided along two lines by organizing committees:

- competition venues (e.g. ice arena, curling rink, velodrome, swimming centre); and
- non-competition venues (e.g. athletes' village, main press centre (MPC), international broadcast centre (IBC)).

Site planning principles, according to Getz (2005), include legibility (clear landmarks, assembly points, pathways, districts), capacity (the maximum number of people, which is usually calculated based on fire and safety regulations, as well as on the desired customer experience), crowd control and management, queuing (avoiding line-ups where possible), traffic and flow (separating types of clients, separating pedestrians from vehicles, avoiding dead-end paths, etc.), and meeting special needs (aurally or visually impaired) and accessibility requirements (e.g. for wheelchairs, for attendants of persons with disabilities). One particular note on crowd control and management (see Getz, 2005 for more information): the term "crowd control" should typically be reserved for police and other law enforcement agencies, whereas crowd management includes security measures, as well as site design and operational factors, which will (hopefully) enhance the various clients' event experience, but does not include force/law enforcement per se.

As well, within a given venue, we will speak of front-of-house (FOH) and back-of-house (BOH). The FOH refers to what the general public can see, such as ticket booths, security checkpoints, concessions, concourse areas. The BOH is the operational area, as well as where athletes and officials, media, and dignitaries enter. These groups typically do not mix between each other and even less so with the general public in the FOH for the larger sports events. Accreditation (i.e. security clearance for specified venues/zones) is needed for the BOH area. Each client group (i.e. athletes, media, and dignitaries) will have their own areas with their own security checkpoints, toilets/locker rooms, lounge/working areas, and seating.

In the sport management literature, researchers have been interested in the link between large-scale facilities development in cities and the hosting of major sports events (e.g. Barghchi *et al.*, 2009; Augustin, 2009; Chalkley and Essex, 1999). The Olympic Games have been referred to as a *spatial event*, that is, as an event which cities want to host in order to increase their city's "attractiveness through the construction of a number of lodging, transport and communication facilities which contribute to urban transformation" (Augustin, 2009: 303). Such Games are seen as a way to fast-track urban regeneration, reimaging, growth, and other civic strategies (e.g. Chalkley and Essex, 1999; Mason and Duquette, 2008; Whitson and Macintosh, 1993, 1996).

While venues as a legacy of the Games will be explored in Chapter 15, some pertinent information for venue/site planning research includes building venues despite not succeeding in obtaining a bid (i.e. a bid as impetus for capital projects; Alberts, 2009), a case study of the 2010 World Cup, examining stadia building and urban development (Maennig and Du Plessis, 2009), and examining the link between building sports facilities and sports tourism (Elcock, 2005). There has also been research examining the economics and pricing of sport facilities and services (e.g. Berrett *et al.*, 1993), and quite a few researchers are interested in the public subsidizing of facilities debate, with the studies' findings seemingly indicating that public subsidies are not the best approach (e.g. Murray, 2009; Whitson *et al.*, 2000).

Absent from the sport event management literature is an examination of the venues themselves. However, we can find studies on this topic in publications outside the traditional sport management literature. For example, Greasley (2008) examined the role of facility design simulation for storage issues in the textile industry. The simulation was argued to be successful as it could consider attribute values for the facility as well as show queuing levels (for the individual product level). Greasley also found that simulation allowed for the initiation of helpful discussions about facility operations. In turn, Tarricone (1994: 34) presented what was the 1996 Atlanta Olympic Games' construction principles: "1. Use existing facilities. 2. Maximize the legacy. 3. Leave no net cost to taxpayers. 4. Consider postuse master plans. 5. Use temporary facilities." These principles can also be seen in how Vancouver approached its venue planning for the 2010 Olympic Winter Games; it used existing facilities (e.g. for figure skating, for the MPC); it wanted to maximize the legacy (e.g. by updating current venues, providing much-needed community venues); it stayed on budget; it considered post-use or legacy (e.g. turning the long-track speed skating venue into a community multi-use venue); and it used temporary facilities (e.g. for the Whistler ceremonies). Nevertheless, there is much room for future research in sport event management focusing on the venues and site planning.

Operations and logistics

Second, venue *operations* refers to the actors, procedures, and systems of the competition or non-competition venue coming together within a set of spatial and temporal constraints to offer different services to different client groups (Beis et al., 2006). As Beis et al. (2006) explained, venue operations during an Olympic Games is characterized by a high volume of demand for services from a multitude of different groups in a very short period of time (e.g. 17 days) and in very specific locations (the venues), with the demands being often lacking in stated specific requirements.

Getz (2005) suggested that there are three operations-related subsystems: (1) *Customer-oriented systems* (crowd control and management, customer service, queuing issues, traffic flow, parking, accessibility issues, etc.); (2) *Producer- and supplier-oriented systems* (managing participants, the media, performers, and VIPs; building/maintaining the infrastructure; contingency planning); and (3) *Communication systems* (equipment, accreditation, hosting, and procedures for the media, as well as performance scheduling).

Regarding the actual operations planning process, Getz (2005) presented a three-step process. First, there are factors to consider, notably programming (e.g. activities, nature of the programme), experiential (e.g. theme, desired atmosphere), management (e.g. budget, human resources, needs of stakeholders, crowd size), site/venue (e.g. capacity, risks, accessibility, flexibility, costs, legal constraints), and other constraints (e.g. political constraints). Second, operational goals and policies are set. Third, venue settings (e.g. design, decor), food and beverage (e.g. choosing vendors, setting up health procedures), degree of service quality (information, staff, hospitality, special needs, evaluation), and technical support, which is when the traffic flow/parking, recycling and waste, security and emergency response, communications, comfort, and utilities are prepared.

In terms of *logistics*, it refers to the timely coordination of materials and people on a given site, both for delivery or commissioning and for take-down or decommissioning. Logistics can also include permits for access to venues and procurement/supply-chain management (Getz, 2005; Van der Wagen and Carlos, 2005). For example, logistics will be involved in the planning of when a venue will be taken over by the organizing committee and then coordinate the various FAs' arrivals of people and materials. Project management tools come in quite handy here.

Within the broader literature, operations and logistics are usually found within the topic of facility management. Studies within facilities management have notably focused on (1) facility ownership and managers; (2) facility location; (3) facility components; (4) facility attendance and satisfaction; (5) green management/sustainability; and (6) risk and security. We will discuss each in turn, reserving risk management and security for Chapter 11.

Facility ownership and managers

As Fenich and Bordelon (2008) explained, there are three options for facility ownership: public, private, and QUANGOs (quasi autonomous non-government organizations). Publicly owned facilities are typically found in a branch of the local government; they are sensitive to the specific needs of that community (and sometimes quite politicized entities). Privately owned facilities are your typical for-profit business. QUANGOs try to capitalize on the advantages of the public and private forms of ownership while mitigating the drawbacks. QUANGO facilities are owned by a government body. The government appoints a board to govern the facility; the board sets out the mission and goals of the facility (e.g. attract out-of-town conferences vs. focus on local needs).

In their study of entertainment and convention facilities in seven US cities, Fenich and Bordelon (2008) found no best model for facility ownership, as the ownership choice depends on the needs of the community. However, they did find that two-thirds were QUANGOs, which seemed, according to the interviewees, to be better as the private model "might not always have the best interests of the community in mind" (p. 197) and the public model was seen as inefficient and often prone to political intervention/pressure. QUANGO boards were seen to have at least one representative from the hotel industry and one from the local convention and visitor bureau. Nevertheless, the key seemed to be a good relationship between the facility and the local convention and visitor bureau, as well as having similar or complementary missions and goals. While QUANGO seems to be the dominant form of ownership, interestingly, Alexander and Brown (2006) noted that much of the facilities management literature has been focused on the business aspect. They argued for a community-based facility management, which would assist in local regeneration of infrastructure and services, as well as skills training and employment opportunities. We could therefore infer a support of these authors for the QUANGO ownership structure.

Peiro et al. (1998) argued that facility managers' tasks fall in the following areas: maintenance, operations, marketing, personnel, and finance. Their survey respondents, Spanish sport facility managers, indicated that they perform tasks in all of these areas, though some were seen as less necessary, with differences being found for privately vs. publicly owned facilities. Managers also indicated using troubleshooting for performance problems as they were only "modestly problematic" (p. 1). In turn, Tripolitsioti et al. (2007) suggested that managers of (Greek) youth centres and indoor municipal venues should have the following eight characteristics: proper management techniques, knowledge of sport science, event management skills, public relations skills, computer/research skills, general facilities management skills, governance abilities, and safety/injury prevention knowledge.

Finally, Goyal and Pitt (2007) examined the role of innovation in facility management. Here, innovation includes product, process, organization, management, production, commercial/marketing, and/or service innovation. The supply chain was particularly emphasized in this study. Facility managers (the respondents of the survey) noted that innovation management policies should be part of facility management. Innovations were mainly seen as a result of competition between facilities and were focused mainly on process and business innovations (e.g. well-planned facilities and quality support services) for effective operations. The authors concluded that innovation principles should be a mindset that is incorporated into facility staff's daily schedules for well-performing facilities.

Facility location

A second research avenue has been on facility location. For example, Braid (1991) discussed options for the socially optimal location for congestible facilities (e.g. parks), which are selected by adjacent jurisdictions (e.g. two municipalities), whereas Doerner et al. (2009) suggested location criteria for facilities in tsunami-prone locations such as Sri Lanka. In turn, Chapin (2000) examined the political economy history of sport facility location. He found that sports facilities have been coming back to the city core despite the high cost of land in these areas and the problem of accessibility for such facilities' main client base, the middle and upper classes, who typically live outside the downtown core. While land costs, transportation accessibility, and location of the fan base used to be the main factors in determining facility location, the current trend is one where political factors (read: public funding) come into play as a key factor. Chapin argued that this shift is mainly due to the sports teams seeing this downtown location as becoming profitable due to the access to public funding (e.g. through tax benefits). The author concluded that the time has come to review these tax breaks and relieve the burden placed on the taxpayers, given the little return they receive on their investment.

An emerging area of interest in facility location is the concept of themed sports zones within cities. Themed sports zones are pockets within a city where we find a coming together of multiple sports facilities, to give these "sport cities" coherence and visibility (e.g. for branding purposes). Smith (2010) examined four themed sports zones in Manchester (UK), Cardiff (UK), Doha (Qatar), and Dubai (United Arab Emirates). Smith found that, to be successful, these sports zones have to be pre-planned as such, and not an afterthought of building a new sports facility near an existing one as a convenient branding opportunity. Because this is an emerging area of study, much can still be examined regarding sports zones beyond associating them with branding, such as the logistics behind such an area, the strategic value and return to the city, the management of such areas, etc.

Finally, we have studies examining empty lots/building spaces, and parking spaces. For example, we have seen an increase in informal sport participation such as increasing numbers of people running or people playing football, basketball, or ultimate Frisbee in a local park or empty lot. Bach (1993) argued that these empty lots, parks, etc., can be considered as informal sports facilities, a complement to the built, formal sports facilities. Bach further suggested that urban planners and municipal sport policy-makers should keep in mind these informal spaces in their planning. In turn, there is literature on parking facilities and their revenue generation function (e.g. Burns and Faurot, 1992), as well as simulation models of parking movement (e.g. Young, 1986). We therefore see that examining sport facilities should not only be limited to the formal sport facility itself, but also to informal sport facilities and supporting infrastructure such as parking. This type of research brings us to the next area of research, components within formal facilities.

Facility components

Some researchers are interested in the role that various components play within a facility. For example, McCarthy and Irwin (1998) examined the issue of seat licences within sport facilities. Seat licences allow for event season ticket access for the purchasers and are a popular revenue source for the facility. The authors suggested that there are particular strategies for seat licences in single-use versus multi-use facilities. Besides seat considerations, some studies have focused on signage within venues, including venue signage as a promotional tool for sponsor brand awareness (e.g. Cianfrone and Zhang, 2006) and the negative impact of clutter – that is, of too many sponsor signs within a venue (e.g. Cornwell *et al.*, 2000; Séguin and O'Reilly, 2008). It seems that sponsor venue signage is effective but less so than television commercials, combined promotional tools, and athlete endorsements (Cianfrone and Zhang, 2006). There is also a particular interest in virtual signage, or signage seen during a game but only by the television spectators (e.g. Cianfrone *et al.*, 2006), and its legal ramifications (e.g. Turner and Cusumano, 2000; Mendez, 1999). Virtual signage does not have the same impact on television consumers regarding sponsor brand awareness as do television commercials (Cianfrone *et al.*, 2006). Having virtual signs makes one question who actually owns the rights to the sport event, the sport venue, and the advertising space. Turner and Cusumano (2000) examined the legal relationships between the key actors (sport event organizer, venue operator, broadcaster, and sponsor) and provided suggestions to remedy any potential contract (or other) problems. They argued that virtual signage is a potentially important source of advertising revenue which can no longer be disregarded in sponsorship agreements between all these stakeholders. What this paragraph highlights, however, is an interest in facility components as revenue-generating sources (with an association to marketing, branding, and sponsorship).

Notwithstanding, we did find research in the tourism sector pertaining to KSF for conference centres. Burger and Saayman (2009) suggested that successful conference centres had the following characteristics, which could be translated to major sports events:

■ *Layout and activities*: the conference centre's layout should allow for networking, such as in a large foyer. The facility should also offer services during conferences, such as spousal/children programmes, financial services, tour and airline desks, etc. For major sports events, we could translate this to the layout of the venue, flow of client traffic, and services provided (e.g. concession stands, information desks, ticket booths, medical services).

145 ▪

- *Core operational aspects*: the venue should be attentive to having proper lighting, temperature control/air conditioning, clean amenities, and welcoming staff.
- *Design and evaluation*: associated with the above, the venue's choice of decor (e.g. lighting, furniture, colour, warmth, flowers, linens) should be carefully considered so that attendees can concentrate on the job at hand, but also be comfortable in their environment. Post-conference/event evaluations are also suggested so that the venue may improve itself.
- *Planning*: a successful conference centre will undertake: mission statement, philosophy, and code of ethics formulation; developing a business plan and budget, figuring out what the break-even point is; and regularly reviewing its business strategies. This is similar for major sports event venues.
- *Marketing*: the venue should do market research to understand its target market, run promotions about the conference centre which are appropriate for its product lifecycle (introduction, growth, maturity, saturation, and decline), develop an appropriate price strategy, and use sales promotions as conference centre inducements.
- *Well-trained employees*: this factor includes recruiting the right individuals for the right positions, and training them properly.

Facility attendance and satisfaction factors

One of the more significant bodies of literature relating to facilities focuses on facility attendance and satisfaction. Wakefield *et al.* (1996) examined the factors within a facility related to attendance and satisfaction with the facility. They found that the feeling of being crowded was a major turnoff. This crowding out could result from the feeling of being cramped in your seat (small seats, sitting tightly side-by-side) or of difficulty reaching the seats, the restrooms, or the concessions, thus, of the traffic flow within the venue. Besides building a new facility, these problems could be remedied by larger seats, improved directional signage, and helpful staff. Another factor was the look of the facility or its aesthetics, which includes fresh paint, cleanliness, decor choices. A third factor was parking accessibility and capacity. The final factor was the scoreboard, both in terms of its technology but also its "entertainment" use during times of less interest on the field. Hall *et al.* (2010) examined attendance at sports events in Melbourne, Australia. They found that attendance depends on (1) people having an emotional attachment to the sports event – that is, feeling emotions associated with fun, stirring events, astonishment, and being entertained; and (2) people's perceptions of the quality and accessibility of the facilities, as well as the parking.

Next, there are studies that examine facility attendance and link this with the question of facility subsidizing. Coates and Humphreys (2005), for example, when examining revenue generation, noted that public subsidies of professional sports stadia are not the most efficient way of subsidizing the professional team itself. They also explain how, initially, venues were built to be multi-use; now, they are, unfortunately, mainly single-use (i.e. professional sports). We can extend this argument for major sports events: a post-Games multi-use is not undesirable if it is what best fits the community. For example, the site for long track speed skating during the 2010 Olympic Winter Games, the Richmond Olympic Oval, has been turned into a community, multi-use facility, including exercise areas, an ice rink, badminton courts, volleyball courts, basketball courts, running tracks, gymnastics/tumbling area, meeting rooms, and more. The facility had almost met its goal of 3,000 members in less than a year, and has been operating in the black (Rudd, 2011).

Regarding satisfaction specifically, we find studies, for example, on people with disabilities, men versus women, and volunteers. Sungwon *et al.* (2005) examined facility satisfaction of people with disabilities in South Korea, finding that these individuals were usually dissatisfied with transportation, parking, entrances, passageways, elevators, restrooms, venue (directional) signage, reserved seating, guest services, and administrative services within sport facilities. Thus, the authors argued that governments and sport facility managers should pay particular attention to these areas. In turn, Trail *et al.* (2002) examined gender differences in facility satisfaction of venue characteristics. They found that the overall cleanliness of the venue, the restrooms, the staff, and the audio experience were more important to women than men. Interestingly, they also found that the satisfaction with certain venue factors – specifically parking, venue cleanliness, and audio experience – depended on the type of event being showcased, in this case women's team playing versus men's team playing. Farrell *et al.* (1998) examined the link between volunteer satisfaction and the event competition facility. The authors found that the physical aspects of the facilities (e.g. parking, restrooms, air quality, and traffic flow within the venue) were part of volunteers' overall satisfaction with their sport event experience.

Green management/sustainability

According to the United Nation's World Commission on Environment and Development, sustainable activities are those activities which meet "the needs of the present without compromising the ability of future generations to meet their own needs" (World Commission on Environment and Development, n.d.: 1). These needs involve social, economic, and environmental considerations – the infamous triple bottom line.

A current hot topic in facility management seems to be green management and sustainability. A significant number of studies are being published in this area. We find, for example, studies trying to define and theorize about what sustainability means for facilities, generally, and for the Olympic Games, more specifically. Lindsay Smith (Smith, L., 2009) examined the concept of sustainability within the conference industry. She provided an overview of the history of the USA Green Building Council's' LEED (Leadership in Energy and Environmental Design) certification, the need for top management's commitment to sustainable practices, areas to focus on, important metrics, and checklists for planners and vendors. She explained that LEED sets strict guidelines for facilities regarding the sustainability of sites, energy and atmosphere, indoor air quality, water efficiency, and materials and resources. Smith suggested areas to focus on for environmental policies in facilities, including: waste reduction and diversion, energy conservation (both in building mechanics and building operations), and water conservation. To determine the degree of success or performance of a facility regarding sustainability, and hopefully encourage better practices, Smith argued that waste diversion, energy consumption, and water usage are the three key metrics or measurements. She even provided a website where event planners, as well as attendees, could measure their carbon footprint free of charge from the Denver Convention Bureau (www.denver.org/convention/green/carbon-calculator). While this article refers specifically to conference centres, there is a definite parallel with sport event venues.

In turn, Porteshawver (2009) argued that building or renovating facilities with an environmental impact perspective in mind is beneficial to almost all stakeholders involved, despite the fact that current US laws do not require new or renovated facilities to go green – although certain local governments do. Porteshawver suggested that building conventional sport facilities is harmful to the environment – including air quality (through increased traffic in the area), water contamination (affecting the local population and wildlife), and local deforestation – because of the harmful paints, adhesives, solder, etc., used. These conventional sport buildings are also a financial risk for the taxpayer (through the public subsidies) as these buildings get older; they may even become obsolete if other municipalities offer a more luxurious building opportunity. Thus, Porteshawver argued that following green principles (e.g. LEED) when building or renovating will improve, or at least not harm, the local environment, be it people, animals, or natural environment. Saving on energy costs also saves money for the sport organization/team in residence. These sustainable facilities then become less of a financial drain or risk for the taxpayer, assuming that developers, architects, engineers, policy-makers/politicians, and sport organizations/teams work together in this endeavour.

A few studies suggest that the adaptive reuse of buildings, instead of demolition/redevelopment (new construction), is a viable option for following sustainable practices. The Australian building owners surveyed in Bullen's (2007) study support this statement. Love and Bullen's (2009) subsequent study suggests that, while an environmental performance assessment of the existing building is needed to determine its energy improvement needs, and thereby determine whether adaptation or a new construction is needed, adaptation will, more often than not, be the preferred, more viable option. However, following an adaptive reuse strategy means that the clients and their designers will have to "re-examine how their facilities are to be used and [will] require them to embrace whole-life costing and the use of innovative materials and technologies" (Love and Bullen, 2009: 357). Yet, regarding environmental assessments, Diduck and Mitchell (2003) cautioned that they have, at best, a legitimating purpose, and are not – at least in their study – participatory, equitable, or empowering. Nevertheless, Diduck and Mitchell suggested that environmental assessments could be emancipatory, and actually be opportunities for mutual learning between policy-makers and scholars, if involvement is done earlier, participation levels are increased, and decision-making is more open.

Another stream of research deals with barriers to and success factors of sustainable policies and practices. For example, depending on what the public's perception is of environmental policies, this may (or may not) be an issue when determining facility location, which can ultimately place public figures in a difficult situation of going against their stated environmental policies, as Wolsink (2010) noted. In turn, Dubose et al. (2007) analysed statewide green building policies and LEED; the authors presented inhibitors and enablers affecting the success of these green building policies:

- Inhibitors: LEED certification opposition, impact of costs, and resistance to change.
- Enablers: having strong champions, obtaining stakeholder support, and capitalizing on external motivators

148

Regarding barriers or inhibitors to the implementation of comprehensive sustainable facility management policies and practices, Elmualim *et al.* (2009, 2010) noted a lack of consensual understanding and knowledge of sustainability, a lack of focus of organizations and individuals, a lack of commitment from senior management, and time constraints as barriers. To remedy the situation, they suggested that training and skills provision,

> traditionally offered separately to designers and facilities managers, needs to be re-evaluated. Sustainability education and training should be developed to provide effective structures and processes to apply sustainability throughout the construction and FM [facility management] industries coherently and as common practice
>
> (Elmualim *et al.*, 2009: 91)

Elmualim *et al.* (2010: 58) stressed, though, that the most significant barrier is the lack of senior management commitment; senior managers, they argue, should appreciate "the opportunities, threats and need for strategic leadership and direction in driving essential change, and hence further the sustainability agenda".

So what conditions would lead to successful green planning and implementation? Baycan-Levent and Nijkamp (2009) notably suggested municipal administration and citizen involvement/participation are critical. The authors added, though, that there are geographical differences (e.g. between northern, southern and eastern Europe) and that these conditions should be examined as a whole (i.e. not all conditions absolutely need to be met; however, you are more likely to be successful if you meet more of these conditions). Chan and Lee (2009) also argued that there is a relationship between development density and environmental quality. Given this relationship, they offered urban design factors for successful sustainable urban renewal projects: land-use planning, conservation and preservation, quality of life, integrated design, provisions for welfare facilities, and conserving existing properties.

Finally, what is the future of sustainability and facility management? Zhang *et al.* (2010) believe that green building should be seen as a competitive advantage as it allows (for-profit) organizations to build their reputation, reduce construction/operation costs, obtain favourable land prices, and increase the number of possible sources of financing. In turn, Mallen *et al.*'s (2010a) delphi study offers ten competencies related to sustainability and facilities management. Some key competencies include: business acumen and environmental awareness, environment technological advances awareness, sustainability trends awareness, understanding of certification (e.g. LEED) programmes and best practices. Mallen *et al.* suggested that a shift in facilities management thinking needs to occur regarding sustainability; this will then facilitate a responsiveness (i.e. managerial and operational performance) in favour of sustainable practices. We are beginning to see this shift in sport event management. The 2010 Olympic Winter Games, for example, had all its competition venues LEED certified at a minimum of a silver level – the levels from lowest to highest being certified, silver, gold, and platinum. VANOC even collaborated with the Canadian Standards Association to create Z2010: "Canada's first event management standard for business, culture and sport event organizers. Z2010 is based largely on VANOC's Sustainability Management and Reporting System" (The Vancouver Organizing Committee for the 2010 Olympic and Paralympic Winter Games, 2010b: 6).

We encourage sport event management researchers to examine facility management in relation to major sports events. There are a variety of avenues for future research such as: examining competition vs. non-competition venues, planning and logistics, and sustainability. In itself, sustainability has great potential as an area of study in sport event management. Paralleling what Mallen *et al.* (2010a) noted about the paucity of sustainability research in sport management, we suggest that there is a great need for research in sport event management, including definitions, regulations, best practices, and implications for leadership, planning, and other sport event management functions. Finally, another key gap is an understanding of the venuization process – that is, the transition from headquarters to venues. We will begin to explore this topic in the next section, but it is certainly an area that requires further research.

THE PRACTITIONER'S PERSPECTIVE ON VENUES AND VENUIZATION

In this section we will discuss management considerations for venues and FAs, paying particular attention to the sport and sport production FAs.

Venues

Venues are identified as competitive and non-competitive to differentiate between the places where the athletes compete and the places where all other activities related to the event take place. Usually we will see one sport per venue, although that sport can include multiple disciplines and sport competitions going on at one time, and there can be a change-over of one sport for another at some point during the event. There is always an athletes' village of some kind. Non-competition venues can include the athletes' village, airport, training sites, MMC, IBC, hotels serving as accommodations for dignitaries and event officials, etc.

It is necessary to further separate the competition venues into FOH, which is where spectators are located, and BOH, which is for specifically accredited visitors, athletes, media, and workforce (including contractors, suppliers, etc.). This type of delineation and clear separation creates a meaningful boundary to segregate activities relative to the user group – for example, spectators in the stands (FOH) and athletes in their dressing rooms (BOH). It also creates a standard reference for all conversation internally and externally. Training workforce is aided by the use of generally understood terms. Just like enduring businesses, these terms create a language that is quickly and easily understood and becomes a common frame of reference for communicating the volume of information that flows constantly in the preparation and execution of an event.

Each venue is divided into zones which are given both letters and numbers. It is a combination of these letters and numbers that permits access for workforce and visitors to all or some areas of the venue. Access is permitted through an accreditation process (discussed later in this chapter) and includes work considerations (what people need access to in order to do their jobs), security considerations (attempt to restrict traffic, e.g. athlete and VIP areas), media considerations (where the can media have access), and protocol considerations (political, sport, and social).

Another tool that is used extensively in relation to venues is CAD (computer-assisted design). These drawings provide a priceless tool to chronicle the life of all buildings and property associated with an event. They are available to the FAs, allowing individuals and groups to access common, current information, and use it effectively for discussion and decision purposes. Thus, these venue CADs are necessary for FA planning and for coordination between functions. The CADs allow FAs to see the venues virtually as they move through the progressive stages to completion and also to plan without physically being in the spaces. The CADs provide a fluid story of progress from which to work. As Figure 7.1a demonstrates, an aerial photograph of the venue may be good for a basic overview of what the venue will look like, but it does little for the actual planning of the venue. Figure 7.1b (the aerial CAD of the venue), in contrast, provides details of where different functional areas will operate, and even traffic flow. Likewise, Figure 7.1c offers an internal CAD view of a section of the building, again showing where, in this case the Olympic Family, would be situated, so that the protocol FA (e.g. ICS) can plan their services for the dignitaries. It is also important to note that there can and will be many iterations of the CADs (e.g. Vancouver 2010 had six iterations) before the final version is approved. Even then, there may be some last-minute changes to accommodate important guests or to fix unforeseen crowd management or traffic flow issues, for example.

Functional areas

During the time that the venues are being constructed, the FAs are located in other places, typically the organizing committee's headquarters. The reporting structure for the workforce is within their own FA. When the construction is complete, some FAs will move and there will be a new reporting structure. FAs transition to the venues in graduated stages relative to construction completion dates; this is done in coordination with logistics and the timeline of the competition schedule. By Games-time, all FAs in the venue will report to the venue general manager (VGM) for the duration of the Games, as well as to their own FA superiors.

It is worth noting a smooth transition from one office to the other and from one management team to another is dependent on two things – critical path planning and the leadership and management skills of the VGM and associated team. In enduring businesses, people learn to work with the differences in personality and leadership style, and eventually settle into a rhythm. With temporary organizations, the "settling in" time is reduced, and the workforce must adapt quickly. While the venue management team (VMT) is not brand new to the workforce because they too have been located in temporary offices and have conduced regular meetings with all of the FAs that will transition during Games-time into that venue, there is still an adjustment for most people in changing their reporting structure.

The first group to "venuize" is logistics and operations, followed by the VGM and his team, and finally the other FAs in a planned and staggered sequence. The groups that typically move to the venue include: VMT; sport; sport production; EVS; food and beverage (F&B); cleaning and waste; technology; accreditation; press and communications; broadcast; ICS, also known as protocol; security; transportation; medical; and anti-doping. Some of these areas are discussed at greater length in other chapters. Here, we will discuss the VMT; sport; sport production; EVS; F&B, cleaning and waste, logistics and overlay; and accreditation.

(a)

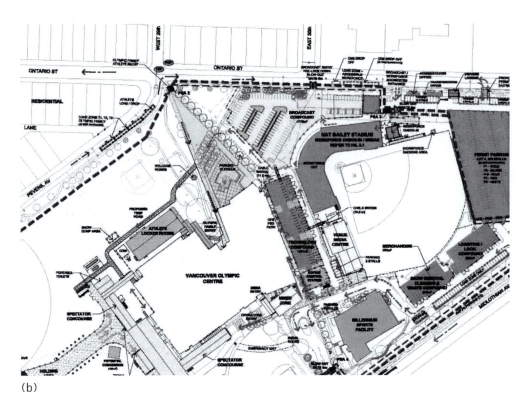

(b)

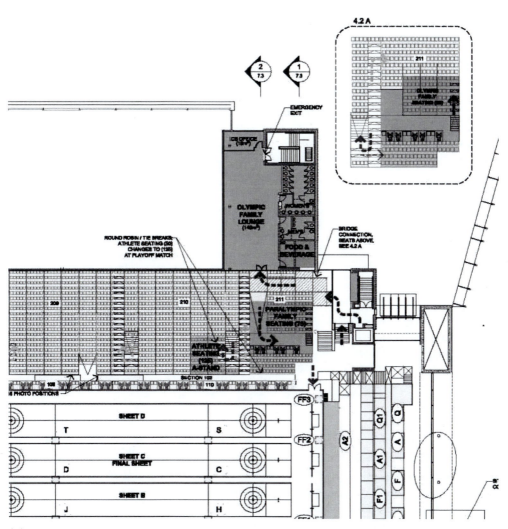

(c)

Figure 7.1 Comparison of a photograph and CADs of Vancouver Olympic Centre (Hillcrest Park) for planning and coordination purposes. Credit: TM/MC © Used under license from the Canadian Olympic Committee, 2011; City of Vancouver.

Venue management team

The VMT is responsible for the management and administration of all activities that occur within and surrounding the venue. All FAs in the venue report to the VGM. The interpersonal and management skills of this team need to be superior because this is the "head office" during Games-times for the FAs on-site. Before the move to the venue, people would have gotten used to one manager (their FA manager); now they must adjust to an additional one. When the blended team connects in a cohesive way, it creates a supportive, reduced-stress environment for everyone to work in. That does not always happen and the collective stress affects both individuals and the venue environment in general. As mentioned in the workforce chapter, just because a person previously worked at a sports event, it does not mean that they have all the requisite skills. There is no performance management to rate individuals at the completion of an event. If the Games were a success, all associated are blanketed with a successful performance. Thus, the VMT's responsibility is essentially one of a coach, to motivate, to lead by modelling behaviour, to intervene quickly when activities or processes have become problematic – perhaps not in the traditional HR sense given the context of major sports event during Games-time, where firing people may not be possible – and to communicate effectively in a direct, consistent, powerful – even fierce (read: "not monkey around") – and confident yet empathic manner, while still doing it in a way that invites respect from the rest of the VTeam.

Event services

EVS is responsible for the flow of people coming into the venue (ingress) and out of the venue (egress). There is substantially more workforce required for this area because their activities are so broad and includes both FOH and BOH. They are the on-the-ground eyes and ears, and can quickly alert other FAs to potential or "in-the-moment" situations or challenges. However, as many EVS staff are outside the venue, they often have less-than-ideal jobs and may not even see any events – contrary to popular belief. Still, they are critical for the successful management of any venue.

Sport

The sport FA is in charge of the technical, field-of-play issues. This includes how many teams/competitors will compete; the structure of the competition; the schedule; the quality of the actual field of play (e.g. the grass, the ice, the water), the field-of-play lines and goal technical questions, and the management of the equipment for the field of play; the decision to go ahead (or not) with an event due to weather or other considerations; the practice session schedule; team arrival, placement/locker and meeting rooms, and departure; coordination/assistance with anti-doping controls and other medical aspects; and so on. While sport and sport production (see below) are central to major sports events (without sport, there would be no major *sports* event), there is unfortunately a lack of research in this area. The logistical issues themselves require analyses to determine best practices; this can be associated with research on facilities management related to multi-venue events, for example. There are also differences associated with indoor versus outdoor sports and venues, including managing the weather factor and its impact on the management of the sport and sport production in that venue.

Sport production

The sport production FA is in charge of the surrounding fan experience associated with what happens on the field of play. This includes fan entertainment before the game, during pauses in the game, and even after the game; the music, images, and information provided on the jumbotrons and scoreboards; the ceremonial aspects (e.g. medal and flower ceremonies on site); and so on. Music, for example, is part of the sound space of a major sports event, which must be imagined, constructed, and managed. This may become difficult for certain sports or countries that have particular cultures or traditions. The presence and impact of the vuvuzelas, a staple of South African football culture, was quite an issue to manage by the organizers at the 2010 FIFA World Cup, as they were perceived to be distracting to non-South African fans, participants, and television spectators (see also Hammond, 2011).

There is a general belief that sport is a spectacle; it is often commercially focused and includes the production of a variety of rituals and social messages using different actors, and varying uses of the concepts of masculinity, pride, chance, and rage (Joseph, 2005). Since the sport spectacle is simultaneously produced and consumed, the production aspect has implications for the manager of the sport FA, the sport production manager, the facility manager or VGM, and the overall event manager, all of whom need to coordinate their efforts for the event to be successful.

One aspect of sport production which is of interest to researchers is fandom (the fans, the spectators, and their experiences and motivations). Fans are important to sport organizations, largely for economic reasons. There are three types of spectators that the sport production manager should consider: the in-venue spectator, the at-home spectator, and the public consumption spectator. This last type is argued to be the best of both worlds: the social interaction from the in-venue (with friends and new acquaintances in the bar, pub, café, or restaurant) and the control of home television viewing (e.g. being able to switch between channels) (Eastman and Land, 1997). The social interaction aspect for both the in-venue and public consumption spectators also includes dealing with your enemies, that is, the fans of the other team(s) or competitor(s). Rival fans appear to experience stimuli (pictures, associations of their favourite) differently (Hillman et al., 2004); this is also linked to the concept of fan identification (Hu and Tang, 2010).

Thus, sport production managers should be cognizant that those attending an event will not all respond in the same way, thereby requiring the sport manager to cater to the different groups. Moreover, given spectators' economic importance, sport organizations should cater to their needs and wants, as well as to consider the costs associated with being a fan (e.g. the cost of tickets, of concession foods and beverages, of merchandise and memorabilia). The degree to which a sport organization (e.g. a sports team, an organizing committee of a major sports event) is perceived to care about its fans can be termed fan orientation. Fan orientation is linked to fan loyalty – that is, repeat purchase (Bristow and Schneider, 2006).

An interesting point to consider from a sport production perspective for spectator attendance (the fans) is that while men usually display more sport fan behaviour (e.g. watching sports, discussing sports, and knowledge of sports) than women, when it comes to sports events, there is no significant difference (Dietz-Uhler et al., 2000). As well, attendance at professional and amateur sports events is dependent on individuals' socio-economic status, with income and education being independent factors (White and Wilson, 1999). Thus, sport production managers need to cater equally to both men and women, their respective likes and dislikes, as well as determine their attendees' socio-economic status to better know with whom they will interact. Fan motivations can be tapped into by sport production managers to build the event experience. Wann *et al.* (1999; Wann, 1995) believed that fan motivation is based on: self-esteem, escape, eustress (the arousing of senses and seeking of stress), entertainment, aesthetic, group affiliation, economic, and family needs.

One key strategy for sport production managers to engage and interact with the fans and spectators at an event is the fan zone or live site. These areas can be in public places (e.g. town squares) or be part of a venue (e.g. a waiting area before entering the venue). They can include live entertainment, such as street performers, and/or entertainment on large television screens. The concepts of fun, entertainment, and peaceful interaction are promoted. As Lauss and Szigetvari (2010: 737) explained of Euro 2008's fan zones, "Fans were offered different roles so that their emotions could be positively channelled, and non-violent, friendly relationships between strangers could flourish. Ties between fans were established both by the macro-architecture of the zones and the type of entertainment offered." At the 2010 FIFA World Cup, Roberts (2010) discussed three types of crowd control in the event-specific public spaces: policing nuisance behaviour, restricting social movement protests, and using volunteer welcome ambassadors (to promote national pride). These three strategies each impacted attendees' (locals and visitors) experiences of the event "space". Management considerations, best practices, and knowledge transfer would be good avenues for future research in this area.

Food and beverage (F&B)

F&B negotiate/provide all of the food and beverages that are required for both FOH (spectator areas) and BOH, which includes all of the workforce, athletes, media, and lounges for accredited guests. They also negotiate/provide F&B for athletes in their village or designated athletes' area, and food for the media in the MPC and IBC. It can be a challenge for this group to maintain both the quality and variety of the food for the duration of an event. Food is important for both sustenance and for the perk factor of obtaining a meal. It can negatively impact athletic performance as well as workforce morale if it is poor or there is not enough, and even catch the attention of the media if the food is questionable. Food provision has evolved for athletes at the Olympic Games over the past century (Pelly *et al.*, 2011). Even today, however, because budget is always a consideration, what F&B would like to provide and the end result may differ. During the 2002 Salt Lake Olympic Winter Games, there were anecdotal stories about the food that was served to VIPs and other accredited guests – hotdogs (which incidentally was the same food provided to athletes throughout the 2011 Pan American Games in Guadalajara, Mexico, Doolittle, 2011). In contrast, at the 2006 Torino Olympic Winter Games, VIPs ate multiple courses of gourmet food and drank a variety of wines in lounges draped in crisp white tablecloths. The 2010 Vancouver Olympic Winter Games saw itself as being in the middle, with a variety of appetizers and soup, and one choice each of red and white wine for the accredited guests lounge.

Cleaning and waste

Cleaning and waste is an essential service for obvious reasons. During Winter sports events, snow removal often becomes a part of this group's duties. Because their area of responsibility extends to a predetermined fenced perimeter surrounding the venue, cleaning and waste workforce members are charged with the safety and access of all traffic – pedestrian and vehicle traffic – into and out of this area. The Games must go on, and this group of people do what is necessary to make that happen in a seamless way. Collection of garbage, cleaning washrooms, lounges, and public areas, and dealing with spills are activities that consume this group. They offer various levels of service – with the quickest response being for the Olympic Family in the case of the Olympic Games – and are increasingly important, especially with the growing interest in sustainability and green initiatives (e.g. recycling).

Logistics and overlay

Logistics is the hub of any event for providing supplies and services to equip and present the "look of the Games". The demands on this FA, despite extensive pre-event planning are often "just-in-time" and simultaneous with other FAs' requests. Inventory moves constantly, and short of cloning themselves, sometimes there are waits and delays. Logistics also works closely with security to ensure that any outside supplies or services are security screened once the venue is locked down for Games-time.

Overlay is the "look of the Games". It is planned before venuization and executed as soon as the venue is turned over to VMT from construction. As Games-time approaches, it includes banners, wrapping of buildings and temporary structures, and signage inside the venues. They must be sensitive to sponsor signage and rights holders' (e.g. the IOC or FIFA) restrictions on what can be left visible relative to brand names on fixtures and other equipment that is not that of a Games sponsor. When budget cuts affect overlay, they have to do more with less to fill spaces, and satisfy many masters regarding the look, including protocol, security, EVS, and rights holders.

Accreditation

Accreditation is in charge of processing accreditation badges. Being accredited means that you have been security cleared. Access into a venue and around it requires accreditation for everyone except spectators – their "accreditation" is the ticket, which grants them access to FOH (after going through security) and a particular seat or general area in the venue. Accreditation is needed for all workforce members, athletes, VIPs, suppliers, contractors, media, sponsors – basically anyone needing BOH access (which includes press tribunes, VIP seating, and athlete seating). Usually, no accreditation means no access. There are also different accreditation cards:

- Basic accreditation: background security check passed but no access has been granted to any BOH venue.
- Regular accreditation: background check has been passed; access is provided to some or all BOH areas in some or all of the venues. Most have this type.

- Day pass: security was not previously approved but venue security has approved and taken responsibility for accompanying the person while they are on venue.
- Upgrade card: the person has basic or regular accreditation but requires an upgrade for a given day to enter a particular venue not indicated on their original accreditation – it is a separate card which is worn along with the basic/regular accreditation. It often must be returned before the person leaves the venue.
- Extras: stickers or other indicators that are attached to a regular accreditation to allow access for a specific event/another venue that the person has not been accredited for. For example, a medical workforce member is required to work at the closing ceremonies rather than their regular, accredited venue.
- Extra passes: these must be accompanied by an accreditation card. For example, an extra pass for access to media transportation if you are not media but need access to that system for a specific (and valid) reason.

There is always a lot of discussion in the planning stages regarding who has access to what zone and there are always disappointments.

The system for accreditation is coded with numbers and letters which correspond to a physical location of an FA and a venue (specific numbers/letters vary from one event owner to the next). For example, having the number 6 and UBC on your 2010 Olympic Winter Games accreditation meant that you had access to the protocol lounge and VIP seating (6) in the University of British Columbia (UBC). There are different levels of accreditation depending on who you are, what you need to do, and where you need to go. Requests are submitted by the FA or stakeholder group (e.g. the delegations for the athletes and media), needs and wants are considered, and the final decision is made by the event's accreditation department according to the event's rights holder's guidelines.

Finally, the athletes' zone is a coveted and protected area (often termed the blue zone in the Olympics for the colour of the zone's accreditation level) where only athletes and their support teams are permitted – and for good reason. In contrast, the rest of the BOH is typically designated red for the non-field-of-play operations. Preparation for an event requires that the physical space be free of unnecessary people, as there is a mental zone that an athlete needs to be in to deliver their best performance. Distractions of media, VIPs, fans, family, etc., can pull focus and may affect ultimate performance. There are layers of "ownership" surrounding the athlete, from coaches, trainers, psychologists, and other medical staff in the local, national, and international organizations that train them, clubs that create the administration frameworks and fund-raise, parents and families that support the athlete, and finally the sponsorship organizations that promote the medal winners. Each person/group feels they deserve access to the athlete; and at an event, it is the mandate of the sport FA, EVS, and security, among others, to ensure that the athlete is protected mentally, physically, and emotionally at all times, in part through accreditation that restricts access.

The importance of sport and sport production and their impact on other functions

Venue teams create daily run sheets, which are detailed schedules that include the precise time allocations for the start and finish of competition, and the operations of every other FA based around the sport schedule. Everything that affects the athlete from medical services, doping control, transportation and accommodation, and changes to ceremonies that will make it better for the athlete will be facilitated by the sport and sport production FAs. Sport is notably responsible for producing the immediate, real-time results, which are distributed to not only to the athletes and delegations, but also the media, dignitaries, the rest of the organizing committee, and even spectators. Sport also chooses, in consultation with the IF, the equipment for the event, like nets, balls – such as The Albert, the official ball of the London 2012 Olympic Games football competition (Associated Press, 2011) – scoreboards, and even the placement of officials, which have an impact on the decisions made by other FAs such as sport production, security, EVS, and press. Likewise, depending on the schedule established by the sport FA and the respective IF, this will impact transportation, workforce, ICS, security, F&B, cleaning and waste, technology, press, anti-doping, medical, sport production, and essentially every other FA in the venue. The technical delegate for a specific sport has the purview to change or postpone a competition or practice due to weather. Strong winds, a thunderstorm, or a snow storm would be examples of situations where changes in the schedule would be warranted. Such changes would not only affect the athletes and the spectators, it would also impact many FAs, including press, security, EVS, ICS, workforce, F&B, transportation, and just as in the previous example, essentially all other FAs that operate during Games-time. Finally, a decision by sport production to add, for example, pre-competition entertainment, would impact the existing schedules of EVS, F&B, workforce, and security, not to mention the coordination and cooperation that is required to execute the change in a seamless manner with all FAs.

CHAPTER SUMMARY

We began this chapter by distinguishing between the concepts of site planning and overlay. We examined site options and distinguished between competition/non-competition venues, as well as FOH and BOH. We considered the difference between crowd control and management, and examined some literature on site planning. We then turned to operations and logistics, and the facilities management literature. We further explored facility ownership and managers, facility location, facility components, facility attendance and satisfaction, and especially green management/sustainability.

From a practitioner's perspective, we defined the venues as competitive and non-competitive and explained the differences. The use of CADs by FAs was also discussed. We also further explored different key FAs and their roles before and during a major sports event, paying particular attention to the venue management team, the FAs' adaptation and reporting structure changes, as well as accreditation basics. Finally, we examined the importance of the sport and sport production FAs and their impact on other functions.

EXPERT CASE: THE CHALLENGE OF MANAGING MULTIPLE VENUES AT THE SAME TIME

In my opinion there is a huge difference between the operational planning of multiple venues and then actually being on-site and simultaneously operating them. It is fair to say that planning for three venues is more challenging than just being in charge of one; however, once you have laid down the basic foundation in developing your FA operating plan, including finalizing all policies and procedures and staff training manuals, as well as completing the more venue-specific dot planning (logistics), staff deployment plan, workforce roster, schedule and rotation plans; tested the signage, client flows, and drop-off location; agreed on a radio fleet map and communication structure, as well as created daily run sheets and checklists; and finally ran table-top and readiness exercises for one stadium, all of the documents and plans can be adapted fairly easily to the others. In most cases only slight amendments have to be made due to physical differences or user constraints, but basically the same principle can be applied uniformly. To put it in more practical terms, the amount of time you need to finalize your planning for one venue does not equal the time you need for the other two. There is a significant amount of resources and time that you save. The real trouble begins when things get progressively operational.

The main challenge you face in the planning phase for multiple venues located in the same precinct is that you are expected to use less resources (e.g. staff, technical equipment, tools, and stationery) than planning for each stadium separately. When procuring and ordering these resources you need to think very operationally and put a strong focus on the competition schedule to anticipate and identify overlaps and common ground. Obviously you benefit from ordering as much mobile equipment as possible (e.g. laptops instead of desktop computers). When projecting these numbers, contingency planning should always be on your mind – for example, at Winter Games, the competition schedule for outdoor venues might change due to weather conditions. Another crucial step is to select the headquarters of operations on-site. Although you need the same basic set up at each stadium, it is vital to have one central office from where all operations will be supervised. It should be conveniently located, and all three stadia should be easily accessible for quick response.

Once this framework exists, the planning for multiple venues is not much more difficult than planning for one, as you benefit from having many similarities and can use collective resources. As previously mentioned, most of the plans can be adapted without too much amendment. It is worth mentioning, though, that within this "economy of scale" lies the risk of underestimating the task ahead: the concurrent set-up and operating in multiple venues at the same time with some of the tasks needing to happen simultaneously. After a successful planning phase, you feel confident that you are on top of things, but when it gets closer to Games-time you have to realize that now is the time for sharing responsibility and relying on others as you simply cannot be physically in all venues at the same time. Building and managing a team that you have trust and confidence in is the key ingredient of successful implementation. It is advisable to pay special attention to an accurate and well-prepared transfer of knowledge to the new staff. Although the venues are similar, for the most part, they will probably have some specific quirks.

The enormous scope of operating multiple venues at the same time becomes apparent when the set-up and venuization processes starts. You might have been able to benefit from adapting plans to all venues once one was completed in the lead time, but now operating three venues literally means three times the effort/trouble. You not only need to manage each venue individually, you also face constraints due to shared resources. At Whistler Olympic Park (WOP) there was only one gate/way into the venue for deliveries, keeping in mind that three times the amount of goods was coming into the precinct. This can be mitigated by preparing a detailed master delivery schedule and integrated installation schedule for the set-up phase. One sole supplier for all venues can result in delays if there are problems at one venue. Hence, prioritizing is key, setting up the main office first.

The common denominators of best practices in project management – like clear communication, effective flow of information, clear hierarchy, well-defined reporting structure, and issue resolution – are vital for the success of event operations. However, if you operate multiple venues at the same time, you really need to take it to the next level. As mentioned earlier, at Games-time we were facing a massive logistical challenge ensuring that we had the right amount of resources at the right venue at the right time. Keeping in mind that due to already extensive vehicle movement in the precinct, deliveries needed to be scheduled thoroughly, with the least impact on existing traffic as possible. Considering many different operational BOH routes, high numbers of spectator pathways FOH, and various accredited client groups, you need to provide a sophisticated and comprehensive wayfinding and signage process which will prove invaluable, particularly for between-venue movement. In the first few days, a significant number of staff should be scheduled to direct and guide clients, and it is recommended that the entire precinct is properly mapped and all sections are well labelled in order to avoid any confusion when arranging meeting points (e.g. for medal presenters).

Putting the spotlight on the internal team management, at the 2010 Vancouver Olympic Winter Games we had one pool of volunteers for the three venues, which meant it was crucial to make sure that all VGMs enforce the rules and regulations exactly in the same way and have at the least a very similar approach when it comes to issue resolution and team management in general, so the volunteers had the most effective guidance possible and did not get confused by different styles of decision-making. Obviously, in this context, extensive debrief sessions and clear communication among the managing team became paramount.

The list of considerations I have provided to operate multiple venues at one location is not exhaustive; however, the most important considerations have been articulated. As a bottom line, the planning for multiple venues demands detailed planning, constant focus, and team effort in every definition of the word team. It can be very exhausting at times, and what mitigates this is a detailed plan with a critical path that allows you to tick all the boxes. Research suggests that attitude contributes 80 per cent to the outcome of activity, and I would concur. If you learn to adjust your attitude in the moment, you will enjoy the ride. I did have a lot of fun – in fact, I would say three times the fun, operating three venues at WOP at the 2010 Vancouver Olympic and Paralympic Winter Games. My experience was unforgettable.

By Christian Akamp, Lead Venue Protocol Manager, LOCOG

Case questions

1 Identify the key considerations when you are managing more than one venue at the same location.

2 How can you mitigate these considerations?

3 What are the reasons for/benefits of having multiple venues at one location?

CHAPTER QUESTIONS

1 What is the difference between site planning, operations, logistics, and overlay? Where does facility management fit in?

2 Define competitive and non-competitive venues. Give examples of who would use each type of venue.

3 How is the CAD used by FAs? Why are they necessary?

4 What is the role of venue management before and during an event?

5 What is the difference between sport and sport production?

FURTHER READING

If you are interested in venues, we recommend the following:

Elliot, J. (2007) Green vs. grey: A comparative energy analysis of two Olympic speed-skating ovals. *Journal of Architectural and Planning Research*, 24, 160–177.

Fried, G. (2009) *Managing Sports Facilities* (2nd edn), Champaign, IL: Human Kinetics.

Klauser, F. (2011) The exemplification of "fan zones": Mediating mechanisms in the reproduction of best practices for security and branding at Euro 2008. *Urban Studies*, 48, 3203–3219.

NOTE

1 There is also a Canadian version, the Canada Green Building Council (see www.cagbc.org); a UK method (the Building Research Establishment Environmental Assessment Method; see www.breeam.org), an Australian method (Green Star; see www.gbca.org.au/green-star); and a Japanese method (the Comprehensive Assessment System for Built Environment Efficiency; see www.ibec.or.jp/CASBEE/english).

Chapter 8

The media

OBJECTIVES

- To understand who the media are in major sports events, what they want, and how they work
- To understand the impact of the media on major sports events and their stakeholders

ILLUSTRATIVE CASE: TODAY'S MAJOR SPORTS EVENTS GARNER HUGE TELEVISION VIEWERSHIP NUMBERS

Major sports events today are geared to the television audience. Those sports events that qualify as mega sports events rake in huge numbers of television spectators. For example, the 2012 edition of American football's Super Bowl (Super Bowl XLVI) attracted 111.3 million viewers above the age of two for that one game (Cutler, 2012b). While that was a record for the Super Bowl, it pales in comparison to the 700 million television spectators for the final of the 2010 World Cup in South Africa, which saw Spain win 1–0 over the Netherlands. While huge, this number in turn pales in comparison to the opening ceremonies of the summer edition of an Olympic Games which can attract over 1.4 billion television spectators worldwide (Miah, 2010). The 2010 Olympic Winter Games attracted approximately 3.8 billion television spectators worldwide during its 17 days (International Olympic Committee, 2010b), whereas the 2010 FIFA World Cup attracted approximately 24 billion television spectators worldwide during the month-long event.

For these events to be broadcast to a worldwide audience, the organizing committee must host the world's media. In 2010 the International Sports Press Association voted the 2010 World Cup (South Africa) as the best press facilities of the year, with the 2010 Olympic Winter Games (Canada) and Wimbledon (Great Britain) coming in second and third, respectively (FIFA.com, 2011).

THE THEORY BEHIND MEDIA

The current success of sport event managers depends, as Emery (2010) noted, on a tripartite relationship between sport, funders, and the media. The media are now a critical part of major sports event management. As Lord Sebastian Coe, Chairman of LOCOG said (quoted in Cutler, 2012a: 1):

> I don't think that a Games has ever been delivered in a media market that has been quite so forensic. In fairness they have made us perform better. Occasionally I say that through gritted teeth but they have. We are not at war with the media. We have a very good and strong relationship with them and occasionally it gets feisty but that is the nature of it. . . . I would rather have a forensic British press. Some-times they do not provide the most enjoyable of experiences but actually I would much rather have a free press than not. And occasionally, and I say occasionally, they come up with some thoughtful observations.

In this section, we will examine what the literature says about what the media are, how the media work, media consumption and representation, the impact of the media, traditional versus new media, and some regulations and restrictions pertaining to the media. While we organize the literature within these different areas of interest, it is important to note that they are not mutually exclusive.

What are the media?

There are different types of media at major sports events. The Olympic Games breaks down the sport event "media" category into: broadcast (television), press (traditional written media and photography), the Olympic News Service (ONS) and Olympic Broadcast Service (OBS), radio, and more recently, new media (all digital and internet-based media including social media, blogging, Twitter, YouTube, Facebook, etc.). The ONS is the organizing committee's in-house news service and is there to collect, manage the production of, and distribute news and information to the Olympic Family, especially the accredited media (mainly broadcast, press, and radio). For example, the ONS will usually obtain "flash" quotes from athletes immediately after their performance, which are then relayed to the media sitting in the MPC; these media can then use the flash quote in their respective news stories. Parent (2008) found the media to be a key issue in the preparation and hosting of major sports events. Media issues mainly relate to media coverage and broadcasting rights. However, the media, in and of themselves, are a stakeholder group to manage, with key interests in visibility, the financial situation of the event, event operations, their interde-pendence with other stakeholders, relationship building and maintenance with other stake-holders, and of course, sport. Essentially, the media want the organizing committee to make their job easy and complete on time, which means: good accommodations, efficient trans-portation, and proper technology and other services (Parent, 2008).

Major sports event spectators in a stadium experience the event "as is", whereas television spectators experience the sports event as a "media event", as the director of the broadcasting network becomes an editor of the event (cf. Cominsky et al., 1977). Media events are also defined as those events which see millions of people suspending their daily lives to tune into a national or international event presented in the media (Rivenburgh, 2002). Some researchers (e.g. Arquembourg, 2006) go so far as stating that media events are the product of the media's constructions, which misrepresent reality. Nevertheless, research which examines other media events – such as tsunamis and other global disasters (e.g. Arquembourg, 2009; Kyriakidou, 2008), United Nations and G8/G20 meetings (e.g. Giffard and Rivenburgh, 2000; McCurdy, 2008), state funerals (e.g. Myers, 2000; Puijk, 2009), and terrorist acts (e.g. Nossek, 2008) – could be translated to the study of major sporting events. Researchers (e.g. Puijk, 2000; Boccia et al., 2010; Naka and Kobayashi, 2010; Papa, 2010a) have argued that today's Olympic Games, as well as their torch relays, should also be considered media events. If the Olympic Games are considered to be media events, then they should "be analysed as a layered series of events of varying 'strength' and meaning" (Puijk, 2000: 309), demonstrating the complexity of studying such events. However, Rivenburgh (2002) questioned the ability of the Olympic Games to sustain its position as a media event in the twenty-first century: while Olympic Games garner increasing broadcasting hours, these hours compete with an increasing number of other international events, increasing numbers of other mega-events (e.g. 9/11 terrorist attacks broadcasts), and increasing numbers of television channels and shows. Still, the Olympic Games and FIFA World Cup are not the only sport media events. Anstead and O'Loughlin (2011) argued that the Twenty20 cricket tournaments can also be viewed as media events (see also Axford and Huggins, 2011).

How do the media work?

There is interest in the broader media-related literature in understanding how the media work. Latham (2010), for example, used the case of the 2008 Beijing Olympic Games to examine the transformations within the Chinese media. To do so, he looked at three areas:

1 The relationship between the media and the government: degree of control from the state, resistance presented by the media.
2 The relationship between national and foreign (international) media: degree of access by foreign media, engagement by national media with the foreign media, acceptance or discrediting of foreign media stances.
3 The emergence of new media and new technologies: impact of the internet, digital television, smart phones, blogging, Facebook, Twitter, etc., as well as examining (old) media habits and their impact on contemporary media agendas and transformations.

The 2008 Beijing Olympic Games were found to have an impact in transforming the Chinese media landscape. The national and international attention that the Olympic Games were bringing to the country resulted in certain events being dealt with more decisively, quickly, and even "sympathetically" (Latham, 2010: 800) by Chinese authorities. Also, while in the past Chinese authority and media professionals believed the Chinese general public to be unaware (ignored, hidden or avoided, whether purposefully so through blocking access or not) of what the foreign media were saying, the discourse has been transformed into one of acknowledgement but also discussion in a way that will reinforce the accepted narrative, even going so far as discrediting the foreign media or limiting its impact. Finally, the emergence and use of new media and technologies for the 2008 Olympic Games demonstrated the interconnectedness between the different forms of media (i.e. they no longer work in isolation) and interaction with the consumers (i.e. sports events are no longer a one-way production of media-to-consumer). Nevertheless, as Latham noted, certain habits – such as the media telling the audience how they should understand what they are seeing – seem to be hard to change (see also Silk, 1999; Silk et al., 2000; Silk and Amis, 2000; Solberg et al., 2009). As such, we see three areas which can be used to examine how the media work in a given country, as well as see the impact an Olympic Games can have on the media landscape in the host country.

Another aspect of how the media work is to understand what is newsworthy. The editor of the *Guardian* in the 1960s, Alastair Hetherington, had seven priorities for news: (1) social, economic, and/or political significance; (2) drama (excitement, entertainment); (3) surprise (unpredictability, newness); (4) personalities (showbiz, royalty); (5) sex, scandal, and/or crime; (6) numbers or scale of the event; and (7) proximity (geographical closeness) (as cited in Venables, 1993; Frost, 2003). Ultimately, Venables (1993; see also Frost, 2003) concluded that there has to be some form of change for there to be news, and security is also a major concern which makes an event newsworthy. Other researchers have also examined what makes an event (in the broad sense) become news. For example,

■ Galtung and Ruge (1965) believed 12 conditions ought to be met for an event to be newsworthy: frequency, threshold (absolute intensity and intensity increase), unambiguity, meaningfulness (cultural proximity and relevance), consonance (predictability and demand), unexpectedness (unpredictability and scarcity), continuity, composition, reference to elite nations, reference to elite people, reference to persons, and reference to something negative.

■ Rosengren (1970) suggested that for international news, newsworthiness is dependent on how important the event is, the physical and/or cultural distance of the event, and how predictable the event is.

■ Shoemaker and colleagues. (Shoemaker and Cohen, 2006; Shoemaker et al., 1991) presented a newsworthiness model combining both event-oriented and context-oriented factors in a two-factor model, whereby social significance and deviance help to explain why a news item would be more newsworthy than another. That is, the more socially significant or important and the more deviant (unusual, unexpected) the event, the more likely it will be newsworthy. Lee and Choi (2009) found that this newsworthiness model is more effective for explaining traditional media coverage of the 2002 FIFA World Cup than online media.

Many of these characteristics – such as meaningfulness, potential for negative reference, unexpectedness, references to elite nations and people, international, and importance/social significance – can also be associated with major sports events, demonstrating why the media love these events. In all these studies, the assumption is that the news value or newsworthiness of an event will predict news coverage, and that news coverage will predict audience attention. Lee (2009) went further, suggesting that news coverage is the mediating variable between newsworthiness and audience attention.

Another concept of interest is media templates. Kitzinger (2000) introduced us to this concept, explaining that media templates serve as a form of narrative or rhetorical shorthand, which helps journalists and audiences make sense of new news stories. They guide public discussion about the topic. Thus, as Kitzinger argued, media templates are useful tools for understanding and analysing how reality is framed by the media "and how media power operates" (p. 61). The media templates used in the article's case illustrate how they "are established and maintained by source strategies, social power relations and journalistic/audience reception processes" (p. 61).

Newsworthiness and media templates are but two aspects examined regarding how the media work. We also find studies examining how the media set agendas (e.g. Barnes *et al.*, 2008), how media influences (e.g. Ritchie *et al.*, 2010), media attitudes (e.g. Viuda-Serrano, 2010), media hypes (e.g. Wien and Elmelund-Præstekær, 2009), and framing by media (e.g. Carey, 1976; Edy and Meirick, 2007; Giffard and Rivenburgh, 2000).

Media coverage of sport and sports events has been an interest for researchers. Falkheimer (2007) examined the 2005 America's Cup pre-regatta in Sweden, noting that media coverage analysis of such an event is often oversimplified. Not only is there a need for developing political and public communication relating to the sports event, but media coverage can differ when one moves from the local to the national media. In turn, Green *et al.* (2002) noted the use of event logos, city images, and icons as tools to increase awareness of the host city through the media coverage. The media are not a passive stakeholder in this process, however. They do have a role to play in constructing these events (Hachleitner and Manzenreiter, 2010). McQuire (2010: 567), for example, suggested that "large screens [in public spaces, live sites, fan zones] have the potential to play a significant role in promoting public interaction", which can justify the live sites for major sporting events.

Accommodations, transportation, and technological services allow the media to properly cover the event. Thus, there is a need to further understand the requirements of the media at major sports events. Notwithstanding, looking at the media more specifically as a group, they can influence the major sporting event, all the way to its core identity and brand. Parent and colleagues (Parent and Foreman, 2007; Parent and Séguin, 2008) argued that once the organizing committee creates its identity and brand, it sends images of itself (about the identity and brand) out to its stakeholders. Some images may be sent directly, but many will go through the media lens, so to speak. As Parent and Foreman's (2007) article highlighted, while the media's job may be to report the facts, that is an ideal world. In reality, the media will transform what it receives into a story it wants to tell (so that it is newsworthy). Thus, there is a possible transformation of the organizing committee image (and therefore identity and brand). The stakeholders will then reflect their own perceptions of the images back to the organizing committee, either directly, or again through the media. The media's presence in this image, identity, and brand feedback loop explains why public relations and communications departments within organizing committees are so important.

There is therefore an intrinsic link between major sports events and the media. Some sports events are seen as more closely linked than others, given the commodification and professionalization of sports such as basketball and football, and the worldwide popularity of the Olympic Games and FIFA World Cup. McTeer and White (2010) argued that the NASCAR racing series is another such sport (event), given its degree of commodification and consumer capitalism which seems to supersede the sport's cultural roots. The authors concluded that the media production's economic logic cannot be separated from the races, which further drives the spectacularization of the sport and its brand.

There have also been some critical examinations of the media themselves. McGregor (1998), for example, questioned the objectivity and power of the media. Many studies have found that in routine context (the everyday), media ownership influences media content (see, for example, Bagdikian, 2000; Herman and Chomsky, 2002; Nasaw, 2000); in times of crisis, however, the influence seems to be more grassroots (Rossman, 2004). The relationship or tension between political control and news management is also of interest (e.g. Wolfsfeld, 1997). In turn, McLeod (1991: 69) stated that "Television has the power to manipulate and to certify, to selectively inform, and to selectively manipulate emotion." Papa (2010a) found that the French media staged or promoted an opposition between Western and Chinese societies during the 2008 Beijing Olympic Games torch relay.

Part of the critical examination includes focusing on the use of language and symbols by the media. Denton (2004) explored these phenomena in relation to the 9/11 attacks in the United States. Many researchers have examined the use of the media to portray national narratives or the media's own national stances/perspectives in their reporting (e.g. Alabarces et al., 2001; Bernstein, 2000; Bloyce et al., 2010; Chwen Chen and Colapinto, 2010; Desmarais and Bruce, 2009; Falcous, 2007; Inthorn 2010; Lee and Maguire, 2009; Min and Zhen, 2010; Naka and Kobayashi, 2010; Papa, 2010b; Pena and De Moragas, 2010; Pena et al., 2010; Wardle and West, 2004). These studies make it clear that the media do have a nationalistic lens. Even when covering terrorist attacks, the media seem to move from their traditional, normative professional frames (which includes a critical perspective and scrutiny of government actions), in favour of a national-patriotic stance which "seeks to re-establish normality and restore order" (Nossek, 2008: 313). Regardless, as Mihelj (2008) noted, conceptualizing the link between nationhood and media phenomena is not as well understood. She suggested that researchers move away from the ceremonial occasions which celebrate national unity towards examining the actual media rituals. Thus, we see a call to examine the media's activities more closely, instead of just focusing on their impacts.

Nevertheless, in the media literature associated with major sports events, we see a particular interest in nationalistic portrayals and perspectives surrounding the 2008 Beijing Olympic Games, with studies comparing China and Brazil, the United States, Japan, South Korea, France, Italy, Spain, and other countries' perspectives on and coverage of the 2008 Games (e.g. Boccia, 2010; Chen and Colapinto, 2010; Chwen Chen and Colapinto, 2010; Lee and Maguire, 2009; Min and Zhen, 2010; Naka and Kobayashi, 2010; Papa, 2010a, 2010b; Pena and De Moragas, 2010; Pena et al., 2010; Tarantino and Carini, 2010). Huang (2010: 833) went further into the Chinese media environment by examining the local and national strategies, arguing that such a study allows one to not only examine local and national media environments, but also "the hidden cultures behind these signs of media ecology". Guojun et al. (2011), for example, noted how China's image may have remained relatively constant (i.e. the 2008 Beijing Olympic Games did not improve the image) of the country, but awareness of the country increased internationally and its image may have become clearer. Preuss and Alfs (2011: 55) suggested that China's signalling efforts were "weakened by several negative news reports".

There is emerging research published on the media and the 2010 FIFA World Cup in South Africa (e.g. Lepp and Gibson, 2011; Maguire, 2011). Also, given the strongly nationalistic perspective and focus on the actual sporting competitions by international media of the 2005 Helsinki IAAF (International Association of Athletics Federations) World Championships (instead of media attention on the host region and economic profit), Nylund (2009) challenged the belief that sport mega-events are effective tools for urban marketing. Yet following the 2010 Olympic Winter Games, Canada was named the number-one country brand in the world for 2010 by New York-based global brand consultant FutureBrand, beating out the United States (Nevin, 2010); thus, there may be a need to qualify the utility of an event for urban marketing as dependent on the actual event (e.g. Olympic Games versus IAAF World Championship). Preuss (2006) contended that the increasing media coverage garnered by a major sports event in turn increases tourism to the host cities, which provides an economic windfall for the host region.

Finally, there is an interest in the concept of globalization associated with the media. Globalization can be defined as the political, socio-cultural, economic, and temporal integration of individuals, products, and services, and even values around the world; this is facilitated through technological, communication, and travel advances (Byers *et al.*, 2012). Jan (2009) suggested that regarding the media, the ways of creating and organizing media (i.e. industry models) is the most popular form of globalization. The International Telecommunications Union and other standards bodies have also, of course, had an impact on the globalization of the media, as does the fact that most countries in the world now have at least a small percentage of their population having (cable or satellite) television and/or using the internet (i.e. penetration of media). This globalization of the media is not solely dominated by American firms; the largest media firms and groups in the world come from the United States, but also France, Germany, Australia, and Japan. We also see some firms choosing to specialize in one area (e.g. ESPN specializes in sports) or in niche markets – we see these firms in the United States, but also in Europe, Canada, East Asia, and Latin America. Some of the key issues regarding the globalization of media include cross-border "data flow, cultural imperialism, media and information flows, and the flow of information, media trade, and effects of national development" (Jan, 2009: 70). With the advent of new media and new technologies, this globalization will likely increase; whether media imperialism (Jan, 2009) continues or the power of the consumer begins to rival the power of the media remains to be seen and studied.

Media consumption and representation

A third general area of interest is media consumption and representation. Some studies focus on media coverage of particular events and their impact on consumption. For example, television viewing, at least of traumatic or stressful events such as the attacks on 9/11, is also found to have an impact on the viewer by increasing their stress and trauma, as Propper *et al.* (2007) noted when studying individuals' dreams following the 9/11 attacks. Also, public involvement in media events, as in the case of the death of Princess Diana, shows the sense of entitlement and sincerity of individuals interviewed and argues for the concept of "intimacy at a distance" as a part of media events (Myers, 2000).

Other studies focus more on the consumers and consumption/representation differences. For example, we find many studies on media's differing and/or supposed bias relating to gender – favouring men over women (e.g. Andrew *et al.*, 2009; Bernstein, 2002; Billings *et al.*, 2006; Capranica and Aversa, 2002; Capranica *et al.*, 2005; King, 2007; Stone and Horne, 2008; Tuggle *et al.*, 2007; Wensing and Bruce, 2003). Duncan (1993), for example, went further by examining the institutional structures behind these media texts relating to gender, focusing on objectification, commodification, and voyeurism. We also find some studies related to media representations of persons with disabilities (e.g. Howe, 2008; Ik Young and Crossman, 2009; Smith and Thomas, 2005; Tanner *et al.*, 2011). Howe's (2008: 148) study on the Paralympic Games' media and their representation of elite athletes with disabilities demonstrates that "Paralympic sports are not yet ready to embrace the old adage that 'any publicity is good publicity'"; instead, there seems to still be some control over the media to produce stories with positive spins. As well, Howe suggested that the media are slowly moving away from the "triumph over tragedy" spin towards more focus on sport for the Paralympic Games; yet, there is still a lack of presence, and even less debate, about the classification system for Paralympic sport, which is central to its habitus.

Besides gender and disabilities, we also see studies on media representations of volunteers and fandom. Lockstone and Baum (2009) examined the media representations of volunteers' experience for the 2006 Melbourne CWG, demonstrating both positive and negative representations by both local and national media. However, the tendency was for more positive and "bland" (p. 52) reporting, highlighting the communications control held by the organizing committee over volunteers. In turn, Bladen (2010) noted differences in how English-language domestic and foreign media represented volunteers at the 2008 Beijing Olympic Games. He explained that Chinese and foreign media often presented conflicting views on volunteers' skills, numbers, identities, motivations, and the impact on the individuals of volunteering. Regarding media representations related to fandom, Lee (2005) argued that the media's focus on the two friendly football games by Real Madrid and Liverpool in Hong Kong diverted readers' attention away from other societal issues occurring at the time (e.g. economic downturn, health epidemics) and made it appear as though the fans were one group instead of highlighting the internal divisions and diverging (more negative) opinions about these events. Moreover, these events were turned into media spectacles, demonstrating the commodification of sport; yet this commodification was not critically discussed in the media. Fandom is also examined in association with other factors, such as:

- Fandom and attendance: Ping-Kun and Chiung-Hsia (2008) argued that in world archery championships, radio coverage and internet communications (website) were the two main media sources influencing fans to attend the event, followed by television advertisements and seeing the event on television. How different media affect fandom and attendance for other major sports events remains to be studied. Pritchard and Funk (2006: 299) suggested that "plotting media use in conjunction with attendance offers a more accurate account of spectator involvement".
- Fandom and sport celebrities: Summers and Johnson Morgan (2008) noted how sports fans are able to separate the negative/bad personal behaviour of sports celebrities depicted in the media, as long as these celebrities continue to do what they are supposed

to do: win and entertain. Ultimately, the authors suggested that public relations professionals working with these celebrities need to build the celebrities' positive images in order to weather negative press and manage fan expectations.

The negative press garnered by sports celebrities behaving badly results in sport organizations needing to consider their ethical and social responsibilities regarding these celebrities (Summers and Johnson Morgan, 2008). Studies are also examining more closely media's representation of ethics and CSR. The media seem to like ethical reporting by companies; they typically provide a positive spin on such stories and include organizational information and labour violations found. Themes associated with public reporting, transparency, corporate responsibility for labour/work conditions, brand accountability, and factory monitoring are also found within media stories about ethics (e.g. Dickson and Eckman, 2008). An interesting case is presented by Wenner (2004), who examined the ethics and conflicts of interest between the media (MTV, CBS) and the NFL regarding the half-time Super Bowl Janet Jackson episode.

There are also media-related studies associated with risk and protests. While the media is an issue category to be dealt with by the organizing committee, it can also be considered a type of risk as the organizing committee has to manage the risk of possible negative coverage (versus positive coverage) by the media (Leopkey and Parent, 2009a). But the media may also be used to examine how the general public views a particular risk issue/event. In such situations, we can seemingly find more information in newspapers than television, as newspapers allow for more comprehensive, detailed coverage, as well as for coverage of more chronic or more local issues/events (Driedger, 2007). Moreover, if we look at the media's coverage of a particular type of risk – protests – the media tend to "portray protests in ways that may undermine [protestors'] social movement agendas" (Smith *et al.*, 2001: 1397). Thus, while media representation of different topics may be growing, readers (and especially researchers using the media as a data source) must look at the media with a critical eye for what they can, do, and do not cover. One aspect that could be examined is media fatigue – the media going all-out on a news story and then reducing and simplifying the event as it drags on over time (see, for example, Schrodt *et al.*, 2005) – and its consequences as well as sport event managers' strategies for avoiding this situation given the importance of the television audience.

Media impacts

Given that the media provide a certain perspective it their representation, they have an impact on a variety of aspects. We have noted the image, identity, and branding processes earlier. However, we also find that the media have an impact on destination image (Chalip *et al.*, 2003), place image, and nostalgia such as for the outdoor hockey game called the Heritage Classic (Ramshaw and Hinch, 2006). The impact of the media in place promotion is not limited to sports events, but also other national or international events, such as political national conventions (Smith, 2005). The tourism benefits are also associated with the media's impact on individuals' interests in travelling to a given destination (e.g. Green *et al.*, 2010). However, this impact is not a given; Euro 2004 seemed to have done little for Portugal in this regard, suggesting a need for more strategic leveraging techniques to derive tourism benefits (Sealy and Wickens, 2008).

The media also have an impact on the emergence or transportation of a given sport (Van Bottenburg and Heilbron, 2006), including commercialization and acquisition of sports teams by media corporations (Gerrard, 2004). As well, the media's coverage of a sports event can have an impact on active participation. The impact of media sport event coverage is linked more to young people's motivation and modelling levels than to the youth's sustained involvement or improvement in the associated sport (Lines, 2007).

Traditional vs. new media

With the advent of new technologies and the popularity of sites such as Facebook and Twitter, an emerging area of interest for media researchers is examining traditional versus new media. Merrin (2002: 369) suggested that "Recent years have seen a renewed interest in Marshall McLuhan's media theory. For many, his description of an electronic society and culture is more recognizable today than it was in his lifetime." The advent of new media has also led to increased attention and involvement by the audience for a given media event (Puijk, 2009). However, this audience comprises different generations, from the parents of baby boomers, to the baby boomers themselves, to the baby busters, and to the children of the baby boomers: generations X, Y, and the millennial generation. There are many books and articles exposing the differences between different generations (see, for example, Della *et al.*, 2008; Getz, 2005; Lancaster, 2002). What we are interested in here are the different generations' views on and use of the media. It is probably not surprising to the reader that Generation Y plays more video games and watches more action or alternative sports (versus traditional league sports like professional basketball or American football) on television than Generation X (Bennett *et al.*, 2006b). Thus, sport event managers need to be conscious of different generations' attitudes, preferences, and uses of different media, which is why there has likely been an exponential increase in the use of internet and mobile technologies by the current major sporting events and their broadcasters. The 2008 Beijing Olympic Games were dubbed the "technology games" by its organizing committee, the 2010 Vancouver Olympic Games saw about half of its broadcasting hours delivered by digital media (e.g. 6,000 hours of broadcast coverage on mobile phones, 1.2 billion web page viewings, and 265 million video views), and the 2012 London Olympic Games are set to break records regarding new media use.

But what is new media? What is social media? What is digital media? Are they all the same? According to the IOC's marketing media guide (International Olympic Committee, 2010d), new media are the digital, mobile, computer, and other technology media platforms such as mobile phones and the internet. Social media would be media designed for social interaction and communication, such as YouTube, Facebook, and Twitter. Digital media is the all-encompassing electronic form of media which allows the creation, transmission, and storage of data in electronic or digital (versus analogue) form. Some researchers use new and social media as a source for their data gathering (e.g. Boccia *et al.*, 2010; Chen and Colapinto, 2010). We also see an adaptation of certain traditional research methods for electronic data, such as the netnography, an online version of ethnography, which can, for example, analyse blogs (see Beaven and Laws, 2007; Berger *et al.*, 2008; Kozinets, 1997, 2002 for more information).

Other researchers study the various aspects of new, social, and digital media, often finding a double-edged sword or paradox in the process. We find that new media allow for both mass and interpersonal (individualized messages to one person) communications, which traditional media cannot do at the same time. Traditional mass and interpersonal communications theories are therefore affected (see Della *et al.*, 2008). Yet the proliferation of messages reaching individuals through new media means that a selection process needs to occur (which messages do we pay attention to?); also, the interactive nature of new media means that there is a possible feedback loop, that individuals can have a greater say in what happens. These changes in the transmission and processing of information therefore have implications for managers wanting to deliver particular messages (Della *et al.*, 2008). This can hold true for other Games stakeholders as well, such as athletes. We see that athletes' use of Twitter allows fans to get an insider perspective, fostering interactivity and relationship building between athletes and fans through the athletes' postings of opinions and comments (Kassing and Sanderson, 2010). Ultimately, though, the use of new, social, and digital media by sport event managers is likely to be associated with revenue generation; as Kjus (2009: 287) noted, "Spectacular events and live content are more essential than ever for extending audience reach and developing new revenues".

Regulations and restrictions

Finally, some research regarding the media has focused on government policy restrictions regarding sport and sports event broadcasting (e.g. Boardman and Hargreaves-Heap, 1999) or lack thereof (e.g. Dyreson, 2005). A particular interest seems to be European laws governing the access to major sports events on pay-TV versus free-to-air TV. Parrish (2008) suggested that the provisions (and revisions) set forth under the European Union's Article 3a Television without Frontiers Directive, whereby member-states can create a list of protected sports events important to society, thereby preventing broadcasters from limiting the events' broadcast, has impacts on the broadcasters, but also on the consumers, sport organizations, and member-states themselves. While such provisions seem to have widespread political support, they raise a number of concerns and questions: (1) the right to free television access; (2) the importance of sport for society; (3) the importance of regulation for European integration, as well as the issue of competence; (4) the dangers of the commercialization of sport; (5) regulations negatively impacting the rights values; (6) regulations negatively impacting the development of a single broadcast services market; (7) the application of such a provision; and (8) the impact on consumers. Of course, not all countries have such provisions; it depends on the degree of state intervention. For example, France and Greece are traditionally seen as interventionist states, whereas the United Kingdom and United States would be non-interventionist states (Parrish, 2008). Studies in the United Kingdom and United States have actually found a need for some form of government policy and/or intervention regarding sports broadcasting rights (cf. Cowie and Williams, 1997; Cox, 1995).

Not only are governments examining different sports events for their importance to society, but they are also examining the content. The US Federal Communications Commission (FCC) has been increasingly restricting indecent material on its airwaves. While this may be relatively easy for broadcasters to control when speaking of taped material (e.g. television series), it is another thing when considering live television, such as sports events. If an athlete, mad at a referee's call, happens to shout a four-letter expletive, technically the broadcaster could face fines, hearings, or (although unlikely) loss of their licence. Examining this issue, Conrad (2008) noted that the FCC has been somewhat reprimanded for such restrictions, especially in cases when the expletive is not meant as degrading or referring to sex or excrement, but as an adjective, such as in the case of Bono, the lead singer of U2, who exclaimed "this is really, really fucking brilliant" in a *Golden Globes* acceptance speech (Conrad, 2008: 184). Yet, the restrictions still apply. Thus, some broadcasters have resorted to means to attempt to pre-empt the airing of such words by, for example, have a slight tape-delay of 5–10 seconds – which is actually rather expensive to do. Conrad suggested sport governing bodies implement their own internal codes of conduct to avoid athletes, coaches, and others using expletives; however, this solution is one that is out of the control of the broadcasters. An alternative would be doing away with the FCC's expletive restriction for broadcasters. However, perhaps more amenable to the FCC and broadcasters would be the creation, Conrad argued, of a sports safe harbour, such as is the case for television shows past a given hour late at night.

Thus, we see that the broader media literature has been examining various aspects of the media, and we do find some research done regarding sports events specifically. We suggest that researchers examine in greater depth the media as a stakeholder, and as a client, to be managed by the organizing committee of a major sports event, including and perhaps contrasting traditional and new media.

THE PRACTITIONER'S PERSPECTIVE ON MEDIA

Without the media, a major sports event would only be major in the minds of the competitors and those who physically attended. The media are integral for two main reasons: (1) the revenues that are generated through the rights to broadcast the event; and (2) the media take events to a global level. Every sports event needs the media, and the layers will depend on the "reach" of the media. Consider the FIFA World Cup and the 32 teams playing 64 matches over the month-long event. Billions of viewers follow these matches and create their own events around the television, smart phone, and computer screen viewing. Soccer/ football has incredible depth and breadth around the world, not to mention the team loyalty that is garnered as a result of the ability of anyone in the world who has access to technology to view the matches and read about them. Many of the viewers may not even watch the sport on a regular basis; however, there is something about a large event which brings the best of the best to compete that attracts first-time and casual observers.

An event like the Olympic Games or FIFA World Cup has so many media outlets, many of which are never obvious or known to the general public; and yet, they play a critical part in how and when the story is told. For the Olympic Games, we can find:

■ OBS: the IOC/in-house recording/feeder broadcaster. Since 2008, the IOC has taken over the basic recording of the events; the feed is then provided to the official broadcasters, which add their logo and other relevant information. At that point the images are transmitted to the viewers.

- ONS: the in-house news service that provides immediate information on the event, the results, and any other additional news. The flash quotes from athletes are taken by ONS staff, as well as other relevant information and results, and fed into the event's intranet (e.g. Info2010 for the 2010 Olympic Winter Games), which can be accessed by organizing committee staff and volunteers, the media (especially those who must stay within the MPC in order to cover more sports at the same time), dignitaries, athletes, delegations, etc. – essentially all those who have BOH access.
- The IOC recognizes five world press agencies for the Olympic Games: Agence France Presse, Associated Press, Reuters, the host country's press (e.g. Canadian Press), and Getty Images (the official photographers for essentially all major sports events).

Where do the media work?

Overall, the media operate both internally and externally during the event. Within a venue, both competitive and non-competitive, there are people and equipment that will report on the sports events, interview athletes post-competition, and create stories that will appear in the moment or are recorded for later viewing. Because the presence of these people is accredited, there are different levels of access depending on who you are and where it has been decided (by the organizing committee and the event owner) you can go.

The MPC houses hundreds of press (written and photographic) journalists who will never be in a venue, as they are often one of only a few from their country and must report on many sports at the same time. In other words, they camp out in the MPC as they cannot be in two places at once. Thus, they rely on the ONS for the soundbites and taglines for their stories. They toil away in a room, perhaps without windows, and report on what has been reported to them – unbeknown to the public that reads the story. The MPC has everything the journalist may need: a workstation, laundry services, F&B services, masseuse, etc., to make their job easier (though they have to pay for these services themselves). There are daily press conferences by the organizing committee and event owner which are held in the MPC. These are attended by both broadcast and press media, depending on the nature of the announcement. There can also be other press conferences: for example by an NOC, which can be held in the MPC.

Typically found near the MPC, the IBC is the broadcast version of the MPC. It is usually the most technologically heavy venue, has the best views of the city, and the most difficult to gain access to; only a broadcast accreditation is acceptable (not even a regular press accreditation will work). The broadcast rights holders of the various countries have their workspace and broadcast centres in this building. Together, the MPC and IBC form the MMC.

Within the individual sports venues, spectators are delivered minute-by-minute coverage through reader boards, video/jumbotrons, and radio (ear buds) that allow them to hear play-by-play commentary. It has become possible to watch an event live, hear it reported, and witness replay all at the same time because of the variety of sources that report and record the events. For the media, venues have, for a lack of a better word, mini media centres in each venue – that is, each competition venue includes a work area with different services for the media. In addition, there is an area called the mixed zone, which is usually a narrow walkway where athletes who exit the field-of-play must go through to allow accredited journalists to interview them immediately following a competition. The athlete may choose not to stop to speak to a journalist, however; one reason might be if the athlete has been randomly chosen for an anti-doping test. (Although there is no access for journalists in the anti-doping area, there will be a breaking story if the athlete tests positive. The testing can take hours, depending on the availability of interpreters and the time it takes for test results.) A journalist can choose to wait around and hope that their contacts within ONS or other accredited journalists with more access can provide them with a scoop. Each competition venue also has a press conference room where winning athletes will speak after their win.

Considerations associated with the media

In order to do their job, the media need to speak to athletes and event organizers. Language can sometimes be an issue. For example, there may be a British journalist who wishes to interview a Chinese athlete, but who does not speak Mandarin. The various venues where the media work will usually (or should) have interpreters. These individuals can be professionals – used especially for the daily event owner and medallist press conferences – or volunteers, who can be used for the mixed zone, other press conferences, anti-doping, medical, security, and any other service requiring interpretation services.

In addition, the media require other services to ensure that they can do their job and offer a favourable view of the event and its organizers. These include their own effective and efficient transportation system between the MPC/IBC and the various competition venues; proper accommodations; access to (rent or purchase) various equipment, products, and services (including phone, computer, internet access) through the rate card system; and up-to-date/fast results system, as well as other event news through an intranet system.

It is also important to note that workforce members are instructed and usually prohibited from speaking to the media about any subject. The reason is obvious – control and accuracy of information is critical because all major sports events have politics. Speaking out of turn or leaking information – especially from inside the organizing committee – can be detrimental to the organizing committee's reputation and can promote false information; however, organizing committees can also be accused of not being transparent by not sharing information with the media – and consequently the world.

The space provided for media varies. Broadcast has generous access because they are located on tribunes (cascading seating with box-like enclosures) in a venue that give them preferential views to the play-by-play of a sport competition. They can also do interviews right in the tribunes if they are successful in gaining permission from the athlete or special guest, who is protected by either protocol or athlete zone control. There is an opportunity, however, to make the request when the person is in transit or to send a note through the protocol manager or sport manager. Once the athlete or guest leaves their zone there is a small neutral area around the exit where the media can potentially get a comment or interview. Otherwise, the media must stick to the mixed zone for athlete access.

If they have the appropriate accreditation, media have access to dedicated transportation which allows them to travel to and from venues. If their accreditation is limited or they have to cover many different competitions at the same time, media can obtain information from the intranet (thanks to internal games news services), on internal television screens (thanks to internal games broadcast services and the host country's broadcaster), or manually, dispensed through a bank of pigeon holes labelled with their names. In this case, information is delivered daily in paper format. For journalists in the MPC, this is often their only source of information because they do not have physical access to other areas. They can essential come to the sports event and remain in just one spot.

Imagine what a challenge it is for a member of the media to break a story today without proprietary access or information. The public is equipped through technology with the ability to capture images as an event unfolds and immediately release it to the world on channels like YouTube, Twitter, Facebook, etc. Cooperation between members of an event's internal and external media is important and increasingly necessary as technology advances. The public's thirst for the instant, for reality, is reflected in the astoundingly positive ratings for these types of shows, and the public's capacity to absorb the reply of both positive and negative pictures is amazing. Technology and the "tastes" of the public have impacted, and in some cases changed, how and by whom stories are "broken". One of the only constants in life and in events is change, and the unknown aspect of what is unknown mentioned in Chapter 4 permeates major sports events.

CHAPTER SUMMARY

In this chapter we examined the media. We started by looking at what the sport event and broader media literatures have studied regarding the media. This included what the media are, how media work, media consumption and representation, the impact of the media, traditional versus new media, and regulations and restrictions pertaining to the media.

From a practitioner's standpoint, we focused our attention on how the media operate during major sports events, including the different types of media and the different locations media work in. We also provided some considerations associated with managing the media, such as what types of services they need to do their job, and why organizing committees often place major restrictions on their staff and volunteers regarding speaking with members of the media.

EXPERT CASE: WHY CARE ABOUT THE MEDIA IN MAJOR SPORTS EVENTS? MEDIA PROCESSES AND IMPACTS?

Broadcasting, print, photographic, and radio media have become integral to the delivery and perceived success of sports events on the scale of the Olympic Games. With the great majority of consumers around the world only having access to the event via the media, event organizing committees have come to the realization that the facilities and resources provided to the media have never before been more extensive, costly, or of greater importance to the event's global success.

In the Olympic world, from the IOC down, there is a distinction made between broadcasters (television) and press (written, photographic). This distinction is made because the needs of the different types of media are different in delivery, but the outcome – providing their consumers with coverage of the event – is exactly the same.

As a baseline, the needs of all media for an event are relatively simple; they have to be able to do their job as easily, cheaply, efficiently, and quickly as possible. Organizing committee broadcast and press operations FAs are tasked with delivering a service to meet these needs in order to keep their client groups happy.

But why does the organizing committee care if the media are happy? Any large sports event is an extraordinarily expensive thing to hold. The investment for the host nation's government is enormous and the potential to recoup those outlays are really very limited. Most organizing committees only aim to break even, and the vast majority make substantial losses. So, with an almost inevitable short-term loss, the only thing that an organizing committee and host nation can aim for is to gain a long-term benefit.

This long-term benefit can only come from the improvement in the host nation's international standing and image. The media are used, whether they realize it or not, to show the world the positives (or negatives if the organizing committee does a poor job) of the host nation. The organizing committee aims to keep the attending media happy so that the reportage is positive and the world is given an impression of the host nation as being a pleasant, well-organized, and generally nice place to visit. If this is achieved, then the event's consumers from around the world will want to visit, invest in, and have a positive outlook about the host nation, which makes the cost of holding the event worthwhile, even if the benefits are difficult to quantify.

The most obvious example of a country using sports events to increase its world standing is Qatar. With the awarding of the 2006 Asian Games, Qatar began its journey to sporting relevance via the hosting of international sports events. In addition to the 2006 Asian Games, Qatar has already won bids to hold/or has hosted the 2011 Asian Cup (football), 2011 Pan Arab Games, and the jewel in the crown, the 2022 FIFA World Cup. Qatar won this bid despite being widely seen as being an unsuitable location for such an event from the perspective of climate, culture, and population density and distribution (Kelso, 2011), some of the factors that saw its bid for the 2016 Olympic Games fail to make the shortlist (BBC Sport, 2008). Qatar's big-money strategy to attract large sports events and the subsequent international attention is the perfect illustration of why organizing committees invest so much in promoting positive media coverage of an event.

On the other hand, the 2010 Delhi CWG shows how poor services to the media and other stakeholders can lead to a negative reflection of the host country. Despite being a global technology powerhouse, problems around the delivery of technology and results systems during the 2010 Delhi CWG cast doubt on the country's hard-won reputation as an emerging power in information technology. A refusal to admit any shortcomings in the event, and a complete disregard for journalists' reasonable requests for statements about the issues of the day, meant the organizing committee officials provided fuel for the fire for allegations of corruption and mismanagement. Unfinished and poorly built stadia and facilities compounded the perception of India being a nation still with a long way to go if it is to be a major player in the world economy. This storyline was further driven by the absence of spectators due to high ticket prices relative to people's incomes, filthy conditions for athletes attending the event, and the near impossibility of finding out what was going on in the sport. This negative reporting and the aftermath of various post-event corruption inquiries in all likelihood means that India will struggle to win a bid for any future major event.

So, with media satisfaction being such a serious concern for host nation organizing committees, how is it facilitated? The first thing the media need so they can do their job is work facilities. In a sports venue, the media need to be able to watch, broadcast, access the participants (athletes, coaches, etc.), and transmit their video/images/text to their audience.

In order to be able to watch and broadcast, the media need, among other things: tribunes, studios, and designated viewpoints (photo positions, broadcast positions). A great deal of planning has to be done to ensure that media are given the best opportunity to deliver quality coverage from event venues, particularly when it comes to the location of photo and broadcast positions. People working within the organizing committee must have a great deal of relevant experience to ensure that these basic aspects of media/broadcast facilities are sufficient.

The media are provided with work areas, which are important; but more important, the media need to have reliable connections to their home bases. The internet is obviously the main vehicle for this connection, so the media require stable, fast, and secure internet access. The cost of internet is a major bone of contention within media circles, as at Olympic Games the internet is a very expensive rate-card item, whereas at the recent FIFA World Cup in South Africa, for example, wireless internet was free for all of the media. With media organizations all over the world currently struggling to survive, exorbitant internet fees may soon be a thing of the past as organizing committees receive serious negative feedback about imposing these charges.

In terms of the production of content – which is after all the whole purpose of the activity – access to the athletes is certainly the most important requirement of the media. Journalists need to speak to the athletes as soon as they leave the field of play, and given the limited opportunities that athletes and media have to interact, good venue design and post-event sequence[1] processes implemented by organizing committees lead to the most being made of these opportunities. Good mixed-zone design, press conference facilities, and logical timings are crucial to facilitating the process.

At most large sports events, organizing committees make a news service operation available to all accredited media. In conjunction with the results service, this internal news agency provides the ingredients that the media need to do their job. The majority of the media spend most of their time chasing their own nation's athletes, and they can only cover so many events in a day. In the case of the Olympic Games, the ONS provides balanced, unbiased, and uncritical coverage of the whole event, allowing a journalist to produce reportage on events that he/she was unable to attend. If a news service is well run, a journalist could potentially cover an entire event without ever setting foot in a sports venue.[2] News services provide quotes, statistics, news, analysis, and schedule information, and serve as a conduit for the organizing committee or IF when they need to communicate directly with the media.

By providing extensive, readily available, and unbiased information about the sport through the news service and results system, organizing committees hope to make the media's reflection on the event generally positive. But media coverage of an event is never completely positive. Organizing committees often try, usually unsuccessfully, to drive agendas in the media by controlling what the news service can and cannot report on. Despite this effort, there are always a set of recurring storylines that find their way into the coverage of an event, no matter how well it is run. For example, the security arrangements of the Games are always at the forefront of media coverage. If event security is visible and well-managed, then the media enjoy pointing to the huge figure that was spent by the host nation; if security is poor and there is a breach, then the media investigate how it was allowed to happen and why the host nation was negligent. This is just one example of a storyline that leaves the organizing committee in a no-win situation; but there are many others that can play out in the same way.

With the internet driving such large contractions in the world's media corporations and also changing the way that consumers access the information, the way large-scale events will be covered in the future is uncertain. The media will always cover the events, but how they do it, and how much money they are willing to spend to do so, will by necessity influence organizing committee media operations. It is entirely possible that the current model, as described above, will not suit the future media paradigm.

By Joel Fitzpatrick, Rugby News Service Project Manager, Infostrada Sports, Rugby World Cup 2011, and Aurelia Ruetsch, Lead Venue Protocol Manager, International Relations – Strategic Programmes Department, LOCOG

Case questions

1   Outline the costs faced by media organizations in attending an event like the Olympic Games and discuss how the organizing committee can encourage favourable coverage by minimizing them.

2   Cite other examples of where media coverage of a major sports event has led to a negative impression of the host nation. Include examples of storylines that led to the negative portrayal of the host nation and the organizing committee.

3   Discuss the role and responsibilities organizing committees have in providing the media with facilities and services to cover the event, and the potential outcomes for the host nation if the services are not seamlessly provided.

CHAPTER QUESTIONS

1   Describe the different forms of media found in a major sports event like the Olympic Games.

2   New, social, and digital media are increasingly utilized by organizing committees and broadcasters of Olympic Games. Thinking about a national sports event that you know, to what extent do, and should, new, social, and digital media be used?

3   Where do the media operate in an Olympic Games and what do they do in these spaces?

4   Why should there be restrictions on who can speak to the media from an organizing committee?

5   What is ONS and why is it important in an Olympic Games setting?

FURTHER READING

If you are interested in media, we recommend the following:

Dayan, D. & Katz, E. (1994) *Media Events: The Live Broadcasting of History*, Cambridge, MA: Harvard University Press.

Hutchins, B. & Rowe, D. (2011) *Sport Beyond Television: The Internet, Digital Media and the Rise of Networked Media Sport*, London: Routledge.

Rowe, D. (2009) Power trip: sport and media. *International Journal of Sport Management and Marketing*, 6: 150–166.

NOTES

1 The post-event sequence determines where the athletes go after competing and in what timeframe. Athletes are usually required to walk through the mixed zone after leaving the field of play. They are not required to stop and speak to the media, but they must follow the post-event sequence.

2 Many media/broadcasters spend the majority of their time in the MPC or IBC. These large complexes are the hub where media can work from 24 hours per day. All the major broadcasters and news agencies/newspapers will also have office space. All media services are centralized at the MPC/IBC.

Chapter 9

Stakeholder relations and protocol

ILLUSTRATIVE CASE: SUCCESSFUL ORGANIZING COMMITTEES SUCCESSFULLY CO-OPT STAKEHOLDERS

Major sports event organizing committees are, by their nature (and lack of time), outsourcing organizations. They typically do not have the in-house expertise or resources and therefore seek other organizations, groups, or individuals (i.e. stakeholders) to assist them or do the work. For example, an OCOG does not have final say on the approval of a field of play (e.g. luge track); that is the purview of the IF. Thus, the OCOG defers such technical decisions to the appropriate IF. Likewise, it does not have the resource capacity to build, by itself, the venues it needs for the sports events to take place. A popular solution to this problem is the creation of Olympic development and/or delivery authorities (such as in the case of London 2012's Olympic Delivery Authority, as well as the London Development Agency), where such partners can include the governments (local, regional, and/or national), the NOC/NPC, construction companies, local tourism boards, as well as the OCOG itself.

Also, to lessen the negative press or impact on OCOG activities, successful OCOGs will co-opt critical (read: often negative) stakeholder groups such as activists and indigenous/aboriginal peoples. For example, SOCOG co-opted Greenpeace into its organization so that it could in effect no longer critique SOCOG. In turn, Vancouver co-opted the four First Nations communities on whose lands the Vancouver 2010 Olympic and Paralympic Games would be hosted. However, Vancouver went a step further: they not only involved them during the planning of the Games, but made them an official partner of the Games by becoming a signee on the MPA (see Government of Canada et al., 2002), which was signed before the bid was even won.

THE THEORY BEHIND STAKEHOLDER RELATIONS AND PROTOCOL

As the above case highlights, the organizing committee needs different individuals, groups, and organizations, broadly termed stakeholders, to assist in and/or undertake certain responsibilities regarding the planning and/or implementation of the event. Being able to co-opt (i.e. bring on board) certain, sometimes "troublesome", stakeholders allows the organizing committee to potentially reduce the risk of a negative impact on its image. All organizations need to deal with a variety of stakeholders; this is the purview of stakeholder management and theory, which we will discuss below. As well, sports event managers have to be cognizant of key protocol issues when they deal with particular stakeholders, such as sport and state/government dignitaries, VIPs, IPPs (international protected persons), and even royalty. These protocol issues can be as simple as knowing how to address a king or prime minister, but also often involve particularly high levels of security and coordination. Yet there is a lack of research regarding protocol. We will examine what does exist in the literature and then examine other stakeholder and protocol issues in the practitioner's section.

Stakeholders and stakeholder management in major sports events

Firms are linked socially and economically – voluntarily or not – with numerous other stakeholders. "The stakeholder view of the corporation recognizes these reciprocal interdependencies, which constitute the stakeholder network of each firm" (Post *et al.*, 2002: 255). We have already presented the key stakeholder groups in past chapters for major sports events (see Chapters 1–2; Figure 2.1).

Freeman (1984) described a stakeholder as any group or person who can impact or who is affected by an organization's actions. More recently, researchers have argued that this definition of a stakeholder is too broad – it, in effect, encompasses all possible constituents. Donaldson and Preston (1995: 85) argued that stakeholders are "persons or groups with legitimate interests in procedural and/or substantive aspects of corporate activity". In turn, Mitchell *et al.* (1997) suggested that groups must possess one or more of the following characteristics to be considered stakeholders: power, legitimacy, and/or urgency. In contrast, Phillips (2003: 135) proposed that "stakeholders are those groups from whom the organization has voluntarily accepted benefits and to whom there arises a moral obligation ... stakeholder status may also be derived from the power to affect the organization and its normative stakeholders". Thus, we see a variety of ways to define what a stakeholder is. Freeman noted that both the types of stakes (equity, economic, influencer) of a constituent and its power source (formal, economic, political) would be important in a stakeholder management process that included the following: determining who surrounds the organization, determining what they want, determining who is more important, determining what needs to be done in order to ensure that the important stakeholders' needs are met. Jones and Wicks (1999: 207) suggested that "the interests of *all* (legitimate) stakeholders have intrinsic value, and no set of interests is assumed to dominate the others", though Phillips (2003) added that the idea of equal value of stakeholders is dependent on fairness, that is, on the obligation owed to each stakeholder based on what it has provided to the organization.

183

Given that organizing committees of major sports events are usually non-profit organizations, it makes sense to take a stakeholder approach to understanding organizing committees and their management, as such organizations need to satisfy multiple stakeholders (not just those holding the purse strings). Thus, we can argue that the ultimate success of a major sports event is determined not by the organizing committee but by its multiple stakeholder groups: by how satisfied they are, by what they perceive as being fair. However, it is not a one-way street. The various stakeholders provide different resources (e.g. financial, human, material, and informational resources) to the organizing committee so that it may undertake its tasks. As well, through their participation in events, stakeholders allow for value co-creation to happen for the organizing committee and themselves (Prebensen, 2010); this is arguably the basic reasoning behind selling event sponsorships (i.e. the benefits that can be accrued to the event as well as the sponsor).

Each stakeholder group has different demands, needs, wants, and interests (see Parent, 2008). For example, governments want a return on their investment, to increase the nation's visibility internationally, and to build national pride. The community wants to have its say in the event, they want it to be accessible, and they are concerned about the quality of the event as it can reflect back on them. Sponsors want a return on their investment. The media want the tools to be available to them and work effectively so that they can do their job (e.g. the transportation system should be functioning properly, as should the computers and internet). The sport organizations are concerned with their sport's technical aspects, the field of play. They also want a piece of the legacy, especially the more local sport organizations. Finally, the delegations want as many of their own as possible to participate in the event, and for the event's services (transportation, accommodations, etc.) to be of quality. There are nine general groups of issues with which a major sports event organizing committee has to deal: financial; human resources; infrastructure, operations, and logistics; legacy; media and visibility; planning and organizing; politics; relationships, interdependencies, and participation; and sport (cf. Parent, 2008). On a more abstract level, we can also talk of stakeholder interests (Reichart, 2003). Stakeholder interests can take the form of affiliative, informational, material, political, and symbolic interests. Table 9.1 provides definitions for these different issues as well as the five stakeholder interests.

Figure 2.1 illustrates how the organizing committee is placed at the centre of the stakeholder hub-and-spoke model. This illustration allows us to highlight the importance of the organizing committee–stakeholder relationship. Such relationships have to be managed, and each has particularities (e.g. based on the different needs, wants, and interests as noted in the preceding paragraph). However, for any given issue (e.g. the choice of a potential venue during the bid phase, and the planning of that venue once the Games are obtained), different stakeholders may be involved and each may need to be managed individually. We can place these stakeholders on a continuum from passively engaged in the issue to actively engaged in the issue. Ponsford and Williams (2010) suggested that as one moves towards more actively engaged stakeholders, there are increasing needs for collaboration between the organizing committee and the stakeholder. Based on their study of the Cypress Mountain venue for the 2010 Olympic Winter Games, they argued that passive stakeholders' main desire is to obtain information about the planning, construction, and operation of the venue, whereas active stakeholders want more comprehensive engagement within the

Table 9.1 Major sports events stakeholder management issues and interests

Stakeholder management issue	Definition
Financial	Refers to obtaining (through grants, sponsorships, ticket sales, merchandising, licensing, and/or other) financial resources and then managing them. Involves both creating the budget and managing/controlling it.
Human resources	Refers to HRM procedures (job descriptions, task analyses, selection, hiring, training) for Games paid staff, secondees, contractors, and volunteers. Also includes leadership, motivation, and team-building aspects.
Infrastructure, operations, and logistics	Refers to the government (city facilities, traffic, public transportation, law enforcement, etc.) and Games (games venues and facilities, technology, medical, security, accommodations, games transportation, accreditation, etc.) activities and services, as well as tourism, travel, and weather issues.
Legacy	Refers to tangible and intangible, positive and negative legacies, such as new facilities, new skills learned, know-how, networks created, positive/negative image/reputation, and trade opportunities.
Media and visibility	Refers to media coverage, broadcasting rights, image and reputation building, and garnering public/corporate support.
Planning and organizing	Refers to planning, decision-making, structure, and other management activities. It also includes determining the organizing committee team's structure, dealing with deadlines, and determining effectiveness and efficiency.
Politics	Refers to the political power plays, power issues, lobbying, ego management, government support, intercity competition, and protocol aspects.
Relationships, interdependencies, and participation	Refers to building and maintaining relationships, negotiating with stakeholders, coordination and communication issues within the organizing committee, divisional and hierarchical linkages, interdependence issues between stakeholders and the organizing committee, accountability, authority, stakeholder participation in decision-making, stakeholder involvement and recognition, ticket availability for stakeholders, fun, and excitement.
Sport	Refers to the technical aspects of the sport competitions, the field of play, the officials/referees, the numbers of competitors, qualification standards, test events, practices, water and other resources for the field of play.
Stakeholder interest	
Affiliative	Refers to the need for belonging to a group, the relationships within and between stakeholder groups.
Informational	Refers to obtaining knowledge, information, and other data that help stakeholders meet their needs and/or monitor others such as the organizing committee.
Material	Refers to the gain/loss of tangible (e.g. financial) benefits and access to resources.
Political	Refers to the internal and external distribution of power and influence (whether political or other). Includes legal and jurisdictional power issues.
Symbolic	Refers to the image, reputation, and other symbols that emerge over time and space for a given organizing committee or stakeholder.

Source: Based on Parent, 2008; Reichart, 2003.

planning, construction, and operation monitoring activities. Ponsford and Williams suggested different strategies for engaging passive and active stakeholders:

- Passive stakeholders: open forums, comment-card systems, displays in public spaces, and organizing committee-led presentations.
- Active stakeholders: public meetings, informal individual stakeholder meetings, open-door (communication) policy, formal liaison committee including both the organizing committee and interested stakeholders, stakeholder involvement in environmental assessments, and venue-owner-led venue walkabouts.

While some of these strategies are specific to venues, the need to use different strategies for different kinds of stakeholders based on the recognition of what their needs are remains key. This differing stakeholder management based on stakeholders' differing needs and wants refers to stakeholder heterogeneity and homogeneity. Just as each individual is different, each organization or group within a given stakeholder group can be different. This difference within a particular stakeholder group is called heterogeneity (the opposite being stakeholder homogeneity). This holds true for major sports event (Parent, 2008). For example, there are differences between ticket buyers – more specifically, between those who are local residents and those who are visitors to the host region. Those individuals who travel specifically to see a sports event usually have a higher level of identification with the "sport subculture" and fan motivation (Snelgrove et al., 2008). We could derive from this finding that organizing committees should tailor their communications (e.g. advertisements) differently when targeting the local residents (e.g. more about the potential legacy of the event) versus the visitors (e.g. focus on the sports presented).

Stakeholder homogeneity/heterogeneity depends on the issues that an organizing committee has to deal with regarding specific stakeholders, as well as the stakeholders' interests. Table 9.2 provides an example of within- and between-stakeholder group heterogeneity. To decrease the degree of heterogeneity within a stakeholder group, a manager could decide to split the organizations, not based on their respective roles (e.g. government, media, sponsor, etc.), but by the benefits the organization wishes to accrue (Wolfe and Putler, 2002). This makes sense for the organizing committee to a certain degree, if one holds to the five stakeholder interests presented above; however, given the number of stakeholders and the number of possible benefits (legacy itself is a broad concept and still under study; see Chapter 15), this may turn out to be more difficult to do for major sporting events than other types of sport organizations. Still, this is an avenue that would require future study.

Part of finding out who the stakeholders are and what they want is determining which stakeholders are more important in order to ensure that their demands and needs are met; this refers to determining stakeholders' relative salience levels. There are many ways to do this, such as those that are primary (essential for survival) versus secondary (not essential; Clarkson, 1995); those that have one or more of power, legitimacy, and urgency (Mitchell et al., 1997); or those that are resource-based, industry structure-based, and socio-political arena-based (Post et al., 2002). Each way of determining stakeholder salience has its merits and its flaws. The key here is to draw-up your list of stakeholders and determine who you see as more important, and why. The more important a stakeholder, the more attention,

Table 9.2 Example of within- and between-stakeholder group heterogeneity

Issue category	Governments				Community			Sport organizations			Media		
	National	Regional	Local	Sponsor	Residents	Aboriginal community	Other community organizations	International	National/regional	Delegations	Broadcaster	Press	Radio
Financial	X	X	X	X	X	X	X	X	X	X	X	X	X
Human resources													
Infrastructure, operations, and logistics								X	X	X	X	X	
Legacy		X	X		X	X	X		X				
Media and visibility	X	X	X	X			X	X	X		X	X	
Planning and organizing													
Politics	X	X						X	X				
Relationships, interdependence, and participation	X		X	X	X	X	X	X	X	X	X		
Sport					X			X	X	X	X		
Interests													
Affiliative				X	X	X	X						
Informational	X	X	X	X	X	X	X	X	X	X	X	X	X
Material	X	X	X	X	X	X	X	X	X	X	X	X	X
Political	X	X	X					X					
Symbolic	X	X	X	X	X	X	X	X	X		X	X	X

Source: Based on Parent (2008).

effort, and resources are likely to be dedicated to this stakeholder. Still, there is danger in disregarding certain groups; activists are often put on the "non-stakeholder" list as they are deemed less important than others. However, disregarding such stakeholders can lead to negative effects such as losing a bid in the case of Toronto's efforts to win the 2000 and 2008 Olympic Games (cf. Lenskyj, 1996, 2000).

The principles of stakeholder theory (whether explicitly stated or not) are increasingly being used to study major sports events, mainly the Olympic Games. Some examples worth reading include the works by Chappelet and colleagues (e.g. Chappelet and Kübler-Mabbott, 2008; Chappelet, 2009; Chappelet, 2011) and Ferrand and colleagues (e.g. Ferrand and Chanavat, 2006; Ferrand and McCarthy, 2008; Ferrand and Stotlar, 2010; Ferrand and Camps I Povill, 2009; Ferrand and Robin, 2009). These studies allow us to understand the various stakeholders within the Olympic Movement. However, we also learn, for example, that we can optimize the interaction between stakeholder groups using relationship marketing, especially when examining the tourism issue (Ferrand and Chanavat, 2006; Ferrand and Robin, 2009), and building stakeholder relationships and networks helps in marketing and branding activities. Ferrand and Stotlar (2010) also correctly pointed out that, when speaking of organizing committees and stakeholders, we should not only examine the dyadic organizing committee–stakeholder relationship, but the broader stakeholder network, which is critical for the success of a major sports event. Studies are also delving deeper into stakeholders' perceptions about different Olympic Games aspects and about other stakeholders. For example, Walker *et al.* (2010) found that 2008 Beijing Olympic Games attendees had positive perceptions about the IOC's CSR efforts when these efforts were perceived to be driven by values and/or stakeholder motives. Consumers had a negative reaction to CSR efforts perceived to be strategically driven. We can deduce from this that the perceived type of motive (e.g. for themselves or for the greater good) behind rights holding sport organizations' and their organizing committees' efforts impacts these organizations' relationships with their stakeholders.

In addition, researchers are starting to examine other Olympic stakeholders. For example, Parent *et al.* (2011) examined the 2010 Olympic Winter Games host governments' coordination issues within and between themselves, as well as strategies used to mitigate them. They found five context-based issues and 11 other types of issues:

- Context based issues: time, geography, funding, other resources, and the political situation of the host region or country.
- Other issues: planning, operational, structure, accountability and authority, power, legal, activation and leveraging, knowledge management, legal, turnover, relationships, and social issues.

To mitigate these issues, Parent *et al.* (2011) suggested the following eight strategies: flexibility, formalized agreements, strategic planning, structural frameworks, communication processes, decision-making frames, engagement, and HRM procedures/principles. Next, VanWynsberghe *et al.* (2011) examined community capacity building at the 2010 Olympic Winter Games. They suggested that binding commitments, precise timing, "and clear consequences for mega-event organizers are necessary for a community-based coalition to build capacity" (p. 370). They further suggested a model of community capacity building that involves three levels – individual, organization, and community – and four dimensions – resources, activities, outcomes, and context.

What an organizing committee is suggested to do is (informally) create a social contract, a social licence to operate, between itself and its stakeholders; by gaining the trust of the stakeholders and being seen as a legitimate organization, one willing to listen to its constituents, the organizing committee is more likely to have positive relationships with its stakeholders (Ponsford and Williams, 2010). Also, these relationships are more likely to be mutually beneficial (e.g. through the exchange of information, material resources, human resources, etc.).

Still, much important work remains to be conducted regarding major sports event organizing committees and their stakeholders. One key avenue of future research is to further examine the broader stakeholder network instead of simply the dyadic organizing committee–stakeholder relationship (cf. Rowley, 1997). Another is to continue to expand our study of the various major sports event stakeholders beyond the Olympic Games setting.

Protocol

A quick literature database search on protocol results in thousands of articles on protocol, but protocol which is associated with technology, computer, wireless, etc., models, algorithms, and processes. This is not what the sport event manager generally understands as protocol. Protocol in our context can be defined as the set of (usually unwritten) rules, procedures, and guidelines dictating proper/generally accepted behaviours (i.e. norms) for dealing with state/diplomatic affairs and individuals for all matters associated with the major sports event. Elaborate protocol is probably best associated with the world's royal families (e.g. royal weddings, coronations, royal funerals). Protocol is therefore often related to kingship, power, and authority (Chatty, 2009).

As there are kings, queens, and other heads of state and government who attend sports events, protocol becomes an important function as it is about tradition, (hopefully mutual) respect, and consideration, and touches on relationships, appearance, and processes (Forni, 2003; Smolinski, 2008; Van der Wagen and Carlos, 2005). In major sports events, we see protocol in how delegations and VIPs are treated when they arrive in the host region, how they are formally welcomed, how they are treated during ceremonies (e.g. opening, closing, victory ceremonies), how VIPs are addressed, who gets to speak, who speaks first, what can be said to declare a Games open, who sits where and besides whom, which flags are to be used/displayed, and how to display them. If protocol is not followed, mayhem or even international incidents can occur. Think of a government (e.g. the House of Commons in the UK, the National Assembly in France, or Congress in the United States); imagine if people didn't wait their turn to speak or know what the protocol was for voting. This could lead to disorder, confusion, pandemonium, and even a breaking up of the government. That is the importance of protocol.

While there may not (yet) be studies specifically examining protocol in major sports events, some studies in the broader management literature can be associated to protocol and help us understand a little more about this area. For example, international executives must act like diplomats in today's globalized business world. Barnum (1989) argued that today's executives, like diplomats, should question their own closely held beliefs, values, and stereotype perceptions, as well as be:

> 1. less competitive and more cooperative, 2. more of a win–win strategist, 3. more aware of geopolitical trends, 4. more future-oriented, and 5. more worldly.... They should learn the rules of etiquette and protocol for formal and informal situations on a country-by-country basis as well.
>
> (Barnum, 1989: 59)

An interesting study by Smolinski (2008) offers some hope of research that examines differences between stakeholders or parties, especially regarding protocol – in this case in a European Union negotiation context. What Smolinski noted is differences in parties' perceptions of selected traits, such as attitudes, interests, power, climate, team organization, communication, concern for protocol, flexibility, emotion, and time sensitivity, among negotiating profiles (p. 247). In this study, concern for protocol is noted on a continuum ranging from informal (e.g. quickly switching to addressing people by their first name, often changing agendas, making many exceptions to rules) to formal (e.g. addressing people by their last name and title, strict following of agendas, rules, and procedures). Not surprisingly, there was a difference found between the European countries surveyed regarding concern for protocol: to illustrate, Slovenians, Estonians, and Slovakians were found to be more concerned with formal protocol than other countries. Thus, we see that a sport event manager hosting tens or hundreds of countries during a major sports event has to be highly aware of protocol perceptions by different countries and therefore what procedures (e.g. how to greet visitors) to follow.

Some studies (Mallon, 1984a, 1984b) examine Olympic rituals during the opening ceremonies, which are (technically) part of Olympic protocol (see Chapter 10 on ceremonies). Qing *et al.* (2010) analysed the 2008 Beijing opening ceremonies; they notably focused on the Olympic rituals of the athletes' entrance parade, the IOC and BOCOG presidents' speeches, the Olympic Flag raising, and the lighting of the Olympic Torch. Throughout the media commentators' comments, these authors noted a dominance of cultural and political references associated with these protocol elements.

Still, there is much room for additional protocol studies, such as its impact on and interdependence with other FAs, and the differences in protocol between different types of sports events. We now turn to the practitioner's perspective and what we can learn from the on-the-ground experience regarding stakeholder relations and protocol.

THE PRACTITIONER'S PERSPECTIVE ON STAKEHOLDER RELATIONS AND PROTOCOL

Let's start with the premise that there is often a big group of stakeholders associated with a major sports event. Every single one of them has a vested interest in the event and they have invested one or more of the following: time, money, and resources. Stakeholders view their contributions based on ROI; in other words, they expect something back and they will monitor, mind, and measure that return from day one to the end of the event. They are not necessarily concerned with the collective – they want their needs, wants, and desires to be accommodated, responded to, and met. Each event has its own set of exceptions, and everyone expects and should be heard. The manager faces the difficult decision of who to accommodate when everyone can't have what they want. Sometimes protocol trumps everything – however, decisions made on the ground, on the run, may not always comply with written or unwritten protocol. Often the people who are on the front line – not the person who made the promise – are in the unenviable position of having to mitigate or resolve an issue or situation. This makes it complicated, and sometimes it is better to ask for forgiveness rather than permission in situations where time is of the essence and a decision must be made immediately, using the facts at hand. This would apply to paid staff before the Games commence and to volunteers during the Games. It is an exception rather than a rule; however, it does happen. Suffice it to say that without the stakeholders, the event would not happen. It is in the best interest of everyone to learn how to say no confidently and gracefully with empathy. It may be the one-hundredth "no" for the manager, but it may be the first for the stakeholder, so it must be handled to avoid or minimize repercussions. It is also helpful to know what promises have been made to whom, as much in advance as possible, so that options can be discussed and put in place before a situation occurs. The interpersonal skills required to handle all of the requests, questions, and comments that stakeholders present is nothing short of being a master at one's craft. Not only does the manager have to handle the stakeholders, they also need to substantiate and explain the decisions they made to other managers and executives. It is not uncommon for an edict to be delivered from an executive to "just make it happen". These demands and edicts are usually understood by the BOH; however, from a public perspective, it can be very suspect when, for example, the number of tickets available to the public has been reduced because of promises that have been made to politicos, sponsors, VIPs, etc.

Sometimes the stakeholder investment is a clear strategic alliance. When the 2010 Olympic Winter Games were won for Vancouver, much of the land that the sport events would be held on belonged to First Nations. It was determined that the most effective way to gain permission to use the land was to include First Nations as a partner with significant representation through board-member representation, programming, and a dedicated pavilion. A lot was agreed to that had to be delivered on. It can be frustrating for those who are charged with fulfilment of this delivery because they did not make the deal; however, they need to make the deal happen.

There are other partnerships that are brilliant in their conception and execution because of the public appeal and reach. An example at the same 2010 Olympic Winter Games was the torch run that travelled thousands of kilometres into hundreds of communities across the country. It galvanized the country because thousands of people ran with it; and that created an acceptance of the Games, an emotional investment and a connection to an event often thousands of miles away yet still in "their" country. The collective energy was important for stakeholders like the media, who want that public watching as much and as often as they are inspired to. The torch relay sponsors basked in the positive exposure that connected them in an almost visceral way to millions of ordinary Canadians who are also consumers (current or potential) for their products and services.

Besides having key stakeholders as partners of the event or fostering partnerships in event-related activities such as a torch relay, stakeholder partnerships can be built through constant communication and information sharing, such as through sponsor conferences or dignitary general assemblies and meetings. Sponsor conferences can occur yearly for update purposes and to build/maintain relationships. General assemblies and meetings increase in frequency as the event draws near and typically culminate with a general assembly of the event rights holding organization's members (e.g. the IOC members) immediately before the event, or with daily meetings with the delegation chefs de mission and assistant chefs de mission during the event. At the major conferences (e.g. the general assembly), it is normal to see the protocol FA involved.

Protocol is a mysterious FA for most people, yet a fundamental one for a major sports event. Protocol helps build and maintain relationships with key event dignitaries (both sport and non-sport). Protocol weaves through all aspects of an event: the order of importance; who is permitted access and where they sit; how they will be greeted; who can interact with them; and even sometimes what languages to offer. There is a level of protocol delivered from the time someone in the Olympic Family (the Olympic protocol umbrella term used to describe the people who require and are entitled to protocol assistance – usually those individuals, groups, and organizations who are the rights holders of the event and core partners like the sport federations and government representatives) arrives until they physically leave the city of the event.

There are two types of dignitaries the protocol FA considers: international and domestic. They include heads of state and heads of government and their representatives (i.e. kings, queens, ambassadors, presidents, and prime ministers); politicians from participating countries and the host country/city, including government ministers and officials; the sports world, which includes the presidents of the event owner, IFs, and NSFs. Following the sport event's protocol technical manual established by the event rights holder (e.g. the IOC), the protocol and accreditation FAs allocate a quota to each country and organization, and decisions are made within these organizations and government bodies as to whom they will send. They always want to send more, and sometimes they just show up with extra people, hoping they can persuade someone in accreditation or protocol to admit these individuals to the venues. There are aides that accompany many of the accredited dignitaries. There is also an assistant assigned to each dignitary that is provided by the organizing committee. This person will have local knowledge and work in tandem with the personal aide of the dignitary.

Each dignitary has a preferred form of address that has been submitted in advance of the event. Some examples include: the crown prince of Norway would be addressed generally as Your Royal Highness; Princess Anne, daughter of Queen Elizabeth II of England, is usually referred to as the Princess Royal; the minister for sport of the same country would generally be addressed as Excellency, or Minister; and a first name alone would be used only if there was permission from the person to be familiar.

At a sports event, the president of the rights holding organization (e.g. the IPC for the Paralympic Games) is the most important person attending, and takes priority over a political head of state. For example, for the Olympic Games, the IOC president is more important than the president of France. This is the protocol; and although there are copious amounts of information communicated to educate and remind politicians of this protocol, they still expect to be treated with priority and exception over anyone else. It is not uncommon to watch the entourage of a politician enter an event and attempt to have everyone in the party accommodated despite the presence of a sport dignitary that would take precedence. It is the single most challenging part of the protocol manager's job on-site at an event. It is important to understand and accept that the IOC and IFs trump global, national, and local politics. The Vancouver 2010 Games were enmeshed and beholden to every level of government in their province and country. When it came to "favour" and preferential seating and services at the Games, the sports organizations took precedence in all protocol situations to the seeming disbelief of Canadian politicians. From venue tours to lounge and seating preference, pecking order was sport first, politicos second.

Once a dignitary enters an event venue, they are greeted by a member of the event's protocol team. With few exceptions, their aides are "parked" in a workforce or parking lot area and are contacted when needed by mobile, text, or from the desk of the dignitaries' lounge, of which there is one in each venue. There is usually not enough space to seat everyone.

There are also levels of access to each venue and event for dignitaries. Some people have accreditation to attend all events, including PEA (prime event access) competitions, while others have restrictions that allow them to see only non-PEA competitions. For these guests there is disappointment, especially if they have been in the venue for the previous competition and now have to leave because the next competition is designated as PEA. All of these decisions about access are determined long before the visitor arrives, and that information has been communicated to each and every accredited guest and can be found on their accreditation card. Still, this seems not to prevent them from attempting to come into a venue without the proper accreditation and expect to be admitted. Again, it is the responsibility of the venue protocol manager to make the decision about whether or not they will accommodate, in discussion with the VMT and security.

The protocol manager must establish relationships with all of the other FAs in a venue so that they can get things done in a timely manner and appear to be solving problems and handling requests in a seamless fashion. For example, the media always has seats for journalists. Dignitary seating is often found in proximity to media seating; this means the protocol manager can negotiate with the press operations manager for the use of these seats if there is a spirit of cooperation between the two FAs. The VMT and security can assist with permissions to admit guests, and with EVS can change the configuration of a seating area within the dignitary section of the venue. F&B can accommodate emergency or special requests if the relationship is there with protocol. Anti-doping and protocol work together closely when protocol is in charge of language services (for anti-doping procedures). Transportation requests from the accredited guests can be handled efficiently and effectively if there is a transportation volunteer in the protocol area. There are typically television screens and computer terminals in every dignitary lounge, so with a friend in technology problems can be fixed quickly by a technician. EVS and protocol need constant communication so that the transition over the invisible line between the public and accredited guests can be crossed effortlessly for the accredited guests. Sport production can assist in minimizing drama before a ceremony with the athletes in a venue if someone does not show up or there is a last-minute substitute – the wrangling of these people is the job of the protocol manager regardless of the fact that sport production is in charge of the event. Flags are an important staple of these ceremonies; when they are correct, no one notices, but if there is a problem, protocol needs direct contact with that FA to correct the situation. Cooperation, compromise, and creative problem-solving happens as a result of communication with all other FAs. Again, the importance of confident, effective, skilful communication from the protocol manager cannot be overstated.

CHAPTER SUMMARY

In this chapter we examined stakeholder relations and protocol. We started by examining stakeholders and stakeholder management within major sports events. The stakeholder groups noted include: the internal organizing committee members, and the external governments, sponsors, community, media, sport federations, delegations, and other stakeholders. We explored different issues that organizing committees must manage when dealing with specific stakeholder groups. We also talked about stakeholder interests, as well as the implications of stakeholder heterogeneity. Depending on the type of stakeholder engagement (passive or active) for a given issue, we presented possible communication strategies for each engagement type. We then explored some of the existing research using stakeholder theory within sports events. Regarding protocol, from a theoretical perspective we highlighted the extreme paucity of research in this area. We defined protocol and explored some research in the broader management literature, which could be associated with the study of protocol in events.

From a practitioner's perspective, we looked at the responsibility to stakeholders once an event commences. The role of protocol as it relates to accredited guests was explored. We further defined some of the important responsibilities of the protocol manager and the competencies that manager needs. We examined the interdependence of protocol with the other FAs in the venue in relation to satisfying the demands of protocol and helping to run the event effectively within that venue for all involved.

EXPERT CASE: HOW TOURISM SET THE BAR FOR PARTNERSHIPS FOR THE 2010 OLYMPIC WINTER GAMES

Because Tourism Vancouver launched the bid to bring the 2010 Olympic and Paralympic Winter Games to Vancouver and Whistler, the organization knew precisely what it was seeking to accomplish from hosting this mega-event.

Not only would the Games bring unprecedented media coverage and international attention to the city, they would also build business for the tourism industry, leave a legacy of much-needed infrastructure, generate significant investment in various tourism sectors, and spawn innovative marketing and partnership opportunities. In other words, the Olympics gave tourism a unique opportunity to do things differently, even unconventionally, with regard to marketing.

As the city's destination marketing organization (DMO), Tourism Vancouver struck up an early relationship with VANOC, offering to handle all spectator accommodation for the

Games, a critical area other host cities have often ignored. Along with Tourism Whistler, Tourism Vancouver presented a memorandum of understanding (MOU) to VANOC, outlining respective roles and responsibilities. However, the MOU was ultimately replaced with that of a third-party that emerged as part of the discussions – Tourism British Columbia. At first, that seemed counter to our best interests.

It was clear that partners are often confused as competitors, and we needed to sort out operating principles if we were to galvanize the tourism industry's limited resources into a formidable force for good. Through a series of subsequent meetings and even a few missteps, the four lead DMOs (Tourism Vancouver, Tourism Whistler, Tourism British Columbia, Canadian Tourism Commission) recognized the need to collaborate rather than compete with each other to realize the full benefits of hosting the Games for key stakeholders and constituents.

Consequently, the DMOs formed the 2010 Tourism Consortium, with oversight vested in a "steering committee". In reference to this consortium, the IOC said they'd never experienced the cohesion of various tourism agencies in full alignment. Given the potential for division, the success of this consortium demanded close adherence to core guiding principles:

- The steering committee members will work together to ensure collaboration and coordination, harnessing the collective resources to achieve more together than by acting individually.
- Steering committee members will be transparent with each other, communicating on a regular basis in an atmosphere of trust and cooperation, informing each other as issues arise, and assuming good intentions of each other.
- Steering committee members will strive to achieve consensus in decision-making, understanding that individual organizations may need to make compromises for the needs of the target customers/audiences. Once a decision has been made, all steering committee members will support it.
- When working on consortium initiatives, steering committee members (or working group members) who are dealing with these groups understand that they are representing the interests of the consortium, not just an individual organization.
- Within this plan and through all Olympic-related activities, organizational strengths are recognized in establishing leadership roles with some organizations (with fewer resources) playing a role as part of the team rather than leading.
- The strengths of each organization will be respected and leveraged, with each taking a leadership role within their core competencies and geographic jurisdictions. All partners should be considered equally important. Steering committee members will agree in advance on who is taking the lead on activities.
- The steering committee and working group members will follow a communications protocol (CP) that will respect the existing CP of each organization within their jurisdictions and to their existing stakeholders and constituents.
- Issues such as communications to stakeholders, announcements and press releases, official spokespeople, how information will flow among organizations involved in the steering committee and among organizations not involved in the steering committee will be included in this protocol.

These principles led to a formal MOU between the Tourism Consortium and VANOC which provided details on the role of the collective DMOs in the execution of Olympic-related tourism initiatives such as visitor experience, marketing, and media relations. Furthermore, it allowed the DMOs to act with one voice and with clear purpose in their collaborative dealings with VANOC.

A key learning from past events (i.e. the 2009 World Police & Fire Games, the 2006 World Junior Hockey Championships, and the 1994 CWG) was that the Vancouver and surrounding communities already had a strong history of community involvement/volunteering, and lots of people wanted to volunteer for events to pad their résumés. History showed us that we simply had to tap into the various communities (e.g. sports teams for sport-specific volunteers). We drew from a large pool of people that were offering their volunteer efforts. We also learned:

- to build the volunteer base from enthusiasm/the participant perspective, and tap into the obvious sources as they are your stakeholders. These obvious sources included their families and their teams and sports (e.g. hockey) community – and involvement was not just for tickets, but to get them to volunteer;
- oftentimes, it takes a personal ask to get the ball rolling; and
- you can tap into community leaders through the network. For example, Vancouver community leader Jim Pattison was asked in the mid-1980s to take over the presidency of Expo '86; this was the catalyst that spun growth for the event.

Tourism is one of the most competitive industries in the world – every part of a country says they are in the tourism business. The information we share might be seen by some as giving away competitive information, but we feel it will serve us well, as did the information we received from past editions of the Olympic Winter Games. We were able to learn a lot from our colleagues in Salt Lake City and Torino; they were accommodating and provided important information. We went there or brought them here to learn from them. One thing we learned in Salt Lake and Park City was that 90 per cent of the Games experience is what happens on the streets. It's not about the sport competition itself, it's not about the Games themselves. A person coming to the Games knows what they are going to get – so most of their "experience" revolves around what happens outside the event – how people live, where to eat, the culture, etc. This informed a lot of what we did during the Games themselves – we had every staff member take shifts to interact with people on the streets – and informed how we set up our visitor information services. In Torino, we learned a lot about the media and how they viewed a Games and what their *modus operandi* was: during the Games period was not the time to sell them on the destination. There was not much action on selling the destination, so Torino put in a ton of things to assist the media. We learned about being prepared and ready for the requests and about having enough people to service the media at our information booths (such as in the MPC). Most people at such an event, including media and sponsors, are there for specific purposes, whereas for the World Police & Fire Games or for hockey championships, there is a lot of free time and you need to be sure you give them a range of options.

The 2010 Tourism Consortium was considered to be a first vis-à-vis the Olympic Games and was applauded by Gilbert Felli, the IOC's executive director for the Games, who stated: "BC and Canada have taken full advantage of the learning from other Olympic and Paralympic Games to vigorously pursue tourism growth." We have shared our learnings and successes with the 2012 London Olympic Games, we are in contact with Sochi and Rio for the 2014 and 2016 Winter and Summer Olympic Games, and we have shared information with the 2015 Toronto Pan American Games. Basically, we are sharing information with anyone asking for information on what we did or advice on how to grow partnerships or develop strategies to help them succeed, which is not common in the industry – it is pretty unique.

A legacy of the Tourism Consortium has been enhanced cooperation and planning and strategic sharing of the various agencies in the years immediately following the Olympic Games. The strongest asset has been that of earned and built up "trust", and a sense that, together, we are more.

By Rick Antonson, President and CEO of Tourism Vancouver & Walt Judas, Vice-President, Marketing Communications & Member Services, Tourism Vancouver

Case questions

1   What contributed to the Tourism Consortium's success?

2   What did the Tourism Consortium learn from past events?

3   Thinking about the tourism organization in your region, what could that tourism organization learn from the Vancouver 2010 Games Tourism Consortium if it were to host a major sports event in your region?

CHAPTER QUESTIONS

1   Describe the major sport event stakeholders, noting also their heterogeneity.

2   What is sport event protocol? Give some examples.

3   Describe a major sports event's group of dignitaries (e.g. who they are, who is more important, what services are offered to them).

4   If you were to design a study on protocol in major sports events, what would be the research question, theoretical framework, and methodology?

5   What, if any, effect do stakeholders have on the protocol manager's job?

FURTHER READING

For more information on stakeholder management and protocol in major sports events, we suggest the following:

Muller, N. (1995) From Athens (1896) to Amsterdam (1928): definitions of ceremonies protocol in accordance with Pierre de Coubertin's ideal. In International Olympic Committee (ed.) *Olympic Ceremonies: Historical Continuity and Cultural Exchange*, Lausanne: International Olympic Committee.

Parent, M. M. & Deephouse, D. L. (2007) A case study of stakeholder identification and prioritization by managers. *Journal of Business Ethics*, 75, 1–23.

Xing, X., Church, A. G., O'Reilly, N., Pegoraro, A., Nadeau, J., Schweinbenz, A., Heslop, L., & Séguin, B. (2008) Olympic Games host and bid city marketing: exploring issue management in the relationships among event stakeholder groups. *International Journal of Sports Marketing & Sponsorship*, 9, 321–335.

Chapter 10

Ceremonies

OBJECTIVES

- To understand the different types of ceremonies which can be found in major sports events
- To understand the symbolism, rituals, and myths associated with ceremonies
- To consider the logistical and protocol issues surrounding major sports event ceremonies

ILLUSTRATIVE CASE: THE 2010 CWG OPENING CEREMONIES

Before the opening ceremonies of the 2010 Delhi CWG in India, the newspapers around the world were filled with negative stories about the organizational capability and readiness of the organizing committee. Before the Games, there were issues with leaking roofs, a collapsed bridge, and faeces in the athletes' village. There were even rumours that delegations would pull out. Some athletes did choose not to attend the Games; but in the end, all delegations went. It seemed so bad that the president of India got personally involved; and with the president of the CGF, Mr Michael Fennel, they pooled their collective resources and political weight to get India "ready" for the opening ceremonies. By the opening ceremonies, all seemed somewhat in place, at least from a building perspective.

The opening ceremonies were found to be highly colourful and quite beautiful, displaying the culture of India in all its splendour. When he spoke, the organizing committee president was booed by the crowd because of seemingly giving India a bad name – there were sponsorship and bribing/favouritism allegations linked to him and key members of his staff. But the president of India was wildly cheered for her efforts when she took to the podium.

During the closing ceremonies, the crowd (composed of residents, dignitaries, the media, and delegations) were in a good mood. They often cheered. There was a sense that this was just the beginning for India. The highly popular Games mascot, Shera the Tiger, was even given an emotional farewell as the mascot toured the stadium during the closing ceremonies.

THE THEORY BEHIND CEREMONIES

As Willi Daume, president of the 1972 Munich Olympic Games, noted, "Not much is actually happening: the teams enter, the Games are declared open according to prescribed ceremony. That's about it. And yet it creates a worldwide effect, enthusiasm and emotion. This fascination is hard to explain" (as quoted by Alkemeyer and Richartz, 1993: 79). We will first examine the different types of ceremonies in major sports events, followed by further analysis of symbolism, rituals, and myths, which can help us understand the different ceremonies in major sports events. We will end this section with other research conducted related to Olympic Games ceremonies.

Types of ceremonies

In the Olympic Games, we find different types of ceremonies: opening and closing ceremonies, medal and flower ceremonies (victory ceremonies), welcoming and flag-raising ceremonies in the athletes' villages for new delegations, and other rituals such as the Olympic Flame (and its torch and torch relay), the post-field-of-play period for the athletes (when they go through anti-doping, the mixed zone, and press conferences) or the welcoming of VIPs.

When international delegations arrive at the athletes' village, there is typically a welcoming ceremony conducted with the "mayor" of the village – often a well-known celebrity and/or past athlete. The delegation's flag is raised, the national anthem heard, and there is an exchange of gifts between the delegation and host (mayor).

The opening ceremonies are the formal ceremonies for the major sports event, and they follow a general script such as the following for the Olympic Games (International Olympic Committee, 2009e):

■ welcoming the head of the event (e.g. the President of the IPC for the Paralympic Games) and the head of state of the host country;
■ raising the host country flag and singing the national anthem;
■ welcoming the athletes through the parade of nations;
■ for the Olympic Games: acknowledging the Games' peaceful intent through a symbolic release of doves;
■ speeches by the organizing committee president and head of the event;
■ official opening of the Games by the head of state of the host country;
■ entrance of the Games flag, raising of the flag, and playing of the Games anthem;
■ athletes' and officials' oaths;
■ entertainment for the spectators;
■ lighting of the Games flame.

In contrast, the closing ceremonies are more of a celebration, a party for the athletes; however, there are a few rituals to follow throughout the course of the evening's entertainment (International Olympic Committee, 2009e):

■ welcoming of the head of the event (e.g. the president of the CGF for the CWG) and of the head of state of the host country;

- raising of the host country flag and singing of the national anthem;
- entrance of the participating nations' flags, followed often by the athletes coming in altogether;
- the final victory/medals ceremony for events completed on that day (if any);
- for the Olympic Games: recognition of newly elected athletes to the athletes commission and recognition of the Games volunteers' efforts;
- for the Olympic Games: playing the Greek anthem;
- lowering the Games flag and handing it over to the next host city/country;
- next host city/country showcase;
- speeches by the organizing committee president and head of the event;
- extinguishing of the Games flame;
- throughout: entertainment for the spectators.

For many sports at the Olympic Games, athletes will receive their medals during an evening ceremony called a victory or medals ceremony, complete with entertainment. The victory/medals ceremony has the following ritual (International Olympic Committee, 2009e):

- introduction of the medal and/or flower presenters;
- introduction of the medallists;
- presentations of the medals and/or flowers to the medallists;
- raising the national flags and playing the gold medallist's national anthem.

If the major sports event has evening victory ceremonies, the athletes will still participate in a ceremony called the flowers ceremony, following their event, where the medallists mount the podium and receive a bouquet of flowers. The Olympic Games' victory/medal ceremonies have paved the way for other major sports events' victory/medals ceremonies, especially in regards to the place and symbolism of the medal podium, the position of the athletes on the podium, and of the dignitaries below the podium giving the medallists their prize (Barney, 1998). What we know today as the victory podium evolved during the early years of the Olympics until the 1932 Olympic Games in Lake Placid (winter) and Los Angeles (summer); interestingly, the protocol during the victory ceremonies, including the flag and anthem, actually came from the First British Empire Games (now called the CWG) in Hamilton (Canada) in 1930 (Barney, 1998).

Symbolism, rituals, and myths

Baron Pierre de Coubertin wanted ceremonies associated with the Olympic Games so as to distinguish them from "mere" world championships; he wanted them to focus on "aesthetics and ritual context of the festival", to have splendour and be powerfully symbolic, as well as provide the Olympic Games with solemnity; they were to be a work of art (Alkemeyer and Richartz, 1993: 79). Olympic ceremonies are full of rituals. A ritual can be defined as "a form of social action in which a group's values and identity are publicly demonstrated or enacted in a stylized manner, within the context of a specific occasion or event" (Islam and Zyphur, 2009: 116).

Alkemeyer and Richartz noted (1993: 80, emphasis in original):

> The central problem of human life is to come to terms with love, power and death, as *ritual* and *myth* (the central points of presentative symbol organization) demonstrate clearly. *Ritual and myth* offer a denouement of this meeting place of individual identities, while at the same time imposing collectively valid standards – but not in the form of instruction. Whereas *myth* informs by visual narration, *ritual* touches the participant both physically and mentally. Included in its gestures are complex, enduring intrinsic values that illustrate and explain.

By the time of the 1988 Seoul Olympic Games, however, the IOC seemed to have moved away from solemnity and ritual and towards a greater emphasis on entertainment (Alkemeyer and Richartz, 1993) – thus we could argue for a move away from the participant towards the spectator and the spectacle (the show), by moving away from ideology. It is a secularization of the ceremony, a removal of the liturgy of the ritual that used to hold the symbolism of the rituals performed (Alkemeyer and Richartz, 1993). The flow of the ritual has been replaced with a series of performances; while this depicts a certain fragmentation of the ceremonies, we do see that it has made the ceremonies more accessible to the audience (Alkemeyer and Richartz, 1993). We have seen, in essence, the commercialization of the Olympic Games ceremonies.

The rituals, myths, and even culture associated with ceremonies are of interest to researchers within and outside of sport. For example, Gordon (2004) examined the rituals associated with cultural politics in Zambia. Boccia (2010) examined the 2008 Beijing Olympic Games Torch lighting ceremony and torch relay ritual, focusing on images and text found within the media. While Boccia (and others) focus on media representations, some researchers examine the ceremonies in and of themselves; what we find is that certain ceremonies, like the lighting of the sports event's flame, are seen as symbols of shared humanity or spontaneous communitas (MacAloon, 1978, 1984), nostalgia (Slowikowski, 1991), and nationalism and commercialism (Sinclair, 2000, 2001). The IOC edited a book examining its own ceremonies and focusing on various parts such as the historical aspect, television, intercultural exchange, the IOC's vision, and the creativity of the ceremonies (e.g. Casanovas, 1995; Chappelet, 1995; Carrard, 1995; Bassat, 1995; MacAloon, 1995). However, it is important to note that rituals do not only apply to the Olympic Games or more generally to major sports events that happen over the course of multiple days. Even single-day events such as the NFL's Super Bowl have rituals; in the case of the Super Bowl, these include the presentation of the athletes, the entertainment (halftime show), and the presentation of the trophy to the winning team.

However, we can go further regarding the study of ceremonies in major sports events and even the actual organizing committees. Understanding that organizational actions can "display a symbolic, expressive element through which beliefs, emotions, and identities can be formed and changed" (Islam and Zyphur, 2009: 114), we can apply Dandridge *et al.*'s (1980) suggestion of using organizational symbolism to study organizations, such as the organizing committee of the major sports event in question. Here, organizational symbolism is defined as "those aspects of an organization that its members use to reveal the unconscious feelings, images, and values that are inherent in that organization" (Dandridge *et al.*, 1980: 77). Organizational symbolism can be seen in:

- the consciously designed or unconsciously invented stories and myths seen as being important factual organizational history;
- the use of organizational ceremonies or ritualized events (e.g. employee banquets, coffee break, lunch routines and rituals);
- the organization's logo;
- the "day-to-day affective and political life of the organization as revealed in the countless anecdotes that are constantly heard around organizations" (p. 77).

The symbols found can be categorized as either verbal, action, or material; and the symbols' functions fall within descriptive, energy controlling, or system maintenance categories (Dandridge *et al.*, 1980). These aspects are also closely associated with organizational culture (see Chapter 5).

In turn, rituals can be seen as a type of symbolic expression (Islam and Zyphur, 2009); they are a way for individuals to feel a sense of communitas, a social bond, or shared membership (Turner, 1969). We can therefore study specific organizational or administrative rituals, which include (Goodsell, 1997):

- explicit rules (e.g. regular/annual events and ceremonies);
- formalistic processes (e.g. budgeting process); and
- expressive programmes (e.g. anti-doping campaigns).

Within the organization, these administrative rituals, according to Goodsell (1997), involve specialized language (such as all the FA acronyms) and active participation by organizational members. Rituals that are geared towards external individuals, groups, or organizations typically use laymen's terms and dramatic forms (Goodsell, 1997). These elements are being applied to enduring organizations; for example, the audit committee's activities can be seen as having ceremonial components, and these rituals can be seen as a ceremonial performance that can offer reassurance to stakeholders such as investors or lenders (Spira, 1999).

Within this perspective, we can therefore view ceremonies as being the context within which we find rituals, which in turn provide individuals with a sense of communitas (cf. Islam and Zyphur, 2009; Trice and Beyer, 1984; Turner, 1969). Thus, using organizational symbolism and ritual analyses could allow researchers to better understand the inner workings of a major sports event organizing committee, its members (participants, paid staff, volunteers, etc.), its various ceremonies, and its relationships with its stakeholders (including the impact that organizational ceremonies and rituals have on these stakeholders). Examining how organizing committees differ to enduring organizations in these aspects would be an interesting future research question.

While focused more on the nation than the organizing committee, Luo (2010) used the concepts of symbolism, rituals, and ceremony to explore how China used the 2008 Beijing Olympic Games opening and closing ceremonies as public rituals in order to achieve a vision of reinvention. Luo does so by showing how this vision was promoted using symbols, but also hindered by the ritualistic context. He explored, for example, the symbolism and perceived meaning of the fireworks in the shape of footprints depicted in the opening ceremonies and the history of China (the idea of bringing the past into the present). Part of this symbolism lies in the spatial arrangement of the city of Beijing and its history. One frustration seen in the Western media was the use of fake footprint fireworks during the actual opening ceremonies, which was perceived as being propaganda by the Chinese. What the analysis showed is how rituals can be analysed, understood, and how risky they can actually be. Others critique the Olympic Games and its opening ceremonies for being hypocritical, rotten, and corrupt. To wit, Tomlinson (2000) came to this conclusion after analysing the Olympic Games opening ceremonies' spectacle, pageantry, melodrama, values, and ideology, suggesting that the true purpose and power of the Games is not to bring the youth of the world together but to transmit cultural, economic, and political messages by the youth to the world (see also Jennings, 2000). This position may not be far off the mark when one thinks of the newly created YOG, where the IOC can now engage with (read: directly tap into) a younger population.

However, we can also inspire ourselves by the research on festivals and how they can be described in order to better understand major sports event ceremonies. Festivals are typically reserved for more culturally based/arts activities, though they engage all the senses (sight, hearing, smell, taste, touch, and movement), like sports events do. As Getz (2005) noted, the event experience is dependent on the setting (the physical place, the sense of place), the people (the participants, audience, and staff/volunteers), and the management systems (the programmes/products offered and the management controls). Thus, programme planning and service quality are important in the event experience and ultimately in the perceived success of the event.

The literature suggests an array of possible elements that combine to make an event experience successful. The presence of rituals and the spectacle are important, as we have been describing so far. Another key element is authenticity. Authenticity here refers to the quality of the audience's experience, whereby if the ceremony is authentic, then the audience has become a willing participant in the ceremony's ritual-like performance. The ceremony is further seen as successful if a sense of communitas or shared bonding is created, especially if this sense of communitas can last beyond the end of the actual ceremony (Uzelac, 2010). Beyond rituals, spectacles, and authenticity, we find other possible elements: the engagement with the senses (and the aesthetics) as noted earlier, the ability for the individual to escape everyday life, the desire for celebration, the presence of protocol, the feeling of hospitality, the opportunity to socialize (and hence build communitas), and the entertainment value. The particular style of the event may also include aspects of sport and physical activity, competition, games, humour, education, and commercial opportunities/activities (for more information, see Getz, 2005). These elements are worth integrating into analyses of major sporting event ceremonies.

Other research on Olympic ceremonies

The Olympic ceremonies have also been used as a research context to study something else. To wit, Hogan (2003) used these ceremonies to examine the national gendered and ethnicized constructions. Silvers and Nelson (2009) argued that you can use the Olympic Games opening ceremonies as a case study to illustrate how the EMBOK (see Chapter 1) can be used to deconstruct and analyse events. They illustrate how the entertainment, programme, and theme elements of the EMBOK's design domain helps analyse the 2006 Torino Olympic Winter Games opening ceremonies. By doing so they were able to understand, assess, and reflect on the opening ceremonies, showing how future (sport) event managers may garner the necessary skills and understanding of such a ceremony.

Another avenue has been the national narratives portrayed in the Olympic ceremonies. Housel (2007) highlighted the multiple national Australian narratives depicted in the 2000 Sydney Olympic Games opening ceremonies, whereas Puijk (1999) presented the Norwegian images and culture found in the 1994 Lillehammer Olympic Winter Games, and Traganou (2010) illustrated the Greek national narratives notably associated with its past and present constituencies and topography within the 2004 Athens Olympic Games. While many believe that the opening ceremonies should present a unified national image or identity to be portrayed to the world, some, such as Traganou, see an opportunity for alternative national identities or renewed national narratives to be portrayed. It is a chance to "stretch the conceptual boundaries of the nation and its relation with Others [sic]" (Traganou, 2010: 236). These national narratives are often discussed in relation to globalization. This applies to studies on mega-events more broadly and their role in sport and media globalization processes, as well as opportunities they offer for intercultural understanding and exchange (e.g. Qing *et al.*, 2010).

Given the nationalistic stance of the opening ceremonies, as well as the media's nationalistic portrayals of the ceremonies, some researchers are questioning the cultural, political, and historical messages portrayed in these ceremonies. Tomlinson (1989) argued that the IOC should put pressure on the organizing committees to focus on its own history and have the athletes play a leading role. The 2004 Athens Olympic Games opening ceremony had many components of the history of the Olympic Games (notably the ancient Olympics), though that is also an intrinsic part of the country's own history. Nevertheless, those opening ceremonies have been noted as one of the more memorable ones, lending some credence to Tomlinson's position. Yet, as Tomlinson (1996) himself noted, the Olympic Games and their ideals are impacted by the historical contexts in which they have been hosted; the Olympic Games are social constructions and productions. On the one hand, the Olympic Games are a globalizing force, where the media and other stakeholders come to expect certain standards (cf. Tomlinson, 1996; Parent, 2008); on the other hand, we have seen these Games – such as in Seoul (1988) and Barcelona (1992) – symbolically suppress differences through the sports events acting "as a form of supra-national global cultural politics" and collapse history into a sort of mythical narrative (Tomlinson, 1996: 597). We therefore see some globalization paradoxes at play, which should be examined further.

Overall, the literature on ceremonies and associated concepts like rituals is relatively sparse within the sport event management literature. What does exist is certainly more qualitative in nature (especially seen in the form of case studies and ethnographic research); few, if any, in-depth quantitative studies have been conducted (Islam and Zyphur, 2009). Research on major sports event ceremonies have typically focused on the symbolism and rituals of the Olympic Games ceremonies, more than other sports events and more than the

205

actual organizational and logistical aspects of the management of such activities. Thus, theory building but also theory testing is certainly needed in this major sports event ceremonies area; moving beyond the Olympic Games setting is also needed. We now look to certain aspects that are important for managers dealing with sport event ceremonies, which have the potential to become areas of research.

THE PRACTITIONER'S PERSPECTIVE ON CEREMONIES

In this section we will discuss logistical issues surrounding key ceremonies and cultural celebrations.

Logistical issues

With Olympic Games, a most fascinating ritual is the transfer of the flame from Greece, which is almost a sacred event (it used to be a sacred event in the ancient Olympic Games). Often what follows that lighting ceremony is a torch relay across the host country that ends in the city where the Games will be held. The power of this ceremonial torch run can galvanize the residents of a country and garner support that advertising cannot. Ownership of the Games happens one person, one community, one province or state at a time, as ordinary citizens pass the flame from one person to the other, and they become connected and committed to the Games. The opportunity to be part of something in a physical way that creates an emotional attachment is often priceless in terms of both loyalty to the Games and patriotism to the host country. Most citizens do not attend the Games but watch them on television or other digital technology. The torch relay can connect a country and its people to the Games in an exponential way. The logistics of this ceremony are extensive, and the workforce faces a relentless schedule of long hours and often unknown challenges because the torch must keep moving and be alight, regardless of the weather conditions, on a schedule to arrive in time for the opening ceremonies.

There are different logistical considerations for different ceremonies. Opening ceremonies are the front door to a major sports event, and consequently, substantial resources, both human and financial, are directed to the planning and execution. There is now a global expectation (at least for the Olympic Games) that the opening ceremonies will be spectacular, and that is what people tune in to watch. That is why the networks pay huge sums of money for the rights to televise. The planning and rehearsal for the opening and closing ceremonies is painstakingly detailed, with precision timing particularly for events that are televised. The television audience for an Olympic Games opening ceremony is in the billions, and the money spent to create the ceremonies is staggering. Allegedly, over US$1 billion was spent by China on their 2008 Beijing opening ceremony, which is equivalent to half the 2010 Olympic Winter Games complete operating budget. If there is a misstep with the ceremonies or the wow factor is not there, the media jump all over it and a cloud falls over the Games before the sports competitions even begin. What it takes to get ready for this moment is nothing short of a miracle. Every piece of the plan must be executed second-by-second to satisfy a myriad of stakeholder expectations – athletes, protocol, special guests, the paying public, sponsors, networks with broadcasting rights, other media, and the very large television audience; and still there will be challenges. Recent challenges during opening ceremonies include: (1) accusations of fakery when the fireworks display appeared part-real and part-pre-recorded, creating a digitally enhanced presentation for the opening ceremonies of the 2008 Beijing Olympic Games (Horne and Whannel, 2012); and (2) one of the four arms of the Olympic cauldron malfunctioning as it was being lit during the opening ceremonies of the 2010 Vancouver Olympic Winter Games. Incidents like these can set a negative tone that then becomes a challenge and can overshadow the Games for their duration. At the end of the day, you have only one chance to make a first impression!

Organizers do look to previous opening ceremonies for ideas and then must make the difficult decision about what to present differently. What aspects of their country and culture would be appropriate and powerful and impactful? What worked in one country will not necessarily be effective for another. Within a country there are typically special interest groups and cultural sensitivities that must also be considered. There is a fine line between presenting the fabric and face of a country and what will "play" to the rest of the world.

As soon as the opening ceremonies are over, the focus is immediately moved to the closing ceremonies for the ceremonies managers. While the stress level is still there, it has reduced because the expectations are not as high and because the closing ceremonies are supposed to have more of a party feel, less of a protocol feel. It is still, however, one last opportunity to leave a positive and lasting memory of the event, especially if there have been negative images portrayed during the event by the media. Sometimes it even provides the gift of mitigation of a misstep or mistake. This is what happened in the example above from the Vancouver 2010 Olympic Winter Games. The malfunction of the arm during the opening ceremony was used in an opening comedic skit during the closing ceremony. It was both humorous and self-deprecating, which showed the world that Canada could laugh at itself. The media picked it up as a positive message, and it transformed the incident from the opening ceremony, leaving the impression of a country that had both humility and a sense of humour.

Another key ceremony, especially for the athletes, is the flower and victory/medals ceremony. In 2002 it was decided to make the medal presentation more of a celebration for all of the athletes at Olympic events, and include more spectators in the ceremony. This resulted in a medal ceremony within a day or two of the end of competition (the victory/medal ceremony) that included entertainment – essentially a party and show surrounding the medals presentations. However, the custom of presenting flowers immediately following the event was retained by the sports that decided to add the victory/medals ceremony. These parties provide the opportunity for athletes to extend their celebration, and it can be another source of revenue for the organizing committee. Perhaps even more important is that more citizens of the host city can feel a part of the event, even though they did not attend the sport competition. They can buy very reasonably priced tickets for the victory/medals ceremonies and see the top athletes in person. This also means that a venue spectator can experience both types of ceremonies over the life of a Games – an immediate flower medal ceremony at the venue and a delayed victory/medal ceremony elsewhere. It has been a positive addition to the list of ceremonies for athletes, the public, and the media because of increased stories and photo opportunities. Winning athletes will actually hear their national anthem played twice if their sport has both the flower presentation immediately following the event and the additional medal ceremonies. It just adds to the experience and memories for all concerned. Still, some sports (e.g. figure skating, ice hockey, and curling) have retained the more traditional way of presenting medals and flowers immediately following the completion of the competition in the venue.

However, the enhanced celebration around medal presentations creates more logistical considerations: an additional venue is prepared, an additional VTeam is needed, entertainers and hosts are essential, F&B for athletes and all other guests, tickets need to be sold, additional workforce are required to ingress and egress the crowd, security must be provided, and internal and external media coverage will be necessary.

Cultural celebrations

Because major sports events have become spectacles beyond sport, we have seen the emergence of cultural celebrations (e.g. the Cultural Olympiad for an Olympic Games) being presented concurrent with the sports event. For Olympic Games, these events are mostly entertainment in nature, although some are educational exhibitions that showcase special interest groups, and history within a culture or country are also presented. They can add or detract from the Games depending on the content and the response of both spectators of the Games and the citizens of the host city. The cultural celebrations create more options for entertainment between competitions and when they are finished for the day, and provide a way to reach additional spectators, those who are not interested in sports. However, as they are often considered secondary to the sport competitions, cultural celebrations often fall victim to budget cuts in times of economic trouble. For other sports events, like the *Jeux de la Francophonie* or the YOG, cultural events are part of the overall event. There can be actual medalling culture events (as in the case of the *Jeux de la Francophonie*) or mandatory cultural activities for the athletes (as in the case of the YOG).

CHAPTER SUMMARY

In this chapter we discussed the management considerations of the different types of ceremonies at major sports events. We examined the concepts of rituals, myths and symbolism within ceremonies. We linked concepts typically associated with festivals, such as communitas and authenticity, with major sports events' ceremonies. We explored research being done regarding ceremonies. From a practitioner's perspective, we delved into logistical considerations for various types of ceremonies, examined cultural celebrations, and noted the importance of protocol at these ceremonies relative to workforce members' tasks and responsibilities.

EXPERT CASE: OPENING AND CLOSING CEREMONIES LOGISTICS COMPARED TO MEDALS CEREMONIES

The opening ceremony was powered by the work of many, the hopes of millions, and financed by the prime broadcaster. The non-negotiables were a spectacle, and precision timing. The two ceremonies bookend the Olympic Games, to set the tone and to finish with a flourish. These ceremonies are covered extensively by the press with relentless commentary that frames public opinion; the audiences both present at the event and watching on television get up at all hours of the night to watch it live; the organizing committee of subsequent Games are taking notes and scrutinizing the ceremonies for ideas; and last but not least, the choreographers of the event have their fingers and toes crossed that the ceremonies will go off without a hitch. Through re-broadcasting and global partnerships, the VTeams are constantly reminded that the opening ceremony would have an audience of 2.5 billion . . . billion! And we had to get it right the first (and only) time. The pressure was on, and became increasingly evident as the opening day approached. The show had been in planning for several years and yet, even once it started, it still seemed a work in progress to those backstage. It almost seemed impossible to ensure that all the teams were in synch with each other, regardless of the number of meetings held. Fortunately, the VTeam was experienced and worked in concert.

Glitches typical of ceremonies of this size were rare, but did happen. An example at the opening ceremonies was a lack of communication between the security team and the production team, resulting in a bus of high-level dignitaries being re-routed to the wrong back-up entrance (and missing the start of the ceremonies). This left a half-empty president's box when the show started exactly on time. Another example was the logistics team being overwhelmed (beyond what they planned to be) when several of the hundreds of truckloads of material arrived at the last minute (meaning plants and fixtures were not delivered to the VIP lounges); the technology team could not tune the dignitaries' large lounge TVs; the construction team could not build the dignitaries' lounges until the last day (with wet paint hardly obvious on opening day).

The overall responsibility of the opening ceremonies, from any perspective, was daunting. The protocol team was responsible for 4,400 seats (and respective VIPs) and three lounges (for 1,800, 300, and 30 people, respectively) with their ensuing catering and fit-out (construction, electrical, technology, plants, furniture). The venue itself was over 20 years old and required significant re-construction. As with any project, there were delays and over-runs. This meant that the lounges and seating areas were not completed on time. In fact, despite our constant moaning, cries for attention, and attempting anything else that might get attention, in the final hours we still had to roll up our sleeves and pile on jobs to an already overloaded group of coordinators. When there were no resources, you did it yourself and grabbed whoever was in the vicinity. My boss and I stickered the seats (all 4,400 of them), which made for a very long evening. We grabbed paintbrushes the day before opening to assist with the painting. We arranged our own florists to come in, and when logistics, security, and accreditation made it too difficult to have them enter the area for last-minute repairs to the lounges, we resorted to giving them some of our opening ceremonies tickets and had them enter the venue as ticketed guests (very early in the day, however, and they were gone by the time the ceremonies started!)

Logistically, the preparations for opening ceremonies were a nightmare. The highest-level VIPs (19 heads of state, other global leaders and ministers) — or rather their advance teams — required specific attention. When the American president was considering attending, there were delegations from the US State Department, Secret Service, and White

House, all expecting separate tours and run-throughs for their leader. Some days, I would wake up after a very late night with 54 voicemails on my mobile phone, mostly from individuals demanding urgent attention. It was impossible to retrieve any messages without being interrupted with a call. I learned to turn off my voicemail very quickly. We also learned to schedule fixed tour times each day (11 a.m. and 2 p.m.) and throw whoever wanted a tour all together quite quickly, much to the consternation of some groups who expected individual attention. These tours had as many as 50 guests at one time, but the fixed-time system worked out well for us, allowing us to focus on getting the lounges and seating areas complete.

Security trumped everything and always had to be addressed. Different screening gates could be open at different times, and internal halls could be blocked if not monitored, leading to the possibility of our guests being stranded in a locked hallway. We had 40 buses coming from several sites, some secure and some not, and they had to be unloaded and guests seated quickly. Our tickets did not indicate a specific seat, but rather included only seating blocks, which assisted in ensuring there were no empty seats for the cameras, and also in getting guests seated quickly; but it also proved problematic when the blocks were not contiguous (or difficult to locate).

The opening ceremony demanded much time and energy. But, there were also almost nightly medal/victory ceremonies and the closing ceremony to consider as they required staff and daily planning. It was in my opinion, these ceremonies that suffered. My colleagues from 19 other venues were required to assist with the opening ceremony before they dispersed back to their individual venues and the mountain of responsibility they entailed. But when the medal ceremonies began, several issues came forward. The presenters, who we were to greet and hold, did not know where we were. The medal presenters' listings had errors. The VIP seating section had been sold to the public. The production team for medals were not as seasoned as those for opening ceremonies. Issues which had not even been envisioned in our practice scenarios developed. A system was gradually put in place to, for example, ensure that the medal presenters (including an Arab crown prince on the first night) were not led into a dark hallway and left in a space standing miserably for an hour while they waited to present their medal. Drivers had to be briefed more fully on exactly which entrance to drop off the presenters. Another seating section had to be located for our guests. The production team had to be assisted in their handling of the presenters – in short, the experience from the opening ceremonies, garnered over months (and years) and one day of excitement, had to be adapted in minutes to fit the realities of the medals/victory ceremonies.

The medal/victory ceremonies and the closing ceremony were much more celebratory in nature – real parties – and were largely free of the protocol and pomp of the opening ceremony. However, they still required the same amount of energy and focus on logistics as the opening ceremony did. Fortunately, the events were popular and well received, and, despite the complexity, relatively error-free. In fact, the closing ceremony made light of the fact that the torch (which rose from the floor missing one leg during the opening ceremony) did not rise properly. This vignette was noted repeatedly as many Canadian's favourite . . . except, of course, the overtime goal in the gold medal hockey game.

It is important to remember that the very nature of the Games is unpredictable; you can't plan for everything (although you try to). The ceremonies and Games-time period involves just-in-time decision-making that requires a different set of competencies because of the magnitude and fallout for the host city, the IOC, athletes, sponsors, and other key stakeholders. It is productive and can be less stressful if you accept and expect the fact that the unexpected will always occur as part of ceremony execution. This acceptance will assist you in discernment with just-in-time decision-making between panic decision-making (read: crisis, unforeseen, unplanned, urgent situations) versus important decision-making (read: take-a-breath, regroup, reframe, and then take action). Impacting, and sometimes exacerbating the situation, is the fact that you have to deal with two different production teams for the same venue, teambuilding in the heat of the action, and having to respect the nature of each type of ceremonies. Some of the most useful skills a ceremonies manager can have are conflict resolution and interpersonal skills – specifically the ability to have timely, fierce conversations that interrogate reality to eliminate assumptions, reveal the facts, and share information. This will ultimately facilitate effective and efficient action in a pressure-cooker of a situation where both experienced and inexperienced managers and stakeholders must work together to accomplish their tasks.

By Robert McDowell, Managing Director, International Governance Associates, Inc.

Case questions

1 What logistical issues were present for the opening ceremony in this case?

2 How is the management of the opening ceremony and medal ceremonies different in this case? How is it similar in this case?

3 What could be done differently next time to mitigate the issues faced in this case for the opening ceremony?

CHAPTER QUESTIONS

1 Describe the different types of ceremonies you can find in the most recent CWG and FIFA World Cup. How do they compare to the Olympic Games ceremonies?

2 Why would certain rituals and symbols depicted during an opening or closing ceremony be considered risky?

3 Compare the rituals and symbols methods for examining ceremonies to the EMBOK framework. What are the pros and cons of each approach? Which do you feel is better?

4 What are the advantages and disadvantages, if any, of a torch relay around the host country; around the world?

5 Why are opening ceremonies so important for a major sports event?

FURTHER READING

If you are interested in ceremonies, rituals, and festivals surrounding major sports events, we suggest examining the sociology and anthropology literatures, as well as the following:

Barney, R. K. & Bijkerk, A. T. (2005) The genesis of sacred fire in Olympic ceremony: A new interpretation. *Journal of Olympic History*, 13, 6–27.

Horne, J. & Whannel, G. (2012) Festival, spectacle, carnival and consumption. In *Understanding the Olympics* (pp. 146–161), London: Routledge.

Islam, G. & Zyphur, M. J. (2009) Rituals in organizations: A review and expansion of current theory. *Group & Organization Management*, 34, 114–139.

Chapter 11

Risk management and security

OBJECTIVES

- To understand the risk management process in major sports events
- To understand security within major sports events
- To present current and potential avenues of research associated with risk management and security within major sports events

ILLUSTRATIVE CASE: 2011 – A HIGH-RISK YEAR FOR THOSE HOSTING SPORTS EVENTS AROUND THE WORLD

The year 2011 was marked by a number of external risks which affected the planning and execution of various major sports events. For example, Mother Nature wreaked havoc on IFs' and local organizing committees' sport event hosting plans:

- Christchurch, Canterbury, New Zealand suffered an earthquake of over magnitude 7 in September 2010, a number of aftershocks, and then another major earthquake of magnitude 6.3 on 22 February 2011. Christchurch's infrastructure was severely affected and nearly 200 people were killed. The International Rugby Board had previously awarded New Zealand with the right to host the 2011 Rugby World Cup. The extent of damage in Christchurch, New Zealand's second largest city, meant that the local organizing committee (RNZ, 2011) made major changes to its schedule, with all seven rugby matches meant for Christchurch being reallocated to other cities since the stadium owner could not guarantee that all necessary repairs to the stadium could be done in time to ensure a safe and secure facility (RNZ, 2011).
- Japan suffered a magnitude 9.0 earthquake on 11 March 2011, which was followed by a significant tsunami, destroying houses, infrastructure, and cities, as well as significantly damaging a nuclear power plant and killing over 15,000 people. Thoughts around the world were on the Japanese people. The ISU was set to have its 2011 World Figure Skating Championships in Japan at the end of March. After some deliberations, and thinking of cancelling the event altogether, the ISU decided at the end of April to move its championships to Russia (Cinquanta and Schmid, 2011).

Also, the Middle East and North Africa were plagued with civil unrest. Egypt, Libya, Tunisia, Yemen, Iran, and Bahrain are notable examples, with some of these countries (e.g. Egypt) seeing governments overthrown. This has meant a period of uncertainty for sports events in this region, which are often publicly funded endeavours. The extent of uncertainty has caused certain IFs to rethink their hosting schedule. For example, Formula 1 decided to cancel its Bahrain race given the unrest in the country, though logistics were cited as the key concern (see Cutler, 2011b). We therefore see that despite the best planning on the part of local organizers, major sports events still face noteworthy, though usually rare, external risks.

THE THEORY BEHIND RISK MANAGEMENT AND SECURITY

> David L. Mair, risk manager for US Olympic Committee Risk & Insurance Man-
> agement, said a special event is anything outside the scope of normal activities that
> has a beginning and an end. No matter what the event, however, the principles are
> the same: risk managers should take care of the people who are going to be there.
>
> (Kehl, 1994: 27)

Today, major sports events typically have a risk and/or security director, officer and/or committee to manage the myriad risks such events can face. A risk can be defined as a dangerous element (Clarke, 2005) or as "uncertainty associated with an outcome" (McKim, 1992: 7). A risk can be caused by individuals' (terrorists, participants, guests, vandals, etc.) actions; supply-and-demand balance fluctuations; environmental hazards (e.g. earthquakes, tsunamis); and unfavourable laws, publicity, or any other external force (Getz, 2005). While these are very broad definitions, a risk has the potential of resulting in (Getz, 2005):

- personal injury to participants, guests, and/or workforce members;
- physical damage to the venue;
- a financial loss and/or legal liability for the managers/owners if and when something goes wrong; and/or
- a loss of reputation and/or future business.

Risk analysis and management have become popular topics in academia; there is even a journal dedicated to risk: *Risk Analysis: An International Journal*. A quick database search will see smoking, diet, influenza, and other health issues as being commonly studied, as well as financial risk, climate change, and terrorism and associated topics (bioterrorism, attacks, etc.). In this book, we take terrorism to mean the ideologically or religiously justified acts committed by a group of individuals who lack the (official) power to change government policies or laws; these acts are geared to maximizing negative psychological impacts on the society and/or government (Toohey and Taylor, 2008).

In this post-9/11 world, security is high-up on the risk awareness scale for sport event managers. In this section, we will examine research associated with risk management and then security more specifically. As Taylor and Toohey (2011: 3259) noted, "safety-related processes and practices are firmly based in compliance-driven risk management".

Risk management

Risk management can be defined as "a proactive process that involves assessing all possible risks to the event and its stakeholders by strategically anticipating, preventing, minimizing, and planning responses to mitigate those identified risks" (Leopkey and Parent, 2009a: 187). There are many different types of risks within major sports events; they can be divided into tangible and intangible types (see Table 11.1). Also, risks can be planned or unplanned. For example, a manager may not automatically plan for the death of an athlete, but they would examine the impact of a new facility construction on the natural environment's destruction. Of the 15 risk categories, Leopkey and Parent (2009a) found that operations were the most common form of risk. However, this may in part be due to the fact that the definition of this category is broad, encompassing many aspects including security, and thus has the potential for many risks.

Regardless of the actual source of the risk, there are different risk management strategies available. Having recourse to legal agreements, contracts, etc., to protect the manager/the event is probably an obvious risk management strategy. The assumption here is that there is implicit risk in participating in an event. Traditional risk literature views athletes participating in sports events as having a responsibility towards their fellow competitors to avoid reckless misconduct. Athletes may be liable for injuries they cause to a fellow competitor (Drowatzky, 1992). Insurance and liability therefore become very important for event managers. This extends not only to athletes but also staff hired, and even sponsorship (Aschkenasy, 1996; Piccarello, 2005). Sport organizations are being forced to put in place procedures to ensure that they can continue to be insured and covered for liability. The more "violent" the sport, the higher the insurance is likely to be (e.g. rugby versus table tennis). Consider the National Hockey League's (NHL) repeated player injury incidents such as Max Pacioretty being checked into the boards and severely injured (broken vertebrae, severe concussion) by Zdeno Chara, and Sydney Crosby's severe concussion at the hands of Victor Hedman during the 2010–2011 season (see, for example, Panesar, 2011). The injuring players would incur game suspensions, but as yet no legal proceedings have been undertaken in these cases; however, in other cases, civil suits have been filed (see Wolohan, 2008). Nevertheless, the NHL has taken steps towards regulating this issue through revising its concussion protocol, reviewing equipment and facilities, and fining players and coaches.

Still, legal strategies are not the only way to deal with risks. Seven risk-management strategies can be considered (see Table 11.1; Leopkey and Parent, 2009b):

1   avoidance
2   diffusion
3   legal
4   prevention
5   reallocation
6   reduction
7   relationship management.

Of the seven strategies, the most commonly used by all stakeholder groups and for all risk categories is reduction (Leopkey and Parent, 2009b). However, different stakeholders

215

Table 11.1 Risk categories and strategies

Type of risk	Risk category	Examples
Tangible	Environment	Pollution, destruction of the natural environment
	Financial	Lack of sponsorship or ticket revenue
	Human resources	Training, sufficient number of paid staff versus volunteers
	Infrastructure	Existing versus new infrastructure
	Legacy	Public availability of new infrastructure post-Games
	Operations	Logistics (such as travel, transportation, food, accommodations), venue/facility management, safety, health and well-being, crowd control, administrative tasks (accreditation, communications), and security
	Organizing	Bureaucracy, legal, organizational change, leadership
	Sport	Officiating issues, number of athletes/teams registered versus showing up
	Threats	Epidemics, personal, terrorism, weather
Intangible	Interdependence	Power hierarchies, partnerships
	Media	Positive vs. negative coverage
	Participation	Public access, ticket availability
	Political	Changes in government, national unrest
	Relationships	Meeting/balancing stakeholder needs and requirements
	Visibility	Ambush marketing, brand, image, reputation, support for the event

Risk-management strategies	Examples
Avoidance	Individual event assessments, risk assessment, research, and evaluation
Diffusion	Creating back-ups, spreading out the risks to others
Legal	Laws, consent forms, insurance, contracts/agreements
Prevention	Rules and regulations, bans, replacements
Reallocation	Transferring the risk or the responsibility for the risk to others
Reduction	Planning (e.g. defining organizational goals), staffing (proper recruitment, training, education), using previous experience and test events, controlling, communication, facility management, proper/limiting accreditation
Relationship management	Stakeholder engagement, cooperation and partnerships, negotiation, meeting stakeholder needs

Source: Based on Leopkey and Parent, 2009a, 2009b.

tend to also use or prefer other strategies. For example, all stakeholder groups seemed to use reduction, allocation, relationship management, and legal strategies, but organizing committees also used diffusion and prevention strategies (Leopkey and Parent, 2009b). More than one strategy can often be used for a given risk category (Leopkey and Parent, 2009b), which means that event managers need to assess the risk, determine the potential impacts (what, who, when, where, why, and how), likelihood of occurrence, degree of impact, and which stakeholders will be involved/impacted, so that a proper strategy can be chosen.

Identifying risks, determining strategies, and implementing them is part of what we call risk analysis/assessment and management. Risk analysis or assessment refers to examining the risks themselves. Sports event managers can ask themselves the following questions to identify risks: (1) what can go wrong (what are the risks)?; (2) what are the consequences?; and (3) what are the likelihoods for each consequence (Henry and Haimes, 2009; Kaplan and Garrick, 1981)? Risk management, in turn, goes further by determining what to do about those risks. Risk analysis is a main concern for sport event managers. Regarding the risk management part of the process, sports event managers can ask the following questions: (1) what are the options for a given risk, what can be done?; (2) what are the tradeoffs (costs, benefits, risks)?; and (3) how does this decision impact future decisions (Haimes, 1991, 2004; Henry and Haimes, 2009). The Mattman model is one way to help analyse risk so that the sports event manager may provide risk reduction recommendations. It is based on the following set of observations (Mattman and Berlonghi, 1987):

1 Event domain and sub-domains: nature of the event, rights holding organization, why it is being held.
2 Designated protectees: who/what requires protection, security.
3 Standard-practice risk reducers: the security measures, precautions, and other procedures that are already in place or offered.
4 Security execution location: location of the event versus fire, health, and other emergency facilities.
5 Calendar and time considerations: date (weekday, weekend, holiday, etc.) and time (morning, afternoon, evening, night) the event is taking place.
6 Environmental conditions: indoor or outdoor event, location (city, inner-city, rural, industrial, natural), and possible weather conditions.
7 Public status and identity of the individuals involved and/or the event itself (e.g. status of the Olympic Games in the world).
8 Degree of controversy of the event, the people involved, and/or the sponsors involved.
9 Level of public awareness: degree of promotion, public relations, media releases, advertising, etc., of the event (i.e. who knows about the event?).
10 Compound stimulant influences: other factors which may increase the risks (e.g. alcohol, drugs, crowding).
11 Maintenance: quality of the venue infrastructure and equipment (e.g. stands, equipment, vehicles, scaffolds).
12 Severity of consequences to the participants, spectators, sponsors, etc.
13 Risk neutralization difficulty.

This model is a good starting point; though, as one can see, it is centred mainly on security and protection concerns, which we know is only part of the types of risks faced by event managers.

Once the sports event manager identifies the various risks, they should also rank them based on their likelihood of occurring, as well as on the degree of impact on the event, the organizing committee, its various stakeholders (participants, spectators, sponsors, governments, etc.). The identification and ranking of possible risks have often been a quantification exercise, thereby discouraging many managers from undertaking this important activity. The probability of occurrence is called the expected value in classical risk theory (McKim, 1992). A given risk's expected value can be compared to other risks' expected values to help managers' decision-making. Sports event managers then have a variety of metrics options (e.g. point-state-transition probability estimates, Poisson event stream) and variables (e.g. time-to-compromise, local device/facility vulnerability, criticality measures), many of which are still being debated in the risk-management literature (see, for example, Henry and Haimes, 2009), to help in decision-making. Most risk analysis models come from other industries, such as computers/technology (e.g. Henry and Haimes, 2009), natural and human hazards (e.g. Hua et al., 2009), including (bio)terrorism (e.g. Parnell et al., 2010). If the reader is interested in such risk analysis modelling, we suggest further exploring the broader risk management literature, as within sport event management there is little of such analysis (Hall et al., 2011 perhaps being an exception).

Ultimately, there is no magic or easy solution, as McKim (1992) noted. One has to be prepared to determine and mitigate risks that they have never encountered (Mattman and Berlonghi, 1987) or that are out of the "ordinary", such as the death of an athlete, spectator or official, an earthquake, a terrorist attack, or a health epidemic. As Sandra Hoffmann (2010: 714) pointed out:

> the results of risk ranking or even technical modeling of a risk generation process are not the only information that is needed to make good risk policy decisions. It also matters how effectively and how inexpensively risk can be reduced. And at an even deeper level, it can be useful to recognize that neither costs nor hazard levels are fixed or naturally occurring values. More often they change as a result of predictable human response to a changing economic environment.

Within the sport management literature, researchers have been interested in examining general risk management in sports events and perceptions of residents and tourists regarding risks. We examine both and then provide some avenues for future research based on risk-related research.

Risk management in sports events

The Olympic Games have been of interest to researchers studying risk management; and the Olympic Winter Games have, not surprisingly, been a particular interest since the winter outdoor conditions are typically of greater concern. The research has generally been descriptive in nature, with types of risks and the process of risk management being presented (e.g. Chang and Singh, 1990; Chappelet, 2001). For the Olympic Winter Games, major risks described have include meteorological/weather risks, financial risks, infrastructure/host region development risks (e.g. white elephants), political risks, transportation risks, legal risks, sponsors/sponsorship and broadcasting risks, image risks, HRM risks, doping risks, health risks, accommodations risks, technology risks, communication risks, transportation risks, and organizational risks (see Chang and Singh, 1990; Chappelet, 2001; Crompton, 1994; Essex and Chalkley, 2004; Jie and Li, 2009). The risk-management process includes looking at past Games information, undertaking brainstorming and SWOT analyses, ranking risks, creating risk management committees and/or managers, and meeting with department managers, senior executives, and board members. Table 11.2

Table 11.2 A comparison of risk identification processes in the Olympic Winter Games

	1988 Calgary Olympic Winter Games Organizing Committee (Chang and Singh, 1990)	2006 Sion Olympic Winter Games Bid Committee (Chappelet, 2001)
Steps	Examine contract and agreement drafts before signing to understand potential liabilities and indemnity provisions	Assisted by Arthur Andersen consultants, carry out a brainstorming session
	Attend meetings focused on risk and responsibility for specific activities	Undertake a SWOT analysis
	Attend monthly executive board, monthly staff, and weekly finance and administration meetings	Classify the 22 identified risks into a 2 × 2 matrix of low/high impact on the Games by low/high probability of occurrence
	Review newspaper articles, facts, information, and financial statements produced by the organizing committee	Compare risks two by two using an electronic vote
	Inspect venues and facilities	Create detailed fact sheets for the risks falling within the high impact and high probability quadrant
	Attend information meetings with department managers	
	Review organizing committee facility contracts	
	Review past Games documentation	
Main risk areas identified	People, property, and public, as well as broadcasting and political risks	Environment, marketing/image, finances, and coordination
Risk management strategies noted	Risk financing programme, loss control programme	Planned step not undertaken: create a risk-management committee as well as have risk managers in each department to manage the identified risks

compares the risk-management process undertaken by the 1988 Calgary Olympic Winter Games Organizing Committee and the 2006 Sion Olympic Winter Games Bid Committee (until the committee was dissolved).

While research in sport event management has typically focused on broader risk types and management processes, some research is beginning on specific risks, such as the risk of sponsorship in major sports events (e.g. Crompton, 1994), including TOP programme sponsors and risk management (e.g. Jie and Li, 2009). However, more is needed in this area, as well as for other risk categories identified in this chapter.

We are also beginning to see a comparison of risk-management processes between the Olympic Games and other major sports events. Jennings and Lodge (2011) provided one of the few studies using a management theory, in this case institutional theory (see DiMaggio and Powell, 1983, 1991; Meyer and Rowan, 1977; Tolbert and Zucker, 1996; Zucker, 1987), to examine the choice of risk-management tools in two different major sports events, the 2012 London Olympic Games, and the 2006 FIFA World Cup in Germany. They suggested that the choice of risk-management tools is dependent on the global field or environment of major sports events, by the particular sport event's specific environment, and by national political systems. This framework, together with institutional theory, allows the authors to examine and explain similarities/differences in tool choice between two different sports events. The national political systems were seen as particularly important for tool choice. What we see is the usefulness of applying a management theory to the comparative analysis of risk management between events in order to move beyond simply describing risks and tools. Certainly, more similar work is needed in our field.

Based on the existing literature (Appenzeller, 2005; Chang and Singh, 1990; Chappelet, 2001; Getz, 2005; Head and Horn II, 1991; Leopkey and Parent, 2009b; Mattman and Berlonghi, 1987; Parent, 2008, 2010), as well as Games experiences, we suggest that the risk-management process can be as follows for major sports events:

1   Identify possible risks that may affect the organizing committee's activities and objectives – this can be done through observations, brainstorming sessions, and SWOT analyses – and determine which risk category each risk is associated with.
2   Identify the consequences of each risk.
3   Rank the risks based on the likelihood of occurrence and degree of severity or magnitude of outcome/impact – this can be done by a ranking system (1 (low) to 5 (high), for example), using matrices, and/or through comparative (two-by-two) voting.
4   Examine possible alternatives (risk-management strategies) to deal with each risk.
5   Select what seems to be the best risk-management strategy – the choice may depend in part on protocol, rights, legal responsibilities, national systems, the type of sport event, and other parameters. Undertake dry-runs/simulate certain risks to determine if the chosen techniques are adequate.
6   Implement the chosen risk-management strategy if and when needed.
7   Monitor the outcomes of the chosen techniques for appropriate resolution of the risk as well as risk-management programme and overall organizing committee effectiveness.

Perceptions of residents and tourists

Residents may be supportive, excited, and feel a sense of national pride for an upcoming major sports event, but, depending on their age, they may have different views on the risks. For example, traffic and transportation risks are often of concern, as is the appropriate degree of security measures to be undertaken. As well, research on the 2012 London Olympic Games has shown that older residents are also concerned with pollution and parking availability, as well as believing that security risks affect attendance (Konstantaki and Wickens, 2010). For other spectators, those travelling to the host region, perceptions of risk depend on gender (and other personal characteristics such as age and nationality) and on the type of tourist (see Qi *et al.*, 2009). For example, the events on 9/11 did not seem to impact the dedicated sports tourist, individuals who travel to a destination specifically to engage in a sport event (passively as a spectator in this case), as Toohey *et al.* (2003) demonstrated in their study on the sports tourists of the 2002 FIFA World Cup in Japan and Korea. Such tourists actually appreciated the increased level of security and safety measures – though the increase could not be to the extent of resulting in the tourists feeling oppressed by the measures.

The literature is consistent in arguing that organizing committee managers need to more effectively and consistently communicate risk-management measures to provide a sense of safety for the spectators. However, organizing committee managers must be cognizant of not overdoing the security/safety measures to avoid the feeling of oppression and constraint (Konstantaki and Wickens, 2010; Toohey *et al.*, 2003). It is important to look at the history or sequence of past events and their limiting factors when looking at building trust in the face of terrorism risks and the need for their associated security and safety measures (cf. Johnson, 2010). Organizing committee members can gain tourists' trust by demonstrating appropriate safety measures, which will help attract the tourists. This positive relationship is the same, if not stronger, than the relationship between the absence of these measures (negative, risky information) and distrust (Eitzinger and Wiedemann, 2008).

Possible future research directions

As we noted above, there is a need for more analytical and comparative analyses of specific risks and risk-management processes/decision-making in different major sports events (cf. Wilson *et al.*, 2011). Some topics to consider include:

- doping in athletes and how to manage such risks for organizing committees (cf. Girginov, 2006; Maennig, 2002; Mroczkowska, 2010);
- institutionalization and democratization of risk management in different cultures (cf. Jennings and Lodge, 2011; Taylor and Toohey, 2011);
- alcohol, drinking as a risk for spectators and other stakeholders (cf. Glassman *et al.*, 2008; Neal *et al.*, 2005);
- media representations of risk and terrorism (cf. Driedger, 2007; Nossek, 2008);
- not only spectator safety but also worker safety (Parnell *et al.*, 2001) could be examined in major sports events, since Vancouver 2010 put that in as a key value and legacy by creating the worker safety programme (Mora, 2010);

- the impact CSR, sustainability, and new international standards (ISO 26000 and ISO 20121 regarding sustainability and social responsibility in events) will have on risk management processes in major sports events (cf. Chappelet, 2009; Husted, 2005);
- the relationship between risk assessment, policy-making, and international relations in the global world of major sports events (cf. McLean *et al.*, 2009).

Each of these potential research avenues can be investigated using qualitative and quantitative methods. However, while quantitative analyses are needed in the sport event management literature, risk should not only be characterized as probabilities and expected values; assessments of uncertainty and scenario-building instruments are needed, which involve qualitative methods (Aven and Renn, 2009).

Security

Seeing security personnel with guns at seemingly every street corner of the 2008 Beijing Olympic Games and the 2010 Delhi CWG should not have come as a surprise to event participants. Security at major sports events has been a concern for over 40 years. The need to address international terrorism started with the 1972 Munich Olympic Games, where members of the Israeli Olympic team were killed by a Palestinian terrorist group, Black September. Those interested in seeing a video of the incident should watch *One Day in September*, a documentary by Arthur Cohn (1999). The fallout and Israeli response is depicted in the movie *Munich* (Spielberg, 2005).

"Montreal's reaction to the Munich massacre became a blueprint for future Olympic Security operations" (Coaffee and Fussey, 2011: 169). The need for high security at the 1976 Montreal Olympic Games explains in part (with facility issues being the other), the resulting government debt for the Games. Nevertheless, since then, host cities and countries have learned from each other, cutting across ideological (e.g. communist versus capitalist countries) and geographical (e.g. Europe, North America, Asia) lines in doing so, and depicting a sort of institutional isomorphism in the process (see Jennings and Lodge, 2011). As Coaffee and Fussey (2011) noted, security costs have continually increased over the years; the 1984 Los Angeles Olympic Games security costs were US$11,627, whereas the 2004 Athens Olympic Games, 20 years later, were US$142,857. By December 2011, the 2012 London Olympic Games security bill was already estimated to be between £533 million and £1 billion (cf. Coaffee and Fussey, 2011; Cutler, 2011c), which shows the post-9/11 impact of terrorism. Most of the security costs are born by the local and national governments through their taxpayers.

While only the most senior major sports event managers will ever be privy (though never quite fully) to governments' security plans, research has provided some descriptive work illustrating the kinds of security measures that are being used (the details of which are highly guarded by security personnel). Coaffee and Fussey (2011) provided details of the kinds of security measures being put in place for the 2012 London Olympic Games; these security measures were designed to be as invisible and unobtrusive as possible. They included:

- surveillance and security started as venue construction began;
- security elements included: visible perimeters/barriers around venues, security land-scaping and crime-reduction features; bridges and other infrastructure strengthening; embedded electronic devices used to scan for explosives; concealment points (e.g. litter bins, drains) hidden or sealed; numberplate recognition; tracking of suspects in the city; and venue lockdowns; and
- table-top or decision-making exercises used to work out logistics.

It is worth taking a moment to explain the concept of venue lockdowns. The moment a given venue has been constructed and overlayed for the event (e.g. construction and logistics personnel have completed their main venue set-ups, the look of the Games has been added, Games personnel have set-up their work areas, security screening areas have been operationalized), a full security sweep by the venue's security commander and his team occurs, after which the venue is locked down. This means that only accredited personnel can enter the venue, after passing through security screening areas. Nothing can be delivered; a local ambulance cannot even come to the venue unless it is first security screened/swept.

What we see from the above is a standardization and normalization of security procedures at major sports events around the world. Today's need for security means that "intense pre-planning" is needed (Coaffee and Fussey, 2011: 178). Still, some argue that the enhanced resilience of new Olympic venues and infrastructure can be seen as a legacy of such Games, which assists in attracting other events/groups in the future; it is also seen as a single long-term crime-reduction strategy (Coaffee and Fussey, 2011). Security as a legacy is also being studied in other events, like the FIFA World Cup; to wit, Eick (2011: 3329) examined FIFA and its 2006 World Cup as a possible "incubator for a 'sustained securitization' of host and post-host cities".

This standardization of security and safety measures extends beyond the Olympic Games. There is notable interest in football because of hooliganism (e.g. Bouchet et al., 2011b; Buford, 1993; Gardiner, 2000; Hall, 2010; Weed, 2002). In England we find the use of command and control centres, such as for the Olympic Games, complete with closed-circuit television (CCTV), staff venue access control using proper accreditation at all times, screening of individuals and cars entering the venue, emergency and evacuation staff training, and risk analyses for the financial, strategic, and operational risks (Hall, 2010). For major football events (e.g. FIFA World Cup, UEFA (Union of European Football Associations) Championship), host countries also screen individuals when they enter the country in order to not allow known hooligans and other criminals or persons of interest into the country. Nevertheless, the British have gone further for football and hooliganism, in that besides government legislation such as the 1989 Football Spectators Act and the 2001 Football Disorder Bill, a football licensing authority and a football intelligence unit have been created (Hall, 2010). American football's premier event, the Super Bowl, is also relevant here, as "the US government has classified the Super Bowl as a 'national special security event'", one in which past violence complacency behaviour has been replaced in this post-9/11 world with terrorist-ready behaviour (Schimmel, 2011: 3277).

While much work on security in sports events has been descriptive in nature, we do find some analytical work also being done. A review of the literature by Giulianotti and Klauser

(2010) resulted in their suggestion of three sets of issues/problems regarding security research in sport mega-events:

1   *Comparison issues between the Northern and Southern Hemispheres*: the increase of Southern Hemisphere countries (whether developed, e.g. Australia, or developing, e.g. Brazil) hosting such events means that we should examine the security risks in the South as compared to the North, and security knowledge and resource (technology, capital) transfers between Northern and Southern countries. It includes developing an in-depth comparative analysis of Northern and Southern countries' approaches to security (and risk) analysis and management. For example, Cornelissen (2011) examined the 2010 FIFA World Cup held in South Africa and its securitization processes.

2   *Event-specific security risks and strategies*: as for general risks, which are to a certain degree event-dependent, security risks and strategies are also relatively event-specific. Thus, understanding the similarities and differences in terrorism, spectator and political violence, and poverty/social division and urban crime's main causes, processes/forms, effects, strategies, symbolism, and indirect consequences will be important in developing the security risk-management literature for major sports events.

3   *Security legacies post-event*: just as event bidders and managers discuss potential venue and infrastructure legacies, security processes in events can also provide legacies related to new security technologies, best practices, government legislation and policies, social transformations (e.g. escorting "undesirable" individuals outside the city limits), social and transsocietal relationship changes (e.g. new relationships created between organizations and law enforcement agencies), and urban redevelopment. These legacies should be examined for the positive and negative consequences (e.g. permanent presence of security cameras in city streets can mean that "Big Brother" is now potentially always watching), as well as the ethical consequences of such legacies.

Examining these avenues of research likely means drawing from a range of theories within sociology and ethics, management and economics, geography, and political studies and urban policy. A variety of theories and (combined) theoretical frameworks could be applied to develop these three research directions. Some such work is beginning. For example, time series computer-generated forecasting models can be used to examine the impact of certain security risks and events (e.g. terrorist attacks like those of 9/11) on a host region's economy. This was the case for Lee *et al.*'s (2010) study of the effects of 9/11 on the Korean economy, Korea being host to the 2002 FIFA World Cup. Their findings demonstrated that the sporting event had a positive impact on the Korean economy, but this impact was smaller than the negative impact of the terrorist attacks, which can in part explain a decrease in the country's tourism industry and economy for that year. As well, researchers are interested in security plans and processes for different editions of the same event (e.g. the London 2012 versus Beijing 2008 versus Athens 2004 Olympic Games – Floridis, 2004; Johnson, 2008; Yu *et al.*, 2009). This would allow a researcher to do a meta-analysis of these articles to determine key lessons and best practices, such as when computer-simulation techniques are useful for security planning and implementation – the answer to this question may be that they are useful early on to develop the plans, and closer to the given event as a training tool for staff (Johnson, 2008).

Moreover, a meta-analysis or a comparative analysis of these articles would highlight the impact of geo-political structures and processes (e.g. UK versus China versus Greece).

Besides those three sets of issues/problems noted above, we add the following:

■ *Spectator and media perceptions*: this set of issues is a relatively popular one for researchers. Attendees at sports events tend to feel safe, and the security measures put in place do not seem to detract (or enhance) spectators' enjoyment of the sports events or from planning to attend a sports event; some attendees are even seen to be openly defiant of security concerns (e.g. Hall *et al.*, 2009; Taylor and Toohey, 2006). Gender (women seem to have more pessimistic risk perceptions, though men believe security measures detract more from their enjoyment), age (older residents seem more pessimistic about security measures affecting attendance), and residents versus travelling tourists (residents seem more aware of security measures but are also less concerned) are three variables that seem to impact perceptions of security risks (Hall *et al.*, 2009; Konstantaki and Wickens, 2010; Taylor and Toohey, 2006, 2007). While we seem to understand spectators' perceptions, there is a need to link the intention to visit with actual visit behaviour; also, we can examine perception of associated security measures such as anti-terrorism legislation. We can also see how implementing different security strategies (whether venue-based or urban) and increasing residents' awareness and resilience can affect/help in event security processes (e.g. Coaffee and Fussey, 2011). Finally, we can also examine other stakeholders' perceptions of security measures, such as athletes/delegations or even the media. Media researchers and sociologists (Crelinstein, 1994; Lenart and Targ, 1995; Simmons and Lowry, 1990) have examined the media's role in and representation/construction of terrorism and pro-/anti-terrorist sentiments. Terrorism falls within what is newsworthy (see Chapter 8) as it is typically unexpected, dramatic, shocking, tragic, and/or incredible. The media have been found to portray terrorism and terrorists as anti-democratic, as contrary to freedom and liberty, as being against economic expansion, especially as it pertains to the United Kingdom and the United States. The media are seen to want to elicit anger, fear, distrust, and a general sense of emotion in the face of terrorism, which ultimately helps the media sell their newspapers and be watched by more individuals (see Atkinson and Young, 2002 for a more in-depth discussion of this topic). As it pertains to security in major sports events, we see the Western countries (e.g. the United States) who are the "victims" of terrorism and hosts of these major sports events being depicted by the media as strong, the safest place to be, and as recovering victims. The terrorists have been in turn depicted as "others" and as enemies of the state (us against them). Still, "Media coverage portrays a general public acceptance of significantly increased security and surveillance with only a few isolated stories reporting that the changes have compromised human rights and or the sport spectator experience", according to Taylor and Toohey (2011: 3259). What do these media depictions mean for sport event managers in charge of securing their event as well as the communications managers? What is the relationship between media's portrayal of terrorism/terrorists and spectators' perceptions? Are there differences for local/national versus international events or spectators (cf. Gartner, 2004)? These are just some questions which remain to be answered in the literature.

- *Assessing security and terrorism risks*: the broader security and terrorism literature identifies different kinds of terrorism risk analysis techniques. For example, probability risk analysis tools such as event trees, influence trees, decision trees, and fault trees, as well as economic assessments, have been used despite criticisms that such tools are not appropriate for evolving and adaptive cases such as terrorism (Akhtar *et al.*, 2010; Brown and Cox Jr, 2011; Ezell *et al.*, 2010). Since terrorists usually know more than the sports event manager does about what will happen, and seek information which will exploit weaknesses in the whole system or event in our case (not just an individual component like a venue), researchers have described infrastructure resilience/terrorist capabilities analyses and other techniques such as "network analysis, computational simulation, information infrastructure, and long-term policy goals" to develop network or whole-system-based strategies, which are suggested to be better alternatives to traditional probability risk analysis tools (Brown and Cox Jr, 2011; Comfort, 2005: 335). With some modifications, however, it may be possible to use more traditional measures for terrorism risk security measures analyses (though this is still debated). To illustrate, Akhtar *et al.* (2010) suggested using an inverse ex-post (economic event) analysis, which can demonstrate the implicit benefits (e.g. implicit costs of lives saved, infrastructure costs) for estimated terror risks and risk changes. Another suggestion is to use a multitude of tools and then draw a conclusion from the overall analysis, since each tool has flaws and deficiencies (Ezell *et al.*, 2010). These suggestions may help justify increased spending on security, though whether to the extent that it has been for major sports events remains questionable and therefore perhaps another avenue for future research, besides determining proper terrorism and security analysis tools and techniques specific to major sports events.
- *The governance of security*: what are the relationships between public, private, and non-profit organizations for security issues in the context of major sports events? What are the consequences of different security governance structures on decision-making and event hosting? What are the performance consequences for these public, private, and non-profit organizations for different security governance structures? Where do finance and politics fit in (cf. Aitken, 2011; Comfort, 2005)? What are the consequences for the general public of these different security governance structures? These are all questions that remain to be answered in the context of major sports events.

While the tendency would be to take a post-positivist approach (see Crotty, 1998) for such studies, as Toohey and Taylor (2008) pointed out, there are other ways to examine risk and security. One way to do so is using the concepts and theories associated with the risk society, a perspective that focuses on society's increasing awareness of individual, local, and global dangers (environmental, terrorist, etc.) and the associated need to develop strategies to mitigate these dangers (Beck, 1992; Toohey and Taylor, 2008). As they emerge, risks are debated publicly and politically for their social, economic, and political consequences. Whether the risk is actually present or absent does not matter; precautionary measures are taken or required of the risk "sponsor" or originator – this is the precautionary principle, and it dominates risk management in the Western world today. It is associated with greater individualism and subjective perceptions of reality, but also greater uncertainty, fear, and anxiety – this is exactly what terrorists play upon (Furedi, 2002; Toohey and Taylor, 2008), and therefore what sport event managers have to deal with when planning their security measures. Thus, we see a vicious cycle composed of terrorism, risk society, precautionary principle, and sport event security (Toohey and Taylor, 2008).

Besides the risk society, we can also take a critical approach (see Alvesson and Deetz, 1996, 2000) to examining security in major sports events. Such a reflexive and reflective approach allows us to ask questions such as "Why does security not work?" or "How can organizing committees truly plan for all worst-case scenarios?". Speight (2010) suggested that it is important for (sport event) managers to find cost-effective to secure susceptible assets, with unspecified risk-based security measures being particularly costly and counterproductive; and, by risk's own nature, the use of past risks may not prove adequate in predicting future risks. Thus, before turning to the practitioner's perspective, in the interest of being critical, we leave the reader with a question to ponder: given the high costs for security (in the billions of dollars for Olympic Games today), is this amount too much or, if nothing happens at the event, then was it worth the cost? Some would argue that it is the cost of doing business when preparing a major sports event (a sunk cost now instead of what used to be more of a discretionary cost). What do you, the reader, believe? Ultimately, when event security documents are declassified in 20–30 years, historians will be able to help answer that question (cf. Gorrell, 2002). Nevertheless, we leave the reader with the following thought from Samatas (2011: 3347):

> post-9/11 Olympic security and surveillance have authoritarian effects, which are dependent on global factors like anti-terrorist and neo-liberal policies, and local factors such as the type of host regime, culture and society. . . . [Such] surveillance systems have an emerging anti-democratic legacy which stretches beyond the hosting of the Olympics.

THE PRACTITIONER'S PERSPECTIVE ON RISK MANAGEMENT AND SECURITY

The mammoth task of providing security for a major sports event defies logic because the sports event manager has to put processes and resources in place to manage the unthinkable – earthquakes, tsunamis, no snow, the death of an athlete, health pandemics, and terrorist assaults (to name but a few). It is important that everyone associated with the sports event feel safe and secure. An individual's role in the event will place the emphasis on security in different ways. An athlete can be a target in several areas – the athletes' village, while en route to or from the event, during competition, medal ceremonies, and in the athlete seating area of any venue. Protocol managers always have their lounges and seating areas populated with politicians, VIPs, and IPPs, and are more often than not in close proximity to both the media and athlete seating. So potential threats to these dignitaries and other key event stakeholder groups are always on security's and protocol's radar, which can add a layer of ever-present stress. Psychologically, it is like a dark blanket that will only be lifted when the Games end and everyone is safely back in their home location. Imagine how difficult it is to ever relax or exhale and the cumulative stress that builds in the body and minds of those carrying this responsibility.

Security is also a part of the language of contracts, MOUs, and agreements – who will be responsible and liable in the event of a security breach? This must be articulated in writing, in advance. Test events are also part of the security language. For example, to test out the 2012 London Olympic Games security system, "U.K. police managed to [unfortunately] smuggle a fake bomb into Olympic Park" only 200 days before the opening ceremonies (Kirka, 2012: 1). This test will have provided valuable information to the organizing committee and those in charge of securing the Games.

While there are known security risks, there is also an aura of "you don't know what you don't know". Everything is put into place to make the athletes, the venues, and the spectators as safe as humanly possible. For example, in each venue there is usually a secret "safe area" that is designated for world leaders and heads of state so they can be quickly sequestered in case of a security threat or emergency. There is an emergency plan for each venue, sometimes over 100 pages long, and everyone in the venue receives training on what to do in case of an emergency before they start their first shift.

While the venues are being constructed and before staff move in, access is freer. After staff move to the venue, human traffic is organized by accreditation, and there is a predetermined "lockdown" date prior to the event. While post-lockdown procedures can be a bit cumbersome for people to go through, it certainly sets the tone for a secure environment. Accreditation, at its core, is a document demonstrating that the person passed a security clearance/background check and provides the areas where the person is allowed access within the venue – thereby limiting both access to the venues to only those who are cleared to do so and within the venues to only those who need to be in a particular area. Moreover, once a staff member moves to their venue, they no longer have access to their previous working environment (i.e. at headquarters). Once lockdown has occurred, venue security "takes over" the venue and everyone responds to their instructions regarding risk management and security procedures. Security is usually strict for both the workforce and all other outside people who are associated with the event.

The number of people required to secure a major sports event is so large that it could not be accomplished without integrating all types of law enforcement, from local police forces, to armed forces, to other law enforcement agencies to international agents protecting IPPs on foreign soil. The coordination and subsequent scheduling involved to create one large policing force is like tuning a symphony. Much practice is required to ensure communication is received clearly and executed with precision. There is no room for error. Moreover, law enforcement agents are human resources, and thus are a finite resource for a country, as are the financial resources needed to create a safe sports event. The human, financial, and even material resources dedicated to a major sports event, its risk and security management, provoke the question: can security for a major sports event at home compromise the country's security/military efforts both at home and abroad? This is a question we leave for the reader to ponder.

Finally, from a risk-management perspective, we also pose the following question for the reader to ponder: in the face of health epidemics, is it the right of the organizing committee to force individuals to have vaccines such as in the case of LOCOG, where 500 Olympic workers were vaccinated against smallpox "to respond to a biological terror attack" at the Games (Cecil, 2012: 1)? Such a risk management situation pins staff's rights and freedom of choice (in Western countries at least) against peer pressure and pressure from higher up to help mitigate risks; does it take away from staff's liberties?

CHAPTER SUMMARY

In this chapter we examined the concepts of risk, risk analysis, and risk management. A risk can be defined as a dangerous element or as uncertainty associated with an outcome. Risk analysis or assessment refers to examining the risks themselves. Risk management is a proactive process; it involves the assessment of all possible risks for a given event and its stakeholders. This is done by strategically planning, anticipating, preventing, and minimizing responses to mitigate the risks identified. We presented 15 risk categories split into tangible and intangible types and eight possible risk-management strategies (see Table 11.1). We also described the risk management process in major sports events. We then examined security, and in particular terrorism. We saw that terrorism-related risks are different than other types of risks since they are adaptive and evolving in nature, and we have incomplete information – in fact the terrorists usually have more information than sports event managers do. Terrorism is also more of a systems-wide risk, instead of being a risk focused on a particular issue (e.g. human resources, finances, or infrastructure). Different best practices, tools, techniques, and assessments (as well as their questioning) were presented. Finally, we examined potential avenues for future research in risk management and security as they pertain to major sports events, including suggesting some non-positivist approaches.

From a practitioner's perspective, we highlighted the needs and psychological effects of security. We also noted how security changes and tightens as Games-time approaches, as do the types of personnel that comprise the security team. Finally, we addressed some administrative considerations.

EXPERT CASE: OLYMPIC GAMES SECURITY PLANNING

Security planning for an Olympic Games is unlike any other major sports event. Multiple sports venues, spread over an expansive geographic area, with simultaneous events occurring at each, add layers of complexity to both security and sport operations.

It is important to separate the sport planning and management role from the security planning and management role. Sport is concerned with the events themselves; the competition, athletes' well-being, rules of the game, and the entertainment and hosting of the spectators of the events. Security is concerned about venue safety and security, the physical security of the athletes and spectators, protection of the venue, and broader concerns related to acts of protest, acts of terrorism, and disaster response.

While the security planning and management can arguably fall under the realm of overall sport planning and management, this is handled much differently at an Olympic Games than it is at a local sports event. As an example, when the Vancouver Canucks or the BC Lions play a game in one of the stadiums in Vancouver, the sport organizations themselves coordinate the sporting event and include private security functions within each venue. The Vancouver Police Department (VPD) will assign officers at each of these events to provide a policing presence within the arena or stadium, specifically to deal with criminal behaviour, and assist on-site security when dealing with unruly spectators or other problems. It is a more efficient deployment model, and reduces the burden on the general patrol officer working out on the street. Given the large number of people within a confined location, and concerns over timely access from external police officers into a venue, this is the most efficient way to deliver policing services within the venue. Deployment numbers and models for the police are based on experience, perceived need depending on the size of the crowd and importance of the game, and a risk assessment of the demands expected of the police. Rock concerts would be one example where the police deployment in the same venue may vary, depending on the band playing, and the type of crowd generally expected for that band.

While local police handle local sporting events, the security needs of an Olympic Games requires a substantially larger police and security response. This is generally done at a national level; and in Canada the Royal Canadian Mounted Police (RCMP) were the national police agency responsible for security at the 2010 Vancouver Olympic Winter Games. The policing structure within the Vancouver region added a layer of complexity to the delivery of this security model, as venues were located in the cities of Vancouver, Richmond, and West Vancouver, along with mountain venues in and around the resort municipality of Whistler. This geographic complexity required the national police force to work alongside and cooperatively with four police departments of jurisdiction (the police department responsible for policing services where the venue is geographically located). To ensure communication across all police agencies, along with the Canadian Forces (CF) who were also a partner agency in securing the remote mountain venues and air space, the Vancouver 2010 Integrated Security Unit (Vancouver2010-ISU) was established, under the command of the RCMP. Representatives from all area police agencies participated in the Vancouver2010-ISU, with many having key leadership roles. It was an integrated policing model that had never been seen before in Canada, and it worked very effectively.

Security needs for an Olympic Games have evolved over the years, and are predicated on past actions at previous Games. The events of the 1972 Munich Olympic Games led to unprecedented security planning and response at the subsequent Games in Montreal in 1976. Since then, global acts of terrorism and political unrest have resulted in ever-increasing risk-management steps being taken in the different host cities, as police agencies work to keep the athletes, visitors, and residents safe. While the events in Munich clearly targeted the athletes within their residence, the urban domain surrounding the venues has also been subject to attack. In 1996, in Atlanta, a bomb exploded in a park, near a medal presentation ceremony, killing one person. While security measures are intensified at and surrounding the venues, delivering a complete security blanket in the hundreds of square kilometres surrounding the region is a near impossible task.

The mandate of the Vancouver2010-ISU was to deliver security to the Olympic venues, in spite of the fact that the venues were situated in the broader community at large. Policing the broader community remained the responsibility of the police of jurisdiction. In the city of Vancouver, the Vancouver2010-ISU coordinated all security planning and management at the stadium (opening and closing ceremonies and medal events), Canada Hockey Place (ice hockey), the Pacific Coliseum (figure skating and short track speed skating), and the Vancouver Olympic Centre (curling). In other words, if it was within the fence line surrounding the venue, it was the Vancouver2010-ISU's responsibility. If it was outside the fences, it was the responsibility of the VPD. Within Vancouver, all of the entertainment district, the bars and restaurants, and the city-organized public events and viewing areas fell under the responsibility of the VPD.

Parallel planning occurred, with overlap and communication between the two policing groups, but there were clear lines of responsibility. While the Vancouver2010-ISU planned for the events in-venue, the VPD planned for security and policing deployment throughout Vancouver. Given the nature of the security systems around each of the venues, with double rows of fencing and electronic intrusion systems and cameras, combined with security screening to get into a venue, it was highly improbable that a protest or large disturbance would occur within a venue. Rather, the protests occurred on the streets outside the venues, and fell to the command and control of the VPD to deal with. The Vancouver2010-ISU only had a situational awareness of what was happening on the streets, as there was no direct threat to the venues themselves.

Within the venues, the security planning was exceptionally complex. The physical security at the venues was unprecedented in Canada. Search teams looking for suspicious devices swept each venue and, once completed, the venue was locked down. Perimeter intrusion detection systems and CCTV systems monitored the entire perimeter of each venue. Screening processes were established for all vehicle and foot traffic (including athletes and visiting dignitaries), ensuring that no prohibited items or unaccredited personnel were brought into the locked-down venue. Those control measures satisfied the security forces within the venue that they were working in a safe environment, and their primary day-to-day focus was on general policing duties within the venue. These duties included many meet-and-greet strategies with the public, but also routine and regular foot patrols around the venue (inside and outside the fence lines) to maintain that secure perimeter.

Venue security was a 24/7 operation, with the venue locked down 3–5 days before the sports event began, and then full-time around-the-clock policing inside the venue until the sports events concluded. Each venue had a sport manager, employed by VANOC and responsible for overseeing the sport event itself. In addition, each venue had a police security commander, overseeing the security operations within the venue. While both worked hand-in-hand, and regularly communicated, security was the paramount concern at the Olympic Games, and should a security event unfold, it would take precedence over the continuation of the sport event.

Preparation for the security of the 2010 Vancouver Olympic Winter Games took years. In the months preceding the Games, command staff received specialized training and numerous exercises and scenarios were conducted, testing all of the venues. These scenarios culminated in a major two-day "Gold Command" simulation exercise, where all levels of the security command structure and security response were put through their paces. It included CF air response, Coast Guard and Marine response, and the use of emergency response teams for hostage-rescue scenarios.

Defining the scenarios to test was done through a process of examining past events at Olympic Games, and consideration for the frequency and seriousness of the event. In any risk-management process, police agencies examine the level of risk in a matrix with the frequency of its occurrence. High-frequency, low-risk events (e.g. a drunk annoying people in the stadium seating area) are events to which police response will be automatic, as it is something police officers deal with on a day-to-day basis. A low-frequency, high-risk event (e.g. a bomb detonated around the security fence at a venue) is something of which there is less experience, and a greater need to exercise, given the scope and history of Olympic Games in the past.

The security demands for the 2010 Olympic Winter Games required in excess of 5,000 police officers dedicated to policing the venues. The Vancouver2010-ISU mobilized police officers from across the country and from many different police forces to ensure sufficient numbers within each venue. For example, at the Vancouver Olympic Centre (curling), there were 137 police officers assigned full-time to that specific venue, providing 24/7 policing services for 17 days. Those officers represented 39 different policing agencies; although the venue itself was located within the city of Vancouver, there was only one VPD officer assigned to this venue – the venue security commander. In fact, there were only nine VPD officers assigned to work within the venues themselves. The remaining VPD personnel were all required to police the urban domain surrounding the venues.

The urban domain policing was over and above the regular policing services the VPD provides to the residents of Vancouver. Additional squads were deployed, including specialized mounted and bicycle units, crowd management units, emergency response teams, and increased foot patrols, to provide a highly visible policing presence in the urban domain. In addition, off-duty Vancouver2010-ISU resources and other regional policing units were occasionally brought in to augment the VPD numbers, ensuring the highest level of security and policing presence in the crowded downtown areas.

Within the venue, it was the responsibility of the venue security commander to build his team and prepare them for their deployment within a very confined space. With officers from across the country, and representing many police departments, it was imperative that all had an understanding of their role within the venue, and their response to actions within it, given the local laws in British Columbia. Venue commanders delivered orientation sessions to all of their personnel, providing expectations and roles and responsibilities to the full workforce. In addition, the human component needed to be managed, as personnel were far from their homes, and frequently had to deal with logistical or personal issues that interfered with their work. Further, in spite of the unique nature of policing an Olympic Games, officers who ordinarily have vast responsibilities in their home departments found themselves in a strange city, guarding a fence line on the night shift, for numerous successive days. While this was novel at the outset, motivating these employees became an ongoing challenge.

Intelligence-led policing was a critical piece of the safety and security of the 2010 Olympic Winter Games. A Joint Intelligence Group worked diligently over the years preceding the Games, building intelligence and information on world events, political unrest, and global issues, ensuring that the best intelligence was available to command staff at the venues. The objective was to inform police decision-making and be better equipped to prevent a potential targeted attack, and target-harden potential areas of attack. This pre-ventative measure proved invaluable, and in the few instances where there were problems with protests and property damage in the urban domain, this intelligence was vital in the successful prosecution of the offenders.

There is no other sport security experience available like delivering security at an Olympic Games. The sense of pride felt when your own country is able to deliver a sports event of this magnitude, without incident, is incredible. This pride is what fuels the police officers and police leaders to strive to succeed, as no one wants something bad to happen in their country, on their watch, with the eyes of the world focused on every move. This is further amplified on a local level, as security and privacy expectation differ here in North America, compared to other parts of the world, where a more oppressive approach to security may be more acceptable.

By Superintendent Daryl Wiebe, Vancouver Police Department

Case questions

1   How is security different for an Olympic Games than other events the region typically hosts?

2   How have security needs evolved over the course of Olympic history?

3   How does security and privacy differ in Canada/North America versus other regions of the world?

CHAPTER QUESTIONS

1   Compare the concepts of risk, terrorism, and security. Should they be considered similar, or are they truly different? Why?

2   What does venue lockdown mean?

3   What types of law enforcement agencies are needed for Games security, and why is there a need for different groups?

4   Think about a sports event you are familiar with. Undertake a risk analysis of the event. Provide potential risk-management strategies for each risk you identify.

5   Pick one of the potential research avenues in risk management presented in this chapter for major sports events. Describe how you would go about examining this topic, providing a research question and methodology in the process.

FURTHER READING

If you are interested in risk management and security, we suggest the following:

Appenzeller, H. (ed.) (2005) *Risk Management in Sport: Issues and Strategies*, Durham, NC: Carolina Academic Press.

Bennett, C. J. & Haggerty, K. D. (eds) (2011) *Security Games: Surveillance and Control at Mega-Events*, Abingdon: Routledge.

Hall, S., Cooper, W., Marciani, L., & McGee, J. (2012) *Security Management for Sports and Special Events*, Champaign, IL: Human Kinetics.

Chapter 12

Technology

OBJECTIVES

■ To understand the different types of technologies that can be involved in the planning and implementation of major sports events
■ To understand the impact of technology on managerial decision-making and processes within major sports events
■ To understand the role technology plays in individual behaviour and performance

ILLUSTRATIVE CASE: FIFA AND ITS EVENTS ON THE CUTTING EDGE OF TECHNOLOGY

New media, such as social media websites and blogs, are changing how we live our lives. For example, the social media website Facebook had over 845 million monthly users by the end of December 2011 (Facebook, 2012) and Twitter has over 100 million active users (Twitter, 2011) worldwide.

This is also true for FIFA. FIFA's 2010 World Cup in South Africa was the biggest live sports event to be broadcast in 3D: over 30 countries around the world had access to 25 of the 64 matches in 3D, thanks to innovative broadcasters and Sony technology (FIFA, n.d.). The 2010 World Cup demonstrated incredible viewing numbers: it had 71,867 broadcast hours over 214 territories, reaching a television audience of 3.2 billion individuals (Kantar-Sport, n.d.), and a total television audience of 40 billion over the course of the month-long event.

Nearly 100 licensees also provided online viewing of matches and 35 licensees provided mobile coverage in over 80 territories, viewing options which were used by millions of fans around the world (KantarSport, n.d.). Fans could also obtain the latest information as it happened on their mobile smartphones and tweet their reactions. FIFA also created an Inter-active World Cup, the latest edition being in 2010 when over 775,000 individuals entered and competed against each other over a six-month period to determine the champion.

At the time of writing FIFA had yet to put video replay cameras in goals for use by offi-cials during matches, thought its president, Sepp Blatter, started to push for this technology in early March 2012 (*Sportsmail Reporter*, 2012). Still, FIFA and its organizing committees do use other technologies for the hosting of World Cups. This includes the latest artificial turf, new advances in stadium design, new technology for increased security, the design and materials used for the official ball, and the material used by the teams and officials for the uniforms and shoes.

As we can see, major sports events are at the forefront of technology use.

THE THEORY BEHIND TECHNOLOGY

We are in the information age, the knowledge economy. Today, our world is shaped by continually emerging new technologies, such as electronic equipment, new materials, the internet, and new media (e.g. Twitter, LinkedIn, Facebook, YouTube, 4G (fourth-generation) mobile smartphones, tablets, etc.). This is also true for sport. Athletes and coaches are continually looking for the newest technologies to help their performance, which have been empirically shown to somewhat increase performance (Haake, 2009), although there is still a significant degree of potential for additional performance improvements (Versluis, 2005); it may have had a greater impact on Paralympic and other athletes with disabilities so far (Prystupa *et al.*, 2006). Major sports event managers are not immune to technological changes either. In fact, it is an intrinsic part of their daily lives. Table 12.1 provides an overview of the different technologies that have emerged to change the event management landscape. Below, we describe in greater detail what research tells us about technology and what types of studies are undertaken under the technology banner.

What is technology?

So, what is technology? It can be material/equipment- (e.g. the latest smartphone or golf club), knowledge-, or process-based (e.g. how to create the best snowboard) (cf. Perrow, 1967). We find technologies at the industry, organizational, work/group, and individual levels (Slack and Parent, 2006). Industry-wide technologies can include new materials, knowledge, processes, standards, or new products (e.g. the speed skating clap skate introduced in the late 1990s). At an organizational level, we can speak of the technology complexity, which differs depending on the unit/small-batch, mass/large-batch, or continuous-process production approach taken (Woodward, 1958, 1965). We can also speak of craft, routine, non-routine, and engineering technology, which differ based on the degree of variability in the task at hand and the degree to which problems are analysable (Perrow, 1967).

Technology can also be used as a *source of coordination* to mitigate task interdependence between departments or groups (Slack and Parent, 2006; Thompson, 1967):

■ Sequential task interdependence, in which the series of tasks must be performed in a particular order. For this, long-linked technology is needed, where the process of the output of one task turns into the input of the next task.
■ Pooled interdependence, in which two or more independent organizations or departments (e.g. governments, sponsors) provide inputs to a linking organization or department (e.g. an organizing committee), requires mediating technologies.

236

Table 12.1 Electronic technologies changing the face of events

Type of technology	When is it useful	Description
Audience response systems and speaker interaction	Marketing and communications, implementation	Mobile texting (SMS), Twitter, web, or audience response system devices that allow for spectator interaction with the event as it is occurring
Bandwidth	Implementation	The more information needs to pass through communication lines at the same time, the higher the bandwidth needed
Basic websites	Marketing and communications, planning	Offers one-way communication from event organizers to stakeholders
Blogs	Marketing and communications, planning, implementation, and wrap-up	An online diary by event organizers or stakeholders (e.g. athletes, spectators)
Desktop computer programs (MS Office Suite, Wordperfect Suite)	Planning, implementation, and wrap-up	The basic writing, numbers, and presentation-based computer programs managers use. Other programs also include project-based programs such as MS Project and publication programs such as Photoshop and MS Publisher.
Digital recording and live streaming media	Marketing and communications, implementation	Digitally recording the event and/or providing a live stream of the event online, or through mobile devices, podcasts, live sites, or other distribution channels
DVDs and CD-ROM media	Marketing and communications, planning	Digitally recorded data (text files, audio, and/or video files) onto discs which can be used for storage purposes or distribution
Electronic judging systems, motion-capture technologies, and other sport decision technology aids	Implementation	Sports such as figure skating now use touch screens and integrated, computerized judging systems to evaluate competitors, and others use motion-capture technologies (e.g. in golf) and "goal-line" technologies/cameras to examine athlete performance and outcome (see www.motiongolf.com and www.goallinetechnology.com for examples)
Email e-blasts	Marketing and communications, planning, implementation, and wrap-up	Emails sent to people who have opted into the receiving of these emails, creating a dialogue between sender and receiver
Event wikis	Marketing and communications, planning, implementation, and wrap-up	Event sites that can be edited by anyone (like Wikipedia), thereby fostering a sense of community

continued

Table 12.1 Continued

Type of technology	When is it useful	Description
Event-specific web sites	Marketing and communications, planning, implementation, and wrap-up	Offers one-way and two-way communications between event organizers and stakeholders for information sharing, announcements, online registration, job applications, results distribution, etc.
Industry information portals	Planning, virtual site selection and research, and for planning purposes	Offers online event management resources and tools (e.g. from the IOC's Olympic Games Knowledge Management (OGKM) site, convention, and tourism bureau)
Mobile technologies	Planning, implementation, wrap-up	3G, 4G, and even 5G smartphones which allow one to do almost everything you do on a computer to be done using your mobile phone (e.g. airline ticket barcodes, viewing podcasts, surfing the web). Also, personal digital assistants (PDAs), which can be used to conduct on-site surveys/evaluations of the event, and GPS (Global Positioning System) systems allow the tracking by spectators and coaches, for example, of athletes running a marathon.
Near field communications (NFC) and radio frequency identification (RFID)	Planning and implementation	Short- or long-range wireless scanning devices which allow for an exchange of information (e.g. using barcodes on tickets and accreditations to verify access credentials of the individual, tollbooth, or parking garage entry badges). Newer technologies, such as credentialling technology (e.g. plastic cards replacing paper tickets and barcodes to track spectators in real time) are seen as more effective.
Online requests for proposals (RFPs)	Planning, virtual site selection, and research	Call for proposals (e.g. from potential hotels) and review of submissions can all be done online.
Podcasts	Marketing and communications, planning, implementation	Audio and video media files which can be played on mobile devices (phones, mp3 players, computers).
Really simple syndication (RSS) feed	Marketing and communications, planning, implementation, and wrap-up	A tool to obtain continually updated information about the latest news, videos, blog entries, etc., from a site

Technology	Phase	Description
Site and room design software	Planning and implementation	Computer-aided designs (CADs) which allows individuals to efficiently design and revise their sites and rooms in 2D and/or 3D.
Social network sites	Marketing and communications, planning, implementation	Offers two-way communications between event organizers and stakeholders.
Tweets	Marketing and communications, planning, implementation, and wrap-up	A short form of blogging through the Twitter website.
Viral videos	Marketing and communications, planning, implementation, and wrap-up	Sharing of content through online videos (e.g. through a YouTube channel).
Virtual signage	Marketing and communications, planning, implementation	The use of video screens, scoreboards, jumbotrons, blue/green-screens, etc., to temporarily display wayfinding, informational, and/or marketing signage for in-venue and/or in-house spectators.
Virtual tours of proposed venues	Planning, for virtual site selection, and research	Offers 3D tailored viewing of potential sites without having to travel to the potential location (see www.virtualvisit.ca for example).
Voice over Internet Protocol (VoIP)	Planning, implementation, and wrap-up	Use of a high-speed internet connection to phone others (vs. traditional landline), such as Skype.
Webinars	Planning and implementation	Web-based seminar or presentation, to which attendees can participate through chats, texting, and/or email, without having to leave the comfort of their office or home.
Wireless and/or wired	Implementation	Requirements for high-speed internet access that is either plugged in (e.g. a stationary desktop) or portable (e.g. mobile phones).

Source: see Birmingham and David, 2011; Fenich, 2012; Johnson, 2010; Mendez, 1999; Santomier and Shuart, 2008; Wyld, 2008 for more information.

- Reciprocal interdependence, in which a group of organizations, units, or individuals all mutually influence each other, requires intensive technology as it is the most complex form of interdependence. Many processes within organizing committees would fall into this category.

Technology can also be described as a *resource* that must be accounted for when doing resource/supply and feasibility studies (Getz, 2005). Existing technologies (e.g. existing light rail systems, ticketing systems) can be used, but new technologies can also be created specifically for the event (e.g. a new results system). New media, in particular, can be used for (Santomier and Shuart, 2008):

- gathering, searching, sorting, distributing, and communicating information;
- designing, editing, and producing; and
- access and display.

Successful projects using new media formats should be simple to use, consider revenue sources, be repeatable, include viral elements, use multiple platforms, and have a fit between the concept/platform and the audience/stakeholders targeted (Santomier and Shuart, 2008). Other, non-electronic technologies, such as new artificial turfs (e.g. Cole, 2004), should also be considered (cost, uses, impacts, etc.) by sport event managers when planning their event.

Technologies can reduce operating costs, increase flexibility, increase control and integration of managerial processes, and provide higher-quality products/services (Child, 1984; Slack and Parent, 2006). It is useful for a range of event management aspects such as communications, transportation, sport services, sport production, planning processes, security and risk management, venue building and overlay, logistics, etc. For example, the venue CADs are a more efficient way to plan and design a venue (versus doing it by hand), but they also serve a coordination function by allowing other FAs to see where they will be and to proceed with their own planning (see Chapter 7 for more details on CADs). Moreover, the internet has allowed knowledge transfer to occur more efficiently between organizing committees, such as the IOC's Olympic Games Knowledge Management (OGKM) website. Technologies have also helped HRM processes, more specifically those associated with general employee development, feedback provision, and annual performance appraisals; in these cases, technology should be seen as a facilitator of the processes (Miller, 2003). Thus, it should not be the technology itself but rather how it is used that impacts outcome or performance (DeSanctis and Poole, 1994; O'Reilly and Knight, 2007; Poole and DeSanctis, 1989).

Technology is also a *force or trend* affecting events as it has led to new leisure pursuits, such as (online) video gaming, and it has affected the way sport event managers work and the performance (effectiveness and efficiency) of sport event organizing committees (Getz, 2005). Event marketers have electronic databases to which they can now turn to promote their product, though Getz (2005) warned us about the privacy issues associated with such databases. Meetings between people around the world can now also be undertaken virtually through videoconferencing and VoIP technology (e.g. Skype), thereby decreasing costs and saving travel time. It has also changed the event-goer's experience through online event information and ticket purchasing, electronic barcode scanning of tickets, security screenings using the latest technology, the use of smartcards as replacements for cash at the event, live streaming of competitions, and immediate downloading of results onto smartphones, etc. If quality sports events should be a sensory experience (sight, smell, taste, touch, and hearing), technology certainly has its place in the creation of the experience. This can include the use of: sound equipment (microphones, speakers, etc.) to play music and for announcers; video screens and jumbotrons for videos and information sharing; computers and timing equipment for results purposes, obtaining results on mobile phones and tablets; pyrotechnics and lasers for entertainment purposes; and so on. There are even an increasing number of sport-and-technology-specific conferences and trade shows popping up around the world, such as Sport and Technology: The Conference (www.sportandtechnology.com) and Sportel Monaco (www.sportelmonaco.com).

Technologies are also a *source of change*, typically an external source of change, which impacts the structure of an organization (Barley, 1986; Bartunek, 1984). Technologies can impact the structure of an industry as well. For example, different product lifecycle achievement levels will have differing impacts on a given industry's structure. Moreover, the industry's own lifecycle will impact the preferred type of technology. To wit, industries that are in decline, "like skiing or yachting, are rather concentrated and tend to focus on process innovations. Fast expanding sectors, like snowboard, mountain bike and cycling, are rather atomized and innovate much more on new product and materials" (Desbordes, 2002: 481). We also see technology changing patterns or structures of interaction between people, such as noticing a decreasing use of telephone (and, we can argue, paper) communications and an increasing use of email communications – this has an impact on the organization's culture, sometimes seen as being less personal or face-to-face (Battenfield and Kent, 2007). Virtual businesses have also changed the nature of communication between businesses and consumers. It used to be business-to-consumer and business-to-business. Now websites allow for consumer-to-consumer communications, businesses, and dealings (O'Beirne, 2012).

Research on technology

Besides the above research examining what technology is and how it can be conceptualized and used, there are other studies focusing on technology. First, some research examines the impact of blogging. For instance, it seems that blogging has not impacted sports journalists as much as media, arts and culture, technology, and finance journalists (Bradshaw, 2008). In addition, different types of bloggers are examined, such as independent bloggers, sport-themed website bloggers, and corporate-sponsored blogging platform bloggers; in the case of the 2006 FIFA World Cup Finals, we see that blogging has democratizing potential and can act as a platform for corporations to tell specific (here, the World Cup) stories (Dart, 2009). Live online (internet) commentary is seen as contributing to the globalization of sport, extending and modifying the sport coverage's symbolic basis; it is argued, however, that online commentary requires more fan identification than regular television commentary (Sandvoss, 2004).

Second, we find studies examining online ticket distribution (e.g. Beaven and Laws, 2007; see Chapter 13 for more information on ticketing) and virtual betting websites. Virtual betting is revolutionizing worldwide wagering; certain sites like Betfair are successful because they take advantage of important technological forces such as (Davies *et al.*, 2005):

- the use of the internet as the main communication medium decreases transaction costs for both the company and the customers;
- innovations like online gaming companies are difficult for governments to regulate;
- innovations like Betfair typically stem from individuals thinking "outside the box";
- following Metcalfe's Law of networks, as the number of customers increases, the market's liquidity increases, and therefore efficiency increases, which in turn increases the utility of the site for the customers;
- following Moore's Law, the increasing power of the computers arriving on the market and the decreasing the costs of these computers offers the company and its customers increasing processing power.

However, these online gaming sites have a number of specific impacts that are also examined. The fact that internet gaming is often anonymous, usually affordable, easily accessible and convenient, lead to disinhibition, can be done frequently, and provides escapism/dissociation, associability, simulation, and interactivity is a concern for researchers (e.g. Braverman *et al.*, 2011). They examined impacts of the preceding factors, such as the issue of workplace internet gambling, protection of vulnerable populations, unscrupulous operators, and electronic cash (Griffiths *et al.*, 2006).

Third, the use and impacts of RFID systems, such as the intelligent local-based information (ILBI) system in events and the broader local tourism industry, are examined. For example, the challenges of implementing an ILBI system at the 2008 UEFA European Football Championships (EURO) 2008 for use by event visitors, but also general tourists a well as locals, were found to include (Peters *et al.*, 2010): time constraints in developing and implementing the programme; a relocation of distribution points from those that were optimal for EURO 2008 to those that would be optimal for regular tourism seasons; and needing initial financial investments. However, unlike GPS (Global Positioning System) or other similar systems, this RFID-based system is free for users, thus giving it a distinct advantage from the user's perspective. Also, the user-tracking and analysis capabilities of these systems can be very useful to the local tourism industry. Nevertheless, systems implementers have to be aware that different tourists and spectators (e.g. short-term vs. long-term tourists) have different informational needs and therefore this issue needs to be factored into the system's development (Peters *et al.*, 2010).

Other electronic technology is also being examined, such as surveillance technology (Giulianotti and Klauser, 2010) and sports decision technology aids (especially to assist referees and officials during a match). Regarding the latter, they are not the be-all-and-end-all answer. Researchers warn that such hawk-eye systems (i.e. a system of multiple high-speed cameras) could inadvertently cause naive viewers to overestimate the ability of technological devices to resolve disagreement among humans because measurement errors are not made salient. For example, virtual reconstructions can easily be taken to show "exactly what really happened".

(Collins and Evans, 2008: 283)

Finally, researchers are beginning to examine the impact of new media technology on marketing and sponsorship. New media provide multiple digital platforms (e.g. virtual signage, Facebook pages, YouTube commercials, fantasy leagues and championships like the one noted in the illustrative case) that can be accessed worldwide. Consumers have become co-producers (Neeley and Judson, 2010; Ryan, 2005). It is argued that a new paradigm of global strategic marketing has emerged because of the new media (Santomier, 2008). However, the race to control the use of such technologies by event stakeholders (e.g. broadcasters, press, athletes, sponsors, etc.) is causing confusion in these stakeholders as the organizing bodies' (e.g. IOC, NOC) social media policies are not coherent/coordinated (Ellis and Séguin, 2011). Nevertheless, research tells us that "communication and technology companies value advertising during online sporting-event broadcasts, because these companies were significantly more visible during the online broadcasts than the television broadcasts" (Pegoraro *et al.*, 2009: 466). Still, there are legal ramifications of virtual advertising for not only the sponsors, but also the event managers, broadcasters, and event facility managers, such as (Turner and Cusumano, 2000):

■ virtual advertising changes traditional relationship structures between sponsors, event organizers, broadcasters, and facility operators by changing existing signage agreements; and
■ global signage capabilities are removed from the event organizer and facility operator and strengthened for the broadcasters.

Remedies for the changes brought about by virtual advertising can include seeking damages for breach of contract or including disclaimers (Turner and Cusumano, 2000).

In sum, not surprisingly, most event management research on technology has focused on the impact of technology on different management areas (e.g. HRM, marketing, ticketing). Certainly, more needs to be done to examine the impact of new media on different management areas, such as planning and sponsorship processes, for the organizing committee as well as other organizations (e.g. parent organizations such as the CGF and its worldwide associations). In addition, it is generally agreed that the nature of sport and sports events is changing; however, how to view the changes in sport, sports events, the athletes, the spectators, and the sport managers' and sponsors' roles is still being debated. For instance, Hutchins *et al.* (2009: 89) believed it is time to think "more about sport as media given the increasing interpenetration of digital media content, sport, and networked information and communications technologies". However, Sheridan (2006: 32) argued that innovations in technology and technique should not compromise "the nature of the good game". Van Hilvoorde *et al.* (2007) cautioned that elite sport is by nature artificial anyway. Still, Smith and Westerbeek (2010) suggested that the new

243

technologies emerging are changing the nature of spectatorship and of the athletes. They concluded that

> The nature of imminent technology will facilitate powerful tribal belonging as it will encourage an unprecedented level of fan-to-fan interaction. In this respect, despite the physical barriers, sport will be accessible to almost anyone with the right technology and the ability to pay for it.
>
> (Smith and Westerbeek, 2010: 344)

We leave it up to the reader and future research to further this debate. However, we provide, in the practitioner's section below, some points to consider.

THE PRACTITIONER'S PERSPECTIVE ON TECHNOLOGY

Technology is an important part of preparing and hosting major sports events. One-quarter of the 2012 London Olympic Games' "overall budget of two billion pounds (US$3.1 billion) has been spent on technology" (Douglas, 2011: 1). This includes both physical resources but also the need to protect the various technological systems from potential (security) risks. In this section, we would like to comment on the use of technology and its limitations.

Use of technology

Because of the volume of people that must be recruited and trained with both generic and job-specific training, technology is part of best practices. It is also essential to managing the workforce of an event. To know that every person has received the same information in the same way in a timely manner gives the organization both the knowledge base and foundation to establish the culture that is required to have people functioning effectively and efficiently in a compressed timeframe. On an ongoing basis, managers cannot possibly spend the same face time with each employee that enduring organizations allow. The ability to deliver ongoing training via technology is priceless. Technology plays a role in every aspect of the HR process for a workforce, including payment of salary. Automatic deposit to the individual's financial institution not only saves time and money, it also eliminates the challenge of the pay-cheque not being received. The power of technology to inform, influence, model, educate, and entertain is still being developed. Suffice to say that it must be a part of the process if there is to be effective group and individual training and ongoing development. Even when geography is a problem, technology such as the Skype program can create enhanced communication by being able to see the other person. Videoconferencing offers large groups the opportunity to share ideas and communicate information in larger group settings. Video is extremely effective because of the adage "a picture is worth 1,000 words". In situations where time is an issue, like orientation, and the audience is diverse relative to job responsibilities, video footage can unite the group in a common goal and emotionally engage the group on a visceral level. This is important and a powerful way to communicate; advances in the quality and ease of use makes it accessible as a training and information tool. With the proliferation of social media, there is a powerful and instant opportunity to communicate with athletes, the workforce, and other participants. Present moment – meaning right now, as-it-is-happening – communication on Facebook and Twitter gives ubiquitous options to information managers and participants who want to share, spread, announce, declare, and comment. It is incumbent on managers to consider the integration of technology, such as new media, into planning and hosting processes for all FAs.

As Games-time approaches, the need for technology changes. And it is not always possible to give everyone their wish list; so people often end up sharing computers or working with equipment that is not necessarily efficient. To mitigate this challenge, a centrally based computer station available for everyone to use can at least provide some access to intranet, internet, and email, which is the preferred method of communication for most people. Still, there are different stakeholder groups that require communication, and the tool and the message need to be matched. Major sponsors need communication regardless of the method – staying in touch means keeping them informed, giving them feedback and connecting by email, mobile phone, videoconferencing, and obviously face-to-face events. During major sports events, mobile phones and radios can be more effective than email as the workforce is communicating in the fast-paced competition environment. Mobile phones are also the preferred method of communication for more sensitive information (such as letting the VMT know that royalty is arriving at the venue). Conversely, email may be more appropriate when larger groups of people in different locations need to be informed about changes, additions, or recent decisions. For the general spectator audience, there are videotrons that can post information in a fairly timely manner. For accredited guests, both face-to-face and written notices in the lounges or private meeting areas are useful. Communicating with the media has predetermined channels and people. Mobile phone and now texting is immediate and creates the best opportunity for a response from the person(s) you need to connect with. The overarching theme around technology bears repetition of a point made earlier in this section – it needs to be appropriate to the situation and the person. It is important to ask people how they would prefer to be contacted. If a manager is unable to satisfy this request, then they should negotiate a best option so that when the time comes that the manager needs help, information, manpower, an answer, or an ear to listen, that the person on the other end is receptive. Finally, as noted earlier, one of the key technologies for a major sports event is the use of CADs. These maps of venues are necessary for FA planning and for coordination between functions.

Limits of technology use

While we live in an age of technology, the individual's skill level and experience varies depending on the equipment and the learning quotient of that person. Add to this the fact that suppliers of technology often contribute, donate, or loan equipment that may not be user-friendly. Immediate and efficient communication is an obvious necessity at a major sports event, and the time available for training is limited. There is a baseline expectation in 2012 that people will be able to navigate and understand technology; and most people answer yes to questions of competency without discerning their real level of competency. This means that the efficiency and effectiveness of the way people communicate on and with technology can and does vary. So expectations need to be realistic and can vary from person to person. While there will be technical support available, it is not their job to, nor do resources allow time for, specific individual training. It can be costly in time, with repercussions to many other people if event managers are not technologically savvy. Testing to ensure that the skills are there may be a good use of time in the initial hiring process as a way of mitigating future problems with efficiency and effectiveness of communication because of technology challenges. It is worthwhile noting that, because technology seems to have insinuated itself into our lives 24/7, younger generations do not see or do not avail themselves of the opportunity to use a balance of media to communicate, including phone and face-to-face. This can result in an overuse of technology, which at times may be inefficient or ineffective for the purpose at hand (e.g. delicate topics, high-profile dignitaries).

It is not always the fault of the user; sometimes it is the equipment that can frustrate or foil operations at an event. This is where the resourcefulness of the people involved comes into play. Do they know how to manually, or with another form of communication, solve the problem? Because of limited resources, it can be like the movie (based on actual events) about Apollo 13. The astronauts had only the mechanical systems and physical resources on board the malfunctioning spacecraft to figure out a way to make it back to earth safely. What was revealed in their efforts and those of the back-on-Earth engineers was not only a solution that saved all their lives, but how success was achieved through teamwork, ingenuity, ability to think outside the box, and the willingness to stay focused on the goal. This is what is required when you work with many different people using multiple types of technology in a fast-paced, high-functioning environment. There must be a willingness on the part of a manager to recognize that answers can and will be found in the moment that may or may not involve technology. We cannot deny that we rely heavily on technology today; but the ability to think our way out of challenges depends on the human qualities of self-control, focus, creativity, patience, and effective interpersonal skills.

CHAPTER SUMMARY

In this chapter we examined what technology is (material, knowledge, process), and its uses and impacts as a resource, a source of coordination, a force or trend, and source of change. We also presented different electronic-based technologies that are impacting major sports events and their managers. Next, we noted some of the research being done regarding technology, including blogging, online gambling, RFID device implementation, and new media and virtual advertising. In doing so, we highlighted some of the confusion, debates, and questions that still need to be answered.

From a practitioner's perspective, we discussed the use of technology and some limitations. Consideration for the preference of type of communication a person wants to receive, knowing a manager's target audience, and accounting for different situational variables were also highlighted as important factors in the choice of technology.

EXPERT CASE: USING TECHNOLOGY FOR WORKFORCE MANAGEMENT IN THE 2010 VANCOUVER OLYMPIC WINTER GAMES

The 2010 Olympic Winter Games in Vancouver required the involvement of approximately 25,000 volunteers and thousands of paid staff and contractors. This case study looks at how technology was used to manage this workforce during such a large-scale sports event.

To better understand the evolving influence of technology, it is useful to contemplate what organizing 25,000 volunteers would have looked like without the availability of electronic tools. Hand-written spreadsheets would have been used, with a single line for each volunteer. This spreadsheet, with 25,000 rows of initial data, would quickly grow as details such as each volunteer's qualifications, assigned position and venue, scheduled shifts, dietary restrictions, and emergency contact information were included. How would this spreadsheet be reproduced and shared, without the presence of photocopiers, scanners, or email? Similarly, how would important updates be communicated quickly? During the 2010 Olympic Winter Games, there were times when heavy fogs rolled into the mountain venues and races needed to be rescheduled. To communicate this message to the volunteers without the use of technology, all the volunteers would have to make the journey to their venue to attend a meeting where they would then receive their new schedules. Would the organizers then reflect these schedule changes on that hand-written spreadsheet? Needless to say, since the first modern Olympic Games in 1896, technology has had a fundamental impact on the way organizing committees plan and manage their workforce. At the 2010 Olympic Winter Games, technology was woven throughout the workforce journey, from when workforce members initially read about the opportunities available to them on a website, to being entertained by the live-video stream of a competition in their break room.

From a practitioner's perspective, technology was an integral element to HR planning several years before the 2010 Olympic Winter Games began. The 2010 Olympic Winter Games website provided a tool to communicate information such as job descriptions, conditions of work, incentives for being involved, and an overview of the application process. The information had global reach and could be updated instantaneously. With the simple click of a button, interested individuals had access to the online application form. The information collected in the application form automatically fed into the application system, where the data could then be easily sorted and filtered for specific purposes. The volunteer application form went "live" two years before the first day of the Olympic Games, which was the same time that the call centre opened up its phone lines to answer questions about the volunteer experience. The 2010 Olympic Winter Games was the first time in Olympic history that paper volunteer applications were non-existent. Phones were not the only piece of hardware in the call centre. Computers were also available, so that if applicants called in to report any changes to their details, the staff could record it directly into the application system. While VANOC had some concern about imposing such a reliance on technology on the volunteers, some of whom had little computer experience, it ultimately decided that information technology education and training could actually be a legacy of the 2010 Olympic Winter Games. By ensuring that adequate technical supports were in place, the general consensus is that the organizing committee was successful in enhancing the computer skills of a large population of volunteers – an impressive feat for an international *sports* event.

After the application and selection process, workforce members participated in various levels of training. Electronic training sessions were available through an online portal. These sessions covered a wide range of topics, including those that, although considered non-essential to the job duties, nevertheless provided a more in-depth understanding of the Olympic Games, such as event history, venue details, and an overview of each sport. Without technology there would not have been the time, human resources, venues nor budget to provide these important supplemental courses. The in-person sessions were enhanced with various audio-visual elements such as PowerPoint presentations, music, and videos. Technology also played a large role behind the scenes in organizing workforce members into the appropriate training sessions through an invitation management system. This system provided the organizing committee with the ability to send out an email to a specific group within the workforce based on their role, or to invite them to a training course. From their personal computers, workforce members could then select a session that best suited their schedule. Once the session had reached its maximum capacity, it would no longer be available for others to select. Closer to the training session date, the invitation management system could generate an attendance list. Once a training session was complete, the system was updated to reflect who had completed the training. It is important to note that once the training system was up and running, it was relatively quick to use. However, implementing such a system required parameters to be defined, template reports to be designed, session information to be input, and user-testing to ensure the program was working properly prior to its launch.

To ensure that thousands of people were not queuing once the uniform and accreditation centre opened its doors, workforce members were invited to collect their accreditation and uniforms in much the same way as the in-person training sessions. In order to expedite the pick-up process, the organizing committee used the website to communicate information such as the sizes, washing instructions, and photos of each of the uniform pieces, and guidelines on how to wear the uniform, which helped to reduce the human resources required to answer such questions. Upon checkout, barcode scanners were used to scan the type and size of each uniform piece in order to help manage the inventory.

Workforce planning for the Olympic Games is complex. The process involves several iterations as information about each of the venue schedules is refined and as each department's service levels are defined. First, departments determined how many people they needed and at what times for each day at each venue. The information was collected centrally and entered into a workforce planning system, which calculated how many volunteers would be needed based on the average shift length and anticipated number of shifts that each person would be working. This information was then passed along to the recruitment team so they knew how many people to recruit into each role. It was particularly important for the F&B team to collect and report this information in aggregate so that they could plan how many breakfasts, lunches, and dinners were required. Similarly, it was important for the transportation team to understand when the first and last buses would need to arrive and depart at each venue. A scheduling system was used to assign individuals to a specific shift. This application facilitated the planning process by taking into account certain pre-determined parameters. For example, it prevented the scheduler from assigning a shift to an individual within eight hours of the end of a previous shift. Once the schedules were finalized, they were "published" so that individuals could see their own schedule by logging into the online portal.

Through the use of technology and careful planning, workforce members showed up knowing how to perform their role, in their uniform with their accreditation, at the right time, and in the right place in order to successfully put on the 2010 Olympic Winter Games. Technology continued to play an integral role during the Games. As workforce members arrived on venue, their accreditation was scanned and they were automatically checked into their shift, which allowed for real-time reporting on any shortages in a particular role. The workforce system could be accessed from the event headquarters. One advantage to this was that the payroll team at headquarters had accurate attendance information and could process salary payments for each of the hourly staff, and monitor these expenses against the budget. Technology also enabled operational communication through the use of radios, mobile phones, group text messaging, and mass emails. Essentially, one message could be communicated to the entire workforce in a matter of seconds.

In addition to operational efficiencies, technology contributed to the morale and sense of community that developed during the 2010 Olympic Winter Games. For the workforce members, it was not uncommon for a few days to go without ever seeing an athlete live, despite being so close to the action. Televisions with live-streaming of the competitions in the break rooms mitigated the possibility of feeling isolated, and were an important tool to engage and inspire the workforce. There was even an opportunity to play Vancouver 2010™, the official video game of the 2010 Olympic Winter Games. Also, bonding continued off-venue as workforce members would go home and "add" their new "friend" to a popular social networking site, Facebook. At the workforce wrap-up party, a photo slideshow played to help reflect the team's accomplishments.

While technological advances have clearly improved the way Olympic Games are organized, managed, and perceived, technology has also presented some challenges for event organizers. First, such customized application systems can be costly and require technological expertise to communicate the needs to the software developers; in the case of the 2010 Olympic Winter Games, these systems were supported by a third party, Atos, a TOP sponsor of the IOC. Second, it was difficult to keep up with the rapid pace of technological developments. At the time of the 2010 Olympic Winter Games, Facebook and Twitter were emerging as social networking tools. The organizing committee could not look to past Olympic Games to see what policies were in place on the appropriate usage of technology, how messages about appropriate usage were communicated in the training programmes, and even how to define appropriate usage. Lastly, it takes significant human resources to monitor the radio system, create video replays, implement the audience response systems, provide real-time statistics reports, and deploy devices such as computers and secure internet connections at each of the venues. The number of workforce in technology-related roles constituted a large portion of the 25,000 volunteers.

By: Bethany Saunders, Venue Human Resources Manager, 2010 Olympic Winter Games

Case questions

1   List five different types of technology used at the 2010 Olympic Winter Games and explain how they each facilitated HRM.

2   What are some technology-related challenges experienced during the 2010 Olympic Winter Games?

3   Blogging and social networking sites, such as Facebook, allow individuals to share their experiences and learn about shared interests. Such bonding can be effective in bringing together a workforce. At the same time, organizers of major sports events are often concerned with privacy (particularly of the athletes), honouring the media rights, and protecting the brand. If you were tasked with developing a policy for the use of blogging and social networking sites for the next Olympic Games, what would be your key messages?

CHAPTER QUESTIONS

1   What is technology?

2   Explain and provide examples of the different types of technologies needed for sequential, pooled, and reciprocal interdependent organizations.

3   What are some of the key technologies needed by sport event managers? What are they used for?

4   For the following client groups, what would be the best form(s) of communication during Games-time, and why? (a) Dignitaries; (b) your work group; (c) other workforce members in the venue; (d) all workforce members across venues; (e) spectators; (f) the media; and (g) key sponsors?

5   Examine the debate regarding the changes brought about by technology on sport, sports events, managers, athletes, etc. Where do you situate yourself in this debate and why?

FURTHER READING

If you are interested in technology and sports events, we suggest the following:

Pearlman, D. M. & Gates, N. A. (2010) Hosting business meetings and special events in virtual worlds: A fad or the future? *Journal of Convention & Event Tourism,* 11, 247–265.

Turner, P. (2007) The impact of technology on the supply of sport broadcasting. *European Sport Management Quarterly,* 7, 337–360.

Viljamaa, K. (2007) Technological and cultural challenges in local innovation support activities: Emerging knowledge interactions in Charlotte's motor sport cluster. *European Planning Studies,* 15, 1215–1232.

Chapter 13

Games-time

OBJECTIVES

- To understand what the Games-time period involves
- To understand the research associated with spectators and attendance, ticketing, crowd management, and volunteer management during a major sports event
- To be aware of other areas of importance during Games-time

ILLUSTRATIVE CASE: PAST GAMES-TIME MISTAKES AT WEMBLEY STADIUM

Games-time event management issues are not a new occurrence. Moreover, what happens in past events has effects for the hosting of future events. For example, Hill (2004) describes the chaos associated with the 28 April 1923 Football Association Cup Final at Wembley Stadium in London, England. The brand new stadium, coupled with the presence of a local team with great support acceding to the final, great access to local train stations where one would have seen 14 "special trains" coming with supporters of the opposing team, and great weather set the scene for the chaos that ensued. There were over 250,000 people (instead of the anticipated 126,000) who descended on Wembley Stadium. The tradition of offering most tickets up for sale at the turnstiles on game day, and the lack of control over crowd movement and entry into the stadium, created havoc. Some people had to climb over the gates – helped by police! – into the already full stadium so they would avoid being crushed to death from the huge crowd behind them outside the stadium. Turnstiles had to be reopened to help ease the crush of people outside, which only further filled the stadium to beyond capacity. It is more luck than proper event management processes that led to only six or seven people being seriously injured and no deaths being recorded.

After the event, the Shortt Committee was tasked with making recommendations on how to conduct future major sports events, covering crowd control and facility layout (e.g. toilets, terrace size, seating), security, and ticketing procedures. These recommendations have been felt in British sports events ever since. Yet these recommendations did not prevent the crushing, asphyxiation, and ultimate death of 96 fans at a 1989 Football

Association Cup semi-final in Sheffield, England (Van der Wagen and Carlos, 2005). We will see whether LOCOG has learned from the past when it uses Wembley Stadium as the host venue for football (soccer) matches.

THE THEORY BEHIND GAMES-TIME

Come Games-time, the organizing committee has venuized; mini organizing committees, sometimes referred to as VTeams, are found in each venue, composed of representatives of the different key FAs (e.g. sport, logistics, EVS, security, overlay, technology, workforce, medical, F&B, cleaning and waste, ICS). Figure 13.1 provides an example of a VTeam organizational chart. As can be seen, it has the main FAs of the larger organizing committee, only re-organized to fit that particular venue's responsibilities and tasks. This type of structure differs from smaller sports events and festivals, which may be fully volunteer-run and comprise a very small committee of, for example, six people: a chair, a secretary, a treasurer, a supply or ancillary services officer, a sales and tickets officer, and a sports/entertainment officer (Shone and Parry, 2004). The size of the VTeam will depend on a number of factors, such as the nature of the competitions to be held (length, prestige, technical expertise required, schedule, number of competitors/teams), the nature of the venue (outdoor, indoor, venue capacity), how services are provided (pavilions, concourse stands, entrance/exit shots, restaurants, staff meal services, etc.), and what FAs are offered by the organizing committee and what is contracted out (see also Shone and Parry, 2004).

The actual Games-time period involves transferring decision-making power to the VTeams' managers so that they may handle crises at the venue level. It is crisis management. Issues that managers deal with include operational, logistics and infrastructure issues (e.g. commissioning of venues, ceremonies, transportation, medical, security, etc.), sport

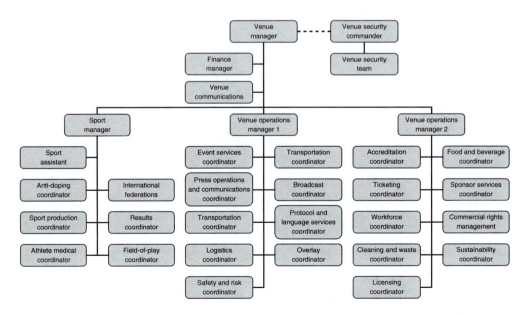

Figure 13.1 Generic Games-time VTeam.

(e.g. field-of-play issues, doping tests, competitor issues, equipment problems, qualification/event standards), HRM issues (e.g. volunteer management, recognition), participation and interdependence, and politics (e.g. ego management, dignitary services) (Parent, 2008). Managers no longer have the time to make decisions; they have to base their decisions on the information at hand, their skills and prior experiences, their gut-feeling, the people around them, the resources they have, and the (crowd management, contingency, emergency, etc.) plans previously created. Decision-making is reactionary in nature as the event velocity is at its highest, where a high-velocity environment means that managers have little or no time to make decisions (Parent, 2010).

Although change is about the only constant when planning and running a major sports event, there is a certain degree of routine which occurs during Games-time. For example, the venue manager or his representative will likely be one of the first people on-site on a given day, along with security. They will obtain information from senior Games management as to issues to deal with within their venue (as well as information on what is occurring elsewhere), they will walk through the venue to ensure all is in place, respond to any crises or problems, transmit information to their FA managers for the day's activities, continue to deal with issues and problems as the day's events occur, take regular meal breaks (if possible), conduct a debrief with FA managers, obtain daily reports from FA managers and transmit their own venue report to senior management, and close down the venue for the night with security personnel on hand (see also Shone and Parry, 2004).

We have already talked about venue management (including accreditation, sport and sport production, F&B, logistics, and cleaning and waste), security and risk management, and technology, all of which are important Games-time functions. In this chapter we focus on other areas to consider during Games-time. This section provides Games-time areas of interest to researchers, namely attendance, ticketing, crowd management, and volunteer management. It also suggests other potential areas of research, namely transportation and athletes.

Attendance

Research falling within the attendance area includes examining, understanding, and measuring event attendance, the tourism-associated question of intention to travel to major sports events, and the link between attendance and risk/terrorism.

Researchers are interested in determining specific attendance factors. We find emotional responses (e.g. passion for/interest in the sport and/or athletes showcased) to the event, the quality/availability of the facilities (e.g. venue accessibility, parking, seat availability), socialization, and event reputation as important predictors of event attendance (Hall *et al.*, 2010; Roy *et al.*, 2010). There is "an emotional and social aspect to attending sporting events, with spectators interested in having fun, being entertained and being comfortable at the event" (Hall *et al.*, 2010: 332), aspects which are associated to the constructs of entertainment and sportscape.

In terms of measuring event attendance motives, it is worth examining the SPEED model by Funk *et al.* (2009). These five motives are thought to help differentiate attendance behaviour, with motives explaining both game attendance (30 per cent of variance) and team commitment (75 per cent variance). This model was developed using Australian Rules Football, a professional sports league; however, it could be transposed for major sports event if the team-based questions (e.g. regarding the esteem felt if one's favourite team wins) could be replaced with favourite athlete or nation. Nevertheless, it would be worth developing an attendance model specific to major sports events, which would be of use for event managers' bidding, planning, and economic-impact analysis activities.

Some research has focused on international travel intentions more specifically. Research has shown that potential spectators will determine whether they travel internationally to see a major sports event according to the following six factors (Chia-Chen, 2010):

1   interest in the sports showcased
2   interest in travel
3   experience of watching live sports events
4   cost, ease of arranging travel plans
5   different cultural experience
6   chance to see famous athletes.

Not surprisingly, the actual travelling aspect and the cultural experience emerge as key differences to the earlier attendance motives discussed. However, we do see that other motives are quite similar, showing a certain "generalizability" of motives across contexts.

Notwithstanding, the Asian experience seems to be a particular attraction for potential spectators wishing to travel internationally. However, the interest in travelling to China, particularly, is dependent on the sports tourists being exposed to positive Chinese cultural images as well as negative event media (Green et al., 2010). Regarding the 2008 Beijing Olympic Games, while pre-event media did not seem to affect tourists' perceptions of Beijing or the 2008 Beijing Olympic Games, perceived personal, cultural, socio-psychological, and violence risks negatively impacted (though not significantly) the intention to travel to Beijing for the Olympic Games; gender, age, and socio-economic status also seem to impact travel intentions (Green et al., 2010; Qi et al., 2009). Importantly, though, these studies did find differences in travel intentions to the country in general versus the host city and Games specifically. It may be worth further exploring these differences between various nation-focused and city-focused intentions to travel for a major sports event.

Next, Toohey and Taylor (2008) expanded on the link between perceived risk/terrorism and travel intentions to Olympic Games. They noted that the 2004 Athens Olympic Games – the first summer Olympic Games after the events of 9/11 – demonstrated resilience, resistance, and even indifference towards potential terrorist threats. Yet there were some indications of risk aversion; these fears may have been tempered by the perception that the organizing committee was placing much effort on wide-ranging risk-management processes and activities.

Ticketing

Within the ticketing topic, researchers focus on different aspects. First, some researchers are interested in ticketing strategies (i.e. pricing, tiers, temporal availability of tickets, quantity of available tickets) and their effect on attendance (e.g. Courty, 2003). In theory, admission prices should impact attendance (e.g. admission prices that are set really high should severely limit attendance, especially if demand is not very high). Findings demonstrate causal relationships between income and attendance, between attendance and admission price, and between income and admission price in the short term. In the longer term, the causal relationship is between admission price and income to attendance (Narayan and Smyth, 2003). Moreover, research is clear that price tiers are important for different reasons (Moe and Fader, 2009): (1) higher-end price tier purchasers tend to buy earlier than low- or mid-priced ticket tiers; (2) higher-end price tier purchasers are more influenced by discounts and premiums; (3) low- and mid-priced tier purchasers are more influenced by the face price value of the tickets; and (4) "there is an exponentially priced schematic to estimate an optimal set of prices to reduce the differential between primary and secondary ticket prices" (Volpano and Bilotkach, 2008: 3), which decreases the risk of lost ticket revenue for the host organization.

However, these studies are typically done in smaller events or non-sport events. Mega sports events like the Olympic Games have such a high demand that they may not follow other event ticketing trends, whereas major sports events like the 2011 Rugby World Cup still have tickets available only a week before the event occurs (cf. Cutler, 2011d); it is typical to see last-minute ticket buying as the general public gets more information and is more confident about the quality of the product. Nevertheless, future research needs to better understand ticket prices in different types of major sports events. Despite people's desire to be spectators at an Olympic Games, we do have evidence to show that mistakes in the ticketing strategy (e.g. use of different phases, ticket offers, and processes) can damage an Olympic Games organizing committee's image and thereby ticket sales and revenues (see Thamnopoulos and Gargalianos, 2002).

This brings us to our second ticket research topic, ticket distribution channels and their impacts. Here, researchers are interested in a combination of aspects which impact fan behaviour and ultimate attendance: pricing, scope of the offer, purchasing mechanisms, technology use, ethics, service quality, and brand fit perceptions of ticket distribution partners. A variety of ticket distribution channels are possible: in person, internet, telephone, mail, fax, and through tourism intermediaries' ticket package bundling (see also Smith, 2007). Regarding the impact of distribution channels on attendance, research findings highlight that (1) attendee behaviour is unpredictable regarding ticket distribution partners' performance; (2) event attendees' ticket distribution depends on availability, convenience, personal services, location, and membership relationship; and (3) host organizations need to carefully manage the ticket distribution process and partners so as to not alienate potential spectators (Beaven and Laws, 2007; Smith, 2007).

A third area of interest is the secondary ticket market, which includes ticket scalping, licensed ticket brokers, fan-to-fan resale, and secondary ticket market websites (e.g. Drayer and Martin, 2010; Happel and Jennings, 2002). Although traditionally depicted in a negative light by event organizers, the secondary ticket market has continued. The issue is that such a market is a lost revenue in ticket sales for event organizers. Some organizations, such as the NFL and VANOC, have tried to provide legitimacy to the secondary ticket market and (hopefully) recoup some of the ticket revenue they would be losing otherwise. For example, VANOC set up a legitimate fan-to-fan ticket resale website. Drayer and Martin (2010) described different legitimacy-building strategies for different segments of the secondary ticket market:

- Scalpers: they attempt to conform to some local values, norm, and ordinance and are selective in their choice of location and buying and/or selling activities so as to not be (completely) out of compliance with local anti-scalping laws. Therefore, scalpers use conformance and selection strategies.
- Brokers: they use conformance and selection strategies like scalpers. However, they also use manipulation and acquisition strategies by granting interviews with local media and by being associated with the National Association of Ticket Brokers, which has strict guidelines for ticket brokers and mediation/complaint processes for ticket buyers.
- Websites: websites are created to conform to local anti-scalping laws, but they also afford anonymity to potential ticket buyers, thereby displaying a certain selectivity. Websites also use manipulation strategies by lobbying for changes in local laws/policies and acquisition strategies through being sponsors of legitimate sport organizations (e.g. the NFL), thereby offering a sort of legitimacy endorsement for the website.

A final area of interest are the anti-scalping laws themselves. However, research is mixed here. More precisely, some findings show that cities which have anti-scalping laws result in ticket prices being on average higher (in this study's case, for baseball and football), thereby perhaps enticing sport organizations to support anti-scalping laws (Depken II, 2000). Yet, earlier findings for the NFL specifically seem to show that prices are lower in cities where anti-scalping laws are present (Williams, 1994). Thus, there is a clear need to further research this area both in terms of the impact of anti-scalping laws on the host organization (especially, in our case, event organizations) and the impact of the legitimization of the secondary ticket market on anti-scalping laws.

Crowd management

Crowd management is seen as a key risk to manage during the event (Van der Wagen and Carlos, 2005). Mitigating queuing impacts is important (cf. Baker and Jones, 2011). Crowd management plans must be created before the event takes place to avoid disastrous situations like the one mentioned in the illustrative case at the beginning of the chapter. Crowd management involves three stages: (1) pre-crisis or pre-event prevention and contingency planning; (2) crisis development – implementation of contingency or emergency plans; and (3) post-crisis evaluation (Getz, 2005). Table 13.1 provides preventative strategies for crowd management. It also includes key strategies for crisis management and emergency responses. These strategies are used to ensure (hopefully) proper, controlled, and orderly evacuation of spectators, guests, and organizing committee staff and volunteers. Such an evacuation is done following an emergency response plan, under the direction of the crisis or risk manager and her team (various administrative, operational, and technical coordinators as needed) (Getz, 2005; Van der Wagen and Carlos, 2005).

Table 13.1 Preventative crowd management strategies

Area of concern	Preventative strategies
Crowd behaviour (e.g. hooliganism)	Review crowd behaviour in similar events held previously
	Review crowd responses to the type of event being showcased (e.g. football versus beach volleyball versus golf)
	Have ticket booths away from the actual venue (re: queuing)
	Consider staggered ticketing entrance
	Introduce safety announcements
	Ensure proper signage to security and medical services
	Set up security screening booths at all entrances
	Place (visible and hidden) security devices and personnel throughout the venue
General admissions areas	Conduct evaluations of all general admissions areas (e.g. mosh pit, terraces) for structural concerns (i.e. engineering, construction) and legal and management concerns (e.g. fire safety, capacity regulations)
	Isolate more critical or "rowdy" areas (e.g. mosh pits) from other spectator areas
	Limit capacity
	Provide easy entrance and exit pathways
	Ban alcohol, cigarettes, drugs, certain clothing or accessories (e.g. chains) and certain behaviours (e.g. body surfing) from such areas
	Station medical services personnel near these areas
	Consider the use of reserved seating
	Consider staggered entrance and exits
Protests and terrorism	Examine past similar events for the likelihood of protests occurring
	Coordinate with law enforcement agencies for all security issues, including protests and terrorism, to ensure proper crowd management
Crisis management and emergency evacuation	Set up a crisis management team for each venue
	Ensure proper communication plans and channels are created and functioning
	Create emergency preparedness plans for each venue, integrating the plan with other venue and FA plans
	Train all managers in key emergency procedures and communication processes

Sources: Getz (2005), Van Der Wagen and Carlos (2005).

Volunteer management

There is a significant literature on volunteer motivation and satisfaction, which may not be surprising given that volunteers typically make up the largest percentage of the workforce of a major sports event, and they are the face of the Games for most visitors. Volunteers provide empathy and a positive relationship with the public, they bring enthusiasm to the organizing committee, and, of course, they are "free" in the sense of not having to pay them a salary (Nichols and Ojala, 2009). However, they are not totally free as the organizing committee has to feed them, sometimes house them, and provide them with oftentimes expensive uniform (see also Solberg, 2003). The event, the organizing committee, the venues, and a multitude of other factors affect volunteer motivation, commitment, and satisfaction. For example, an organization's reputation is thought to have a direct effect on commitment and an indirect effect through satisfaction (Bang, 2009). Thus, much research effort is being undertaken to understand event volunteers, their motives, commitment, and satisfaction (e.g. Allen and Shaw, 2009; Chanavat and Ferrand, 2010; Downward *et al.*, 2005; Downward and Ralston, 2006; Kim *et al.*, 2010; Lockstone and Baum, 2009; MacLean and Hamm, 2007; Nichols and Ojala, 2009; Parent and Slack, 2007; Pauline and Pauline, 2009; Shaw, 2009; Surujlal, 2010; Treuren, 2009; Williams *et al.*, 1995). For more information on volunteers, we direct the reader to Chapter 5.

Some suggestions for future research avenues

What we see is that most research associated with Games-time has focused on the FOH aspect. Yet, as is evident in this book, the BOH is a hugely critical component to the success of an event. Thus, researchers are encouraged to focus on the BOH and on the difference the Games-time context presents for managers and volunteers regarding their decision-making and actions. For example, examining sense-making in such an environment (cf. Bogner and Barr, 2000), performance in a high-velocity environment (cf. Eisenhardt, 1989; Judge and Miller, 1991), determining how to manage stress in such a context (Hede, 2010), examining support and preparedness systems for volunteers and paid staff, whether human, technological, medical, safety, or other (cf. Betlehem and Schaefer, 2010; Carlsson and El Sawy, 2008). As Getz *et al.* (2010) noted, further research is needed in individual and group-level event experience and meaning. These can be linked to service quality models and their assessments (cf. Ko *et al.*, 2011), and other event management-associated processes. Service quality analyses should include aesthetic (visually/artistically pleasing atmosphere, service environment, and ancillary products), functional (clients' perceptions of the service delivery process), and technical (e.g. international delegations' characteristics, athlete performance) dimensions (see Yoshida and James, 2011).

As well, no city, however large or small, seems to be immune to being critiqued for transportation problems during an event. For example, only 48 hours before the opening ceremony, the 2010 Delhi CWG transportation drivers left the organizing committee because they had not been paid their promised salaries. This caused the organizing committee to hire volunteers who did not know anything about the various venues (e.g. their names, their location) or how to get to the venue locations in the convoluted streets of Delhi. Even other volunteers, when asked by the drivers how to get to certain venues, had no idea. Thus, again, more than one dignitary and other Games stakeholder was significantly delayed in getting to certain venues – sometimes, they were driven to the wrong venue. As well, during the 2010 Vancouver Olympic Winter Games, some London media initially criticized Vancouver for transportation line-ups. Yet until the 2012 Olympic Games, there remained major concerns about London's own already stretched public transportation system; also, many Vancouverites experienced shorter-than-normal commutes during Games-time, and most line-ups for public transportation post-competition had less than ten minutes wait-times. In contrast, Auckland, New Zealand experienced transportation problems during the opening game of the 2011 Rugby World Cup; the city's transportation system "struggled to cope with a large estimated crowd of 200,000", with trains, buses, and ferries being stretched or even having to be cancelled (Cutler, 2011e: 1).

Transportation is a key element which stakeholders, especially the media, scrutinize when determining the overall success of an event. It is also a key part of bid books and of knowledge transfer between events. For example, there were concerns during the 2010 Olympic Winter Games bid that the distance between Vancouver and Whistler (where the mountain venues would be) was too great – it was a two-hour drive – and the drive was not very safe. Vancouver bid organizers therefore had to expend significant effort in assuaging concerns and assuring IOC members that the Sea-to-Sky highway would be improved, making it safer and quicker (down to a 90-minute drive).

Transportation, generally speaking, includes air and ground transportation (Cantrav Services Inc. & EMS Event Management Solutions Inc., 2010). Smooth, efficient (quick) airport arrivals and departures are critical; it is also recommended to have a centrally managed flight system to facilitate coordination (Cantrav Services Inc. & EMS Event Management Solutions Inc., 2010). In turn, ground transportation includes both event (internal) transportation systems for dignitaries, athletes, media, and sport officials, as well as public (external) transportation systems of public buses, metros/light rail systems, trains, and cars. Event ground transportation is usually discernible by specific logos/markings on the vehicle and/or special access passes (Cantrav Services Inc. & EMS Event Management Solutions Inc., 2010). It is essential that event drivers be familiar with the local geography and roads and be very well trained or versed in venues and routes.

Organizing committees and local government strategies to decrease traffic congestion during a major sports event include: blocking key streets in and around venues to private vehicles, increasing the number of buses and metros/light rail trains, increasing the number of park-and-ride parking lots, promoting telecommuting and off-hour commuting. Encouraging spectators to use public transportation decreases potential traffic and parking issues, but also facilitates so-called green initiatives. The 2006 FIFA World Cup in Germany had transportation – both increasing the use of public transportation and reducing the effects of transportation on the environment – as a Green Goal Programme principle (Dolles and Söderman, 2010). Such transportation strategies have been found to also be effective for the environment by decreasing carbon emissions/ozone pollution and therefore providing a healthier level of air quality (cf. Friedman *et al.*, 2001). The link between green games/environmental sustainability (including reducing carbon emissions and mitigating climate change) is of interest to transportation researchers, many of whom examine policy processes, strategies, and decision-making in this area (e.g. Batac and Lem, 2008; Black *et al.*, 2002).

Notwithstanding the above information on transportation, sport management researchers have not examined this critical component of major sports event hosting, except in passing – for example, when discussing potential impacts. Given that transportation is part of what stakeholders use to determine the success of an event, it is important to empirically examine

259

transportation so that more efficient and effective methods can be garnered for future events. Researchers in other fields are looking at transportation and sustainability, tourism, travel times, and system efficiency, to name but a few key areas (Boilé, 2002; Jeon and Amekudzi, 2005; Jeon *et al.*, 2010; Khadaroo and Seetanah, 2007; Susilo and Dijst, 2010). These are areas which could be juxtaposed to major sports events.

Finally, where are the athletes and their perceptions in all of this? There is still very little research focusing on athletes' perceptions of Games-time management. An exception to this is the work by MacIntosh and Nicol (2012). These authors surveyed athletes at the 2010 Delhi CWG during and after the event. They found that

> ceremonies (e.g. opening), ancillary areas (e.g. fitness facility) and sport venues (e.g. environment) in particular were rated by the athletes as positive. Certain aspects of the Games were identified as requiring improvements such as accommodations (e.g. housekeeping, laundry) and communication (e.g. wireless availability). Further, despite high scores for security, athletes also reported feeling uneasy about additional travel outside of the athletes' village.
>
> (MacIntosh and Nicol, 2012: 12)

In addition, Trauer *et al.* (2003) examined Masters' Games athletes. They found that Masters' athletes' motives – namely the serious competitors who are there to be challenged and the Games enthusiasts who are there more for the social involvement and personal preferences – can impact how Games organizers plan their event. That is, for the Masters' Games specifically, the population of athletes were predominantly Games enthusiasts, which means that Masters' Games organizers should emphasize the social interaction opportunities such as activities in the Games Village, instead of going after official IF sanctioning. This situation would be the opposite in higher-profile events like the Olympic Games, where the dominant athlete population is the serious competitor. Still, Trauer *et al.* did find that even the Games enthusiasts expect proper sport competition procedures (e.g. accurate time-keeping, results/record management and keeping). The poor quality of some of these procedures has been found to be stressors for young athletes – housing issues, lining-up for food, transportation problems, and extreme heat/weather were all found to be organization-based stressors (Kristiansen and Roberts, 2010). The media were also found to be a stressor for elite athletes, even Olympic-level athletes. Kristiansen *et al.* (2011) noted Olympic athletes' use of coping strategies for dealing with media demands at the 2010 Olympic Winter Games; they found that the delegation's supporting personnel needed to employ motivational strategies to assist athletes so that they could focus on the task at hand (performing). Nevertheless, much still needs to be examined from the athletes' perspectives for Games-time management and operations.

THE PRACTITIONER'S PERSPECTIVE ON GAMES-TIME

As the opening of the Games approaches, there is a physical move to the venues where competition will take place, and that can be traumatic for several reasons. A cohesive FA unit has functioned to get to this point, and now many people will have to move to a new space.

They will miss the familiarity, support, and camaraderie of the tight knit unit that got them this far. The event has started and with that comes the only constant: change, change, change. There is a change in reporting structure concurrent with the move and a change of management (from FA to venue), which has its own way of doing things, and that requires adjustment. The challenge is lack of time to ponder these changes – the train is moving and the manager just has to jump on. Everyone's energy has jumped to the next level, and the tempo quickens to create a velocity akin to a roller coaster you cannot exit until the ride stops. It's full-speed ahead – all the training and simulation exercises are in the past. It is present-moment living, with no safety net from here onwards. There is so much to absorb that the manager cannot possibly keep notes. Instead, they learn to commit to memory the layout of the venue – what separates the FOH from the BOH – the dozens and dozens of names of people they will need to rely on and communicate with frequently when the Games commence, and they file under R for Remember all the ad hoc comments – the non-sequiturs that occur in the course of the dozens of conversations managers have each day.

Each VMT provides a daily run sheet which details minute-by-minute of all the activities in the venue for that day for all FAs, including venue opening times for staff and spectators, competition times, deliveries, transportation and ticketing windows, etc. That means everyone starts on the same page. These run sheets are an invaluable tool to both coordinate activities and communicate effectively with other FAs and anyone externally who is implicated in activities in the venue, including competition, of course. They are an imperative and the blueprint for what is supposed to happen each day.

However, other aspects also come to the forefront during Games-time for managers, including: transportation, volunteer management, egos, observer programmes, and generally surviving the Games-time period. Each is described below.

Transportation

Transportation is always a logistics nightmare – getting everyone in and out of the venue safely and in a timely manner. Parking real estate is usually at a premium; there are typically three tiers of parking for the larger sports events. One for buses that carry the media, one for VIPs/dignitaries, and one for athletes; in addition, there is usually an area for high-level IPPs that is separate and secret, for people like presidents, who must be able to enter and exit in a completely secure manner. And if there is room, sometimes there is a small on-site area designated for a few workforce and accredited guests that drive themselves and have a work reason for needing the flexibility of parking for a personal vehicle. For the most part, workforce travels on the transportation that the spectators and general public use, or get dropped off blocks from the actual venue because of security and traffic management restrictions. Getting to the event usually takes more time after the event commences. This transportation consideration adds another layer of stress for the workforce member who is already putting in insanely long days to deliver the Games.

The city transportation systems should work in cooperation with the organizing committee's internal Games transportation system to coordinate the various clients' transportation needs during Games-times. Regular bus and train schedules are adjusted with extended hours, additional vehicles/trains, and changed routes as necessary to accommodate competition schedules and traffic. City streets have dedicated lanes for vehicles that have passes that have been issued prior to the event. Only authorized vehicles travel in them. This assists in ensuring that designated people, particularly the athletes, do not have to fight regular traffic; workforce required at remote locations can be transported in a timely manner, usually in buses, to meet shift requirements; and staff can travel predictably between venues. Routes should be designed to be point-to-point instead of circuitous. Such changes are great for people involved and interested in a major sports events; however, in some regions not everyone is enamoured with sport or the changes to their routines, so city planners have to minimize impacts to the people where and when possible.

There is a major logistical problem with Games transportation: it is the fact that it cannot be fully tested – unlike test events which allow for the testing of a venue and its internal operations during a sports competition, usually held the year before the major sports event. Certain tests and estimates can be made for transportation; but the lack of the full in-flow of people, the activity of multiple venues occurring at the same time, and the desire to not disrupt the residents more than absolutely necessary all result in the first real test of the integrated (Games and public) transportation coming on the first day of the event. This is why we often see transportation problems in a new event that are then corrected over the next few days.

Vehicles transporting athletes, media, and some VIPs are usually termed "clean" vehicles. That does not relate to a car wash. It means that the vehicle has been swept by security teams at one venue to be safe and specifically pre-arranged passenger(s) have been cleared to ride in it to another venue without having to stop and be (re)screened. It also means that this vehicle cannot accept any unauthorized passengers, it cannot stop en route – it must go from point A and not stop until it gets to point B. As a contrast, a "dirty" vehicle would be a necessary vehicle like a fire truck or a delivery truck that has not been security checked but is a necessary vehicle for the Games for a specific (usually one-time) purpose. It is just not possible to secure every single vehicle in the city, so decisions are made to keep world leaders safe. Although everyone entering a venue (except spectators) has had a background check, things can still happen – hence the security screenings and risk-management procedures.

All access routes to the city, including airports, train stations, bus terminals, and harbour facilities, must be ready for the flood of people who don't usually arrive in such a concentrated manner. They tend to come in waves and tax all the resources, including the facilities and their staff, as well as the workforce of the Games. There are the spectators, dignitaries, athletes, and the media who all expect to have their transportation needs accommodated immediately upon arrival.

Is all of this disruption worth it to the Games city? This is a question that has been pondered by sport managers, politicians, and academics. There is no clear answer. Each city can point to things that would not have happened without the Games, and that begs the questions: did they need it in the first place? Can you translate pride of country, positively affecting a culture, creating lasting memories, new shiny buildings, and highways? In esoteric terms, in philosophical terms, yes; in cold, hard cash, that's a different story, and very subjective to the person or group who is doing the translation. Suffice it to say there are perceived benefits that sell the event, typically a legacy in buildings, roadways, memories, and bragging rights.

Volunteers

It has been stated previously in this book that a major sports event does not happen without volunteers, and the operative word here is volunteers. The recruiting, training, and "uni-forming" of the volunteers takes place before Games-time, and the challenges and benefits have been iterated repeatedly to prepare people mentally and emotionally for a once-in-a-lifetime experience for most. That does not prevent attrition once the Games start. Several factors for attrition can be blamed, such as: personal unforeseen emergencies, boredom with the job, or they don't like their job. Even though they are not paid, it is more delicate to deal with "de-hiring" or firing a volunteer than a paid employee. There is public percep-tion, public relations to consider. Each person must be left with their dignity, and once they have been assigned to an FA, it is really difficult and sometimes impossible from an adminis-tration perspective to reassign them. So managers need to be creative in either adjusting their duties and responsibilities to better suit the person or getting them to de-hire them-selves. It is an art to manage volunteers, and managers want them to have a positive Games experience because they are giving time, money, and talent to the Games.

Egos

Anytime there is a competitive environment, there are egos, and because they cannot be controlled, they need to be managed. It starts with my ego and I have to let go of it, and then move on from there. The most effective way to manage ego is to make an effort to understand the "currency" of the person displaying the ego. What do they value and what are they afraid of losing if their ego is not satisfied? Just this shift in attitude changes perspec-tive, and the ego will feel like it is being heard and understood – especially when you cannot give the ego what it wants. The second effective strategy is to focus on what can be done. When a person listens, rephrases, and asks questions, the other person feels heard and knows there is a genuine attempt to understand. This builds a foundation – by first accept-ing what someone is telling you as their truth, and then attempting to find out more about why they feel this way. A conversation without resistance can take place. What we know about conflict resolution is that we all have ego, and what we want first is to be heard and understood. It is how someone feels after they leave a conversation that matters as much or sometimes even more than the resolution.

Observer programmes

There is a programme that impacts venues and FAs of a major sports event called the observer programme. It is a generous reach-out and invitation to organizing committees that will be holding future editions of the event, as well as potential candidate cities, to attend and "observe" – to learn what they can that would be helpful in their planning. It is an offer that is embraced. It is most often a delegation of people, and their expectations vary from reasonable to unreasonable for the manager who needs to host them on a particular day, regardless of how busy it is. This adds another layer of duties for managers, as well as stress since managers attempt to deal with their fast-paced, always-changing environment, while balancing emergencies and special requests from their clients, and answering observer questions, doing tours, and generally informing the observer group. Still, it is an important part of the knowledge transfer process for a major sports event. In order to minimize the impact of observer groups come Games-time, FA managers could direct the observer group to "less busy" venues to spare the other venues, or they can do a rotation to spread the impact between venues. The boundaries around when and how observer groups could visit might be revisited to reduce the burden on Games staff and simultaneously satisfy the desire to be helpful to future Games by sharing information. For example, restricting numbers to only one or two individuals per FA may be more manageable than having to host a group at the same time.

Surviving the Games-time period

Based on our collective Games experience, we offer our nine personal strategies for not only surviving the Games, but for staying present in the moment during the Games, so that the manager (and volunteer) does not miss one of the most amazing experiences they could ever have.

1 *Prepare one's personal life.* Pay bills, stock up on a month's worth of food in the refrigerator/ freezer, arrange for caretaking of pets, children (and even partners), etc. Such pre-planning will alleviate the work to do at home when the workforce manager returns home after a long day.

2 *Surrender to the moment*, to the change, to the fast pace, to not having all the answers, to unreasonable requests, to not knowing, to the tiredness, to the noise, to the "what is". This allows one to be as effective as they can be – the acceptance lowers the volume and reduces the mind chatter in one's head. Just accepting what is allows one to deal with the moment rather than mentally fighting what has already occurred. It is personal power one gains from surrendering – an oxymoron perhaps that one can get power from surrendering, but true nonetheless.

3 *Be in the moment and stay in the moment.* Deal with what is happening right now, not analysing the why – that is past – move to the present, what needs to happen now. Being in the moment keeps one grounded – it allows one to return to at least neutral, as one shifts their mind chatter and emotions back to the task at hand. The focus that comes from being in the present moment is invaluable.

4 *Breath deep and often* – just keep breathing. Yoga can help a person learn to breathe. This gives oxygen to the body and allows the person to manage emotions. Breathing helps a person calm down and at that same time conserve energy.

5 *Make water one's beverage of choice.* Our body is an electromagnetic circuit and water cleanses, giving instant energy, with no "sugar" hangovers. Every time we need something – an emotional fix, some energy, or just to quench a thirst – we can get it if we choose to drink water. Drinking coffee has a dehydrating effect on the body and there is an energy crash after the affects of the caffeine wear off.

6 *Restart the day if it is not going well.* Letting go of what is not working, and reframing a situation to look at the positive, shifts everything in a person's mind to a new place. It is

a mind trick to let go of the negative and start in a neutral or more positive mind space. It can be even more impactful if a person's intentions are verbally announced – telling people that your day has begun again helps to reinforce that it's okay to let go and begin again. There is just so little time during Games-time that dwelling on negatives is unproductive for the workforce member and for the event.

7 *Be grateful* for being a participant rather than an observer; for being chosen out of all the people who applied for this position; for being part of the "rarefied air" of a major sports events with elite athletes, dignitaries, and special guests. This can instantly remind one of what is working in their life and provide a calmer, clearer space to deal with whatever the day brings.

8 *Know that every emotional response is a choice.* We cannot control what presents itself; however, we can choose our reaction or response. We can choose how we are going to feel. A person feels more personally powerful by taking control of their emotional response. Despite the fact that there are hundreds of things we cannot stop or control in a day, we can always choose our response to what happens to us. It takes practice and then it becomes a habit to stop, breathe, and choose an emotional response. This simple act of "choosing" takes the stress from the emotional body and places it in the thinking body, where power and action reside.

9 *Trust one's self and enjoy the ride.* The manager has planned what they can, volunteers have been trained. The manager must trust in the efforts put in so far and enjoy the experience (whatever it may bring).

CHAPTER SUMMARY

In this chapter we examined the structure of VTeams and Games-time decision-making. We explored research focused on the Games-time period, namely attendance, ticketing, crowd control, and volunteer management. We also suggested some future research avenues in regards to transportation and athletes.

We went into greater depth in the Games-time period within the practitioner's perspective. Here, we explored what it looks like from the BOH as the Games starts; who and what is affected once the Games begin; how the demands of workforce change and some strategies for dealing with the constant change. We focused on transportation, egos, volunteer management, observer programmes, and tips for surviving the Games-time period.

EXPERT CASE: VANCOUVER INTERNATIONAL AIRPORT – INTERNATIONAL CLIENT SERVICES ARRIVALS AND DEPARTURES

The timeframe required for operation at Vancouver International Airport (YVR) was double in comparison to the sports venues. Soft arrivals began two weeks before the beginning of the Olympic Games, and continued throughout the Games up until the closing ceremony. Departures were infrequent throughout the Games, with 90 per cent of the departures occurring on the two days following the closing ceremony. With that said, scheduled staff and volunteers were consistent throughout the Games and during pre- and post-Games.

There were many parts to the operations at the airport. Most attention was given to security, followed by customer service and satisfaction, and overall communication. The beginning stages of planning encompassed designing, building and issuing schedules, communication of VANOC operations with the existing operations and business of the YVR airport, learning and training VANOC staff and volunteers about customs and border policies for Canada, and reviewing and analysing arrival and departure data.

Operations at YVR were much different than the individual sporting venues, in that YVR was already a fully functioning business operation. The relationship that was solidified between VANOC and YVR was between all FAs of VANOC and YVR to ensure safe, efficient, and professional arrivals and departures (i.e. Customs and Border Control, Airport Security, Airport information and volunteer programme, VANOC transportation, VANOC volunteers, VANOC logistics in equipment transport, and escorting of VIP status clients).

To begin the merging of both entities, VANOC managers had to work very closely with an already functioning business and policy infrastructure at YVR during their planning. This required a lot of approval and adjustment of the VANOC plans. In many respects, knowing how established the YVR systems were enabled a smoother operation come Games-time. The requirements for VANOC were to then carry out the already-in-place systems and blend the Games-specific systems. For this we had very thorough training sessions and daily updates to any and all changes that occurred.

ICS were responsible for the arrivals and departures of the Olympic Family (IOC members, heads of state or government, TOP sponsors, NOC presidents and secretary generals), excluding athletes and the media. Our operation was completely dependent on information provided by the clients into the arrivals and departures system. The information had been requested many weeks in advance, but often there was not information for specific clients until days or hours prior to their arrival. Based on arrival information, scheduled volunteers were assigned to greet clients and personally guide them through the airport, customs hall, and baggage claim to their assigned transportation.

Problems that arose were all managed with a huge effort in communication. These issues were: delayed or cancelled flights, "no show" of the expected client, and missed connection of the VANOC volunteer with the client. When any of these issues did occur, we made adjustments to scheduling, assigning of the volunteers to clients, or called upon our partnership resources with YVR. One issue in particular that required delicate management was working with a Games partner, Airline, and their VIP programme. A few times we had "run-ins" with the airline concierge and the ICS volunteers in regards to who was going to assist the client. This was resolved by VANOC volunteers being asked to assist the paid airline employee, and then step in to continue with service once the airline employee fulfilled their obligation.

Security at the airport was the main focus, regardless of the activities or energy of the Games. It was of utmost importance that VANOC staff and volunteers operated within the security systems consistently to avoid any issues of revoking of privileges. This also required a constant update of communication between VANOC, YVR, and CBSA (Canada Border Services Agency). To ensure a limit to potential issues, we padded the schedules of volunteers in terms of being ready to receive the clients, and time between clients. Also, constant updating of information with all three partners was needed (e.g. when a high-level client was arriving, VANOC as well as YVR and CBSA were updated on the information to ensure a smooth arrival without security issues).

Departures were much more organic in operation. VANOC had the flight departure information, but without knowing when the clients were to arrive at the airport for check-in. This was overcome by positioning the ICS volunteers at all the main entrances to greet and offer assistance to *all* passengers entering through those doors. We distributed the flight departure information within the ICS volunteers so they could keep attention on those clients arriving to the airport in advance of 2–3 hours before their flights. It became relatively systematic to watch for VANOC-sponsored vehicles dropping off clients, to then be greeted by an ICS volunteer, and assisted to the check-in desk at the airport. Post-security accompaniment was not offered on departures except in special cases.

In the case of V1 or V2 clients (those with personal cars), we did have more information and formal procedure for their departures from YVR. If a police escort was involved, YVR concierge and security, as well as CBSA, were notified of their arrival to the airport for their flight departure. VANOC would work in conjunction with these parties to ensure a smooth curb greet and escort through the security points to the gate or airline lounge. In almost all cases these greets were seamless and a great sense of accomplishment in communication and execution of services.

How can an organizing committee ensure high success of arrivals and departures of Games clients? By having a detailed vision of how the operation should look; practising the procedures prior the Games is hugely beneficial. This allows time to adjust and communicate those changes with all the partners involved. Changes were constant; therefore communicating those changes was also constant and imperative.

How can the level of engagement of the volunteers and VANOC staff be maintained at a high level? It was important to let the volunteers know they were the ambassadors not only for the Olympic Games, but also for their city. They took pride in making sure the client's first moments upon arrival were positive and mirrored in their departures. Being able to make changes and adjustments with fluidity and confidence was also emphasized and pivotal in the success of the airport operations.

How does the end of the Games feel? When I arrived for my shift time, my colleague had already implemented a system based on the earlier day activities. The volunteers were stationed strategically at all the entryways greeting all Olympic guests and clients. I remember getting a five-minute debrief to catch up on how things were working, and feeling a sense of "wow". The wow came because of the ease of how the airport was functioning with 25,000 passengers departing, and a bit of an anti-climatic feeling from all the energy and time spent troubleshooting, planning, and practising for this big day. But it was because of that preparedness that all the staff and volunteers could look at one another, give a few high fives and smile, saying "Okay, we could do that again!"

By Leah Hill, Co-manager of ICS at YVR

Case questions

1 How do you coordinate and merge organizing committee policies and procedures to existing policies and procedures in an organization like an airport?

2 What are strategies to resolve coordination issues between an organizing committee and the existing organization (here, the airport)?

3 Why is the airport so important in terms of Games planning and success?

CHAPTER QUESTIONS

1 What issues are dealt with during Games-time?

2 Examine the anti-scalping laws in your area. What impact do they have on event management and event ticket systems? How have past events in your area dealt with the secondary ticket market?

3 Discuss transportation – the different kinds, the pros and cons during a sports event.

4 How can a manager deal with ego (their own and others) during Games-time?

5 Name four strategies that could assist with managing your emotions and stress during Games-time.

FURTHER READING

For further reading on the Games-time period, we suggest the following:

Chernushenko, D., van der Kamp, A., & Stubbs, D. (2001) Transportation: Cut the traffic; breathe easier. In D. Chernushenko (ed.), *Sustainable Sport Management: Running an Environmentally, Socially and Economically Responsible Organization* (pp. 190–199), Ottawa: Green & Gold Inc.

Farrell, J. M., Johnston, M. E., & Twynam, G. D. (1998) Volunteer motivation, satisfaction, and management at an elite sporting competition. *Journal of Sport Management*, 12, 288–300.

Sherry, E., Karg, A., & O'May, F. (2011) Social capital and sport events: Spectator attitudinal change and the Homeless World Cup. *Sport in Society*, 14, 111–125.

Chapter 14

Closure

OBJECTIVES

■ Understand the various components forming the wrap-up mode of a major sports event
■ Understand the issues associated with undertaking an economic impact analysis
■ Understand differences between one-off and recurring events during the wrap-up mode

ILLUSTRATIVE CASE: A MULTITUDE OF REPORTS DUE FOR BOTH THE ORGANIZING COMMITTEE AND MAJOR STAKEHOLDERS

There is a multitude of reports that are written after a major sports event is hosted. For OCOGs, the IOC now requires a final report to be submitted; however, it also requires the OCOG to participate in a transfer of knowledge process where reports are written by different sports and different divisions or FAs and presented during a debriefing session to the next Host City. The more detailed and the higher the quality of the report, the better and more useful the transfer of knowledge can be.

Stakeholders often also write reports to determine key learnings for the next time (if there is one) the given organization will be involved in the endeavour. For example, the marketing departments of Games sponsors often prepare reports for the rest of the organization and other interested parties (e.g. stockholders). Governments also prepare reports and usually undertake audits on spending and outcomes. For example, the Office of the Commissioner of Official Languages prepared a report of the 2010 Olympic Winter Games in Vancouver on the OCOG's and Canadian federal government departments' French/English language efforts (see Office of the Commissioner of Official Languages, 2010). As well, for the 2010 Delhi CWG, the Indian federal government auditor's report revealed that the final Games budget was 16 times higher than initial estimates, going from US$270 million to US$4.1 billion; yet only US$35 million were generated as revenues. The report also revealed that the organizing committee was rife with favouritism, bias, and flaws, especially regarding authority, decision-making delays, accountability, procurement/tender decisions, and unity of command (Cutler, 2011f).

THE THEORY BEHIND CLOSURE

Closing down an organizing committee of a one-time major sports event is an unavoidable, pre-determined fact. Closing the organizing committee falls within the wrap-up mode (Parent, 2008). This mode officially begins the moment the closing ceremonies have concluded and can last for up to a year. The wrap-up mode includes the following activities:

■ *Debriefing and evaluation*: attending debriefing sessions (e.g. for the benefit of the next host of the Games), and undertaking and/or responding to evaluation procedures (see the next subsection). As part of the debriefing sessions, stakeholders may offer their perspectives and evaluations of the event, based on participant observations (e.g. observer programmes). Such activities allow for knowledge transfer to occur; however, they must be incorporated into the culture of the organizing committee, as a learning organization, for these activities to be truly beneficial. (We will speak more about knowledge transfer and learning organizations in Chapter 15.)

■ *Decommissioning (closing) the venues and the FAs*: this involves taking down all temporary buildings, logistics, and looks; turning the venue into its post-Games function (e.g. from a speed skating oval to a community-used multi-sport, physical activity, and business/entertainment venue in the case of the 2010 Vancouver Olympic Winter Games' Richmond Olympic Oval); and wrapping-up the final activities of each FA (such as thanking and recognizing the efforts of staff and volunteers, providing final receipts for reimbursement, preparing final accounts and reports, making any final presentations to stakeholders, dealing with any lawsuits or contract problems, etc.).

■ *Final report(s) and closing the books (for one-time events)*: while these are prepared post-Games, some of the work should already have begun during the Games, if not before. For example, FA managers and venue managers prepare daily reports for their respective superiors. These reports are used to track the goings-on during the Games and manage issues as needed, but they are also aggregated post-Games into the FA's final report, which in turn is incorporated into the overall organizing committee's final reports to event rights holders (e.g. FISU in the case of the Universiades) and primary funders (e.g. host governments).

■ *Managing the legacies*: transferring all remaining tangible legacies (e.g. revenues, sport and non-sport equipment, venues) to the respective legacy management bodies, whether that be a formal legacy management organization (e.g. in the case of funding) or venue owners. We will discuss legacy in greater depth in Chapter 15.

Once these tasks are completed, the organizing committee can cease to exist. Throughout the wrap-up mode, organizing committees will face a number of issues; however, legacy, operations, and HR issues dominate (Parent, 2008).

In the following subsections we examine the research associated with the wrap-up mode and closing of a sports event. The research can be divided into the following themes: event evaluation, economic impact analyses, and provision of some considerations for sports events of a recurring nature. We end the section by providing some future research avenues.

Event evaluation

As event researchers (e.g. Hall, 1992; Masterman, 2009; Parent, 2008) have noted, the wrap-up mode is important as it involves key areas of event evaluation and knowledge transfer; it also helps in the professionalization of the (sport) event industry. This is why we are seeing an increasing number of event books include a chapter on event evaluation or a related topic with similar messages regarding evaluation, decommissioning venues, and completing administrative activities (cf. Shone and Parry, 2004; Van der Wagen and Carlos, 2005). Authors, such as Masterman (2009), Getz (2005), Shone and Parry (2004), and Van der Wagen and Carlos (2005) have discussed different periods of evaluation with specific types of evaluations associated at each point, which we summarize and integrate here:

1   *Pre-Games research*: Here, we find evaluations by the bid committee and key stakeholders (to see if a bid should go forward, for example), and by the organizing committee to determine what their stakeholders need. Therefore, we find formative evaluations such as needs assessments, feasibility studies, market research, stakeholder input, and situation and SWOT analyses being used.

2   *Pre-Games evaluation*: Here, we find iterative, continuous, formative evaluations, which examine progress in relation to stated objectives, milestones, and budgets. Such monitoring is critical to ensure that all FAs are on time, are coordinating among themselves where needed, and will be ready come the opening ceremonies. Monitoring and control systems during this period include both preventative and feedback controls to ensure that the event is on course. Therefore, we find formative and process evaluations such as market research, committee meetings, stakeholder input/feedback, certification audits and quality control procedures (e.g. for quality standards), staff supervision, and benchmarking.

3   *Games-time evaluation*: Here, we find evaluations which ensure that the event is happening as it should, that issues and complaints are dealt with, and that the event is still on track to become successful. We speak of operational control during this period. Therefore, we find process-oriented evaluations such as daily meetings, quality-control procedures, direct/participant observations (like secret shoppers), staff supervision, immediate client feedback (e.g. because of complaints), and daily FA and venue reports.

4   *Post-Games evaluation*: Here, we find evaluations that examine the event's outcomes, impacts, value and legacies, efficiency, and effectiveness. This is done immediately after the event, as well as over the long term (six months later, a year later, two years later, etc.) to determine the extent and impact of the event's legacies (tangible and intangible, direct and indirect, positive and negative). Therefore, we find summative evaluations such as self-evaluations by and performance evaluations of staff/volunteers (though these are often not undertaken for one-off events, unfortunately), formal debrief meetings, key stakeholder evaluations (e.g. sponsor feedback, media coverage, security stakeholder group review, customer and tourist satisfaction surveys – see Bresler (2011) as an example), formal final reports and financial audits (there should have been annual financial audits as well), legacy valuations, and economic impact analyses. A stakeholder approach to evaluating the event is ideal as they are the ones who will determine the ultimate success (of failure) of the event.

The types of evaluations noted above can be undertaken using both qualitative and quantitative approaches. For example, budget tracking is typically done using quantitative numbers, whereas knowing what stakeholders need or how the venuization of an FA is going would be more qualitative. In order to properly undertake evaluations, they must be planned for ahead of time (Masterman, 2009; Van der Wagen and Carlos, 2005); thus, they need to be incorporated into the early planning period, when objectives are set and resources are allocated. In addition, debriefs and evaluations are more successful for future events if both the successes and failures are considered (see Ellis and Davidi, 2005; Ellis *et al.*, 2006). During the debriefing and evaluation period event organizers should be able to answer the question "Did we meet our goals?" (to determine the event's effectiveness). To this, we could add the question "Did we satisfice (i.e. satisfy and suffice) our stakeholders?" (to determine stakeholders' satisfaction and the degree to which event organizers sufficiently met the needs of their stakeholders).

Another perspective one can take to evaluate an event's performance is to use a project management approach, specifically the Project Performance Scorecard (PPS). The PPS includes an evaluation of stakeholders (what is important to them, degree of involvement), project process (from beginning to end), benefit (business values and gains), quality (meeting and going beyond the stated objectives, efficiency, reliability, functionality, etc.), learning and innovation (knowledge capabilities garnered from the project), and use (how the project process results are being used) (Barclay and Osei-Bryson, 2009).

Within both the event management and project management literatures, we see a consideration of stakeholders' perspectives. However, it is not only event organizers who undertake evaluations; the stakeholders themselves (e.g. sponsors, host governments, and other event funders/partners) also undertake evaluations so that they may see the benefits of their contribution, as well as establish key learnings for the next time (if they think that there should be a next time). Stakeholders will determine what the event was worth to them; this can be done using economic impact analyses (see below), total revenue brought in by the event, ROI, consumer surplus and existence values (i.e. willingness-to-pay for benefits and willingness-to-accept costs), effectiveness and efficiency, project safety and security, sponsorship potential, media value, impact on the local/national sportscape, and network and psychic benefits (felt by individuals and the community) (cf. Crompton, 2004c; Getz, 2007; Ludwig and Karabetsos, 1999; Sugden and Tomlinson, 1996; Toor and Ogunlana, 2010). Based on their own evaluations, some stakeholders may choose to change their processes; for example, host governments may formalize or modify an existing event hosting policy (see Leopkey *et al.*, 2010). Residents' experiences of an event may also impact future support if benefits thought to accrue to the host region are perceived to "bypass those most in need" in favour of those of higher economic status (cf. Briedenhann, 2011: 5)

To determine stakeholders' experiences, perceptions, and satisfaction regarding the event, as well as event effectiveness, strengths, weaknesses, and improvements, Nguyen and Menzies (2010) suggested that stakeholders be queried regarding:

1 *visible elements*: the physical environment or sportscape of the event and facilities (e.g. aesthetics, layout, functionality, accessibility, toilets, seating, and cleanliness);

2   *interaction elements*: the social environment or stakeholders' interactions with the event (e.g. atmosphere, friendliness and helpfulness of staff and volunteers); and

3   *management elements*: the management, marketing, and all other event actions (e.g. accreditation process, ticketing process, merchandise, and licensing opportunities).

Part of determining the effectiveness (and efficiency, i.e. the degree to which resources are used to meet the objectives) of the management elements includes the aspects of communication and coordination which enable the sharing of knowledge for more effective and efficient processes, as well as the degree of shared knowledge, which assists in the initial coordination and communication processes (Adenfelt, 2010). Thus, shared knowledge/ knowledge sharing, coordination, and communication are interdependent in relation to management processes and the ultimate perceived effectiveness and efficiency of the event.

Based on these evaluations and all other information at hand regarding the event (sports results, financial accounts, etc.), event managers will decide what exactly to include in the final reports and prioritize which stakeholders should receive the final reports (e.g. rights holders vs. sponsors vs. governments vs. media) (Masterman, 2009). Final reports themselves are rather large documents; for an Olympic Games it often includes three volumes of significant size. As noted above, however, it is ultimately the stakeholders who determine the success of the event based on each stakeholder's perceived satisfaction with the event. Thus, even in the summarizing of the evaluations and writing of the final report(s), a subjective element is included as event organizers will want to showcase the best of the event (often foregoing the negative) in order to positively influence stakeholder perceptions of the event's outcome(s).

Economic impact measurements

Part of the event's outcome(s) often includes an economic impact analysis. The idea is to translate into economic form the benefits accrued from hosting a major sports event in the region. Most information is garnered from visitor surveys. Information is collected regarding who came (demographic data), for how long, how much they spent, where they spent it, as well as information on the region (e.g. gross domestic product (GDP)). The benefits can take the form of (Masterman, 2009):

■   *direct effects*: increased profits and wages for local businesses and residents due to increased expenditures by event tourists;

■   *indirect effects*: ripple effect of the tourists' expenditures to the workers and businesses supplying those accruing the direct costs;

■   *induced effects*: the (re-)spending of additional income received due to the increased tourists' expenditures.

To illustrate what may go into an economic analysis, Table 14.1 demonstrates the inputs and outputs of the Canadian Sport Tourism Alliance and Conference Board of Canada's Sport Tourism Economic Assessment Model (STEAM, Canadian Sport Tourism Alliance, 2011). In turn, Table 14.2 provides an overview of three common methods for evaluating

Table 14.1 Inputs and outputs of STEAM

Inputs	Outputs
Information, demographics on participants, spectators, media, and VIPs	Gross domestic product (GDP)
Capital input	Wages/salaries
Operating input	Employment (full-time/year jobs)
	Direct and total taxes
	Industry output

Source: Canadian Sport Tourism Alliance (2011).

the economic impact of an event: input–output analysis (IOA), computable-general-equilibrium model (CGE), and cost–benefit analysis (CBA).

Economic impact analyses have been fraught with methodological problems and critiques as they have typically been overinflated and often used for political purposes (see Andersson *et al.*, 2008; Barget and Gouguet, 2010; Crompton, 1995, 1999, 2001, 2004b; Fourie *et al.*, 2011; Getz, 2007; Gratton *et al.*, 2000; Gratton *et al.*, 2006; Késenne, 2005; Lee and Taylor, 2005; Madden, 2006; Masterman, 2009; Mitchell and Carson, 1993; Mondello and Rishe, 2004; Preuss, 2005; Taks *et al.*, 2011; Wilson, 2006). Examples of problems with these measures include: the measuring of direct effects may be "gross" effects instead of "net" effects; multipliers of economic impact of an expense are often over-exaggerated; leakages are sometimes forgotten or minimized; the use of expenditure multipliers is unjustified if the purpose is to examine ultimate income benefits (thus needing rather to use income multipliers); and the need to consider that not all tourists are alike – you need to consider time-switchers, avoiders, runaways, home stayers, casuals, pre-event tourists, changers, and post-event tourists (i.e. all those being displaced before, during, and after the event) (Getz, 2005; Matheson and Baade, 2007; Preuss, 2005).

Ex-post analyses are complicated, and ex-ante economic analyses are even more difficult to undertake. Readers should be wary of politicians, media, and even bid committees providing suggested economic impacts of the potential hosting of an event (Masterman, 2009). In fact, in an ex-post economic analysis of the 1971 to 2001 Super Bowls, Matheson and Baade (2007) found that Super Bowls accrued, on average, US$92 million in income gains, a figure approximately *one-quarter* what the NFL claimed. Moreover, the type of event may also impact the actual analysis; that is, it would be wrong to assume that if we host a FIFA World Cup, we would have the same positive impacts as hosting an Olympic Games. To wit, Sterken's (2007) ex-post analysis of the impact of the summer Olympic Games and FIFA World Cups between 1964 and 1998 showed that while there may be a positive impact for the Olympic Games, this did not hold true for the FIFA World Cup. Moreover, Chengli *et al.* (2011: 11) found that the economic impact of Olympic Games of the 15 host countries of the past 24 Summer and Winter Olympic Games "is only significant in terms of certain parameters (i.e. gross domestic product performance and unemployment) in the short term".

Despite these issues, potential funders (e.g. governments) of events, and even the general public, often require bid organizers to provide an estimate of the potential economic impact

Table 14.2 A comparison of economic analysis approaches

Approach	Description	Good points	Criticism
Input–output analysis (IOA)	Describes financial flows, regional economic inflow from other regions/nations.	Politician- and media-friendly output (provides an economic number)	Does not measure the efficiency of the actual event (i.e. value produced vs. value consumed)
	Most frequently used (though most frequently criticized as well)		Difficult to argue that money is more efficiently spent in this tourism endeavour than other industries
	Uses multipliers to convert total expenditures (direct, indirect, induced) into a net amount (minus leakages of monies not remaining in the local economy), which produces an estimate of job creation (employment)		Does not measure local economic flow between residents
			Does not consider the value for the local residents
	It is about economic effects and market values		Misuse of the multiplier (overestimation (sometimes even deliberate), incorrect use of the turnover multiplier, double-counting costs–income for suppliers) which inflate the result
	Regional multipliers (what is the value added of monies coming into the region because of the event) used to measure direct and indirect effects		Inaccurate to assume that increased local expenditures automatically means jobs must be created by local businesses
	Displacement effects		Opportunity costs (displacement of tourists) are a problem
			Not a dynamic model
			Assumes a linear economic development without capacity constraints or crowding out considerations, nor any elastic supply curves

continued

Table 14.2 Continued

Approach	Description	Good points	Criticism
Computable-general-equilibrium model (CGE)	Comprises sub-models describing the neighbouring regional economies, capital market, and labour market	An evolution of the IOA	Economic adaptation assumption is doubtful for shorter-term organizations (i.e. of smaller events)
	Regional metrics (info on multiple industries, households, imports/exports, and regional government)	More inclusive than the IOA	Assumes linear relations, which means providing an average cost analysis; yet most events would be more appropriately measured using a marginal analysis
	Links to other neighbouring regions and federal government		
	Same kind of inputs as IOA but they are treated as "demand-side shocks" on the regional economy (on employment, GDP, particular industries, and imports/exports), with the effects being measured by the CGE		
	Expenditures as "shocks" can include: Games operations, Games venue constructions, Games visitor expenditures, and induced tourism expenditures		
	Consumers choose services/goods based on preference but are constrained by personal income		
	Producers choose inputs to minimize production costs		
	Substitutions are possible between regions		
	Markets are seen as interdependent		
	It is about economic efficiency and market values		
	Long-term modeling		

Cost–benefit analysis (CBA)	Assessment of costs and benefits based on welfare changes (including political)	Ambitious: almost impossible to have a perfect CBA as it is extremely difficult to consider *all* effects and assign correct values to *all* resources (tangible and intangible) and benefits accrued (tangible and intangible)
	All resources should be included (not only those traded on the market)	The benefit side is dependent on the subjective assessment of the value of the pleasure and excitement felt by spectators
	All individuals impacted in any way (directly or indirectly) are considered	Results are not as politician- and media-friendly because they are not "hard" economic numbers like the IOA
	Based on comparing created value vs. value of resources used	
	It is about economic efficiency and welfare values	
	Examples of tangible costs considered: capital and construction costs, salaries and other employment costs	
	Examples of tangible benefits considered: sponsor and investor expenditures (e.g. for activation/leveraging), new facilities/venues (if externally funded), positive media coverage providing tourism gains, economic growth, increased trade, increased tourism capacity for future gains (e.g. new hotels), retained resident expenditures (though controversial)	
	Examples of intangible costs considered: traffic jams and congestion, noise, parking problems, crime and prostitution, demonstrations	
	Examples of intangible benefits considered: national/regional pride, attitude changes towards politicians/organizations, increased interest from investors, extraordinary experiences, increased cultural activity, increased social capital	
	To measure some of these intangibles, the contingent valuation method may be used (degree of willingness-to-pay for benefits and willingness-to-accept costs) which gives an estimate of the value of an experience in monetary terms	

Sources: Anderson et al. (2008), Arcodia and Whitford (2006), Barget and Gouguet (2010), Crompton (2001), Getz (2007), Madden (2006), Masterman (2009), and Mitchell and Carson (1993).

before they support the event (Getz, 2005). To partly resolve this disconnect between the ex-ante "attractiveness" of the IOA and its methodological problems, in comparison to the "unattractiveness" yet more accurate CBA, it has been suggested to supplement the ex-ante IOA and incomplete CBA with a qualitative legitimacy test for the event, which would comprise questions pertaining to (1) social, environmental, and economic undesirable effects of the event (e.g. hooliganism, pollution) and means to mitigate these effects; (2) the perceived quantification of the event by individuals, particularly for taxpayers; (3) prioritization of public funds into the event versus another industry or activity; (4) the perceived excess costs of the event beyond what is stated (Barget and Gouguet, 2010).

As Getz (2005) noted, we cannot or should not assume that: (1) all major sports events create economic benefits; (2) organizers need to justify the economic benefits to obtain funding for their event (it could, instead, be a statement on the expected number of tourists and what they could spend on the event); (3) all visitors are the same (see earlier); (4) all new facilities built for an event are benefits (questions to answer here include: How much did they cost anyway? Who paid for the facility? How will it be used post-event?); (5) events create lots of employment opportunities (in fact, most "opportunities" are for volunteers, secondees, and part-time work); (6) we can include all visitor expenditures in calculations of benefits (only after considering leakage, time-switchers, displacements, etc.); and (7) multipliers must be used (not all models require multipliers, they are fraught with assumption problems, and you may only need tourists' direct expenditures on the event to give a sense of the economic impact).

Points to consider for recurring events

The general process of closing down an event can also be followed by recurring event (e.g. Wimbledon, Calgary Stampede, and Boston Marathon) managers, although these managers do not undertake the full close-down of the organization as they hope to continue the event the following year. They will undertake debrief and evaluation sessions so that two important questions may be answered by recurring event organizers: (1) Did the event meet its objectives?; and (2) What can we improve for the next edition? (cf. Shone and Parry, 2004). They will decommission the venue(s) and complete administrative duties such as providing final accounts of revenues and expenditures for that edition of the event. The remaining legacies will be kept by the managers for (re-)use during the next edition of the event the following year (Shone and Parry, 2004). The learnings drawn from this year's event are then (hopefully) applied to the following year. Some points to consider when drawing lessons learned – and this can be useful for one-off events as well in their knowledge transfer – include: (1) the lessons drawn must be of benefit to the organizers themselves; (2) the evaluation and lesson-learning process must start from the beginning (not only be done as an after-thought post-event); (3) lessons should be linked to future actions for the following year's event; and (4) event "leaders must hold everyone, especially themselves, accountable for learning" (Darling et al., 2005: 84).

Possible future research directions

While the wrap-up has not been extensively examined in the sport event management literature, the economic impact has been and will likely continue to be so. One aspect that has not been scrutinized is the impact of the ending of a Games and its organizing committee on former employees and volunteers. VANOC expended a significant amount of effort in preparing its employees for the next phase of their life through résumé workshops, job opportunity notices, etc., but, as the psychology literature shows (e.g. Beike *et al.*, 2009; Bell and Taylor, 2011), there is still a sense of loss, a bereavement period. In addition, there is work being undertaken relating to the cognitive (re-)construction of stressful or negative events and closure processes (e.g. Boals *et al.*, 2011; Foley *et al.*, 1997; Habermas and Berger, 2011); given that major sports events are a stressful, adrenaline-pumping environment, it would be interesting to examine cognitive narrative constructions by organizing committee employees and volunteers.

These topics warrant future research, as does more investigation on the overall post-Games period and event evaluation. For example, research in India in the engineering field has revealed that the structure of an organization (e.g. hierarchical versus heterarchical – that is, more localized control, self-organizing, has a greater learning culture, changing roles as a function of circumstances) impacts the perceived effectiveness (here, functioning) of the organization (Bhargava and Sinha, 1992); to what extent does this hold for major sports events organizing committees as compared to other types of organizations? In addition, Ko *et al.* (2011) developed a measurement scale for event quality in spectator sports called the SEQSS; as it was done using a single sport, it may be worth examining transferability of the measurement in a multi-sport setting.

Finally, there is emerging research examining evaluations specific to environmental, green, and sustainability initiatives (Hartungi, 2010; Laing and Frost, 2010; Mallen *et al.*, 2010b); how these should be integrated (not conducted separately) into and benefiting the major sports event evaluation process is worth investigating given the emerging dominance of "green" or "sustainable" Games like Vancouver 2010 and London 2012. Noting the paucity of developmental event evaluation processes from the outset of the event conceptualization, Ma *et al.* (2011) proposed a monitoring framework that includes sustainability issues, and therefore is one example of such a study. The framework was developed with host residents and other stakeholders of the 2009 Kaohsiung World Games. It includes quantitative tools for measuring economic, social, and environmental impacts, and qualitative tools for the following evaluation criteria:

- *sustainable economy*: consumer habits, employment, and investments;
- *sustainable society*: social equality, human habitat and settlement, sustainable sport event hosting policies, community-wide participation, and health protection; and
- *sustainable environment*: sports facilities, transportation, water, waste, energy, conservation areas, and biodiversity.

THE PRACTITIONER'S PERSPECTIVE ON CLOSURE

The executive team and a small group of workforce members are critical to the closing of a major sports event. The intellectual property coupled with their personal observations and experience will influence, inspire, inform, and educate future organizing committees. Notwithstanding, it positions each of them to leverage their event experience in their personal and business lives. The motivation for them to stay focused until the books are actually closed could be a challenge unless the leader is still fired up; and considering the physical and mental drain the leader has experienced, this can be a distinct challenge. It is important to have as much process decided and created in advance so that the questionnaires, debriefs, and evaluation activities capture all necessary and useable information in the answers. Details of how the debriefing and evaluations will be conducted need to be thought out in advance. It contributes to efficiency for both the people who are responding to the questions and providing suggestions, so that the organizing committee can preserve this information for future organizing committees. It will also help to ensure more complete answers so that explanations that are required for the turnover process of facilities to cities, communities, and governments can take place in a more seamless way.

Having a professional business coach or someone with coaching skills, or an individual trained in research methods, can be invaluable to the process of debriefing and evaluation. Often, there are second and third questions that need to follow an initial question to prompt memory and/or trigger memories for respondents. If there is not a human involved in the process, some important and valuable information may be lost. A coach or researcher can read body language, voice inflections and language in a particular way to interrogate the reality of what is being said, which will ultimately affect the quality of feedback that is received. When people feel heard and understood, they will dissolve barriers to allow more transparent communication, revealing and sharing in an unguarded and prolific way. Often, it just takes another question, a rephrasing of what they have said, or some gentle encouragement to uncover the "gold" in their thoughts and memories. The IOC seemed to heed this call by having stakeholder focus groups led by researchers to evaluate the first editions of the summer and winter YOG. Feedback from athletes, coaches, and chefs de mission will hopefully improve future editions of the event.

Next, there may also be legal issues that were partially resolved – enough to allow the event to proceed – but which still have loose ends that could have residual consequences. These must be dealt with swiftly, employing masterful interpersonal skills. The rise of sponsorship protection/anti-ambushing laws is likely a signification part of the legal department's pre-Games, Games-time, and post-Games workload. This explains why the legal team is almost the last one to turn out the lights.

Media representatives scramble to answer the question of whether the sport event lost money, made money, or broke even (even if that result is usually still months away). The media also provide final thoughts on the event, establishing a reputation that will last for a long time, and one which the organizing committee – since it will soon cease to exist – is at pains to change. Positive messaging to the media is therefore critical so that the organization appears transparent with what information is immediately available while also being willing to share as soon as possible the final verdict on the numbers and any other relevant information (e.g. sustainability reports).

Most workforce members leave on the last day of the Games. It is abrupt and final. There is no office to go back to as everything was moved when the FAs venuized in preparation for the event. All of the activity during the event should hopefully have been chronicled in the daily reports; however, there is sometimes no one left to create a final report or evaluate the activities and summarize experiences and observations. To illustrate, the venue manager will have a couple of days to compile the overall summary; however, it will lack the individual contribution of the managers from all of the FAs that have been disbanded. While workforce employees have known that the end will come, there is no amount of conversation and written material that can adequately prepare a person for the feelings and thoughts that flood like a tsunami, fast and furiously, when the doors close – when the last sport event is completed and the spectators and athletes have exited the facility after the closing ceremony. It is indescribable; and the emotional wake can remain for days, weeks, and even months after the experience. This is sometimes referred to as the post-Games blues. There are certainly exit strategies that have been extended and facilitated for people to transition to new jobs, or at least to begin the process of job hunting, such as: one-on-one coaching and information meetings with HR managers, seminars on the closure process and next steps (e.g. résumé writing), contact information for potential employers, and obtaining written reference letters from superiors.

More recently, however, social and new media have provided a new forum for résumé posting, job searching, and networking. Facebook, for example, allows a person to instantly change their status and begin job prospecting conversations, as well as keep in touch with former Games colleagues; LinkedIn, a professional portal that "links" like-minded people, also facilitates (past and future) connections. Recognition plaques and certificates authenticate the experience for the individual and future employers. There is almost always a one-year anniversary event to look forward to. However, the fact remains that, in a moment, one of the most exhilarating, exciting, and challenging experiences of a person's life has ended. It will be very difficult to match or exceed the adrenalin rush, the collegial intimacy, the personal satisfaction of contribution, and the legacy that this event experience has delivered on a visceral, very individual level (unless one decides to become a Games gypsy and start the process all over again!)

CHAPTER SUMMARY

In this chapter we find that most research associated with the closure of a major sports event or the wrap-up mode fall under the economic impact analysis theme. Regarding economic impact analyses, we discussed different approaches and their numerous methodological problems. From a broader event evaluation perspective, we examined the four main periods: pre-Games research, pre-Games evaluation, Games-time evaluation, and post-Games evaluation. We stressed the importance of incorporating stakeholders' perceptions into the evaluation as they ultimately determine the success (or failure) of the event. We noted that stakeholders have their own event evaluations to do as well. We also examined the activities found during the wrap-up mode. We provided some differences between one-off and recurring events regarding the wrap-up mode, and offered suggestions for future research associated with closing a major sports event.

From a practitioner's standpoint, we went beyond the logistics of closing the doors to think about the leadership and legal aspects. We also explored the importance of debriefing and evaluation processes. Finally, we stressed the emotional wake that is created because of the abrupt finish for most of the workforce members on the last day of the event.

EXPERT CASE: CSPR'S POST-OLYMPIC AND PARALYMPIC WINTER GAMES STORY

Corporate Strategy and Partner Relations (CSPR) division was initially responsible for all municipal, provincial, federal, and aboriginal government partners. In particular, CSPR was in charge of honoured guests who would be attending the Games on behalf of their governments. This included, for the first time, a historic partnership with the Lil'wat, Musqueum, Squamish, and Tsleil-Waututh nations, as the Games were being held within their traditional and shared territories. This marked the first time in history that indigenous peoples were recognized by the IOC as official partners in the hosting of an Olympic Games.

As VANOC began to streamline operations in preparation for the Games, it was important to ensure that the strongest possible resources were accountable for areas where synergies could be found. CSPR therefore took on the responsibility for managing the Olympic Family (which included international heads of state), venue protocol, language services, and flags.

Key deliverables during Games-time for the Olympic Family included: Olympic information desks in the Olympic Family hotels; and planning and managing all official pre-Games and Games-time meetings and events, including project reviews, coordination commission meetings, governing board meetings, daily coordination meetings, and the IOC session. CSPR was also in charge of Olympic Family lounges and seating areas at each venue, arrivals and departures at airports, medal and flower presenter wrangling (i.e. finding the presenters and getting them to the medal ceremony area), and interpretation (professional, volunteer, and over the phone).

It is important to note that when dealing with high-level heads of state, a key aspect of the task is to make sure these guests have proper access to all of the Olympic venues, that their transportation is seamless, and that they have seats waiting for them upon arrival at venues. Sometimes very popular sports events or medal rounds led to some difficult decisions regarding seating capacity and security. As a result of strong pre-planning, together with coordinated in-venue teams, CSPR managed these expectations well.

CSPR faced some key challenges both pre-Games and during Games-time. Pre-Games, the executive vice-president changed three times, which delayed some planning during the transfer of knowledge. Increased budgetary gaps company-wide required some creative solutions for affordable programmes and space. Additionally, dealing with government partners happened VANOC-wide, and this meant being at odds with another FA on how to proceed to solve a problem encountered by a stakeholder. CSPR doubled in size in the few months before the Olympic Games began, which meant integrating new staff and quickly getting up to speed on the new job requirements within the expanded function. When the Games finally arrived, the deliverables were so front-end heavy that the group was already tired when the opening ceremony started.

By the time the flame was extinguished in Whistler at the end of the Paralympic closing ceremony, much of the planning to close down CSPR had already been initiated. The CSPR staff complement was reduced first after the end of the Olympic Winter Games, and then further reduced by the end of the Paralympic Winter Games. Some of the minute tasks involved in closing down the function included what to do with all of the extra volunteer gifts, participation medals, plush mascot toys, and the like – CSPR had been allocated far more gifts than we had volunteers. We also had to clarify the check-in process for phones, cars, laptops, and other "personal" items – is it at the venue level or are these items returned to the FA manager?

Ideally, a wrap-up lunch or dinner with the whole team after the Olympics would be useful as this is likely the last interaction the team will have in its entirety. In fact, the last day for many of CSPR's team was the night the Olympics ended, and others had moved on by the time the Paralympics were over. CSPR hosted a team dinner in Whistler for its entire staff complement, which provided a nice moment of closure for the team. Additionally, a thank you letter or certificate was sent out to team members, as well as a post-Games contact list of all team members.

The OGKM reports had to be completed. These were legacy and knowledge transfer reports for the next OCOG. They were completed pre-Games, during the Games, and post-Games. The reports consisted of describing the various challenges faced, the response to these challenges, and some of the things CSPR would have liked to change if the opportunity had arisen.

At the end of the Games, had budget permitted, CSPR would have liked to do a follow-up with each of the Canadian government partners to discuss lessons learned from their experience. For the provinces and territories, our partners wanted help to prove that they had received good value for their investment with VANOC. As the budget did not permit on-site visits, email communications went out to the partners to find out how their Games-time experience went. CSPR was able to follow-up in person with the federal government. There was a high degree of satisfaction with the overall outcome of the Games, but they suggested that collaboration between themselves and VANOC should have begun far earlier than five years prior to the Games – which was when CSPR was formed.

The closing-down venue protocol part of CSPR was a little different from the rest of CSPR. It is important to determine in advance who will leave after the Olympics and who will stay on for the Paralympics. Many of the venues for the Olympics were different during the Paralympics. This typically takes some adjusting and some negotiating to get it right. There typically wouldn't be any need for a final report from each of the venues, as venue managers should have been sending daily updates to their director. The head of venue protocol should have compiled a final report that would include the daily reports from each venue. Finally, the FA should take care to collect key documents from the planning stages – including training manuals, PowerPoint slide decks, key reports and presentations, venue operating plans, business plans, etc.

It should be noted that the government partner experience will differ from Games to Games, depending upon the number of parties involved and how these parties interact with each other and an OCOG. What are their expectations for their heads of state or government leaders? Should the CSPR function be as large and varied in tasks as it is?

VANOC, towards the end of the Games, placed great trust and confidence in CSPR's assistance in solving a wide range of issues – something made possible because of the strength of the trust relationships established by the CSPR team and leadership. As crises hit – such as the passing of an athlete, the late arrival of dignitaries, and the protests at the opening ceremony – CSPR was able to convene and assist in managing a collaborative response to these issues with the main operation centre.

What is critical, however, is that the organizing committee recognize the importance of the CSPR function – or whatever it may be called – early enough in the process to ensure all stakeholders are appropriately engaged and that their expectations can be tempered as early as possible in the process. Many of these conversations are highly sensitive, involving political figures, and ensuring people are able to "save face" and can be seen to be part of a win will go a long way in ensuring broader cooperation on other issues that may be pain points for the OCOG.

Personal perspectives

Many people say working for an Olympic Games is the opportunity of a lifetime, and I agree. But what happens after the flame is extinguished is a completely different experience. Being one of the last remaining in my FA at the end of the Games was certainly a big change from the norm. By the time my last day rolled around, it was the middle of April – nearly two months removed from the close of the Olympic Games. Even that small amount of distance from the closing ceremony gave me the opportunity to look back rather fondly on the entire experience and be glad that I made it through in one piece, as there were obviously some very stressful days. What I was less prepared for was saying goodbye on an almost daily basis to colleagues whose end dates came before mine. I met some incredible people in the year and a half working at VANOC and I left grateful that I met them, for the crazy journey we took together, and for the amazing experiences that I will never forget. – *Melissa*

One of the most difficult things about being one of the last to leave is that there is a remarkable sense of loss following several years of build-up to a euphoric moment with a wonderful team. For me, there were two particularly difficult parts to the departure process – the sense that something had come to an end – and would never again happen; and the knowledge that while we had done an incredible job, there, as always, remained some unfinished business – we didn't have a chance to formally close out with many of our partners, and much of the reporting we had hoped to do was not done because the budget situation did not allow for people to stay on. It is not often one is in a role that tests every aspect of one's ability – but at the end of it all, the skill that mattered most was being able to ensure things were finished off as well as possible, knowing full well that the day after the last day at Vancouver 2010, nothing would be the same. – *Taleeb*

By Taleeb Noormohamed, President and CEO – Serebra Learning Corporation; and Melissa Harder, Manager, Special Projects – Serebra Learning Corporation

Case questions

1   Describe the key steps involved in closing down a function like CSPR.

2   Games are themselves organisms that require nurturing – and the teams involved are no different. Because of the synergistic relationships expected between governments and the OCOG, what other methods could be used to integrate and advance collaborative efforts while recognizing the importance of differing needs between stakeholders? What steps could be taken at earlier stages in Games planning to ensure expectations are managed and collaborative alternatives to problems developed?

3   Given the divergent needs of an OCOG and governments, is it reasonable to expect governments to put their own needs aside in favour of a collective approach where the OCOG is primary? Why?

CHAPTER QUESTIONS

1   What is the wrap-up mode, when does it occur, and what does it include?

2   Describe and critique the different methods for determining the economic impact of an event.

3   How would you integrate environmental/green/sustainability evaluation measurements into the overall event's wrap-up and evaluation processes?

4   What is the role of leadership during the closure process?

5   From an organizational standpoint, what can be done to assist the transition of workforce from event closing to the next chapter in their lives?

FURTHER READING

For further reading on aspects associated to closure (evaluations, stakeholder perspectives), we suggest the following:

Chelladurai, P. (1987) Multidimensionality and multiple perspectives of organizational effectiveness. *Journal of Sport Management*, 1, 37–47.

Prebensen, N. K. (2010) Value creation through stakeholder participation: A case study of an event in the High North. *Event Management*, 14, 37–52.

Preuss, H. (ed.) (2007) *The Impact and Evaluation of Major Sporting Events*, Abingdon: Routledge.

Chapter 15

Legacy and sustainability

OBJECTIVES

■ To distinguish between legacy, leveraging, and other related concepts
■ To understand the challenges of planning, managing, and evaluating legacy
■ To understand the concepts of sustainability and CSR as they pertain to major sports events
■ To understand knowledge management and transfer processes

ILLUSTRATIVE CASE: REVISITING LEGACIES OF PAST OLYMPIC GAMES

The focus on legacy is typically on current (or future) Olympic Games for the potential legacies these events can bring to the host regions and countries, with (usually flawed) ex-ante economic analyses leading the charge and an increasing interest in social and environmental legacies emerging. However, some long-finished Olympic Games are still or even only beginning to demonstrate key benefits. For example, the 1976 Montreal Olympic Games allowed the province of Quebec to lead Canada and the other provinces in terms of "amateur" sport funding, with the result being that a large percentage (sometimes even a majority) of the Canadian delegations in the more recent past were Quebecers. The 1988 Calgary Olympic Winter Games left a legacy for all future OCOGs of the TOP programme sponsors. As well, the facilities left behind after 1988 are now providing fruitful ground for the training of winter sport athletes. Next, an unexpected legacy for the 1992 Barcelona Olympic Games has been that it has become the convention capital of the world. Finally, Innsbruck (Austria) was able to use the venues built for the 1964 and 1976 Olympic Winter Games when it hosted the 2012 Winter YOG, thereby substantially decreasing the cost of hosting the first Winter YOG and demonstrating a positive legacy stemming from events hosted over 40 years ago.

THE THEORY BEHIND LEGACY AND SUSTAINABILITY

Legacy is an increasingly popular topic for event researchers. There is also some branching into the concepts of sustainability, CSR, and knowledge management and transfer. We will therefore examine the legacy phenomenon, spending time on issues and challenges, and legacy planning, management, and evaluation. We will also provide an overview of the link with sustainability, CSR, and leveraging. Finally, we will look at the concept of knowledge management and transfer.

The legacy phenomenon

Event legacy is a concept that emerged in the event/sport event management literature in the late 1980s and early 1990s and alludes to what the hosting of events brings to and leaves behind in the local region. Prior to this time, other terms such as impacts (Getz, 1997; Hall, 1992; Hiller, 1998; Ritchie, 1984), outcomes (Hiller, 2002), and effects (Holmes and Shamsuddin, 1997) were seen throughout the literature.

The increased importance of the term stems from bidders, organizers, and event owners' needs to justify the expenditure of scarce resources on the perceived gigantisms and excesses associated with hosting a major sports event. Although other events such as the World's Fair in New Orleans (e.g. Dimanche, 1996), and sports events including the CWG (e.g. Smith and Fox, 2007; Matheson, 2010) and the FIFA World Cup (e.g. Gratton and Preuss, 2008; Preuss, 2007a) have been examined, there tends to be a stronger research focus on Olympic Games-related impacts (e.g. Cashman, 2006; Girginov, 2011; Gold and Gold, 2007; Ritchie, 2000; Vigor et al., 2004).

Much attention has been paid to the outcomes associated with hosting sports events as the diversity of the concept also provides a platform for its investigation in a variety of disciplines, including history, anthropology, sociology, media, disability, environmental, and urban studies (e.g. Gold and Gold, 2007; Smith and Fox, 2007). Legacy has been generally defined in dictionaries as something handed down by a predecessor; a long-lasting effect of an event or process; or the act of bequeathing or gifting (Pearsall, 1999). Although there continues to be a lack of agreement on the definition of the concept, within the field of sport event management, a common but broad view of the term is reflected in the following definition: legacy is "all planned and unplanned, positive and negative, intangible and tangible structures created by and for a sport event that remains for a longer time than the event itself" (Preuss, 2007b: 86). Table 15.1 illustrates the differences between similar terms seen in the literature.

Since first appearing in sport event management discourse, legacy has evolved as a concept reflecting the general benefits and impacts associated with hosting a sports event to proactively planned sustainable long-term legacies (Leopkey and Parent, 2012). Both positive and negative legacies have been identified (Cashman, 2006; Leopkey and Parent, 2012; Lenskyj, 2002; Mangan, 2008; Preuss, 2007b). For example, positive legacies can include new infrastructure, urban revival, enhanced international reputation, increased tourism, business opportunities, heightened community spirit, improved public welfare, as well as education and volunteer training opportunities. Negative legacies linked to hosting have also surfaced, such as: high construction costs, debt, white elephants (i.e. unused facilities), temporary crowding, loss of permanent visitors, evictions, housing issues, redistribution of funding for social programmes, reduced public access to facilities, and strenuous use of local resources (Leopkey and Parent, 2012; Lenskyj, 2002; Preuss, 2007a; Smith, A., 2009).

287

Table 15.1 Legacy-related concepts

Term	Dictionary definition*	As discussed in the literature
Legacy	Gift, handed down from the past, long-lasting effect	Anything leftover following the hosting of a (sport) event
Leveraging	Exertion of force, power to influence	Optimizing economic and/or social benefits from hosting and enhancing the effect of hosting (e.g. Beesley and Chalip, 2011)
Impacts	Influencing, effecting, force exerted by a new concept or technology	Immediate outcomes, changes related to the event (e.g. Getz, 2007, Robinson et al., 2010)
Outcomes	Final product or end result, that which results from something	Consequences of intended and unintended legacies (e.g. Jinxia and Mangan, 2008)
Effects	Something produced by a cause, result, or consequence of something	Influence of an action, enhancing impact of the event (e.g. Xing and Chalip, 2008; Turco, 1994)
Heritage	Transmitted from the past or handed down; the outcome of an action	Accumulated capital of the past arriving in the present (e.g. MacAloon, 2008)

Note
* Definitions from the *Concise Oxford Dictionary* (Pearsall, 1999).

While many event stakeholders continue to view legacy from an economic or physical infrastructure point of view, there is common acknowledgement that other forms of legacy do exist (e.g. Cashman, 2006; Minnaert, 2012; Ritchie, 2000; Swart et al., 2011). There is tourism (e.g. Fourie and Spronk, 2011), sport participation (e.g. Frawley and Cush, 2011; Funk et al., 2011), political impacts (e.g. Heere et al., 2011), environmental impacts (e.g. Jin et al., 2011), national unity/pride (e.g. Ndlovu-Gatsheni, 2011b), and network building/evolution (e.g. Sallent et al., 2011).

A variety of event legacy classifications have also been provided in the literature (e.g. Cashman, 2006; Chappelet, 2006). For example, Ritchie (1984) suggested six types of impacts for hallmark (major sport and cultural) events. These were economic (e.g. expenditures), tourism/commercial (e.g. awareness, reputation), physical (e.g. facilities, the environment), socio-cultural (e.g. regional traditions), psychological (e.g. local pride), and political (e.g. political propaganda, image). In contrast, Leopkey and Parent (2012) summarized the legacy information found in the Olympic bids and final reports into 13 different but interconnected, tangible and intangible types of event legacies linked to the hosting of an Olympic Games. These were:

- cultural legacies: cultural programming and opportunities;
- environmental legacies: environmentally friendly architecture/engineering designs, policies, and education programmes;
- educational/informational legacies: legacies associated with the desire to increase one's personal development; to gain experience and/or knowledge; and/or to develop research and governance capacity/processes;

- financial/economic: increased number of jobs, tourism, hosting and marketing opportunities, incoming funding to the region, etc.;
- image legacies: increased national/international awareness, enhanced host destination/region image;
- nostalgia-based legacies: those legacies associated with personal experiences, memories of the event;
- Olympic Movement legacies: those legacies associated with the Olympic Family's values, desires, and wants, such as having an influence on the youth and global harmony;
- political legacies: policies and policy development instruments;
- psychological legacies: those personal emotions as well as community-wide thoughts/feelings of (national) pride and enthusiasm;
- social issues: legacies impacting the general population (the residents) and/or special populations such as health issues, social progress, homelessness, new opportunities and civic engagement;
- sport: sport facilities, sport development, sport participation;
- sustainability: those legacies which have a long-term planning perspective, and are environmental friendly and/or economically viable; and
- urban legacies: building of facilities, rejuvenation of sport facilities, and improvements in municipal transportation infrastructure, services, planning, and recreation spaces.

Besides the Olympic Movement, the other legacy types could easily be found in other types of major sports events; instead of the Olympic Movement, we could use "event values" as a broader term to encompass values associated with other types of major events (e.g. the Francophone culture for the *Jeux de la Francophonie*). In addition, within sustainability we could include social issues, as well as financial/economic legacies and environmental legacies. In fact, there are suggestions that the literature may be moving from speaking of legacy to being more about sustainability (and leveraging). Finally, while physical and financial legacies may be more commonly discussed and studied in the literature, it has been argued that, in fact, the more valuable – yet hard to measure (i.e. intangible) – types of legacies are social and psychological in nature (Ritchie, 2000).

Finally, Chappelet (2012) summarized the concept of legacy and proposed key aspects/types of legacies in the following definition:

All that remains, be it:

- tangible and intangible
- territorial (geography-based) and individual (personal)
- sport and non-sport

can be considered by:

- the local population
- the urban regime
- the owner(s) of the event

289

can be considered:

- during the bidding and organizing phases
- between one and ten years post-event
- more than ten years post-event

as a consequence of the event:

- positive versus negative
- related versus non-related
- intended versus non-intended.

Legacy issues and challenges

There are many issues and challenges associated with delivering an effective event legacy. These include the fact that legacy is commonly discussed as a positive end-result. Of course, this positive perspective varies based on the perspectives of the different event stakeholders. Some researchers (e.g. Gratton and Preuss, 2008; Mangan, 2008) believe this occurs for several reasons: (1) it avoids blame by the public and provides evidence why hosting is beneficial for the city; (2) it justifies the use of public resources on event infrastructure (i.e. ROI); and (3) positive legacies motivate other cities to bid for and host events in the future.

Moreover, event legacy has been considered an "elusive, problematic, and even dangerous word for a number of reasons" (Cashman, 2006: 33), including questions of legacy semantics (MacAloon, 2008). Namely, words for the same concept vary across languages, thereby resulting in heightened ambiguity surrounding legacy. For example, in English the word legacy has been adopted, whereas in French it is common to see *héritage* or *legs* used to describe equivalent concepts related to coming from the past to the present or leaving a legacy for the future. However, MacAloon (2008: 2067) criticized this approach, saying:

> this superficial comparison conceals an important statistical difference in the semantic weighting of the two terms in ordinary speech. In actual usage, the French term is more encompassing and more weighted in more contexts toward the accumulated capital of the past arriving in the present, while the English term is more narrowly specified — for example, through its legal referents — and tilted towards the present's contribution to the future.

In addition, the word is commonly articulated or planned for without being formally defined. There is also a belief that legacy benefits automatically flow to a community post-event; however, it has been agreed that proper legacy planning is required to ensure effective legacy maintenance post-Games (Ritchie, 2000; Shipway, 2007). Not only was legacy originally looked at as a side issue and frequently postponed due to lack of time during the lead-up and hosting of the event (Cashman, 1999), but organizing committees generally disband within a short period following the wrap-up of an event (Mangan, 2008; Parent, 2008). It also takes time and resources to measure the true impact of legacy, sometimes upwards of 30 years, as noted in the illustrative case at the beginning of this chapter. To wit,

Dimanche (1996) noted how mega-event impacts can be both short and long term and may change (i.e. negative in the short term but positive in the long term as in the case of the 1984 Louisiana World Fair in New Orleans). As well, perceptions of legacy impacts can change over time, as Balduck *et al.*'s (2011) study of resident perceptions of the Tour de France's social legacy impacts demonstrates. Finally, "the diversity and scope of events is such that it is difficult, if not impossible, to progress beyond research into case-specific, tangible and measurable impacts of events" (Sharpley and Stone, 2012: 351); legacy is context, culture, and politically dependent (cf. Beesley and Chalip, 2011; Cornelissen *et al.*, 2011).

Legacy planning and management

Common belief is that hosting sports events can help transform a host city or region in a variety of ways, including heightened image, increased tourism, and urban regeneration. Urban regeneration, for example, includes transportation, supply, and industrial restructuring in a host region, but also economic (re)growth, which is often led by property development (Pacione, 2012). Nevertheless, economic impact analysis and other studies examining physical legacies remain inconclusive. Still, there is a push for garnering positive legacies. To do so successfully depends on the amount of strategic planning undertaken by the host organization to realize these potentials (Cashman, 2006; Mangan, 2008). Legacy planning is important as it serves to help prepare organizers on how to realize targeted event-related benefits and to deliver sustainable legacies. Girginov (2011: 2) positioned Olympic legacy planning as

> a forward thinking exercise with clear developmental goals performing a range of political, economic and social functions ... [and] therefore, represents a developmental project which holds both a promise to accomplish something that does not exist and the uncertainty of how this future state is going to be delivered.

Moreover, Girginov (2011) suggested that this process is shaped through the collective action of state, market, and society.

Shipway (2007) argued that the delivery of an effective legacy starts in the planning stage. Leopkey and Parent (2011) suggested that it starts even before that, when candidate cities are deciding to formally bid. Following an investigation of the Sydney 2000 and Vancouver 2010 Olympic Games, Leopkey and Parent (2011) identified four legacy governance phases that occur during the event-hosting cycle: conceptualization, planning and implementation, transfer, and post-Games governance. The purpose and timeline of each phase is described in Table 15.2. An important point to notice from Table 15.2 is that legacy planning should occur before the bid for a major sports event is completed – by the host region – and legacy management will continue long after the major sports event's organizing committee has ceased to exist.

Following an investigation of the legacy proposals for the 2014 Glasgow CWG, Matheson (2010) identified key risks in the legacy planning process. These included the economic environment surrounding the delivery of the event, the longevity and quality of the key Games-related partnerships, and finally ongoing political and community support throughout the legacy process.

291

Table 15.2 Legacy governance phases

Legacy phase	Purpose	Timeline
Legacy conceptualization	Develop the legacy vision for the event	Begins before the bidding of the major sports event
Legacy planning and implementation	Outline and exercise the legacy vision	Occurs during the planning and implementation modes of the organizing committee
Legacy transfer	Distribute and transfer assets	Occurs during the wrap-up mode of the organizing committee
Post-Games legacy governance	Monitor and manage Games legacy over the long term	Occurs after the organizing committee has ceased to exist

Source: Adapted from Leopkey and Parent (2011).

Legacy evaluation

Following the planning and implementation of the legacy vision, evaluation of the event-related legacies is crucial for proper long-term governance. Cashman (2006: 14) noted that "outcomes should be related back to the stated aims. Assessment introduces the twin notions of accountability and sustainability. If Olympic promises can't be delivered, they represent empty rhetoric and may also contribute to the problem of gigantism".

Gratton and Preuss (2008: 1925) suggested that "the measurement of a legacy should start with the changes events create". The business of trying to understand and measure legacy and event impacts has been contested throughout the literature (see Chapter 14; Gratton and Preuss, 2008; Preuss, 2007b). The issue of measurement is extremely complex, and there is no right formula or method that has been widely accepted. Still, Dickson et al. (2011) proposed a framework for evaluating Olympic legacies. They suggested the use of a radar framework to create legacy profiles of an event for different types of legacies following their analysis of the existing literature. The radar is proposed to include six dimensions: cost, planning, structure, tangibility, timeframe, and spatial impact. Types of legacies which can be put into the radar composed of these six dimensions include: sport; economics; infrastructure; information and education; public life, politics, and culture; symbols, memory, and history; social capital; environmental; legal; urban development; and destination image.

Some researchers (see Pentifallo, 2010) believe that there are key elements (e.g. environment, economics, brand awareness, image) or indicators across all events that remain constant in the context of a mega-event, while others have argued that it is not useful to have a general template for planning and measuring event legacy as there are fundamental differences that exist between developed and developing countries (e.g. Cornelissen, 2010). The fact that event legacies occur in different cities and at different times heightens both the uniqueness and complexity of event legacies; and as such, it is very difficult to use benchmarks to predict and identify potential legacies (Preuss, 2007b). Difficulties also arise when trying to measure legacy from a top-down approach as "event-related changes need to be isolated from general metropolitan development" (Preuss 2007b: 215). This proves challenging as many intangible types of legacy exist beyond the direct economic growth resulting from hosting, and as such a holistic, multidimensional view of measuring legacy must be applied in order to understand the complete picture (Preuss, 2007b). The bottom-up approach that takes into consideration all (both hard and soft) alterations of structure resulting from the event to measuring legacy is proposed as an alternative solution (Preuss, 2007b). However, despite this encompassing approach, there are still obstacles to overcome, including: differentiating between net legacy and gross legacy; determining the value of legacy (i.e. judging if it is negative or positive, which is made more difficult because of the multi-stakeholder perspective); and, finally, the measurement of legacy over the long term (Preuss, 2007b).

One event evaluation tool that was recently developed in order to measure the overall impacts of hosting on the region is the Olympic Games Impact (OGI) programme. In 2000, the IOC launched the OGI project in order to provide a consistent methodology for measuring Olympic Games-related impacts. The tool includes over 120 indicators for economic, social, and environmental impacts (Gratton and Preuss, 2008). A new OGI is created for each edition of the Games and lasts over a 12-year period, from the bid stage until two years following the conclusion of the event. OCOGs are responsible for providing results in four reports. A baseline report is submitted to the IOC prior to the selection of the host city (e.g. Vancouver's baseline report was submitted in 2001) (OGI-UBC, 2010). Next, a pre-Games report is provided once the city is selected, and provides any relevant updates to the contextual data. This is followed by a Games-time report that focuses on Olympic-event data and a post-Games report that summarizes the overall impacts of the event (OGI-UBC, 2010). The OGI project associated with the Vancouver 2010 Games is the first full OGI project to be undertaken throughout the entire Games lifecycle. Criticisms of this tool exist, including its longevity and post-Games evaluation, as it ends two years after the event, which is considered too soon to see the full effects or measure the longer-term legacies of an event (Gratton and Preuss, 2008).

In sum, there are numerous key points to consider when evaluating legacy (refer also to Chapter 14). To wit, it would take 15–30 years to measure the true legacy of one major sports event; however, difficulties with this longitudinal approach also exist, including commitments of time and research resources required for studying the net legacy benefits. Also, most of the current event impact research focuses on the economic impacts (including tourism, employment, and infrastructure) and typically lacks measurement indicators on environmental and social impacts of the events. Some researchers (e.g. Preuss, 2007b) have argued that the huge figures of economic impacts are not event legacy because, in the long run, both the event demands and the leakage of money influx most likely return to equilibrium income of pre-event levels. To complicate matters further, three different types of multipliers can be used to assess economic impact (sales created, employment, or household income change) and whichever one will benefit the purpose and funder/backer of the study will generally be utilized; essentially, the choice is a political one. Needless to say, event evaluations are a complicated matter, and it is important to understand that there is no simple answer to the question of impacts an event may have on its host. Additionally, pre-event evaluations have been criticized by many authors (e.g. Gratton and Preuss, 2008; Kasimati, 2003) for their biases in trying to provide favourable results, their use of secondary data, and their narrow focus on only the planned, positive, tangible legacy dimensions.

Sustainability

Many cities bidding for or hosting major sports events have started using sustainability and sustainable development in addition to the concept of legacy in order to justify the ROI of public monies invested in the hosting and delivery of the event (Smith, A., 2009). These concepts are intertwined within the sport event management literature (Horton and Zakus, 2010). This is especially evident within the Olympic Movement, where the terms are sometimes used interchangeably. As Cornelissen *et al.* (2011: 307) noted, legacy should "integrate triple bottom-line principles" (these principles being traditionally associated with sustainability and CSR).

The concepts of sustainability and sustainable development became popular in the 1980s. A widely accepted definition of sustainable development comes from the Brundtland Commission of the United Nations: "Sustainable development is development that meets the needs of the present without compromising the ability of future generations to meet their own needs" (United Nations Conference on Environment and Development (UNCED), 1987: 43). Furrer (2002: 2) further described it as "a path of socio-economic development that would be financially balanced, socially equitable, ethically responsible and adequately integrated in the long-term ecological balance of the natural environment".

Three pillars of sustainability – social, economic, and environmental – have often been discussed in the literature. Horton and Zakus (2010) suggested further division of the pillars was necessary, and deconstructed the social pillar by adding a "human" element (e.g. humanity, sport for all) to the mix. Since the emergence of the concept, changes in its focus are evident. To wit, in the 1980s and 1990s, attention was placed on the environmental pillar; the late 1990s saw an increased interest in the growth and economic side; and since 2000 the inclusion of the social dimension has led to a convergence of all three. Tarradellas (2003) purported that sustainable development is the responsibility of all collective actors in the field, and that each one has a role to ensure the progress and protection of the environment. Furthermore, sustainable development is a dynamic process that will continue to change and become more refined as our knowledge increases and concepts are reinvestigated (Furrer, 2002).

Inspired by the UNCED *Agenda 21*, in 1999 the IOC created their own version of *Agenda 21* that details their actions and plans towards sustainable development in the movement. The *Olympic Movement's Agenda 21: Sport For Sustainable Development* is based on three fundamental goals: improving socio-economic conditions, conservation and management of resources for sustainable development, and strengthening the role of major groups (Tarradellas, 2003; VanWynsberghe *et al.*, 2011). As a result, it became more important for OCOGs to think about sustainability. In the beginning, OCOGs mainly focused on environmental concerns (e.g. SOCOG); but overall Games planning has evolved to include economic and social aspects (e.g. Turin in 2006 and Vancouver in 2010). These aspects are especially strong for the 2012 London Olympic Games. More specifically, the IOC's *Agenda 21* has resulted in the development of OCOG policies that guide stakeholder engagement, long-term planning, accessibility, equity, and healthy communities (i.e. the sustainable development of the host communities/countries) (Horton and Zakus, 2010).

Several event sustainability standards and measurement approaches have also been adopted within the event-hosting sphere. Vancouver, in cooperation with the Académie Internationale des Sciences et Techniques du Sport (AISTS), developed the Sustainable Sport and Event Toolkit as a tool for sport organizations to help incorporate the concepts of sustainability into their organizational strategies and event planning (Vancouver 2010 and AISTS, n.d.). A number of local, national, and international management and sustainability conventions were incorporated into this initiative including: ISO standards 14001–14006, Global Reporting Initiative (GRI) G3, IOC *Agenda 21*, IOC Guide on Sport, Environment, and Sustainable Development, British Standards Institute 8900–8901, the United Nations Environment Programme, and the Vancouver 2010 Sustainability Management and Reporting System (Vancouver 2010 and AISTS, n.d.). Additionally, the UBC established a Centre for Sport and Sustainability (CSS) in conjunction with the 2010 Vancouver Games to help capture and transfer knowledge on how sport can create sustainable benefits locally, regionally, and internationally (UBC CSS, n.d). VanWynsberghe *et al.* (2011) suggested that sustainability mandates are now essential parts of the event delivery process. LOCOG, the IOC, and UEFA have created the GRI Event Organizers Sector Supplement; this supplement offers guidelines for the reporting of sustainability activities (see Global Reporting Initiative, 2011). The GRI Event Organizers Sector Supplement is recognized by the IOC as an appropriate standard for the reporting of Olympic Games sustainability and social responsibility activities (International Olympic Committee, 2011a). The ISO 26000/ISO 20121 sustainability and social responsibility standards were also created with the assistance of LOCOG (Pelham, 2011).

In addition, the Network for Business Sustainability (NBS) released the top ten sustainable business strategies for 2011. They included the following findings:

1 innovation and employees drive profit;
2 marketing of CSR internally can help retain talented employees;
3 CSR has the potential to stimulate performance;
4 the market will react to positive and negative sustainability-related news;
5 positive stakeholder relations aid performance;
6 prioritization of sustainability programming is important;
7 involvement in social indices affects share price;
8 "green" isn't always positive;
9 functionality is more important than ethics; and
10 increased giving by employees is linked to heightened loyalty (NBS, 2011).

Research on sustainability has taken off in the urban studies area related to hosting events. To illustrate, Essex and Chalkley (2004) looked at mega-events as a tool for urban and regional regeneration, Frey *et al.* (2008) investigated the sustainability reporting and the impact of sport events on local development, and Smith (2007) provided principals for hosts on how to maximize sustainable regeneration legacy resulting from hosting large-scale sports events. In addition, research has been conducted on the delivery of sustainable legacies (e.g. Vigor *et al.*, 2004), and more specifically sustainable sport and sport development legacies (Coalter 2004; Girginov and Hills, 2009; Lindsey, 2008), social, educational/cultural legacies (e.g. Smith, A., 2009), and health legacies (Shipway, 2007).

295

Finally, Theodoraki (2010) identified six challenges threatening sustainability in the Olympic Movement. These included event owner bureaucratization (i.e. the external control exerted over the OCOG by the IOC); isomorphism resulting in (1) increased difficulty in changing existing practices, and (2) continuation of similar behaviours over time; inflation of event expectations which lead to OCOGs always trying to deliver the best Games ever; centralization of host government stakeholders; supply chain interdependence; and whitewashing of event impact assessments.

Corporate social responsibility

The concepts of sustainability and CSR are closely linked, sometimes being used interchangeably. Here, CSR refers to the discretionary and voluntary relationships an organization (or organizing committee) has with its community and societal stakeholders (cf. Frederick, 1994; Waddock, 2004; Walker and Parent, 2010). It is associated with the triple bottom line of economic, social, and environmental activities. Within major sports event and sport organizations, there are a variety of CSR-related activities. For example, the IOC has activities focusing on sport for all, development through sport, education through sport, environment and sport, peace through sport, and women and sport (International Olympic Committee, 2011b). The CGF – led by the efforts of CWG Canada – have development through and of sport initiatives mainly in Africa and Central America. SportAccord even has an office dedicated to CSR called the Sports' Social Responsibility Department; SportAccord has advocacy, facilitation, knowledge sharing, and training services/tools services for its members associated with six special projects: Sport and the Environment; Sport and Child and Youth Development; Sport and Health; Sport and Gender; Sport and Peace; and Sport and Persons with Disabilities. SportAccord is also part of creating common CSR standards (SportAccord, 2010).

Yet there continues to be definitional issues with the CSR construct. For example, Carroll (1991, 1999) suggested a pyramid of CSRs. At the base are the economic responsibilities – an organization must be profitable. Next, there are legal responsibilities – an organization must obey the laws of the land. Third, there are the ethical responsibilities – an organization should be ethical. At the top of the pyramid are the philanthropic responsibilities – an organization should be a "good corporate citizen". In contrast, others divide CSR into three related concepts: CSR_1 (corporate social responsibility); CSR_2 (corporate social responsiveness); and CSR_3 (rectitude – which has been replaced in the literature by corporate citizenship or CC) (see Frederick, 1994; Walker and Parent, 2010). While CSR_1 has moral undertones, CSR_2 is seen as more proactive; CSR_2 can be seen as explicit, forward-looking actions dealing with external stakeholder and social or public policies (Walker and Parent, 2010). In turn, CC is an extension of CSR_1, being the more legal, cultural, community embedded, and global dimension; it is about being a "good corporate citizen" (Walker and Parent, 2010).

Gallagher and Goodstein (2002) argued that CSR/organizational ethics should include the following elements:

1   *Integrity* in the focal organization's mission and core values;
2   *Responsibility* towards stakeholders; and
3   *Institutional reflection* on decisive choices with potentially broad implications.

Within sport management, we see geography, business operations, and stakeholder influences determine the type of CSR undertaken by an actor. For example, professional sports teams (the micro/meso geographical levels) seem to focus on CSR_1, while professional sports leagues (the macro level) focus on CSR_2 and, perhaps more importantly for this book, sport governing bodies and organizations/corporations (the macro and supra levels) focus on CC (Walker and Parent, 2010).

Next, CSR is also associated with marketing and sponsorship. We can see it in the decisions to sponsor the Olympic Games (e.g. Kang and Stotlar, 2011), in the use of corporate support instead of the traditional exclusive sponsorship of events (e.g. Séguin et al., 2010), or in cause-related marketing (e.g. Irwin et al., 2003).

In addition, consumers have certain perceptions or attributions regarding the CSR efforts of an organization. These can be stakeholder-driven (society/community-focused), values-driven (socially motivated), or strategic-driven (profit-related or seen as serving the organization itself) (Ellen et al., 2006; Walker et al., 2010). A study on the 2008 Beijing Olympic Games found that consumers' awareness of Olympic CSR activities favourably impacted values- and stakeholder-driven attributions, providing in turn positive impacts on reputation and patronage. However, increased awareness did not positively impact strategic-driven attribution; on the contrary, if these rather negative attributions were increased in some way, this led to decreased patronage and a negative impact on reputation (Walker et al., 2010).

There also seems to be a relationship between CSR and media representations of bid and organizing committees. More precisely, Carey et al. (2011) found that CSR and community development focus are different between the traditional (e.g. Western, developed) and non-traditional (e.g. Eastern, developing) bid/candidate cities, which results in the media providing different portrayals of the traditional and non-traditional bid/candidate cities. The extent to which this can be applied to event organizing committees remains to be seen. Nevertheless, we could hypothesize that this differing portrayal can have an impact on other stakeholders' perceptions of the organization (the bid city in this case).

Finally, there is some emerging research on the concepts of "greenwashing" and "green fatigue". Greenwashing essentially refers to false advertising about an organization's environmental initiatives, where marketers misuse environmental principles in their marketing initiatives, leading consumers to not be able to trust the advertisement (Kärnä et al., 2001). Emerging research cautions organizations/industries who create environmental-friendliness policies and charters as they can be perceived as greenwashing by certain stakeholder groups, such as conservation groups/organizations, activists, consumers/clients, and the general population (cf. George, 2003; Ramus and Montiel, 2005). Seven sins have been suggested as part of greenwashing (TerraChoice, 2012):

1   The sin of *the hidden tradeoff*: tradeoff between "green" claims and the (industrial) processes to get the "green" end-product.
2   The sin of *no proof*: unsubstantiated claims.
3   The sin of *vagueness*: broad or poorly defined claims (e.g. "all-natural" products are not equivalent to good products since there are poisonous naturally occurring products as well).

297

4   The sin of *worshiping false labels*: the misleading impression of having third-party endorsement where there is none in actuality.

5   The sin of *irrelevance*: unhelpful or unimportant claims, such as CFC (chlorofluorocarbon)-free products, when CFCs have been banned by law.

6   The sin of *lesser of two evils*: while a product within a category may be relatively greener than its counterparts, the sin lies in not looking at the greater category (e.g. fuel-efficient or hybrid trucks and sport utility vehicles).

7   The sin of *fibbing*: false claims such as stating a product is "Energy Star" certified when it is not.

Nevertheless, there is evidence to suggest that independent sustainability ratings "could act to deter 'greenwashing' and encourage virtuous firms to preserve ... their CSR practices" (Parguel *et al.*, 2011: 15). In turn, a related concept to greenwashing, green fatigue, refers to a sense of disillusionment or apathy towards green sustainability efforts. This can be due to a variety of reasons, such as feeling as though no one else is really making an effort, still seeing climate changes (e.g. glaciers melting) despite one's efforts, overstimulation/over-exposure or over-marketing of the green concept and initiatives, etc. (cf. *The Independent*, 2007; Parguel *et al.*, 2011). In sum, there is evidence in the broader management world of greenwashing and green fatigue; it would therefore be important for sport event researchers to examine this issue, given the increasing importance of sustainability, green initiatives, and CSR in major sports events. A critical perspective is also needed on this issue regarding the degree to which purported green Games are truly green or environmentally sustainable (see, for example, Hayes and Horne, 2011).

Leveraging

Leveraging is typically seen as a marketing/relationship marketing concept where sponsors will activate or leverage their event sponsorship to gain as much ROI as possible (e.g. Stokes, 2005). However, leveraging can also more broadly refer to the use by event stakeholders (particularly local businesses, sponsors, governments, and community organizations/members) of a major sports event being hosted in order to reap certain benefits. These benefits, which range from a local to an international scope, can include increased tourism, a new or more positive destination brand or image, increased economic activity and trade, cultural insights, networking and relationship building, and increased pride and social capital to name a few (cf. Kellett *et al.*, 2008; O'Brien, 2006; Snelgrove and Wood, 2010; Ziakas and Costa, 2010). We often see leveraging discussed in relation to destination marketing and branding and event marketing (e.g. Chalip and Costa, 2005; Devine *et al.*, 2010; Fong-Yi, 2010; Green, 2001; Harrison-Hill and Chalip, 2005; Sealy and Wickens, 2008; Snelgrove and Wood, 2010).

Leveraging is facilitated when sport organizers and the destination's managers (tourism organizations, local businesses, commerce boards/bureaus, local governments, etc.) network to build relationships and alliances. In the past, local businesses usually failed to recognize an event's leveraging opportunities (Chalip and Leyns, 2002); efforts from the last few years (such as in Vancouver for the 2010 Olympic Winter Games; see also the expert case study in Chapter 9), however, are starting to turn this around in practice and in the interest of event leveraging researchers.

Whereas legacy is sometimes argued to be more passive – although researchers are calling for more active pre-event legacy planning – leveraging is seen as more strategic and proactive. Also, moving from a focus on an event's direct impacts and outcomes (legacy) to one where stakeholders use an event to garner their own benefits (leverage) is seen as "a subtle, yet significant paradigm shift" (O'Brien, 2006: 240). The hope is that major sports event managers become a party to the event's leveraging efforts so that longer, more sustainable business outcomes, benefits, and ROI can be garnered (O'Brien, 2006).

There are two main types of leveraging discussed in the literature: economic or business leveraging and social leveraging. Their opportunities, strategic objectives, and means are presented in Table 15.3. Regarding economic/business leveraging, we know that networking is key, as are legitimacy – the institutionalization or sanctioning of relationships and stakeholders – and the temporal dimension (O'Brien, 2006). The event has a finite timeline but it takes time to build relationships and legitimize them. Moreover, businesses garner leveraging benefits by using standard promotional/themed tactics (Chalip and Leyns, 2002). However, a certain degree of coordination is needed for business leveraging to occur,

Table 15.3 Economic/business and social event leveraging

Type of leveraging	Opportunity	Strategic objective	Means
Economic/business	Event visitors and trade	Maximize total trade and revenues	Foster visitor spending
			Increase length of visitor stays
			Retain expenditures from the sport event
			Enhance business relationships
	Event media	Enhance the host region's image/brand	Enhance business relationships
			Promote the host region image/brand through event advertising/reporting
			Use the sport event in advertising/promoting
Social	Communitas	Focus sport event stakeholders' attention on specific social issues	Fit the event with the specific social issues
			Fit the values of the specific social issues with local sport subcultures
			Increase length of visitor stays
			Entice engagement with the specific social issues
	Event media	Establish or change the community agenda related to specific social issues	Promote social issues through event advertising/reporting
			Use the sport event in issue-related publicity

Source: Based on Chalip, 2004; O'Brien, 2007; O'Brien and Chalip, 2008.

a coordination which business leaders hope will come from an existing body (versus a new actor) so as to not add another layer of bureaucracy (Chalip and Leyns, 2002).

Regarding social leveraging, as Chalip (2006: 109) put it:

> Anthropological work on events demonstrates that their celebratory nature engenders a liminoid space that can foster social value, particularly through a sense of communitas. In order to enable and amplify liminality and communitas, event organisers and host community planners should foster social interaction and prompt a feeling of celebration by enabling sociability among event visitors, creating event-related social events, facilitating informal social opportunities, producing ancillary events, and theming widely.

It is believed that if a strategic approach is taken to the impending hosting of a major sports events, benefits can be maximized and negative impacts minimized, which will lead to social leveraging (Balduck et al., 2011). Social leveraging will allow for social capital to be built (Ziakas and Costa, 2010), and social capital can bring attitudinal change (Sherry et al., 2011), and therefore (hopefully) social change. The means uses for building liminality and communitas (i.e. social leveraging) include:

- enabling sociability
- creating sport event-related social events
- facilitating informal social opportunities
- producing ancillary events
- theming widely.

The means will help social interaction and increase feelings of celebration (Chalip, 2006; O'Brien and Chalip, 2008).

To garner benefits through event leveraging, part of the strategic approach can and should include the concept of event portfolios. In our context, an event portfolio means that the major sports event is included in a host region's larger, strategically driven portfolio of events (sport- and culture-based). The event portfolio can be a way to coordinate the organizing committee's and other stakeholders' leveraging (and legacy) efforts (cf. Ziakas and Costa, 2011).

Much remains to be examined regarding business and social leveraging and related concepts such as event portfolios. We encourage researchers to begin to fill the many gaps which still exist. For example, just examining event portfolios results in many questions emerging, such as: "the nature and character of event portfolios, investigating event interrelationships, explicating inter-organisational relationships of events networks and learning how to build community capacity in event portfolio management" (Ziakas and Costa, 2011: 409).

Knowledge management and transfer

Cashman (2006) discussed two different perspectives for how to view the concept of legacy, first from the view of the host city or region's experiences related to hosting, and second from a transfer-of-knowledge view within the Olympic Movement (i.e. know-how, experience, and best practices shared between event hosts). Knowledge management and transfer principles stem from the knowledge-based view of the firm, proponents of which believe that organizations exist to create, apply, and transfer knowledge within and between them, with knowledge being seen as the key resource to a sustained competitive advantage (cf. Kogut and Zander, 1992). But what is knowledge? It can (Crossan *et al.*, 1999; Kogut and Zander, 1992; Winter, 1987; Zander and Kogut, 1995):

- be found in the form of information or know-how/experience;
- stem from products, people, processes, or relationships;
- be tacit or explicit – with tacit (the intangible) being more difficult to transfer and thus the key to a sustained competitive advantage;
- be held at the individual, group, or organizational levels.

Knowledge has different characteristics. It can be (Winter, 1987; Zander and Kogut, 1995) described as:

- codifiable or articulable – how much knowledge can be encoded and, as such, more easily transferred;
- teachable – the degree to which staff members can be trained in this knowledge;
- complex – how different results can occur based on different combinations of skills and competencies;
- system dependent – how much the knowledge is dependent on the experience of the group of people around the table/in the organization;
- having observable products – to what level can competitors copy the resulting product?

The key is finding ways to transfer the tacit knowledge, in our case from one event to the next. Event-related records come in many forms, including: archival files, reports, serials, memorabilia, audio-visual, images, photos, art, electronic sources, and other formal or informal documents such as plans (Cashman, 2000). However, people, such as Games gypsies – those individuals moving from one event to the next – also hold much of the important tacit knowledge in terms of both information and know-how. Nevertheless, as Beesley and Chalip (2011: 323) noted, "knowledge must first be localised"; knowledge transfer is affected by cultural and political borders.

The complexity of hosting mega-events like the FIFA World Cup or the Olympic Games has led to the increased awareness of the benefits of prior experiences and knowledge transfer as they help facilitate the success of the FA's activities, such as logistics, marketing, and accreditation required to deliver a sport event (Cashman, 2000; Toohey and Halbwirth, 2002).

While some research has examined knowledge management and knowledge transfer from within the realm of sports events, much of it stems from experiences at the 2000 Sydney Olympic Games, as until then there were few formal standards established which helped transfer information from city to city (Cashman, 2000; Halbwirth and Toohey, 2001; Toohey and Halbwirth, 2002). A formal agreement between SOCOG and the

301

IOC ensured the transfer of know-how in both written and oral forms to future organizing committees (Toohey and Halbwirth, 2002). This information subsequently formed the foundations for an Olympic management guide and knowledge management system (the OGKM).

A major problem that has been identified with past Olympic hosts is the fact that due to strict timelines and budget limitations, "less important processes" such as conservation of records and other archival material were shelved. For example, several previous hosts, including Moscow (1980) and Albertville (1992) are unaware of the status of their archives and their locations are unknown (Toohey and Halbwirth, 2002). Although the sharing of information is not an irregular occurrence in organizations, special issues that affect the organization of a mega-event such as the Olympic Games include: the complexity of Games delivery; the dynamic environment in which there were constant changes in operations; the fixed timeline and the finite ending of the project (Toohey and Halbwirth, 2002). This is particularly important for events where there are new organizing committees formed in each host city, and for events with restricted budgets and staff.

Relatively new to the management and knowledge discourses is the use of knowledge management as a business strategy. The concept of knowledge management varies widely and has a variety of different origins, including technology, organization behaviour, sociology, education, management, and information science. Halbwirth and Toohey (2001) identified four elements that support the implementation of a successful knowledge management project: (1) information infrastructure; (2) organizational culture; (3) designing and implementing knowledge management processes; (4) creating knowledge assets and the learning organization. These elements were evident in the Sydney case. First, SOCOG inherited an established knowledge-based culture from the Sydney Olympic Bid Committee that had already established a resource library and records management system (Toohey and Halbwirth, 2002). Explicit and tacit knowledge on Games delivery was also available to SOCOG through the many staffers who worked at previous OCOGs, such as Atlanta (i.e. Games gypsies). Cashman (2008) calls this phenomenon of the continuing presence of OCOG staff, volunteers, and consultants at subsequent Olympic Games independent from each other "the Olympic caravan"; we broaden the term to Games gypsies to include other major sports events. SOCOG's formal information management strategy included the establishment of an organization-wide information management system, a terminology codification system, and an aligned records and archives approach (Toohey and Halbwirth, 2002). They also created an internal (intranet) information system called Athena, to provide a shared work environment for staff.

Much remains to be examined regarding this topic in major sports events, such as the role of Games gypsies, the impact of the local/national culture on the knowledge management and transfer system, and the overall process for different types of major sports events.

THE PRACTITIONER'S PERSPECTIVE ON LEGACY AND SUSTAINABILITY

In this section we will discuss some key points associated with the questions of legacy and sustainability, as well as knowledge transfer.

The question of legacy and sustainability

From the practitioner's perspective, legacy and sustainability are at times so synonymous that it can be very challenging to distinguish, especially when examining the definitions presented earlier in the chapter. From a managerial standpoint, we wonder about the need by academics to continue to separate the terms when managers are using them interchangeably. A question for academics to ponder, therefore, is whether or not legacy and sustainability today are one and the same. From a manager's perspective, they look like the same thing, both asking the same question – what do major sports events bring and what do they leave behind?

What does a major sports event leave behind for a community that is tangible? During the bid phase, there is emphasis on what the community and country will have in terms of infrastructure that was not there before – building and facilities that are left after the closing ceremony. Yet, the answer to the question of major sports event legacy is continually being reviewed in an almost forensic manner, because legacy can be translated in so many different ways, especially when we consider intangible aspects. Measuring tangible legacy in the form of buildings and transportation systems can be fraught with the argument that they would have been built anyway or, alternatively, were they really needed? The cost of maintaining these structures can become a burden, so is that a positive or negative legacy, or positive in the short term and negative in the long term, or vice versa?

Questions that are asked and not easily answered include: Did we need the buildings? At what cost? Would they have been built anyway on a different timeline but built just the same? What was the cost to the environment? Are there lost opportunities? Are there negative impacts such as reduced or banned access during the time of the actual building of the venues and the execution of the Games to the residents and businesses? Did the Games pollute despite attempts to be green? Is the cost to operate and maintain villages built for the athletes a burden on the residents of the Games communities? These questions have been and will continue to be wrestled to the ground before, during, and after many sports events by journalists, environmentalists, politicians, ordinary citizens, etc.

There are answers, but whether they are satisfactory answers is another question. Suffice to say that the communities who hosted will forever have that legacy of memories from all the visitors and athletes that were part of the events. What is the value of that legacy? Certainly, the bragging rights and opportunity to be considered for other sports events or a training location for future champions can be considered. National/local pride, skills development, and networking should also be considered, however. Notwithstanding, measuring the effect on the environment now and in the future is less clear because there is still not consensus on global warming and size of footprint in the countries around the world.

Moreover, how do you accurately reconcile the financial impact of a major sports event when you have to estimate the number of people and the value of the visit of the people who did not visit the city because they could not afford to come during the Games? Conversely, how do you determine or estimate the number of people and their dollar value of a visit to the site of previous Games? How do you set up the accounting to reflect the financial, psychological, and emotional costs of a major sports event to the residents, disenfranchised, and businesses that were adversely affected because they could not get to work or afford to be part of the event, people who were relocated to another area to make room for buildings, or events or business owners and operators whose access to their business was closed off or reduced? Conversely, how do you measure the positive effects and translate into dollars the wonderful memories, the bragging rights, the pride, the network and skills developed, the once-in-a-lifetime opportunity to be vicariously or peripherally involved as a spectator to ancillary events around the Games or through technology? How do you measure the legacy and value of the inspiration that is created in the mind and heart of a future Olympian, or even on a smaller scale and equally important, in the psyche of a young person who decides that they are going to become involved in sports? Is it a legacy of a major sports event when people who have been involved as participants or paid staff or volunteers in previous sports events have a positive experience as they relive or revisit their experience, which releases endorphins in their body which acts in a chemical way to boost their immune system and thereby reduces their need for health care? Albeit this is a far-reaching idea, and that is the point. Legacy can be translated in myriad ways, and it is an aspect of major sports events that will continue to be studied and debated and written about for years to come. The key consideration is that the benefits must outweigh the negatives, but translating benefits is very subjective and therefore must be answered by each individual, each stakeholder.

Knowledge transfer and Games gypsies

There is a formal process for transferring knowledge that is part of an OCOG's responsibility. The challenge with this process is that most people are finished on the last day of the Games, which means that all information requested may not have been sent. The people left compiling the legacy information get what they get and it may be lacking in detail and description. Despite the fact that English is the universal language of sport, it is used and understood through the perception and level of language knowledge of every recipient. This means that the quality of the knowledge transferred can vary as can the usability of the information received.

A very real and equally important transfer of knowledge takes place with the Games gypsies because they carry with them valuable on-the-job experiences, information that may not have been recorded, their perspective on successes and failures, and the reason for these. They are a precious resource; and an organization is fortunate if they can in fact hire a Games gypsy. While their familiarity with sport event management processes is valuable, they have also created a network of relationships that they can personally leverage, which would otherwise not be available to the new sport event organizing committee. This network can be tapped in many ways: attracting people to consider working once again for a sports event; as an information resource by recalling their experience to assist with creating best practices; or information gathering in their network to answer questions or attract like-minded people as a workforce or resource. The value and leveraging of personal connections can never be overestimated!

CHAPTER SUMMARY

In this chapter we examined the burgeoning area of major sports event legacy and its associated concepts. While relatively new, this area of research is growing exponentially. We examined issues and challenges associated with the legacy concept, as well as legacy planning, management, and evaluation. Next, we considered the concepts of sustainability and CSR. We noted how the ideas of greenwashing and green fatigue are emerging. In addition, we reviewed emerging areas of importance associated with legacy: event leveraging and knowledge management and transfer. From a practitioner's perspective, we offered some thought-provoking legacy questions to debate. We also briefly discussed the ways and means of transferring knowledge, the challenge that may result, and the significance of Games gypsies.

EXPERT CASE: LEGACY AND SUSTAINABILITY AT THE 2010 VANCOUVER OLYMPIC AND PARALYMPIC WINTER GAMES

Canada has played host to numerous top international multi-sport events over the past century, including several editions of the CWG, the Pan American Games, and both the Summer and Winter Olympic Games. Most recently, Vancouver/Whistler hosted the Olympic and Paralympic Winter Games in February and March 2010, respectively. Planning for the Vancouver 2010 Games started in the mid to late 1990s, when Vancouver first sought to win the Canadian rights to bid for the 2010 Winter Olympic Games. On 2 July 2003, Vancouver was officially selected by the IOC to host the XXI Winter Olympic Games.

The Vancouver Games represent the first Games that have been affected throughout the entire planning process by the increased prevalence of the term "legacy" and its inclusion in the Olympic Charter. In 2003 the IOC cemented the existence of the term in Olympic discourse by including it in the Olympic Charter, with a focus on favourable changes felt by hosts (Chappelet, 2008). Official candidature questionnaires now ask specifically about the expected legacy of the event on the city as a result of winning the bid (Leopkey and Parent, 2011). As such, the Vancouver candidature saw many unprecedented directions in legacy planning during the bid and planning phases of the Games. Not only did the Vancouver legacy vision include improvements to existing as well as new infrastructure, such as the Sea-to-Sky Highway and the Canada Line rail link between the airport and downtown, but they also sought to have increased involvement of the local First Nations, and heightened focus on sustainability in their Games planning and implementation.

Moreover, Vancouver was the first candidate city to create a legacy organization separate from the bid committee, which was responsible for legacy development associated with the bidding and potential hosting of the Games. The organization, 2010 Legacies Now, was to remain active even if the city did not win the right to host (a direction that many bid committees are now following; for example, Chicago 2016 with World Sport Chicago). The original purpose of the organization was to leverage support for sport development, increase community capacity, and to ensure community outreach throughout the province of British Columbia as a result of the bid (2010 Legacies Now, n.d.a). Once Vancouver won the right to host in 2003, 2010 Legacies Now expanded their programming beyond just sport and recreation to include other social aspects, including arts, volunteerism, healthy living, and literacy development (2010 Legacies Now, n.d.a). In order to build on the successes of 2010 Legacies Now, following the conclusion of the Games, it evolved into a philanthropy organization called LIFT, which applies venture finance and business strategies to charitable investments in order to continue advancing positive social change across the country and internationally (LIFT, n.d.).

Following suggestions made by previous hosts such as Sydney, an MPA was formulated and signed by all major Games partners in the country prior to the final city selection by the IOC. Part of this document outlined the foundations of the legacy planning, responsibilities, and post-Games governance. Legacy-related initiatives included the Legacy Endowment Fund (LEF), the Games Operating Trust (GOT), the Amateur Sport Legacy Fund (ASLF), and the Whistler Legacies Society (WLS). The CAN$110 million (value at time of establishment) LEF made up of equal contributions by the federal and provincial host governments was founded to guarantee operational costs for local facilities (e.g. Richmond Oval, WOP, and Whistler Sliding Centre) and sport development funding both before and after the Games. The fund is governed by the GOT; the trust would have also been responsible for the ASLF (made up of 60 per cent of the operating surplus of VANOC); however, this was not realized as VANOC declared almost a year after the Games that their CAN$1.9 billion operations budget broke even (CBC, 2010). The trust is championed by an eight-member board of directors, and was appointed by and is representative of many of the MPA signatories. The WLS, now known as Whistler Sport Legacies (WSL), owns and operates the Olympic venues that are located in Whistler (Whistler Sliding Centre, WOP, and the Whistler Athletes' Centre), and their goal is to maintain a sustainable Olympic playground (WSL, n.d.).

Not only was legacy an important element of the Vancouver bid, but so too was the concept of sustainability. VANOC's commitment to sustainability was related to the management of "social, economic, and environmental impacts and opportunities of [the] Games to produce lasting benefits, locally and globally" (2010 Legacies Now, n.d.b: para. 1). In order to provide regular information about the progress of their sustainability initiatives as well as a way to publicly benchmark their overall progress, VANOC produced five sustainability reports over the lifecycle of the event, with the final edition covering the decommissioning of the event and dissolution of the organizing committee post-Games. Additionally, two other independent projects measuring the impacts of the Games were ongoing throughout the delivery of the event. A comprehensive impact study by PriceWaterhouseCoopers was also jointly commissioned by the provincial and federal governments in order to investigate the direct and indirect socio-economic impacts on the country from 2003–2013 (PCH, 2009). The IOC's OGI requirement for VANOC was led by the UBC, and measured a variety of socio-cultural, economic, and environmental indicators in order to assess the event's overall sustainability (OGI-UBC, 2010). The UBC also established the CSS, which brings together researchers to focus on sport and sustainability-related research; specific focuses include the economy and infrastructure, social development and impact, health, urban renewal and ecological change, and public policy and planning (UBC CSS, n.d.).

By Becca Leopkey, Doctoral Candidate, Olympic legacy expert

Case questions

1 Describe the similarities and differences between the concepts of legacy and sustainability for the Vancouver 2010 Games.

2 How do other events such as the FIFA World Cup, the Asian Games, or the Pan American Games compare to Vancouver Games in terms of legacy and sustainability? What about future editions of the Olympic Games (e.g. London 2012, Sochi 2014, Rio 2016, PyeongChang 2018)?

3 How do you think the concepts of legacy and sustainability will evolve in the future?

CHAPTER QUESTIONS

1 Why is legacy a consideration/concern when planning and hosting a major sports event?

2 Examine the different ways to categorize legacy. Draw a conceptual map showing the relationships between the different types proposed.

3 Looking at your area, who should be in charge of conceptualizing legacies from the hosting of a potential major sports event, and who should be in charge of managing the event's legacies post-event? Why?

4 How could event organizers and partners (key stakeholders) use the NBS 2011 top ten sustainable business strategies in the context of a major sports event?

5 Why is transfer of knowledge important for major sports events?

FURTHER READING

If you are interested in legacy and associated concepts, we recommend the following:

Babiak, K. & Wolfe, R. (2006) More than just a game? Corporate social responsibility and Super Bowl XL. *Sport Marketing Quarterly*, 15, 214–222.

Case, R. (2012) Event impacts and environmental sustainability. In S. J. Page & J. Connell (eds), *The Routledge Handbook of Events* (pp. 362–384), London: Routledge.

Smith, A. (2010) Leveraging benefits from major events: Maximising opportunities for peripheral urban areas. *Managing Leisure*, 15, 161–180.

Chapter 16

Other considerations

OBJECTIVES

- To understand that there are concepts and forces which pervade the whole sport event context
- To explain how the concepts of power, ethics, culture, change management, and communication impact major sports events and their managers
- To understand similarities and differences between major sports events (one-off vs. recurring vs. para-events)

ILLUSTRATIVE CASE: CORRUPTION SEEMS RAMPANT IN THE INTERNATIONAL MAJOR SPORTS EVENTS WORLD

The year 2011 was a banner one for corruption within major sports events at the international level. The chairman of the 2010 CWG, Suresh Kalmadi, was arrested following allegations of corruption around the event (Cutler, 2011i). He subsequently served a nine-month sentence for having supposedly inflated "tenders worth millions of dollars for equipment used" at the Games (Cutler, 2012c: 1). A state auditor noted in 2011 that the Games were "deeply flawed, riddled with favouritism and bias" (as quoted by Cutler, 2012c: 1).

In turn, Orlando Silva, the Brazilian sports minister resigned following corruption allegations for his involvement in both the 2014 FIFA World Cup and the 2016 Rio Olympic Games (Cutler, 2011h). In addition, the International Boxing Association began investigating allegations of large pay-outs in return for guarantees that Azerbaijan boxers would be awarded gold medals during the 2012 London Olympic Games (Cutler, 2011g). These are but three examples of the level of corruption found within major sports events.

OTHER AREAS WHICH SHOULD BE CONSIDERED AS PART OF MANAGING MAJOR SPORTS EVENTS

In this chapter we present some theories and considerations that do not necessarily fall specifically within any of the earlier chapters as they pervade all of them. More precisely, we want to spend a little time on the concepts of power, ethics, culture, change management, and communication. We also want to briefly discuss commonalities and differences between major sports events – that is, between one-off and recurring events, and between able-bodied and para-events. Unlike the preceding chapters, we will not separate the theory from the practitioner's perspective; instead, we will integrate our experiences and perspectives to stimulate discussion and discourse around these areas by both researchers and practitioners.

Power

A sociological concept, power has been used in the examination of organizations within and outside of sport (through organization theory and critical perspectives, e.g. Bachmann, 2001; Bakan, 2004; Brass and Burkhardt, 1993; Fligstein and Brantley, 1992; Green, 2004; Hoye and Cuskelly, 2003; Ibarra, 1993; Klein, 1998; McCambridge, 2004; Murray *et al.*, 1992; Ocasio, 1994; Pitter, 1990; Riess, 1981; Steen-Johnsen and Hanstad, 2008; Sugden and Tomlinson, 1998; Wolfe *et al.*, 2002). Power is also used when examining major sports events, notably related to international events, the Olympic Games, and the IOC (e.g. Gupta, 2009; Kidd, 1988; Lenskyj, 2000; Senn, 1999). Max Weber was one of the first to focus on power and differentiate it from authority. Power itself is typically defined as an actor's (individual, group, or organization) ability to make another actor do something they would not otherwise do regardless of their resistance; in contrast, authority relates to orders that are voluntarily obeyed (with no resistance) (Gerth and Mills, 1946; Weber, 1947). As Parent (2006) noted, research typically examines power using one of three approaches: structural, behavioural, or personal.

Structural approaches are usually associated with power, authority, and control within an organization. Here, power is acquired by an actor when another actor is dependent on it. Etzioni's (1964) coercive (use of violence, restraint, force), utilitarian (use of financial, human, material, or other physical resources), and normative (use of symbolic resources which do not fall within the other two categories) forms of power can also be seen as associated with dependence of one actor on another's resources in this case, given the latter's power over the former. For organization theory researchers using this approach, power has typically been examined by looking at who controls the organizations and what are the consequences. Theories such as resource dependence theory (cf. Ulrich and Barney, 1984) and structural contingency (cf. Hickson *et al.*, 1971) fall within this structural approach to power. Taking a different route, Davis and Thompson (1994) used a social movement approach involving the examination of interests, political opportunity structure, social infrastructure, and mobilization to examine how and why shareholders can take control of a large corporation (i.e. to examine their power). They focus on both formal and informal influences. Yet as Fligstein and Brantley (1992) found, it does not matter who controls the organization; organizational factors, such as the CEO's background, industry growth, and product strategy, are the factors that seem to have a greater effect on organizational performance.

The behavioural approach has a more micro perspective and focuses on individuals' behaviours in relation to power. Here, power is found when "the mere expectation of power can be enough to have someone do something that they would not otherwise do" (Parent, 2006: 218). The third conceptualization of power, the personal approach, is associated with an individual's own characteristics, such as the power "given to" a charismatic leader. These individual-based approaches to power can be found within French and Raven's (1959) sources of power, which include:

- coercive power: based on an individual's ability to punish another;
- expert power: based on an individual's special set of abilities, skills, knowledge or competencies;
- legitimate power (associated with Weber's (1947) authority): acquired through an individual's position;
- referent power: associated with an individual's charisma;
- reward power: based on one individual's ability to control another individual's rewards.

In contrast, Lukes (1974) saw power not only as an actor's (person, group, or organization) ability to impose their will on another actor (his first dimension), but also as the actor's ability to thwart an issue from being raised (in a meeting, for example; his second dimension), and even as latent conflict (his third dimension). These second and third dimensions demonstrate an actor's power to stop a decision from being taken or from even being discussed in the first place (keeping it latent). This power can be exercised through encouragement, inducement, and/or persuasion (Fletcher, 1992; Lukes, 1974). To study power, Lukes suggested researchers examine (1) the relevant counterfactual (i.e. what an actor would have done in the absence of another actor's power); and (2) the mechanisms allowing an actor to exercise power over another actor.

There are other approaches to power and all of them have their respective strengths and weaknesses. Regardless of the specific definition/reference used for power, we can see that information is power. It can create a set of skills, competencies, and knowledge, giving an actor referent power; it can be a source of utilitarian power; and it can allow a stakeholder to thwart a discussion or even prevent one from happening if it is not the stakeholder's desire to do so, as former IOC president Juan Antonio Samaranch was known to do (see Pound, 2004). This concept of information as power can be viewed as a double-edged sword. When a person is informed about a subject, they have the initial advantage when in the presence of an uninformed listener. The informed person can further enhance their position if they have specific personal experiences to include in their conversation. A second layer to this situation is if the presentation skills of the speaker are good. In the face of facts, experience, and masterful communication of a subject, the uniformed listener is left bereft. This is important in the context of a fast-paced, high-velocity, high-performance business environment like a major sports event. Time is of the essence; and the person who has the information and experience can communicate authentically and passionately from experience, and factually will have more power in the conversation, and usually win.

To gain power, an actor's network of relationships is also important. We know from network theory research that: who you know (an actor's social capital) matters (Burt, 2000); that the actor's position within a network of relationship can give him power by allowing the actor to mediate the flow of information, communication, and other resources (Burt, 2000; Granovetter, 1973; Rowley, 1997); and that good alliances will provide increased status, which helps performance (Podolny, 1993, 1994). This is also true in the old-boys, tight-knit community that is major sports events. Major sports event managers need to leverage relationships just to tread water and stay in the game. Loyalty, tenure of relationships, and "markers" (favours owed) can trump information in power-struggle situations. When you have pre-existing relationships with people in positions of power/ influence/knowledge, they should be nurtured. Life is not fair and the business of sport is not fair! At the end of the day, the way someone feels or their history with a person can be the determining factor in securing agreement/approval or not. If a person is given preference or the benefit of the doubt, or defended regardless of the facts because of a positive pre-existing relationship, it is what it is. It can also happen in reverse, where we do not support, refer, or accept a person or their ideas because of a pre-existing negative experience or impression. We are not always rational, and are often subjective in how we treat others.

When power is exercised, there is an element, big or small, of politics. The politics of sports may be much less blatant than political politics. It is nonetheless a significant aspect of many of the decisions that are made in the managing and delivering of major sports events. While the operative word is sport – at least that is the face of it – what prefaces and leads, behind that face of sport, is an administrative team that could sometimes be described as a machine that is responsible for delivering sport. The administrative body is comprised of individuals who each have their own set of attitudes and beliefs, personally leveraged relationships, individual and collective agendas, and likes and dislikes. They vote individually, which is where the politics start. They can, have been, and likely continue to be vulnerable to influence, bribery, flattery, and personal gain. Where an event is held is as much about the politics as it is about the place. There is so much perceived financial, social, and political gain, notwithstanding the bragging rights, that politics cannot be avoided. Behind closed doors, deals are made – that's politics. Decisions are made unilaterally by majority vote – that's politics. Individuals with charisma and personal power are used as front people to push an agenda – that's politics. Money is promised in return for future considerations – that's politics. People can be selected for their positions based on their political leverage within the sport, business, or political affiliations.

We cannot consider power without considering ego. There is a difference between ego and ego drive. For our purposes, we will use commonly accepted definitions:

- Ego is defined as a person's sense of self-esteem or self-importance.
- Ego drive is the need of one individual to persuade another to a particular point of view and feel satisfaction in having done so.
- Ego and ego drive are part of every person.

Let's add EQ (emotional intelligence) to this. In the last 20 years, social scientists and psychologists have examined EQ. In 1985 Daniel Goleman's book *Emotional Intelligence* brought the term to the masses. The definition that is most practical for us is from Mayer (2009:1): emotional intelligence "represents an ability to validly reason with emotions and to use emotions to enhance thought". How does this relate to major sports events? Ego and ego drive are at the heart of why people want to participate as athletes; why a particular city is chosen; why business wants to be a stakeholder; why people want to work or volunteer at these events; why the public wants to attend; why media wants to report; why the events have grown to include culture and entertainment; why people become Games gypsies. The EQ of each person who participates will determine the effectiveness, efficiency, and amount of collateral damage and emotional wake that is a consequence of their words and actions as they move through their conversations.

From a research point of view, the political and sociological perspectives are popular. Questions relate to whether or not decision-making within and surrounding the bid committee and the organizing committee are political in nature and who is impacted. The general (and repetitive) consensus is that yes, the event and its processes are, at least in part, political, and this can have a negative impact on the more distal (non-powerful) stakeholders. Lenskyj and others (e.g. Lenskyj, 1992, 1996, 2000; Whitson and Macintosh, 1993, 1996) have brought awareness to the impact of major sports events on low-income and other disadvantaged groups. This begs the question: now what? We know that politics are involved, so what happens now: do we try to decrease the political nature? Do we advocate for more transparency in processes (cf. Chappelet and Kübler-Mabbott, 2008; Mason et al., 2006)? Moreover, for event managers and researchers, an important question becomes: how can such political processes be controlled (if possible) and/or manipulated for the benefit of the event manager and/or the non-powerful stakeholders (be they residents, unions, employees, etc.)?

Ethics

Ethics is the "analytical, scientific study of the theoretical bases of moral action"; in turn, morals relate to a person's "actual customs or manners", technically referring to the person's actions as being described as right/wrong, virtuous/vicious, good/bad (Lumpkin et al., 2003: 4). Associated to morals are values, which can be defined as "those people, actions, and things that are worthwhile to us" (DeSensi and Malloy, 2006: 375). This area of study is quite broad and well-developed within the fields of management and sport management. Within management, we see ethics often associated with stakeholder theory, CSR, the environment, HRM, social networks, or technology (e.g. Banerjee et al., 1998; Carroll, 1996; Coates, 2004; Cordeiro, 2003; Everett et al., 2006; Gallagher and Goodstein, 2002; Greenwood, 2002; Hall and Rosson, 2006; Harting et al., 2006; Hepler et al., 2003; Hwang et al., 2009; Jones, 1995; Phillips, 2003; Rasche and Esser, 2006; Wempe, 2005; Wicks and Freeman, 1998; Wijnberg, 2000). In sport management, we see ethics notably examined in association with sponsorship and ambush marketing (e.g. Crompton, 1993, 2004a; Danylchuk and MacIntosh, 2009; Mazanov and Connor, 2010); athlete participation in able-bodied versus para-events (e.g. Edwards, 2008); athlete doping (e.g. Kaufman et al., 2010; Koenig, 1995; Mignon, 2003); athlete sex testing (e.g. Ritchie, 2003; Wiederkehr, 2009); spectator behaviour (e.g. Case et al., 1987); student-athlete academic corruption (e.g. Kihl and Richardson, 2009; Kihl et al., 2008); secondary ticket sales (e.g. Drayer and Martin, 2010); technology and media (e.g. Moles et al., 2001; Numerato, 2009); and match fixing and fair play (e.g. Hill, 2010; McLaren, 2008). We will therefore only highlight some key aspects of the concept, encouraging the reader to read further into this topic should it be of interest, before examining specific ethical issues examined within major sports events.

A person with a "good" character would be defined as one who has the qualities of (Likona, 1991):

- moral knowing: decision-making, knowing moral values, moral awareness, moral reasoning, perspective taking, and self-knowledge;
- moral feeling: conscience, empathy, humility, loving the good, self-esteem, and self-control; and
- moral action: competence, habit, and will.

Ethical behaviour is about knowing and believing, valuing (including both values and principles), and acting. As Lumpkin *et al.* (2003) argued, to think ethically means to have the ability to be consistent, impartial, and exercise reflective thinking (based on the person's clear, moral, and non-moral values). They further argue that Kantian ethics (Kant, 1997) – those based on Kant's philosophy – are seen as a worldwide standard for reasonableness and rationality. A key principal of Kantian ethics is the concept of universality, where one's moral judgements should be founded upon universal rules (i.e. applicable to all individuals in the same way) and one should treat others with respect. Besides Kantian philosophy, existential philosophy – driven in large part by Jean-Paul Sartre (1957, 1966) – focuses mainly on the concepts of authenticity, dread, freedom, and responsibility. Both of these approaches can be used by event leaders and managers in their daily workings within a major sports event organizing committee.

Mediating the relationship between beliefs, values, principles, and actions are the written and unwritten rules. Written rules and principles should ideally be written in the negative form (e.g. I will not lie – a principle referring to the value of honesty) as it covers all situations/cases/issues of concern for the organization or individual (DeMarco and Fox, 1990). Codes of conduct are popular documents for organizations, including organizing committees, to provide ethical guidelines. VANOC created a code of conduct which included clauses on conflicts of interest, honesty and integrity, fairness and dignity, fiscal responsibility and accountability, sustainability and environmental stewardship, performance, diversity, inspiration, discrimination and harassment, inclusiveness, and confidentiality and privacy (The Vancouver Organizing Committee for the 2010 Olympic and Paralympic Winter Games, n.d.).

The Canadian Centre for Ethics in Sport suggested the following as unethical threats to sport: doping, violence, parents behaving badly, weak community sport governance, lack of access and inclusion, and negative behaviours in professional sports (e.g. match fixing, doping) (Canadian Centre for Ethics in Sport, 2011). Unfortunately, unethical, corrupt behaviour has been found at the highest levels of international major sport event organization. Books and articles have been written on this subject (e.g. Hill, 2008; Jennings, 2000; Mason *et al.*, 2006), and many cases are widely known, such as Canadian sprinter Ben Johnson's doping during the 1988 Seoul Olympic Games or the 2002 Salt Lake City scandal which broke in 1999 (see Hamilton, 2010).

IFs are trying to counter the ongoing corruption. For example, the IOC created an ethics commission, whereas FIFA has an ethics committee and recently added a good governance committee and three task forces, which examine FIFA statutes changes, ethics committee changes, and ways to "make FIFA more transparent" (Cutler, 2011j: 1). Still, the degree to which these committees will be effective remains to be seen. In contrast, academics are calling for more accountability (Chappelet and Kübler-Mabbott, 2008; Mason et al., 2006). For example, Mason et al. (2006) suggest that the IOC include key stakeholders (e.g. corporate partners, media) in its management and control functions, and notably create a board to oversee the IOC's operations, which would have sanctioning authority over IOC members. Still, one issue remains: these organizations are independent, international, private (as in not publicly owned) organizations, which means that there is no legal require- ment for these organizations to do anything they do not want to do. Money is arguably the driving factor. Having said this, the normative, ethical behaviour of the manager should still influence these organizations' processes and actions, meaning that being successful (e.g. gaining financial and reputational resources) should not come at the expense of ethical behaviour.

There is an axiom that you bring yourself wherever you go. If a person is driven by values, this is the compass that directs their leadership, regardless of the organization. In enduring organizations, there is a permanent culture defining the boundaries and constants in the organizational structure that allows an individual to assess their behaviour and decisions over a protracted period of time. With short-term organizations, there can be conflicts for values-driven managers. They know what the right thing to do is, and they may not be able to follow through. For example, regarding protocol for a major sports event, the athlete should come first, second all of the leaders of the sport, with politicians being third in the pecking order. There are pages of guidelines for protocol, and yet the politicians who attend events often ignore or refuse to acknowledge these guidelines. A manager is faced with having to make value decisions in the moment that may contradict both values and protocol. They must reframe the situation to fit the circumstance rather than sticking to their values. In other circumstances, values may be sacrificed to "ceremony" or an executive or board edict. These contradictions to a manager's values will sap energy and can be de- motivating. If they insist on sticking to their values, there could be consequences. There are so many stakeholders, and decisions to keep a person or to cut losses quickly and fire them comes at the forefront of the list of consequences. Compromise of a manager's values is a given in this ego-driven, politically charged environment.

Culture

While we talked about organizational culture in Chapter 5, on the workforce, we would like to spend a little time to discuss the impact of national, local, and sport cultures on the organizing committee and the event. Societal culture, the values and beliefs of a society or nation, impacts how individuals in that society work and think. It is therefore logical to believe that societal culture can impact the workings of a major sports event organizing committee in that society, versus another. To illustrate, a major sports event hosted in China would likely be fundamentally different to ones hosted in South Africa or Greece or Mexico or the United States. Each culture has its beliefs; for example, some cultures will be pushing the planning to almost seem ahead of schedule (like China did for the 2008 Olympic Games) whereas others have a culture that seems more last-minute from the outside (e.g. Latin America, Greece). To wit, in reference to the significant and worrying (for the IOC notably) delays seen during the lead-up to the 2004 Athens Olympic Games, the Greek ambassador to Canada noted: "I know my people and we do it our way. Our way always works out in the end. If it gives you a heart attack, that's your problem" (Cleary, 2002: A13). We can also extend this thinking within a country. Different regions in a country (e.g. Sicily vs. Rome vs. Piedmont in Italy) have different feels, different characteristics, and different ways of doing. Spain (with its Catalan nation), Canada (with its Québec province), and the UK (with Scotland) are cases in point. Thus, the culture of the local, host region can also impact the organizing committee. To illustrate, the 2010 Olympic Winter Games were hosted in Vancouver, British Columbia, Canada, situated between the Pacific coast and the Rocky Mountains. The west coast of Canada is known as more laid-back; and the fluid landscape of mountains and oceans contributed to the relaxed business-casual attire choice within the organization, meetings often starting about five minutes late, and the influence of the blue and green waves on the look-feel of the publications. In contrast, Curi *et al.* (2011: 140) illustrated Rio's (Brazil) approach to the Fifteenth Pan American Games, which was to erect walls around the stadia to hide "the unsightly parts of the city, that is, the poor neighborhoods and favelas. This wall could be seen as a BRIC way of organizing mega-events."

Next, sport subculture is suggested to impact event promotion, social event leveraging, and visitor spending for the host community (Green, 2001; O'Brien, 2007). So can it not also impact the individuals/groups working in a major sports event organizing committee, especially those working for a given sport (i.e. within the sport division and in that sport's venue)? For example, it is logical to believe that a sport like curling, whose culture is associated with a drinking, laid-back, even fun attitude (such as the Norwegian curling team's chequered outfits during the 2010 Olympic Winter Games), will be transposed into the working attitudes and behaviours of those event managers working in the sport division on curling or in the curling venue, in contrast to, perhaps, a more "rigid", structured sport like figure skating or speed skating.

As Higham and Hinch (2003) suggested, the sport, space, and time elements of an event impact tourists of that event. We can extend the idea to say that the type of sport(s), the space, or context/location of the event, and the time of its hosting make the event unique but also impact the organizing committee and its members (i.e. choice of vision, mission, goals, look-feel, operating procedures, etc.). Nevertheless, what we suggest here still needs to be empirically examined. Examining economic, political, and social effects on the Global South and BRIC countries, as well as image building of events/host regions in the Global South (e.g. Dupont, 2011; Steinbrink *et al.*, 2011) are fruitful areas to critically examine Western constructs associated with planning and hosting major sports events and their legacies.

Change management

In a major sports event organizing committee, the only constant is change. Workforce members need to expect that changes will occur essentially daily. Change can be planned (e.g. the move from headquarters to the venues) or unplanned (e.g. the sudden resignation of a vice-president). There are other types of changes as well (Greenwood and Hinings, 1996):

- Radical change, also known as frame bending, refers to busting loose from an existing orientation and organizational transformation.
- Convergent change refers to the fine tuning of an existing orientation.
- Evolutionary change is change that occurs slowly, over time.
- Revolutionary change occurs swiftly and affects most or all parts of the organization simultaneously.

Revolutionary change may be seen when a major outside force for change – be that technological, people-based, structure and systems-based, or products and services-based (McCann, 1991; Slack and Parent, 2006) – such as a worldwide economic recession affects the overall organizing committee and drastic measures need to be taken quickly. However, a major sports event organizing committee is more likely to see convergent, evolutionary changes as it has set a number of goals and objectives under the broad umbrella of its purpose (to prepare and host a major sports event). Thus, it will tweak its course along the way to ensure it meets its purpose.

Change within organizing committees can be examined following a contextualist approach – that is, examining the content (the what), context (the why), and process (the how) of change (Child and Smith, 1987; Pettigrew, 1985, 1987). From a content perspective, we note that organizing committees have structural changes; they move from a headquarters-centred organizational structure during the planning phase to a venue-centred structure during Games-time, and then back to a headquarters-centred structure during the wrap-up mode (see Chapter 3 for more information) (Parent and Séguin, 2010). As the organizing committee moves through its planning and implementation modes, other changes also occur, especially in regards to its growth in human resources. Other resources, namely financial, infrastructure, and informational, also have organizing committee-wide impacts (Parent and Séguin, 2010). From a context perspective, internal politics, external access to resources, and changes in the host country/region's and/or IF/NSF political landscape are sources of change for the organizing committee.

From a process perspective, Parent and Séguin (2010) argued that change needs to become a routine within an organizing committee. A routine is a recognizable and repetitive pattern of action, and it can be a "source of change as well as stability. [It has an] inherent capability . . . to generate change merely by [its] ongoing performance" (Feldman and Pentland, 2003: 94). A routine can be either ostensive (i.e. abstract, principle, or generalized idea) or performative (i.e. a specific action taken by a particular actor at a specific time and place). Ostensive routines can be prospectively, or retrospectively used to determine "what should be [done] or [what] should have been done, respectively", whereas the performative routines are "the actual enactment or implementation of ostensive routines" (Parent and Séguin, 2010: 6). Artefacts allow us to see the ostensive and performative routines. Ostensive routine artefacts could include policies and procedures, forms, checklists, and rules; whereas, performative routine artefacts focus on performance indicators (e.g. work/timesheets). As performance can differ from the plans (ostensive routines), it is important to differentiate between the two types of routines. According to Parent and Séguin (2010), to plan for the unexpected during Games-time, organizing committees establish ostensive routines (policies, procedures, contingency plans, daily run sheets, etc.) during the planning mode. They then put these plans into action during Games-time through performative routines. Performative routines continue during the wrap-up mode as organizing committee members have to enact the legacy management plans created previously, as well as undertake the report writing and closing down of the organization.

Individuals often resist change because of self-interest, lack of trust, or understanding about the implications, different assessments of the consequences, or the costs of the change (Slack and Parent, 2006). It is therefore important that organizing committees, their leaders, and managers properly manage the constant changes their workforce will face. Strategies which help organizing committees manage change include: choosing leaders who can "get the job done", creating ostensive and performative routines that allow the development of a capacity and capability for change, being flexible (adaptable and able to change, and flexible during the planning process), and paying particular attention to strategic and contingency planning, as well as communication within and outside the organizing committee (Parent and Séguin, 2010).

In the face of change, good leaders are masters at shifting. Kevin Cashman (2001) presented five change mastery shifts:

1 *From problem focus to opportunity focus.* Effective leaders tend to perceive and to focus on the opportunities inherent in change
2 *From short-term focus to long-term focus.* Effective leaders don't lose sight of their long-term vision in the midst of change.
3 *From circumstance focus to purpose focus.* Effective leaders maintain a clear purpose regardless of immediate circumstances.
4 *From control focus to adaptability focus.* Effective leaders understand constant control is not possible, but adaptability allows them and others to flow with change.
5 *From doubt focus to trust focus.* Effective leaders are more secure in themselves; they possess a sense that they can handle whatever may come their way.

The organizing committee leader's management of the continual change means that they have realistic expectations. They also under-promise and over-deliver. Good event managers are those who accept, expect, and thrive on the constant changes. In other words, they are built for the fast-paced, high-velocity, high-performance environment.

Communication

Given that there are individuals and organizations from different cultures and traditions working within the context of a given edition of a major sports event, being aware of communication components and processes is critical. The communication process (sender, message, medium, receiver) was described in Chapter 6. A communication can be written or verbal. Regardless, there needs to be a connection for it to be termed a communication. Otherwise, it is a monologue or a dissertation. To make that connection, there must be something in the information to which the listener/receiver can relate. Mehrabian (1981) expressed the components of a verbal communication and the impact percentage on the communication:

- 55 per cent of a verbal communication is non-verbal: gestures, body language, appearance, and facial expressions.
- 38 per cent of a verbal communication is vocal: speed, tone, pitch, voice inflection, intonation, pronunciation, enunciation, and accent.
- 7 per cent of a verbal communication is verbal: choice of words and vocabulary.

Considering this information, it is more important how we say what we say, and what we say non-verbally, than the words or vocabulary that we use. So it is those people who infuse passion, authenticity, empathy, honesty, and sincerity into their communication that are most effective.

A person's personality profile and the type of person they are also contribute to how many different types of people a speaker can appeal to. A skilled speaker will be able to understand and accept different personality types and adapt their communication to connect with all types. All things being equal – education, experience, and competencies – the most important asset a leader or manager can have is strong interpersonal skills. We need only to look at those leaders that have persuaded humanity to good (e.g. Ghandi, Nelson Mandela) and evil (e.g. Hitler, Saddam Hussein) through their exceptional ability to speak to and with people. Event managers who treat people individually, take time to listen and value input from others, include some fun and humour, and use please and thank you as value acknowledgements will frequently encourage an environment of cooperation, camaraderie, and calm, thereby providing an environment which fosters quality communication.

Parallels and differences with recurring events and Para-games

Regardless of the type of sport event, cultural event, celebration, or festival, and regardless of the size of the event, the foundation remains the same. That is, the core principles of leading, setting-up, planning, workforce management, marketing, venue management, media, stakeholder relations and protocol, ceremonies, risk management and security, technology, Games-time, closure, and legacy and sustainability management should remain the same.

However, there are some differences, which sometimes can be seen as benefits for recurring events. For festivals, hallmark events, and other types of recurring events, certain procedures and issues become routine; recurring event managers can have, for example, a routine ready and vetted from past years for the venuization process. In addition, these event managers can learn from mistakes and apply lessons learned the following year to improve that event. Moreover, such events are usually more closely tied to the community, creating the opportunity to develop long-term relationships with the local government and residents; attending these events can become a tradition for local residents (Getz, 2005), allowing them to become embedded within the community and more sustainable. The long-term relationship building is also a benefit for the recurring event organizing committee's relationship with sponsors; recurring events offer the option of having a multi-year contract, providing greater sponsorship options (e.g. over a number of events) either at a stable sponsorship level or with options to increase (or decrease) support over the years. This multi-year characteristic of recurring events allows both the event and sponsor to build recognition, and to build a brand for the event, the community, and the sponsor.

In turn, a certain distinction needs to be made between able-bodied and Para games. Contrary to popular belief, the rights may or may not be held by the same organization. For example, the rights for the Olympic Games and Paralympic Games are held by the IOC and the IPC, respectively, which are two distinct, separate organizations. This explains in part why the two events are not held simultaneously but instead consecutively. In contrast, the CWG includes both able-bodied and para sport competitions held during the same period. When able-bodied and para events are held separately, the para event is typically smaller in size: there are fewer athletes, fewer countries represented, fewer media, and fewer sports. While less media and recognition often means less sponsorship (and therefore fewer resources), this smaller size does not necessarily have only negative drawbacks. Having the same organizing committee undertake both events allows a re-use of the able-bodied event's resources (venues, workforce, etc.), it can feel more intimate in atmosphere, and it can feel more like a party. Moreover, the Paralympic Games have evolved over their 60 years of existence from burgeoning awareness, to a rise in prominence, to transcendence in their impact on disability, sport, and society (Legg and Steadward, 2011). Still, it is true that para events have different logistical needs which require changes in venue fit-out in between the two events. In addition, workforce members' energy often wanes after the able-bodied event, so members have to consciously wind themselves back up and leaders must make extra efforts to motivate their subordinates. This is why having some new workforce blood is good for the para event. Nevertheless, the workforce members now essentially know what to expect and what to do; thus, they have routines as guidelines to assist them in being effective and efficient.

CHAPTER SUMMARY

In this chapter we discussed some aspects which pervade the overall planning, implementation, and wrap-up of a major sports event. We saw that there are three approaches to power (structural, behavioural, and personal), along with the concepts of ego, ego drive, and EQ. We examined ethical principles and discussed the idea that ethical behaviour is about knowing, believing, valuing (including both values and principles), and acting. We also examined the idea of culture (e.g. national and sport) and suggested that type of sport(s), the space or context/location of the event, and the time of its hosting make the event unique but also impact the organizing committee and its members. Next, we offered suggestions for leaders to manage the change that is pervasive within major sports event organizing committees, as well as the all-important communication process. Finally, we examined some key differences between able-bodied and para major sports events, as well as recurring events.

EXPERT CASE: XIX CWG IN DELHI, INDIA: A MEETING GROUND OF SPORT AND CULTURE

Originally known as the British Empire Games when the first athletic competitions were hosted in the city of Hamilton in the Province of Ontario, Canada in 1930, the most recent edition of what is now the CWG was held in the city of Delhi, India on 4–14 October 2010.

Future hosts of the Games include Glasgow, Scotland in 2014, and the Gold Coast Australia in 2018. The CWG is a large major multi-sports event that takes place every four years, in which elite athletes compete in both able-bodied and para sport events across an 11–12-day programme. Athletes compete as individuals (e.g. in athletics, wrestling) and as members of team sports (e.g. rugby sevens, netball, and hockey) while representing their country.

The title and property holder of the Games, the CGF, is based in the UK. The CGF board plans, organizes, and is involved in the decision-making with respect to direction of the Games mission, vision, and movement. Six geographical regions have delegations involved in the Games (Africa, the Americas, Asia, the Caribbean, Europe, Oceania). Each region has a vice-president who acts as a representative on the CGF board, and each country within that region also has a CGA (e.g. Canada, Australia).

Like other major multi-sports events, the focus of operations for the property holder (i.e. CGF) is on delivering a well-run event which features, in their case, celebrations of sporting excellence and culture. The XIX Games included a record 4,352 athletes from all 71 Commonwealth nations and territories (e.g. Sri Lanka, New Zealand, Wales, Jamaica, Kenya, Canada). Such diversity of delegations from different nations and territories creates a very inter-cultural environment both in and outside the field of play.

Every transaction between athletes, coaches, trainers, administrators, and other stakeholders during the Games, to some degree, involves expression of one's own values and beliefs. Personal values and beliefs can be shaped in part from the cultural norms within a person's country of origin; among other factors such as religion and upbringing. The transactions between stakeholders from different cultures are likely to shed light on cultural ways of doing things. For example, it is highly plausible that in some cultures, a more formalized, planned approach to organizing is expected, in contrast to other cultures which rely predominantly on the relationships that need to develop in order to get work done. While such a contention is highly dependent on context, and generalizing is often problematic, the links between a person's values and beliefs system, within the context of their culture from which they are born and raised, makes for an interesting discussion within sport event management.

To illustrate, the use of the word "culture" can connote many different meanings. In order to understand what is meant by "culture", we must first recognize the various meanings and interpretations of the word itself. From a more anthropological view, culture can mean the attributes of a group within a relatively defined and given boundary of that group's environment (artefacts can help describe how people lived). Another common use of the word is the comparison between "cultures"; for example, the culture of the Americas is vastly different from the culture of Asia. Further, another variation of the word is "cultured", a term which can describe a person's involvement in literature, art, music, cuisine, and other diversified aspects. As well, the term "organizational culture" is used to describe the values, beliefs, and assumptions deemed important within organizational life (some would use it to denote "how things are done around here"). At the XIX Games, the word culture could be used to describe these areas for the Indian organizing committee.

Some contend that a person's geographical up-bringing (or country of birth) can influence organizational culture and how the working environment functions. For example, at the XIX Games it would be assumed that the way by which the Indian organizing committee went about operating the Games can provide a "window" into some of the values and beliefs within the country. Consider that during the opening, medal, and closing ceremonies etc., expressions of food, dance, song, and ritual composed aspects of the Indian way of life. Extending this further, the colours used in the Games logo, the symbol and mascot (the Tiger), and special sporting and cultural heroes were all a part of the Indian organizing committee's plan to tell the world what these Games represent.

The XIX Games in Delhi were a perfect opportunity to explore how athletes and other stakeholders from the various countries experience the same event. The Games provided a meeting ground for stakeholders of sport throughout the Commonwealth. Leading up to the Games, the Indian organizing committee came under a fair bit of international media scrutiny, led by CGAs from Canada, England, and New Zealand (to name a few). Indeed, these CGAs were very clear that the amenities needed to be world class and that only a few weeks before the Games some were not ready. This highlighted one of the areas whereby intercultural management is an applicable area of study.

For the CGF, three core values help guide decision-making regarding the sporting events – humanity, equality, and destiny. A part of the larger mission is to ensure that athletes experience a world-class Games. During the XIX Games, the survey I helped construct to empirically examine the athletes' experience considered many facets that were developed in consultation with the CGF Athletes Representative and CGF board members. These facets of the athletes' experience were identified as: (1) athletes village environment (e.g. fitness centre, transportation in village); (2) food services (e.g. quality, availability); (3) sporting venues (e.g. training facilities, competition management); (4) travel (e.g. transfer to village, accreditation); (5) games security (e.g. presence, confidence); (6) ceremonies (e.g. opening, medal); (7) communications (e.g. wireless access, chef de mission availability); and (8) medical (e.g. confidence in staff, anti-doping information). Additionally, three items were used to assess the overall athlete experience (e.g. "overall, I would assess my experience as . . ."; "I have let my family and friends know my overall experience has been . . ."). A Likert scale was created in which 1 = very poor; 2 = poor; 3 = satisfactory; 4 = good; and 5 = excellent, which anchored the survey. In addition, four open-ended questions were included which asked participants to (1) indicate and describe any immediate concerns; (2) identify whether they had any suggestions on how to improve future Games; (3) identify and describe one thing above all else not related to their athletic event which contributed to their enjoyment; and (4) to suggest ways for the CGF to improve the opening ceremonies.

When analysing the athlete data, significant multivariate effects were found based on the respondent's geographical region. Specifically, differences were found based on the region for the factors of transportation, accommodations, sporting venues, and overall experience. For transportation, respondents in Oceania had a significantly lower mean score than Africa, Asia, the Caribbean, and Europe, which indicated their experience with this factor was less favourable. Further, the Americas also had a lower mean score for transportation than Asia, the Caribbean, and Europe. For the factor of accommodations, respondents in Oceania again had a lower mean score than all other regions, and athletes from the Americas had lower mean scores than Africa, Asia, the Caribbean, and Europe. Results also showed that for the factor "sport venues", respondents from Oceania again had lower mean scores than Asia and the Caribbean. Lastly, in regards to overall experience, respondents from Europe had higher mean scores than Africa and Oceania.

321

What does such information tell us?

Upon further inspection, it is interesting that in large part the respondents from the Oceania region rated many factors lower than other regions (e.g. transportation, accommodations, sport venues). In regards to the factor of accommodations, it is possible that the towers in which the athletes from the Oceania region were staying had specific problems above other regions' towers, or that they experienced service problems above those of other regional athletes. It was clear that for this cohort of athletes, these factors could be improved for future Games. It is also plausible that hosting the CWG in Melbourne in 2006 may have also shaped expectations for these athletes going into the XIX Games (particularly those athletes from Australia). This "hangover effect" (for lack of a better phrase) may be something which occurs for athletes at each subsequent Games if their country was the previous host. It would be interesting to examine such phenomena in future Games with the athlete delegation from the previous host country.

Indeed, for the property rights holder, such evaluations undertaken can expose differences in the potential areas in need of improvement for specific regional athletes. Identifying these areas can aid in the creation of strategic initiatives built into the planning process by various CGAs leading up to future events. For the CGF, such knowledge can also assist in strengthening their vision and mission by demonstrating their commitment to athletes from across the Commonwealth.

The findings from this survey demonstrated that athletes had different experiences, which is not that surprising. In future athlete research, consideration should also be given to how "expectations" can shape experiences. In addition to examining expectations and experiences more closely, further research should also consider different stakeholders of sport events (e.g. officials) and how they experience the Games. Clearly, all of these stakeholders need to be managed by the organizing committee. The bottom line is that people do not share the same focus on what is important, nor do they place the same importance on all factors. Consequently, further exploration into these factors based on regional differences is needed with a larger sample size to gain a deeper appreciation of the cultural differences and how they shape the athlete experience.

By Dr Eric MacIntosh, PhD, Associate Professor, School of Human Kinetics, University of Ottawa

Case questions

1   Why might we expect to have differences in experiences across the various countries and regions? What can managers do about these differences?

2   What is the hangover effect?

3   How is culture expressed during Games?

CHAPTER QUESTIONS

1   What could be some of the positive and negative consequences of relationship leveraging within major sports events?

2   Why are ethics important for sport event managers?

3   Think of your favourite major sports event. If it were to be held in your city, describe the kind of societal, national, local, and sport cultures that would impact the organizing committee.

4   How can a leader prepare his team for the changes that will occur over the course of the workforce members' tenure with the organizing committee?

5   What are the similarities and differences between one-time major sports events and recurring events?

FURTHER READING

For further readings on some of the topics in this chapter, we suggest the following:

Amirtash, A. M. (2005) Iran and the Asian Games: The largest sports event in the Middle East. *Sport in Society*, 8, 449–467.

Scott, S. (2002) *Fierce Conversations: Achieving Success at Work & in Life, One Conversation at a Time*, New York: Penguin Group.

Shogan, D. (2007) *Sport Ethics in Context*, Toronto: Canadian Scholars' Press Inc.

Chapter 17

Conclusion

OBJECTIVES

■ To reflect on the theoretical knowledge we have about major sports event

■ To reflect on some trends and best practices

■ To provide future directions for organizing committees of major sports events and interested researchers

ILLUSTRATIVE CASE: 2012 YOG LABORATORY FOR YOUTH AND INNOVATION (YOGINN) AND OTHER STUDIES BENEFITING RESEARCH AND PRACTICE

YOGINN was created within the Innsbruck University's Institute for Sports Science. Its goal is to ensure the sustainability of not only the YOG, but also the academic partnership that has been created between Innsbruck University and the 2012 YOG. Other universities are also involved in this research project, which is designed to understand various aspects of the YOG, such as the Culture and Education Program, the volunteers, youth leaders, athletes, parents, and coaches. There are also the standard IOC secondee and observer programmes found at the YOG like the Olympic Games. The information garnered from these research and practitioner activities will assist the current and future YOG Organizing Committees such as Nanjing (China) 2014 and Lillehammer (Norway) 2016, as well as the future OCOGs such as Sochi (Russia) 2014, Rio (Brazil) 2016 and PyeongChang (South Korea) 2018.

In this book we set out to use the 2010 Olympic Winter Games and other major sports events to discuss the key areas that lead to hosting successful major sports events and what the research tells us about these areas. As the reader may have seen, some chapters are longer than others (e.g. planning, marketing), which demonstrates the greater emphasis placed on these areas from a research and/or practitioner perspective. Other areas (e.g. technology) have shorter chapters, usually demonstrating the lack of research associated with these areas. To conclude this book, we want to reflect on the existing theoretical aspects, and examine recurring themes and best practices. Finally, we will provide some reflections on future trends, both theoretical and practical.

THEORETICAL REFLECTIONS

In researching this book we found some areas are well developed in the literature or on their way to being so. This is notably the case for marketing and sponsorship, economic impact, and volunteer management. This is not to say that these areas do not need any further analysis. On the contrary, numerous questions remain for these different areas, such as:

- marketing, sponsorship, branding, look-feel:
    - the impact of new media on sponsorship contracts and policies, branding, and look-feel;
    - the interrelationship between the various marketing concepts (sponsorship, branding, relationship marketing, look-feel, stakeholders, etc.); and
    - current trends within events and marketing such as action sports marketing, cause-related marketing, legal aspects, etc.
- workforce management:
    - determining how volunteers (and their skills and knowledge) can be retained from one major sports event to another within a given host region and between different editions of a given sports event;
    - determining how individuals who travel to a given region to volunteer can be targeted to become future tourists to the region or rest of the country (which therefore includes a question about the working relationship between an organizing committee and the local/national tourism organizations);
    - examining the proper hiring procedures for event employees to gain that elusive fit;
    - examining event staff characteristics to establish profiles;
    - examining the characteristics and motivations of Games gypsies.

Moreover, there are other areas which are lacking in research, notably in regards to ceremonies, athletes/sport, transportation, media, venues and venuization processes, post-games wrap-up procedures, and more. Future research questions associated with these areas can include (but are certainly not limited to):

- How to improve the experience of all the various stakeholders (e.g. athletes, media, dignitaries, sponsors) and not just spectators during ceremonies, sports competitions, and associated event activities?
- How are ceremonies and sport production decisions affected by the local/regional and national/international contexts, as well as the sports presented in the given event?
- What are best practices regarding efficient and effective transportation, sport production, sport, venuization and venue management, etc.?
- How can lower-level employees and volunteers be involved and contribute to the post-games evaluation and wrap-up process?
- How can and do new media change established planning, implementation, and wrap-up activities and procedures?

- What is the relationship between the concepts associated with legacy (e.g. leveraging, impacts, outcomes, sustainability, and CSR) and is there a typology or taxonomy which can simplify the varied terminology?
- What is the place of major sports events in a host region's long-term master plan in relation to smaller and recurring events (sport or otherwise)? This could include further examination of the event portfolio concept.

As can be seen in the book, each area of an event has a multitude of concepts associated with it. It should also have become obvious to the reader that there is significant overlap between areas. For example, volunteer management is a workforce consideration (HRM), but also falls within planning, venuization, Games-time, and wrap-up activities. Technology is an intrinsic part of planning, venue management, venuization, workforce management, marketing, communications, sponsorship, sport and sport production, media, ceremonies, risk management and security, Games-time, and wrap-up procedures.

As well, theories are being borrowed from other domains to help explain event processes. For example, theories associated with motivation, commitment, and satisfaction are being used to help explain volunteer behaviour. However, as of yet, there is no true sport event-based theory. Whether or not the reader believes there should be a "theory" of major sports events remains a philosophical question to debate – one we encourage the reader to reflect upon. Notwithstanding, once sport event concepts and theories are established and properly grounded, it will be possible to integrate the various issues into a more comprehensive view of sports events. Following Whetten (1989), if researchers increasingly use questions answering not only the what but also the how, why, who, when, and where, we will be able to provide the domain (subject of the theory), theoretical assumptions and explanations, and the temporal and contextual factors providing the boundaries of the theory. Therefore, we encourage researchers to move beyond "what" questions to other types of questions as well.

In order to begin this process of creating sport event-specific theory, we created a conceptual map of the various concepts discussed in this book. We reviewed every chapter and pulled out recurring concepts to demonstrate their association with the given chapter topic. We placed these conceptual relationships in a matrix (in an Excel file) and then had the network analysis computer software programs UCINET 6.2 and NetDraw 2 (Borgatti, 2002; Borgatti et al., 2002) determine the visual network depiction of this analysis. Figure 17.1 provides a basic overview of this relationship, and Figure 17.2 provides a further analysis of the network using the concepts of:

- centrality: which nodes have the greatest number of lines (so are connected to the greatest number of concepts), are closer to a greater number of concepts, can have greater linking ability between other concepts, and are more important than others – shown as being relatively bigger nodes (i.e. degree, closeness, betweenness, and Eigenvector centrality, respectively; see Wasserman and Faust, 1994; Bonacich, 1972).
- the K-core (Wasserman and Faust, 1994): which nodes can be seen as part of a clique, and the degree of coreness of the nodes – shown as nodes of the same shape.

Figure 17.1 Conceptual map of major sports event concepts.

It is important to note that these figures and the concepts represented are not the final, ultimate illustration for all major sports events, nor are the relationships depicted set in stone, for many reasons. First, the field of major sports events is growing exponentially; with this comes the constant examination and establishment of new concepts and new associations between these concepts. As well, the choice (name, depth/detail, etc.) of concepts to include remains a subjective one (e.g. if we left something out of the book, it would not be represented in the figure, despite someone else believing it to be a core concept). Next, this book is about the management of major sports events; thus, the figures' lens follows this particular approach. Finally, what is presented in the book is partly a function of what is available in the literature; thus, greater prevalence of certain areas may influence the presence of certain concepts. Therefore we present the figures as relative, subjective depictions of the "world" of major sports events.

Notwithstanding the above, we do notice some interesting points and clustering (groups of associations). For example, for major sports events' management, the most important areas (those with the highest centrality and coreness) seem to be: HR, media, venues, legacies and sustainability, planning, stakeholders, Games-time, and risk management. Other important concepts seem to include: sport, leadership, technology, marketing, communications, financial, bidding, ceremonies, relationships, and wrap-up and closure. Additional

Figure 17.2 Relative importance of major sports event concepts.

concepts which have a significant degree of coreness include image and identity, tourism, spectators and fans, politics, government, and organizing. This is not to say that other areas are less important for major sports event managers (or researchers), simply that the identified areas are more closely associated. The K-core measure also provides the ability to create a dendogram that can provide cliques or association groupings for the concepts. Figure 17.3 provides a visual depiction of possible cliques and concept associations.

We encourage researchers to examine the conceptual maps and clusters presented here, build their own, and use the illustrated relationships found in these figures as starting points for potential research questions. We hope that this will catalyse theorizing/theory building associated with major sports events. Moreover, future research should build on the largely descriptive aspect of current research and popular books (e.g. Burbank *et al.*, 2001; Lenskyj, 2000; Yarbrough, 1996) in order to not only describe but also explain and then (perhaps) predict behaviour and event success since, ultimately, failure to host a successful event is unthinkable given the wide repercussions of such an event. Furthermore, research seems to have focused, for better or for worse, a great deal on the Olympic Games (and to a lesser extent on the FIFA World Cup). But there are so many other major sports events that can and should be studied, such as: the Asian Games, Cricket World Cup, World Police & Fire Games, Masters Games, North American Indigenous Games, Arctic Winter Games,

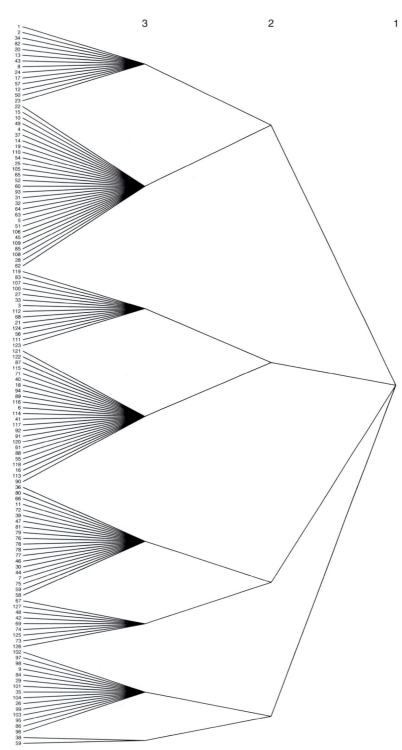

		3	2	1
Events	1			
Sport	2			
Stakeholders	34			
Risk management	82			
Marketing	20			
Venues	13			
Ceremonies	43			
HR	8			
Planning	24			
Legacies and sustainability	17			
Games-time	57			
Media	12			
Technology	50			
Bidding	23			
Politicians	22			
Tourism	15			
Image and identity	10			
Ethics and morals	49			
Community	4			
Milestones	37			
Financial	14			
Natural environment	19			
Leveraging	110			
Communication	54			
Implementation	25			
Destination marketing	105			
Visibility	65			
Ambush marketing	52			
Accountability	60			
Internet and new media	93			
Government	31			
Globalization	32			
Interdependence	64			
Participation	63			
Impacts and outcomes	5			
CSR	51			
Cause marketing	106			
Terrorism and violence	45			
Look-feel	109			
Legal	85			
Awareness	108			
Decision-making	28			
Activists	62			
Entertainment	119			
Language	83			
Loyalty	107			
Rituals	100			
Culture	27			
Project management	33			
Festivals	3			
Logistics	112			
Dignitaries	68			
Politics	21			
Communitas	124			
Protocol	56			
Experience-spectacle	111			
Authenticity	123			
Live sites	121			
Accommodations	122			
Accreditation and access	87			
Event services	115			
Branding	71			
Operations	40			
Delegations	18			
Athletes	94			
Transportation	89			
Cleaning and waste	116			
Economic impact	6			
Signage	114			
Venuization	41			
CADs	117			
Merchandise and licensing	92			
Food and beverages	91			
Field-of-play	120			
Infrastructure	61			
Security	88			
Venue management	55			
Sport production	118			
Spectators and fans	16			
Crowd management	113			
Tickets	90			
Skills and competencies	36			
Recruitment	80			
Support	66			
Change	11			
Adaptation	72			
Organizing	39			
Rewards and recognition	47			
Trust and respect	81			
Training	79			
Modelling	76			
Alliance	78			
Growth	78			
Figurehead	77			
Relationships	46			
Commitment	30			
Power and control	44			
Resources	7			
Mentoring	75			
Performance	59			
Team building	58			
Social issues	67			
Relationship marketing	127			
Networking	48			
Gypsies	42			
Effectiveness and efficiency	69			
Knowledge	74			
Power	125			
Learning	73			
Pride	126			
Values	102			
Fairness and justice	97			
Best practices	98			
Symbols	9			
Health	84			
Satisfaction	29			
Myths	101			
Sponsorship	35			
Reputation	104			
Motivation	26			
Conflict management	99			
Momentum	103			
Hiring	95			
Evaluation	86			
Integration	96			
Wrap-up and closure	38			
Leadership	59			

Figure 17.3 Concept clusters.

329

Maccabiah Games, and the host of world championships. These events are, more often than not, more likely to be a good fit with a broader range of cities around the world; smaller events can also more easily be hosted by many more cities around the world than the Olympic Games, and thus have more applicability for a greater number of sport event managers.

RECURRING THEMES AND FUTURE DIRECTIONS

In this section, we provide some reflections on what we feel are recurring themes or links between different parts of the book (that is, on the management of major sports events), interweaving these with managerial best practices and future research suggestions.

The Games must go on

One of the key messages that we want the reader – both the practitioner and researcher – to remember is that the Games must go on. Regardless of what one manager may or may not do (or have the ability to do), the Games will go on. Extremely rarely do major sports events get pulled from a host city, though it does happen. To wit, while the IOC had major concerns about Athens' readiness for the 2004 Olympic Games, it did not pull the event, nor did the CGF pull the 2010 CWG from Delhi. However, the 2005 FINA World Aquatics Championships were pulled from the host city of Montreal, Canada, only six months before the event was supposed to take place, due in no small part to major concerns about the progress of the event's facilities – a concern which had been noted for some time. Upon strong lobbying efforts, however, the city's mayor managed to regain the right to host the event one month later. In contrast, facility and political concerns have not been enough for FIFA to pull the 2014 FIFA World Cup from Brazil.

Understanding that the Games must go on will hopefully reduce some stress in managers fretting over the state of their function or the abilities of one of their employees or volunteers. These issues will be managed/resolved somehow. It also helps to remember that most people (clients, stakeholders) do not know what should happen at the event as it is their first major sports event. Thus, the expectations can be managed. This is the case of most host government officials, the community, and even many of the organizing committee's workforce members. Those who do know and have set expectations – whether formally or informally noted – include the athletes/delegations, sport organizations/federations, and the media representatives whose beat is sport and/or major sports events.

Still, the community are a wildcard as to how they will react. Ideally, the organizing committee needs to use an ONS-like group of marketing/communications within its organization or the event owner's to present data on the impact of the event on the community not only after the event but during the event. However, from an empirical perspective, not every sport organization has the data or the capacity to get such data. Of those who do, the data are often fraught with methodological or analytical problems (such as economic impact analyses). Thus, looking to past hosts for some of the intangible impacts, or the benefits of tangible impacts over a 20- or 30-year period, may be a fruitful avenue for managers.

It's about the experience

In order to produce a successful major sports event, there are needs that must be met, such as:

- efficient and effective transportation;
- proper (meeting established standards) venues, facilities, infrastructure, and services (e.g. F&B, dignitary lounges, and seating);
- proper security and risk management;
- preceding the sports event with other events (e.g. torch relay), attractions (e.g. culturally themed activities) to galvanize the host region and country, to build momentum and pride in the local and national spectators/residents;
- having gathering places (e.g. live sites, celebration sites) with appropriate – but not excessive – security for locals; and
- satisficing key stakeholders' (e.g. event owner, IF/NSF, host governments, and sponsors) expectations.

It is ultimately about the experience. The experience is based on the unique combination of people, space or place, and time. The event and its associated activities (e.g. live sites) should be designed to make people feel like they are part of the event, that they contribute to the event, even if they only watch on television. Interestingly, the spectacle-experience nodes in Figures 17.1 and 17.2 are not central, dominant in research. Perhaps the managerial link between those concepts seen as central in the research and the experience-spectacle is worth further examination.

Notwithstanding, part of the experience involves innovation. Innovation, of course, can come in the form of new technologies (e.g. use by media representatives, as well as athletes, of social and digital media) or new ways of doing things. The transportation shuttle system and Culture and Education Program of the 2012 Winter YOG noted above would be considered innovations for the Olympic Movement, as would the mixed gender, mixed NOC, and other new events presented at the YOG (both summer – Singapore 2010 – and winter – Innsbruck 2012). These innovations serve to (hopefully) enhance the client's (spectator, athlete, media, dignitary, or other) experience of the event, thereby enhancing satisfaction and the perceived success of the organizing committee and its event.

Organizational, strategic, and human resources management

First, planning activities are understandably at the core of managing a major sports event. Event managers need to get event stakeholders on the same page for the event's objectives to be achieved. All decisions should lead to the objectives. Events are increasingly stating that the athlete is at the centre of their mission (e.g. London 2012 Olympic Games). If these events use the athlete as the central aspect, then other "goals" like bilingualism, cultural and sport development, the spectator experience, etc., can end up becoming secondary. For example, the 2010 Olympic Winter Games' CEO had the athlete at the centre of his motivations, which placed decisions about bilingualism for other clients (spectators, dignitaries, etc.) in second (or worse) place, and led to a backlash by the media, government, and spectators on the lack of French during its opening ceremonies.

Second, an event is deemed successful if there are no perceived management problems occurring. Yet the perceived degree of planning occurring within the organizing committee will likely not be accurate from the outside. Many mistakes, problems, and challenges can and will occur inside the organizing committee, in the BOH; as long as they do not "leak" to the outside or FOH, the organizing committee can continue its efforts. This lack of transparency is not necessarily negative. While the Western world wants to stay apprised of the goings-on of an organizing committee's efforts, and this information helps keep stakeholders engaged, a lack of transparency in certain areas can avoid mayhem, reduce potential stress for certain groups, and even be legally mandated. To illustrate, had the spectators, athletes, and media known about a potential strike on the eve of the quarter-finals of the *2001 Jeux de la Francophonie's* most popular sport, there would have been confusion, stress (especially with the athletes and the rest of the organizing committee), decreased morale, and a general sense of chaos that would have been difficult to manage. Another example relates to most opening ceremonies details being known to only a very small number of individuals within the organization, despite efforts from other organizing committee members, governments, media, etc., to find out what will happen. Likewise, details of security plans are often only known by the security agencies and a select few top managers of the venues and organizing committee. As well, it is not uncommon for individuals who have never done a major sports event to say after the event that had they known what it would involve at the beginning, they may not have accepted to be part of the event, even if it was an experience of a lifetime. Thus, there can also be an intrusion of "too much information" in the decision-making processes of certain groups. As such, an event's executive team have the unenviable position of needing to balance the needs and requirements of information sharing versus withholding to keep stakeholders engaged, trusting, but not scare them off.

Third, there is a need to empower lower-level employees and volunteers so that the Games can occur successfully. To do this, the organizing committee's structure should be as flat as possible, at least come Games-time. The flatter the organizing committee's and VTeam's structures, the better communication can flow. Decisions can be made more quickly because individuals have the authority to do so, and little bureaucracy gets in the way of efficient and effective decision-making.

Fourth, HRM comes in at this point. HR managers must pick people and teams who collectively (e.g. in an FA) possess a combination of maturity, experience, skills, work ethic, self-directedness, ability to make decisions quickly and confidently, can accept responsibility, and can manage differences and different situations. The selection decisions will be moderated by those individuals who have already been selected/hired, prior "debts", protectionism, and loyalty to certain individuals, groups or organizations, among others. Still, how do you ferret out the required individuals? One option the HR manager has is behavioural description interviewing, in which scenarios are given to candidates to describe how they would handle a given situation, and where candidates can substantiate their characteristics and prior successes based on specific experiences or examples.

Individuals and their motivations

At the individual (staff, volunteer) level, the physical toll is the most obvious outcome of an event. Working long hours, eating not-so-great food, having to make just-in-time decisions, and generally living in a state of stress and adrenaline for weeks or months is a unique experience. Managers' and volunteers' emotional reactions while they perform their responsibilities is a potential area of future study. While some individuals find the event experience draining and choose to not do another event, others, who we term Games gypsies, seem to thrive on the adrenaline rush. Perhaps they feed off the adrenaline rush, become addicted to it, and therefore seek new events to repeat the experience. These individuals seem to rise to the occasion, time and time again. They have a passion for events. What makes a person become a Games gypsy? These individuals are an important source of knowledge that can be transferred from one event to the next and therefore become an important group to study in relation to the management of major sports events.

In addition, "must" is a wonderful master. When we *have* to do something, are pushed to the wall, we find ways to do things; we become creative, resourceful, and resilient beyond what we can imagine. "Must" gives a manager or volunteer the requisite skills for the next time. And the reason for doing the next event is because it will be different. This difference or newness is due to the different people, space/place, and time. The challenge, the draw, can be irresistible; this is perhaps another motivation for Games gypsies' continual move from one event to the next.

Future directions

Finally, we offer some paths for future research directions:

- Look for the patterns in successes, failures, execution, and challenges of the event to understand how major sports events work and how they can become more effective and efficient.
- Look to the Games gypsies for knowledge transfer, HRM choices, motivations, and behaviours (e.g. when they drop off the event bandwagon, what impacts them?).
- Look to the athlete – their motivations, their drive for competition – for the relevance of the event and its leveraging.
- Look to the event owners for the event structures, decisions, and future trends (e.g. importance of sustainability, the degree of possible innovation).
- Look to the community for the relevancy of wanting to bid/host events for the experience-spectacle. There is also nothing like relatives or important guests coming to town to motivate someone to clean their house or undertake renovations.
- Look to the media for their influence on images, reputation, brand, and momentum; understand their reasons and motivations. Some media questions also include: at what point do media consumers (e.g. newspaper readers) abandon the media's perspective to form their own images of the event? How can event managers bring the media in to the organizing committee's planning in a productive way?

- Look to the past in terms of people, space/place and time to understand the present and the future regarding decisions by the community, spectators, the media, athletes, sponsors, governments, and other stakeholders. Demographics, financial issues, and motivations (political, social, etc.) can assist in this understanding. Where do stakeholders' disparate or differing perspectives converge? What are the common intersections, especially those that the organizing committee can control or manage? If finances (cf. Parent, 2008) are a core juncture of event management practices, what can managers do from the outset regarding structure, stakeholder relationship management, marketing and branding, communications and public relations, athlete expectations, and other key areas to manage the financial issue?
- Look to the local, regional, national, and international governments and sponsors for the right funding structure balance, ownership, leveraging opportunities, and event impacts.

Finally, we would suggest that to research events, to truly understand them, one must have the inside knowledge of this often closed world; and this inside knowledge comes from working inside them (as a manager, volunteer, observer, or other).

CHAPTER SUMMARY

We hope that the book has offered practitioners the keys and knowledge to produce the proverbial "best Games ever", and that researchers are inspired to go in new directions, to develop sport event management theory. We have provided in this final chapter some recurring trends and thoughts for both the practitioner and the researcher, such as: understanding that the event will go on; that it is about the experience; that organizational, strategic, and human resource management are central; and that individuals and motivations are key. We also suggest managers and researchers look to the different stakeholders – their characteristics, motivations, behaviours – and the past, and gain major sports event experience in order to understand major sports event management theory and practice.

DISCUSSION AND THOUGHT-PROVOKING QUESTIONS

1   Describe a key area in which further investigation is needed, providing three examples of research questions. For each research question, provide a short description of an appropriate methodology.

2   How can managers use the theory and information garnered from research on major sports events?

3   What could a major sports event management theory look like?

4   Does major sports event management need its own theory or theories? Why or why not?

5   What would the sports landscape look like without major sporting events? What would the cascading effect be to the social, political, cultural, and academic sectors of our world?

FURTHER READING

We provide some additional readings to help the reader reflect on major sports events theory and practice:

Bacharach, S. B. (1989) Organizational theories: Some criteria for evaluation. *Academy of Management Review*, 14, 496–515.

Emery, P. (2010) Past, present, future major sport event management practice: The practitioner perspective. *Sport Management Review*, 13, 158–170.

Yeoman, I., Robertson, M., & Smith, K. (2012) A futurist's view on the future of events. In S. J. Page & J. Connell (eds), *The Routledge Handbook of Events* (pp. 507–525), London: Routledge.

Glossary

Accreditation   A badge held by a lanyard, demonstrating that the individual has been cleared by security to enter the event venue (usually for back-of-house access), and typically provides the venue(s) and area(s) or zone(s) to which the individual has been granted access.

Ambush marketing   A purposefully planned action (effort, campaign, etc.) by an organization to indirectly associate itself to an event for some benefit (e.g. commercial gain or name recognition) but that has not paid for the right to be an official sponsor of the event.

Bid considerations   The internal, process, and external factors to evaluate when deciding to bid for an event and preparing the bid documents. Bid considerations also include questions to ask oneself and issues to manage during the bid.

Bid phase   The period when an individual, group, or organization proposes to host an event (for informal bid processes) or competes for the right to host a given edition of an event (for formal bid processes).

Computer-assisted designs (CADs)   Drawings which chronicle the layout and life of all buildings and property associated with an event.

Crowd management   Security measures, site design, and operational factors regarding the crowd (e.g. ingress and egress, queuing, crisis management and emergency response strategies) to enhance the various clients' event experiences. It does not include force/law enforcement per se (this is crowd control).

Culture   The values and beliefs of a society, nation, sport, organization, or subgroup demonstrated through means of stories, rituals, artefacts, symbols, myths, heroes, rites, ceremonies, language, physical setting, power structures and hierarchy, dress codes, member behaviour, etc.

Economic impact analysis   Putting into economic form the direct, indirect, and induced benefits accrued from hosting a major sports event in the region.

Ego   A person's sense of self or self-importance.

Ethics   The scientific and analytical study of the theoretical bases of a person's moral action, where morals refer to the actual customs or manners.

Event brand   The tangible (e.g. distinct logo, look, name), intangible (e.g. values) and emotional elements that identify the event to its various stakeholders and distinguish it from other events.

Event ceremonies   The various celebrations found as part of a major sports event, which can include torch/flame, welcoming, flag raising, opening, victory/medals/flower, and closing ceremonies. These form the aesthetic and ritual context for the sports event.

Event rights holder   The event's owner

Feasibility study   An analysis of the community's, city's, region's, and/or country's capability to host a given event (e.g. facility review/assessment, event fit-out requirements, transportation capability, accommodations/hosting capability, sport expertise, and economic impact analyses and projections).

Financial planning   The determination of the event's goals and objectives, the strategic planning process, the operational and budgeting decisions, and the monitoring and control activities undertaken by the event owner and bid/organizing committee.

Functional area   An organizing committee department structured around a key task such as food and beverage, construction, sport, or protocol

Games-time period   The period beginning with the operational opening of the various venues and the transferring of decision-making power to the venue teams' managers so that they may handle crises at the venue level. It concludes at the end of the closing ceremonies.

Human resource management (HRM)   The coherent, strategic approach to managing the workforce members of an organizing committee who work together towards the common goal of preparing and executing the event. Planning, staffing, performance appraisals, rewards systems, and organizational justice are parts of HRM.

Leader   The top management individual or group of individuals who, together, have the political/networking, business/management, and sport/event skills to set up and run an organizing committee, and be the figurehead(s) of the event. Lower-level managers and experienced volunteers can also be seen as leaders because of their knowledge and experience.

Legacy   A planned or unplanned, tangible or intangible, positive or negative structure created by and/or for a major sports event which remains post-event.

Leveraging   A stakeholder's use of the event's hosting to optimize economic and/or social benefits and enhance the effects of hosting.

Main press centre (MPC)   The main venue for the written and photographic press where daily press conferences occur and all competition results and out-of-competition information can be found for the world's press members who are accredited to be part of the event. Together with the International Broadcast Centre, the main press centre forms the main media centre.

Major sports event   A planned (pre-determined lifecycle), temporary, special event that can be single- or multi-sport, one-off or recurring, have high attendance (participants and/or spectators), and media attention. They include recurring hallmark (events tied to a place), large-scale, and mega-events.

Media   The broadcast (television), press (traditional written media and photography), radio, and new media (all digital and internet-based media), along with event-specific media such as the Olympic Broadcast Service or Olympic News Service, found associated with a sports event.

Mixed zone   Usually a narrow walkway where athletes who exit the field of play must go through to allow accredited journalists (broadcast, press, and then others) to interview them immediately following a competition. The athlete may choose whether or not to stop to speak to the media.

New technologies   Emerging technology such as electronic equipment, new materials, the internet, and new media (e.g. Twitter, LinkedIn, Facebook, YouTube, 4G mobile smartphones, tablets, etc.).

Organizational symbolism   Those aspects used by the organization's members to demonstrate or expose the values, images, and feelings inherent to that organization.

Organizing committee   The group of individuals who work together towards the common goal of preparing and executing the sports event within a structured hierarchical system; the organization is typically incorporated as a non-profit organization.

Planning mode   The first operational mode of the organizing committee that includes the development of the business plan, operational plan, and divisional plans (including the bid and transition phases).

Project management   An approach to sport event management which focuses on the fact that sports events have pre-defined start and end dates. It involves developing and tracking the work breakdown structure, milestones, float, Gantt, and PERT charts, and the critical path.

Protocol   The set of (usually unwritten) rules, procedures, and guidelines dictating proper/generally accepted behaviours (i.e. norms) for dealing with state/diplomatic affairs and individuals for all matters associated with the major sports event.

Risk   A planned or unplanned dangerous element or uncertain aspect of an outcome caused by an individual and/or external force.

Risk management   The proactive process involving the assessment of all possible risks to the event and its stakeholders, and mitigating those risks by strategically planning responses, anticipating, minimizing, and preventing, the identified risks.

Ritual   Within the context of a specific event, a social action where we find a public demonstration/enactment or symbolic expression of a group's values and identity in a stylized manner.

Satisfice   The degree to which an event and its organizing committee satisfy and suffice the event's stakeholders.

Sponsorship   The provision of a cash and/or value in-kind fee that is paid to the event owner or organizing committee in exchange for the right to use the name/logo (or other aspect) of the event in its commercial activities, as well as access to the event itself.

Sport event lifecycle   This includes the planning (bid, business plan, operational plan, divisional plans), implementation (venue plans, venuization, Games-time), and wrap-up (decommissioning of venues, final report writing, legacy management) of an event.

Stakeholder   The different individuals, groups, and organizations who assist in and/or undertake certain responsibilities regarding the planning and/or implementation of the event, or who are impacted by the organizing committee's actions.

Stakeholder management   The process of identifying the stakeholders that are involved with the event and a particular manager, characterizing the stakeholders (needs, wants, desired degree of engagement, etc.), prioritizing them, and implementing strategies to manage them.

Sustainability   Post-event legacy associated with the triple bottom-line (social, economic, and environmental) principles.

Technology   Material/equipment-, knowledge-, or process- based, found at the industry, organizational, work/group, or individual levels; it can be conceptualized as a resource, a source of coordination, a force or trend, or a source of change.

Venue   A facility or site that serves as the sports event's competition or non-competition setting.

Venue lockdown   When the venue has been constructed and overlayed for the event, a full security sweep by the venue's security commander and his team occurs, after which the venue is locked down. This means that only appropriately accredited individuals and vehicles can enter the venue after passing through security screening areas.

Venue team (VTeam)   A kind of mini organizing committee found in each venue, composed of representatives of the different key functional areas, and headed by a venue general manager and his venue management team.

Venuization   the transferring of divisional plans to venue plans, including the workforce members' transition from headquarters to the various venues.

Volunteer   The short- or long-term unpaid workforce members of the organizing committee who have their own set of motivations, commitments, and satisfaction factors.

Workforce   The paid staff, secondees, consultants, contractors, and volunteers who make up the human resources of the organizing committee.

Wrap-up mode   The process that begins the moment the closing ceremonies have concluded. It can last up to one year. It includes debriefing and evaluating, decommissioning, writing the final reports and closing the books, and managing the legacies.

Bibliography

2010 Legacies Now (n.d.a) *Our History*. Online. Available at http://2010andbeyond.ca/#/our-history (accessed 27 December 2011).

2010 Legacies Now (n.d.b) *VANOC Sustainability Report*. Online. Available at www.2010legaciesnow.com/vanoc_sustainability (accessed 27 December 2011).

2011 World Police & Fire Games (2011) *2011 New York World Police & Fire Games: Information Kit*, Fort Totten, NY: Author. Online. Available at http://2011wpfg.org/News/PressRoom/PressKit/tabid/214/Default.aspx (accessed 2 March 2012).

Aaker, D. A. (1991) *Managing Brand Equity: Capitalizing on the Value of a Brand Name*, New York: The Free Press.

AccountingStudy.com (n.d.) *Accounting Study Guide*. Online. Available at http://accountinginfo.com/study/fs/fs-comp-101.htm (accessed 27 February 2012).

Adams, J. S. (1963) Toward an understanding of inequity. *Journal of Abnormal Social Psychology*, 67, 422–436.

Adams, J. S. (1965) Inequity in social exchange. In L. Berkowitz (ed.), *Advances in Experimental Social Psychology* (Vol. 2, pp. 267–299), New York: Academic Press.

Adenfelt, M. (2010) Exploring the performance of transnational projects: Shared knowledge, coordination and communication. *International Journal of Project Management*, 28, 529–538.

Aitken, R. (2011) Financializing security: Political prediction markets and the commodification of uncertainty. *Security Dialogue*, 42, 123–141.

Akhtar, J., Bjørnskau, T., & Veisten, K. (2010) Assessing security measures reducing terrorist risk: Inverse ex post cost–benefit and cost-effectiveness analyses of Norwegian airports and seaports. *Journal of Transportation Security*, 3, 179–195.

Alabarces, P., Tomlinson, A., & Young, C. (2001) Argentina versus England at the France '98 World Cup: Narratives of nation and the mythologizing of the popular. *Media, Culture and Society*, 23, 547–566.

Alberts, H. C. (2009) Berlin's failed bid to host the 2000 Summer Olympic Games: Urban development and the improvement of sports facilities. *International Journal of Urban and Regional Research*, 33, 502–516.

Alexander, K. & Brown, M. (2006) Community-based facilities management. *Facilities*, 24, 250–268.

Alexander, R. H. (1995) The economic impact of licensing logos, emblems and mascots. *Journal of Legal Aspects of Sport*, 5, 28–34.

Alkemeyer, T. & Richartz, A. (1993) The Olympic Games: From ceremony to show. *Olympika: The International Journal of Olympic Studies*, 2, 79–89.

Allen, J. B. & Shaw, S. (2009) "Everyone rolls up their sleeves and mucks in": Exploring volunteers' motivation and experiences of the motivational climate of a sporting event. *Sport Management Review*, 12, 79–90.

Alvesson, M. & Deetz, S. (1996) Critical theory and postmodernism approaches to organizational studies. In S. Clegg, C. Hardy, & W. R. Nord (eds), *Handbook of Organization Studies* (pp. 191–217), Thousand Oaks, CA: Sage Publications.

Alvesson, M. & Deetz, S. (2000) *Doing Critical Management Research*, Thousand Oaks, CA: Sage Publications.

Alvesson, M. & Kärreman, D. (2007) Unraveling HRM: Identity, ceremony, and control in a management consulting firm. *Organization Science*, 18, 711–723.

American Marketing Association. (2007) *Definition of Marketing*. Online. Available at www.marketingpower.com/AboutAMA/Pages/DefinitionofMarketing.aspx (accessed 26 October 2011).

Andersson, T. D., Armbrecht, J., & Lundberg, E. (2008) Impact of mega-events on the economy. *Asian Business and Management*, 7, 163–179.

Andrew, D. P. S., Seungmo, K., O'Neal, N., Greenwell, T. C., & James, J. D. (2009) The relationship between spectator motivations and media and merchandise consumption at a professional mixed martial arts event. *Sport Marketing Quarterly*, 18, 199–209.

Anstead, N. & O'Loughlin, B. (2011) Twenty20 as media event. *Sport in Society*, 14, 1340–1357.

Apostolopoulou, A. & Papadimitriou, D. (2004) "Welcome home": Motivations and objectives of the 2004 Grand National Olympic Sponsors. *Sport Marketing Quarterly*, 13, 180–192.

Appenzeller, H. (2005) Risk management in sport. In H. Appenzeller (ed.), *Risk Management in Sport: Issues and Strategies* (2nd edn, pp. 5–10), Durham, NC: Carolina Academic Press.

Arcodia, C. & Whitford, M. (2006) Festival attendance and the development of social capital. *Journal of Convention and Event Tourism*, 8(2), 1–18.

Armstrong, G. & Kotlar, P. (2005) *Marketing: An Introduction* (7th edn), Upper Saddle River, NJ: Pearson Education, Inc.

Armstrong, K. L. (1998) Ten strategies to employ when marketing sport to Black consumers. *Sport Marketing Quarterly*, 7, 11–18.

Armstrong, K. L. (2008) Consumers of color and the "culture" of sport attendance: Exploratory insights. *Sport Marketing Quarterly*, 17, 218–231.

Armstrong, M. (2003) *A Handbook of Human Resource Management Practice* (9th edn), Sterling, VA: Kogan Page Limited.

Armstrong-Doherty, A. J. (1996) Resource dependence-based perceived control: An examination of Canadian interuniversity athletics. *Journal of Sport Management*, 10, 49–64.

Arquembourg, J. (2006) From international events to global events: The outward signs of a worldwide sensitivity. *HERMES*, 46, 13–21.

Arquembourg, J. (2009) Who did the tsunami happen to? An analysis of the media account of events as part of a process in collective understanding. *Global Media and Communication*, 5, 389–404.

Aschkenasy, J. (1996) To insure or not to insure? Special events beg the question. *Risk Management*, 43, 66–69.

Associated Press (2011, 24 July) *2012 Olympic Soccer Ball to be Called "The Albert"*. Online.

341

Available at http://sports.espn.go.com/espn/wire?section=oly&id=6798691 (accessed 9 March 2012).

Atkinson, M. & Young, K. (2002) Terror games: Media treatment of security issues at the 2002 Winter Olympic Games. *Olympika: The International Journal of Olympic Studies*, 11, 53–78.

Augustin, J. P. (2009) Les Jeux Olympiques, l'événement spatial par excellence (The Olympic Games, the quintessential spatial event). *Bulletin de l'Association des Géographes Français*, 86, 303–311.

Aven, T. & Renn, O. (2009) The role of quantitative risk assessments for characterizing risk and uncertainty and delineating appropriate risk management options, with special emphasis on terrorism risk. *Risk Analysis: An International Journal*, 29, 587–600.

Avolio, B. J. & Gardner, W. L. (2005) Authentic leadership development: Getting to the root of positive forms of leadership. *The Leadership Quarterly*, 16, 315–338.

Avolio, B. J. & Yammarino, F. J. (1990) Operationalizing charismatic leadership using a levels-of-analysis framework. *Leadership Quarterly*, 1, 193–208.

Axford, B. & Huggins, R. (2011) Cricket for people who don't like cricket? Twenty20 as expression of the cultural and media zeitgeist. *Sport in Society*, 14, 1326–1339.

Bach, L. (1993) Sports without facilities: the use of urban spaces by informal sports. *International Review for the Sociology of Sport*, 28, 281–297.

Bachmann, R. (2001) Trust, power and control in trans-organizational relations. *Organization Studies*, 22, 337–365.

Bagdikian, B. H. (2000) *The Media Monopoly*, Boston, MA: Beacon.

Bakan, J. (2004) *The Corporation: The Pathological Pursuit of Profit and Power*, Toronto: Penguin Books.

Baker, T. & Jones, S. A. (2011) The inevitable queue: Exploring the impact of wait time at sporting events. *International Journal of Sports Marketing & Sponsorship*, 13, 49–59.

Balduck, A.-L., Maes, M., & Buelens, M. (2011) The social impact of the Tour de France: comparisons of residents' pre- and post-event perceptions. *European Sport Management Quarterly*, 11, 91–113.

Banerjee, D., Cronan, T. P., & Jones, T. W. (1998) Modeling IT ethics: A study in situational ethics. *MIS Quarterly*, 22(1), 31–60.

Bang, H. (2009) The direct and indirect influences of sporting event organization's reputation on volunteer commitment. *Event Management*, 13, 139–152.

Bang, H., Won, D., & Kim, Y. (2009) Motivations, commitment, and intentions to continue volunteering for sporting events. *Event Management*, 13, 69–81.

Barclay, C. & Osei-Bryson, K. (2009) Toward a more practical approach to evaluating programs: The multi-objective realization approach. *Project Management Journal*, 40(4), 74–93.

Barget, E. & Gouguet, J.-J. (2010) Hosting mega-sporting events: Which decision-making rule? *International Journal of Sport Finance*, 5, 141–162.

Barghchi, M., Omar, D. B., & Aman, M. S. (2009) Cities, sports facilities development, and hosting events. *European Journal of Social Sciences*, 10, 185–195.

Barley, S. (1986) Technology as an occasion for structuring: Evidence from observation of CT scanners and the social order of radiology departments. *Administrative Science Quarterly*, 31, 78–109.

Barnes, M. D., Hanson, C. L., Novilla, L. M. B., Meacham, A. T., McIntyre, E., & Erickson, B. C. (2008) Analysis of media agenda setting during and after Hurricane Katrina: Implications for emergency preparedness, disaster response, and disaster policy. *American Journal of Public Health*, 98, 604–610.

Barney, R. K. (1998) The great transformation: Olympic victory ceremonies and the medal podium. *Olympika: The International Journal of Olympic Studies*, 7, 89–112.

Barnum, C. F. (1989) The making of a global business diplomat. *Management Review*, 78, 59–60.

Barros, C. P., De Barros, C., Santos, A., & Chadwick, S. (2007) Sponsorship brand recall at the Euro 2004 soccer tournament. *Sport Marketing Quarterly*, 16, 161–170.

Barth, M. E. (2006) Including estimates of the future in today's financial statements. *Accounting Horizons*, 20, 271–285.

Bartunek, J. M. (1984) Changing interpretive schemes and organizational restructuring: The example of a religious order. *Administrative Science Quarterly*, 29, 355–372.

Basefsky, M., Post, A., Maxwell, J. L., & Turner, B. G. (2004) What are the five most important qualities of an effective leader? *American Water Works Association Journal*, 96, 34–36.

Bass, B. M. (1990a) *Bass and Stogdill's Handbook of Leadership: A Survey of Theory and Research*, New York: Free Press.

Bass, B. M. (1990b) From transactional to transformational leadership: Learning to share the vision. *Organizational Dynamics*, 18, 19–31.

Bass, B. M. & Avolio, B. J. (1990a) The implications of transactional and transformational leadership, team, and organizational development. *Research in Organizational Change and Development*, 4, 231–272.

Bass, B. M. & Avolio, B. J. (1990b) Transformational leadership and organizational culture. *International Journal of Public Administration*, 17, 541–554.

Bassat, L. (1995) The creativity of the Barcelona '92 Olympic ceremonies. In International Olympic Committee (ed.), *Olympic Ceremonies: Historical Continuity and Cultural Exchange* (pp. 241–250), Lausanne: International Olympic Committee.

Batac, T. & Lem, L. (2008) Transportation strategies to mitigate climate change. *Leadership and Management in Engineering*, 8, 124–131.

Battenfield, F. L. & Kent, A. (2007) The culture of communication among intercollegiate sport information professionals. *International Journal of Sport Management and Marketing*, 2, 236–251.

Baycan-Levent, T. & Nijkamp, P. (2009) Planning and management of urban green spaces in Europe: Comparative analysis. *Journal of Urban Planning and Development*, 135, 1–12.

BBC Sport (2005) *Rivals for 2012: Paris*, London, BBC Sport. Online. Available at http://news.bbc.co.uk/sport2/hi/other_sports/olympics_2012/4233055.stm (accessed 24 November 2010).

BBC Sport (2008, 4 June) *Four on 2016 Olympics Short-List*. Online. Available at http://news.bbc.co.uk/sport2/hi/olympics/7435215.stm (accessed 16 September 2011).

Beaven, Z. & Laws, C. (2007) "Never let me down again": Loyal customer attitudes towards ticket distribution channels for live music events – a netnographic exploration of the US leg of the Depeche Mode 2005–2006 World Tour. *Managing Leisure*, 12, 120–142.

Beck, U. (1992) *Risk Society: Towards a New Modernity* (M. Ritter, trans.), London: Sage Publications.

Beesley, L. G. & Chalip, L. (2011) Seeking (and not seeking) to leverage mega-sport events in non host destinations: The case of Shanghai and the Beijing Olympics. *Journal of Sport & Tourism*, 16, 323–344.

Beike, D. R., Markman, K. D., & Karadogan, F. (2009) What we regret most are lost opportunities: A theory of regret intensity. *Personality and Social Psychology Bulletin*, 35, 385–397.

Beis, D. A., Loucopoulos, P., Pyrgiotis, Y., & Zografos, K. G. (2006) PLATO helps Athens win gold: Olympic Games knowledge modeling for organizational change and resource management. *Interfaces*, 36 (1), 26–42.

Bell, E. & Taylor, S. (2011) Beyond letting go and moving on: New perspectives on organizational death, loss and grief. *Scandinavian Journal of Management*, 27, 1–10.

Bennett, G., Cunningham, G., & Dees, W. (2006a) Measuring the marketing communication activations of a professional tennis tournament. *Sport Marketing Quarterly*, 15, 91–101.

Bennett, G., Sagas, M., & Dees, W. (2006b) Media preferences of action sports consumers: Differences between Generation X and Y. *Sport Marketing Quarterly*, 15, 40–49.

Berger, I. E., O'Reilly, N., Parent, M. M., Séguin, B., & Hernandez, T. (2008) Determinants of sport participation among Canadian adolescents. *Sport Management Review*, 11, 277–307.

Bernstein, A. (2000) "Things you can see from there you can't see from here": Globalization, media, and the Olympics. *Journal of Sport & Social Issues*, 24, 351–369.

Bernstein, A. (2002) Is it time for a victory lap? Changes in the media coverage of women in sport. *International Review for the Sociology of Sport*, 37, 415–428.

Berrett, T., Slack, T., & Whitson, D. (1993) Economics and the pricing of sport and leisure. *Journal of Sport Management*, 7, 199–215.

Berry, A. & Jarvis, R. (2006) *Accounting in a Business Context*, London: International Thomson Business Press.

Betlehem, J. & Schaefer, J. (2010) Emergency medical preparedness during the 2006 World Cup in Frankfurt, Germany. *Disasters*, 34, 155–163.

Bhargava, S. & Sinha, B. (1992) Prediction of organizational effectiveness as a function of type of organizational structure. *Journal of Social Psychology*, 132, 223–231.

Bhattacharjee, S. & Rao, G. (2006) Tackling ambush marketing: The need for regulation and analysing the present legislative and contractual efforts. *Sport in Society*, 9, 128–149.

Billings, A. C., Craig, C. C., Croce, R., Cross, K. M., Moore, K. M., Vigodsky, W., & Watson, V. G. (2006) "Just one of the guys?" Network depictions of Annika Sorenstam in the 2003 PGA Colonial Tournament. *Journal of Sport & Social Issues*, 30, 107–114.

Birmingham, J. & David, M. (2011) Live-streaming: Will football fans continue to be more law abiding than music fans? *Sport in Society*, 14(1), 69–80.

Bisson, M. (2010) *Qatar 2022 World Cup Bid Reveals New Stadium Plans and Cooling Technologies*. Online. Available at www.worldfootballinsider.com/Story.aspx?id=33206 (accessed 24 February 2011).

Black, D. & Peacock, B. (2011) Catching up: Understanding the pursuit of major games by rising developmental states. *International Journal of the History of Sport*, 28 (16), 2271–2289.

Black, J. A., Paez, A., & Suthanaya, P. A. (2002) Sustainable urban transportation: Performance indicators and some analytical approaches. *Journal of Urban Planning and Development*, 128(4), 184–209.

Bladen, C. R. (2010) Media representation of volunteers at the Beijing Olympic Games. *Sport in Society*, 13, 784–796.

Bloyce, D., Liston, K., Platts, C., & Smith, A. (2010) Pride of the Lions: A sociological analysis of media coverage of the 2005 tour from the perspective of the Four Home Nations. *Sport in Society*, 13, 448–469.

Bluedorn, A. (1991) Three modern classics: A very special book review section. *Journal of Management*, 17, 489–509.

Boals, A., Banks, J. B., Hathaway, L. M., & Schuettler, D. (2011) Coping with stressful events: Use of cognitive words in stressful narratives and the meaning-making process. *Journal of Social and Clinical Psychology*, 30, 378–403.

Boardman, A. E. & Hargreaves-Heap, S. P. (1999) Network externalities and government restrictions on satellite broadcasting of key sporting events. *Journal of Cultural Economics*, 23, 165.

Boccia, L. V. (2010) Brazil: Cultural enchantment – the Beijing Olympic Games torch lighting ceremony and torch relay. Brazil's warm-up coverage. *International Journal of the History of Sport*, 27, 1534–1548.

Boccia, L. V., Argolo, L. D. T. E., Leandro, P. R., Gomes, J. F., & Fonseca, P. (2010) Brazil: Beijing changes the way mega-media events are presented – perspectives of 2008 Beijing Olympic Games. *International Journal of the History of Sport*, 27, 1759–1777.

BOCOG (2008) *Accreditation*, Lausanne: International Olympic Committee.

Bogner, W. C. & Barr, P. S. (2000) Making sense in hypercompetitive environments: A cognitive explanation for the persistence of high velocity competition. *Organization Science*, 11, 212–226.

Boilé, M. P. (2002) Evaluating the efficiency of transportation services on intermodal commuter networks. *Transportation Quarterly*, 56, 75–91.

Bonacich, P. (1972) Factoring and weighting approaches to status scores and clique identification. *Journal of Mathematical Sociology*, 2, 113–120.

Borgatti, S. P. (2002) *Netdraw Network Visualization*, Harvard, MA: Analytic Technologies.

Borgatti, S. P., Everett, M. G., & Freeman, L. C. (2002) *Ucinet for Windows: Software for Social Network Analysis*, Harvard, MA: Analytic Technologies.

Bouchet, P., Bodet, G., Bernache-Assollant, I., & Kada, F. (2011a) Segmenting sport spectators: Construction and preliminary validation of the Sporting Event Experience Search (SEES) scale. *Sport Management Review*, 14, 42–53.

Bouchet, P., Castel, P., & Lacassagne, M.-F. (2011b) Comment analyser les relations déviantes potentiellement violentes ou discriminatoires dans le spectacle sportif au stade? *Sport Science Review*, 20, 137–165.

Bourgeon, D. & Bouchet, P. (2001) La recherche d'expériences dans la consommation du spectacle sportif. *Revue Européenne de Management du Sport*, 6, 1–47.

Bradshaw, P. (2008) When journalists blog: How it changes what they do. *Nieman Reports*, 62(4), 50.

Braid, R. M. (1991) The locations of congestible facilities in adjacent jurisdictions. *Regional Science and Urban Economics*, 21, 617–626.

Branham, L. (2004) *The 7 Hidden Reasons Employees Leave: How to Recognize the Subtle Signs and Act Before it's too Late*, New York: AMACOM.

345

Brass, D. J. & Burkhardt, M. E. (1993) Potential power and power use: An investigation of structure and behavior. *Academy of Management Journal*, 36, 441–470.

Braverman, J., LaBrie, R. A., & Shaffer, H. J. (2011) A taxometric analysis of actual internet sports gambling behavior. *Psychological Assessment*, 23(1), 234–244.

Bresler, N. C. (2011) Tourist considerations in hosting a mega sport event: 2010 FIFA World Cup in South Africa. *South African Journal for Research in Sport, Physical Education & Recreation (SAJR SPER)*, 33, 17–33.

Bridges, B. (2011) The making of a modest mega-event: Hong Kong and the 2009 EastAsian games. *International Journal of the History of Sport*, 28, 2384–2397.

Briedenhann, J. (2011) Economic and tourism expectations of the 2010 FIFA World Cup: A resident perspective. *Journal of Sport & Tourism*, 16, 5–32.

Bristow, D. N. & Schneider, K. C. (2006) An investigation of the customer orientation of professional sports organizations: Development of the Sports Fan Orientation Scale (SFOS). *Journal of Hospitality and Leisure Marketing*, 15, 27–44.

Brown, G. G. & Cox Jr., L. A. (2011) How probabilistic risk assessment can mislead terrorism risk analysts. *Risk Analysis: An International Journal*, 31, 196–204.

Brown, M. T. (2003) An analysis of online marketing in the sport industry: User activity, communication objectives, and perceived benefits. *Sport Marketing Quarterly*, 12, 48–55.

Bryman, A. (1992) *Charisma and Leadership in Organizations*, London: Sage Publications.

Buford, B. (1993) *Among the Thugs*, London: Random House.

Bullen, P. A. (2007) Adaptive reuse and sustainability of commercial buildings. *Facilities*, 25, 20–31.

Burbank, M. J., Andranovich, G. D., & Heying, C. H. (2001) *Olympic Dreams: The Impact of Mega-Events on Local Politics*, London: Lynne Rienner.

Burger, E. & Saayman, M. (2009) Key success factors in managing a conference centre in South Africa. *South African Journal for Research in Sport, Physical Education & Recreation (SAJR SPER)*, 31, 15–28.

Burns, J. (1978) *Leadership*, New York: Harper & Row.

Burns, M. R. & Faurot, D. J. (1992) An econometric forecasting model of revenues from urban parking facilities. *Journal of Economics and Business*, 44, 143–150.

Burt, R. S. (2000) The network structure of social capital. *Research in Organizational Behaviour*, 22, 345–423.

Burton, N. & Chadwick, S. (2009) Ambush marketing in sport: An analysis of sponsorship protection means and counter-ambush measures. *Journal of Sponsorship*, 2, 303–315.

Byers, T., Slack, T., & Parent, M. M. (2012) *Key Concepts in Sport Management*, London: Sage Publications.

Canadian Centre for Ethics in Sport (2011) *Threats to Sport*. Online. Available at www.cces.ca/en/home (accessed 27 October 2011).

Canadian Sport Tourism Alliance (2011) *STEAM (Sport Tourism Economic Assessment Model)*. Online. Available at http://canadiansporttourism.com/industry-tools/steam-sport-tourism-economic-assessment-model.html (accessed 8 August 2011).

Cantrav Services Inc. & EMS Event Management Solutions Inc. (2010) *Success Through Knowledge, Resources and Relationships: Games IQ*, Vancouver: Author.

Capranica, L. & Aversa, F. (2002) Italian television sport coverage during the 2000 Sydney

Olympic Games: A gender perspective. *International Review for the Sociology of Sport*, 37, 337–349.

Capranica, L., Minganti, C., Billat, V., Hanghoj, S., Piacentini, M. F., Cumps, E., & Meeusen, R. (2005) Newspaper coverage of women's sports during the 2000 Sydney Olympic Games: Belgium, Denmark, France, and Italy. *Research Quarterly for Exercise & Sport*, 76, 212–223.

Carey, J. (1976) How media shape campaigns. *Journal of Communication*, 26, 50.

Carey, M., Mason, D. S., & Misener, L. (2011) Social responsibility and the competitive bid process for major sporting events. *Journal of Sport and Social Issues*, 35, 246–263.

Carlsson, S. A. & El Sawy, O. A. (2008) Managing the five tensions of IT-enabled decision support in turbulent and high-velocity environments. *Information Systems and e-Business Management*, 6, 225–237.

Carrard, F. (1995) The Olympic message in ceremonies: The vision of the IOC. In International Olympic Committee (ed.), *Olympic Ceremonies: Historical Continuity and Cultural Exchange* (pp. 23–28), Lausanne: International Olympic Committee.

Carroll, A. B. (1991) The pyramid of corporate social responsibility: Toward the moral management of organizational stakeholders. *Business Horizons*, 34, 30–48.

Carroll, A. B. (1996) *Business and Society: Ethics and Stakeholder Management* (3rd edn), Cincinnati, OH: South-Western College Publishing.

Carroll, A. B. (1999) Corporate social responsibility: Evolution of a definitional construct. *Business & Society*, 38, 268–295.

Carron, A. V. & Chelladurai, P. (1981) Dynamics of group cohesion in sport. *Journal of Sport Psychology*, 3, 123–139.

Case, B. W., Greer, H. S., & Lacourse, M. G. (1987) Moral judgement development and perceived legitimacy of spectator behavior in sport. *Journal of Sport Behavior*, 10, 147–156.

Case, R., Dey, T., Hobbs, S., Hoolachan, J., & Wilcox, A. (2010) An examination of sporting event direct-spending patterns at three competitive levels. *Journal of Convention & Event Tourism*, 11, 119–137.

Casanovas, J. M. (1995) Ceremonies within the framework of sporting events. In International Olympic Committee (ed.), *Olympic Ceremonies: Historical Continuity and Cultural Exchange* (pp. 257–260), Lausanne: International Olympic Committee.

Cashman, K. (2001) *Leadership from the Inside Out: Becoming a Leader for Life*, Provo, UT: Executive Excellence Publishing.

Cashman, R. (1999) Olympic legacy in an Olympic city: Monuments, museums and memory. In *Fourth International Symposium for Olympic Research* (pp. 107–113), London, Ontario, Canada.

Cashman, R. (2000) Olympic scholars and Olympic records: Access and management of the records of an Olympic Games. In *Fifth International Symposium for Olympic Research* (pp. 207–214), Sydney, Australia.

Cashman, R. (2006) *The Bitter-Sweet Awakening: The Legacy of the Sydney 2000 Olympic Games*, Sydney: Walla Walla Press.

Cashman, R. (2008) The Australian Olympic caravan in Beijing: Ninth International Symposium for Olympic Research, Beijing, China, August 2008. In R. Barney, M. Heine, K. Wamsley, & G. MacDonald (eds), *Pathways: Critiques and Discourse in Olympic Research* (pp. 509–519), Ontario: The International Centre for Olympic Studies.

347

Časlavova, E. & Berka, P. (2005) The financial management of sports clubs in the Czech Republic. *Kinesiology*, 37, 204–213.

CBC (2010, 17 December) *Vancouver Olympics Broke Even: VANOC*. Online. Available at www.cbc.ca/news/canada/british-columbia/story/2010/12/17/bc-vanoc-final-report.html (accessed 27 December 2011).

Cecil, N. (2012, 11 January) Britain stockpiles anthrax vaccine against Olympic attack. *London Evening Standard*. Online. Available at http://politics.standard.co.uk/2012/01/britain-stockpiles-anthrax-vaccine-against-olympic-attack.html (accessed 10 April 2012).

Chalip, L. (1992) The construction and use of polysemic structures: Olympic lessons for sport marketing. *Journal of Sport Management*, 6, 87–98.

Chalip, L. (2004) Beyond impact: A general model for sport event leverage. In B. W. Ritchie & D. Adair (eds), *Sport Tourism: Interrelationships, Impacts and Issues* (pp. 226–252), Clevedon: Channel View.

Chalip, L. (2006) Towards social leverage of sport events. *Journal of Sport & Tourism*, 11, 109–127.

Chalip, L. & Costa, C. A. (2005) Sport event tourism and the destination brand: Towards a general theory. *Sport in Society*, 8, 218–237.

Chalip, L. & Leyns, A. (2002) Local business leveraging of a sport event: Managing an event for economic benefit. *Journal of Sport Management*, 16, 132–158.

Chalip, L., Green, B. C., & Hill, B. (2003) Effects of sport event media on destination image and intention to visit. *Journal of Sport Management*, 17, 214–234.

Chalkley, B. & Essex, S. (1999) Urban development through hosting international events: A history of the Olympic Games. *Planning Perspectives*, 14, 369–394.

Chan, E. H. W. & Lee, G. K. L. (2009) Design considerations for environmental sustainability in high density development: A case study of Hong Kong. *Environment, Development and Sustainability*, 11, 359–374.

Chanavat, N. & Ferrand, A. (2010) Volunteer programme in mega sport events: The case of the Olympic Winter Games, Torino 2006. *International Journal of Sport Management & Marketing*, 7, 241–266.

Chanavat, N., Martinent, G., & Ferrand, A. (2010) Brand images causal relationships in multiple sport event sponsorship context: Developing brand value through association with sponsees. *European Sport Management Quarterly*, 10, 49–74.

Chang, P. C. & Singh, K. K. (1990) Risk management for mega-events: The 1988 Olympic Winter Games. *Tourism Management*, 11, 45–52.

Chapin, T. (2000) The political economy of sport facility location: An end-of-the-century review and assessment. *Marquette Sport Law Review*, 10, 361–382.

Chappelet, J. (1995) From Moscow (1980) to Lillehammer (1994): Ceremonies and the televised spectacle. In International Olympic Committee (ed.), *Olympic Ceremonies: Historical Continuity and Cultural Exchange* (pp. 153–156), Lausanne: International Olympic Committee.

Chappelet, J.-L. (2001) Risk management for large-scale events: The case of the Olympic Winter Games. *European Journal for Sport Management*, 8(Special Issue), 6–21.

Chappelet, J.-L. (2006) The tale of three Olympic cities – forecast for Torino on basis of Grenoble and Innsbruck. Torino 2006 – XX Winter Olympic Games Symposium, 9 February 2006, Turin, Italy.

Chappelet, J.-L. (2008) Olympic environmental concerns as a legacy of the Winter Games. *The International Journal of the History of Sport*, 25, 1884–1902.

Chappelet, J.-L. (2009) Corporate social responsibility: A new frontier for the IOC. In P. Rodriguez, S. Kesenne & H. Dietl (eds), *Social Responsibility and Sustainability in Sports* (pp. 17–29), Oviedo: Universidad de Oviedo.

Chappelet, J.-L. (2011) Strategic management and planning. In L. Robinson & D. Palmer (eds), *Managing Voluntary Sport Organisations* (pp. 51–69), London: Routledge.

Chappelet, J.-L. (2012, 12 January) *Mega Sports Event Legacy: The Case of Innsbruck*. Keynote presentation at the 4th International Sport Business Symposium, Innsbruck, Austria.

Chappelet, J.-L. & Kübler-Mabbott, B. (2008) *The International Olympic Committee and the Olympic System: The Governance of World Sport*, Abingdon: Routledge.

Chatty, D. (2009) Rituals of royalty and the elaboration of ceremony in Oman: View from the edge. *International Journal of Middle East Studies*, 41, 39–58.

Chelladurai, P. (1999) *Human Resource Management in Sport and Recreation*, Champaign, IL: Human Kinetics.

Chen, C. C. & Colapinto, C. (2010) The run-up to the Beijing Olympics in Switzerland and Italy. *International Journal of the History of Sport*, 27, 1461–1472.

Cheng-Li, H. & Mien-Ling, C. (2009) The effect of attitudes towards the budgetary process on attitudes towards budgetary slack and behaviors to create budgetary slack. *Social Behavior & Personality: An International Journal*, 37, 661–671.

Chengli, T., Huai-Chun, L., & Hsiou-Wei, L. (2011) The economic benefits of mega events: A myth or a reality? A longitudinal study on the Olympic Games. *Journal of Sport Management*, 25, 11–23.

Chia-Chen, Y. (2010) Factors that influence international fans' intention to travel to the United States for sport tourism. *Journal of Sport & Tourism*, 15, 111–137.

Child, J. (1984) *Organization: A Guide to Problems and Practice* (2nd edn), London: Chapman.

Child, J. & Smith, C. (1987) The context and process of organizational transformation: Cadbury Limited in its sector. *Journal of Management Studies*, 24, 565–593.

Choi, Y. S. & Yoh, T. (2011) Exploring the effect of communication channels on sponsorship effectiveness: a case study of Super Bowl XLII. *International Journal of Sport Management and Marketing*, 9, 75–93.

Chwen Chen, C. & Colapinto, C. (2010) Beijing Olympics between media, sport and politics: Perspectives from the Swiss and Italian media. *International Journal of the History of Sport*, 27, 1694–1716.

Cianfrone, B. A. & Zhang, J. J. (2006) Differential effects of television commercials, athlete endorsements, and venue signage during a televised action sports event. *Journal of Sport Management*, 20, 322–344.

Cianfrone, B., Bennett, G., Siders, R., & Tsuji, Y. (2006) Virtual advertising and brand awareness. *International Journal of Sport Management and Marketing*, 1, 289–310.

Cinquanta, O. & Schmid, F. (2011, 24 March) *ISU World Figure Skating Championships 2011*. Online. Available at www.sportcentric.com/vsite/vcontent/content/news/0,10869,4844-203666-220889-18885-312988-news-item,00.html (accessed 16 June 2011).

Clarke, K. S. (2005) On issues and strategies. In H. Appenzeller (ed.), *Risk Management in Sport: Issues and Strategies* (2nd edn, pp. 11–22), Durham, NC: Carolina Academic Press.

Clarkson, M. B. E. (1995) A stakeholder framework for analyzing and evaluating corporate social performance. *Academy of Management Review*, 20, 92–117.

Cleary, M. (2002, 26 April) Envoy vows Greece will be ready for 2004 Games. *The Ottawa Citizen*, p. A13.

Close, A. G., Finney, R. Z., Lacey, R. Z., & Sneath, J. Z. (2006) Engaging the consumer through event marketing: Linking attendees with the sponsor, community, and brand. *Journal of Advertising Research*, 46, 420–433.

Coaffee, J. & Fussey, P. (2011) Olympic security. In J. R. Gold & M. M. Gold (eds), *Olympic Cities: City Agendas, Planning, and the World's Games, 1896–2016* (2nd edn, pp. 167–179), Abingdon: Routledge.

Coalter, F. (2004) Stuck in the blocks? A sustainable sporting legacy. In A. Vigor, M. Mean, & C. Tims (eds), *After the Gold Rush: A Sustainable Olympics for London* (pp. 91–108), London: IPPR and Demos.

Coates, B. E. (2004) Corporate culture, corporate mischief, and legislated ethics: The Sarbanes–Oxley Act. *Journal of Public Affairs*, 7, 39–58.

Coates, D. & Humphreys, B. R. (2005) Novelty effects of new facilities on attendance at professional sporting events. *Contemporary Economic Policy*, 23, 436–455.

Cobbs, J. & McKelvey, S. (2009) The practice of brand extension through licensing: The Spalding challenge. *Sport Management Review (Elsevier Science)*, 12, 185–192.

Cohn, A. (1999) *One Day in September* [Movie], Culver City, CA: A Passion Pictures Production.

Cole, M. D. (2004) Turf wars heat up as technology enhances artificial playing surfaces. *International Fiber Journal*, 19(5), 14–16.

Collins, H. & Evans, R. (2008) You cannot be serious! Public understanding of technology with special reference to "hawk-Eye". *Public Understanding of Science*, 17, 283–308.

Comfort, L. K. (2005) Risk, security, and disaster management *Annual Review of Political Science*, 8, 335–356.

Cominsky, P., Bryant, J., & Zillmann, D. (1977) Sports: The medium is the stadium commentary as a substitute for action. *Journal of Communication*, 27(3), 150–153.

Conger, J. A. & Kanungo, R. N. (1987) Toward a behavioral theory of charismatic leadership in organizational settings. *The Academy of Management Review*, 12, 637–648.

Conrad, M. (2008) "Fleeting expletives" and sports broadcasts: A legal nightmare needs a safe harbor. *Journal of Legal Aspects of Sport*, 18, 175–205.

Copeland, R., Frisby, W., & McCarville, R. (1996) Understanding the sport sponsorship process from a corporate perspective. *Journal of Sport Management*, 10, 32–48.

Cordeiro, W. P. (2003) Should business ethics be different in transitional economies? *Journal of Business Ethics*, 47, 327–334.

Cornelissen, S. (2010) Using mega-events sustainability indicators to inform legacy practice: Lessons from South Africa. In C. Pentifallo, *Sport Mega-Events, Sustainability, and Impact Assessment Summary Report* (pp. 11–14). Proceedings from the UBC Centre for Sport and Sustainability Invitational Think Tank, 18 February 2010, Vancouver, Canada: UBC Centre for Sport & Sustainability.

Cornelissen, S. (2011) Mega event securitisation in a third world setting: Glocal processes and ramifications during the 2010 FIFA world cup. *Urban Studies*, 48, 3221–3240.

Cornelissen, S., Bob, U., & Swart, K. (2011) Towards redefining the concept of legacy in relation to sport mega-events: Insights from the 2010 FIFA world cup. *Development Southern Africa*, 28, 307–318.

Cornwell, T. G., Relyea, G. E., Irwin, R. L., & Maignan, I. (2000) Understanding long-term effects of sports sponsorship: Role of experience, involvement, enthusiasm and clutter. *International Journal of Sports Marketing & Sponsorship*, 2, 127–143.

Costa, C., Chalip, C., Green, C., & Simes, C. (2006) Reconsidering the role of training in event volunteers' satisfaction. *Sport Management Review*, 9, 165–182.

Council of Europe (n.d.) *Common European Framework of Reference for Languages: Learning, Teaching, Assessment (CEFR)*. Online. Available at www.coe.int/t/dg4/linguistic/CADRE_EN.asp (accessed 27 February 2012).

Courty, P. (2003) Ticket pricing under demand uncertainty. *Journal of Law and Economics*, 46, 627–652.

Cowie, C. & Williams, M. (1997) The economics of sports rights. *Telecommunications Policy*, 21, 619–634.

Cox, P. M., II (1995) Flag on the play? The siphoning effect on sports television. *Federal Communications Law Journal*, 47, 571–591.

Crelinstein, R. (1994) The impact of television on terrorism and crisis situations: Implications for public policy. *Journal of Contingencies and Crisis Management*, 2, 61–72.

Crompton, J. L. (1993) Sponsorship of sport by tobacco and alcohol companies: A review of the issues. *Journal of Sport & Social Issues*, 17, 148–167.

Crompton, J. L. (1994) Benefits and risks associated with sponsorship of major events. *Festival Management & Event Tourism*, 2, 65–74.

Crompton, J. L. (1995) Economic impact analysis of sport facilities and events: Eleven sources of misapplication. *Journal of Sport Management*, 9, 14–35.

Crompton, J. L. (1999) The economic impact of sports tournaments and events. *Parks & Recreation*, 34, 142–150.

Crompton, J. L. (2001) Public subsidies to professional team sport facilities in the USA. In C. Gratton & I. P. Henry (eds), *Sport in the City: The Role of Sport in Economic and Social Regeneration* (pp. 15–34), London: Routledge.

Crompton, J. L. (2004a) Sponsorship ambushing in sport. *Managing Leisure*, 9, 1–12.

Crompton, J. L. (2004b) Beyond economic impact: An alternative rationale for the public subsidy of major league sports facilities. *Journal of Sport Management*, 18, 40–28.

Crompton, J. L. (2004c) Conceptualization and alternate operationalizations of the measurement of sponsorship effectiveness in sport. *Leisure Studies*, 23, 267–281.

Crossan, M. M., Lane, H. W., & White, R. E. (1999) An organizational learning framework: From intuition to institution. *Academy of Management Review*, 24 (3), 522–537.

Crotty, M. (1998) *The Foundations of Social Research: Meaning and Perspective in the Research Process*, Thousand Oaks, CA: Sage Publications.

Crow, D. & Hoek, J. (2003) Ambush marketing: A critical review and some practical advice. *Marketing Bulletin*, 14, 1–14.

Curi, M., Knijnik, J., & Mascarenhas, G. (2011) The Pan American Games in Rio de Janeiro 2007: Consequences of a sport mega-event on a BRIC country. *International Review for the Sociology of Sport*, 46, 140–156.

Cuskelly, G., McIntyre, N., & Boag, A. (1998) A longitudinal study of the development of organizational commitment amongst volunteer sport administrators. *Journal of Sport Management*, 12, 181–202.

Cutler, M. (2011a) *London Olympic Schedule Unveiled*. Online. Available at www.sportbusiness. com/news/183087/london-olympic-schedule-unveiled?utm_source=sbinsl&utm_medium=email&utm_campaign=feb16 (accessed 18 February 2011).

Cutler, M. (2011b, 16 June) *Bahrain Struck Off 2011 F1 Calendar for Good*. Online. Available at www.sportbusiness.com/news/183790/bahrain-struck-off-2011-f1-calendar-for-good (accessed 16 June 2011).

Cutler, M. (2011c, 16 December) *Military Called in to Boost London 2012 Security*. Online. Available at www.sportbusiness.com/news/184824/military-called-in-to-boost-london-2012-security (accessed 19 March 2012).

Cutler, M. (2011d, 31 August) *Rugby World Cup Organisers Still Confident Over Ticket Sales*. Online. Available at www.sportbusiness.com/news/184224/rugby-world-cup-organisers-still-confident-over-ticket-sales (accessed 31 August 2011).

Cutler, M. (2011e, 12 September) *McCully Calls for Action After Transport Chaos on Rugby World Cup Opening Night*. Online. Available at www.sportbusiness.com/news/184289/mccully-calls-for-action-after-transport-chaos-on-rugby-world-cup-opening-night (accessed 22 March 2012).

Cutler, M. (2011f, 8 August) *Auditor Report Hits Out at "Deeply Flawed" Delhi Games Preparations*. Online. Available at www.sportbusiness.com/news/184112/auditor-report-hits-out-at-deeply-flawed-delhi-games-preparations (accessed 8 August 2011).

Cutler, M. (2011g, 23 September) *AIBA to Probe Corruption Allegations*. Online. Available at www.sportbusiness.com/news/184368/aiba-to-probe-corruption-allegations (accessed 27 October 2011).

Cutler, M. (2011h, 27 October) *Brazil Rocked by Resignation of Sports Minister Silva*. Online. Available at www.sportbusiness.com/news/184563/brazil-rocked-by-resignation-of-sports-minister-silva (accessed 27 October 2011).

Cutler, M. (2011i, 26 April) *Ex-Commonwealth Games Chief Kalmadi Arrested on Corruption Allegations*. Online. Available at www.sportbusiness.com/news/183520/ex-commonwealth-games-chief-kalmadi-arrested-on-corruption-allegations (accessed 27 October 2011).

Cutler, M. (2011j, 24 October) *FIFA President Blatter Unveils Reforms*. Online. Available at www.sportbusiness.com/news/184538/fifa-president-blatter-unveils-reforms (accessed 27 October 2011).

Cutler, M. (2012a, 12 March) *British Media an Asset to London 2012 Preparations – Coe*. Online. Available at www.sportbusiness.com/news/185215/british-media-an-asset-to-london-2012-preparations-coe (accessed 12 March 2012).

Cutler, M. (2012b) *Super Bowl Breaks TV Records Yet Again*. Online. Available at www.sportbusiness.com/news/185053/super-bowl-breaks-tv-records-yet-again (accessed 12 March 2012).

Cutler, M. (2012c) *IOC Seeks Clarification on Kalmadi*. Online. Available at www.sportbusiness. com/news/184990/ioc-seeks-clarification-on-kalmadi (accessed 26 March 2012).

Dandridge, T. C., Mitroff, I., & Joyce, W. F. (1980) Organizational symbolism: A topic to expand organizational analysis. *Academy of Management Review*, 5, 77–82.

Danylchuk, K. E. & MacIntosh, E. (2009) Food and non-alcoholic beverage sponsorship of sporting events: The link to the obesity issue. *Sport Marketing Quarterly*, 18(2), 69–80.

Darling, M., Parry, C., & Moore, J. (2005) Learning in the thick of it. *Harvard Business Review*, 83(7–8), 84–92.

Dart, J. J. (2009) Blogging the 2006 FIFA World Cup Finals. *Sociology of Sport Journal*, 26, 107–126.

Davies, M., Pitt, L. F., Shapiro, D., & Watson, R. (2005) Betfair.com: Five technology forces revolutionize worldwide wagering. *European Management Journal*, 23, 533–541.

Davis, G. F. & Thompson, T. A. (1994) A social movement perspective on corporate control. *Administrative Science Quarterly*, 39, 141–173.

Dawson, M. (2011) Putting cities on the map: Vancouver's 1954 British Empire and Commonwealth Games in comparative and historical perspective. *Urban Geography*, 32, 788–803.

Deci, E. L. & Ryan, R. M. (1985) *Intrinsic Motivation and Self-Determination in Human Behavior*, New York: Plenum.

Deci, E. L. & Ryan, R. M. (2002) *Handbook of Selfdetermination Research*, New York: University of Rochester Press.

Deci, E. L., Connell, J. P., & Ryan, R. M. (1989) Self-determination in a work organisation. *Journal of Applied Psychology*, 74, 580–590.

Della, L. J., Eroglu, D., Bernhardt, J. M., Eedgerton, E., & Nall, J. (2008) Looking to the future of new media in health marketing: Deriving propositions based on traditional theories. *Health Marketing Quarterly*, 25, 147–174.

DeMarco, J. P. & Fox, R. M. (1990) *Moral Reasoning: A Philosophic Approach to Applied Ethics*, New York: Harcourt Brace.

Denton, J. R. E. (2004) Language, symbols, and media. *Society*, 42, 12–18.

Depken II, C. A. (2000) Fan loyalty and stadium funding in professional baseball. *Journal of Sports Economics*, 1, 124–138.

DeSanctis, G. & Poole, M. S. (1994) Capturing the complexity in advanced technology use: Adaptive structuration theory. *Organization Science*, 5, 121–147.

Desbordes, M. (2002) Analysis of the innovation phenomena in the sports equipment industry. *Technology Analysis & Strategic Management*, 14, 481–498.

Desmarais, F. & Bruce, T. (2009) The power of the local in sports broadcasting: A cross-cultural analysis of rugby commentary. *International Journal of Sport Communication*, 2, 129–145.

DeSensi, J. T. & Malloy, D. C. (2006) Ethical challenges in sport management. In J. B. Parks, J. Quarterman, & L. Thibault (eds), *Contemporary Sport Management* (3rd edn, pp. 375–388), Champaign, IL: Human Kinetics.

Dessler, G. & Cole, N. D. (2010) *Human Resource Management in Canada* (11th edn), Toronto: Pearson Education Canada.

Devine, A., Bolan, P., & Devine, F. (2010) Online destination marketing: Maximising the tourism potential of a sports event. *International Journal of Sport Management & Marketing*, 7, 58–75.

Dickson, M. A. & Eckman, M. (2008) Media portrayal of voluntary public reporting about corporate social responsibility performance: Does coverage encourage or discourage ethical management? *Journal of Business Ethics*, 83, 725–743.

Dickson, T. J., Benson, A. M., & Blackman, D. A. (2011) Developing a framework for evaluating Olympic and Paralympic legacies. *Journal of Sport & Tourism*, 16(4), 285–302.

Diduck, A. & Mitchell, B. (2003) Learning, public involvement and environmental assessment: A Canadian case study. *Journal of Environmental Assessment Policy and Management*, 5, 339–364.

Dierendonck, D. V. (2011) Servant leadership: A review and synthesis. *Journal of Management*, 37, 1228–1261.

Dietz-Uhler, B., Harrick, E. A., End, C., & Jacquemotte, L. (2000) Sex differences in sport fan behavior and reasons for being a sport fan. *Journal of Sport Behavior*, 23, 219–231.

DiMaggio, P. J. & Powell, W. W. (1983) The iron cage revisited: Institutional isomorphism and collective rationality in organizational fields. *American Sociological Review*, 48, 147–160.

DiMaggio, P. J. & Powell, W. W. (1991) The iron cage revisited: Institutional isomorphism and collective rationality in organizational fields. In W. W. Powell & P. J. DiMaggio (eds), *The New Institutionalism in Organizational Analysis* (pp. 63–82), Chicago, IL: University of Chicago Press.

Dimanche, F. (1996) Special events legacy: The 1984 Louisiana World's Fair in New Orleans. *Festival Management & Event Tourism*, 4, 49–54.

Doerner, K. F., Gutjahr, W. J., & Nolz, P. C. (2009) Multi-criteria location planning for public facilities in tsunami-prone coastal areas. *OR Spectrum*, 31, 651–678.

Doherty, A. J. (1997) The effect of leaders' characteristics on the perceived transformational/ transactional leadership and impact on interuniversity athletics administrators. *Journal of Sport Management*, 11, 275–285.

Doherty, A. J. & Danylchuk, K. E. (1996) Transformational and transactional leadership in interuniversity athletics management. *Journal of Sport Management*, 10, 292–309.

Dolles, H. & Söderman, S. (2010) Addressing ecology and sustainability in mega-sporting events: The 2006 football World Cup in Germany. *Journal of Management and Organization*, 16, 587.

Donaldson, T. & Preston, L. E. (1995) The stakeholder theory of the corporation: Concepts, evidence, and implications. *Academy of Management Review*, 20, 65–91.

Doolittle, R. (2011, 30 October) *Pan Am Games Report Card from Guadalajara*. Online. Available at www.thestar.com/sports/panamgames/article/1078367-pan-am-games-report-card-from-guadalajara (accessed 7 March 2012).

Douglas, S. (2011, 10 October) *London 2012 Safe from Cyber Attacks, Say Officials*. Online. Available at http://news.yahoo.com/london-2012-safe-cyber-attacks-officials-170024098.html (accessed 19 March 2012).

Downward, P. & Ralston, R. (2006) The sports development potential of sports event volunteering: Insights from the XVII Manchester Commonwealth Games. *European Sport Management Quarterly*, 6, 333–351.

Downward, P., Lumsdon, L., & Ralston, R. (2005) Gender differences in sports event volunteering: Insights from Crew 2002 at the XVII Commonwealth Games. *Managing Leisure*, 10, 219–236.

Drayer, J. & Martin, N. T. (2010) Establishing legitimacy in the secondary ticket market: A case study of an NFL market. *Sport Management Review*, 13, 39–49.

Drengner, J., Jahn, S., & Zanger, C. (2011) Measuring event–brand congruence. *Event Management*, 15, 25–36.

Driedger, S. M. (2007) Risk and the media: A comparison of print and televised news stories of a Canadian drinking water risk event. *Risk Analysis: An International Journal*, 27, 775–786.

Drowatzky, J. N. (1992) Assumption of risk in sport. *Journal of Legal Aspects of Sport*, 2, 92–100.

Dubose, J. R., Bosch, S. J., & Pearce, A. R. (2007) Analysis of state-wide green building policies. *Journal of Green Building*, 2, 161–177.

Duncan, M. C. (1993) Beyond analyses of sport media texts: an argument for formal analyses of institutional structures. *Sociology of Sport Journal*, 10, 353–372.

Dupont, V. D. (2011) The dream of Delhi as a global city. *International Journal of Urban and Regional Research*, 35, 533–554.

Dyreson, M. (2005) Aggressive America: Media nationalism and the "war" over Olympic pictures in sport's "golden age". *International Journal of the History of Sport*, 22, 974–989.

Eastman, S. T. & Land, A. M. (1997) The best of both worlds: sports fans find good seats at the bar. *Journal of Sport & Social Issues*, 21, 156–178.

Edwards, S. D. (2008) Should Oscar Pistorius be excluded from the 2008 Olympic Games? *Sport, Ethics & Philosophy*, 2, 112–125.

Edy, J. A. & Meirick, P. C. (2007) Wanted, dead or alive: Media frames, frame adoption, and support for the war in Afghanistan. *Journal of Communication*, 57, 119–141.

Eick, V. (2011) Lack of legacy? Shadows of surveillance after the 2006 FIFA World Cup in Germany. *Urban Studies*, 48, 3329–3345.

Eisenhardt, K. M. (1989) Making fast strategic decisions in high-velocity environments. *Academy of Management Journal*, 32, 543–576.

Eitzinger, C. & Wiedemann, P. (2008) Trust in the safety of tourist destinations: Hard to gain, easy to lose? New insights on the asymmetry principle. *Risk Analysis*, 28, 843–853.

Elcock, Y. (2005) Sports tourism in Barbados: The development of sports facilities and special events. *Journal of Sport & Tourism*, 10, 129–134.

Ellen, P. S., Webb, D. J., & Mohr, L. A. (2006) Building corporate associations: Consumer attributions for corporate socially responsible programs. *Journal of the Academy of Marketing Science*, 34, 147–157.

Ellis, D. & Séguin, B. (2011) Virtual Games: Olympic sponsorship and new media. Paper presented at the 19th European Association for Sport Management Conference, Madrid, Spain.

Ellis, D., Gauthier, M. E., & Seguin, B. (2011a) Ambush marketing, the Olympic and Paralympic Marks Act and Canadian national sports organisations: Awareness, perceptions and impacts. *Journal of Sponsorship*, 4, 253–271.

Ellis, D., Scassa, T., & Seguin, B. (2011b) Framing ambush marketing as a legal issue: An Olympic perspective. *Sport Management Review*, 14, 297–308.

Ellis, S. & Davidi, I. (2005) After-event reviews: Drawing lessons from successful and failed experience. *Journal of Applied Psychology*, 90, 857–871.

Ellis, S., Mendel, R., & Nir, M. (2006) Learning from successful and failed experience: The moderating role of kind of after-event review. *Journal of Applied Psychology*, 91, 669–680.

Elmualim, A., Czwakiel, A., Valle, R., Ludlow, G., & Shah, S. (2009) The practice of sustainable facilities management: Design sentiments and the knowledge chasm. *Architectural Engineering and Design Management*, 5, 91–102.

Elmualim, A., Shockley, D., Valle, R., Ludlow, G., & Shaw, S. (2010) Barriers and commitment of facilities management profession to the sustainability agenda. *Building and Environment*, 45, 58–64.

Emery, P. R. (2002) Bidding to host a major sports event: The local organising committee perspective. *The International Journal of Public Sector Management*, 15, 316–335.

Emery, P. (2010) Past, present, future major sport event management practice: The practitioner perspective. *Sport Management Review*, 13, 158–170.

Essex, S. & Chalkley, B. (2004) Mega-sporting events in urban and regional policy: A history of the Winter Olympics. *Planning Perspectives*, 19, 201–232.

Etzioni, A. (1964) *Modern Organizations*, Englewood Cliffs, NJ: Prentice Hall.

Evans, M. G. (1970) The effects of supervisory behavior on the path–goal relationship. *Organizational Behavior and Human Performance*, 5, 277–298.

Everett, J., Neu, D., & Rahaman, A. S. (2006) The global fight against corruption: A Foucaultian, virtues-ethics framing. *Journal of Business Ethics*, 65, 1–12.

Ezell, B. C., Bennett, S. P., Von Winterfeldt, D., Sokolowski, J., & Collins, A. J. (2010) Probabilistic risk analysis and terrorism risk. *Risk Analysis: An International Journal*, 30, 575–589.

Facebook (2012) *Fact Sheet*. Online. Available at http://newsroom.fb.com/content/default.aspx?NewsAreaId=22 (accessed 19 March 2012).

Fairley, S., Kellett, P., & Green, B. C. (2007) Volunteering abroad: Motives for travel to volunteer at the Athens Olympic Games. *Journal of Sport Management*, 21, 41–57.

Falcous, M. (2007) The decolonizing national imaginary promotional media constructions during the 2005 Lions Tour of Aotearoa New Zealand. *Journal of Sport & Social Issues*, 31, 374–393.

Falkheimer, J. (2007) Events framed by the mass media: Media coverage and effects of America's cup preregatta in Sweden. *Event Management*, 11, 81–88.

Farmer, S. M. & Fedor, D. B. (1999) Volunteer participation and withdrawal: A psychological contract perspective on the role of expectations and organizational support. *Nonprofit Management and Leadership*, 9, 349–367.

Farrell, J. M., Johnston, M. E., & Twynam, G. D. (1998) Volunteer motivation, satisfaction, and management at an elite sporting competition. *Journal of Sport Management*, 12, 288–300.

Feldman, M. S. & Pentland, B. T. (2003) Reconceptualizing organizational routines as a source of flexibility and change. *Administrative Science Quarterly*, 48, 94–118.

Fenich, G. G. (2012) *Meetings, Expositions, Events, and Conventions: An Introduction to the Industry* (3rd edn), Upper Saddle River, NJ: Prentice Hall.

Fenich, G. G. & Bordelon, B. M. (2008) Is there an optimal type of ownership and organizational structure when developing convention and entertainment facilities? *Journal of Convention & Event Tourism*, 9, 182–198.

Ferrand, A. & Camps I Povill, A. (2009) Le marketing Olympique. *Revue Juridique et Économique du Sport*, 92, 7–44.

Ferrand, A. & Chanavat, N. (2006) Le marketing territorial événementiel. In J.-L. Chappelet (ed.), *Les Politiques Publiques d'Accueil et d'Organisation d'Événements Sportifs* (pp. 72–85), Paris: L'Harmattan.

Ferrand, A. & McCarthy, S. (2008) *Marketing the Sports Organisation: Building Networks and Relationships*, Abingdon: Routledge.

Ferrand, A. & Robin, J. (2009) Les stratégies de marketing relationnel associées aux événements sportifs majeurs comme support au développement touristique des villes. *Revue Europeenne de Management du Sport*, 24, 154–168.

Ferrand, A. & Stotlar, D. K. (2010) Introduction: New perspectives in sport event marketing. *International Journal of Sport Management & Marketing*, 7, 145–155.

Fiedler, F. E. (1967) *A Theory of Leadership Effectiveness*, New York: McGraw-Hill.

Fiedler, F. E. (1978) The contingency model and the dynamics of the leadership process. In L. Berkowitz (ed.), *Advances in Experimental Social Psychology* (pp. 59–112), New York: Academic Press.

FIFA (n.d.) *FIFA E-Activity Report 2010*. Online. Available at www.fifa-e-activityreport.com (accessed 27 September 2011).

FIFA.com (2011, 3 February) *Media Vote FIFA World Cup as Best Press Facility of 2010*. Online. Available at www.fifa.com/aboutfifa/federation/news/newsid=1376385.html (accessed 10 March 2011).

Filo, K., Funk, D. C., & Hornby, G. (2009) The role of website content on motive and attitude change for sport events. *Journal of Sport Management*, 23, 21–40.

Fleishman, E. A. & Harris, E. F. (1962) Patterns of leader behavior related to employee grievances and turnover. *Personnel Psychology*, 15, 43–56.

Fleishman, E. A., Harris, E. F., & Burtt, H. E. (1955) *Leadership and Supervision in Industry*, Columbus, OH: Ohio State University, Bureau of Educational Research.

Fletcher, J. K. (1992) A poststructuralist perspective on the third dimension of power. *Journal of Organizational Change Management*, 5, 31–38.

Fligstein, N. & Brantley, P. (1992) Bank control, owner control, or organizational dynamics: Who controls the large modern corporation? *American Journal of Sociology*, 98, 280–307.

Floridis, G. (2004) Security for the 2004 Athens Olympic games. *Mediterranean Quarterly*, 15, 1–5.

Foley, M. A., Foley, H. J., Durso, F. T., & Smith, N. K. (1997) Investigations of closure processes: What source-monitoring judgments suggest about what is "closing". *Memory and Cognition*, 25, 140–155.

Fong-Yi, L. (2010) Exploring consumer schemata of destination and sports event brands: the case of Kaohsiung City and the 2009 World Games. *International Journal of Sport Management & Marketing*, 7, 267–281.

Forni, P. M. (2003) *Choosing Civility: The 25 Rules of Considerate Conduct*, New York: St. Martin's Griffin.

Fourie, J. & Spronk, K. (2011) South African mega-sport events and their impact on tourism. *Journal of Sport and Tourism*, 16, 75–97.

Fourie, J., Siebrits, K., & Spronk, K. (2011) Tourist displacement in two South African sport mega-events. *Development Southern Africa*, 28, 319–332.

Fraser, A. (2005) *Unlikely Victory*, London: BBC Sport. Online. Available at http://news.bbc.co.uk/sport2/hi/other_sports/olympics_2012/4658035.stm (accessed 24 November 2010).

Frawley, S. & Cush, A. (2011) Major sport events and participation legacy: The case of the 2003 Rugby World Cup. *Managing Leisure*, 16, 65–76.

Frederick, W. C. (1994) From CSR1 to CSR2. *Business and Society*, 33, 150–164.

Freeman, R. E. (1984) *Strategic Management: A Stakeholder Approach*, Boston, MA: Pitman.

French, J. R. P. J. & Raven, B. (1959) The bases of social power. In D. Cartwright (ed.), *Studies in Social Power* (pp. 150–167), Ann Arbor, MI: University of Michigan Press.

Frey, M., Iraldo, F., & Melis, M. (2008) *The Impact of Wide-Scale Sport Events on Local Development: An Assessment of the XXth Torino Olympics through the Sustainability Report*. Online.

357

Available at http://papers.ssrn.com/sol3/papers.cfm?abstract_id=1117967 (accessed 13 December 2011).

Friedman, M. T., Parent, M. M., & Mason, D. S. (2004) Building a framework for issues management in sport through stakeholder theory. *European Sport Management Quarterly*, 4, 170–190.

Friedman, M. S., Powell, K. E., Hutwagner, L., Graham, L. M., & Teague, W. G. (2001) Impact of changes in transportation and commuting behaviors during the 1996 Summer Olympic Games in Atlanta on air quality and childhood asthma. *JAMA: Journal of the American Medical Association*, 285, 897–905.

Frisby, W. (1986) Measuring the organizational effectiveness of national sport governing bodies. *Canadian Journal of Applied Sport Sciences*, 11, 94–99.

Frost, C. (2003) *Reporting for Journalists*, London: Routledge.

Frow, N., Marginson, D., & Ogden, S. (2010) "Continuous" budgeting: Reconciling budget flexibility with budgetary control. *Accounting, Organizations and Society*, 35, 444–461.

Funk, D. C. (2008) *Sport Marketing: Consumer Behaviour in Sport and Events – Marketing Action*, Jordan Hill: Routledge.

Funk, D. C., Filo, K., Beaton, A. A., & Prichard, M. (2009) Measuring the motives of sport event attendance: Bridging the academic–practitioner divide to understanding behaviour. *Sport Marketing Quarterly*, 18, 126–138.

Funk, D. C., Mahoney, D. F., Nakazawa, M., & Hirakawa, S. (2001) Development of the Sport Interest Inventory (SII): Implications for measuring unique consumer motives at sporting events. *International Journal of Sports Marketing and Sponsorship*, 3, 291–316.

Funk, D. C., Mahoney, D. F., & Ridinger, L. L. (2002) Characterizing consumer motivation as individual difference factors: Augmenting the Sport Interest Inventory (SII) to explain level of spectator support. *Sport Marketing Quarterly*, 11, 33–43.

Funk, D. C., Ridinger, L. L., & Moorman, A. M. (2003) Understanding consumer support: Extending the Sport Interest Inventory (SII) to examine individual differences among women's professional sport consumers. *Sport Management Review*, 6, 1–32.

Funk, D. C., Jordan, J., Ridinger, L., & Kaplanidou, K. (2011) Capacity of mass participant sport events for the development of activity commitment and future exercise intention. *Leisure Sciences*, 33, 250–268.

Furedi, F. (2002) *Culture of Fear*, London: Continuum.

Furrer, P. (2002) *Sustainable Olympic Games: A Dream or Reality?* Online. Available at www.omero.unito.it/web/Furrer%20(eng.).PDF (accessed 13 December 2011).

Gallagher, J. A. & Goodstein, J. (2002) Fulfilling institutional responsibilities in health care: Organizational ethics and the role of mission discernment. *Business Ethics Quarterly*, 12, 433–450.

Galtung, J. & Ruge, M. H. (1965) The structure of foreign news. *Journal of Peace Research*, 2, 64–91.

Gardiner, S. (2000) Keeping football hooliganism in check. *Solicitors Journal*, 144, 655–657.

Gardner, W. L. and Avolio, B. J. (1998) The charismatic relationship: A dramaturgical perspective. *Academy of Management*, 23, 32–58.

Gartner, S. S. (2004) Making the international local: The terrorist attack on the USS Cole, local casualties, and media coverage. *Political Communication*, 21, 139–159.

George, A. A. (2003) Managing ski resorts: Perceptions from the field regarding the sustainable slopes charter. *Managing Leisure*, 8, 41–46.

Gerrard, B. (2004) Media ownership of teams: The latest stage in the commercialisation of team sports. In T. Slack (ed.), *The Commercialisation of Sport* (pp. 247–266), London: Routledge.

Gerth, H. H. & Mills, C. W. (eds) (1946) *From Max Weber: Essays in Sociology*, Oxford: Oxford University Press.

Getz, D. (1997) The impacts of mega events on tourism: Strategies for destinations. In M. Andersson (ed.), *Conference Proceedings: The Impact of Mega Events*, 7–8 July, Ostersund, Sweden: Mid Sweden University.

Getz, D. (1998) Trends, strategies and issues in sport event tourism. *Sport Marketing Quarterly*, 7, 8–13.

Getz, D. (2005) *Event Management & Event Tourism*, Elmsford, NY: Cognizant Communication Corp.

Getz, D. (2007) *Event Studies: Theory, Research and Policy for Planned Events*, Burlington, MA: Elsevier.

Getz, D. & Fairley, S. (2003) Media management at sports events for destination promotion: Case studies and concepts. *Event Management*, 8, 127–139.

Getz, D., Andersson, T., & Carlsen, J. (2010) Festival management studies. *International Journal of Event and Festival Management*, 1, 29–59.

Giannoulakis, C., Wang, C. H., & Gray, D. (2008) Measuring volunteer motivation in mega-sporting events. *Event Management*, 11, 191–200.

Gibson, H., McIntyre, S., Mackay, S., & Riddington, G. (2005) The economic impact of sports, sporting events, and sports tourism in the U.K.: The DREAMTM Model. *European Sport Management Quarterly*, 5, 321–332.

Giffard, C. A. & Rivenburgh, N. K. (2000) News agencies, national images, and global media events. *Journalism and Mass Communication Quarterly*, 77, 8–21.

Gillon, P. (2011) Olympic system: Toward a geopolitical approach | Une lecture géopolitique du système Olympique. *Annales de Géographie*, 119, 425–448.

Girginov, V. (2006) Creating a corporate anti-doping culture: The role of Bulgarian sports governing bodies. *Sport in Society*, 9, 252–268.

Girginov, V. (2011) Governance of London 2012 Olympic Games legacy. *International Review for the Sociology of Sports*, 1–16. doi: 10.1177/1012690211413966.

Girginov, V. & Hills, L. (2009) The political process of constructing a sustainable London Olympics sports development legacy. *International Journal of Sport Policy*, 1, 169–181.

Giulianotti, R. & Klauser, F. (2010) Security governance and sport mega-events: Toward an interdisciplinary research agenda. *Journal of Sport & Social Issues*, 34, 49–61.

Gladden, J. M. & Milne, G. R. (1999) Examining the importance of brand equity in professional sports. *Sport Marketing Quarterly*, 8, 21–29.

Gladden, J. M., Milne, G. R., & Sutton, W. A. (1998) A conceptual framework for evaluating brand equity in Division I college athletics. *Journal of Sport Management*, 12, 1–19.

Glassman, T., Dodd, V., Sheu, J. J., Miller, M., Arthur, A., & Book, E. (2008) Winning isn't everything: A case study of high-risk drinking the night of the 2006 national championship football game. *Journal of Alcohol and Drug Education*, 52, 31–48.

Global Reporting Initiative. (2011) *Event Organizers*. Online. Available at www.globalreporting. org/ReportingFramework/SectorSupplements/Events (accessed 29 November 2011).

Gold, J. R. & Gold, M. M. (2007) *Olympic Cities: City Agendas, Planning, and the World's Games, 1896–2012*, New York: Routledge.

Goleman, D. (1985) *Emotional Intelligence: Why It Can Matter More Than IQ* (10th edn), New York: Bantam Dell.

Goodsell, C. T. (1997) Administration as ritual. *International Journal of Public Administration*, 20, 939–961.

Gordon, D. (2004) The cultural politics of a traditional ceremony: Mutomboko and the performance of history on the Luapula (Zambia). *Comparative Studies in Society and History*, 46, 63–83.

Gorrell, M. (2002) Security at the games. *Olympic Review*, 27, 45–47.

Goslin, A. (1996) Human resource management as a fundamental aspect of a sport development strategy in South African communities. *Journal of Sport Management*, 10, 207–217.

Government of Canada, Government of British Columbia, City of Vancouver, Resort Municipality of Whistler, Canadian Olympic Committee, Canadian Paralympic Committee *et al.* (2002) *Multiparty Agreement for the 2010 Winter Olympic and Paralympic Games*. Online. Available at www.canada2010.gc.ca/role/gc/mpa/MPA-e.PDF (accessed 16 March 2012).

Goyal, S. & Pitt, M. (2007) Determining the role of innovation management in facilities management. *Facilities*, 25, 48–60.

Grady, J., McKelvey, S., & Bernthal, M. (2010) From Beijing 2008 to London 2012: Examining event-specific Olympic legislation vis-à-vis the rights and interests of stakeholders. *Journal of Sponsorship*, 3, 144–156.

Graen, G. B. & Uhl-Bien, M. (1991) The transformation of professionals into self-managing and partially self-designing contributions: Toward a theory of leadership making. *Journal of Management Systems*, 3, 33–48.

Graen, G. B. & Uhl-Bien, M. (1995) Relationship-based approach to leadership: Development of leader–member exchange (LMX) theory of leadership over 25 years – applying a multi-level, multi-domain perspective. *Leadership Quarterly*, 6, 219–247.

Granovetter, M. (1973) The strength of weak ties. *American Journal of Sociology*, 78, 1360–1380.

Gratton, C. & Preuss, H. (2008) Maximizing Olympic impacts by building up legacies. *The International Journal of the History of Sport*, 25, 1922–1938.

Gratton, C., Dobson, N., & Shibli, S. (2000) The economic importance of major sports events: A case-study of six events. *Managing Leisure*, 5, 17–28.

Gratton, C., Shibli, S., & Coleman, R. (2006) The economic impact of major sports events: A review of ten events in the UK. *The Sociological Review*, 54(s2), 41–58.

Gratton, L. (1994) Implementing strategic intent: Human resource processes as a force for change. *Business Strategy Review*, 5, 47–66.

Greasley, A. (2008) Using simulation for facility design: A case study. *Simulation Modelling Practice and Theory*, 16, 670–677.

Green, B. C. (2001) Leveraging subculture and identity to promote sport events. *Sport Management Review*, 4, 1–19.

Green, B. C., Costa, C., & Fitzgerald, M. (2002) Marketing the host city: Analyzing exposure generated by a sport event. *International Journal of Sports Marketing & Sponsorship*, 4, 335–353.

Green, B. C., So Youn, L., Won Jae, S., & Yongjun, S. (2010) Effects of cultural exposure through pre-event media. *Journal of Sport & Tourism*, 15, 89–102.

Green, B. C., Murray, N., & Warner, S. (2011) Understanding website useability: an eye-tracking study of the Vancouver 2010 Olympic Games website. *International Journal of Sport Management & Marketing*, 10, 257–271.

Green, M. (2004) Power, policy, and political priorities: Elite sport development in Canada and the United Kingdom. *Sociology of Sport Journal*, 21, 376–396.

Greenleaf, R. K. (2002) *Servant Leadership: A Journey into the Nature of Legitimate Power and Greatness* (25th anniversary edn), New York: Paulist Press.

Greenwood, M. R. (2002) Ethics and HRM: A review and conceptual analysis. *Journal of Business Ethics*, 36, 261–278.

Greenwood, R. & Hinings, C. R. (1996) Understanding radical organizational change: Bringing together the old and the new institutionalism. *Academy of Management Review*, 21, 1022–1054.

Griffiths, M., Parke, A., Wood, R., & Parke, J. (2006) Internet gambling: An overview of psychosocial impacts. *UNLV Gaming Research & Review Journal*, 10, 27–39.

Gripsrud, G., Nes, E., & Olsson, U. H. (2010) Effects of hosting a mega-sport event on country image. *Event Management*, 14, 193–204.

Grohs, R. & Reisinger, H. (2005) Image transfer in sports sponsorships: An assessment of moderating effects. *International Journal of Sports Marketing and Sponsorship*, 7, 42–48.

Guest, D. E. (1998) Is the psychological contract worth taking seriously? *Journal of Organizational Behavior*, 19, 649–664.

Guardian (2010, 15 June) World Cup 2010: FIFA detains 36 female Holland fans for "ambush marketing". Online. Available at www.guardian.co.uk/football/2010/jun/15/holland-ambush-marketing-fifa-dresses (accessed 15 December 2011).

Guiltinan, J. P. (1987) The price bundling of services: A normative framework. *Journal of Marketing*, 51, 74–85.

Guojun, Z., Go, F., & Kolmer, C. (2011) The impact of international TV media coverage of the Beijing Olympics 2008 on China's media image formation: a media content analysis perspective. *International Journal of Sports Marketing & Sponsorship*, 12, 319–336.

Gupta, A. (2009) The globalization of sports, the rise of non-Western nations, and the impact on international sporting events. *International Journal of the History of Sport*, 26, 1779–1790.

Gustafson, R. (2001, 5 April) Product brands look set to gain new advantage. *Marketing*, p. 20.

Gwinner, K. P. (1997) A model of image creation and image transfer in event sponsorship. *International Journal of Sports Marketing and Sponsorship*, 14, 145–158.

Gwinner, K. P. & Eaton, J. (1999) Building brand image through event sponsorship: The role of image transfer. *Journal of Advertising*, 28, 47–57.

Gyongyi, F. S. & Krawczyk, Z. (1982) Social role of sports events in Poland and Hungary. *International Review of Sport Sociology*, 17, 23–47.

Haake, S. J. (2009) The impact of technology on sporting performance in Olympic sports. *Journal of Sports Sciences*, 27, 1421–1431.

Habermas, T., & Berger, N. (2011) Retelling everyday emotional events: Condensation, distancing, and closure. *Cognition and Emotion*, 25, 206–219.

Hachleitner, B. & Manzenreiter, W. (2010) The EURO 2008 bonanza: Mega-events, economic pretensions and the sports–media business alliance. *Soccer and Society*, 11, 843–853.

361

Hackman, J. R., Oldham, G., Janson, R., & Purdy, K. (1975) A new strategy for job enrichment. *California Management Review*, 17, 57–71.

Haimes, Y. Y. (1991) Total risk management. *Risk Analysis*, 11, 169–171.

Haimes, Y. Y. (2004) *Risk Modeling, Assessment and Management*, Hoboken, NJ: John Wiley and Sons.

Halbwirth, S. & Toohey, K. (2001) The Olympic Games and knowledge management: A case study of the Sydney Organizing Committee of the Olympic Games. *European Sport Management Quarterly*, 1, 91–111.

Hall, C. M. (1989) The definition and analysis of hallmark tourist events. *GeoJournal*, 19, 263–268.

Hall, C. M. (1992) *Hallmark Tourist Events: Impacts, Management and Planning*, London: Belhaven Press.

Hall, C. M. (2001) Imaging, tourism and sports event fever: The Sydney Olympics and the need for a social charter for mega-events. In C. Gratton & I. P. Henry (eds), *Sport in the City: The Role of Sport in Economic and Social Regeneration* (pp. 166–183), London: Routledge.

Hall, J. & Rosson, P. (2006) The impact of technological turbulence on entrepreneurial behavior, social norms and ethics: Three Internet-based cases. *Journal of Business Ethics*, 64, 231–248.

Hall, J., O'Mahony, B., & Viecelli, J. (2010) An empirical model of attendance factors at major sporting events. *International Journal of Hospitality Management*, 29, 328–334.

Hall, S. A. (2010) An examination of British sport security strategies, legislation, and risk management practices. *Sport Journal*, 13, 3.

Hall, S. A., Marciani, L., Phillips, D., & Cunningham, T. (2009) Spectator perceptions of security management at a NASCAR (National Association for Stock Car Auto Racing) event. *Sport Journal*, 12, 1.

Hall, S. A., Fos, P. J., Marciani, L., & Lei, Z. (2011) Value modeling in sport security planning: Setting priorities in security efforts at large spectator events. *International Journal of Sport Management*, 12 (2), 191–207.

Hallmann, K. & Breuer, C. (2010) Image fit between sport events and their hosting destinations from an active sport tourism perspective and its impact on future behaviour. *Journal of Sport & Tourism*, 15, 215–237.

Halpin, A. W. (1957) The observed behavior and ideal leaders behavior of aircraft commanders and school superintendents. In R. M. Stogdill & A. E. Coons (eds), *Leader Behaviors: Its Description and Measurement* (pp. 65–68), Columbus, OH: Ohio State University, Bureau of Business Research.

Halpin, A. W. & Winer, B. J. (1957) A factorial study of the leader behavior descriptions. In R. M. Stogdill & A. E. Coons (eds), *Leader Behaviors: Its Description and Measurement* (pp. 39–51), Columbus, OH: Ohio State University, Bureau of Business Research.

Hamilton, T. A. (2010) The long hard fall from Mount Olympus: The 2002 Salt Lake City Olympic Games bribery scandal. *Marquette Sports Law Review*, 21, 219–240.

Hammond, N. (2011) The disharmonious honking of the vuvuzelas: homogenization and difference in the production and promotion of the 2010 Soccer World Cup in South Africa. *Soccer & Society*, 12, 46–55.

Hanlon, C. & Cuskelly, G. (2002) Pulsating major sport event organizations: A framework for inducting managerial personnel. *Event Management*, 7, 231–243.

Hanlon, C. & Stewart, B. (2006) Managing personnel in major sport event organizations: What strategies are required? *Event Management*, 10, 77–88.

Happel, S. K. & Jennings, M. M. (2002) Creating a futures market for major event tickets: Problems and prospects. *Cato Journal*, 21, 443–461.

Harrison-Hill, T. & Chalip, L. (2005) Marketing sport tourism: Creating synergy between sport and destination. *Sport in Society*, 8, 302–320.

Harting, T. R., Harmeling, S. S., & Venkataraman, S. (2006) Innovative stakeholder relations: When "ethics pays" (and when it doesn't). *Business Ethics Quarterly*, 16, 43–68.

Hartungi, R. (2010) Evaluation of sustainable development projects: Participatory approach. *International Journal of Sustainable Development*, 13, 362–373.

Hayes, G. & Horne, J. (2011) Sustainable development, shock and awe? London 2012 and civil society. *Sociology*, 45, 749–764.

Head, G. L. & Horn II, S. (1991) *Essentials of Risk Management*, Malvern, PA: Insurance Institute of America.

Hede, A. (2010) The dynamics of mindfulness in managing emotions and stress. *The Journal of Management Development*, 29, 94–110.

Heere, B., Chiyoung, K., Yoshida, M., Nakamura, H., Ogura, T., & Kyu Soo, C. (2011) The impact of World Cup 2002 on the bilateral relationship between South Korea and Japan. *Journal of Sport Management*, 26, 1–45.

Henry, M. H. & Haimes, Y. Y. (2009) A comprehensive network security risk model for process control networks. *Risk Analysis: An International Journal*, 29, 223–248.

Hepler, J. A., Neumann, C. M., & Rossignol, A. M. (2003) Environmental compliance and ethics: A case study at a facility of the US army corps of engineers in Oregon. *Environmental Practice*, 5, 134–145.

Herman, E. S. & Chomsky, N. (2002) *Manufacturing Consent: The Political Economy of the Mass Media*, New York: Pantheon.

Hersey, P. & Blanchard, K. H. (1984) *Management of Organizational Behavior*, Englewood Cliffs, NJ: Prentice Hall.

Herzberg, F. (1968) One more time: How do you motivate people? *Harvard Business Review*, 46, 53–62.

Herzberg, F., Mausner, B., & Snyderman, B. (1959) *The Motivation to Work*, New York: John Wiley and Sons.

Hickson, D. J., Hinings, C. R., Lee, C. A., Schneck, R. E., & Pennings, J. M. (1971) A strategic contingencies theory of intraorganizational power. *Administrative Science Quarterly*, 16, 216–229.

Higham, J. E. S. & Hinch, T. D. (2003) Sport, space, and time: Effects of the Otago Highlanders franchise on tourism. *Journal of Sport Management*, 17, 235–257.

Hill, D. (2008) *The Fix: Soccer and Organized Crime*, Toronto: McClelland & Stewart Ltd.

Hill, D. (2010) A critical mass of corruption: Why some football leagues have more match-fixing than others. *International Journal of Sports Marketing & Sponsorship*, 11, 221–235.

Hill, J. (2004) "The day was an ugly one": Wembley, 28th April 1923. *Soccer & Society*, 5, 152–168.

Hiller, H. (1998) Assessing the impact of mega-events: A linkage model. *Current Issues in Tourism*, 1, 47–57.

363

Hiller, H. (2002) Towards a science of Olympic outcomes: The urban legacy. In M. de Moragus, C. Kennett, & N. Puig (eds), *The Legacy of the Olympic Games 1984–2000* (pp. 102–109), Lausanne: IOC.

Hillman, C. H., Cuthbert, B. N., Bradley, M. M., & Lang, P. J. (2004) Motivated engagement to appetitive and aversive fanship cues: Psychophysiological responses of rival sport fans. *Journal of Sport and Exercise Psychology*, 26, 338–351.

Hoeber, L. (2010) Experiences of volunteering in sport: Views from Aboriginal individuals. *Sport Management Review*, 13, 345–354.

Hoek, J. & Gendall, D. (2002) Ambush marketing: More than just a commercial irritant. *Entertainment Law*, 1, 72–91.

Hoffmann, S. (2010) Ensuring food safety around the globe: The many roles of risk analysis from risk ranking to microbial risk assessment. *Risk Analysis: An International Journal*, 30, 711–714.

Hogan, J. (2003) Staging the nation: Gendered and ethnicized discourses of national identity in Olympic opening ceremonies. *Journal of Sport & Social Issues*, 27, 100–123.

Holmes, R. A. & Shamsuddin, A. F. M. (1997) Short- and long-term effects of World Exposition 1986 on US demand for British Columbia tourism. *Tourism Economics*, 3, 137–160.

Hooijberg, R., Hunt, J. J., & Dodge, G. (1997) Leadership complexity and development of the leaderplex model. *Journal of Management*, 23, 375–408.

Horne, J. & Whannel, G. (2012) Festival, spectacle, carnival and consumption. In *Understanding the Olympics* (pp. 146–161), London: Routledge.

Horton, P. & Zakus, D. (2010) How green will my (Lea) valley be? Olympic aspirations: Rhetoric or reality. *The International Journal of the History of Sport*, 27, 2677–2709.

House, R. J. (1971) A path–goal theory of leader effectiveness. *Administrative Science Quarterly*, 16, 321–339.

House, R. J. (1977) A 1976 theory of charismatic leadership. In J. G. Hunt & L. L. Larson (eds), *Leadership: The Cutting Edge* (pp. 189–207), Carbondale, IL: Southern Illinois Press.

House, R. J. & Aditya, R. (1997) The social scientific study of leadership: Quo vadis? *Journal of Management*, 23, 409–473.

Housel, T. H. (2007) Australian nationalism and globalization: Narratives of the nation in the 2000 Sydney Olympics' opening ceremony. *Critical Studies in Media Communication*, 24, 446–461.

Howe, P. D. (2008) From inside the newsroom: Paralympic media and the "production" of elite disability. *International Review for the Sociology of Sport*, 43, 135–150.

Hoye, R. & Cuskelly, G. (2003) Board power and performance within voluntary sport organisations. *European Sport Management Quarterly*, 3, 103–119.

Hu, A. W.-L. & Tang, L.-R. (2010) Factors motivating sports broadcast viewership with fan identification as a mediator. *Social Behavior & Personality: An International Journal*, 38, 681–689.

Hua, L., Apostolakis, G. E., Gifun, J., VanSchalkwyk, W., Leite, S., & Barber, D. (2009) Ranking the risks from multiple hazards in a small community. *Risk Analysis: An International Journal*, 29, 438–456.

Huang, Y. (2010) A study of Guangdong TV's Olympics coverage strategy. *Sport in Society*, 13, 833–839.

Humphreys, B. R. & Prokopowicz, S. (2007) Assessing the impact of sports mega-events in transition economies: EURO 2012 in Poland and Ukraine. *International Journal of Sport Management and Marketing*, 2, 496–509.

Husted, B. W. (2005) Risk management, real options, corporate social responsibility. *Journal of Business Ethics*, 60, 175–183.

Hutchins, B., Rowe, D., & Ruddock, A. (2009) "It's fantasy football made real": Networked media sport, the internet, and the hybrid reality of MyFootballClub. *Sociology of Sport Journal*, 26, 89–106.

Hwang, D., Golemon, P., Chen, Y., Wang, T., & Hung, W. (2009) Guanxi and business ethics in Confucian society today: An empirical case study in Taiwan. *Journal of Business Ethics*, 89, 235–250.

Ibarra, H. (1993) Network centrality, power, and innovation involvement: Determinants of technical and administrative roles. *Academy of Management Journal*, 36, 471–501.

Ik Young, C., & Crossman, J. (2009) "When there is a will, there is a way": A quantitative comparison of the newspaper coverage of the 2004 Summer Paralympic and Olympic Games. *International Journal of Applied Sports Sciences*, 21, 16–34.

Ilies, R., Morgeson, F. P., & Nahrgang, J. D. (2005) Authentic leadership and eudaemonic well being: Understanding leader–follower outcomes. *The Leadership Quarterly*, 16, 373–394.

Independent. (2007, 20 September) Have you got green fatigue?, *The Independent*. Online. Available at www.independent.co.uk/environment/green-living/have-you-got-green-fatigue-402971.html# (accessed 26 March 2012).

Innsbruck 2012 (2011, December) *Innsbruck 2012 Spectator Guide*. Online. Available at www.innsbruck2012.com/uploads/cd_page_element/1207997961/YOG2012_Spectators_Guide_.pdf (accessed 7 March 2012).

International Olympic Committee (2008) *International Olympic Committee Marketing Report: Beijing 2008*. Online. Available at http://view.digipage.net/?userpath=00000001/00000004/00040592 (accessed 27 February 2012).

International Olympic Committee (2009a) *Revenue Sources and Distribution*. Online. Available at www.olympic.org/ioc-financing-revenue-sources-distribution?tab=1 (accessed 18 February 2011).

International Olympic Committee. (2009b) *Beijing 2008*. Online. Available at www.olympic.org/beijing-2008-summer-olympics (accessed 19 September 2011).

International Olympic Committee. (2009c) *Salt Lake City 2002*. Online. Available at www.olympic.org/salt-lake-city-2002-winter-olympics (accessed 19 September 2011).

International Olympic Committee. (2009d) *Sydney 2000*. Online. Available at www.olympic.org/sydney-2000-summer-olympics (accessed 19 September 2011).

International Olympic Committee (2009e) *Technical Manual on Ceremonies*, Lausanne: Author.

International Olympic Committee (2010a) *Beijing 2008*, Lausanne: Author.

International Olympic Committee (2010b) *International Olympic Committee Marketing Report: Vancouver 2010*. Online. Available at http://view.digipage.net/?id=iocvancouver2010 (accessed 12 March 2012).

International Olympic Committee. (2010c) *Successful Singapore Youth Olympic Games Come to a Close*. Online. Available at www.olympic.org/yog-presentation?articleid=97704 (accessed 19 September 2011).

365

International Olympic Committee (2010d) *IOC Marketing: Media Guide – Vancouver 2010.* Online. Available at www.olympic.org/Documents/Reports/EN/IOC-MEDIAGUIDE-2010-EN.pdf (accessed 3 April 2011).

International Olympic Committee. (2011a) *XIII Olympic Congress Copenhagen – Follow-up,* Lausanne: Author.

International Olympic Committee. (2011b) *Olympism in Action.* Online. Available at www.olympic.org/olympism-in-action (accessed 27 November 2011).

Inthorn, S. (2010) Europe divided, or Europe united? German and British press coverage of the 2008 European Championship. *Soccer & Society,* 11, 790–802.

Irwin, R. L., Lachowetz, T., Cornwell, T. B., & Clark, J. S. (2003) Cause-related sport sponsorship: An assessment of spectator beliefs, attitudes, and behavioral intentions. *Sport Marketing Quarterly,* 12, 131–139.

Islam, G. & Zyphur, M. J. (2009) Rituals in organizations: A review and expansion of current theory. *Group & Organization Management,* 34, 114–139.

Jago, L. K. & Shaw, R. N. (1998) Special events: A conceptual and definitional framework. *Festival Management & Event Tourism,* 5, 21–32.

Jago, L. K. & Shaw, R. N. (1999) Consumer perceptions of special events: A multi-stimulus validation. *Journal of Travel & Tourism Marketing,* 8, 1–24.

Jago, L. K., Chalip, L., Brown, G., Mules, T., & Ali, S. (2003) Building events into destination branding: Insights from experts. *Event Management,* 8, 3–14.

James, J. D. & Ridinger, L. L. (2002) Female and male sport fans: A comparison of sport consumption motives. *Journal of Sport Behaviour,* 25, 260–278.

Jan, M. (2009) Globalization of media: Key issues and dimensions. *European Journal of Scientific Research,* 29, 66–75.

Jarvis, N. & Blank, C. (2011) The importance of tourism motivations among sport event volunteers at the 2007 world artistic gymnastics championships, Stuttgart, Germany. *Journal of Sport and Tourism,* 16, 129–147.

Jennings, A. (2000) *The Great Olympic Swindle: When the World Wanted its Games Back,* London: Simon & Schuster.

Jennings, W. & Lodge, M. (2011) Governing mega-events: Tools of security risk management for the FIFA 2006 World Cup in Germany and London 2012 Olympic Games. *Government and Opposition,* 46, 192–222.

Jeon, C. M. & Amekudzi, A. (2005) Addressing sustainability in transportation systems: Definitions, indicators, and metrics. *Journal of Infrastructure Systems,* 11, 31–50.

Jeon, C. M., Amekudzi, A. A., & Guensler, R. L. (2010) Evaluating plan alternatives for transportation system sustainability: Atlanta Metropolitan Region. *International Journal of Sustainable Transportation,* 4, 227–247.

Jermier, J. M. (1996) A path–goal theory of leadership: A subtextual analysis. *Leadership Quarterly,* 7, 311–316.

Jie, D. & Li, Z. (2009) The Olympic Partners: Benefit, risk and risk management. *Journal of Wuhan Institute of Physical Education,* 43, 29–33.

Jin, L., Zhang, J. J., Ma, X., & Connaughton, D. P. (2011) Residents' perceptions of environmental impacts of the 2008 Beijing green olympic games. *European Sport Management Quarterly,* 11, 275–300.

Jinxia, D. & Mangan, J. A. (2008) Beijing Olympics legacies: Certain intentions and certain and uncertain outcomes. *The International Journal of the History of Sport*, 25, 2019–2040.

Johnson, B. (2010) Trust and terrorism: Citizen responses to anti-terrorism performance history. *Risk Analysis*, 30, 1328–1340.

Johnson, C. W. (2008) Using evacuation simulations for contingency planning to enhance the security and safety of the 2012 Olympic venues. *Safety Science*, 46, 302–322.

Johnson, G. & Scholes, K. (2002) *Exploring Corporate Strategy* (6th edn), London: Prentice Hall.

Johnson, J. (2010) The power of plastic. *Athletics Administration*, 45(7), 22–23.

Jones, T. M. (1995) Instrumental stakeholder theory: A synthesis of ethics and economics. *Academy of Management Review*, 20, 404–437.

Jones, T. M. & Wicks, A. C. (1999) Convergent stakeholder theory. *Academy of Management Review*, 24, 206–221.

Joseph, J. (2005) Sport as Spectacle. *Berkshire Encyclopedia of World Sport*, 4, 1499–1504.

Judge, W. Q. & Miller, A. (1991) Antecedents and outcomes of decision speed in different environmental contexts. *Academy of Management Journal*, 34, 449–463.

Judge, W. Q. & Zeithaml, C. P. (1992) An empirical comparison between the board's strategic role in nonprofit hospitals and in for-profit industrial firms. *Health Services Research*, 27, 47–64.

Jun, J. W. & Lee, H. (2008) Impact of events on the brand Germany: Perspectives from younger Korean consumers. *Event Management*, 11, 145–153.

Jung, B. (2004) The evolution of leisure and sport participation in Poland. *International Journal of the History of Sport*, 21, 727–741.

Kaczynski, A. T. & Crompton, J. L. (2006) Financing priorities in local governments: Where do park and recreation services rank? *Journal of Park & Recreation Administration*, 24, 84–103.

Kaler, J. (2006) Evaluating stakeholder theory. *Journal of Business Ethics*, 69, 249–268.

Kang, K. J., & Stotlar, D. (2011) An investigation of factors influencing decision making for participation in the Olympic Partners sponsorship: A case study of Samsung. *International Journal of Applied Sports Sciences*, 23, 225–250.

Kant, I. (1997) *Critique of Practical Reason* (M. Gregor, trans.), Cambridge: Cambridge University Press.

KantarSport. (n.d.) *2010 FIFA World Cup South Africa: Television Audience Report*. Online. Available at www.fifa.com/mm/document/affederation/tv/01/47/32/73/2010fifaworldcupsoutha fricatvaudiencereport.pdf (accessed 27 September 2011).

Kaplan, S. & Garrick, B. J. (1981) On the quantitative definition of risk. *Risk Analysis*, 1, 11–27.

Kaplanidou, K. (2007) Affective event and destination image: Their influence on Olympic travellers' behavioural intentions. *Event Management*, 10, 159–173.

Kärnä, J., Juslin, H., Ahonen, V., & Hansen, E. (2001) Green advertising: Greenwash or a true reflection of marketing strategies? *Greener Management International*, 33, 59–70.

Kasimati, E. (2003) Economic aspects and the summer Olympics: A review of related research. *International Journal of Tourism Research*, 5, 433–444.

Kassing, J. W. & Sanderson, J. (2010) Fan–athlete interaction and Twitter tweeting through the Giro: A case study. *International Journal of Sport Communication*, 3, 113–128.

Katz, D., Maccoby, N., Gurin, G., & Floor, L. (1951) *Productivity, Supervision, and Morale among Railroad Workers*, Ann Arbor, MI: University of Michigan Survey Research Center.

Katz, D., Maccoby, N., & Morse, N. (1950) *Productivity, Supervision, and Morale in an Office Situation*, Ann Arbor, MI: University of Michigan Institute for Social Research.

Katz, R. L. (1955) Skills of an effective administrator. *Harvard Business Review*, 33, 33–42.

Kaufman, K. R., Kaufman, N. D., & Sciancalepore, J. (2010) L'Affaire Jessica Hardy: Doping violations and the Olympics – ensuring qualification and competition by clean athletes. A commentary. *Open Sports Medicine Journal*, 4, 29–33.

Keegan, A. & Den Hartog, D. N. (2004) Transformational leadership in a project-based environment: A comparative study of the leadership styles of project managers and line managers. *International Journal of Project Management*, 22, 609–617.

Kehl, J. L. (1994) The everyday nature of special events risk. *Risk Management*, 41(6), 27.

Keller, R. T. (2006) Transformational leadership, initiating structure, and substitutes for leadership: A longitudinal study of research and development project team performance. *Journal of Applied Psychology*, 91, 202–210.

Kellett, P., Hede, A.-M., & Chalip, L. (2008) Social policy for sport events: Leveraging (relationships with) teams from other nations for community benefit. *European Sport Management Quarterly*, 8, 101–121.

Kelso, P. (2011, 9 January) Qatar has 11 years to vindicate FIFA's strange decision to hand them 2022 World Cup. *The Telegraph*. Online. Available at www.telegraph.co.uk/sport/football/international/8249265/Qatar-has-11-years-to-vindicate-Fifas-strange-decision-to-hand-them-2022-World-Cup.html (accessed 16 September 2011).

Kemp, S. (2002) The hidden workforce: Volunteers' learning in the Olympics. *Journal of European Industrial Training*, 26, 109–116.

Keogh, F. & Fraser, A. (2005) *Why London Won the Olympics*, London: BBC Sports. Online. Available at http://news.bbc.co.uk/sport2/hi/other_sports/olympics_2012/4618507.stm (accessed 24 November 2010).

Késenne, S. (2005) Do we need an economic impact study or a cost–benefit analysis of a sports event? *European Sport Management Quarterly*, 5, 133–142.

Khadaroo, A., & Seetanah, B. (2007) Research note: Does transport infrastructure matter in overall tourism development? Evidence from a sample of island economies. *Tourism Economics*, 13, 675–684.

Kidd, B. (1988) The philosophy of excellence: Olympic performances, class, power, and the Canadian state. In P. J. Galasso (ed.), *Philosophy of Sport and Physical Activity: Issues and Concepts* (pp. 11–31), Toronto: Canadian Scholars' Press.

Kihl, L. A. & Richardson, T. (2009) "Fixing the mess": A grounded theory of a men's basketball coaching staff's suffering as a result of academic corruption. *Journal of Sport Management*, 23, 278–304.

Kihl, L. A., Richardson, T., & Campisi, C. (2008) Toward a grounded theory of student-athlete suffering and dealing with academic corruption. *Journal of Sport Management*, 22, 273–302.

Kim, N. S. & Chalip, L. (2004) Why travel to the FIFA World Cup? Effects of motives, background, interest and constraints. *Tourism Management*, 25, 695–707.

Kim, M., Won, D., & Harrolle, M. G. (2009) Influences of gifts on perspective volunteers: A conjoint analysis approach. *International Journal of Sport Management*, 10, 51–67.

Kim, M., Kim, M. K., & Odio, M. A. (2010) Are you proud?: The influence of sport and community identity and job satisfaction on pride of mega-event volunteers. *Event Management*, 14, 127–136.

King, C. (2007) Media portrayals of male and female athletes: A text and picture analysis of British national newspaper coverage of the Olympic Games since 1948. *International Review for the Sociology of Sport*, 42, 187–199.

Kirka, D. (2012, 9 January) *UK Police Smuggle Fake Bomb onto Olympic Site*. Online. Available at http://ca.sports.yahoo.com/olympics/news?slug=capress-oly_london_2012_200_days-16234042 (accessed 19 March 2012).

Kitzinger, J. (2000) Media templates: Patterns of association and the (re)construction of meaning over time. *Media, Culture and Society*, 22, 61–84.

Kjus, Y. (2009) Everyone needs idols: Reality television and transformations in media structure, production and output. *European Journal of Communication*, 24, 287–304.

Klein, G. (1998) *Sources of Power: How People Make Decisions*, Cambridge, MA: MIT Press.

Konstantaki, M. & Wickens, E. (2010) Residents' perceptions of environmental and security issues at the 2012 London Olympic Games. *Journal of Sport & Tourism*, 15, 337–357.

Ko, Y. J., Zhang, J., Cattani, K., & Pastore, D. (2011) Assessment of event quality in major spectator sports. *Managing Service Quality*, 21, 304–322.

Koenig, E. (1995) Criticism of doping: The nihilistic side of technological sport and the antiquated view of sport ethics. *International Review for the Sociology of Sport*, 30, 247–261.

Kogut, B. & Zander, U. (1992) Knowledge of the firm, combinative capabilities, and the replication of technology. *Organization Science*, 3, 383–397.

Koo, G. Y., Quarterman, J., & Flynn, L. (2006) Effect of perceived sport event and sponsor image fit on consumers' cognition, affect, and behavioural intentions. *Sport Marketing Quarterly*, 15, 80–90.

Kotlar, P. (1980) *Principals of Marketing*, Englewoods Cliffs, NJ: Prentice-Hall.

Kozinets, R. V. (1997) I want to believe: A netnography of the X-Philes' subculture of consumption. *Advances in Consumer Research*, 24, 470–475.

Kozinets, R. V. (2002) The field behind the screen: Using netnography for marketing research in online communities. *Journal of Marketing Research*, 39, 61–72.

Kristiansen, E. & Roberts, G. C. (2010) Young elite athletes and social support: Coping with competitive and organizational stress in "Olympic" competition. *Scandinavian Journal of Medicine & Science in Sports*, 20, 686–695.

Kristiansen, E., Hanstad, D. V., & Roberts, G. C. (2011) Coping with the media at the Vancouver Winter Olympics: "We all make a living out of this". *Journal of Applied Sport Psychology*, 23, 443–458.

Kuhnert, K. W. & Lewis, P. (1987) Transactional and transformational leadership: A constructive/developmental analysis. *Academy of Management Review*, 12, 648–657.

Kyriakidou, M. (2008) Rethinking media events in the context of a global public sphere: Exploring the audience of global disasters in Greece. *Communications*, 33, 273–291.

Lacey, R., Close, A. G., & Finney, R. Z. (2010) The pivotal roles of product knowledge and corporate social responsibility in event sponsorship effectiveness. *Journal of Business Research*, 63, 1222–1228.

Ladkin, D. & Taylor, S. S. (2010) Enacting the "true self": Towards a theory of embodied authentic leadership. *The Leadership Quarterly*, 21, 64–74.

Laing, J. & Frost, W. (2010) How green was my festival: Exploring challenges and opportunities associated with staging green events. *International Journal of Hospitality Management*, 29, 261–267.

Laios, A., Theodorakis, N., & Gargalianos, D. (2003) Leadership and power: Two important factors for effective coaching. *International Sports Journal*, 7, 150–154.

Lancaster, L. C. (2002) *When Generations Collide*, New York: Harper Paperbacks.

Lantos, G. P. (2011) *Consumer Behaviour in Action: Real-life Applications for Marketing Managers*, New York: M.E. Sharpe, Inc.

Latham, K. (2010) China's media viewed through the prism of the Beijing Olympics. *Sport in Society*, 13, 797–812.

Lauss, G. & Szigetvari, A. (2010) Governing by fun: EURO 2008 and the appealing power of fan zones. *Soccer & Society*, 11, 737–747.

Lee, C. K. & Taylor, T. (2005) Critical reflections on the economic impact assessment of a mega-event: The case of 2002 FIFA World Cup. *Tourism Management*, 26, 595–603.

Lee, C. K., Moon, S., & Mjelde, J. W. (2010) Disentangling the effects on the Korean economy of the 9/11 terrorist attacks from the short-run effects of hosting the 2002 World Cup, using the CGE model. *Tourism Economics*, 16, 611–628.

Lee, F. L. F. (2005) Spectacle and fandom: Media discourse in two soccer events in Hong Kong. *Sociology of Sport Journal*, 22, 194.

Lee, J. H. (2009) News values, media coverage, and audience attention: An analysis of direct and mediated causal relationships. *Journalism and Mass Communication Quarterly*, 86, 175–190.

Lee, J. H. & Choi, Y. J. (2009) News values of sports events: An application of a newsworthiness model on the World Cup coverage of US and Korean media. *Asian Journal of Communication*, 19, 302–318.

Lee, J. W. & Maguire, J. (2009) Global festivals through a national prism: The global–national nexus in South Korean media coverage of the 2004 Athens Olympic Games. *International Review for the Sociology of Sport*, 44, 5–24.

Lee, M. S., Sandler, D. M., & Shani, D. (1997) Attitudinal constructs towards sponsorship: Scale development using three global sporting events. *International Marketing Review*, 14, 159–169.

Legg, D. & Steadward, R. (2011) The Paralympic Games and 60 years of change (1948–2008): Unification and restructuring from a disability and medical model to sport-based competition. *Sport in Society*, 14, 1099–1115.

Legg, D., Fay, T. E. D., Hums, M. A., & Wolfe, E. L. I. (2009) Examining the inclusion of wheelchair exhibition events within the Olympic Games 1984–2004. *European Sport Management Quarterly*, 9, 243–258.

Lenart, S. & Targ, H. (1995) The media war against Nicaragua. *Peace Review*, 7(3–4), 347–353.

Lenskyj, H. J. (1992) Whose sport? Whose tradition? Canadian women and sport in the twentieth century. *The International Journal of the History of Sport*, 9, 141–150.

Lenskyj, H. J. (1996) When winners are losers: Toronto and Sydney bids for the summer Olympics. *Journal of Sport & Social Issues*, 20, 392–410.

Lenskyj, H. J. (2000) *Inside the Olympic Industry: Power, Politics and Activism*, Albany, NY: State University of New York Press.

Lenskyj, H. (2002) *The Best Olympics Ever? Social Impacts of Sydney 2000,* New York: State University of New York.

Leopkey, B. & Parent, M. M. (2009a) Risk management issues in large-scale sporting events: A stakeholder perspective. *European Sport Management Quarterly,* 9, 187–208.

Leopkey, B. & Parent, M. M. (2009b) Risk management strategies by stakeholders in Canadian major sporting events. *Event Management,* 13, 153–170.

Leopkey, B. & Parent, M. M. (2011, September) Governing the Olympic Games from the perspective of the host city: A look at the Sydney 2000 and Vancouver 2010 models. Paper presented at *European Association of Sport Management* Conference, Madrid, Spain.

Leopkey, B. & Parent, M. M. (2012) Olympic Games legacy: From general benefits to sustainable long term legacy. *International Journal of the History of Sport,* 29. Online. Available at www.tandfonline.com/doi/abs/10.1080/09523367.2011.623006 (accessed 27 December 2011).

Leopkey, B., Mutter, O., & Parent, M. M. (2010) Barriers and facilitators when hosting sporting events: exploring the Canadian and Swiss sport event hosting policies. *International Journal of Sport Policy,* 2, 113–134.

Lepp, A. & Gibson, H. (2011) Reimaging a nation: South Africa and the 2010 FIFA World Cup. *Journal of Sport & Tourism,* 16, 211–230.

Levermore, R. (2011) Sport-for-development and the 2010 Football World Cup. *Geography Compass,* 5(12), 886–897.

LIFT (n.d.) About Us. Online. Available at www.liftpartners.ca/who-we-are/about-us (accessed 27 December 2011).

Likona, T. (1991) *Educating for Character,* New York: Bantam.

Lindsey, I. (2008) Conceptualizing sustainability in sports development. *Leisure Studies,* 27, 279–294.

Lines, G. (2007) The impact of media sport events on the active participation of young people and some implications for PE pedagogy. *Sport, Education & Society,* 12, 349–366.

Lockstone, L. & Baum, T. (2009) The public face of event volunteering at the 2006 Commonwealth Games: The media perspective. *Managing Leisure,* 14, 38–56.

Lockstone, L., Smith, K., & Baum, T. (2010) Volunteering flexibility across the tourism sector. *Managing Leisure,* 15, 111–127.

Love, P. & Bullen, P. A. (2009) Toward the sustainable adaptation of existing facilities. *Facilities,* 27, 357–367.

Ludwig, S. & Karabetsos, J. D. (1999) Objectives and evaluation processes utilized by sponsors of the 1996 Olympic Games. *Sport Marketing Quarterly,* 8(1), 11–19.

Lukes, S. (1974) *Power: A Radical View,* London: MacMillan.

Lumpkin, A., Stoll, S. K., & Beller, J. M. (2003) *Sport Ethics: Applications for Fair Play* (3rd edn), New York: McGraw-Hill Higher Education.

Luo, J. (2010) "Betwixt and between": Reflections on the ritual aspects of the opening and closing ceremonies of the Beijing Olympics. *Sport in Society,* 13, 771–783.

Lyberger, M. R. & McCarthy, L. (2001) An assessment of consumer knowledge of, interest in, and perceptions of ambush marketing strategies. *Sport Marketing Quarterly,* 10, 130–137.

Ma, S. C., Egan, D., Rotherham, I., & Ma, S. M. (2011) A framework for monitoring during the planning stage for a sports mega-event. *Journal of Sustainable Tourism,* 19, 79–96.

MacAloon, J. J. (1978) Religious themes and structures in the Olympic movement and the Olympic Games. In F. Landry & W. A. R. Orban (eds), *Philosophy, Theology and History of Sport and of Physical Activity* (pp. 161–169), Miami, FL: Symposium Specialists.

MacAloon, J. J. (1984) Olympic Games and the theory of spectacle in modern societies. In J. J. MacAloon (ed.), *Rite, Drama, Festival, Spectacle: Rehearsals Toward a Theory of Cultural Performance*, Philadelphia, PA: Institute for the Study of Human Issues.

MacAloon, J. J. (1995) Olympic ceremonies as a setting for intercultural exchange. In International Olympic Committee (ed.), *Olympic Ceremonies: Historical Continuity and Cultural Exchange* (pp. 29–43), Lausanne: International Olympic Committee.

MacAloon, J. J. (2008) "Legacy" as managerial/magical discourse in contemporary Olympic affairs. *The International Journal of the History of Sport*, 25, 2060–2071.

McCambridge, R. (2004) Underestimating the power of nonprofit governance. *Nonprofit and Voluntary Sector Quarterly*, 33, 346–354.

McCann, J. E. (1991) Design principles for an innovating company. *Academy of Management Executive*, 5, 76–93.

McCarthy, L. M. & Irwin, R. L. (1998) Permanent seat licenses (PSLs) as an emerging source of revenue production. *Sport Marketing Quarterly*, 7, 41–46.

McCartney, G. & Osti, L. (2007) From cultural events to sport events: A case study of cultural authenticity in the dragon boat races. *Journal of Sport & Tourism*, 12, 25–40.

McCarville, R. E. & Copeland, R. P. (1994) Understanding sport sponsorship through exchange theory. *Journal of Sport Management*, 8, 102–114.

McCarville, R. E., Flood, C. M., & Froats, T. A. (1998) The effectiveness of selected promotions on spectators' assessments of a nonprofit sporting event sponsor. *Journal of Sport Management*, 12, 51–62.

McCrory, P. (2002) "The unfriendly games". *British Journal of Sports Medicine*, 36, 79.

McCurdy, P. M. (2008) Inside the media event: Examining the media practices of dissent! At the hori-zone eco-village at the 2005 G8 Gleneagles Summit. *Communications*, 33, 295–311.

McDaniel, S. R. (1999) An investigation of match-up effects in sport sponsorship advertising: The implications of consumer advertising schemas. *Psychology and Marketing*, 16, 163–184.

McDonald, P. (1991) The Los Angeles Olympic Organizing Committee: Developing organizational culture in the short run. In P. J. Frost, L. F. Moore, M. R. Louis, C. C. Lundberg, & J. Martin (eds), *Reframing Organizational Culture* (pp. 26–38), Newbury Park, CA: Sage Publications.

McGregor, A. (1998) Ruralness, development and democracy: Media, myths and the creation of meaning at Lake Cowal, New South Wales. *Australian Geographer*, 29, 191–203.

McGregor, D. (1960) *The Human Side of Enterprise*, New York: McGraw-Hill.

McKelvey, S. & Grady, J. (2008) Sponsorship program protection strategies for special sport events: Are event organizers outmaneuvering ambush marketers? *Journal of Sport Management*, 22, 550–586.

McKim, R. A. (1992) Risk management: Back to basics. *Cost Engineering*, 34(12), 7–12.

MacIntosh, E. W. & Nicol, L. (2012) The athlete's event experiences of the XIX Commonwealth Games in Delhi, India. *International Journal of Event and Festival Management*, 3, 12–29.

McLaren, R. H. (2008) Corruption: Its impact on fair play. *Marquette Sports Law Review*, 19, 15–38.

McLean, C., Patterson, A., & Williams, J. (2009) Risk assessment, policy-making and the limits of knowledge: The precautionary principle and international relations. *International Relations,* 23, 548–566.

MacLean, J. & Hamm, S. (2007) Motivation, commitment, and intentions of volunteers at a large Canadian sporting event. *Leisure/Loisir: Journal of the Canadian Association for Leisure Studies,* 31, 523–556.

McLennan, K. (1967) The manager and his job skills. *Academy of Management Journal,* 3, 235–245.

McLeod, J. R. (1991) The seamless web: Media and power in the post-modern global village. *Journal of Popular Culture,* 25, 69–75.

McQuire, S. (2010) Rethinking media events: Large screens, public space broadcasting and beyond. *New Media and Society,* 12, 567–582.

McTeer, W. G. & White, P. G. (2010) Winston/NEXTEL Cup: The triumph of the spectacle. *International Journal of Sport Management & Marketing,* 8, 93–105.

Madden, J. R. (2006) Economic and fiscal impacts of mega sporting events: A general equilibrium assessment. *Public Finance and Management,* 6, 346–394.

Madison, M. (2009) *More on Trademarks, Ambush Marketing, and International Soccer.* Online. Available at http://madisonian.net/2009/08/07/more-on-trademarks-ambush-marketing-and-international-soccer/ (accessed 15 December 2009).

Maennig, W. (2002) On the economics of doping and corruption in international sports. *Journal of Sports Economics,* 3, 61–89.

Maennig, W. & Du Plessis, S. (2009) Sport stadia, sporting events and urban development: International experience and the ambitions of Durban. *Urban Forum,* 20, 61–76.

Maguire, J. (2011) Invictus or evict-us? Media images of South Africa through the lens of the FIFA World Cup. *Social Identities,* 17, 681–694.

Mahony, D. F. & Howard, D. R. (2001) Sport business in the next decade: A general overview of expected trends. *Journal of Sport Management,* 15, 275–296.

Mallen, C., Adams, L., Stevens, J., & Thompson, L. (2010a) Environmental sustainability in sport facility management: A Delphi study. *European Sport Management Quarterly,* 10, 367–389.

Mallen, C., Stevens, J., Adams, L., & McRoberts, S. (2010b) The assessment of the environmental performance of an international multi-sport event. *European Sport Management Quarterly,* 10, 97–122.

Mallon, B. (1984a) The history of the opening ceremonies. *Olympic Review,* 199, 333–337.

Mallon, B. (1984b) Independent views: the history of the opening ceremonies. *Olympic Review,* 200, 449–450.

Mangan, J. A. (2008) Prologue: Guarantees of global goodwill – post-Olympic legacies. Too many limping white elephants? *The International Journal of the History of Sport,* 25, 1869–1883.

Mangan, J. A. (2011) The new Asia: global transformation, regional ascendancy, and metaphorical modernity. *International Journal of the History of Sport,* 28, 2229–2239.

Mangan, J. A., Ok, G., & Park, K. (2011) From the destruction of image to the reconstruction of image: a sports mega-event and the resurgence of a nation – the politics of sport exemplified. *International Journal of the History of Sport,* 28, 2339–2364.

Maslow, A. H. (1943) A theory of human motivation. *Psychological Review*, 50, 370–396.

Maslow, A. H. (1954) *Motivation and Personality*, New York: Harper & Row.

Mason, D. S. & Duquette, G. H. (2008) Urban regimes and sport in North American cities: Seeking status through franchises, events and facilities. *International Journal of Sport Management and Marketing*, 3, 221–241.

Mason, D. S., Thibault, L., & Misener, L. (2006) An agency theory perspective on corruption in sport: The case of the International Olympic Committee. *Journal of Sport Management*, 20, 52–73.

Mason, R. B. & Cochetel, F. (2006) Residual brand awareness following the termination of a long-term event sponsorship and the appointment of a new sponsor. *Journal of Marketing Communications*, 12, 125–144.

Masterman, G. (2004) *Strategic Sports Event Management: An International Approach*, Oxford: Elsevier.

Masterman, G. (2009) *Strategic Sports Event Management: Olympic Edition*, Oxford: Butterworth-Heinnemann.

Masterman, G. (2009) *Strategic Sports Event Management: Olympic Edition*, 2nd edn, Oxford: Butterworth-Heinnemann.

Matheson, C. (2010) Legacy planning, regeneration, and events: The Glasgow 2014 Commonwealth Games. *Local Economy*, 25, 10–23.

Matheson, V. A. (2009) Economic multipliers and mega-event analysis. *International Journal of Sport Finance*, 4, 63–70.

Matheson, V. A., & Baade, R. A. (2007) Padding required: Assessing the economic impact of the Super Bowl. In H. Preuss (ed.), *The Impact and Evaluation of Major Sporting Events* (pp. 41–62), Abingdon: Routledge.

Mattman, J. W. & Berlonghi, A. E. (1987) The Mattman model: The risks of special events. *Risk Management*, 34(10), 60–65.

Mayer, J. D. (2009) *What is Emotional Intelligence (EI)?* Online. Available at www.unh.edu/emotional_intelligence/ei%20What%20is%20EI/i%20definition.htm (accessed 29 December 2011).

Maynard, S., Powell, G. M., & Kittredge, W. (2005) Programs that work: A strategic plan at the core of public recreation financial management – a case study of Gwinnett County, Georgia. *Journal of Park & Recreation Administration*, 23, 115–128.

Mazanov, J. & Connor, J. (2010) The role of scandal and corruption in sports marketing and sponsorship. *International Journal of Sports Marketing & Sponsorship*, 11, 183.

Meenaghan, T. (1998) Ambush marketing: Corporate strategy and consumer reaction. *Psychology and Marketing*, 15, 305–322.

Mehrabian, A. (1981) *Silent Messages: Implicit Communication of Emotions and Attitudes*, Belmont, CA: Wadsworth.

Mei, D. (2009) Job satisfaction among volunteers of the 2007 Special Olympics World Summer Games. *Asian Journal of Physical Education & Recreation*, 15, 29–34.

Mendez, H. Y. (1999) Virtual signage: The pitfalls of "now you see it, now you don't". *Sport Marketing Quarterly*, 8, 15–21.

Merkel, U. & Kim, M. (2011) Third time lucky!? PyeongChang's bid to host the 2018 Winter Olympics – politics, policy and practice. *International Journal of the History of Sport*, 28, 2365–2383.

Merrin, W. (2002) Implosion, simulation and the pseudo-event: A critique of McLuhan. *Economy and Society*, 31, 369–390.

Meyer, J. P. & Allen, N. J. (1991) A three-conceptualization of organizational commitment. *Human Resource Management Review*, 1, 61–89.

Meyer, J. P. & Herscovitch, L. (2001) Commitment in the workplace: Towards a general model. *Human Resource Management Review*, 11, 299–362.

Meyer, J. W. & Rowan, B. (1977) Institutionalized organizations: Formal structure as myth and ceremony. *American Journal of Sociology*, 83, 340–363.

Meyer, J. P., Allen, N. J., & Smith, C. A. (1993) Commitment to organizations and occupations: Extension and test of a three-component conceptualization. *Journal of Applied Psychology*, 78, 538–551.

Meyer, J. P., Stanley, D. J., Herscovitch, L., & Topolnytsky, L. (2002) Affective, continuance, and normative commitment to the organization: A meta-analysis of antecedents, correlates, and consequences. *Journal of Vocational Behavior*, 61, 20–52.

Miah, A. (2010, 12 February) The opening ceremony of the Olympic Games. *The Huffington Post*. Online. Available at www.huffingtonpost.com/andy-miah/the-opening-ceremony-of-t_b_459071.html (accessed 12 March 2012).

Mignon, P. (2003) The Tour de France and the doping issue. *International Journal of the History of Sport*, 20(2), 227–245.

Mihelj, S. (2008) National media events: From displays of unity to enactments of division. *European Journal of Cultural Studies*, 11, 471–488.

Miller, J. S. (2003) High tech and high performance: Managing appraisal in the information age. *Journal of Labor Research*, 24, 409–424.

Min, W. & Zhen, X. (2010) Mirroring the Olympic Games: The Beijing 2008 Olympic Games in the American media. *International Journal of the History of Sport*, 27, 1794–1808.

MindTools (2012) *Project Management Tools*. Online. Available at www.mindtools.com/pages/main/newMN_PPM.htm (accessed 27 February 2012).

Minnaert, L. (2012) An Olympic legacy for all? The non-infrastructural outcomes of the Olympic Games for socially excluded groups (Atlanta 1996–Beijing 2008). *Tourism Management*, 33, 361–370.

Mintzberg, H. (1979) *The Structuring of Organizations*, Englewood Cliffs, NJ: Prentice Hall.

Mitchell, R. C. & Carson, R. T. (1993) *Using Surveys to Value Public Goods: The Contingent Valuation Method*, Washington, DC: Resources for the Future/John Hopkins University Press.

Mitchell, R. K., Agle, B. R., & Wood, D. J. (1997) Toward a theory of stakeholder identification and salience: Defining the principle of who and what really counts. *Academy of Management Review*, 22, 853–886.

Miyazaki, A. D. & Morgan, A. G. (2001) Assessing market value of event sponsoring: Corporate olympic sponsorships. *Journal of Advertising Research*, 41, 9–15.

Moe, W. W. & Fader, P. S. (2009) The role of price tiers in advance purchasing of event tickets. *Journal of Service Research*, 12, 73–86.

Moles, J. B. M., Pruneau, J., & Pigeassou, C. (2001) The implication of new technologies for "television sports": learning ethics or shame on the unethical. *Loisir & Societe*, 24, 223–244.

Mondello, M. J., & Rishe, P. (2004) Comparative economic impact analyses: Differences across cities, events, and demographics. *Economic Development Quarterly*, 18, 331–342.

Montemayor, E. F. (1995) Situation or person? Contrasting the effects of budget constraints and individual values on pay-for-performance norms. *Journal of Psychology*, 129, 531.

Moorman, A. & Greenwell, C. (2005) Consumer attitudes of deception and the legality of ambush marketing practices. *Journal of Legal Aspects of Sports*, 15, 183–211.

Mora, M. (2010) Vancouver 2010 passes on safety torch for future Olympics. *Canadian Occupational Safety*. Online. Available at www.cos-mag.com/Training/Training-Stories/Vancouver-2010-passes-on-safety-torch-for-future-Olympics.html (accessed 12 February 2010).

Morrison, E. W. & Robinson, S. L. (1997) When employees feel betrayed: A model of how psychological contract violation develops. *Academy of Management Review*, 22, 226–256.

Mowday, R. T., Porter, L. W., & Steers, R. M. (1982) *Employee–Organization Linkages: The Psychology of Commitment, Absenteeism, and Turnover*, New York: Academic Press.

Mowen, A. J., Kerstetter, D. L., Trauntvein, N. E., & Graefe, A. R. (2009) What factors shape visitor support for the privatization of park services and amenities? *Journal of Park & Recreation Administration*, 27, 33–45.

Mroczkowska, H. (2010) The structure of values and the risk of their loss under conditions of differentiated probability of doping control. *Polish Journal of Sport & Tourism*, 17, 15–19.

Mullin, B. J., Hardy, S., & Sutton, W. A. (1993) *Sport Marketing*, Champaign, IL: Human Kinetics.

Mullin, B. J., Hardy, S., & Sutton, W. A. (2000) *Sport Marketing* (2nd edn), Champaign, IL: Human Kinetics.

Mulvey, J. M. & Shetty, B. (2004) Financial planning via multi-stage stochastic optimization. *Computers and Operations Research*, 31, 1–20.

Murray, D. (2009) Reflections on public funding for professional sports facilities. *Journal of the Philosophy of Sport*, 36, 22–39.

Murray, V., Bradshaw, P., & Wolpin, J. (1992) Power in and around nonprofit boards: a neglected dimension of governance. *Non Profit Management Leadership*, 3, 165–182.

Myers, G. (2000) Entitlement and sincerity in broadcast interviews about Princess Diana. *Media, Culture and Society*, 22, 167–185.

Naka, M. & Kobayashi, N. (2010) A quantitative and qualitative analysis of Japanese television news coverage of the Beijing Olympics opening ceremony. *International Journal of the History of Sport*, 27, 1778–1793.

Narayan, P. K. & Smyth, R. (2003) Attendance and pricing at sporting events: Empirical results from Granger Causality Tests for the Melbourne Cup. *Applied Economics*, 35, 1649–1657.

Nasaw, D. (2000) *The Chief: The Life of William Randolph Hearst*, New York: Houghton Mifflin Harcourt.

NBS (2011) *Top 10 CSR Research Findings of 2011*. Online. Available at http://nbs.net/news-events/top-10-csr-research-findings-of-2011 (accessed 13 December 2011).

Ndlovu-Gatsheni, S. J. (2011a) Pan-Africanism and the 2010 FIFA world cup in South Africa. *Development Southern Africa*, 28, 401–413.

Ndlovu-Gatsheni, S. J. (2011b) The World Cup, vuvuzelas, flag-waving patriots and the burden of building South Africa. *Third World Quarterly*, 32, 279–293.

Neal, D. J., Sugarman, D. E., Hustad, J. T. P., Caska, C. M., & Carey, K. B. (2005) It's all fun and games … or is it? Collegiate sporting events and celebratory drinking. *Journal of Studies on Alcohol*, 66, 291–294.

Neeley, L. & Judson, K. M. (2010) Technology segmentation for marketing: Entrepreneurial approaches to intercollegiate athletics. *International Journal of Sport Management and Marketing*, 7, 4–20.

Nelson, K. B. (2009) Enhancing the attendee's experience through creative design of the event environment: Applying Goffman's dramaturgical perspective. *Journal of Convention & Event Tourism*, 10, 120–133.

Nevin, M. (2010) *Canada Named No. 1 Country Brand in the World: Tourism Leads Results*. Online. Available at http://mediacentre.canada.travel/content/ctc_news/canada-number-one-country-brand-index-futurebrand (accessed 31 March 2011).

Nguyen, S. N. & Menzies, J. (2010) Event effectiveness: Analysing the perceptions of key stakeholders of the Lexmark Indy 300/Champ Car event, Gold Coast. *International Journal of Sport Management and Marketing*, 8, 106–130.

Nichols, G. & Ojala, E. (2009) Understanding the management of sports events volunteers through psychological contract theory. *Voluntas*, 20, 369–387.

Nichols, L. (2011a, 30 September) *Strip Bar Warned over RWC Tactics*. Online. Available at www.stuff.co.nz/business/5707640/Strip-bar-warned-over-RWC-tactics (accessed 15 December 2011).

Nichols, L. (2011b, 28 September) *Wellington Retailers Defy All Blacks Ad Ban*. Online. Available at www.stuff.co.nz/dominion-post/news/5694387/Wellington-retailers-defy-All-Blacks-ad-ban?comment_msg=posted#post_comment (accessed 15 December 2011).

Nord, W. R. & Durand, D. E. (1978) What's wrong with the human resources approach to management? *Organizational Dynamics*, 6, 13–25.

Nossek, H. (2008) "News media"–media events: Terrorist acts as media events. *Communications*, 33, 313–330.

Nufer, G. & Bühler, A. (2010) How effective is the sponsorship of global sports events? A comparison of the FIFA World Cups in 2006 and 1998. *International Journal of Sports Marketing and Sponsorship*, 11, 303–319.

Numerato, D. (2009) The media and sports corruption: An outline of sociological understanding. *International Journal of Sport Communication*, 2, 261–273.

Nylund, M. (2009) Mega-sporting events and the media in attention economies: National and international press coverage of the IAAF world championships in Helsinki 2005. *Nordicom Review*, 30, 125–140.

O'Beirne, C. (2012) Information technology and communications technology and its use in sport business. In L. Trenberth & D. Hassan (eds), *Managing Sport Business: An Introduction* (pp. 338–349), New York: Routledge.

O'Brien, D. (2006) Event business leveraging The Sydney 2000 Olympic Games. *Annals of Tourism Research*, 33, 240–261.

O'Brien, D. (2007) Points of leverage: Maximizing host community benefit from a regional surfing festival. *European Sport Management Quarterly*, 7, 141–165.

O'Brien, D. & Chalip, L. (2008) Sport events and strategic leveraging: Pushing towards the triple bottom line. In A. Woodside & D. Martin (eds), *Advancing Tourism Management* (pp. 318–338), Cambridge, MA: CABI Publishing.

Ocasio, W. (1994) Political dynamics and the circulation of power: CEO succession in US industrial corporations. *Administrative Science Quarterly*, 39, 285–312.

Office of the Commissioner of Official Languages (2010) *Raising our Game for Vancouver 2010: Final Report on the Vancouver 2010 Olympic and Paralympic Winter Games.* Online. Available at www.ocol-clo.gc.ca/docs/e/stu_etu_games_jeux_e_02_2011.pdf (accessed 23 March 2012).

OGI-UBC (2010) *Olympic Games Impact Study: A Backgrounder.* Online. Available at www.ogi-ubc.ca/about.asp (accessed 27 December 2011).

Oliver, R. (2011) Toronto's Olympic aspirations: A bid for the waterfront. *Urban Geography*, 32, 767–787.

O'Reilly, N. & Knight, P. (2007) Knowledge management best practices in national sport organisations. *International Journal of Sport Management and Marketing*, 2, 264–280.

O'Reilly, N. & Séguin, B. (2009) *Sport Marketing: A Canadian Perspective*, Scarborough, ON: Nelson Education Ltd.

O'Reilly, N., Nadeau, J., Seguin, B., & Harrison, M. (2007) In-stadium sponsorship evaluation of a mega-sponsee: The 2004 Grey Cup. *International Journal of Sports Marketing and Sponsorship*, 8, 179–198.

Organ, D. W., Podsakoff, P. M., & MacKenzie, S. B. (2006) *Organizational Citizenship Behavior: Its Nature, Antecedents, and Consequences*, Thousand Oaks, CA: Sage Publications.

Organizing Committee Commonwealth Games 2010 Delhi (2010) *Executive Management.* Online. Available at www.cwgdelhi2010.org/executive_management (accessed 13 December 2010).

O'Sullivan, P. & Murphy, P. (1998) Ambush marketing: The ethical issues. *Psychology and Marketing*, 15, 349–366.

Ozaralli, N. (2003) Effects of transformational leadership on empowerment and team effectiveness. *Leadership & Organization Development Journal*, 24, 335–344.

Ozturk, M. A., Kozub, F. W., & Kocak, S. (2004) Impact of sponsorship on companies that supported the 2002 Salt Lake City Winter Paralympics. *International Journal of Sports Marketing and Sponsorship*, 5, 282–295.

Pacione, M. (2012) The role of events in urban regeneration. In S. J. Page & J. Connell (eds), *The Routledge Handbook of Events* (pp. 385–400), London: Routledge.

Panesar, K. (2011, 15 March) *Head Shots at NHL GM Meetings in Florida: Are the Winds of Change Blowing?* Online. Available at www.habsaddict.com/2011/03/head-shots-at-nhl-gm-meetings-in.html (accessed 5 July 2011).

Papa, F. (2010a) France: A conflict of values? The Olympic torch relay in Paris – the mass media were on cue. *International Journal of the History of Sport*, 27, 1452–1460.

Papa, F. (2010b) France: The Beijing Olympics 2008 – revisiting history to build a new future? *International Journal of the History of Sport*, 27, 1675–1693.

Papadimitriou, D. & Apostolopoulou, A. (2009) Olympic sponsorship activation and the creation of competitive advantage. *Journal of Promotion Management*, 15, 90–117.

Parent, M. M. (2006) Organization theory in sport management. In P. Bouchet & C. Pigeassou (eds), *Management du Sport: Actualités de la Recherche et Perspectives* (pp. 211–225), Clapiers, France: AFRAPS.

Parent, M. M. (2008) Evolution and issue patterns for major-sport-event organizing committees and their stakeholders. *Journal of Sport Management*, 22, 135–164.

Parent, M. M. (2010) Decision making in major sport events over time: Parameters, drivers, and strategies. *Journal of Sport Management*, 24, 291–318.

Parent, M. M. (2012) Describing the Olympic Games Knowledge Transfer Stakeholder Network.

Paper presented at the 4th International Sport Business Symposium, Innsbruck, Austria. Online. Available at www.uibk.ac.at/isw/unterlagen/pdf-management-symposium/hall-1-keynotes/1-8_describing-the-olympic-games-knosledge-transfer-stakeholder-network.pdf (accessed 20 February 2012).

Parent, M. M. & Deephouse, D. L. (2007) A case study of stakeholder identification and prioritization by managers. *Journal of Business Ethics*, 75, 1–23.

Parent, M. M. & Foreman, P. O. (2007) Organizational image and identity management in large-scale sporting events. *Journal of Sport Management*, 21, 15–40.

Parent, M. M. & Séguin, B. (2007) Factors that led to the drowning of a world championship organizing committee: A stakeholder approach. *European Sport Management Quarterly*, 7, 187–212.

Parent, M. M. & Séguin, B. (2008) Toward a model of brand creation for international large-scale sporting events: The impact of leadership, context, and nature of the event. *Journal of Sport Management*, 22, 526–549.

Parent, M. M. & Séguin, B. (2010) Change as routine? Understanding organizational change in Canadian major sporting events. In A. Ferrand, C. Legrand, & B. Séguin (eds), *International Federation of Scholarly Associations of Management*, Paris, France: IFSAM.

Parent, M. M. & Slack, T. (2007) Structural factors influencing the volunteer–professional staff relationship in large-scale sporting events. In M. M. Parent & T. Slack (eds), *International Perspectives on the Management of Sport* (pp. 229–245), Burlington, MA: Elsevier.

Parent, M. M., Beaupré, R., & Séguin, B. (2009a) Key leadership qualities for large-scale sporting events: A case study of the World Aquatics Championships. *International Journal of Sport Management & Marketing*, 6, 367–388.

Parent, M. M., Olver, D., & Séguin, B. (2009b) Understanding leadership in major sporting events: The case of the 2005 World Aquatics Championships. *Sport Management Review*, 12, 167–184.

Parent, M. M., Séguin, B., Gagné Côté, D., Leblond, O., & Laperle, K. (2009c) Un modèle pour des alliances stratégiques dans le cadre de la gestion d'événements sportifs au Canada. In S. Carayannopoulos (ed.), *Administrative Sciences Association of Canada Conference*, Niagara Falls, ON: Wilfrid Laurier University. Online. Avalailable at http://luxor.acadiau.ca/library/ASAC/v30/TourismAndSportManagement/Papers/ParentSeguinCoteLeblondLaperle.pdf (accessed 23 February 2012).

Parent, M. M., Rouillard, C., & Leopkey, B. (2011) Issues and strategies pertaining to the Canadian governments' coordination efforts in relation to the 2010 Olympic Games. *European Sport Management Quarterly*, 11, 337–369.

Parent, M. M., Eskerud, L., & Hanstad, D. V. (2012) Brand creation in international recurring sports events. *Sport Management Review*, 15, 145–159.

Parguel, B., Benoît-Moreau, F., & Larceneux, F. (2011) How sustainability ratings might deter "greenwashing": A closer look at ethical corporate communication. *Journal of Business Ethics*, 102, 15–28.

Parker, L. D. (2008) Boardroom operational and financial control: An insider view. *British Journal of Management*, 19, 65–88.

Parmenter, G. (2000) *Accreditation* (p. 7), Lausanne, Switzerland: International Olympic Committee.

Parnell, G. S., Frimpon, M., Barnes, J., Kloeber Jr, J. M., Deckro, R. F., & Jackson, J. A. (2001) Safety risk analysis of an innovative environmental technology. *Risk Analysis: An International Journal*, 21, 143–156.

Parnell, G. S., Smith, C. M., & Moxley, F. I. (2010) Intelligent adversary risk analysis: A bioterrorism risk management model. *Risk Analysis: An International Journal*, 30, 32–48.

Parrish, R. (2008) Access to major events on television under European Law. *Journal of Consumer Policy*, 31, 79–98.

Pauline, G. & Pauline, J. S. (2009) Volunteer motivation and demographic influences at a professional tennis event. *Team Performance Management*, 15, 172–184.

Payne, M. (1998) Ambush marketing: The undeserved advantage. *Psychology and Marketing*, 15, 323–366.

PCH (2009, 5 November) *PricewaterhouseCoopers Report Shows 2010 Winter Games Creates Jobs, Stimulate Economy*. Online. Available at www.pch.gc.ca/eng/1294862468773/1294862468775 (accessed 27 December 2011).

Pearsall, J. (ed.) (1999) *The Concise Oxford Dictionary* (10th edn), Oxford: Oxford University Press.

Pegoraro, A., O'Reilly, N. J., & Giguere, M. (2009) Online and off-line advertising during March madness: Which companies drive consumers to the web? *International Journal of Sport Communication*, 2, 466–483.

Peiro, J. M., Ramos, J., Gonzalez, P., Rodrigez, I., Tordera, N., Martinez-Tur, V., & Whitely, W. (1998) Situational distinctions in organizations: The case of sport facility management. *Journal of Park & Recreation Administration*, 16, 1–24.

Pelham, F. (2011) Sustainable event management: The journey to ISO 20121. In J. Savery & K. Gilbert (eds), *Sustainability and Sport* (pp. 43–49), Champaign, IL: Common Ground.

Pelly, F. E., O'Connor, H. T., Denyer, G. S., & Caterson, I. D (2011) Evolution of food provision to athletes at the summer Olympic Games. *Nutrition Reviews*, 69, 321–332.

Pena, E. F. & De Moragas, M. (2010) Spain: Media focus on the geopolitical issues of a major sporting event. *International Journal of the History of Sport*, 27, 1501–1509.

Pena, E. F., De Moragas, M., Lallana, I., & Rezende, A. (2010) Spain: The power of a mega event which eclipses criticism. *International Journal of the History of Sport*, 27, 1634–1674.

Pentifallo, C. (2010) *Sport Mega-Events, Sustainability, and Impact Assessment. Summary Report*, Vancouver: UBC Centre for Sport & Sustainability. Online. Available at http://css.ubc.ca/events/think-tank-1/think-tank-1-summary-report (accessed 26 March 2012).

Perrow, C. (1967) A framework for the comparative analysis of organizations. *American Sociological Review*, 32, 194–208.

Peters, L. H., Hartke, D. D., & Pohlmann, J. T. (1985) Fielder's contingency theory of leadership: An application of the meta-analysis procedures of Schmidt and Hunter. *Psychological Bulletin*, 97, 274–285.

Peters, M., Piazolo, F., Koster, L., & Promberger, K. (2010) The deployment of Intelligent Local-Based Information Systems (ILBI): A case study of the European Football Championship 2008. *Journal of Convention & Event Tourism*, 11, 18–41.

Pettigrew, A. M. (1985) *The Awakening Giant: Continuity and Change in Imperial Chemical Industries*, Oxford: Blackwell.

Pettigrew, A. M. (1987) Context and action in the transformation of the firm. *Journal of Management Studies*, 24, 649–670.

Phillips, R. (2003) *Stakeholder Theory and Organizational Ethics*, San Francisco, CA: Berrett-Koehler Publishers, Inc.

Phillips, R., Freeman, R. E., & Wicks, A. C. (2003) What stakeholder theory is not. *Business Ethics Quarterly*, 13, 479–502.

Piccarello, C. M. (2005) Terrorism, tourism, and torts: Liability in the event of a terrorist attack on a sports or entertainment venue. *Villanova Sports & Entertainment Law Journal*, 12, 365–392.

Pineno, C. J. & Tyree, L. M. (2006) Appropriate budget accounts and activity-based costing for decision making in non-profit organizations: A comparative study. *Competition Forum*, 4, 354–370.

Ping-Kun, C. & Chiung-Hsia, W. (2008) Impact of media coverage of the 42nd World Archery Championships on audience attendance and purchases. *Sport Journal*, 11, 64–71.

Pipan, T. & Porsander, L. (2000) Imitating uniqueness: How big cities organize big events. *Organization Studies*, 21, 1–27.

Pitter, R. (1990) Power and control in an amateur sport organization. *International Review for the Sociology of Sport*, 25, 309–322.

Pitts, B. G. (1998) An analysis of sponsorship recall during Gay Games IV. *Sport Marketing Quarterly*, 7, 11–18.

Pitts, B. G. (2002) Examining sport management scholarship: A historical review of the *Sport Marketing Quarterly*. *Sport Marketing Quarterly*, 11, 84–92.

Pitts, B. G., & Stotlar, D. K. (1996) *Fundamentals of Sport Marketing*, Morgantown, WV: Fitness Information Technology.

PMBOK (2012) *PMBOK Guide and Standards*. Online. Available at www.pmi.org/PMBOK-Guide-and-Standards.aspx (accessed 27 February 2012).

Podolny, J. M. (1993) A status-based model of market competition. *American Journal of Sociology*, 98, 829–872.

Podolny, J. M. (1994) Market uncertainty and the social character of economic exchange. *Administrative Science Quarterly*, 39, 458–483.

Pons, F., Laroche, M., Nyeck, S., & Perreault, S. (2001) Role of sporting events as ethnoculture's emblems: Impact of acculturation and ethnic identity on consumers' orientation towards sporting events. *Sport Marketing Quarterly*, 10, 231–240.

Ponsford, I. F. & Williams, P. W. (2010) Crafting a social license to operate: A case study of Vancouver 2010's Cypress Olympic venue. *Event Management*, 14, 17–36.

Poole, M. S. & DeSanctis, G. (1989) Use of group decision support systems as an appropriation process. Paper presented at the 22nd Annual Hawaii International Conference on System Sciences, Hawaii, USA.

Porsander, L. (2000) Translating a dream of immortality in a (con)temporary order. *Journal of Organizational Change Management*, 13, 14–29.

Porteshawver, A. B. (2009) Green sports facilities: Why adopting new green-building policies will improve the environment and the community. *Marquette Sports Law Review*, 20, 241–265.

Portlock, A. and Rose, S. (2009) Effects of ambush marketing: UK consumer brand recall and attitudes to official sponsors and non-sponsors associated with the FIFA World Cup 2006. *International Journal of Sports Marketing and Sponsorship*, 10, 271–286.

Post, J. E., Preston, L. E., & Sachs, S. (2002) *Redefining the Corporation: Stakeholder Management and Organizational Wealth*, Stanford, CA: Stanford University Press.

Pound, R. W. (2004) *Inside the Olympics: A Behind-the-Scenes Look at the Politics, the Scandals, and the Glory of the Games*, Mississauga: John Wiley and Sons.

Prebensen, N. K. (2010) Value creation through stakeholder participation: A case study of an event in the High North. *Event Management*, 14, 37–52.

Preuss, H. (2005) The economic impact of visitors at major multi-sport events. *European Sport Management Quarterly*, 5, 281–301.

Preuss, H. (2006) Impact and evaluation of major sporting events. *European Sport Management Quarterly*, 6, 313–316.

Preuss, H. (2007a) FIFA World Cup 2006 and it legacy on tourism. *Trends and Issues in Global Tourism 2007*, 3, 83–102.

Preuss, H. (2007b) The conceptualization and measurement of mega-sport event legacies. *Journal of Sport and Tourism*, 12, 207–227.

Preuss, H. & Alfs, C. (2011) Signaling through the 2008 Beijing Olympics: Using mega sport events to change the perception and image of the host. *European Sport Management Quarterly*, 11, 55–71.

Preuss, H., Séguin, B., & O'Reilly, N. (2007) Profiling major sport event visitors: The 2002 Commonwealth Games. *Journal of Sport and Tourism*, 12, 5–23.

Pritchard, M. P. & Funk, D. C. (2006) Symbiosis and substitution in spectator sport. *Journal of Sport Management*, 20, 299–321.

Propper, R. E., Stickgold, R., Keeley, R., & Christman, S. D. (2007) Is television traumatic? Dreams, stress, and media exposure in the aftermath of September 11, 2001. *Psychological Science*, 18, 334–340.

Prystupa, E., Prystupa, T., & Bolach, E. (2006) Developmental trends in sports for the disabled: The case of the summer Paralympics. *Human Movement*, 7, 77–83.

Puijk, R. (1999) Producing Norwegian culture for domestic and foreign gazes: The Lillehammer Olympic opening ceremony. In A. M. Klausen (ed.), *Olympic Games as Performance and Public Event: The Case of the XVII Olympic Games in Norway* (pp. 97–136), New York: Berghahn Books.

Puijk, R. (2000) A global media event? Coverage of the 1994 Lillehammer Olympic Games. *International Review for the Sociology of Sport*, 35, 309–330.

Puijk, R. (2009) Intense media coverage. *Communications*, 34, 1–20.

Qi, C. X., Gibson, H. J., & Zhang, J. J. (2009) Perceptions of risk and travel intentions: The case of China and the Beijing Olympic Games. *Journal of Sport & Tourism*, 14, 43–67.

Qing, L., Boccia, L. V., Chunmiao, H., Xing, L., Fu, Y., & Kennett, C. (2010) Representing the opening ceremony: Comparative content analysis from USA, Brazil, UK and China. *International Journal of the History of Sport*, 27, 1591–1633.

Rafoss, K. R. & Troelsen, J. (2010) Sports facilities for all? The financing, distribution and use of sports facilities in Scandinavian countries. *Sport in Society*, 13, 643–656.

Ralston, R., Lumsdon, L., & Downward, P. (2005) The third force in events tourism: Volunteers at the XVII Commonwealth Games. *Journal of Sustainable Tourism*, 13, 504–519.

Ramshaw, G. & Hinch, T. (2006) Place identity and sport tourism: The case of the Heritage Classic Ice Hockey event. *Current Issues in Tourism*, 9, 399–418.

Ramus, C. A. & Montiel, I. (2005) When are corporate environmental policies a form of greenwashing? *Business and Society*, 44, 377–414.

Rasche, A. & Esser, D. E. (2006) From stakeholder management to stakeholder accountability: Applying Habermasian discourse ethics to accountability research. *Journal of Business Ethics*, 65, 251–267.

Rasmus, J. (2009) Speculative capital, financial crisis and emerging epic recession. *Critique*, 37, 31–49.

Rehorick, S., Johannsdottir, K., Parent, M., & Patterson, D. (2011) *Using the Common European Framework of Reference for Evaluating Language Volunteers for the Vancouver 2010 Olympic and Paralympic Winter Games*. Online. Available at www.ecml.at/LinkClick. aspx?fileticket=th5EFNLwtXU%3d&tabid=174&language=en-GB (accessed 27 February 2012).

Reichart, J. (2003) A theoretical exploration of expectational gaps in the corporate issue construct. *Corporate Reputation Review*, 6, 58–69.

Rice, R. W. (1978) Construct validity of the least preferred coworker score. *Psychological Bulletin*, 85, 1199–1237.

Richelieu, A. (2004) Building the brand equity of professional sports teams. In B. G. Pitts (ed.), *Sharing Best Practices in Sport Marketing* (pp. 3–21), Morgantown, WV: Fitness Information Technology.

Riess, S. A. (1981) Power without authority: Los Angeles' elites and the construction of the coliseum. *Journal of Sport History*, 8, 50–65.

Ritchie, B. W., Shipway, R., & Chien, P. M. (2010) The role of the media in influencing residents' support for the 2012 Olympic Games. *International Journal of Event and Festival Management*, 1, 202–219.

Ritchie, I. (2003) Sex tested, gender verified: Controlling female sexuality in the age of containment. *Sport History Review*, 34, 80–98.

Ritchie, J. R. B. (1984) Assessing the impact of hallmark events: Conceptual and research issues. *Journal of Travel Research*, 23, 2–11.

Ritchie, J. R. B. (2000) Turning 16 days into 16 years through Olympic legacies. *Event Management*, 6, 155–165.

Ritchie, J. R. B. & Smith, B. H. (1991) The impact of a mega-event on host region awareness: A longitudinal study. *Journal of Travel Research*, 31, 3–10.

Ritchie, W. J., Anthony, W. P., & Rubens, A. J. (2004) Individual executive characteristics: Explaining the divergence between perceptual and financial measures in nonprofit organizations. *Journal of Business Ethics*, 53, 267–281.

Rivenburgh, N. K. (2002) The Olympic Games: Twenty-first century challenges as a global media event. *Culture, Sport, Society*, 5, 31–50.

RNZ (2011, 31 March) *Christchurch Matches Rescheduled after Quake*. Online. Available at www.rugbyworldcup.com/destinationnewzealand/news/newsid=2041723.html#christchurch+ma tches+rescheduled+after+quake (accessed 16 June 2011).

Robbins, S. P. (1997) *Managing Today!* Upper Saddle River, NJ: Prentice Hall.

Roberts, D. (2010) Durban's future? Rebranding through the production/policing of event-specific spaces at the 2010 World Cup. *Sport in Society*, 13, 1486–1497.

Robinson, P., Wale, D., & Dickson, G. (2010) *Events Management*, Cambridge, MA: CABI.

Robson, L. M. (2011) A demographic study of event planners. *Journal of Convention & Event Tourism*, 12, 45–52.

Rosengren, K. E. (1970) International news: Intra and extra media data. *Acta Sociologica*, 13, 96–109.

Rossman, G. (2004) Elites, masses, and media blacklists: The Dixie Chicks controversy. *Social Forces*, 83, 61–79.

Rousseau, D. M. (1989) Psychological and implied contracts in organizations. *Employee Responsibilities and Rights Journal*, 2, 121–139.

Rousseau, D. M. (1998) The "problem" of the psychological contract considered. *Journal of Organizational Behavior*, 19, 665–671.

Rousseau, D. M. & McLean Parks, J. (1993) The contracts of individuals and organizations. In L. L. Cummings & B. M. Stow (eds), *Research in Organizational Behavior* (Vol. 15, pp. 1–47), Greenwich, CT: JAI Press.

Rowley, T. J. (1997) Moving beyond dyadic ties: A network theory of stakeholder influences. *Academy of Management Review*, 22, 887–910.

Roy, D. P. & Cornwell, T. B. (2003) Brand equity's influence on responses to event sponsorships. *Journal of Product & Brand Management*, 12, 377–393.

Roy, D. P. & Cornwell, T. B. (2004) The effects of consumer knowledge on responses to event sponsorships. *Psychology & Marketing*, 21, 185–207.

Roy, D. P. & Graeff, T. R. (2002/2003) Influences on consumer responses to Winter Olympic sponsorship. *International Journal of Sports Marketing and Sponsorship*, 4 (4), 355–375.

Roy, D. P., Goss, B. D., & Jubenville, C. B. (2010) Influences on event attendance decisions for stock car automobile racing fans. *International Journal of Sport Management and Marketing*, 8, 73–92.

Rudd, P. (2011) Vancouver Olympics leave a legacy of gain and financial pain. *The Seattle Times*. Online. Available at http://seattletimes.nwsource.com/html/restlessnative/2014280249_restless20.html (accessed 19 February 2011).

Rugby New Zealand 2011 Ltd (2011) *Team 2011 Volunteers*. Online. Available at www.rugby-worldcup.com/destinationnewzealand/volunteers.html (accessed 19 September 2011).

Ryan, T. J. (2005) Marketing mix. *SGB*, 38(12), 22.

Sallent, O., Palau, R., & Guia, J. (2011) Exploring the legacy of sport events on sport tourism networks. *European Sport Management Quarterly*, 11, 397–421.

Samatas, M. (2011) Surveillance in Athens 2004 and Beijing 2008: A comparison of the Olympic surveillance modalities and legacies in two different Olympic host regimes. *Urban Studies*, 48, 3347–3366.

Sander, M. & Altobelli, C. F. (2011) Virtual advertising in sports events: Does it really work? *International Journal of Sports Marketing & Sponsorship*, 12, 225–239.

Sandler, D. M. & Shani, D. (1989) Olympic sponsorship vs. "ambush" marketing: Who gets the gold? *Journal of Advertising Research*, 29, 9–14.

Sandler, D. M. & Shani, D. (1993) Sponsorship and the Olympic Games: The consumer perspective. *Sport Marketing Quarterly*, 2, 38–43.

Sandvoss, C. (2004) Technological evolution or revolution? Sport online live internet commentary as postmodern cultural form. *Convergence*, 10(3), 39–54.

Santomier, J. P. (2008) New media, branding and global sports sponsorship. *International Journal of Sports Marketing and Sponsorship*, 10, 15–28.

Santomier, J. P. & Shuart, J. A. (2008) Sport new media. *International Journal of Sport Management and Marketing*, 4, 85–101.

Sartre, J.-P. (1957) *Existentialism and Human Emotions*, New York: The Wisdom Library.

Sartre, J.-P. (1966) *Being and Nothingness*, New York: Washington Square Press.

Scassa, T. (2008) Faster, higher, stronger: The protection of Olympic marks leading up to Vancouver 2010. *University of British Columbia Law Review*, 41, 34–68.

Scassa, T. (2011) Ambush marketing and the right of association: Clamping down on references to that big event with all the athletes in a couple of years. *Journal of Sport Management*, 25, 354–370.

Schimmel, K. S. (2011) From "violence-complacent" to "terrorist-ready": Post-9/11 framing of the US Super Bowl. *Urban Studies*, 48, 3277–3291.

Schneider, G. and Bradish, C. L. (2006) Location, location, location: The marketing of place and Super Bowl XL. *Sport Marketing Quarterly*, 15, 206–213.

Schrodt, P. A., Gerner, D. J., & Yilmaz, Ã. (2005) Methods meet policy: Transnational monitoring of the Israel–Palestine conflict. *International Studies Perspectives*, 6, 235–251.

Schwarz, E. C. & Hunter, J. D. (2008) *Advanced Theory and Practice in Sport Marketing*, London: Butterworth-Heinemann.

Sealy, W. & Wickens, E. (2008) The potential impact of mega sport media on the travel decision-making process and destination choice: The case of Portugal and Euro 2004. *Journal of Travel and Tourism Marketing*, 24, 127–137.

Séguin, B. & O'Reilly, N. J. (2008) The Olympic brand, ambush marketing and clutter. *International Journal of Sport Management Marketing*, 4, 62–84.

Séguin, B., Lyberger, M., O'Reilly, N., & McCarthy, L. (2005) Internationalizing ambush marketing: The Olympic brand and country of origin. *International Journal of Sport Marketing and Sponsorship*, 6, 216–229.

Séguin, B., Parent, M. M., & O'Reilly, N. (2010) Corporate support: A corporate social responsibility alternative to traditional event sponsorship. *International Journal of Sport Management & Marketing*, 7, 202–222.

Senn, A. E. (1999) *Power, Politics and the Olympic Games*, Champaign, IL: Human Kinetics.

Shamir, B. & Howell, J. M. (1999) Organizational and contextual influences on the emergence and effectiveness of charismatic leadership. *Leadership Quarterly*, 10, 257–283.

Shani, D. & Sandler, D. M. (1998) Ambush marketing: Is confusion to blame for the flickering of the flame? *Psychology & Marketing*, 15, 367–383.

Shank, M. D. (2005) *Sport Marketing: A Strategic Perspective* (3rd edn), Upper Saddle River, NJ: Pearson Education Inc.

Sharpley, R. & Stone, P. R. (2012) Socio-cultural impacts of events: Meanings, authorized transgression and social capital. In S. J. Page & J. Connell (eds), *The Routledge Handbook of Events* (pp. 347–361), London: Routledge.

Shaw, S. (2009) "It was all 'smile for Dunedin!'": Event volunteer experiences at the 2006 New Zealand Masters Games. *Sport Management Review*, 12, 26–33.

Sheridan, H. (2006) Tennis technologies: De-skilling and re-skilling players and the implications for the game. *Sport in Society*, 9, 32–50.

Sherry, E., Karg, A., & O'May, F. (2011) Social capital and sport events: spectator attitudinal change and the Homeless World Cup. *Sport in Society*, 14, 111–125.

Shipway, R. (2007) Sustainable legacies for the 2012 Olympic Games. *The Journal of the Royal Society for the Promotion of Health*, 127, 119–124.

Shoemaker, P. & Cohen, A. (2006) *News Around the World: Content, Practitioners, and the Public*, New York: Routledge.

Shoemaker, P., Danielian, L. H., & Brendlinger, N. (1991) Deviant acts, risky business and US interests: The newsworthiness of world events. *Journalism and Mass Media Quarterly*, 68, 781–795.

Shone, A. & Parry, B. (2004) *Successful Event Management*, London: Thomson.

Shonk, D. J. & Chelladurai, P. (2008) Service quality, satisfaction, and intent to return in event sport tourism. *Journal of Sport Management*, 22, 587–602.

Silk, M. (1999) Local/global flows and altered production practices: Narrative constructions at the 1995 Canada Cup of Soccer. *International Review for the Sociology of Sport*, 34, 113–123.

Silk, M. & Amis, J. (2000) Institutional pressures and the production of televised sport. *Journal of Sport Management*, 14, 267–292.

Silk, M., Slack, T., & Amis, J. (2000) Bread, butter and gravy: An institutional approach to televised sport production. *Culture, Sport, Society*, 3, 1–21.

Silvers, J. R. & Nelson, K. B. (2009) An application illustration of the Event Management Body of Knowledge (EMBOK) as a framework for analysis using the design of the 2006 Winter Olympics opening ceremonies. *Event Management*, 13, 117–131.

Simmons, B. & Lowry, D. (1990) Terrorists in the news, as reflected in three news magazines. *Journalism Quarterly*, 67, 692–696.

Sinclair, J. (2000) More than an old flame: National symbolism and the media in the torch ceremony of the Olympics. *Media International Australia Incorporating Culture & Policy*, 97, 35–46.

Sinclair, J. (2001) Nationalism and commercialism in the Olympic torch ceremony. *Australian Journal of Communication*, 28, 73–84.

Singapore 2010 Youth Olympic Games. (2010) *Blazing the Trail: Official Report*, Singapore: Author.

Skinner, B. F. (1974) *About Behaviorism*, New York: Alfred A. Knopf.

Slack, T. & Parent, M. M. (2006) *Understanding Sport Organizations: The Application of Organization Theory* (2nd edn), Champaign, IL: Human Kinetics.

SLOC (2002) *Human Resources: Volunteers*, Lausanne: International Olympic Committee.

Sloman, J. (2000) *Staffing the Games*, Lausanne: International Olympic Committee.

Slowikowski, S. S. (1991) Burning desire: Nostalgia, ritual, and the sport-festival flame ceremony. *Sociology of Sport Journal*, 8, 239–257.

Smith, A. (2006) Tourists' consumption and interpretation of sport event imagery. *Journal of Sport & Tourism*, 11, 77–100.

Smith, A. (2007) Large-scale events and sustainable urban regeneration: Key principles for host cities. *Journal of Urban Regeneration and Renewal*, 1, 178–190.

Smith, A. (2009) Theorising the relationship between major sport events and social sustainability. *Journal of Sport & Tourism*, 14, 109–120.

Smith, A. (2010) The development of "sports-city" zones and their potential value as tourism resources for urban areas. *European Planning Studies*, 18, 385–410.

Smith, A. & Fox, T. (2007) From "event-led" to "event-themed" regeneration: The 2002 Commonwealth Games legacy programme. *Urban Studies*, 44, 1125–1143.

Smith, A. & Thomas, N. (2005) The "inclusion" of elite athletes with disabilities in the 2002 Manchester Commonwealth Games: An exploratory analysis of British newspaper coverage. *Sport, Education & Society*, 10, 49–67.

Smith, A. C. T. & Westerbeek, H. (2010) "From enhancement to engagement": Reflections on the future of sport consumption. *Sport in Society*, 13, 344–353.

Smith, J., McCarthy, J. D., McPhail, C., & Augustyn, B. (2001) From protest to agenda building: Description bias in media coverage of protest events in Washington, DC. *Social Forces*, 79, 1397–1423.

Smith, K. A. (2007) The distribution of event tickets. *Event Management*, 10, 185–196.

Smith, L. (2009) Sustainability of an industry: Green buildings and green events. *Journal of Green Building*, 4, 63–89.

Smith, M. F. (2005) Spotlight events, media relations, and place promotion: A case study. *Journal of Hospitality & Leisure Marketing*, 12, 115–134.

Smolinski, R. (2008) How was the fifth European Union enlargement actually negotiated? A comparative analysis of selected traits. *International Negotiation*, 13, 247–283.

Snelgrove, R. & Wood, L. (2010) Attracting and leveraging visitors at a charity cycling event. *Journal of Sport & Tourism*, 15, 269–285.

Snelgrove, R., Taks, M., Chalip, L., & Green, B. C. (2008) How visitors and locals at a sport event differ in motives and identity. *Journal of Sport & Tourism*, 13, 165–180.

Solberg, H. A. (2001) Finding a price policy that maximises the ticket revenues at sporting events: A focus on price bundling. *European Sport Management Quarterly*, 1, 300–319.

Solberg, H. A. (2003) Major sporting events: Assessing the value of volunteers' work. *Managing Leisure*, 8, 17–27.

Solberg, H. A., Hanstad, D. V., & Steen-Johnsen, K. (2009) The challenges of producing popular sports contests: A comparative study of biathlon and cross-country skiing. *International Journal of Sports Marketing & Sponsorship*, 10, 171–189.

Spears, L. C. (1995) *Reflections on Leadership: How Robert K. Greenleaf's Theory of Servant-leadership Influenced Today's Top Management Thinkers*, New York: John Wiley and Sons.

Speed, R. & Thompson, P. (2000) Determinants of sports sponsorship response. *Psychology and Marketing*, 28, 226–238.

Speight, P. (2010) Why security doesn't work. *Journal of Applied Security Research*, 5, 234–270.

Spielberg, S. (2005) *Munich* [film], Willowday, Canada: Universal Pictures and Dreamworks Pictures.

Spira, L. F. (1999) Ceremonies of governance: Perspectives on the role of the audit committee. *Journal of Management and Governance*, 3, 231–260.

SportAccord (2010) *Sports' Social Responsibility Map*. Online. Available at http://sportaccord.com/en/services/index.php?idIndex=33&idContent=14523 (accessed 4 January 2012).

Sportcal.com (2010) *World Cup Heading to Middle East for the First Time As Qatar Wins 2022 Bidding Race*. Online. Available at http://racefor.sportcal.com/Bidding/MediaRelease.aspx?CompanyID=41569 (accessed 24 February 2011).

Sport Canada (2008) *Federal Policy for Hosting International Sport Events*. Online. Available at www.pch.gc.ca/pgm/sc/pol/acc/2008/accueil-host_2008-eng.pdf (accessed 28 February 2012).

Sports Illustrated (2010) Qatar's 2022 World Cup bid. *Sports Illustrated*. Online. Available at http://sportsillustrated.cnn.com/multimedia/photo_gallery/1009/soccer.2022.world.cup.stadiums.qatar/content.1.html (accessed 24 February 2011).

Sportsmail Reporter (2012, 2 March) *Blatter Pushing Hard for Technology As FIFA Chief Aims to Avoid Repeat of Lampard Blunder.* Online. Available at www.dailymail.co.uk/sport/football/article-2109354/Sepp-Blatter-pushing-hard-goal-line-technology.html#ixzz1pawS8Jbr (accessed 19 March 2012).

Steen-Johnsen, K. & Hanstad, D. (2008) Change and power in complex democratic organizations: The case of Norwegian elite sports. *European Sport Management Quarterly*, 8, 123–143.

Steinbrink, M., Haferburg, C., & Ley, A. (2011) Festivalisation and urban renewal in the Global South: Socio-spatial consequences of the 2010 FIFA World Cup. *South African Geographical Journal*, 93, 15–28.

Sterken, E. (2007) Growth impact of major sporting events. In H. Preuss (ed.), *The Impact and Evaluation of Major Sporting Events* (pp. 63–77), Abingdon: Routledge.

Stogdill, R. M. (1948) Personal factors associated with leadership: A survey of the literature. *Journal of Applied Psychology*, 25, 35–71.

Stogdill, R. M. (1974) *Handbook of Leadership: A Survey of Theory and Research*, New York: Free Press.

Stokes, R. (2005) Relationship marketing during Rugby World Cup 2003: A comparative analysis of public and private sector sponsors. *International Journal of Sports Marketing & Sponsorship*, 7, 49–56.

Stone, J. & Horne, J. (2008) The print media coverage of skiing and snowboarding in Britain: Does it have to be downhill all the way? *Journal of Sport and Social Issues*, 32, 94–112.

Stotlar, D. K. (2001) *Developing Successful Sport Marketing Plans*, Morgantown, WV: Fitness Information Technology.

Strigas, A. D. & Jackson Jr, E. N. (2003) Motivating volunteers to serve and succeed: Design and results of a pilot study that explores demographics and motivational factors in sport volunteerism. *International Sports Journal*, 7, 111–123.

Sugden, J. & Tomlinson, A. (1996) What's left when the circus leaves town? An evaluation of World Cup USA 1994. *Sociology of Sport Journal*, 13, 238–258.

Sugden, J. & Tomlinson, A. (1998) Power and resistance in the governance of world football: Theorizing FIFA's transnational impact. *Journal of Sport and Social Issues*, 22, 299–316.

Summers, J. & Johnson Morgan, M. (2008) More than just the media: Considering the role of public relations in the creation of sporting celebrity and the management of fan expectations. *Public Relations Review*, 34, 176–182.

Sungwon, B., Kyoungtae, K., Jackson, E. N., & Park, K.-Y. (2005) Utilization of sports facilities by physically disabled consumers in South Korea: Are they satisfied? *ICHPER – SD Journal*, 41, 14–19.

Surujlal, J. (2010) Volunteer motivation in special events for people with disabilities. *African Journal for Physical, Health Education, Recreation & Dance*, 16, 460–474.

Susilo, Y. O. & Dijst, M. (2010) Behavioural decisions of travel-time ratios for work, maintenance and leisure activities in the Netherlands. *Transportation Planning and Technology*, 33, 19–34.

Swart, K., Bob, U., Knott, B., & Salie, M. (2011) A sport and sociocultural legacy beyond 2010: A case study of the Football Foundation of South Africa. *Development Southern Africa*, 28, 415–428.

Tait, R. (1996) The attributes of leadership. *Leadership & Organization Development Journal*, 17, 27–31.

Taks, M., Kesenne, S., Chalip, L., Green, B. C., & Martyn, S. (2011) Economic impact analysis versus cost benefit analysis: The case of a medium-sized sport event. *International Journal of Sport Finance*, 6, 187–203.

Tanner, S., Green, K., & Burns, S. (2011) Media coverage of sport for athletes with intellectual disabilities: The 2010 Special Olympics national Games examined. *Media International Australia*, 140, 107–116.

Tarantino, M. & Carini, S. (2010) The good, the fake and the cyborg: The broadcast and coverage of Beijing 2008 Olympics in Italy. *International Journal of the History of Sport*, 27, 1717–1738.

Tarradellas, J. (2003) The Olympic Games and the sustainability. In M. de Moragus, C. Kennett, & N. Puig (eds), *The Legacy of the Olympic Games 1984–2000* (pp. 74–82), Lausanne: IOC.

Tarricone, P. (1994) Pregame show. *Civil Engineering*, 64(8), 34–37.

Taylor, J. & Bowers, D. G. (1972) *The Survey of Organizations: A Machine Scored Standardized Questionnaire Instrument*, Ann Arbor, MI: University of Michigan, Institute for Social Research.

Taylor, T. & Toohey, K. (2006) Impacts of terrorism-related safety and security measures at a major sport event. *Event Management*, 9, 199–209.

Taylor, T. & Toohey, K. (2007) Perceptions of terrorism threats at the 2004 Olympic Games: Implications for sport events. *Journal of Sport & Tourism*, 12, 99–114.

Taylor, T., & Toohey, K. (2011) Ensuring safety at Australian sport event precincts: Creating securitised, sanitized and stiffling spaces? *Urban Studies*, 48, 3259–3275.

TerraChoice (2012) *The Seven Sins*. Online. Available at http://sinsofgreenwashing.org/findings/the-seven-sins (accessed 4 January 2012).

Thamnopoulos, Y. & Gargalianos, D. (2002) Ticketing of large scale events: The case of Sydney 2000 Olympic Games. *Facilities*, 20, 22–33.

Theodoraki, E. (2001) A conceptual framework for the study of structural configurations of organising committees for the Olympic Games (OCOGs). *European Journal for Sport Management*, 8, 106–124.

Theodoraki, E. (2010) Institutional challenges to Olympic Games sustainability. In C. Pentifallo, *Sport Mega-Events, Sustainability, and Impact Assessment Summary Report* (pp. 15–16). Proceedings from the UBC Centre for Sport and Sustainability Invitational Think Tank, 18 February 2010, Vancouver: UBC Centre for Sport & Sustainability. Online. Available at http://css.ubc.ca/events/think-tank-1/think-tank-1-summary-report (accessed 26 March 2012).

Thoits, P. & Hewitt, L. (2001) Volunteer work and well-being. *Journal of Health and Social Behavior*, 42, 115–131.

Thompson, J. D. (1967) *Organizations in Action*, New York: McGraw-Hill.

Thompson, K. (2011, 28 April) *TEDxBelfast – Ken Thompson – The Habits of High Performing Teams*. Online. Avalaible at www.youtube.com/watch?v=KNNWLj-3wx0 (accessed 24 October 2011).

Tkaczynski, A. & Rundle-Thiele, S. R. (2011) Event segmentation: A review and research agenda. *Tourism Management, 32,* 426–434.

Tolbert, P. S. & Zucker, L. G. (1996) The institutionalization of institutional theory. In S. Clegg, C. Hardy & W. R. Nord (eds), *Handbook of Organization Studies* (pp. 175–190), Thousand Oaks, CA: Sage Publications.

Tomlinson, A. (1989) Representation, ideology and the Olympic Games: A reading of the opening and closing ceremonies of the 1984 Los Angeles Olympic Games. In R. Jackson & T. McPhail (eds), *The Olympic Movement and the Mass Media: Past, Present and Future Issues* (pp. 7/3–7/11), Calgary, Canada: Hurford Enterprises.

Tomlinson, A. (1996) Olympic spectacle: Opening ceremonies and some paradoxes of globalization. *Media, Culture and Society, 18,* 583–602.

Tomlinson, A. (2000) Carrying the torch for whom? Symbolic power and Olympic ceremony. In K. Schaffer (ed.), *The Olympics at the Millennium: Power, Politics, and the Games* (pp. 163–183), Piscataway, NJ: Rutgers University Press.

Toohey, K. & Halbwirth, S. (2002) Information and documentation in the Olympic Games. In *University Lectures on the Olympics,* Barcelona: Centre d'Estudis Olimpics (UAB). Online. Available at http://olympicstudies.uab.es/lec/pdf/toohey.pdf (accessed 26 March 2012).

Toohey, K. & Taylor, T. (2008) Mega events, fear, and risk: Terrorism at the Olympic Games. *Journal of Sport Management, 22,* 451–469.

Toohey, K., Taylor, T., & Lee, C. K. (2003) The FIFA World Cup 2002: The effects of terrorism on sport tourists. *Journal of Sport Tourism, 8,* 167–185.

Toor, S. & Ogunlana, S. (2010) Beyond the "iron triangle": Stakeholder perception of key performance indicators (KPIs) for large-scale public sector development projects. *International Journal of Project Management, 28*(3), 228–236.

Torino 2013 World Masters Games (2009) *50,000 athletes in Torino for the 2013 World Masters Games.* Online. Available at www.torino2013.org/public/comunicato_eng.pdf (accessed 9 November 2010).

Traganou, J. (2010) National narratives in the opening and closing ceremonies of the Athens 2004 Olympic Games. *Journal of Sport and Social Issues, 34,* 236–251.

Trail, G. T. & James, J. D. (2001) The motivation scale for sport consumption: Assessment of the scale's psychometric properties. *Journal of Sport Behavior, 24,* 108–127.

Trail, G. T., Anderson, D. F., & Fink, J. S. (2002) Examination of gender differences in importance of and satisfaction with venue factors at intercollegiate basketball games. *International Sports Journal, 6,* 51–64.

Trauer, B., Ryan, C., & Lockyer, T. (2003) The South Pacific Masters' Games – Competitor involvement and games development: Implications for management and tourism. *Journal of Sport Tourism, 8,* 270–283.

Treuren, G. (2009) The associative-supportive motivation as a factor in the decision to event volunteer. *Leisure/Loisir: Journal of the Canadian Association for Leisure Studies, 33,* 687–711.

Trice, H. M. & Beyer, J. (1984) Studying organizational cultures through rites and ceremonials. *Academy of Management Review, 9,* 653–669.

Tripolitsioti, A., Moudakis, K., Konstantinakos, P., & Theodorikakos, P. (2007) The management competencies of the directors of youth centres and indoor facilities in the municipalities. *Biology of Exercise, 3,* 47–58.

Tsuji, Y., Bennett, G., & Zhang, J. (2007) Consumer satisfaction with an action sport event. *Sport Marketing Quarterly*, 16, 199–208.

Tuggle, C. A., Huffman, S., & Rosengard, D. (2007) A descriptive analysis of NBC's coverage of the 2004 Summer Olympics. *Journal of Sports Media*, 2, 53–75.

Turco, D. M. (1994) Event sponsorship: Effects on consumer brand loyalty and consumption. *Sport Marketing Quarterly*, 3(3), 35–37.

Turner, P. (2007) The impact of technology on the supply of sport broadcasting. *European Sport Management Quarterly*, 7, 337–360.

Turner, P. & Cusumano, S. (2000) Virtual advertising: Legal implications for sport. *Sport Management Review*, 3, 47–70.

Turner, P. & Westerbeek, H. M. (2004) Network relationships in the bidding process for major sporting events. *International Journal of Sport Management*, 5, 335–356.

Turner, V. W. (1969) *The Ritual Process*, Chicago, IL: Aldine.

Twitter (2011, 21 September) *Twitter Blog*. Online. Available at http://blog.twitter.com (accessed 27 September 2011).

UBC CSS (n.d.) *About*. Online. Available at http://css.ubc.ca/about-2/ (accessed 27 December 2012).

Uhrich, S. & Koenigstorfer, J. (2009) Effects of atmosphere at major sports events: A perspective from environmental psychology. *International Journal of Sports Marketing & Sponsorship*, 10, 325–344.

Ulrich, D. R. & Barney, J. B. (1984) Perspectives in organizations: Resource dependence, efficiency, and population. *Academy of Management Review*, 3, 471–481.

UNCED (1987) *Our Common Future*, Paris: UN.

Uzelac, G. (2010) National ceremonies: The pursuit of authenticity. *Ethnic and Racial Studies*, 33, 1718–1736.

Van Bottenburg, M. & Heilbron, J. (2006) De-sportization of fighting contests: The origins and dynamics of no holds barred events and the theory of sportization. *International Review for the Sociology of Sport*, 41, 259–282; 479–480; 485; 491.

Vancouver 2010 & AISTS (2008) *Sustainable Sport and Event Toolkit (SSET)*. Online. Available at http://events.whistler.com/downloads/Sustainable%20Sport%20and%20Event%20Toolkit.pdf (accessed 17 February 2012).

Vancouver Organizing Committee for the 2010 Olympic and Paralympic Winter Games. (n.d.) *VANOC: Human Resources – Policy and Procedures. Code of Conduct*, Vancouver: Author..

Vancouver Organizing Committee for the 2010 Olympic and Paralympic Winter Games (2003) *Bid Book*. Online. Available at www.vancouver2010.com/en/OrganizingCommittee/AboutOrganizingCommittee/BidHistory/BidBook (accessed 26 March 2006).

Vancouver Organizing Committee for the 2010 Olympic and Paralympic Winter Games (2007) *Business Plan and Games Budget*. Online. Available at www.linkbc.ca/torc/downs1/2010_Olympics.pdf (accessed 31 August 2009).

Vancouver Organizing Committee for the 2010 Olympic and Paralympic Winter Games (2009) *Updated Budget*. Online. Available at www.vancouver2010.com/dl/00/08/78/2009budget_28d-qb.pdf (accessed 6 December 2010).

Vancouver Organizing Committee for the 2010 Olympic and Paralympic Winter Games (2010a) *VANOC Annual Report: Consolidated Financial Statement*. Online. Available at www.fin.gov.bc.ca/reports/2010_VANOC_Financial_report_English.pdf (accessed 28 February 2012).

Vancouver Organizing Committee for the 2010 Olympic and Paralympic Winter Games (2010b) *Vancouver 2010 Sustainability Report: 2009–2010*, Vancouver: VANOC. Online. Available at www.2010legaciesnow.com/fileadmin/user_upload/About_Us/VANOC/SUS-1261_Sustainability_Report_09–10.pdf (acccessed 24 February 2011).

Van der Wagen, L. & Carlos, B. R. (2005) *Event Management for Tourism, Cultural, Business, and Sporting Events*, Upper Saddle River, NJ: Pearson Prentice Hall.

Van Hilvoorde, I., Vos, R., & De Wert, G. (2007) Flopping, klapping and gene doping: Dichotomies between "natural" and "artificial" in elite sport. *Social Studies of Science*, 37, 173–200.

VANOC (2010) *Accreditation*, Lausanne: International Olympic Committee.

VanWynsberghe, R., Kwan, B., & Van Luijk, N. (2011) Community capacity and the 2010 Winter Olympic Games. *Sport in Society*, 14, 370–385.

Vassout, D. (2009) *Pringles Ambush Marketing at Wimbledon*. Online. Available at www.vanksen.com/blog/pringles-ambush-marketing-at-wimbledon (accessed 15 December 2011).

Venables, J. (1993) *What is News?* Huntingdon: ELM Publications.

Versluis, C. (2005) Innovations on thin ice. *Technovation*, 25, 1183–1192.

Vigor, A., Mean, M., & Tims, C. (eds) (2004) *After the Gold Rush: A Sustainable Olympics for London*, London: IPPR and Demos.

Viuda-Serrano, A. (2010) A diplomatic mission: Spain and the 1948 London Olympics. *International Journal of the History of Sport*, 27, 1080–1103.

Volpano, L. & Bilotkach, V. (2008) A case study: How to rationalise concert entertainment ticket pricing. *Journal of Revenue and Pricing Management*, 7, 3–6.

Vroom, V. H. (1964) *Work and Motivation*, New York: John Wiley and Sons.

Vroom, V. H., & MacCrimmon, K. R. (1968) Toward a stochastic model of managerial careers. *Administrative Science Quarterly*, 13, 26–46.

Waddock, S. (2004) Parallel universes: Companies, academics, and the progress of corporate citizenship. *Business and Society Review*, 109, 5–42.

Wadongo, B. I., Edwin, O., & Oscar, K. O. (2010) Managerial roles and choice of performance measures in the Kenyan five-star hotels using a cross-sectional correlational design. *Managing Leisure*, 15, 17–31.

Wakefield, K. L., Blodgett, J. G., & Sloan, H. G. (1996) Measurement and management of the sportscape. *Journal of Sport Management*, 10, 15–31.

Walker, M. & Parent, M. M. (2010) Toward an integrated framework of corporate social responsibility, responsiveness, and citizenship in sport. *Sport Management Review*, 13, 198–213.

Walker, M., Heere, B., Parent, M., & Drane, D. (2010) Social responsibility and the Olympic Games: The mediating role of consumer attributions. *Journal of Business Ethics*, 95, 659–680.

Walters, G. (2011) Bidding for international sport events: How government supports and undermines national governing bodies of sport. *Sport in Society*, 14 (2), 208–222.

Walumbwa, F. O., Avolio, B. J., Gardner, W. L., Wernsing, T. S., & Peterson, S. J. (2008) Authentic leadership: Development and validation of a theory-based measure. *Journal of Management*, 34(1), 89–126.

Wang, E., Chou, H. W., & Jiang, J. (2005) The impacts of charismatic leadership style on team cohesiveness and overall performance during ERP implementation. *International Journal for Project Management*, 23, 173–180.

Wann, D. L. (1995) Preliminary validation of the sport fan motivation scale. *Journal of Sport and Social Issues*, 19, 377–396.

Wann, D. L., Schrader, M. P., & Wilson, A. M. (1999) Sport fan motivation: Questionnaire validation, comparisons by sport, and relationship to athletic motivation. *Journal of Sport Behavior*, 22, 114–139.

Wardle, C. & West, E. (2004) The press as agents of nationalism in the Queen's Golden Jubilee: How British newspapers celebrated a media event. *European Journal of Communication*, 19, 195–214.

Wasserman, S. & Faust, K. (1994) *Social Network Analysis: Methods and Applications*, New York: Cambridge University Press.

Weber, M. (1947) *The Theory of Social and Economic Organization*, New York: Free Press.

Weed, M. E. (2002) Football hooligans as undesirable sports tourists: Some meta-analytical speculations. In S. Gammon & J. Kurtzman (eds), *Sport Tourism: Principles and Practices* (pp. 35–52), Eastbourne: Antony Rowe Ltd.

Wempe, B. (2005) In defense of a self-disciplined, domain-specific social contract theory of business ethics. *Business Ethics Quarterly*, 15, 113–135.

Wenner, L. A. (2004) Recovering (from) Janet Jackson's breast: Ethics and the nexus of media, sports, and management. *Journal of Sport Management*, 18, 315–334.

Wensing, E. H. & Bruce, T. (2003) Bending the rules: Media representations of gender during an international sporting event. *International Review for the Sociology of Sport*, 38, 387–396.

Westerbeek, H., Turner, P., & Ingerson, L. (2002) Key success factors in bidding for hallmark sporting events. *International Marketing Review*, 19, 303–322.

Whetten, D. A. (1989) What constitutes a theoretical contribution? *Academy of Management Review*, 14, 490–495.

Wien, C. & Elmelund-Praestekaer, C. (2009) An anatomy of media hypes: Developing a model for the dynamics and structure of intense media coverage of single issues. *European Journal of Communication*, 24, 183–201.

Williams, A. T. (1994) Do anti-ticket scalping laws make a difference? *Managerial and Decision Economics*, 15, 503–509.

Williams, P. W., Dossa, K. B., & Tompkins, L. (1995) Volunteerism and special event management: A case study of Whistler's Men's World Cup of Skiing. *Festival Management & Event Tourism*, 3, 83–95.

Wilson, J. (2000) Volunteering. *Annual Review of Sociology*, 26, 215–240.

Wilson, R. S. (2006) The economic impact of local sport events: Significant, limited or otherwise? A case study of four swimming events. *Managing Leisure*, 11, 57–70.

Wilson, R. S., Winter, P. L., Maguire, L. A., & Ascher, T. (2011) Managing wildfire events: Risk-based decision making among a group of federal fire managers. *Risk Analysis: An International Journal*, 31, 805–818.

Winter, S. G. (1987) Knowledge and competence as strategic assets. In D. J. Teece (ed.), *The Competitive Challenge* (pp. 159–184), Cambridge, MA: Ballinger.

White, P. & Wilson, B. (1999) Distinctions in the stands: an investigation of Bourdieu's "habitus", socioeconomic status and sport spectatorship in Canada. *International Review for the Sociology of Sport*, 34, 245–264.

Whitson, D. & Macintosh, D. (1993) Becoming a world-class city: Hallmark events and sport franchises in the growth strategies of Western Canadian cities. *Sociology of Sport Journal*, 10, 221–240.

Whitson, D. & Macintosh, D. (1996) The global circus: International sport, tourism, and the marketing of cities. *Journal of Sport and Social Issues*, 20, 278–295.

Whitson, D., Harvey, J., & Lavoie, M. (2000) The Mills report, the Manley subsidy proposals, and the business of major-league sport. *Canadian Public Administration*, 43, 127–156.

Wicks, A. C. & Freeman, R. E. (1998) Organization studies and the new pragmatism: Positivism, anti-positivism, and the search for ethics. *Organization Science*, 9, 123–140.

Wiederkehr, S. (2009) "We shall never know the exact number of men who have competed in the Olympics posing as women": Sport, gender verification and the Cold War. *International Journal of the History of Sport*, 26, 556–572.

Wijnberg, N. M. (2000) Normative stakeholder theory and Aristotle: The link between ethics and politics. *Journal of Business Ethics*, 25, 329–342.

Wolfe, R. A. & Putler, D. S. (2002) How tight are the ties that bind stakeholder groups? *Organization Science*, 13, 64–80.

Wolfe, R. A., Meenaghan, T., & O'Sullivan, P. (2002) Power and sports networks. *Journal of Business Research*, 55, 611–622.

Wolfsfeld, G. (1997) Fair weather friends: The varying role of the news media in the Arab–Israeli peace process. *Political Communication*, 14, 29–48.

Wolohan, J. T. (2008, October) Civil actions: Ice hockey injury not result of willful behavior, court rules. *Athletic Business*. Online. Available at http://athleticbusiness.com/articles/article.aspx?articleid=1877&zoneid=28 (accessed 5 July 2011).

Wolsink, M. (2010) Contested environmental policy infrastructure: Socio-political acceptance of renewable energy, water, and waste facilities. *Environmental Impact Assessment Review*, 30, 302–311.

Woodward, J. (1958) *Management and Technology*, London: Her Majesty's Printing Office.

Woodward, J. (1965) *Industrial Organization: Theory and Practice*, London: Oxford University Press.

World Commission on Environment and Development (n.d.) *Our Common Future, Chapter 2: Towards Sustainable Development*. Online. Available at www.un-documents.net/ocf-02.htm (accessed 4 March 2011).

WSL (n.d.) *Our Mission*. Online. Available at www.whistlersportlegacies.com/about/mission (accessed 27 December 2011).

Wyld, D. C. (2008) The chips are in: Enhancing sports through RFID technology. *International Journal of Sports Marketing and Sponsorship*, 9, 135–150.

Xing, X. & Chalip, L. (2006) Effects of hosting a sport event on destination brand: A test of co-branding and match-up models. *Sport Management Review*, 9, 49–78.

Xing, X. & Chalip, L. (2009) Marching in the glory: Experiences and meanings when working for a sport mega-event. *Journal of Sport Management*, 23, 210–237.

Xing, X., Church, A. G., O'Reilly, N., Pegoraro, A., Nadeau, J., Schweinbenz, A., Heslop, L., & Séguin, B. (2008) Olympic Games host and bid city marketing: Exploring issue management in the relationships among event stakeholder groups. *International Journal of Sports Marketing & Sponsorship*, 9, 321–335.

Yarbrough, C. R. (2000) *And They Call Them Games: An Inside View of the 1996 Olympics*, Macon, GA: Mercer University Press.

Yoshida, M. & James, J. D. (2011) Service quality at sporting events: Is aesthetic quality a missing dimension? *Sport Management Review*, 14, 13–24.

Young, W. (1986) A model of vehicles movements in parking facilities. *Mathematics and Computers in Simulation*, 28, 305–309.

Yu, Y., Klauser, F., & Chan, G. (2009) Governing security at the 2008 Beijing Olympics. *International Journal of the History of Sport*, 26, 390–405.

Yukl, G. A. (1971) Toward a behavioral theory of leadership. *Organizational Behavior and Human Performance*, 6, 414–440.

Yukl, G. A. (1981) *Leadership in Organizations*, Englewood Cliffs, NJ: Prentice Hall.

Yukl, G. A. (2002) *Leadership in Organizations* (5th edn), Upper Saddle River, NJ: Prentice-Hall Inc.

Yukl, G. A. (2010) *Leadership in Organizations* (7th edn), Upper Saddle River, NJ: Prentice-Hall Inc.

Yukl, G. A. & Mahsud, R. (2010) Why flexible and adaptive leadership is essential. *Consulting Psychology Journal: Practice and research*, 62, 81–93.

Zander, U. & Kogut, B. (1995) Knowledge and the speed of the transfer of organizational capabilities. *Organization Science*, 6, 76–92.

Zhang, X., Shen, L., & Wu, Y. (2010) Green strategy for gaining competitive advantage in housing development: A China study. *Journal of Cleaner Production*, 19, 157–167.

Ziakas, V. & Costa, C. A. (2010) "Between theatre and sport" in a rural event: Evolving unity and community development from the inside-out. *Journal of Sport & Tourism*, 15, 7–26.

Ziakas, V. & Costa, C. A. (2011) Event portfolio and multi-purpose development: Establishing the conceptual grounds. *Sport Management Review*, 14, 409–423.

Zucker, L. G. (1987) Institutional theories of organization. *Annual Review of Sociology*, 13, 443–464.

Index